Phil Kelly

INTERNATIONAL BUSINESS AND MANAGEMENT

Phil Kelly

INTERNATIONAL BUSINESS AND MANAGEMENT

SOUTH-WESTERN
CENGAGE Learning

Australia • Brazil • Japan • Korea • Mexico • Singapore • Spain • United Kingdom • United States

SOUTH-WESTERN
CENGAGE Learning™

International Business and Management
Phil Kelly

Publishing Director: John Yates

Publisher: Tom Rennie

Development Editor: James Clark

Content Project Editor: Dan Benton

Manufacturing Manager: Helen Mason

Senior Production Controller: Maeve Healy

Marketing Manager: Anne-Marie Scoones

Typesetter: KGL India

Cover design: Design Deluxe Ltd, Bath, UK

Text design: Design Deluxe Ltd, Bath, UK

For product information and technology assistance, contact **emea.info@cengage.com**.

For permission to use material from this text or product, and for permission queries, email **clsuk.permissions@cengage.com**

British Library Cataloguing-in-Publication Data
A catalogue record for this book is available from the British Library.

ISBN: 978-1-84480-784-0

Cengage Learning EMEA
Cheriton House, North Way, Andover, Hampshire SP10 5BE

Cengage Learning products are represented in Canada by Nelson Education Ltd.

For your lifelong learning solutions, visit
www.cengage.co.uk

Purchase e-books or e-chapters at:
http://estore.bized.co.uk

Printed by Seng Lee Press, Singapore
1 2 3 4 5 6 7 8 9 10 – 11 10 09

Dedicated to Toby, Jacob and Ben and Mum
(Phyl Kelly 24th August 1945 to 6th December 2008)

Brief contents

Contents

Part I

International business and management 2

1 An introduction to international business and management 4

Part II

Planning for international business 38

2 Analyzing the global business environment 40

3 International and global strategy 74

4 Behaving responsibly around the world 104

Part V

International business 482

Preface

Introduction

Inspired by international business practice experience in 20 different countries, advising large international and domestic organizations, I have moved on to teach international business in three different UK universities, including assignments in Hong Kong and Singapore. Throughout teaching these courses, however, I have found shortfalls with most international business textbooks: they simply do not reflect the knowledge required by most managers working in contemporary worldwide international organizations. Such textbooks emphasize theories that are often out of date, difficult to apply, or too specialized for the majority of managers working in international organizations. They seem to devote too much text to certain subject areas to the detriment of others resulting in knowledge gaps and a narrow coverage of international business and management. Furthermore, they often reflect the academic and traditional bias of the writer, who typically may focus exclusively on the strategic or the 'hard' management subjects.

Despite wide recognition of the resource-based view of strategy, many textbooks fail to integrate subject areas that would result in the creation of dynamic business capabilities and therefore a sustainable competitive advantage. They give insufficient coverage to the management of intangible resources such as people, knowledge, information and technology. They focus on what the strategist or CEO should know (doing the right things) but not what the everyday manager should know (doing things right, efficiently). This textbook has been written to address these needs directly, and give students and lecturers alike, a more relevant, contemporary international business and management text.

The aim of this book

The overall aim of this book is to equip student readers with the knowledge that will allow them to prosper in their future careers within international organizations. As a strong grounding in international business will ensure that the international organization has the dynamic capabilities, in terms of resources and competencies, to survive and prosper in an uncertain and constantly changing world.

To achieve this aim the book focuses on the strategic importance of resources, core competencies and dynamic capabilities required to attain a sustainable competitive advantage. By balancing the importance of resources and capabilities with the practical concept of turning strategy into action, through the effective and efficient management of resources, the text demonstrates how such competencies and capabilities can be created. An issue addressed throughout is how managers can develop strategic capabilities within international organizations, enabling them to create value for customers, shareholders, society and themselves.

The text is broadly influenced by the internal resource-based, and the external competitive industry perspectives and also taken an eclectic and multidisciplinary approach, drawing on both classic and new theory from strategy, operations management, marketing, information systems, finance, human resource management and the specific literature on international business and management. The strategic role of HR in developing people is recognized as a source of competence difficult for competitors to imitate. Also discussed is knowledge management, the learning organization, HR practices and business processes. As is the important role of information resources and technology and how enterprise systems, business intelligence, knowledge management systems and e-business and e-commerce systems support people and contribute to business strategies. These topics of human and information technology resources are also considered in terms of the specific primary activities of operations management, logistics, marketing and sales. The role of finance and the management of financial resources in the international organization are also covered alongside their supporting systems. Throughout the text employee behaviour is considered from productive and ethical standpoints, emphasizing the key role of leadership. Recognizing globalization and change, we also provide tools and frameworks to analyze international organizational surroundings both internally and externally and explain how change can be managed in order to align the organization with its customers and environment.

Who should use this book?

This book has been written for students taking courses in international business at undergraduate level in the second and third years of a business degree programme. It is also relevant for MBA students studying business for the first time and international organizations in particular. In addition to the overall focus on international business and management, relevant general management concepts are explained and the book explores how they are applied in the international context. While many aspects of international business management are fundamentally the same as management at the national level, once managers are required to operate across national boundaries they face differing problems and opportunities.

Perspectives on international business and management

Many traditional international texts see international business as the study of transactions taking place across national borders for the purpose of satisfying the needs of individuals and organizations. The popular literature tends to focus more on external factors such as the environment, sales and marketing and adopts the term 'international business' (IB). The IB texts include more on the 'hard' areas of business, i.e. marketing, operations management, strategy, and finance as well as covering international economics and trade and the various trading blocs in the world. An alternative model is often presented under the international management (IM) label. The IM books tend to focus more on the 'softer' management aspects of global business, organizational behaviour, human resource management, negotiating and cultural differences. These texts cover information systems and technological issues superficially. Despite there being numerous international management/ business textbooks on the market, they are lacking in several fundamental ways. Some are almost exclusively strategic, others tend to be overly functional (focusing on traditional subject areas such as sales and marketing, HR, finance) i.e. not integrated – the traditional approach to business education. Almost all of the leading books devote insufficient attention to coverage of processes and the application of information systems and technology to global challenges.

Leading books pay little attention to the use of internet technologies to access global markets. Furthermore, they tend to lack a European or Asian focus. In order to develop an integrative understanding of global business there should be a tight integrated flow between chapters. The need for an integrated understanding of business issues derives from several contemporary business problems. An integrated understanding of business supports horizontal strategies whereby organizations seek out synergistic benefits across aspects of their multinational enterprise. The need for integration is also borne out of the process view of organizations, a need to be responsive and customer focused. Today's business student must see the organization as more than simply a collection of functional parts. Important capabilities are created from the way in which people (including skills and know-how), information, financial and physical resources are tied together. Business and management as a subject area is distinctive in that it is interdisciplinary, drawing upon a wide range of base disciplines from 'hard to soft' sciences.

Distinctive features

International *business and management* – is an integrated multidisciplinary textbook emphasizing the need to develop agile companies that can meet changing customer needs in a timely and profitable manner. International management should take a supply chain and value system perspective, identifying how organizations can operate more effectively and efficiently at a global level; using their resources such as information, people, knowledge, technology and finances to achieve their goals and compete in the global marketplace. Recent years have brought sweeping changes in the way organizations apply information technology to solve complex problems that are common in increasingly competitive and global business environments. All organizations today create sustainable value from leveraging their intangible assets – human capital; databases and information systems; responsive, high-quality processes; customer relationships and brands; innovation capabilities; and culture. Effective resource management can deliver competitive advantage; organizations must manage people, information, knowledge and technological resources along with tangible goods and materials if they are to be responsive, innovative, effective and efficient. This is a text containing theory about managing international organizations. Special features of this text include:

- A multidisciplinary/integrated and holistic treatment of international management problems.
- A refreshing, European perspective with Asian case studies included.
- A focus on the use of technology in the international organization – how organizations use information and IT to support global operations and deliver competitive advantage.
- A focus on the practice of managing business operations across countries. The book contains the explicit knowledge required by those in charge of running an international business.
- Coverage of horizontal strategies, business process reengineering, enterprise systems and resource sharing required to develop agile companies.
- Focus on the use of Internet technologies to conduct global business.
- Comprehensive coverage of supply chain and value system issues.
- Numerous contemporary case studies.

How to use this book

This book is organized in five parts:

1 an introduction to international business and management;
2 international strategy;
3 human resource management;
4 managing information and technical resources; and
5 international business and trade (see figure).

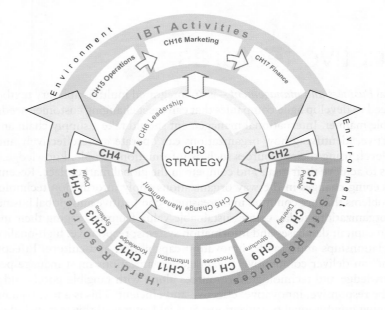

Part 1, an introduction to international business and management, identifies what constitutes an international organization, why they exist and how they are derived. Different types of international organization are considered alongside the activities they undertake. This forms a basis for explaining how resources are used effectively and efficiently, so that organizations can compete and attain their goals, thus performing in a desirable manner.

Part 2, has a strategic focus, introducing the factors which shape what the organization will do and where it will do it (purpose and scope). Part 2 is more about the need to be effective through an analysis of the environment and stakeholder needs and the wisdom of its leaders, managers and employees. This part discusses how international organizations compete and achieve their goals through efficient use of resources and the selection of markets in which to offer their products and services.

Parts 3 and 4 focus on efficiency and act as the building bricks used by strategists seeking to create sustainable competitive advantages, whereas in Part 2 the focus is on challenges associated with organizational behaviour and the use of human resources. Chapter 7 focuses on human capital as a source of sustainable competitive advantage and considers the problems associated with managing people worldwide. Chapter 8 considers diversity and managing multicultural groups of all sizes, understanding how to work with people who may seem different. In Chapter 9 we consider the need to organize human resources, to divide, allocate, coordinate and control activities so that the organizational goals can be achieved. Chapter 10 (business processes) continues to focus on work design, turning attention to the structuring of work tasks enabling efficiency gains and an ability to be responsive while attaining time-based advantages. Part 3 builds on earlier coverage of human resources as this part considers how information and knowledge resources can be managed. Manual or knowledge-based work activities can be enabled by ICT and the organization coordinated and controlled through the free flow of information resources. Furthermore, synergies and scale benefits may accrue for the international organization which takes learning from one part and utilizes it in another. These technologies, discussed in Chapters 13 and 14, unify an organization and enable it to operate across boundaries.

The final part of the book (Part 5), focuses on business, creating, marketing and selling organizational outputs. Operations management, marketing and sales are the internal customers and users of the resources discussed in Parts 3 and 4 of the book. They enable the organization to pool its resources and execute the activities that result in customer satisfaction and revenue generation. Finally, in Chapter 17 we consider the management of financial resources worldwide.

About the author

An international business practitioner, researcher and lecturer, Dr Phil Kelly has worked for a range of international and domestic companies in 20 different countries, advised Asia's highest-paid CEO, managed a successful international consultancy, has a doctorate in business administration from Manchester Business School and now teaches international business and management at the Liverpool Business School. Committed to teaching international business and management, Phil has conducted research into teaching multicultural MBA groups, has an MA in teaching and learning in higher education and in 2008 delivered a lecture on multicultural teaching at the higher education academy conference under the international theme. An experienced educator he has worked in three UK universities, taught in a variety of countries, and is an examiner for other universities, a leading UK institution and the GSM association. He has addressed and chaired over 30 international conferences and has authored and edited management reports for the *Financial Times*.

Acknowledgements

I would like to take this opportunity to thank all of those individuals whose insight, time and hard work have contributed to this book. I want to thank James Clark, the Development Editor, Cengage Learning, for his patience, support and management of the project. Thanks also to publishers Jennifer Pegg and Tom Rennie. Special thanks go to all of those in the formal review process; their feedback and suggestions for improvement helped shape the book. Numerous individuals contributed towards the thinking behind the book through conversations, conferences, seminars and writings. I have greatly benefited from the views and experiences of international business educators and practitioners from around the world. Our appreciation goes to many individuals including: staff from Liverpool Business School (LBS) based within the Faculty of Business & Law, Ian Lovegrove; Yvonne Moogan; Francis Muir; Lindsey Muir; Jack O'Farrell; Roger Pegum; Maureen Royce; and Lihong Zhang; Bill Kirwan of Dublin Business School; Jon Pike of the European College of Business and Management; Shuaib Masters, FTC Kaplan, Steve Fowler and staff at the Institute for Risk Management (IRM).

I would also like to thank the LJMU international business students and staff for trialling aspects of the text. I am grateful to a variety of companies and publishers for permission to reproduce copyright material and acknowledgements are given as and when we use such material throughout the text. Likewise I thank the various organizations providing case study materials.

Phil Kelly
July 2008

Review acknowledgements

The publishers and the author would like to thank the following reviewers for their constructive feedback at proposal and draft review stage:

Jens Graff	Umeå University
Irene Greaves	University of Central Lancashire
Carla Millar	University of Twente
David Pollard	Leeds Metropolitan University
Shameen Prashantham	University of Glasgow
Yuxin Xiao	University of Aberdeen

Walk through tour

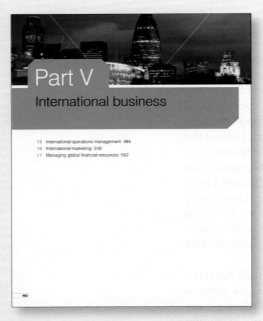

Part openers divide the chapter into clearly defined groups, arranged to help your understanding of the subject.

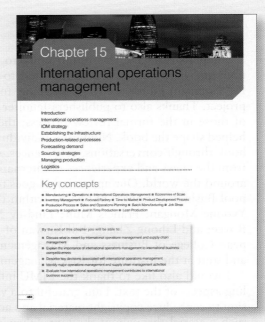

Chapter openers introduce key concepts within each chapter and set out learning objectives.

Active learning cases preface every chapter, providing practical insights into how international business issues affect real-life companies and industries.

Look back and look ahead arrows cross-reference different sub-topics throughout the book, showing how issues can cut across diverse areas of international business.

Stop & think boxes urge readers to critically assess their understanding of the topic under discussion at key points in every chapter.

Each chapter concludes with a **summary of key learning points,** a set of **review questions** and **references** to key texts and research.

About the website

Visit the *International Business and Management* companion website at **www.cengage.co.uk/kelly** or **www.cengage.com** to find valuable teaching and learning material including:

For students

- Student podcasts
- A glossary of terms
- Multiple choice questions to test your learning
- Links to relevant sites on the World Wide Web

For lecturers

- A secure, password-protected site with teaching material
- A downloadable version of the full Instructors' Manual including solutions to questions
- PowerPoint slides for chapters and figures, to be used in your lectures
- Additional case studies

List of figures

List of cases

Part I

International business and management

Part 1 contains a single chapter – An introduction to international business and management, which aims to describe the nature and composition of international organizations and examine why they exist. We start with a case study of one of Europe's largest international organizations (Nestlé). The case study highlights several important concepts such as the environment and globalization, strategy, corporate social responsibility, change and leadership – all of which are considered in detail throughout the second part of the book. In Chapter 1 we introduce the fundamental challenges faced by the international organization and discuss the major assumptions that guide resultant decisions and behaviour.

International organizations are considered as a bundle of resources, scattered around the globe and brought together by shared goals, common assumptions and the need to perform in a manner that assures such goals are met. In meeting goals international organizations must be both effective and efficient in the way resources are utilized. Perhaps the most important assumption governing business activities and the organization and utilization of resources concerns the way the organization interprets the worldwide marketplace. The international organization may adopt a convergence and integrated view – the world is a single market – or divergent view – the world is a collection of many (country) markets. Through the opening case study we examine Nestlé's market assumptions and then market assumptions of other organizations throughout the book. We will note implications for strategy, organizational structure, processes and activities and systems. For example, one problem faced by all international organizations concerns the use of information resources and technology. Should this be standardized and integrated on a worldwide scale or should each subsidiary or country operation manage their information resources and technology? Similar problems may be framed with regard to organizational culture, structure and other systems within the international organization. Assumptions about performance also impact upon organizational activities and the way resources are used. Whereas some organizations see their role solely in terms of maximizing shareholder wealth, others may take a wider perspective and will consider a broader set of stakeholders when making business decisions; they may strive to create shared value for society. We can understand a great deal about organizations from an understanding of their basic assumptions.

Later in Chapter 1 we distinguish between international business and international management and the associated strategic perspectives of market positioning and the resource-based view. Assumptions about how best to compete and win business – to choose where best to compete or what best to compete with – impact upon strategy, resource allocation and utilization decisions. Finally, we conclude this part of the book with arguments about what should be studied in the field of international business and management and discuss why this particular coverage is appropriate. Overall, Part 1 sets the scene for subsequent parts of the book.

Chapter 1

An introduction to international business and management

Introduction

The international organization

International organizational performance

What to study and why: international business and management

Key concepts

- International organization ■ Multinational companies ■ Value chain ■ Value system
- Internationalization ■ Centralization ■ Integration ■ Globalization
- Operational effectiveness ■ Strategy ■ International trade ■ Capabilities
- Resource-based view ■ Competences

By the end of this chapter you will be able to:

- Distinguish between types of international organizations

- Explain the difference between international business (IB) and international management (IM)

- Explain what is meant by globalization and its impact upon organizations worldwide

- Distinguish the generic methods used to deliver sustainable superior international organizational performance

- Describe the trade theories typically associated with the economic activities of international business

- Describe the resource-based view (RBV) and explain its relationship with productive activities and sustainable competitive advantage

Active learning case

Nestlé

Switzerland is home to six of the largest companies in Europe, one of which is Nestlé – ranked third in the FT2008 list. Nestlé is today the world's leading food company, with a 135-year history and operations in virtually every country in the world – their success is built, in part, on a recognition that their 'principal assets are not office buildings, factories, or even brands. Rather, it is the fact that we are a global organization comprised of many nationalities, religions, and ethnic backgrounds all working together in one single unifying corporate culture.'

In 2008, at the 141st Annual General Meeting of Nestlé – Chairman and CEO Peter Brabeck-Letmathe commented on the company's performance. Nestlé's sales topped the 107 billion Swiss francs mark in 2007, with more than 100 billion Swiss francs (approx. 60 billion Euros) of this total generated in food and beverages – 'Given the difficult environment in which this performance was achieved, it is nothing short of remarkable' he argued. Commenting on performance he noted that objectives had been met, sales had grown by almost 10 per cent and net profit by 16 per cent resulting in an increased dividend to shareholders. The chairman argued that, the results did not come about by chance. He attributed 'this enviable situation' to a clearly defined strategy, flexible structures and brand power, which have enabled Nestlé to maintain the trust and loyalty of consumers and the 'commitment and professionalism' of Nestlé employees. Nestlé has evolved into the kind of company whose growth and performance depend essentially on its capacity for leveraging their know-how; making the very best out of their huge intellectual assets and resources and ensuring that information is shared with partners and within their communities. Nestlé give value to the research process; Nestlé work increasingly with universities, other research institutions and third-party companies. They believe R&D is vital in order to maintain an innovation pipeline to keep them ahead of competitors. Aside from attention to strategic and structural issues, the company also introduced new technology that enabled them to manage their business in a more efficient manner, thus driving down costs and increasing operating margin. Many efficiency gains had been attained through Project GLOBE (Global Business Excellence) which presented the company with a means for managing both the complexity resulting from the diversity of their consumers and the operational efficiency the company strives to achieve.

GLOBE is a business re-engineering programme with the primary goals of implementing a series of Business Excellence initiatives, managing data on a global level and standardizing working practices through implementation of enterprise systems – standardizing how Nestlé operates around the world. The project, through structural changes at the global level, is attributed with transforming Nestlé – making it more flexible. Centralizing and unifying structures in purchasing, production and factory management has enabled the company to reduce production costs by benefiting from the scale and scope of activities. Rather than operate in a scattered

www.nestle.com

Nestlé Headquarters in Vevey, Switzerland

Nestlé, headquartered in Switzerland, was founded in 1866 by Henri Nestlé and is a nutrition, health and wellness company. Sales for 2007 were CHF 107.6 bn, with a net profit of CHF 10.6 bn. Nestlé employ around 276 050 people and have factories or operations in almost every country in the world. The company's priority is to bring the best and most relevant products to people, wherever they are, whatever their needs, throughout their lives.

Nestlé demonstrate a deep understanding of the local nature of nutrition, health and wellness; Nestlé know that there is no one single product for everyone – their products are tailored to suit particular tastes and habits. Today Nestlé are present in different markets within the following: coffee, water, other beverages, dairy and infant nutrition.

manner, country by country, Nestlé have opted to present themselves to suppliers, customers and commercial partners as a single entity, with the increased weight and authority this implies. Downstream, in customer interactions however, Nestlé are decentralized. 'We continue to believe that there is no such thing as a global consumer, and this is why we absolutely must take local preferences and habits into account. It is this respect of cultural and ethnic or religious differences that enables us to maintain the trust of consumers throughout the world. Our marketing and communication activities are carefully evaluated to ensure that they conform to the sensibilities of our local consumers. This is the key to our success.' In order for Nestlé to succeed as a company the Chairman believes good governance and the implemention of a long-term strategy are vital. He argues that sustainable success requires an extra step – 'the creation of long-term value is not conceivable without consideration of criteria such as economic viability, social equality and ecological sustainability'. In recent years Nestlé have been developing a concept they call the 'creation of shared value'. It is not enough to create value for shareholders only. In the interests of the development of the company as a whole, it is essential to involve consumers, employees, suppliers and communities in this process. For a business to be successful in the long term it has to create value, not only for its shareholders but also for society. Simply stated, in order to create value for their shareholders and company, Nestlé need to create value for the people in the countries where they are present.

The company has undergone transformational change over the preceding decade. To make a success of this change, Nestlé had to specify what they wanted to be as a company and how they would achieve this. Nestlé has evolved from food and beverage to a global leader in nutrition, health and wellness. In their mind, the transformation concerned a move from 'super-tanker' (classic multinational) to 'an agile fleet of businesses'. Looking to the future and long-term sustainable performance Nestlé emphasize the need for highly efficient, low-cost operations and operational efficiency in particular. Nestlé also discuss the need to differentiate themselves and to harness the skills and competencies of their people. They perceive a need to reduce working capital, manage inventories, simplify structure and leverage scale and skill. Furthermore, Nestlé recognize a need to develop and deploy a host of capabilities – to have people equipped with the tools necessary for them to perform and execute the business strategy. In particular the company recognizes a need to create an ability to anticipate change and act fast 'with good information'. To help sustain future performance Nestlé believes it has four main competitive advantages: their brands and broad product portfolio, a leading R&D capability (that focuses on delivering benefits to consumers), geographic presence (spread, infrastructure and local understanding) and people (culture, values and attitude). Moving forward they see a need to deliver the strategy and build upon their competitive advantage.

www.nestle.com

Websites and resources:
Dullforce (2008), FT Global 500 method and background, www.ft.com accessed 28 June 2008
http://www.nestle.com/SharedValueCSR/People/Introduction/Introduction.htm accessed 28 June 2008
Chairman's address by Mr Brabeck-Letmathe, at the Nestlé SA Annual General Meeting Lausanne, Switzerland, April 10, 2008 presented on the Nestle website, www.nestle.com/MediaCenter/ accessed 28 June 2008
http://www.nestle.com/SlideShows/20080226_LDN/nestle_final.html accessed 28 June 2008

A range of Nestlé products

Introduction

We start this chapter and the book with a recognition that international business is vast and a significant source of opportunity (and threat) for many organizations. The statistics are abundant but we will try to limit them here to just a few. In any event, as soon as attempts to collate the statistics are complete, the numbers seem to change drastically by the next count. Consequently, a simple appreciation of the key measures will suffice and should convince the reader that the knowledge contained within this textbook is important and relevant to the contemporary manager. Many now see the world as a single and growing market (now worth approximately $50 trillion per year). Not only have we witnessed growth in world GDP and the world population (from approximately 5 to almost 7 billion in the past 20 years – with a total labour force of almost half this figure) but we have also witnessed growth in international trade and investment and resource flows of many types between countries (see the UNCTAD Handbook of Statistics which provides essential data for analyzing world trade, investment, international financial flows and development). In an era when half of the world's biggest economic entities are multinational corporations (that is to say many of our larger international organizations now produce more than some countries); where labour is increasingly mobile across borders and ICT enables companies to overcome barriers in time, distance and language the contemporary manager simply cannot afford to remain parochial, ethnocentric, or not in constant pursuit of competitive advantage. To do so, is to be disadvantaged.

Gross domestic product (GDP) the total value of all goods and services produced by a country in one year

Ethnocentric a belief that home nationals are superior

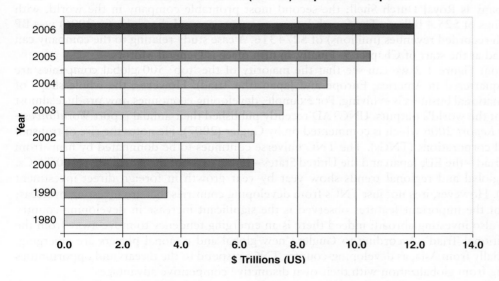

International Trade (World) Exports & Imports

Figure 1-1

Growth of international trade (Source: UNCTAD 2008)]

There has been significant growth (recently in excess of 10 per cent per year) in international trade over the past three decades, see Figure 1-1. Cross-border trade now amounts to over $10 trillion. However, it is not just goods and services that flow between countries, so too do finances, people, technology, knowledge and other resources. Consumers and investors not only buy and sell across country boundaries but also invest in other countries (see foreign direct investment (FDI) – over $1 trillion is invested overseas each year). Organizations undertake FDI for a variety of reasons such as setting up offices, manufacturing, operations and distribution facilities. Additionally, in some cases, trade takes place using electronic channels (see e-business/commerce). Online shopping is now valued in the $trillions (Forrester Research estimated worldwide net commerce of $6.8 trillion in 2004); not surprising when we consider there to be around 1 billion Internet users worldwide.

At this point, we might ask why international business has grown so much over the past 10–20 years. There are many explanations for the growth of international business. The (social, political and economic) pursuit of 'free trade' has also eroded barriers and borders. This has been further enabled through the wide scale adoption of ('open') information and communication technologies (ICT) which enable trade, communication and collaboration – eroding barriers in time, space and language and integrating financial, political and legal systems. Liberalization has not only resulted in increased mobility of people as workers and migrants but also in the movement of capital, goods and services. Consumers want choice, quality and low-cost products sourced from around the world. E-commerce and the MNC now bring the world to the doorsteps of businesses and consumers everywhere. With the phenomenal growth of e-commerce, anyone can be open for business on an international level 24 hours a day, no matter where the business is physically located. In other words, one location can serve the business needs over the entire globe.

Transnational corporation (TNC) an enterprise that controls assets of other entities in economies other than its home economy, usually by owning a certain equity capital stake. UNCTAD compiles key data on TNCs

Companies may now not only import and export more easily but can also establish their operations overseas. The production of goods and services by transnational corporations (TNCs) outside their home countries grew more rapidly in 2006 than in the previous year (UNCTAD 2007c). The sales, value added and exports of some 78 000 TNCs and their 780 000 foreign affiliates are estimated to have increased by more than 10 per cent. They also accounted for the equivalent of 10 per cent of world GDP and one-third of world exports. Of the top 100 TNCs, 58 belonged to six industries: motor vehicles (11), petroleum (10), electrical and electronic equipment (10), pharmaceuticals (9), telecommunications (9), and electricity, gas and water services (9). The largest company in the world, Wal-Mart Stores, employs 1.9 million people worldwide and had revenues (millions) of $351 139 in 2006. Though not the biggest in 2006, the oil giant Exxon Mobil remained the most profitable company in the world, with $39.5 billion in earnings. Europe's biggest company is Royal Dutch Shell; the second most profitable company in the world, with earnings of $25.4 billion. The fourth largest company around the globe (in 2006) was BP which recorded revenues (millions) of $274 316. A case study relating to the company can be read at the start of Chapter 9. Finally, in fifth place is General Motors.

From Figure 1-2 we can see that the majority of the 'top' 500 global companies are headquartered in America, Europe and Japan (the Triad). However, the whole shape of international business is evolving. For example, developing economies now produce almost half of the world's outputs. UNCTAD recently published their annual report *World Investment Report 2006* which is commented on by Gugler (2007). He notes the rise of transnational corporations (TNCs). The TNC universe continues to be dominated by firms from the Triad – the EU, Japan and the United States – home to 85 of the world's top 100 TNCs. The global and regional trends show year by year growth in foreign direct investment (FDI). However, it is not just TNCs from developing countries that are investing overseas; one of the important features observed is the significant increase in developing-country firms also investing abroad; indeed there is an emerging tendency to move away from the 'traditional Triad'. According to Gugler, 'new global and regional players are emerging, especially from Asia, as developing-country TNCs respond to the threats and opportunities arising from globalization with their own distinctive competitive advantages'.

Their outward expansion is driven by various factors. *Market-oriented factors* push developing-country TNCs out of their home countries or pull them into host countries and rising costs of production in the home economy – especially labour costs – are a particular concern for TNCs from East and South-East Asian countries, such as Malaysia, the Republic of Korea and Singapore. There are also competitive pressures on developing-country firms (e.g. from low-cost producers), pushing them to expand overseas and in some cases, government policies in both the home and host countries influence decisions on outward FDI. For example, Chinese TNCs regard their government's policies as an important push factor in their internationalization. According to the report, in addition to these factors, two other major developments drive developing-country TNCs abroad. The first is the rapid growth of many large developing countries such as China and India. The second is a behavioural change among TNCs, which increasingly realize they are operating in a global economy, not a domestic one, forcing them to adopt an international vision.

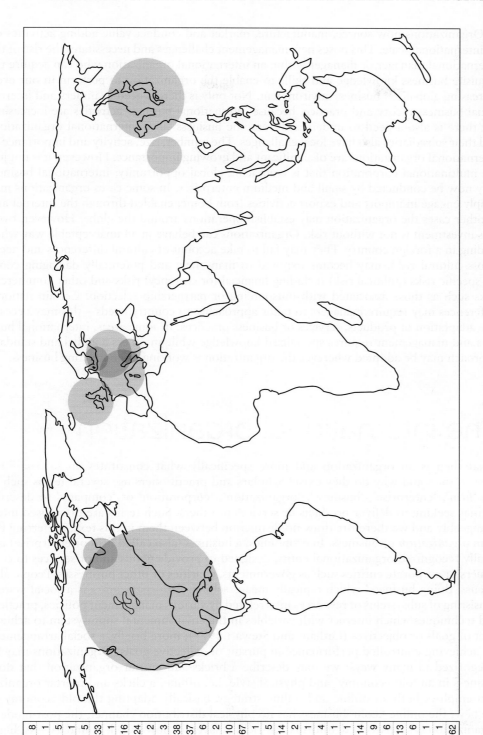

Australia	8
Austria	1
Belgium	5
Belgium/Netherland	1
Brazil	5
Britain	33
Britain/Netherlands	1
Canada	16
China	24
Denmark	2
Finland	3
France	38
Germany	37
India	6
Ireland	2
Italy	10
Japan	67
Malaysia	1
Mexico	5
The Netherlands	14
Norway	2
Poland	1
Russia	4
Saudi Arabia	1
Singapore	1
South Korea	14
Spain	9
Sweden	6
Switzerland	13
Taiwan	6
Thailand	1
Turkey	1
United States	162

Figure 1-2

Location of global 500 companies (Adapted from Fortune Global 500 data)

Organizations now source, manufacture, market and conduct value adding activities on an international scale. This poses new management challenges and necessitates the rise of the international manager or manager within an international organization who can acquire the requisite business knowledge and skills to enable the organization to perform in our ever-increasing globalized business environment. Not only is there a need to understand international business theory and practice, because international business activities are increasing, but there is also a need to understand domestic business since international organizations and their subsidiaries also have local challenges. The number, size, activity and importance of international organizations are of significant and growing importance. However, it is not just the multinational corporation that is embracing global opportunity; international business may now be conducted by small and medium enterprises. In some cases organizations may simply engage in import and export activities from home, enabled through the Internet and in other cases the organization may establish operations around the globe. However, overseas investment is not without risk. Organizations can behave in an unacceptable way when trading in a foreign country. They may fail to take account of cultural differences and needs (cross-cultural risk), may become exposed to many new and potentially damaging country specific risks (political risk) including financial (or currency) risks and other commercial risks such as those associated with outsourcing or partnership selection. Certain national differences may require managers to tailor approaches to country needs – this may necessitate adaptation of products, services or business practices. In some areas, international business and management requires specialized knowledge while in others a global and standard approach may be adopted wherever the organization is working or conducting business.

The international organization

International organization any organization that engages in international trade, investment or offers products or services outside their home country

What then is an organization and more specifically what constitutes an international organization and why do they exist? Scholars and practitioners use several terms such as the 'firm', 'enterprise', 'business', 'organization', 'corporation' or 'company' to describe entities seeking to deliver products or services to others. Such terms are often used interchangeably and we therefore draw no distinction between them in this text, preferring the term *organization* or business. In economics, a business (also called firm or enterprise) is a legally recognized organizational entity, designed to provide goods and/or services to consumers or corporate entities such as governments, charities or other businesses. People also discuss 'doing business' which typically means selling. An organization is a social system consisting of subsystems of resources interrelated by various management policies, practices and techniques which interact with variables in the environmental suprasystem to achieve a set of goals or objectives (Luthans and Stewart 1977); more briefly, a social arrangement for achieving controlled performance in pursuit of collective goals. Organizations may be categorized in many ways: we may describe a bricks-and-mortar organization that does business in an 'old-economy' and physical style, i.e. offline; a clicks-and-mortar organization employs both an offline and online strategy, basically adapting the old economy to the new; the online '.com' business has no physical distribution channel; the post-modern organization is a networked, information-rich, delayered, downsized, boundary-less, high-commitment organization employing highly skilled, well-paid, autonomous knowledge workers; and finally, the virtual organization is an organization which uses information and communications technology to allow it to operate without clearly defined physical boundaries between different functions, it provides customized services by outsourcing production and other functions to third parties (Chaffey 2007).

Organization a social arrangement for achieving controlled performance in pursuit of collective goals

Organizational studies, organizational behaviour, and organizational theory are related terms for the academic study of organizations, examining them using the methods of economics, sociology, political science, anthropology, communication studies, and psychology. The study of the structure, functioning and performance of organizations and the behaviour of groups and individuals within them is captured under the banner of 'organization theory' (Pugh 1997) or organizational behaviour (OB) – (Huczynski and

Organizational behaviour the study of the structure, functioning and performance of organizations, and the behaviour of groups and individuals within them

Buchanan 2007). In discussing organizations, scholars and practitioners discuss 'organizational capability' (competence), an organization's capacity to deploy resources for a desired end result. Organizations may be small, medium or large in size. A small to medium-sized enterprise (SME) may be defined in terms of number of employees, turnover or size of the balance sheet. The European Commission revised its definition of an SME in 2003. The following enterprise categories are identified by headcount and turnover:

Size	Headcount	Turnover
Micro	<10	< 2 million
Small	<50	< 10 million
Medium	<250	< 50 million

Statistics for 2006 published by the Department of Trade and Industry (DTI) Small Business Service (SBS) Statistics Unit show that out of 4.5 million businesses in the UK, 99.3 per cent were small firms with fewer than 50 employees.

From our discussions above, it is clear that there are many types of organization, which, as a result, may be classified in many ways. One of the most common focuses on the primary profit-generating *activities* of a business: *agriculture and mining* businesses are concerned with the production of raw material, *manufacturers* produce products, *service businesses* offer intangible goods or services, *retailers and distributors* act as intermediaries ('middle-men') in getting goods produced by manufacturers to the intended consumer, *financial* businesses include banks and other companies that generate profit through investment and management of capital, *information* businesses generate profits primarily from the resale of intellectual property, *utilities* produce public services, *real estate* businesses generate profit from the selling, renting, and development of properties and *transportation* businesses deliver goods and individuals from location to location. We may also classify organizations according to where they do business, at home (domestic) or overseas (international). Some international organizations are based in their home country and export or import goods to and from other countries while other companies locate operations in other countries. Multinational companies are organizations that behave in their foreign markets as if they were local companies. Some scholars identify with the 'Multinational enterprise' (MNEs) – a company headquartered in one country but having operations or subsidiaries in other countries.

A further way of categorizing and understanding international organizations is based on an analysis of how the organization adds value. Value is essentially what something is worth, the amount customers are willing to pay for a product or service. Added-value is the difference between the amount customers are willing to pay for a product minus the costs of inputs and transformational activities used to create that product or service (offering). There are three main factors that influence the value equation: input costs (supply-side), transformation costs and the amount the buyer is willing to pay for products or services on the demand side (based on perceived product benefits) relative to competing products. Porter (1985) identified the value chain as a means of analyzing an organization's strategically-relevant activities. Value chain analysis helps the organization identify core competencies and distinguish those activities driving competitive advantage. The chain, see Figure 1-3, consists of five primary activities and four support activities. The nine activity groups are:

Primary activities:

1 Inbound logistics: materials handling, warehousing, inventory control, transportation.
2 Operations: machine operating, assembly, packaging, testing and maintenance.
3 Outbound logistics: order processing, warehousing, transportation and distribution.
4 Marketing and sales: advertising, promotion, selling, pricing, channel management.
5 Service: installation, servicing, spare part management.

Multinational company a company headquartered in one country but having operations or subsidiaries in other countries

Value chain a model for analysis of how supply chain activities can add value to products and services delivered to the customer and thus add a margin of value to the organization

Figure 1-3

Value chain

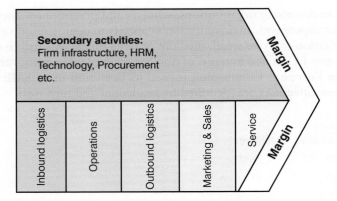

Support activities:

6 Firm infrastructure: general management, planning, finance, legal, investor relations.

7 Human resource management: recruitment, education, promotion, reward systems.

8 Technology development: research and development, IT, product and process development.

9 Procurement: purchasing raw materials, lease properties, supplier contract negotiations.

A value chain is a chain of activities. Products pass through all primary activities of the chain in order and at each activity the product gains some value. The chain of activities gives the products more added value than the sum of added values of all activities. Thus the value chain presents a tool to decompose organizations into their parts and then focus attention on these decomposed activities. The idea of the value chain is based on the process view of organizations (discussed further in Chapter 10), the idea of seeing a manufacturing (or service) organization as a system, made up of subsystems each with inputs, transformation processes and outputs (discussed further in Chapter 5).

The value chain concept has been extended beyond individual organizations. An organization's value chain is part of a larger system including the value chains of upstream suppliers and downstream channels and customers. Porter calls this series of value chains the **value system**, shown conceptually in Figure 1-4. Other scholars may refer to this as a value network or supply chain. Linkages exist not only in a firm's value chain, but also between value chains.

Value system the supply chain within which an organization's value chain is located, i.e. includes producers, suppliers, distributors, and buyers

→ Supplier Value Chain → Firm Value Chain → Channel Value Chain → Buyer Value Chain

Figure 1-4

Value system

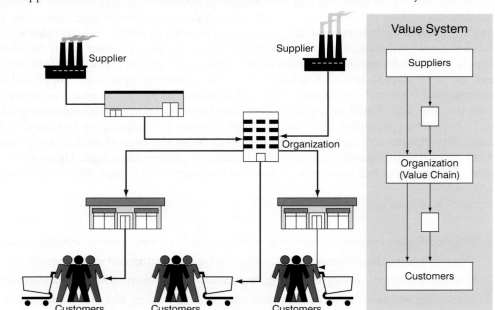

As noted thus far, one way an organization can attain its profit goal is through creating offerings that are of value to customers. This presents two possible strategies for business. The organization can increase value-add by reducing its costs and by differentiating its products so that customers are willing to pay a premium price for them. Consequently, the manager may seek to identify opportunities to raise willingness to pay and to reduce input costs. In the case of cost leadership, transformational activities will be analyzed with a view to making them more efficient and in the case of differentiation the organization will analyze activities in search of opportunity to do things differently that might increase willingness to pay. In general, a company should search through its organization and eliminate activities that generate costs without creating commensurate willingness to pay. Performing activities that increase the value of goods or services to consumers is termed value creation. There are other ways to add value or make profit without the need for transformational activities; the simple act of buying in one place or time and selling in another for example. Arbitrage is about profit from a price discrepancy. Value chain analysis is a well known strategic concept which enables organizations to establish how value is being added within a business. The whole enterprise is 'broken down' into key 'support' and 'primary' activities which are then compared with competitive 'benchmarks' representing best practice. Value chain analysis describes the activities within and around an organization, and relates them to an analysis of the competitive strength of the organization. Therefore, it evaluates which value each particular activity adds to the organization's products or services. Porter argues that the ability to perform particular activities and to manage the linkages between these activities is a source of competitive advantage; linkages are crucial for corporate success. The linkages are flows of information, goods and services, as well as systems and processes for adjusting activities.

Value creation performing activities that increase the value of goods or services to consumers

Example

The Coca-Cola Company value chain and system

Suppliers include those business partners who supply their system with materials including ingredients, packaging, and machinery, as well as goods and services. Inbound, the company receives ingredients and packaging and in some cases the ingredient may come from a concentrate plant. The ingredients are mixed in the manufacturing process and may be bottled (bottling plant) or produced in tins. Goods are stored in warehouses as a part of the outbound logistics process and later transported to customers (retail outlets and restaurants) or vending machines and coolers. From here they are made available to consumers. Goods and 'outlets' are branded for marketing purposes.

Customers include large, international chains of retailers and restaurants, as well as small, independent businesses.

© Luke Peters / Alamy

Thus far we have defined what is meant by the term organization and considered the different types of organization, focusing on the international and multinational organization. We have also considered how companies organize their activities in order to add value. We might now consider why organizations exist in the first place – *organizational purpose*. The theory of the firm consists of a number of economic theories which describe the nature of the firm (company or corporation), including its existence, its behaviour and its relationship with the market. The traditional 'theory of the firm' assumes that profit maximization is the goal of the commercial organization. More recent analyses suggest that sales maximization or market share, combined with satisfactory profits, may be the main purpose of large industrial corporations. Furthermore, while traditional views recognized only the shareholder as the focus of organizational goals, more recently, organizations have considered society as a key stakeholder.

Organizations exist in a wider environment, explored in the next chapter, where they typically compete with other organizations for revenues. If the costs of doing business are less than the amount customers are willing to pay for the organization's goods and services the organization makes profit which may be retained or distributed to shareholders. Companies typically arrange themselves to achieve their purpose (see Chapter 9). Common functions include: accounting, human resources, marketing and sales, operations and production, customer service, procurement, strategic sourcing, purchasing, research and development (R&D), information systems and technology, communications/public relations, administration and internal audit; the way that they utilize their resources and the markets within which they select to operate may give such organizations a competitive advantage over rivals, resulting in revenue. Among the performance measurements for organizations is the triple bottom line.

Triple bottom line

Look forward
See chapter 4

The triple bottom line (or 'TBL', '3BL', or 'people, planet, profit') captures an extended range of values and criteria for measuring organizational success; economic, environmental and social. The concept of TBL demands that a company's responsibility is to 'stakeholders' rather than shareholders. In this case, stakeholders refers to anyone who is influenced, either directly or indirectly, by the actions of the organization. People (human capital) pertains to fair and beneficial business practices toward labour and the community and region in which a corporation conducts its business; planet (natural capital) refers to sustainable environmental practices and profit (not limited to the internal profit made by a company or organization) is the bottom line shared by all commerce – the economic benefit enjoyed by the host society.

The triple bottom line idea proposes that an organization's licence to operate in society comes not just from satisfying stakeholders through improved profits (the economic bottom line), but by also improving its environmental and social performance. As such, it encompasses environmental responsibility, social awareness and economic profitability. We revisit the concept of TBL in Chapter 4, behaving responsibly. Thus far we have identified what an international organization is and why it exists. In the next section we consider *how* the international organization comes into existence.

Internationalization

A company may offer its goods and services solely in its domestic market or wider in a global market. Clearly there is more opportunity associated with the latter but not all organizations become multinational. Multinationals appear to be concentrated in industries characterized by high ratio of R&D relative to sales, tend to have high values of intangible assets, are often associated with new or technologically-advanced and differentiated products and are often relatively old, large and more established organizations within their sector. The domestic organization, headquartered at home, must decide whether or not to become a multinational organization and if not, will decide whether or not to export its goods and services (from production facilities at home). According to Dunning (1977) cited in Brakeman *et al.* (2006: 91) three conditions need to be satisfied in order for a firm to become a multinational, summarized in the OLI acronym:

OWNERSHIP ADVANTAGE – derived from organization specific capabilities, competences or resources that give a competitive edge over rivals (for example knowledge capital can be transported at low cost to foreign production facilities). If an organization owns a resource that can generate revenue in another country then it makes sense to do so providing there are no extraordinary costs associated;

LOCATION ADVANTAGE – is associated with specific countries; low-skilled production processes may be fragmented and based in low wage countries for example. This advantage recognizes that scarce resources are not in existence everywhere and may only be found in certain countries, thus accessing them may provide an advantage over other countries; and

INTERNATIONALIZATION ADVANTAGE makes it more profitable for an organization to undertake foreign production itself, rather than licensing it to a foreign organization.

In the previous paragraph we introduced arguments as to why an organization might seek to establish operations overseas but we have not yet explained how the international organization comes into existence. Some organizations are 'born global', others evolve over time. Vernon (1966) presented a stage model to explain this. Describing a life cycle model of internationalization, in the first stage, new products are initially developed for sale in the domestic market. In the second stage, exports start to develop to foreign markets where consumers have the same preferences and incomes as at home. In the third stage, as the foreign markets start to grow, the firm might establish a subsidiary abroad, to produce closer to the destination markets, implying that exports to the markets will fall and finally, in the fourth stage, as the foreign subsidiaries master the production process they might begin to export their products back to the initial home market, creating re-import of the same product. Since the introduction of Vernon's model a number of other scholars have presented explanations as to how organizations internationalize. A related issue is *foreign entry modes*. Organizations may enter foreign countries and markets in a variety of ways. The multinational must choose between non-equity (exporting, licensing or franchising) and equity (greenfield investments, acquisitions or alliances) modes of entry. They must determine the desired level of ownership in the case of equity entry, choosing between wholly or partially owned and must analyze the advantages and disadvantages of buying an existing foreign entity or establishing a foreign operation from scratch. A more detailed explanation is given in Chapter 2.

Look forward
See chapter 2

Internationalization the gradual process of taking organizational activities into other countries

Subsidiary a company for which a majority of the voting stock is owned by another company, usually referred to as the parent company – a wholly or partially owned company that is part of a large corporation. A foreign subsidiary is a separately incorporated entity under the host country's law. A subsidiary's financial results are carried on the parent company's books

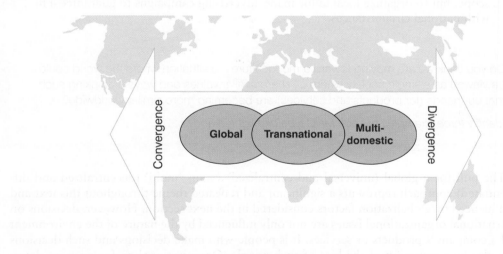

Figure 1-5
Convergence or divergence?

So far we have discussed the idea of internationalization, noting that not all organizations become multinational. However, we should not treat 'multinational' as a simple term. Multinationals are not always the same. The most popular classification of multinationals in the international business literature is probably Bartlett and Ghoshal's technology of strategic postures: global, multidomestic and transnational, see Figure 1-5. Multinationals may be:

Global organizations which promote a convergence of consumer's preferences and strive to maximize standardization of production, which makes centralization and integration profitable. They benefit from home country specific advantages and export these abroad by creating *replicas* of the parent company. Strategic decisions

Global organization an organization which trades internationally as if the world were a single and boundaryless entity

Centralization consolidation of power under central control

Integration the extent to which units in an organization are linked together, and their respective degree of independence

on marketing and production tunnel down to the subsidiaries, so that the latter have little discretion to adapt to local circumstances. Global companies possess firm-specific advantages, mostly characterized by home country specificities that do not need to be complemented by the exploration of the host country advantages. These firm specific advantages are therefore not bound to a particular host location and artificially transferable to foreign locations, thus overcoming any natural or unnatural market imperfections in foreign markets. In short, the global MNC sees the world as a single market with little need to do things differently wherever it operates. The focus is on integration as opposed to differentiation (see Lawrence and Lorsch 1967).

Multidomestic organization an organization that trades internationally as if the world were a collection of many different (country) entities

Multidomestic organizations, by contrast, develop strategies for national responsiveness. Due to significant competitive differences between countries, the multidomestic strategy is determined by cultural, political and social national characteristics. The primary objective is the adapting of marketing and production strategies to specific local customer needs and government requirements. Products and policies conform to different local demands and the investor activities are usually tied to the buyer's location, which create incentives for the development of competitive advantages that are bound to a particular location. Responsiveness to different national markets requires the relation of a local country specific knowledge and the latter's efficient integration into local business networks. Whereas the global MNC is logically a single entity, the multidomestic is a collection of 'companies' each focused on the specific needs of the country within which they operate.

Transnational enterprises an international organization that standardizes certain aspects of its activities and output while adapting other aspects to local differences

Transnational enterprises (TNE) operate a balanced combination of the multidomestic and global strategies. Although activities and resources may differ from country to country (decentralization), particular activities are coordinated and executed globally (centralization). For example, a transnational enterprise might decide to carry out research and development centrally to make economies of scale and scope, but to organize local tailor-made advertising campaigns to guarantee a fit with national circumstances.

STOP & THINK

Do you think we are moving toward a monoculture – a situation where the world could be viewed as a single society where all share similar values and ways of thinking such that our needs (for products and services) are becoming more similar worldwide?

Identify three examples of each MNC type highlighted above.

The pull for a global (universal and centralized) versus 'multi' (decentralized and differentiated) approach represents a significant and repeated theme throughout this text and is influenced by globalization factors considered in the next section. However, decisions on international organizational issues are not only influenced by the nature of the environment and a company's products or services. It is people who make decisions and such decisions may also be a reflection of the bias of such people. Organizational preferences are determined by the nature of the offerings, cost and the preferences of key decision – makers in the company. For example Perlmutter (1969:11) identifies 'Three primary attitudes among international executives toward building a multinational enterprise':

- ethnocentric (home country) attitude (home nationals are superior);
- polycentric (host country) host country cultures are different; and
- geocentric (world oriented), superiority is not equated with nationality.

Perlmutter's three attitudes represent a further key theme running through this text. Such attitudes impact upon strategic decision-making, human resource management (HRM), organizational structure and enterprise system strategies, discussed later. Thus far we have identified types of international organization and how and why organizations internationalize. One reason for internationalization is globalization and in the next section we consider the impact of globalization on organizations.

Globalization

More flexible international trade; one aspect of globalization

Globalization, the opposite of protectionism (policies reflecting the belief that domestic manufacturers and workers need to be safeguarded from foreign competition), refers to the growing interdependency between nations and organizations through international trade and factor mobility (integration). A variety of meanings have been attached to the concept. For some it is the extension of operations' supply chain to cover the whole world (Slack, Chambers, and Johnston 2007); a trend away from distinct national economic units and towards one huge global market (Hill 2006); the increase of international trading and shared social and cultural values (Chaffey 2007) and the intensification of worldwide social and business relationships which link distant localities in such a way that local happenings are shaped by distant events, and vice versa (Huczynski and Buchanan 2007). Hill (2006) discusses the globalization of markets, 'moving away from an economic system in which national markets are distinct entities, isolated by trade barriers and barriers of distance, time, and culture, and towards a system in which national markets are merging into one global market'. He also discusses the globalization of production, a trend by individual firms to disperse parts of their productive processes to different locations around the globe, thus taking advantage of differences in cost and quality of factors of production.

Globalization growth and integration to a global or worldwide scale

Globalization and the globalization process mean different things to different people. Many have discussed the concept of cultural globalization, i.e. whether there is a global culture or set of universal cultural variables; economic globalization considers the increased interdependence of national economies and the trend towards greater integration of goods, labour and capital markets; geographical globalization refers to the idea of compressed time and space as a result of reduced travel times between locations and the rapid (electronic) exchange of information. Knowledge and production previously confined to certain geographical areas may now cross borders and be made available because of the rapid transfer of information and transport innovations. Consequently some argue that location no longer matters. Despite this, some argue that geography is becoming more, not less, important. Institutional globalization is typified through organizations such as the international Monetary Fund (IMF), World Bank and World Trade Organization (WTO) which seek to make markets more flexible and demolish international barriers to trade.

Scholars also discuss the concept of political globalization and the relationship between the power of markets and multinational organizations versus the nation state. As a result of globalization, the international organization faces the global–local dilemma. This relates to the extent to which products and services may be standardized across national boundaries or need to be adapted to meet the requirements of specific national markets; we briefly touched upon this issue as a central theme in the previous section.

Economic globalization has significantly increased the competitive pressure on enterprises in many sectors. This comes as a result of, among other factors, the emergence of new, lower-cost producers, fast-changing demand patterns, increased market fragmentation and shortened product life cycles. In such an environment, innovation (either in terms of business processes or of final products and services) becomes crucial for the long-term competitiveness and survival of enterprises. Many scholars and practitioners comment on the use of information and knowledge to produce economic benefits and enable the organization to meet its goals. Often, such discussions go hand-in-hand with discussion on the role of ICT and talented human resources in organizations. However, it should be noted that ICT typically represents a tangible and easily imitated resource while knowledge is intangible and therefore more difficult to imitate. Furthermore, knowledge has a related and interconnected human capital aspect to it. Many describe today's global economy as one in transition to a 'knowledge economy', as an extension of the 'information society', where knowledge resources such as know-how, expertise, and intellectual property are

Innovation development of new products, processes, organizations, management practices, and strategies

more critical than other economic resources such as land and natural resources. Consequently, knowledge management is a critical activity in the international organization.

The United Nations Conference on Trade and Development (2007) produced the Information Economy Report 2007–2008. Suggesting the world economy is increasingly driven by technological innovations they argue ICTs affect productivity and growth; ICT can be applied in, for example, marketing or communication, supply chain management, knowledge management, recombining existing technologies and product development. If organizations are to seize the opportunities and address emerging global challenges, they will have to harness those innovations and the associated knowledge. Among other things, ICT enables knowledge creation and diffusion, supporting enterprise competitiveness – enabling faster cross-border knowledge dissemination. It is easy, almost trivial, to explain the many ways in which adopting ICTs can improve business performance, particularly by allowing companies to operate differently and at lower costs, and also to bring new products to the market. ICT enables new ways of working at the international level – providing opportunity to support value chain fragmentation. New services have been generated by ICT in the form of e-commerce that lead to greater economic efficiency. The use of ICT for business processes can also contribute to income generation and increased labour productivity. ICT can reduce the cost of transactions and increase market access.

As the number of broadband subscribers continues to grow rapidly worldwide and the number of employees using the Internet in their daily work continues to grow, the benefits of having an intranet or extranet, which are often the first steps towards the automated integration of business processes also grows. Whereas in the past innovation revolved around concepts of mass production, economies of scale and corporate-dominated research and development, in the last three decades of the twentieth century this was replaced, to a large extent, by an emphasis on economies of scope, exploiting the benefits of interconnected flexible production facilities, and greater flexibility and decentralization of research and development. UNCTAD (2007) consider the role played by information and communication technologies (ICTs), which are generally considered to have been the prime mover in the powerful wave of innovation transforming the global economy over the last quarter of the 20th century.

International organization performance

In the previous section we focused on what an international organization *is* and to some extent considered *why* they exist and how international organizations come into existence. The purpose and goals (to be explored further in Chapter 3) of such organizations varies dependent upon whether they are established to make profit for their owners or to deliver public or charitable services. A key aim of this book is to provide the reader with knowledge that may be used in order to help the international organization within which they work to perform well and attain goals. Performance relates to organizational purpose (mission); reflects achievements relative to the resources used by the organization (how well the organization manages its resources); and must be considered within the environment in which the organization does its work (adaptability). Organizational performance must integrate the concepts of 'effectiveness' and 'efficiency'. That is, the international organization must be able to meet its goals (effectiveness) and to do so with an acceptable outlay of resources (efficiency). The organization must be able to develop and implement strategies which will ensure performance over extended periods of time. In summary, the performance of international organizations can be considered in three broad areas: performance in activities which support the mission (effectiveness), performance in relation to the resources available (efficiency), and performance in relation to long-term viability or sustainability (ongoing relevance). However, it is worth remembering that organizational performance is a broad construct and may include productivity (quantity and effort), employee satisfaction (the extent to which workers are satisfied with their work and conditions), client or customer satisfaction and quality dimensions.

The international organization may be considered a success when the objectives or goals of the organization and its evaluators are fulfilled. One generic objective for the international organization is the pursuit of sustainable superior performance; superior means greater than the performance of comparable organizations, such as competitors and sustainable means to carry on such superior performance over a long period. There are many ways by which the international organization can achieve superior performance such as through the possession of sustainable competitive advantages. The main task for managers would then be to find strategies to create, renew, and maintain competitive advantages. For this reason, the literature has mainly focused on competitive advantage as the *dependent* variable for organizational performance and we discuss this in more detail later. Superior performance is often conceived in terms of abnormal profits and is about the organization outperforming its industry. At any moment in time, the international organization may be described in one of four possible states of performance:

■ superior performance;
■ eroding superior performance;
■ improving inferior performance; and
■ worsening inferior performance.

Operational effectiveness and strategy are both essential to superior performance but they work in very different ways (Porter 1996). A company can outperform rivals in the long run, only if it can establish a difference that it can then preserve. It must deliver greater value to customers or create comparable value at a lower cost, or do both. Delivering greater value allows a company to charge higher prices and greater efficiency results in lower costs. Ultimately, all differences between companies in cost or price derive from the hundreds of activities required to create, produce, sell, and deliver their products or services (refer back to the value chain). Cost is incurred by performing activities, and cost advantage arises from performing particular activities more efficiently than competitors. Similarly, differentiation arises from both the choice of activities and how they are performed. Activities, then, are the basic units of competitive advantage, argues Porter (1996). Overall advantage or disadvantage results from all a company's activities. Decomposing the organization into its core activities and processes is also useful when analyzing the international organization. Decisions can then be made about where such activities will take place and who and what resources will be required to complete the activity.

Operational effectiveness (and efficiency) is about performing similar activities better (through operational improvements) than rivals perform them. Improvements can be made in productivity, quality, or speed (see e.g. total quality management (TQM), continuous improvement, benchmarking, time-based competition, outsourcing, partnering, reengineering and change management). Such initiatives change *how* international organizations perform activities in order to eliminate inefficiencies, improve customer satisfaction and achieve best practice. Some companies are able to get more out of their resources than others because they eliminate wasted effort, employ more advanced technology, motivate employees better, or have greater insight into managing particular activities or sets of activities.

Operational effectiveness refers to any number of practices that allow a company to better utilize its resources, resulting in differences in profitability among competitors because relative cost positions and levels of differentiation are directly affected. However, few companies have competed successfully on the basis of operational effectiveness over an extended period. One important reason for this is the speedy dissemination of best practices. Competitors can quickly *imitate* management techniques, new technologies, input improvements, and superior ways of meeting customers' needs. The most generic solutions – those that can be used in multiple settings – diffuse most rapidly. The more benchmarking companies do, the more they look alike. The more that rivals outsource activities to, often the same or similar

Operational effectiveness performing similar activities better than rivals perform them

companies, the more generic those activities become. When rivals invest in the same technologies or best practices, the resulting major productivity gains are captured by customers and equipment suppliers, not retained in superior profitability. As rivals imitate one another's improvements in quality, cycle times, or supplier partnerships, strategies converge to the point where no one can win. Competition based on operational effectiveness alone is mutually destructive, halted only by limiting competition. This may lead to the simple approach, to buy up rivals. In such a case, the remaining companies in an industry are those that outlasted others, not companies with real advantage.

Strategy the creation of a unique and valuable position

Competitive **strategy** is about being different and *strategic positioning* means performing activities which differ from rivals' activities, or performing similar activities in different ways (Porter 1996). Strategy is the creation of a unique and valuable position, involving a different set of activities. The essence of strategic positioning is to choose activities that are different from rivals' activities. Positioning can be based on:

- producing a subset of an industry's products or services (variety);
- serving most or all the needs of a particular group of customers (targeting a segment of customers); or
- segmenting customers who are accessible in different ways.

Although their needs are similar to those of other customers, the best configuration of activities to reach them is different (access-based positioning). Access can be a function of customer geography or customer scale – or of anything that requires a different set of activities to reach customers in the best way. Whatever the basis – *variety*, *needs*, *access*, or some combination of the three – positioning requires a tailored set of activities because it is always a function of differences on the supply side; that is, of differences in activities.

Choosing a unique position, however, is not enough to guarantee a *sustainable* advantage. A valuable position will attract imitation by others. Positioning choices determine not only which activities a company will perform and how it will configure individual activities, but also how activities relate to one another. While operational effectiveness is about achieving excellence in individual activities, or functions, strategy is about combining (fitting together) activities. Imitators then find it more difficult to copy systems of related and interdependent activities. The whole matters more than any individual part. Competitive advantage grows out of the entire system of activities. The fit among activities substantially reduces cost or increases differentiation. Strategic fit among many activities is fundamental not only to competitive advantage but also to the sustainability of that advantage. It is harder for a rival to match an array of interlocked activities than it is merely to imitate a particular sales-force approach, match a technology, or replicate a set of product features. Positions built on *systems* of activities are far more sustainable than those built on individual activities. The more a company's positioning rests on activity systems the more sustainable its advantage will be. Such systems, by their very nature, are usually difficult to untangle from outside the company and therefore hard to imitate.

Improving operational effectiveness ('*how*' work activities are undertaken) is a necessary part of management, but it is not strategy. Managers must clearly distinguish operational effectiveness from strategy (how the organization will compete and use its resources and scope: the '*what*' and the '*where*'). Both are essential, but the two agendas are different. The operational agenda involves continual improvement everywhere. There are no trade-offs. The operational agenda is the proper place for constant change, flexibility, and relentless efforts to achieve best practice. In contrast, the strategic agenda is the right place for defining a unique position, making clear trade-offs, and tightening fit. It involves the continual search for ways to reinforce and extend the company's position. A company must continually improve its operational effectiveness and actively try to shift the productivity frontier. At the same time there needs to be ongoing effort to extend its uniqueness while strengthening the fit among its activities. In this book we devote Part 2 to *strategy* and the remaining parts to *operational effectiveness*. However, the remaining parts are also used to inform and enable strategy. Collectively they contain the explicit knowledge to help generate sustainable superior performance in the international organizations within your place of work. Returning to this chapter, next we introduce international trade and discuss revenue and profit derived from international business. Later we consider the way an organization utilizes and manages its resources in order to create products and services for trade.

What is international business (IB)?

We can think of companies in many ways: the business they do and the outputs they produce and the ways or methods used to create such outputs. In previous sections we have presented arguments for the internationalization of organizations and described a variety of forms such organizations may take. We also noted that organizations provide goods and services to others and in some cases they are exchanged for money which generates revenue to the organization. International trade concerns the purchase, sale, or exchange of goods and services across national borders and is a source of revenue for the international organization. International trade may be analyzed at the country, organization or consumer levels. There are a number of benefits associated with international trade. For example, consumers are presented with a greater choice of goods and services; goods may become cheaper and there may be quality differences. There is a tendency in the literature to associate 'trade' with 'businesses' and next we identify and explain several theories of international trade.

$$\text{Profit} = \text{Revenue} - \text{Costs}$$

Organizations with profit goals will consider potential market size and the potential for revenue. They will also consider the cost of value adding activities and serving the market. Given that the world typically contains more prospective customers than any given country it is not surprising to learn that the world, as a market, tends to offer more opportunity – but how much? There are many ways to measure the size and performance of an economy. The present world economy (total GDP) is approximately $50 trillion – see Figure 1-6. This figure gives a feel for the opportunity space presented to businesses worldwide. We have identified the top ten countries (economic entities) by GDP. Interestingly though, many MNCs' annual sales are greater than the GDP of many countries. This not only makes them very powerful but also makes them significant customers in business-to-business commerce. Approximately half of the world's top 100 economic entities are now companies.

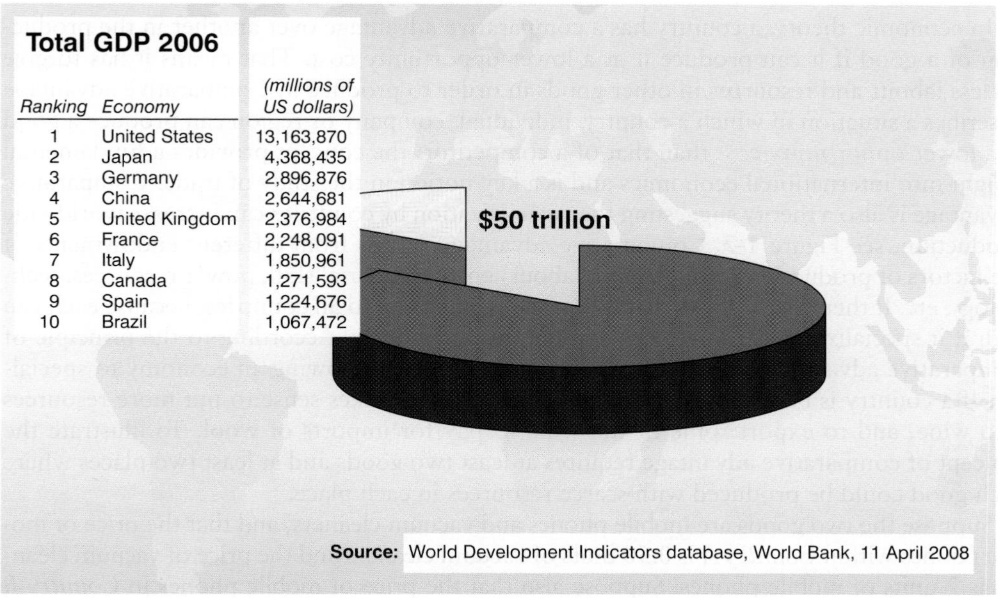

Revenue amount generated from sale of goods or services, or any other use of capital or assets, associated with the main operations of the organization – before any costs or expenses are deducted

International trade the purchase, sale, or exchange of goods and services across national borders

Figure 1-6

The world economy (Source: World Development Indicators database, World Bank 11 April 2008)

Total GDP 2006

Ranking	Economy	(millions of US dollars)
1	United States	13,163,870
2	Japan	4,368,435
3	Germany	2,896,876
4	China	2,644,681
5	United Kingdom	2,376,984
6	France	2,248,091
7	Italy	1,850,961
8	Canada	1,271,593
9	Spain	1,224,676
10	Brazil	1,067,472

$50 trillion

Source: World Development Indicators database, World Bank, 11 April 2008

Globalization through increased competition forces companies to locate particular operations (activities and resources) in those places where they can be performed most efficiently. Organizations do this by relocating production facilities to other countries or by outsourcing certain activities to companies in other countries. In the next paragraph we explore trade theory which provides further insights into *what* business occurs *where* and *why*.

Theories of international trade seek to explain why trade occurs and how it can benefit the different parties to an exchange. One of the first theories that attempts to explain why *nations* should engage in international trade is mercantilism. This economic trade theory explained how countries accumulate financial wealth by encouraging exports and discouraging imports. Nations believed they could increase their wealth by maintaining a trade surplus (as opposed to a trade deficit), i.e. conditions where the value of export was greater than the value of imports.

Governments actively intervened in international trade to maintain a trade surplus. This was achieved by banning or restricting (through tariffs or quotas) imports and subsidizing domestic producers while encouraging exports. In the 18th and early 19th century the theories of absolute and comparative advantage emerged. Absolute advantage describes the ability of a country to produce goods more efficiently than any other country. The theory of absolute advantage views international trade as a positive not a zero (as in the case of mercantilism) sum game. A country with an *absolute advantage* can produce a greater output of goods or services than other countries using the same amount or fewer resources. Under this theory, a country should concentrate on producing the goods in which it holds an absolute advantage. It can then trade with other countries to obtain the goods it needs but does not produce. While this theory shows the gains from international trade, it raises the problem of what a country should do when it does not hold an absolute advantage in the production of any product.

English economist, David Ricardo developed the theory of comparative advantage which suggests that trade is still beneficial even if one country is less efficient in the production of two goods, as long as it is less inefficient in the production of one of the goods. This theory states that a country specializes in producing the goods that it can produce more efficiently than any other goods. The absolute and comparative advantage theories, focusing on the productivity of the production process for a particular good, remained popular until the 20th century but were problematic in their main focus on labour as opposed to other resource types and their lack of consideration of transportation costs and transportation problems.

If a foreign country can supply us with a commodity cheaper than we ourselves can make it, better buy it off them.

(Smith 1776)

In economic theory, a country has a comparative advantage over another in the production of a good if it can produce it at a lower opportunity cost. That means it has to give up less labour and resources in other goods in order to produce it. Comparative advantage describes a situation in which a country, individual, company or region can produce a good at a lower opportunity cost than that of a competitor; the concept provides a fundamental insight into international economics and is a key notion in the study of trade. Comparative advantage is also a theory suggesting that specialization by countries can increase worldwide production, see Figure 1-7. Comparative advantage results from different endowments of the factors of production (capital, land, labour) entrepreneurial skill, power resources, technology, etc. It therefore follows that free trade is beneficial to all countries, because each can gain if it specializes according to its comparative advantage. According to the principle of comparative advantage, the gains from trade follow from allowing an economy to specialize. If a country is better at making wine than wool, it makes sense to put more resources into wine, and to export some of the wine to pay for imports of wool. To illustrate the concept of comparative advantage requires at least two goods and at least two places where each good could be produced with scarce resources in each place.

Suppose the two goods are mobile phones and vacuum cleaners, and that the price of mobile phones within *Country A* is 0.50 units of vacuum cleaners and the price of vacuum cleaners is 2 units of mobile phones. Suppose also that the price of mobile phones in *Country B*

Mercantilism an economic philosophy advocating that countries should simultaneously encourage exports and discourage imports

Absolute advantage a country has an absolute advantage in the production of a product when it is more efficient than any other country at producing it

Comparative advantage the name for the ability of one business entity to engage in production at a lower opportunity cost than another entity. Comparative advantage, rather than absolute advantage, is useful in determining what should be produced and what should be acquired though trade.

Opportunity cost benefit, profit, or value of something that must be given up to acquire or achieve something else. Since every resource (land, money, time, etc.) can be put to alternative uses, every action, choice, or decision has an associated opportunity cost

Adam Smith, widely acknowledge as 'the father of economics'

is 1.5 units of vacuum cleaners and the price of vacuum cleaners is 0.60 units of mobile phones. Then we can say that Country A has a comparative advantage in producing mobile phones and Country B has a comparative advantage in producing vacuum cleaners. It follows that in a trading relationship Country A should allocate at least some of its scarce resources to producing mobile phones and Country B should allocate at least some of its scarce resources to producing vacuum cleaners, because this is the most efficient allocation of the scarce resources and allows the price of mobile phones and vacuum cleaners to be as low as possible.

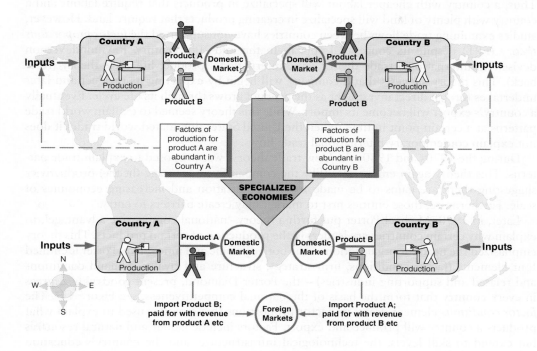

Figure 1-7

Comparative advantage

If countries either completely or partially specialize production according to their comparative advantage, they can reap the gains from specialization in terms of achieving higher total production and welfare levels (Brakeman et al. 2006). Multinational organizations have had the opportunity to benefit from the comparative advantage of different countries, be they technology driven or factor abundance driven, to reduce the total costs of production, particularly through the ever more popular method of *fragmentation* (slicing up the value chain) in which different parts (activities) of the production process are located in different countries (refer to Chapter 15), see Figure 1-8.

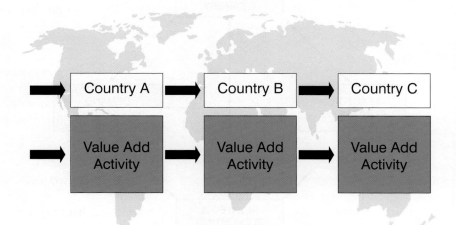

Figure 1-8

Value chain fragmentation

Factor proportions theory a trade theory suggesting countries produce and export goods which require abundant resources (factors) and import goods that require resources in short supply

Early in the 20th century an international trade theory emerged which focused attention on a country's resources. The factor proportions (Heckscher-Ohlin) theory is a trade theory suggesting that countries produce and export goods that require resources (factors) which are abundant and import goods that require resources in short supply. Whereas earlier theories focused on *productivity*, the factor proportions theory suggests a country specializes in producing and exporting goods using the factors of production that are most abundant and thus cheapest. Input resources (factors) include labour, land and capital equipment. Thus, a country with cheaper labour will specialize in products that require labour and a country with plenty of land will specialize in creating products that require land. However, studies examining trade flows between countries have not supported the *factor proportions theory* (FPT) despite its conceptual appeal. In the mid-20th century, Raymond Vernon devised an international trade theory – the international product life cycle theory (refer back). This theory suggests that a company will begin by exporting its product and later undertakes foreign direct investment as the product grows through its life cycle. Eventually a country's export will become its import. While this theory seemed to explain world trade patterns at a certain point in time (when the United States dominated world trade) it does not explain contemporary international trade flows.

During the 1970s and 1980s the 'new trade theory' was proposed to explain trade patterns. This theory again emphasizes (like the comparative advantage theory) productivity suggesting there are gains to be made from specialization and increasing economies of scale. Furthermore, those entities first to market may create barriers to entry.

Later, in 1990, Michael Porter put forth a theory, 'national competitive advantage', to explain why certain countries are leaders in the production of certain products. This theory emphasized the need for organizations to be both dynamic and innovative. Porter identified four elements (factor conditions, firm strategy, structure and rivalry, demand conditions and related and supporting industries) – the Porter Diamond, present to varying degrees in every country that form the basis of the national competitiveness, see Figure 1-9. The *factor conditions* element draws on factor proportions theory and is used to explain what products a country will produce and export. Factors include labour and natural resources but extend to skill levels, the technological infrastructure, and the country's education system and research and development capabilities. Porter argues that sophisticated buyers in the home market are also important to national competitive advantage in a product area (*demand conditions*) as such buyers drive companies to develop products and services which satisfy their needs. Furthermore, a *country industry* characterized by high degrees of competition and rivalry will help those companies compete against imports and develop a presence in foreign markets.

Figure 1-9

The Porter Diamond

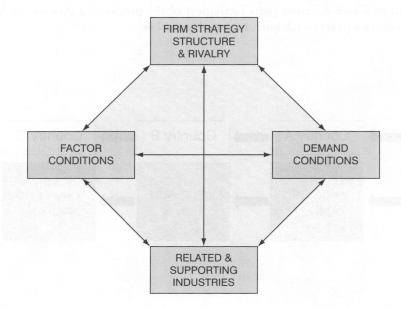

Whereas mercantilism encouraged protectionism, later theories favoured free trade; free trade is simply trade in the absence of barriers. However, for many reasons international trade is not always without barriers. Historically, governments have intervened in trade through initiatives that seek to either promote or restrict international trade. They may do this in order to please voters, protect jobs, protect and preserve national security, in response to unfair trade and to protect infant industries. Trade may be promoted through the use of subsidies, export financing and special government agencies or restricted through tariffs (taxes and duties), quotas (a restriction on the amount of a good that can enter or leave a country during a certain period), embargos and local content requirements. The purpose of local content requirements is to force companies from other countries to use local resources in their production processes – particularly labour. Over the past 50 years, through a variety of treaties and agreements, countries have set out to collectively encourage free trade. Many argue that the erection of barriers to competition results in less competitive organizations and industries, greater job losses, and lower standards of living than would be the case under free trade.

Thus far we have explained international trade according to access to resources and other advantages. There are challenges associated with trade across country borders. For example, distance related barriers to trade exist. While some studies do not consider location to be important, others find distance to be very important, i.e. the position of a country relative to other countries determines its market potential. The *gravity model of international trade flows* looks more closely at the link between distance and trade. Large countries with a common language and sharing a common border are more likely to trade with one another while landlocked countries and those with cultural differences are less likely to trade with one another. Furthermore, the presence of transportation costs and other trade barriers impact upon international trade flows. Companies engaged in international trade, when a transaction involves a buyer and a seller from two countries, must confront several problems such as the choice of currency to use, the form of payment and payment terms. There may also be a need to assess customer risk and conduct credit checks.

In this section we have focused on *economic activity* (international business) and explained why it is not evenly spread across space – with some countries producing a lot more than others and some countries specializing in what they produce. Much of the theory presented in this section is presented as a foundation for other parts of the book, the final chapter (finance) in particular. Economic activity and the international business literature is more focused on inputs and outputs, markets and industries and advantage from strategic positioning – all in all the focus of attention is much more on those things external to the organization. This represents an important part of the international organizational picture but it is not the whole picture. Having outlined what is meant by IB we now turn our attention to international management (IM), which focuses more on the *productive activities* of the international organization. It is a more internal focus though there is an overlap with IB. However, IM focuses more on achieving operational effectiveness and efficiency through the way resources are used, human resources motivated, organized, made knowledgeable, technologically enabled and coordinated through business processes and best practice. In short, IM considers the transformational activities taking place within the international organization and how value is actually added. Collectively, IM and IB seek to ensure the organization generates revenue, attains goals and performs in an efficient, sustainable and superior manner.

IM: leveraging and resource capabilities

While the focus of the previous section was economic activity (inputs and outputs), this section focuses on productive activity (the transformational and value adding activities and processes). Scholars and practitioners alike strive continuously to perfect our knowledge of what makes some organizations perform better than others. Generally they focus upon the effects of industry and *positioning* versus *organization* factors on performance variability. Leverage reflects the extent to which resources are utilized in the international

Free trade trade in the absence of barriers

International trade transactions between a buyer and a seller, each from different countries

Transformational activities at an oil refinery add value to crude oil

organization; leverage is using given resources in such a way that the potential positive outcome is magnified. Earlier we discussed IB in terms of positioning, business and trade. Management is more concerned with the effective utilization and coordination (leveraging) of resources and activities to achieve defined objectives with maximum efficiency. To that end there is a focus on getting things done with the aid of people and other resources (technological, financial, material, intellectual or intangible). At a simple level we might consider IB to be about those activities that take place at the interface of the organization and interaction with customers and markets and IM to be about leveraging internal resources in order to attain organizational goals. Adopting this approach, the book is structured with both IB and IM in mind for the strategy part; IM is more the focus in parts three and four while IB is the focus of the final part.

Factors of production resources, such as land, labour and capital used to produce goods and services

The term factors of production relates to the key factors (resources) which contribute towards making goods and delivering services – the resources organizations use to create what customers want. Common factors identified so far include: land, labour, capital and enterprise. For a manufacturing company, typical factors engaged will be; management and employees, raw materials, plant and equipment. For example, a company like Coca-Cola has sites (production, bottling and warehouse facilities) based on physical land; employs skilled production, sales and marketing labour, purchases in its raw materials (ingredients) and makes use of labour and machinery to create its products. The shareholders and directors take the risk of bringing the operation together, and employ directors and managers to ensure the success of the enterprise.

Figure 1-10

Value add process (activities and resources)

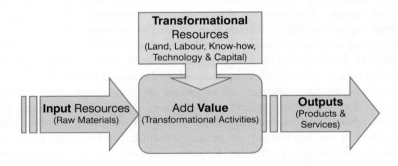

Wernerfelt (1984) explored the usefulness of analyzing organizations from the resource (input and transformational process) side rather than from the product (output) side. For the organization, resources and products are 'two sides of the same coin'. Most products require the services of several resources and most resources can be used in several products. Looking at organizations in terms of their resources has a long tradition in economics; however, analysis is typically confined to categories such as labour, capital, and land. The idea of looking at organizations as a broader set of resources goes back to the seminal work of Penrose (1959). Wernerfelt (1984) argued that we can identify types of resources which can lead to

Resource productive assets owned by the organization

high profits. He discussed resources and profitability; by a resource he meant anything which could be thought of as a strength or weakness of a given organization. More formally, an organization's resources at a given time could be defined as those (tangible and intangible) assets which are tied semi-permanently to the organization. Examples of resources are:

- brand names;
- in-house knowledge of technology;
- employment of skilled personnel;
- trade contacts;
- machinery;
- efficient procedures;
- capital; etc.

Wernerfelt posed the question: 'Under what circumstances will a resource lead to high returns over longer periods of time?' To analyze a resource for its potential for high returns, one has to look at the ways in which an organization with a strong position can influence the acquisition costs or the user revenues of an organization with a weaker position.

The resource-based (RBV) theory is the perspective on strategy stressing the importance of capabilities (sometimes known as core competences) in determining sustainable competitive advantage. The resource-based approach has been attributed to several scholars (Penrose 1959 and Wernerfelt 1984) perhaps more notably Barney (1991). The fundamental principle of the RBV is that the basis for competitive advantage of an organization lies primarily in the application of the bundle of valuable resources at its disposal. The bundle of resources, under certain conditions, can assist the organization, sustaining above average returns. Such resources must be valuable (costing less than discounted future cash flows) and must enable the achievement of goals. Which resources matter? Resources within the RBV are generally broken down into two fundamental categories:

1 tangible resources; and
2 intangible resources.

Tangible resources include those factors containing an accounting value as recorded in the organization's balance sheet. Intangible resources, on the other hand, include those factors that are non-physical (or non-financial) in nature and are rarely, if at all, included in the organization's balance sheet. Intangible resources can be defined as either assets or capabilities. If the intangible resource is something that the organization 'has', it is an asset. If the intangible resource is something the organization 'does', it is a capability. Thus, resource constructs may be conceptualized as:

1 tangible resources which include:
   a financial assets; and
   b physical assets;
2 intangible resources – assets which include:
   a intellectual property assets;
   b organizational assets; and
   c reputational assets; and
3 intangible resources that are capabilities (Galbreath and Galvin 2004).

The central proposition of the RBV is that not all resources are of equal importance in contributing to organization performance (Barney 1991). The resource-based literature describes resources in terms of their value, rareness, inimitability and non-substitutability (VRIN).

■ Valuable

■ Rare

■ Imitability

■ Non-substitutability

Organizational assets may be (intangible) assets that can resist the imitation efforts of competitors. Organizational assets (e.g., culture, HRM policies, and organization structure) contribute order, stability, and quality to the organization. Some scholars suggest that without strong organizational assets, the organization will weaken productivity, deliver poor quality products and services and will have inferior human talent. Organizational assets may be difficult to duplicate. Although not legally protected by property rights, reputation is argued to be an important and sophisticated asset; reputation is built, not bought, suggesting that it is a non-tradable asset that may be much more difficult to duplicate than tangible assets. Capabilities, as ultimately reflected by the organization's know-how, are argued to be the principal source of organizational performance; the productivity and performance of any organization is solely dependent upon the know-how of its employees. Lastly, the ability to build and maintain relationships external to the organization is not only essential for competitive success; it is largely reflective of the knowledge-generating, knowledge-sharing and learning ability of the organization. In other words, building and maintaining external relationships is critical for the organization and largely consists of a 'collective', organization-wide effort of the know-how of a variety of employees and managers.

Although intangible assets may be resistant to competitor duplication, capabilities are viewed as a 'superior' intangible resource. Furthermore, intangible assets have been described as resources that are created as a result or outcome of capabilities. Thus, capabilities can be considered a higher-order and more important resource. Consequently, the RBV literature largely favours *capabilities* as the most important determinant of organization *performance*.

Galbreath and Galvin (2004) discovered that while RBV theory largely associates organizational performance with intangible resources, empirically the association may not always hold true. They found that some intangible resources do seem to account for additional significant effects on performance and therefore may be valuable, rare, inimitable and non-substitutable; however, this was not the case in all of the expected predictions. One explanation may be that the strength of some resources is dependent upon interactions or combinations with other resources and therefore no single resource – intangible or otherwise – becomes the most important for organization performance. This argument is central to the structure and content of this book.

As was noted earlier, dominant theories about the sources of competitive advantage cluster around the internal or external environment (see next chapter). The dominant paradigm in the 1980s was the *competitive forces approach* developed by Porter which focused on the external environment. The key aspect of the firm's environment is the industry or industries within which it competes. Industry structure strongly influences the competitive rules of the game as well as the strategies available to firms. In the competitive forces model, five industry-level forces – entry barriers, threat of substitution, bargaining power of buyers and suppliers, and rivalry among industry incumbents – determine the inherent profit potential of an industry. The approach can be used to help the firm find a position in an industry from which it can best defend itself against competitive forces or influence them in its favour.

A related approach, referred to as a *strategic conflict approach* (e.g. Shapiro 1989), is similar in its focus on product market imperfections, entry deterrence, and strategic interaction. Teece, Pisano and Shuen (1997) refer to latter approaches as 'models of strategy emphasizing the exploitation of market power'. Later, the 'resource-based perspective,' was proposed, with an internal focus, emphasizing firm specific capabilities as the fundamental determinants of organizational performance. This perspective represents a strategy model emphasizing efficiency. The resource-based (RBV) approach sees organizations with superior systems and structures being profitable, not because they engage in strategic investments that may deter entry and raise prices above long-run costs, but because they have markedly lower costs, or offer markedly higher quality or product performance. Organizations which are able to accumulate resources and capabilities that are rare, valuable, non-substitutable, and difficult to imitate will achieve a competitive advantage.

Teece, Pisano and Shuen (1997) build on the efficiency-based approach, introducing the concept of dynamic capabilities to address changing environments (discussed in the next chapter). This approach emphasizes the development of management capabilities, and difficult-to-imitate combinations of organizational, functional and technological skills. The term 'dynamic' refers to the capacity to renew competences so as to achieve congruence with the changing business environment. Certain innovative responses are required when time-to-market and timing are critical, the rate of technological change is rapid, and the nature of future competition and markets difficult to determine. The term 'capabilities' emphasizes the key role of strategic management in adapting, integrating, and reconfiguring internal and external organizational skills appropriately, as well as resources, and functional competences to match the requirements of a changing environment. Organizations rely increasingly on information technologies, including process, knowledge, and communication technologies, to enhance their agility (Sambamurthy, Bharadwaj and Grover 2003).

Dynamic capabilities the firm's ability to integrate, build, and reconfigure internal and external competences to address rapidly changing environments

Competences when firm-specific assets are assembled in integrated clusters spanning individuals and groups so they enable distinctive activities to be performed

Agility is the ability to detect and seize opportunities for innovation by assembling necessary assets, knowledge, and relationships with speed and surprise. As contemporary international organizations face intense rivalry, globalization, and time-to-market pressures, agility is considered to be an imperative for business success. Agile organizations sense opportunities for competitive action continually in their product-market spaces and gather together the necessary knowledge and assets for seizing those opportunities. Agility underlies organizational success in continuous enhancement and redefinition of value creation, capture, and competitive performance through innovations in products, services, channels, and market segmentation.

The convergence of computing, communications, and content technologies offers international organizations significant opportunities for enhancing agility. Contemporary organizations make significant investments in information technologies (such as web services, data warehousing, customer relationship management, or supply chain management technologies) to leverage the functionalities of these technologies in shaping their business strategies, customer relationships, and extended enterprise networks. In particular, the disruptive forces of digitization, unbundling of information and physical value chains, and disaggregation of organizational infrastructures for customer relationship, manufacturing, procurement, and supply chain fulfilment have heightened the significance of IT in enabling agile competitive moves. Dynamic capabilities permit organizations to combine flexibly different IT and business resources and stimulate competitive actions through innovations in products, services, and channels.

Agility the ability to detect and seize opportunities for innovation by assembling necessary assets, knowledge, and relationships with speed and surprise

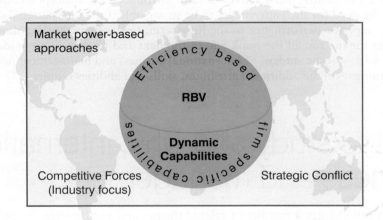

Figure 1-11

Sources of (sustainable) competitive advantage

The different approaches to strategy and the attainment of superior and sustainable organizational performance discussed thus far, see Figure 1-11, view differently the sources of *wealth creation* and the essence of the strategic problem faced by international organizations. The competitive forces framework sees the strategic problem in terms of industry structure, entry deterrence, and positioning. Game-theoretic models view the strategic problem as one of interaction between rivals with certain expectations about how each other will behave.

Resource-based perspectives have focused on the exploitation of firm-specific assets. Each approach asks different, often complementary questions. The approaches discussed are generally considered to be complementary and practitioners must work out which frameworks are appropriate for the problem in hand. Mindless devotion to one approach to the neglect of all others is likely to generate strategic blindspots. Teece, Pisano and Shuen (1997) argue that winners in the global marketplace are organizations who can demonstrate timely responsiveness and rapid and flexible product innovation, coupled with the management capability to coordinate and redeploy internal and external competences effectively. They advance the argument that the competitive advantage of organizations lies with its managerial and organizational processes (the way things are done), shaped by its specific asset position (resources to hand), and the available paths (strategic alternatives). The organization's processes and positions collectively encompass its competences and capabilities.

Building on this evolution of approaches to strategy, Dyer and Singh (1998) highlight that the search for competitive advantage, from an RBV perspective, has focused on those resources housed *within* the organization. According to the RBV, an individual company should attempt to protect, rather than share, valuable proprietary know-how to prevent knowledge spillovers, which could erode or eliminate competitive advantage. However, an organization's critical resources may extend beyond its boundaries. A *relational view* considers the network as the unit of analysis, not the individual organization, and advocates the benefits of collaboration, i.e. interorganizational linkages. Organizations can generate revenues by leveraging the complementary resource endowments of an alliance partner. A pair or network of organizations can develop relationships resulting in sustained competitive advantage. Analysis by Dyer and Singh (1998) suggests that although looking for competitive advantage within organizations and industries has been (and is still) important, a singular focus on these units of analysis may limit the explanatory power of the models developed to explain organizational level profitability.

In summary, thus far, we have looked at the composition and workings of international organizations and why they exist. We have described *economic* and *productive* activities at the international level and the need to make efficient use of resources when undertaking such activities and adding value to organizational outputs. We have noted the need for such organizations to attain goals and considered the performance of international organizations. From a competitive perspective we have introduced the concept of advantage and recognized the need for such advantages to be sustainable if the international organization is to deliver superior performance in the long term. Discussions thus far should serve as a foundation for the rest of the book and in the next and final section we identify, more specifically, *what* it is the student of international business and management needs to study and will comment on the additional attributes, skills and abilities required.

Complementary resource endowments distinctive resources of alliance partners which collectively generate greater rents than the sum of those obtained from the individual endowments of each partner

What to study and why: international business and management

Throughout this chapter a number of related themes and perspectives on global business activities have emerged that are integrated throughout this book. The 'global' issue represented the first theme, the pursuit of and methods to attain sustainable competitive advantage a second. Related to this was the RBV (internal) versus market-based (external) focus of organizations. We also discussed decision makers in international organizations and their predisposition to simply replicate the way things are done at home (ethnocentric) or adopt a polycentric approach – based upon a belief that host country cultures are different and as such local people are better placed to make business decisions. At the heart of the themes is integration and differentiation.

At this point we ask, what is it that the scholar of international business and management should know? In some cases this may be defined by some certifying institution such as in the case of the MBA or business studies student and in other cases it will be governed by what the practitioner needs to know in order to ensure the superior and sustainable performance of their international organization. Business and management as a subject area is distinctive in that it is *interdisciplinary*, drawing upon a wide range of base disciplines from 'hard' to 'soft' sciences. The European Quality Link (EQUAL), the European association of national accrediting bodies, the Association of MBAs (AMBA), the Association to Advance Collegiate Schools of Business (AACSB International), the Association of Business Schools (ABS) and the Quality Assurance Agency (QAA) in the UK have all contributed to ideas on the content of an MBA through benchmark standards. In its work on the

MBA *benchmarks*, the QAA built upon the previously agreed ABS and EQUAL European MBA guidelines and AACSB International criteria. They suggested all masters graduates should be able to demonstrate relevant knowledge and understanding of *organizations* (internal aspects, behaviours and cultures, structures, operations and management), the external *context* in which they operate and *how they are managed* (leadership and management, processes, procedures and decision-making). Additionally, students should have an understanding of *change* management. To ensure relevance in today's global economy, the subject must be set within an international perspective. All of which are covered in depth in this text.

International Business (IB)

Globalization & the Environment
Culture
Monetary Systems
Internationalization &
Market Entry Strategies
Sales & Marketing
Operations Management
Finance
Strategy
Ethics
International Economics & Trade

International Management (IM)

HRM
Organization Structure
Managing Difference
OB
Knowledge Management
CSR
Leadership
Change Management

Information Systems and Technology (EB | EC | ES)
Business Processes

Figure 1-12

Contrasting IB and IM topics

Not all business textbooks are the same. Concepts of international business management clearly vary. While many aspects of international business management are fundamentally the same as management at the national level, many agree that once managers are required to operate across national boundaries they face differing problems and opportunities. While this might be so, the manager in the international organization is likely to need to understand management both at home and abroad. Many scholars see international business as the study of transactions taking place across national borders for the purpose of satisfying the needs of individuals and organizations.

The popular literature tends to focus more on external factors such as the environment, sales and marketing and adopts the term 'international business' (IB). Such texts are more likely to focus on marketing, operations management, strategy, finance, international economics and trade and the various trading blocs in the world. An alternative model is often presented under the international management (IM) label. The IM books tend to focus more on the 'softer' management aspects of global business, OB, HRM, negotiating and cultural differences. Only slight coverage of information systems and technology issues is presented in such texts, see Figure 1-12. Authors also vary in how they treat the subjects with some treating them as totally different, others see one as a subset of the other, While others see them overlapping or effectively the same – using the terms interchangeably, see Figure 1-13.

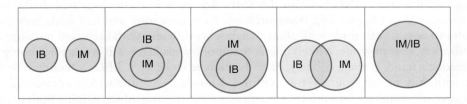

Figure 1-13

Alternative definitions of the relationship between IB and IM

Despite there being numerous international management/business textbooks on the market, they are wanting in several fundamental ways. Some are almost exclusively strategic, others tend to be overly functional (focusing on *traditional* subject areas such as sales and marketing, HR, finance), i.e. not integrated – the traditional approach to business education. Almost all of the leading books are severely lacking in coverage of *processes* and the application of *information systems* and *technology* to global challenges. Leading books lack attention to SMEs and the use of Internet technologies to access global markets. Furthermore, they tend have a bias towards an American focus. In order to develop an integrative understanding of global business there should be a tight integrated flow between chapters. The need for an integrated understanding of business issues derives from several contemporary business problems. An integrated understanding of business supports horizontal strategies and the RBV whereby organizations seek out synergistic benefits across aspects of their multinational enterprise. The need for integration is also borne out of the process view of organizations, a need to be responsive and customer focused. As Porter (1996) and others have observed, today's business student must see the organization as more than simply a collection of functional parts.

The scope of *international management* should include all aspects associated with the *practice* of managing business operations and strategy within and across countries. Any contemporary text should contain the explicit knowledge required by those tasked with running an international business. The emphasis is less on the economics of trade and the detail of the external environment and more on the need to position and develop agile companies that can meet changing customer needs in a timely and profitable manner. International management should take a supply chain and value system perspective, identifying how organizations can operate more effectively and efficiently, at a global level. Such a textbook should focus on how organizations use their assets such as information, people, knowledge, technology and finances to achieve their goals and compete in the global marketplace. Recent years have brought sweeping changes in the way organizations apply information technology to solve complex problems that are common in increasingly competitive and global business environments. All organizations today create sustainable value from leveraging their intangible assets – human capital; databases and information systems; responsive, high-quality processes; customer relationships and brands; innovation capabilities; and culture. Effective resource management can deliver sustainable competitive advantage; organizations must manage people, information, knowledge and technology resources along with tangible goods and materials if they are to be responsive, innovative, effective and efficient.

We therefore believe there is a clear need for a hybrid textbook, focused on *international business and management*. As highlighted in the preface, the aim of this book is to present an integrative text: integrating business and management perspectives, operations with strategy, functional and horizontal perspectives, enabling the reader to take a multidisciplinary and problem-oriented view of work within the international organization. In many ways, this book reflects the resource-based view and the market or institution based view of organizations. The *scope* of this book is business conducted both at home and overseas by international organizations, i.e. business around the globe. The scope includes both an external (marketing, sales, and environmental forces) and internal (leveraging resources and capabilities for sustainable advantage) focus, grounded in strategy and operations. We believe that global business, studied from an IB and IM perspective, is the most stimulating, demanding and pertinent subject offered by contemporary business schools.

Knowledge of global business and managing internationally is of use not only to the manager in the large MNC but also the SME. Advances in technology (see digital business considered in Chapter 14), transportation, communication and free trade now mean that almost anyone can trade with almost anyone worldwide. With increased mobility and globalization, it is now more likely the contemporary manager will work for a company not headquartered in their country, may themselves work in a different country or will work with, buy or sell from overseas entities. Knowledge is now widely considered as a key source of advantage for both the organization and the individual, helping both to meet their respective goals. The knowledge of international business and international management contained within this text will help the reader become a better manager bringing rewards for their organizations, society and themselves.

In the preface we highlighted our model for studying IB and IM through this text, see Figure 1-14. The first main part of the text focuses on strategic challenges and is followed by two parts that focus on the 'soft' and 'hard' resources, representing the internal environment of the international organization. Studying the use of such resources enables attention to be directed at operational effectiveness and doing the right things efficiently. Furthermore, such knowledge will enable the bundling of resources to create sustainable advantages. In the final part of the book we consider the international business and trade activities: operations, marketing and the management of financial resources worldwide.

Figure 1-14

Model for studying IB and IM

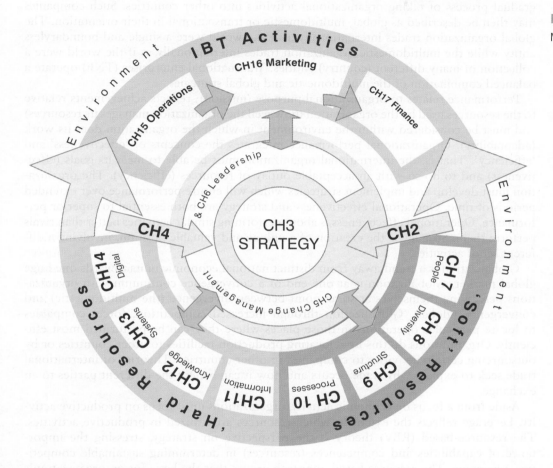

Acting with this knowledge the reader should be better placed to consider the needs of international organizations, determine unique and valuable positions; the means to achieve objectives and determine how to compete successfully in particular markets. Furthermore, they should be able to enhance operational effectiveness and efficiency and contribute to sustainable and superior organizational performance. However, it is important to note that explicit knowledge alone will not result in success. The international manager must have the requisite leadership and managerial skills, abilities and attributes (see Chapter 6). A selection of the required skills may be developed by completing the activities accompanying this book and possibly reinforced in the classroom. In particular, the reader might develop their report writing, presentation and other communication skills; problem solving and group work, IT and information management skills.

Summary of key learning points

As an introductory chapter, we set out to outline the need for the international organization, describe their features, how international organizations come to be and why they exist. We also considered the activities undertaken by them in creating and adding value. An international organization is any organization engaging in international trade, investment or offering products or services outside its home-country. We noted the growing importance of such organizations, many of which are now larger economic entities than many countries. Such organizations can be categorized in many ways and may be analyzed according to the activities they perform. The choice of activities and the way resources are used provide the organization with advantages that may help it compete.

Some organizations are born global, others evolve over time; internationalization is the gradual process of taking organizational activities into other countries. Such companies may then be described as global, multidomestic or transnational in their orientation. The global organization trades internationally as if the world were a single and boundaryless entity while the multidomestic organization trades internationally as if the world were a collection of many different (country) entities. Transnational enterprises (TNE) operate a balanced combination of the multidomestic and global strategies.

Performance relates to organizational purpose (mission); reflects achievements relative to the resources used by the organization (how well the organization manages its resources) and must be considered within the environment in which the organization does its work (adaptability). Organizational performance integrates the concepts of 'effectiveness' and 'efficiency'. That is, the international organization must be able to meet its goals (effectiveness) and to do so with an acceptable outlay of resources (efficiency). The organization must develop and implement strategies which will ensure performance over extended periods of time. Operational effectiveness and strategy are both essential to superior performance. Operational effectiveness is about performing similar activities better than rivals perform them. Strategy is the creation of a unique and valuable position, involving a different set of activities.

Globalization is a trend away from distinct national economic units towards one huge global market. Globalization is at one end of a convergence continuum with organizations perceiving themselves at some point between divergence (the multidomestic) and convergence (global). Globalization through increased competition, forces companies to locate particular operations in those places where they can be performed most efficiently. Organizations do this by relocating production facilities to other countries or by outsourcing certain activities to companies in other countries. Theories of international trade seek to explain why trade occurs and how it can benefit the different parties to an exchange.

Aside from a focus on economic activity, organizations must focus on productive activity. Leverage reflects the extent to which resources are utilized in productive activities. The resource-based (RBV) theory is the perspective on strategy, stressing the importance of capabilities and competences (resources) in determining sustainable competitive advantage. The resource-based approach argues that the basis for an organization's competitive advantage lies primarily in the application of the bundle of valuable resources at its disposal. The bundle of resources, under certain conditions, can assist the organization, sustaining above average returns. Such resources need to be valuable and enable the achievement of goals. In dynamic environments, organizations must create, innovate and develop their capabilities constantly and be able to detect and seize opportunities as they present themselves.

Review questions

Nestlé

Review the opening case study:

1 Select a Nestlé product and use the value chain framework to describe the primary value adding activities.

2 Describe the value system for the product analyzed in part (1).

3 Explain how Nestlé might add and create value from its activities.

4 Consider the convergence and divergence debate and its impact upon Nestlé. Would you describe Nestlé as a global, multidomestic or transnational company?

5 Identify the activities Nestlé has chosen to standardize – why do you think they were selected? Identify the activities Nestlé has chosen to decentralize – why do you think they were selected?

6 How has globalization affected Nestlé over the past decade? What further impact will it have over the next decade?

7 With regard to the knowledge economy, evaluate how Nestlé make use of information and knowledge resources. Next consider Nestlé's standardization of their IT and information infrastructure – do you consider this to be a good thing to do? How has project GLOBE helped Nestlé?

a Identify the major resources used by Nestlé to transform raw materials into finished goods.

b Which resources may provide Nestlé with a sustainable competitive advantage?

8 Explain how operational effectiveness leads to improved organizational performance in Nestlé.

9 Evaluate how Nestlé competes: what is its competitive strategy?

10 Why does Nestlé emphasize agility and innovation?

References

Amit, R. and Zott, C. (2001) 'Value Creation in E-Business', *Strategic Management Journal*, Special Issue, 22(6/7):493–520.

Argyris, C. (1957) 'The Individual and Organization: Some Problems of Mutual Adjustment', *Administrative Science Quarterly* 2(1):1–24.

Barney, J. (1991) 'Firm Resources and Sustained Competitive Advantage', *Journal of Management* 91(17):1:99–120.

Brakeman, L., Garretsen, H., Marrewijk, C. and Witteloostuijn, A. (2006) *Nations and Firms in the Global Economy*, Cambridge: Cambridge University Press.

Chaffey, D. (2007) *E-Business and E-Commerce Management* (3 ed), Harlow: Prentice Hall.

Criscuolo, P., Haskel, J. and Slaughter, M. J. (2005) 'Global Engagement and the Innovation Activities of Firms', National Bureau of Economic Research (NBER), NBER Working Paper No W11479, Available at SSRN: http://ssrn.com/abstract=760172.

Dyer, J. H. and Singh, H. (1998) 'The Relational View: Cooperative Strategy and Sources of Inter-organizational Competitive Advantage', *The Academy of Management Review* 23(4):660–679.

Forester Research, http://web.archive.org/web/20020210142542/http:/www.forrester.com/ER/Press/ForrFind/0,1768,0,00.html.

Fortune Global 500: available from www.money.cnn.com/magazines/fortune/global500/2007/index.html, accessed 8 May 2008.

Galbreath, J. and Galvin, P. (2004) *Which Resources Matter? A Fine-Grained Test of the Resource-Based View of the Firm*, Academy of Management Proceedings, 1–6.

Garvin, D. (1993) 'Building a Learning Organization', *Harvard Business Review*, July–August 1993:78–91

Gugler, P. (2007) 'World Investment Report 2006. FDI from Developing and Transition Economies: Implications for Development. United Nations, New York and Geneva (2006)', *International Business Review* 16(4):528–530.

Hill, C. (2006) *International Business* (6 ed) New Jersey: McGraw Hill.

Huczynski, A. and Buchanan, D. (2007) *Organizational Behaviour* (6 ed), Harlow: FT Prentice Hall.

Lawrence, P. R. and Lorsch, J. W. (1967) 'Differentiation and Integration in Complex Organizations', *Administrative Science Quarterly* 12(1):1–47.

Luthans, F. and Stewart, T. (1977) 'A General Contingency Theory of Management', *Academy of Management Review* 2:181–195.

Peng, M. W. (2008) *Global Business*, Mason: South-Western Cengage Learning.

Penrose, E. G. (1959) *The Theory of the Growth of the Firm*, New York: Wiley.

Perlmutter, H. (1969) 'The Tortuous Evolution of the Multinational Corporation', *Columbia Journal of World Business* 69(4)(1):9–19.

Porter, M. E. and Millar, V. E. (1985) 'How information gives you a competitive advantage', *Harvard Business Review*, July–August 63:149–174.

Porter, M. E. (1996) 'What Is Strategy?', *Harvard Business Review*, 74(6):61–78.

Pugh, D. S. (1997) 'Organization Theory' (4 ed), Harmondsworth: Penguin.

Sambamurthy, V., Bharadwaj, A. and Grover, V. (2003) 'Shaping Agility Through Digital Options: Reconceptualising The Role Of Information Technology In Contemporary Firms', *MIS Quarterly*, June 2003 22(2):237–263.

Shapiro, C. (1989) 'The theory of business strategy', *RAND Journal of Economics*, Spring 1989, 20(1):125–137.

Slack, N., Chambers, S. and Johnston, R. (2007) *Operations Management* (5 ed), Harlow: Financial Times Press.

Teece, D. J., Pisano, G. and Shuen, A. (1997) 'Dynamic Capabilities and Strategic Management', *Strategic Management Journal* (August 1997) 18(7):509–533.

UNCTAD. (2007) 'Information Economy Report 2007–2008 Science and technology for development: the new paradigm of ICT', United Nations – New York and Geneva, 2007, available from www.unctad.org/ecommerce, UNCTAD/SDTE/ECB/2007/1.

UNCTAD. (2007b) 'Trade and Development Report, 2007', United Nations Publication – Report Unctad/TDR/2007.

UNCTAD. (2007c) 'World Investment Report 2007: Transnational Corporations, Extractive Industries and Development', United Nations Publication.

UNCTAD. (2008) 'The UNCTAD Handbook of Statistics 2006–7', United Nations, TD/STAT.31.

Vernon, R. (1966) 'International Investment and International Trade in the Product Cycle', *The Quarterly Journal of Economics* (May, 1966) 80(2):190–207.

Wernerfelt, B. (1984) 'A Resource-based View of the Firm', *Strategic Management Journal* (April–June 1984) 5(2):171–180.

Wise, R. (1999) 'Why things go better at Coke', *Journal of Business Strategy* (January–February 1999) 20(1):15–20.

Suggestions for further reading

Journals

International Business Review

The journal provides a forum for academics and professionals to share the latest developments and advances in knowledge and practice of international business. It aims to foster the exchange of ideas on a range of important international subjects and to provide stimulus for research and the further development of international perspectives. IBR is the official journal of European International Business Academy (EIBA) www.elsevier.com/locate/ibusrev.

Part II

Planning for international business

International organizations are resource systems continuously interacting with their environment – a source of opportunity, threat and constraint. The environment provides the organization with a purpose, and shapes its mission and goals. It governs what the organization will do (activities) and how it will do it. An understanding of both external and internal environments (Chapter 2), the requirements of significant stakeholders and the preferences and senior decision-makers shape the organizational strategy – where and how to compete, and the identification and application of required resources. In Chapter 2 we consider how strategy is developed and implemented. Chapter 3 (International and global strategy) seeks to answer fundamental questions such as: in which markets and geographical areas will we compete, how will we compete and what resources and capabilities do we require. Strategy is concerned with how the international organization achieves its aims and goals. Stakeholders, other than investors, must be considered when formulating strategy and conducting business activities. In Chapter 4 we consider how organizations can behave responsibly when operating worldwide. Once strategy has been formed or strategic decisions made, changes must take place. Change is necessary in a dynamic environment and various theories of change are explored in Chapter 5. We explore what can be changed and how the international organization can accomplish change. Finally, in Chapter 6 we recognize the role of leaders and managers in strategy, ethical and change management and behaving responsibly. They play a key role in planning, designing, allocating resources, coordination, control, setting direction and motivating.

The challenge of strategic management is to understand complex issues facing organizations and develop the capability for long-term organizational success. The aim of this section is to develop the reader's knowledge of the need and means to align the organization with its environment so its resources can be developed and deployed to meet its goals.

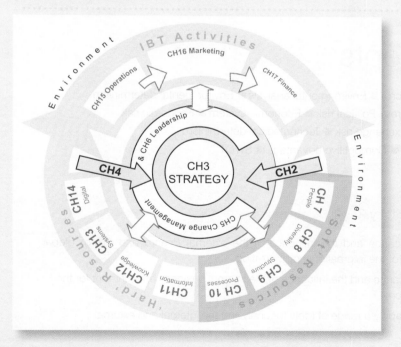

The overall aim of this book is to ensure the international organization has the resources and competencies (dynamic capabilities) to survive and prosper in an uncertain and constantly changing world. To survive and prosper an organization needs to address the challenges it faces from the environment. In particular it must be capable of delivering against the critical success factors that arise from demands and needs of its customers. The strategic capability to do so is dependent on international organizational resources, competencies and capabilities.

Chapter 2

Analyzing the global business environment

Introduction

External (macro) environment

Industry (micro) environment

The internal environment

Contingency and environmental perspectives

Positioning versus resource-based perspective

Key concepts

- Environment (macro/micro) ■ Environmental analysis ■ Environmental determinism
- Political system ■ Culture ■ Political risk ■ Economic system ■ Economic risk
- Technology ■ Foreign exchange risk ■ Technological determinism
- Ecological environment ■ Competitive advantage ■ SWOT

By the end of this chapter you will be able to:

- Understand the significance and the influence of the external (macro and micro) global business environment for the international organization

- Understand the significance and the influence of the internal business environment for the international organization

- Critically evaluate and apply a range of tools for analyzing the internal and external environment

- Explain the concepts of strategic fit and alignment

- Distinguish between the positioning and resource-based perspectives

Active learning case

European airline industry

Since 1919 countries have held sovereign rights over the airspace of their territory; national governments being responsible for the regulation of the industry. In 1944 many countries made attempts to set the rules on economic rights in aviation. The United States wanted operating freedom (an 'open skies' policy) for its airlines under a multilateral agreement. The UK and other larger European countries whose industries had been devastated by the war proposed the formation of an international authority, one which would regulate capacity and fares on routes, thereby giving their aviation industries a chance to rebuild. Agreement was reached on some issues such as the right to fly over a third country's airspace while on an agreed service and for the airline to land in a third country for fuel and maintenance but not pick up or discharge traffic.

The internal *European* market was a rather different story. While the European carriers were engaged in moderate competition in transatlantic travel, the domestic scheduled market was still very heavily regulated through bilateral agreements until the mid-1980s.

The European airlines were mainly public airlines or majority government owned. They enjoyed the duopolistic situation created by the bilateral agreements and prevented new entry in the intra-European market. Through these bilateral agreements, the airlines pooled revenues and shared capacity, thus eliminating any competition between themselves on these routes. The European Commission (EC) had recommended opening aviation to competition as early as 1972, but strong objections put back this discussion until 1979 when it published the Civil Aviation Memorandum. The larger European nations were very reluctant until the mid-1980s to abandon the protected status of their national carriers by advocating more liberal competition policies. These governments directly or indirectly subsidized their carriers, the extent of which varied from country to country. Financial assistance was provided to:

1 compensate airlines for the imposition of a public service obligation;
2 develop and operate domestic services;
3 provide service to economically underdeveloped regions;
4 encourage the acquisition and operation of specific airplanes (Airbus in Europe); or
5 simply to cover an airline's operating loss.

Further, the governments often used their airlines as a means to boost employment. New competitors found stringent laws, designed to protect these national airlines, a significant barrier to entry. This resulted in inefficiency within the industry.

In 1986, British Airways (BA), a persistent poor performer, was sold to the private sector, thus joining Swissair as the only other privately owned airline in Europe. With declining profitability in its European operations, BA signed a marketing agreement with United Airlines. It integrated United's flight schedules and networks in America with BA's transatlantic services to American cities. The agreement enabled the airlines to share passengers and increased the quality of service for time-conscious business travellers. As a result, BA's utilization of available seating capacity (load-factor) on the transatlantic sector increased by almost 40 per cent. This helped BA in its turnaround.

easyJet airline company limited

The first easyJet flight, departed for Glasgow from Luton airport in November 1995. In terms of e-commerce, the firm sold its first seat online in April 1998. EasyJet PLC is engaged in the provision of airline service on short-haul and medium-haul point-to-point routes principally within Europe. The company's subsidiaries include easyJet Airline Company Limited, easyJet Switzerland SA, easyJet Aircraft Company Limited, easyJet Sterling Limited and easyJet Leasing Limited. For the fiscal year ended 30 September 2007, easyJet plc's revenue increased 11 per cent to £1.8bn. The company employs over 5000 people. EasyJet's main competitor is Ryanair.

Ryanair was Europe's original low fares airline, first flying in 1985. A pioneering European discount airline, Ryanair Holdings offers low-fare, no-frills air transportation. Ryanair is engaged in the provision of a scheduled airline service across a European route network. The company recorded revenues of 2.2bn (£1.8bn) during the fiscal year ended March 2007, an increase of 32.2 per cent over 2006. Like easyJet, the company employs over 5000 people.

That same year the EC Commissioner, threatened to take the 12 major airlines to the European Court for operating an illegal cartel in violation of the competition rules of the Treaty of Rome. European transport ministers met in Brussels to agree on a package to free competition. Further liberalization talks ended in 1992 where after ten years of hard negotiations, the EC finally agreed on issues that would create a more competitive environment in European skies. Thus the European airline industry entered a critical phase of reorganization with the economic integration of Europe.

The European airline industry differs significantly in structure from that in the United States. Due to the relatively small size of the market, substitutes for air travel are significant. The train and car are feasible alternatives in Europe given the shorter distances and the one- to two-hour prior-to-departure check-in requirements for international travel. The price on most routes has been consistently higher than prices charged for similar distances in the United States. The 'liberalization' movement began in Europe in an effort to end these monopolies and bring prices down to more competitive levels. Further, the European airline industry was found to be inefficient relative to US carriers (Captain and Sickles 1997).

Deregulation by the EU paved the way for new entrants and new strategies. Several European 'no-frills' airlines started with the characteristics of: low fares, no on-board meals, no allocated seats, often using regional airports and lower staffing costs. Initially expected to attract mainly leisure travellers, much of the demand turned out to be from business travellers who resent paying premium fares to travel within Europe. The 'no-frills' operators significantly undercut the big carriers and focused mainly on high volume, short-haul, point-to-point trips. Low fares are achieved through savings in distribution costs (intermediary margins) reduced through technology enabled e-tickets and online bookings; removing catering services; standardizing the fleet of aircraft and using regional airports instead of the major hubs. Companies like easyJet and Ryanair adopted such models, threatening established carriers such as BA.

Airlines rely on key inputs such as aircraft, fuel and labour in order to operate. The airline industry in Europe is characterized by strong *supplier* power (Boeing and Airbus manufacture of aircraft globally), as yet, there is no viable substitute for jet fuel (though there is presently much research into jet biofuels). The air industry in Europe has been deregulated to a certain extent, which makes it more attractive for new entrants, although the bureaucracy and large financial outlay involved in setting up an airline serve as a *barrier* to new companies. Not only may a new company require considerable capital, access to good distribution channels may be difficult. The large number of individual consumers in this market weakens *buyer* power, as the impact on an airline of losing one customer is insignificant. Switching from one player to another does not incur any additional costs and customers are therefore free to shop around for the best deal on their particular journey. On the whole this industry is highly price sensitive and the majority of customers are keen to find the lowest priced ticket for their journey (though differentiation of services is used to compete in certain segments such as the lucrative business travel class).

Buyer power is increased by the presence of online booking sites that allow customers to compare and contrast tickets according to price and other journey attributes. In response to the ease of switching from one player to another, many airlines offer loyalty schemes thus increasing switching costs and locking in customers. As the airline industry is labour-intensive, staffing costs

©iStockphoto.com/Mitja Bezenšek

are substantial, and contribute significantly to an airline's total costs. Airline fuel is not taxed. However, airlines have little control over rising fuel prices. Infrastructure in some parts of Europe is lagging behind the growth in air traffic. Congestion at major international airports means that 'slots' at certain airports (the right to take-off or land at a particular time) have become an important commodity for many airlines. This creates difficultly for a new airline aiming to negotiate primetime slots at busy airports and can result in it being restricted to offering flights only at off-peak times, or having to fly to airports further away from popular destinations.

The main substitutes for airlines are other forms of transport; road, rail and marine. As distances between European destinations can be relatively small, flights may be short in duration, and the time taken to reach the airport and check in can make the overall journey times similar to rail travel. Also, some consumers may see the greater environmental impact of air travel as a significant disadvantage compared with rail. However, for longer journeys rail travel may be comparatively time-consuming and rail fares often compare unfavourably with budget airfares, reducing the threat of this substitute. Overall, the threat of substitute modes of travel is moderate.

Websites and resources:

(1) Captain, P. F. and Sickles, R. C. (1997) 'Competition and Market Power in the European Airline Industry: 1976–90', *Managerial and Decision Economics* (May 1997) 18(3):209–225.

(2) www.ryanair.com/site/EN/about.php?page=About&sec=story.

Introduction

In the previous chapter we outlined the value-adding activities of the international organization which typically converts inputs into outputs (products and services) in order to make a profit or meet other goals. However, it does not function in a vacuum; it has to act and react to what happens outside (the situation it finds itself in). Factors outside the organization are known as external factors or influences. These will affect the main internal functions of the business and possibly the business objectives and strategies. The business environment is divided into the external and internal environment. The internal environment consists of all resources and capabilities found within the organization which influence the organization's ability to act (to create outputs). The analysis of the business environment allows the organization and its employees to understand the context within which they operate and strategy is developed and implemented. It is important to note, however, that environments are not static but constantly changing.

Understanding the global business environment and its economic, social and political influences is crucial to success in today's international business world. Since the comments of Emery and Trist, more than 40 years ago, we have witnessed great change in the environment of many industries and organizations; the opening case study serving as just one example. The Internet, globalization, increased social mobility, the erosion of boundaries, mobile telephony and increased privatization are factors affecting the global business environment. These changes impact upon organizations, influencing *how* they work and *what* they produce. According to the UK Quality Assurance Agency for Higher Education, the external context encompasses a wide range of factors including economic, ethical, legal, political, sociological and technological, together with their effects at local, national and international levels upon the strategy, behaviour and management of organizations.

The external environment is complex and its future uncertain yet managers must attempt to make sense of it if they are to identify opportunities and threats and respond appropriately. Similarly, through comparisons within the multinational organization and with competitors in the micro environment, the organization can identify its strengths and weaknesses. Through an understanding of such factors the organization can compete and fulfil customer needs more effectively and efficiently. Various models exist to help managers make sense of their environment and will be reviewed throughout this chapter. One of the first challenges is to recognize the enormity of factors in the business environment and therefore decompose it into manageable parts. Environmental variables are factors that affect the organization, but are beyond the *direct* or positive control of the organization.

The external environment may be divided into layers, see Figure 2-1. The macro environment is the wider environment of social, legal, economic, political and technological influences (forces). The macro environment contains the more general factors likely to affect organizations in a similar manner whereas at the industry level the factors are of more specific concern to a specific set of organizations. The micro environment is the immediate (industry) environment including customers, competitors, suppliers and distributors. One of the main factors affecting most international organizations is the degree of competition faced. Greater influence is likely to come from the actions of competitors and the behaviour of customers or prospects. Markets change rapidly through the entrance of new competitors, technologies, legislation and evolving customer needs. Aside from considering the macro and industry (micro) external business environment, the organization must also analyze the internal environment; resources and capabilities (refer back to the previous chapter – 'leveraging and resource capabilities').

Earlier we observed that the environment was constantly changing. Yet the environments of some industries change more than others. Emery and Trist (1965) presented a typology describing four kinds of organizational environment from placid at one extreme to turbulent at the other. Similarly, two dimensions of the environment were identified by Duncan (1972). The simple-complex dimension is defined as the number of factors taken into consideration in decision-making (environmental complexity); the more factors, the higher the complexity. The static-dynamic dimension is viewed as the degree to

Business environment the totality of factors, internal and external, which may influence the organization's achievement of its goals

Environmental variables factors that affect the organization

Macro environment the wider environment of social, legal, economic, political and technological influences in which the organization is situated

Micro environment the immediate environment including customers, competitors, suppliers and distributors in which the organization is situated

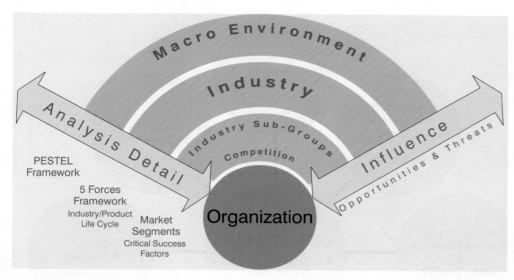

Figure 2-1

Layers of the international organization business environment

which these factors in the decision unit's environment remain basically the same over time or are in a continual process of *change* (environmental dynamism); the greater the pace of change, the more dynamic the environment. Similarly, environmental uncertainty describes the degree of unpredictable turbulence and change in the external political, economic, social, technological, legal and ecological context within which an organization operates; the more the dimensions of the external context are interrelated, the higher the environmental uncertainty.

Environmental dynamism is a widely-explored construct in the organization theory and strategic management literature. This construct has a growing importance according to the degree of instability or turbulence of such key operating concerns as market and industry conditions as well as more general technological, economic, social, and political forces, see Figure 2-2. The ability of an organization to adapt to changing environmental circumstances is a key to organizational survival while effectiveness of the adaptive response is dependent on aligning the response to the environmental circumstances faced by the organization. As firms have limited control over the external environment, their success depends upon how well they adapt to it. A firm's ability to design and adjust its internal variables to take advantage of opportunities offered by the external environment, and its ability to control threats posed by the same environment, help determine its success.

There are many ways to analyse and assess the environment. Environmental analysis is the process of assessing and interpreting the information gathered through environmental scanning (continuously monitoring the environment). Such analysis is considered within this chapter which is organized with Figure 2-1 in mind. First, considering the macro environment and methods to analyze it, we then move on to consider the environment at the more specific industry and industry sub-group level. The internal environment is then considered and we conclude the chapter with a brief discussion about the relationship between the internal and external environment, contingency theory and differing perspectives on the environment. This chapter provides a building block for the study of international and global strategy – considered in the next chapter – and the challenges associated with its implementation; it also acts as a foundation for the remainder of the book. To provide structure and aid learning, this chapter is organized into four main sections:

- macro environment;
- micro environment;
- the internal environment; and
- contingency.

Environmental dynamism the pace of change in relevant factors external to the organization; the greater the pace of change, the more dynamic the environment

Environmental uncertainty the extent of ambiguity in the external environment

Environmental analysis the process of assessing and interpreting the information gathered through environmental scanning

Environmental scanning the process of collecting information about the forces in the environment

Figure 2-2

Environmental influences on the international organization

External (macro) environment

Making sense of the macro environment poses a significant challenge. However, there are diagnostic frameworks that help break it down into more manageable components (environmental variables) that can be investigated. PESTEL (*see* also PEST, SLEPT, STEP and PESTLE) analysis is a common technique for analyzing the general external environment of an organization in terms of the political, economic, socio-cultural, technological, environmental and legal aspects, see Figure 2-3. Organizations undertake the process of continuously monitoring the environment so that they can respond accordingly; in some cases the analysis of the external environment may be described as an external audit. From an international organizational perspective it is important to recognize that legal, economic and sociocultural factors exist within each country. Consequently, the environment of the international organization is more diverse and complex. Not all factors will influence the organization's industry and the analyst must identify the more important factors, understand the implications and then act accordingly – typically adapting the organization's strategy, structure, practices, systems, culture, products and services.

We consider each of the PESTLE factors next before focusing on the micro business environment of the international organization. We will consider what each variable is and why the organization needs to be aware of it.

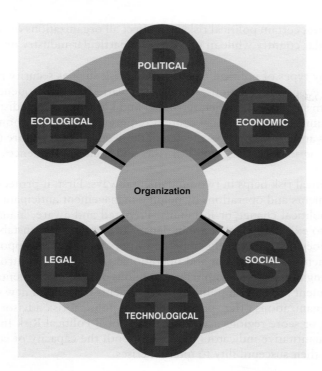

Figure 2-3
PESTLE factors

Political environment

Governments can grant access to markets and rescind such permission at any time. Governments formulate policy toward international trade and vary in the degree to which they may intervene in order to protect or help their domestic organizations competing at home or abroad. The policies individual countries adopt affect the size and probability of markets and may create unfair competition; acts of government create winners and losers in the marketplace. However, political behaviour can be a source of efficiency and market power particularly in international contexts. All organizations, to some extent, are exposed to political risk and forces – it is intrinsic to international business.

Political systems (the structures, processes and activities by which any nation governs itself) may be a source of opportunity or threat. Within countries, it is the political ideology (set of integrated beliefs, theories and doctrines) that may direct the actions of society. The political system may be described in a number of ways, typically on a continuum between democracy and totalitarianism (such as communism, theocratic or secular totalitarianism). Systems exist on a continuum where power is centralized (with the government) at one extreme and decentralized at the other. A totalitarian regime is characterized by the centralization of power, an imposed authority (typically supported through a powerful military). Even within democracies, different beliefs exist. Conservatives (rightwing) seek to minimize government activities while maximizing private ownership of business, while liberals might prefer greater government involvement (leftwing). In some cases a country's religious leaders are also its political leaders – a system labelled theocracy. In other cases, a particular ethnic group within the country may impose its will on others – a system known as tribal totalitarianism.

When undertaking business in different countries, the international organization will *adapt* to meet the demands of the local political system. For example, the law may be considered more vague or non-existent in totalitarian nations. In such countries, more emphasis may be placed on how individual bureaucrats interpret the law making business dealings more risky. Political risk arises from a variety of sources such as an unstable political system, policy change, conflict, poor political leadership or poor relations with other countries. Managers must be aware of how political risk can affect their organization and

Political ideology a set of doctrines or beliefs that form the basis of a political system

Democracy Political system in which government is by the people, exercised either directly or through elected representatives

Totalitarianism form of government in which one person or political party exercises absolute control over all spheres of human life and opposing political parties are prohibited

Political risk the chance that politically induced events will adversely affect the profit and other goals of a business organization

trade. In some cases, certain political risks will affect all organizations operating in or trading with a particular country while in other cases a particular industry or small-group may be threatened.

There are many types of political and associated risk such as security risks, corruption, civil protest and economic sanctions. There are a variety of consequences (business impacts) arising from such risk. Conflict, terrorism and kidnapping may disrupt business operations and revenue generation; local content requirements impact upon labour cost and quality of outputs and profits may be affected in the event of asset seizure (see confiscation, expropriation or **nationalization**). Political risks and their consequences are summarized in Figure 2-4.

Managing political risk helps in two fundamental ways. First, it protects new and existing global investments and operations by helping management anticipate the business risk implications of political change or instability. Prepared and aware, management is more likely to be able to exit markets that are in danger of growing too unstable. Where short-term instability does not dampen the appetite to pursue long-term opportunity, management can implement risk mitigation and operational oversight to control against shocks. Second, monitoring political risk within target regions or across continents, see Figure 2-5, can help management hone in on political developments that reveal new opportunities.

A variety of organizations offer specialized global political risk advisory and consulting services and rank or score regions according to a Global Political Risk Index – a range of qualitative and quantitative indicators to measure both the capacity of countries to withstand shocks and their susceptibility to internal crises.

Nationalization changing something from private to state ownership or control

Figure 2-4

Political risks and their impact

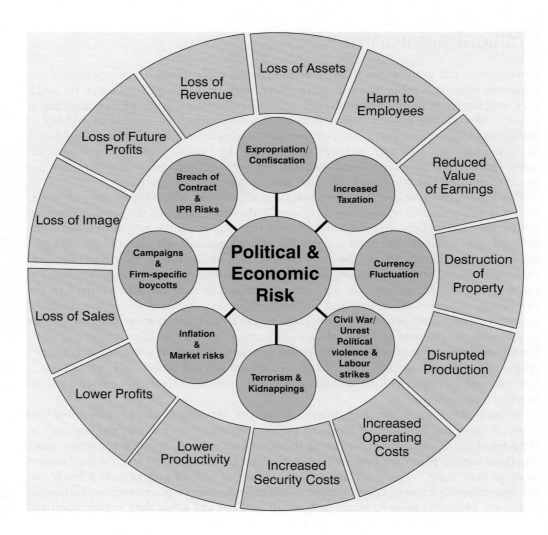

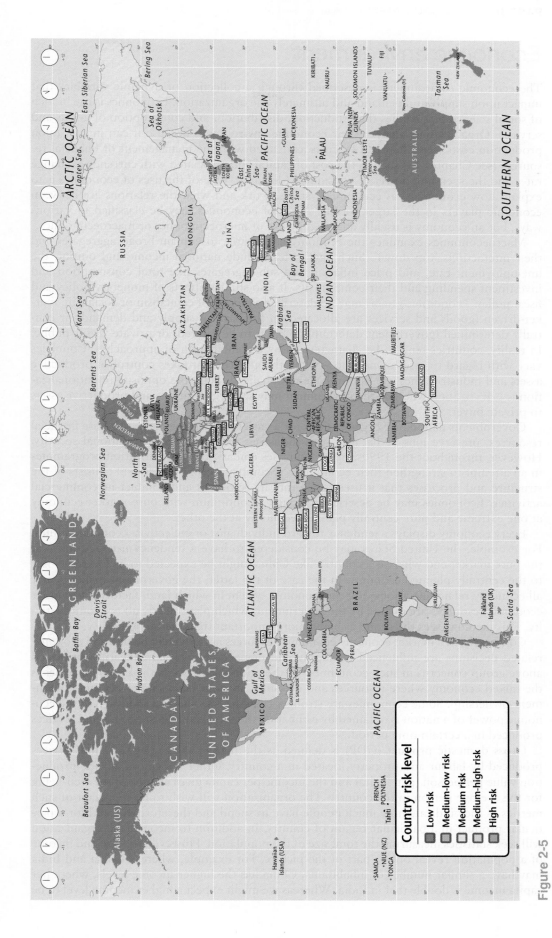

Figure 2-5

Adapted from Political and economic risk map (Copyright Aon Corporation)

Country risk level

- Low risk
- Medium-low risk
- Medium risk
- Medium-high risk
- High risk

Economic environment

The economic environment is described through a collection of dynamic variables that impact upon supply and demand and ultimately the organization. Economics is the branch of social science that studies the production, distribution, and consumption of goods and services. Organizations analyze their economic environment because it can impact upon production costs (see Chapter 14), costs associated with the management of financial resources (see Chapter 16) such as the cost of capital and associated with currency exchange rates and the spending power of consumers (demand). One of the uses of economics is to explain how economies, as economic systems, work and what the relations are between economic players in the larger society. Areas of economics may be classified in various ways, but an economy is usually analyzed by use of microeconomics or macroeconomics.

Macroeconomics examines the economy as a whole to explain broad aggregates and their interactions 'top down'. Such aggregates include national income and output, the unemployment rate, and price inflation and sub-aggregates like total consumption and investment spending and their components. It also studies effects of monetary policy and fiscal policy. Economic systems may be described in terms of capitalism or socialism, market-driven (goods and services are allocated on the basis of supply and demand) or centrally determined (government determines what is to be offered) or private versus public. In reality, countries tend to be characterized by a combination of approaches. Countries vary with regard to asset ownership – when the government takes control of productive assets and industries they are said to have nationalized them; the opposite of nationalization is privatization whereby the government may sell organizations and productive assets to private buyers.

Economic system a set of methods and standards brought by which a society decides and organizes the ownership and allocation of economic resources

Privatization the sale by the government of organizations and productive assets to private buyers

Governments nationalize organizations for a variety of reasons such as to raise financial resources, preserve jobs or because such industries may be critical to national security. However, throughout the 1990s, many countries embarked on privatization programmes in an attempt to strengthen their economies. A country's economic system consists of the structure and processes that it uses to allocate its resources and conduct its commercial activities. Economies may be described through a continuum with pure market economy at one extreme and pure centrally planned economy at the other.

Every economy displays a tendency toward individualist or collectivist economic values. For example, the United States may be considered to have a tendency oriented more at the pure market end whereas a country like China might be expected to be located closer to the centrally planned economy. In the case of the latter, the government makes nearly all economy related decisions; it is an economic system in which land, factories and other economic resources are owned by the government, which plans nearly all economic activity. This ideology sees the group as being more important than the individual.

Conversely, in a market economy economic resources are privately owned and economy related decisions are influenced by supply and demand. Individual concerns are placed above group concerns in such economies. At the midpoint between these two extremes is the mixed economy where resources and decisions are split between private and government ownership. Some economies are stronger than others. The best indicator of the economic power of a nation is obtained by estimating the total value of the goods and services produced in a certain time period.

Gross domestic product (GDP) is defined as the market value of goods and services produced by labour and property located in a country. Other indicators include production value per person (per capita) and the income per capita gives an idea of the well-being for the average person in the country. The organization will wish to be cognizant of such metrics as they indicate how much people have to spend and therefore demand for a particular product in a particular region of country. In addition to income, the organization will seek statistics measuring the total size of the population. However, the size and income of a population reveal only a part of the picture. For example, whereas China and India may have a similar number of inhabitants, China has the higher income levels, where per capita income is double that in India. Whereas we might expect a higher income level to be associated with the purchase of more luxurious items, people only start to purchase certain items once their individual income level has passed a certain threshold level. For example, in an analysis of China and India, people start to buy mobile telephones when their income is at least $3000 (approximately). Consequently, while the Chinese per capita income was found to be 70 per cent higher than Indian per capita income the market for mobile telephones in China was not twice as large as in India (the total income comparison), but more than 23 times as large.

In many ways, the economic systems of countries are becoming similar. Through the establishment of transnational rules, treaties, policies, agreements and law, countries are now more economically intertwined (economic integration) with one another, engaging in more international trade than ever before. Economic integration impacts upon business activity; in some cases creating trade (countries may focus in areas where they have a comparative advantage) and in other cases diverting it (members of the group may cease trading with non-members, favouring each other). The degree of economic integration varies from simple (free trade agreements/areas) through the elimination of trade barriers (common market) to full economic or political union where policies are unified across members and a common governing body exists. International organizations, MNCs in particular, adapt their strategies to benefit from integration, locating operations or forming strategic alliances and acquisitions that enable access to such markets.

When trading with another country, products and services may be purchased with currency from a country which is foreign to the producer. To exchange one currency for another in international transactions, organizations rely on the foreign exchange market – a market in which currencies are bought and sold and their prices determined; one currency is converted into another at a specific exchange rate. However, the presence of foreign currency in international transactions exposes organizations to risk when there is a delay between the sale and payment. If the exchange rate of the foreign currency drops during this period then the value of any payment, relative to the organization's home country will fall (meaning of course that it will receive less money). The practice of insuring against potential losses that result from adverse changes in exchange rates is called currency hedging. As we have seen, unfavourable movements in exchange rates can be costly for international organizations.

Exchange rates affect business activities, they affect the demand for a company's products in the global marketplace (a weak currency has the affect of lowering prices, making the country's export more appealing) and can be used to increase margin when workers are paid in a country with a weak currency yet products are sold in a country with a strong currency. As was indicated earlier, organizations trading across country borders must manage foreign exchange risk. Foreign exchange risk, also known as 'currency risk' or 'exchange-rate risk', is the risk that changes in exchange rates will harm the profitability of a business transaction. The organization faces foreign exchange risk when the financial benefits or costs of an international transaction can be adversely affected by exchange rate fluctuations. It is not just transactions that may be at risk from foreign exchange rate fluctuations. There are also translation and economic exposures. As part of reporting its results, the multinational must integrate the financial statements of its subsidiaries into a set of consolidated financial statements (see Chapter 17). Currency translation involves converting the financial statements of foreign subsidiaries into the currency of the home country. Translation exposure is the extent to which the reported consolidated results and balance sheets of a corporation are affected by fluctuations in foreign exchange values.

Foreign exchange risk the chance of a loss due to an adverse movement in exchange rates

Socio-cultural environment

The social or socio-cultural factors in the macro environment typically include social values, attitudes and beliefs, demographic trends, lifestyle preferences and skills availability. When organizations operate internationally they need to understand how people in other countries may differ; the international organization must operate in different countries

Socio-cultural the common behavioural influences of stakeholders on organizations

Courtesy of Blair Castle, Perthshire

Scottish bagpipers; one example of national culture on display

Culture shared ways of thinking and behaving (uniformity)

Figure 2-6
Elements of culture

Power distance (PD) The extent to which the less powerful members of institutions and organizations within a country expect and accept that power is distributed unequally. (A score of 100 represents a large power distance country)

Uncertainty avoidance (UA) The extent to which the members of a culture feel threatened by uncertain or unknown situations. (A score of 100 represents a country with high uncertainty avoidance)

Individualism (Ind) Individualism pertains to societies in which the ties between individuals are loose: everyone is expected to look after themselves. Collectivism as its opposite pertains to societies in which people from birth onwards are integrated into strong cohesive in-groups. (A score close to 100 represents an individualist country)

Masculinity (Mas) Masculinity pertains to societies in which social gender roles are clearly distinct as opposed to overlapping. (A score of 100 represents a more masculine country)

where the inhabitants may differ to those of their home markets. The construct used to describe such differences is termed (national) culture and cultural differences can create problems within the business environment. Differences in culture (fit) may necessitate changes to business practices, management styles, products and services. Differences in societies arise through education, religion, language and social systems inculcating values and meanings that become shared by the country's people (see the elements of culture in Figure 2-6). Differences may also arise as a result of the country's location, physical environment, geography and climate. The environment is a source of challenge shared by inhabitants who develop similar coping behaviours. The degree of difference between two countries impacts upon the extent of adaptation required by an international organization. The organization, therefore, needs to have some awareness of the differences. To that end, a variety of frameworks exist to measure national culture. Such frameworks (see for example Hofstede 1984) typically decompose the complex construct of culture into several dimensions. Dimensions vary and are dependent upon the level of culture being analyzed. Typically, dimensions at the national and pan-national level are value-based. Dimensions at the organizational or sub-group level may include attitudes but are more likely to focus on behaviour and practice rather than on constructs directly related to the way we think.

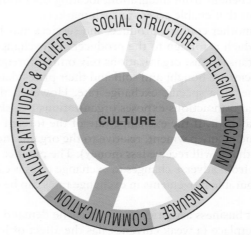

The starting point in comparing different cultures concerns how to define culture and the cultural dimensions to study (Javidan and House 2001). There is no standard definition of culture and no universal set of cultural dimensions. There are potentially many ways that cultures can be different. In Table 2-1 we present an outline of different cultural dimensions and a simplified explanation of possible behavioural consequences based on the landmark work of Hofstede – who studied how values in the workplace are influenced by culture. He analyzed a large database of employee values scores collected by IBM between 1967 and 1973 covering more than 70 countries, from which he first used only 40 and later extended the analysis to 50 countries and 3 regions. From the initial results, and later additions, Hofstede developed a model that identifies five primary dimensions to assist in differentiating national cultures:

- power distance (related to the problem of inequality);
- uncertainty avoidance (related to the problem of dealing with the unknown and unfamiliar);
- individualism – collectivism (related to the problem of interpersonal ties); and
- masculinity – femininity (related to emotional gender roles).

Later he added the fifth dimension:

- long- versus short-term orientation (related to deferment of gratification).

Despite arguments that suggest some aspects of culture cannot be measured or compared, or that the differences between countries is diminishing, the study and its findings have been widely embraced and continue to be used by many.

The cultural dimensions proposed by Hofstede can be used, in conjunction with other information, to evaluate cultural differences and therefore predict any needy adaptation by the international organization. The extent of cultural adaptation will depend on the closeness of the cultural 'fit' between countries.

More recently, Javidan and House (2001) present important findings from the GLOBE project designed to enhance global managers' cultural acumen. GLOBE not only adopted the dimensions paradigm, they also started from Hofstede's choice of five (Hofstede 2006). For conceptual reasons they expanded these to nine. The nine dimensions served as the basis for the culture questions in the GLOBE questionnaire. The GLOBE project was designed as a replication and elaboration of the Hofstede study. We include the data from Hofstede's study (scores of cultural dimensions) for reference throughout the book. It is important to remember, however, that the values have been generalized for the whole population and should not be used to infer the values of any particular individual from a specific country.

Table 2-1

Dimensions of national culture

Dimension	Consequences
Power distance	Societies that are high on PD tend to expect obedience towards superiors and clearly distinguish between those with status and power and those without it. In countries with a high power score (discipline), superiors are supposed to initiate contact and subordinates will follow command without question (rule orientation). Organizations in such countries tend to be bureaucratic, tall hierarchies with consequences of slower decision-making. In low PD countries, an employee is more likely to challenge-the-boss. A belief or attitude such as 'The boss knows best' may result in negative behaviour such as not speaking out about problems. High PD cultures are like military machines while in lower PD cultures, employees of organizations are more likely to think like owners.
Uncertainty avoidance	Societies that are high on uncertainty avoidance have a stronger tendency toward orderliness and consistency, structured lifestyles, clear specification of social expectations, and rules and laws to cover situations. In contrast, the people of countries where there is strong tolerance of ambiguity and uncertainty are used to less structure in their lives and are not as concerned about following rules and procedures. Hofstede lists characteristics of high uncertainty avoidance such as fear of failure, less risk-taking, a belief in expertise, a preference for clear requirements and instructions, and orientation to rules, and lower readiness to compromise.
Individualism	On the individualist side we find societies in which the ties between individuals are loose: everyone is expected to look after themselves and their immediate family. On the collectivist side, people from birth onwards are integrated into strong, cohesive in-groups, often extended families which continue protecting them in exchange for unquestioning loyalty. Members of collectivist cultures are more likely to favour group decision-making, value harmony and will engage in face saving behaviours; members of individualist cultures emphasize autonomy, self-respect and independence. Individual achievement is highly valued in individualistic cultures.
Masculinity	Countries with the least gender-differentiated practices tend to accord women a higher status and a stronger role in decision-making. They have a higher percentage of women participating in the labour force and more women in positions of authority. Men and women in these cultures tend to have similar levels of education. In contrast, countries reported to have high degrees of gender differentiation tend to accord men higher social status and have relatively few women in positions of authority.
Future orientation	Countries with a strong future orientation, such as Singapore, Switzerland, and the Netherlands, are associated with a higher propensity to save for the future and longer thinking and decision-making time frames. Countries with weak future orientation, such as Russia, Argentina, and Italy, are associated with shorter thinking and planning horizons and greater emphasis on instant gratification.

Table 2-2

Scores of cultural dimensions
(by country)

Country	Ind	PD	UA	MAS	
Argentina	46	49	86	56	
Australia	90	36	51	61	
Austria	55	11	70	79	
Belgium	75	65	94	54	
Brasil	38	69	76	49	
Canada	80	39	48	52	
Chile	23	63	86	28	
Colombia	13	67	80	64	
Denmark	74	18	23	16	
Finland	63	33	59	26	
France	71	68	86	43	
Germany	67	35	65	66	
Great Britain	89	35	35	66	
Greece	35	60	112	57	Avoid Uncertainty
Hong Kong	25	68	29	57	
India	48	77	40	56	
Iran	41	58	59	43	
Ireland	70	28	35	68	
Israel	54	13	81	47	
Italy	76	50	75	70	More Masculine
Japan	46	54	92	95	
Mexico	30	81	82	69	
Netherlands	80	38	53	14	
New Zealand	79	22	49	58	
Norway	69	31	50	8	
Pakistan	14	55	70	50	
Peru	16	64	87	42	Large Power Distance
Philippines	32	94	44	64	
Portugal	27	63	104	31	
Singapore	20	74	8	48	
South Africa	65	49	49	63	
Spain	51	57	86	42	
Sweden	71	31	29	5	
Switzerland	68	34	58	70	
Taiwan	17	58	69	45	
Thailand	20	64	64	34	
Turkey	37	66	85	45	Individualist
USA	91	40	46	62	
Venezuela	12	81	76	73	
Yugoslavia	27	76	88	21	

Constructs such as those presented as culture dimensions (see Table 2-1), research data (see Table 2-2), personal observations and conversations with others can all be used to build profiles about other cultures. Such profiles enable employees to anticipate the differences that may be encountered when working with people from other cultures; they help a person from one culture develop an understanding of another and may help workers anticipate management styles and different ways of doing business in other cultures. We discuss working in other countries and cultures in Chapter 8.

While, thus far, we have emphasized country differences, to some extent, people from certain countries are more similar than those of more distant countries. Many scholars have argued for similarities among national cultures and attempted to simplify the classification process. Identifying clusters of countries sharing similar cultural values that might affect business practices can reduce work in analysis and design activity. The GLOBE research team identified ten cultural clusters. Clusters can be used when formulating strategy – the degree of similarity or difference may impact upon market entry methods, selection of countries in which to conduct business and decisions about whether practice is likely to be transferred, or created. Hofstede (1984, 1997) groups both countries and related values and attitudes; specifically, he notes a correlation between the two dimensions of power distance and individuality (despite believing them to be conceptually different). He notes that most high power distance countries are also low individualism countries (i.e. collectivist) and vice versa, but there are exceptions. He argues against collapsing the two into one dimension. Additionally, he notes that power distance and uncertainty avoidance will interact. For simplicity, we have clustered Hofstede's national culture dimensions – see Figure 2-7 Countries that score high on PD also tend to score high on collectivism (see Table 2-2). Such countries typify the 'East' and South America. At almost the opposite is the 'West' with typically a low PD and high Ind scores. Similarly, many high PD countries seem to score low on uncertainty avoidance.

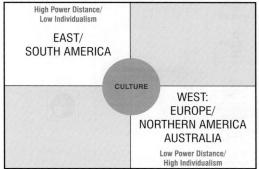

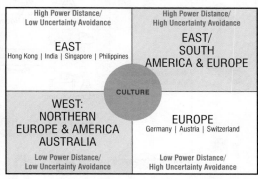

Figure 2-7

Simplified view of East and West clusters (Adapted from Hofstede (1984: 159))

Technological environment

Technology is a broad concept that literally means the application of science, especially to industrial or commercial objectives; for most people technology represents electronic or digital products and systems (such as communication devices, machines, computers, robots, etc.). Like culture, it is a factor that features in all aspects of the business environment – external and internal. Technological *change* may result in new ways of behaving

Technological environment those forces that affect the technology used by the organization and which can create new products, new markets, and new opportunities

Technology a broad concept that literally means the application of science, especially to industrial or commercial objectives

both at work and at home and can raise productivity, improve and change the way we communicate and may impact upon mechanisms of trade affecting how we buy and sell goods and services, see Figure 2-8.

Aside from impacting upon business practice itself, new technology may also feature within products and services. The application of new technologies in any of these areas may result in new opportunities and threats for the international organization. Technology may be transferred from outside the organization or from within. For example, international organizations, the multinational in particular, may transfer the benefits of technologies developed in-house to their subsidiaries (intra-organizational transfer). Technology may also be transferred externally through franchises, licences, and joint ventures. Different technologies impact upon work in different ways, changing the nature of work and therefore may impact upon the organization and structuring of work. The relationship between technology and work is captured in a theory known as technological determinism. Technological determinism (considered in Chapter 9) is a contingency theory arguing that technology determines aspects of organizational structure, i.e. it should be possible to predict aspects of organizational structure from knowledge of the organization's technology – *see also* structural determinism – contextual factors impose certain constraints upon the structural choices managers make (Child 1997). Valentin (2001) identifies potential effects of technological developments suggesting they may:

- bring about direct substitutes for end-products;
- catalyze societal changes that affect life styles and shopping patterns;
- spawn environments that lift constraints;
- alter cost structures; and
- create substitutes for industrial processes.

It has been argued that some jobs (work tasks) have been eliminated as a result of technology (replacement) while in some cases it has created jobs. Similarly, it has been argued

Technological determinism the argument that technology can be used to explain internal aspects of the organization

Figure 2-8

Technology and work

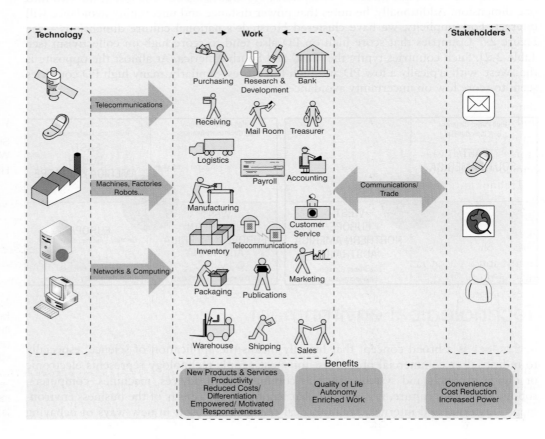

that technology can deskill work while others have argued that it increases demand on people at work. Technology can impact on both the physical and mental aspects of work. During the industrial revolution, machines typically replaced the physical activities of people and were sometimes applied to boring and repetitive work. In many cases, low-paid manual work is more easily automated, however it is much more difficult to substitute technology for people in jobs that require more complex problem-solving abilities. During the information revolution, technology primarily through information systems and communications sought to replace some thinking tasks while assisting people with others.

Technological change in conjunction with broader political and economic change led to the delayering and downsizing of organizations throughout the 1990s. In many cases, technology has been used to enrich work, empowering people and enabling group work. Overcoming both time and distance problems it has changed the nature of work through tele- and home-working; developments in computing and telecommunications have made such options more viable. Tele- or home-working may benefit the organization in many ways. The organization requires less office space thus reducing building and utility costs; the employee may be more motivated through flexibility and autonomy, and may witnesses a reduction in their personal work-related costs (transportation to and from work and possibly childcare). Such workers may be more time-rich, possibly saving several hours per week in travel time (improving the quality of life). Such time savings may be shared to benefit both employer and employee alike. Furthermore, the organization requires less supervisory control and employees typically report increased efficiency and productivity due to less distraction. There are, however, downsides as home workers or tele-workers often feel isolated and may not share the typical attitudes, assumptions and beliefs developed through the organizational culture.

Through technology, customer and broader stakeholder interactions with the organization are also changed. Either through the use of Internet or telecommunications (data or voice), the customer may interact with the organization without the need to be physically present at the organization's offices during their opening hours. Customers may make use of e-commerce systems or call centres to communicate electronically with the organization. Whereas, historically, a customer may have been shunted around the organization in order to find an employee who could answer the customer query, the contemporary organization makes use of information systems such as customer relationship management, supply chain management and enterprise resource planning software to enable call centre employees access to the information they require to solve customer problems (see Chapter 13). Telecommunications coupled with such systems enable call centres to be located almost anywhere in the world thus making use of and exploiting lower wage rates and skill shortages. Furthermore, technology may be used to monitor and control the work of employees. In the case of outsourcing and off-shoring, technology poses *threats* to some (domestic employees and trade unions) and *opportunities* to others (host country and foreign country employers and foreign employees).

Technology is not without its downside. At the organizational level, companies may suffer competitive disadvantage where competitors acquire superior technology. In this case, the organization's lack of technology is a weakness and the company is threatened by competitor actions. At a micro level, the organization's technology and intellectual property may be copied or stolen – see digital copies. Text or anything else can now be produced almost infinitely at next to zero cost. Furthermore, the organization's technology assets may be threatened, particularly those relating to its information systems and IT. In many cases, organizations are critically dependent upon such technology.

Call centre a physical place where customer and other telephone calls are handled by an organization, usually with some degree of computer automation

Intellectual property a generic term used to describe designs, ideas and inventions – covers patents, trade marks, designs and copyright

Legal systems in the environment

Thus far we have outlined the political, economic, socio-cultural and technological aspects of the macro environment. In this section we touch briefly on the legal environment and the key factors that may influence the international organization. The main focus is on laws and legal systems. However, given the vast and specific nature of law and complexity

Legal system System of rules that regulate behaviour and the processes by which the laws of a country are enforced and through which redress of grievances is obtained

of international law we simply identify the main types of legal systems worldwide. A legal system is the set of laws made and enforced to control the actions of people and organizations. Countries' legal and political systems are interwoven. Laws may limit or open up opportunity, govern the conduct of business operations and manifest in the way business is performed. Organizations are required to obey the law otherwise they are likely to incur costs. Legal systems may be categorized in a number of ways and vary from country to country. Common law is used to describe a legal system based on precedent; civil law is based on written rules and theocratic law is based upon religious teachings. Legal-system-forces may influence or manifest in product safety and reliability, intellectual property protection, antitrust regulations and taxation. Examples of laws affecting the international organization include: copyright and patent laws, minimum wage, work safety and environmental protection laws. In some countries, legislation is used to ensure good corporate governance.

STOP & THINK

Individually or in groups, discuss the impact of laws and regulations on the airline industry. You might also consider other industries such as telecomms or media.

In the ongoing public debate on globalization outlined in the introductory chapter, concerns have been expressed about the economic, social and environmental impacts of deepening international trade and investment ties and about the activities of the multinational enterprises (OECD 2001). These concerns focus on a variety of issues including labour relations, human rights, environment, corruption, control of technology and consumer protection. The high profile of this debate means that most multinational enterprises now pay close attention to public perceptions of their activities in the societies in which they operate. Globalization has also brought with it additional management challenges for organizations in an area that has come to be called 'legal compliance'.

Multinational enterprises are often present in dozens of jurisdictions covering many legal and regulatory areas. These companies need to keep themselves informed about the regulations affecting them and must take steps to ensure that they comply with law and regulation. Compliance can be quite complex, especially when the enterprise's operations straddle a variety of regions and business cultures. Thus, compliance with law and regulation is often not a straightforward task, especially for multinational enterprises. Organizations have attempted to respond to public concerns and to the growing challenge of 'legal compliance' in a globalizing business environment. New management techniques have emerged. Some 20 years ago organizations began issuing policy statements (or codes of conduct) that set forth their commitments in various areas of business ethics and legal compliance. A second step was the development of management systems designed to help them comply with these commitments and the emergence of standardized management systems. A new management discipline has emerged involving professionals that specialize in regulatory, legal and ethical compliance. More recently, steps have been taken to formulate standards providing guidance for business reporting on non-financial performance. We consider the issues of business ethics, legal compliance and corporate social responsibility in Chapter 4 and corporate governance in Chapter 17.

Ecological environment

Industrial waste can impact upon other companies and individuals, not just nature

The ecological environment is concerned with the use of natural resources (inputs), pollution (outputs), global warming and similar issues. Concerns may affect the organization's production processes (Chapter 15), customer buying habits and customer perception of the company or product (Chapter 16). In recent times there has been considerable concern about the effects of pollution (greenhouse gases and acid rain) and the depletion of natural resources (rain forests and the ozone layer). Carbon dioxide emissions from industry and the CFCs from their products have contributed to global warming and a myriad of secondary consequences. Such environmental problems result from economic activity. The production and consumption of goods and services can generate spillover effects impacting upon the wider population and not just producers and consumers. However, many organizations do not fully consider the wider social costs of their business activities.

When shareholder returns are the primary goal, the organization may be less likely to spend revenue (decreasing margin) in taking action to curtail environmental damage. Furthermore organizations may be reluctant to pass on the costs of such initiatives to consumers which may result in a need to raise prices and become less competitive. Industrial waste from production processes can also impact upon other companies and individuals – not just nature. In short, there may be negative consequences of economic activity and in some cases the organization responsible may not be motivated to put right any harm caused.

Being more environmentally friendly and responsible (Chapter 4) often causes the organization to incur a cost and it is this that acts as a disincentive to action. In some cases, organizations may be less inclined to incur such costs when they compete with less environmentally conscious competitors from the developing world. The pressure for the international organization to act in the interests of the ecological environment may come from customers, the government, other stakeholders or from within the organization itself. The organization may voluntarily set goals and standards for environmentally responsible behaviour. For example easyJet have an environmental code, based on three promises:

1 to be environmentally efficient in the air;
2 to be environmentally efficient on the ground; and
3 to lead in shaping a greener future for aviation, for example: through carbon offsetting and shaping future aircraft design.

Alternatively, companies may be encouraged to act more responsibly through the activities and influence of government in the form of taxes, fines, grants, regulation and legislation. The tax mechanism can be used to impose extra costs on both producers and consumers (polluter pays). The effect of the tax is to increase the cost of production and reduce the output of pollutants. Grants can be used as an incentive to reduce pollution, waste and emissions and encourage environmentally friendly behaviour. Regulations can be used in a variety of ways such as to prohibit certain activities (abstraction or disposal), to set minimum and maximum limits for the abstraction of particular natural resources and discharge of pollutants and prescribe appropriate technology and activities.

Environmental standards, regulations and penalties can create barriers to entry (see Porter's five forces to be discussed later), facilitate the search for substitute inputs and may spawn new business opportunities. Furthermore, in the future, organizations that are based in heavily regulated countries (early movers) may be in position to gain competitive advantage over organizations operating under less regulation. Not only may such companies gain from positive consumer perceptions, they may also accumulate experience. In some cases regulation will occur at the national level while in other cases environmental issues are being tackled on a regional and global scale (see for example the United Nations or European Union). Such organizations, aside from protecting human health, typically have goals to preserve, protect and improve the quality of the environment and to ensure a prudent and rational utilization of natural resources. Not only may the government have the power to influence organizations, pressure may also be exerted by the consumer, media, insurers and pressure groups.

Organizations and their industries vary in the extent of environmental damage they cause. Whereas agriculture, mining and chemicals are likely to have a high impact, tourism, packaging, and electronics a moderate impact, the likes of advertising, education and government will have a lower impact. Not only do we observe variation in the impact but also in the responses available to organizations. In some cases the organization may simply comply (minimal response) with regulations; in other cases the organization will go further, taking a positive and proactive stance towards environmental issues (green organizations). It is possible for international organizations to locate in less regulated, developing countries in order to escape tougher environmental legislation. However, there is a danger that consumers and other stakeholders consider this to be an example of the organization trying to avoid their environmental responsibilities.

Many companies subscribe to self-regulation schemes and make information available to the public, principally by an environmental policy statement together with clear targets and goals needed to meet the policy. Environmental issues are becoming increasingly important in consumer buying decisions a matter we consider in Chapter 4 and in Chapter 16 on marketing in Part V. Consumers may avoid products that cause environmental damage or unnecessary waste or use scarce resources or resources likely, through their depletion, to impact on other animals. In some cases the customer may be prepared to pay a higher price or seek out those organizations which they believe to be ethical.

Thus far we have presented and explained the PESTLE framework used to diagnose and make sense of the macro external environment. In this first section we have focused on the more general factors that can impact upon organizations and their activities. In the next section we focus on the more specific factors in the micro environment.

Industry (micro) environment

Micro environment: the immediate environment within a defined industry

The last section demonstrated the importance of the macro factors in the external business environment, but such factors are only of relevance if they impact upon the industry and the organization. In this section we focus on the influences (forces) that are closer to the organization, the micro environment – the immediate environment including customers, competitors, suppliers and distributors and seek to develop an understanding of the *industry context*. Not all industries are the same with some being inherently more profitable than others, some more complex and others more dynamic. The term industry is sometimes used to describe a very precise business activity (e.g. mobile telecomms) or a more generic business activity (e.g. telecomms or the car industry), a particular kind of commercial enterprise. If a company participates in multiple business activities, it is usually considered to be part of the industry in which most of its revenues are derived.

When analyzing competition within an industry from an international perspective, two types of industry are revealed. In *multidomestic* industries competition in each country (or small group of countries) is essentially independent of competition in other countries, i.e. there is a particular industry present in many countries but competition occurs on a country-by-country basis. The international industry becomes a collection of essentially domestic industries – hence the term multidomestic. At the other end of the spectrum are global industries. A global industry is an industry in which a firm's competitive position in one country is significantly influenced by its position in other countries. In such cases rivals compete against each other on a truly worldwide basis (Porter 1986). As a part of environmental analysis, the organization should seek to identify, as precisely as possible, the market it is operating within. We discuss this further in Chapter 16 and introduce the concept of segmentation to assist with this task.

Industry competition

In the opening case study we described the European airline industry. While a PESTLE analysis would help make sense of the macro business environment it would not provide the detailed understanding needed to compete in the industry. Consequently, in this section we consider tools such as the five forces framework and industry life cycle to enable a more detailed understanding of the business environment.

The first stage of industry analysis is to identify the key elements of the industry's structure: the suppliers, the competitors and the customers and their relative bargaining power. In order to predict the future profitability of an industry, we must consider levels of competition and identify the trends that are changing the industry's structure. We must then consider how these structural changes will affect the five forces of competition. The actions of competitors will often be among the strongest influences on the organization. Porter's five forces framework can help in identifying the sources of competition in an industry. An organization must confront:

> **Five forces framework** a model that describes the interaction of external influences (forces) within an industry that present threats and opportunities for an organization

1 rivalry of competitors within its industry;

2 threat of new entrants;

3 threat of substitutes;

4 the bargaining power of customers; and

5 the bargaining power of suppliers – together these determine competition in an industry or market.

The competitive forces model is used to describe the interaction of external influences, specifically threats and opportunities that affect an organization's strategy and ability to compete. It uses concepts developed in Industrial Organization (IO) economics to derive the forces that determine the competitive intensity and therefore attractiveness (the overall industry profitability) of a market. An 'unattractive' industry is one where the combination of forces acts to drive down overall profitability. They consist of those forces close to a company that affect its ability to serve its customers and make a profit.

The ultimate profit potential of an industry is governed by the collective strength of the five forces; organizations in certain industries typically earn high profits while organizations in other industries may earn relatively low profits; the weaker the forces collectively, however, the greater the opportunity for better performance. Some scholars believe the corporate strategist's goal is to find a position in the industry where his or her company can best defend itself against these forces or can influence them in its favour (we return to issues of positioning later). The organization must probe below the surface and analyze each force. For example, what makes the industry vulnerable to entry by new competitors (that will steal market share and reduce opportunity) and what determines the bargaining power of suppliers or customers (that may increase costs or reduce margins)? Knowledge of these underlying sources is used by the organization to inform action.

New entrants to an industry bring new capacity, the desire to gain market share, and often considerable resources. However, they may face barriers to entry such as economies of scale, capital requirements, the need for access to distribution channels and political limitations. The threat of entry changes, as these conditions change. Suppliers can exert bargaining power on participants in an industry by raising prices or reducing the quality of purchased goods and services. Powerful suppliers can thereby squeeze profitability out

Figure 2-9
Competitive force (Adapted from Porter 1979)

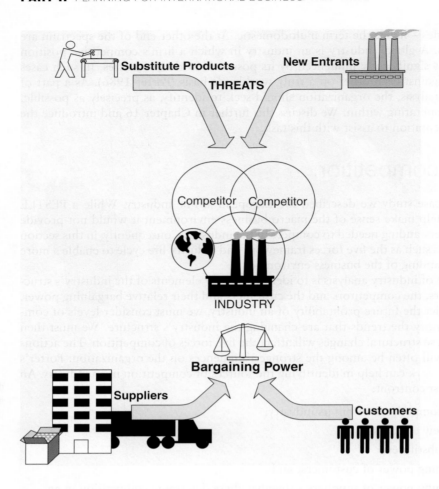

Rivalry the act of competing – a quest to secure an advantage over another

of an industry. A company can improve its strategic posture by finding suppliers or buyers who possess the least power to influence it adversely. Rivalry among existing competitors takes the familiar form of jockeying for position – using tactics like price competition, product introduction and advertising. Intense rivalry is related to the presence of a number of factors:

- competitors are numerous or are roughly equal in size and power;
- industry growth is slow;
- the product or service lacks differentiation or switching costs;
- fixed costs are high or the product is perishable; and
- exit barriers are high.

Average industry profitability is influenced by both potential and existing competitors. Assessing industry attractiveness includes an analysis of entry barriers such as the scale of investment required, the cost and time to establish a brand name and differentiated products. Analysis extends to consideration of substitution threats which may be affected by switching costs. The five forces framework focuses an industry's potential for profit. Next we must determine how such profit is shared between the different organizations competing in that industry. To do this we must identify the key success factors – who the customers are and what their needs are, and how they choose between competing offerings. We must understand what customers want and what the organization must do in order to survive competition. Competitive analysis involves the systematic collection and analysis of public information about rivals (competitive intelligence) in order to predict and determine their future behaviour. Strategic analysis should not be restricted to the present actions of competitors. The organization should also think through future competitive behaviour – competitors do not stand still. Forecasting what they may do in the future enables the organization to contemplate moves that maintain or enhance their competitive position.

McGahan (2000) argues that improved corporate performance hinges on understanding how industries evolve and that the main frameworks currently in use for this purpose are the five forces and the product life cycle models. The five-force framework provides an approach for determining the financial performance of an industry, and thus its attractiveness for investors, at a specific point in time. The product life cycle (PLC) framework is based on the idea that industries move through periods of emergence, shake-out, maturity and decline. McGahan believes that rigorous analysis of industry evolution is necessary to anticipate when different kinds of opportunities are likely to emerge over time. Analyzing industry evolution can generate compelling insights into emerging opportunities, which may reveal critical weaknesses in the organization's old approaches.

The first analytical step involves taking a snapshot of the current environment:

- Is the industry structurally attractive?
- What approaches have been used to balance buyer power and supplier power?
- How do partnerships and strategic alliances influence relationships?
- Are there significant switching costs for customers, incumbents, or suppliers?
- Has rivalry generated excess capacity in key activities?

After analyzing industry structure, evaluate the competitive position of the organization relative to its direct rivals.

- Does it hold a competitive advantage or disadvantage?

Managers should understand the nature of competition within their industry so that they understand how attractive it might be to others and what their position is within it. It is important to recognize that the five forces and market conditions change over time.

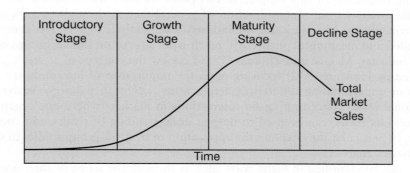

Figure 2-10
Product life cycle

For most international organizations, the external environment is in a constant state of change. The industry life cycle is used to describe change within an industry (see Figure 2-10). Producers introduce their offerings as the industry emerges, however, sales are initially small and products less well known. New industries tend to begin in high income countries. It takes time for the customer base to grow until saturation is reached (maturity stage) whereupon any demand is wholly for replacement. Finally the industry enters decline as it is challenged by new industries and customer-needs change.

The different stages of the industry life cycle place differing demands on organizations. Changes in demand growth and technology over the cycle have implications for industry structure, competition, and the sources of competitive advantage. Creativity and innovation in the form of product development are responsible for the *birth* of the industry. With time comes a greater emphasis on process innovation. In the *introduction* phase, products may be of a poorer quality and more costly to produce. Low demand necessitates short production runs and the use of more specialized distribution channels. As demand grows in other countries, they are serviced initially by exports. Customers tend to be high income early adopters, probably located in advanced countries. At this stage there may be few

Industry life cycle a theory linking the intensity of competition in a particular market with the time since the breakthrough innovation that made that market possible

competitors. There is increased demand in the growth phase placing pressure on production processes and often leading to capacity shortages. Geographical scope is likely to increase as customers are likely to emerge in more places, yet with the increased demand comes increased competition. Competitors will seek to develop their brand and will design the product with quality and manufacturer in mind. Competitors start to consider standardization and process innovation.

Once the industry reaches the *maturity* stage, customers are more knowledgeable and have increased bargaining power. This may result in organizations lowering prices, particularly if the product becomes commoditized. Consequently organizations tend to differentiate through branding and other tactics. Repeat buying is likely, forcing organizations to focus on customer relationship management. Increased competition is likely to result in overcapacity and a focus on price is likely to result in the selection of different manufacturing processes that emphasize longer production runs or flexibility. The value chain is more likely to be fragmented, with aspects of production located in developing countries (international migration of production).

Mature industries tend to be more stable and efficiency goals are likely to be met through bureaucracy. Thus in such organizations we are more likely to observe higher degrees of centralization, well-defined roles (specialization) and a more vertical hierarchy. Efficiency is achieved through standardized routines and tight control. Finally as the industry enters *decline*, differentiation and innovation become unprofitable and increased overcapacity is observed. This may result in the pursuit of cost reduction strategies and price-based competition (price wars), thus the intensity and nature of competition changes during the course of the industry life cycle; rivalry increases with time, as do the number of competitors and there is a shift to price-based competition. With rivalry comes a reduction in margin. Industry evolution poses a significant challenge to the international organization as strategy, structure and contingent systems must be adapted to meet change.

From the beginning of this chapter to this point we have increased the detail of environmental analysis from a consideration of general factors through to a focus on the specific environment. In some cases the industry level analysis may be too general and a more detailed and meaningful picture will result from a focus on similar groups operating within an industry. McGee and Thomas (1986) review the concept of strategic groups (a term coined by Hunt in 1972) focusing upon the importance of intra-industry strategic groupings in understanding differences across firms *within* an industry. Analysis at the organizational level, concentrating on interactions in markets where one organization's action affects its rivals, can be used to deepen understanding of rivalry and competitive advantage. In particular they explore the application of strategic group studies to strengths and weaknesses analysis.

Groups can be identified in many ways such as through the scope of their activities or the way in which they use their resources. For example, in the case of the MBA industry we might identify groupings such as teaching (typically former polytechnics) or traditional (more research oriented) universities and profit-making business schools. Analysis of this type enables the organization to distinguish its most direct competitors and the basis of their competitive rivalry.

Organizations may also consider macro environmental forces specific to or may consider opportunities outside of their group. Aside from a need to understand competitors in relation to opportunity and threat, the international organization must also understand its actual and potential customers and their respective needs. We discuss such issues in Chapter 16. Influences and changes in the environment may impact upon customer needs, creating new opportunities and threats alike. This may then drive organizations to create the required capabilities, products and services.

Within this section we have investigated the external environment and considered a number of diagnostic frameworks to help the international organization make sense of it. The international organization may either routinely, through scanning, or occasionally gather and assess international market-information in order to support decision-making and action. Information is typically used to determine demand (is there an opportunity?),

Strategic groups a collection of organizations within an industry with similar strategic characteristics, following similar strategies or competing on similar bases

Look forward
See chapter 16, p. 525

assess risk (is it safe?) and help with specific finance, marketing or operational activities. Many organizational processes rely on information about external forces, for example:

- internationalization process (investment decisions/capital budgeting);
- strategy formulation process (opportunities and threats);
- leadership process;
- change management process (adaptation);
- marketing process (local issues affecting standardization and differentiation);
- knowledge management process (impact of culture);
- production process (facilities location, sourcing decisions, infrastructure for the supply chain);
- HRM process (hiring practice, motivation, rewards, payroll);
- finance and accounting (standards for reporting).

Such processes are investigated in subsequent chapters. We described the PESTLE framework used to analyze the macro environment and the five forces framework to investigate the micro environment. Recognizing such environments to be in a constant state of change we also discussed the life-cycle model as a means to help understand how industries and products evolve. Having investigated the factors and analytical tools used in the external environment we now turn our attention to the internal environment of the international organization. However, as you will see, the internal environment is partly understood with reference to the external environment.

The internal environment

International success can be realized by focusing on the organization, rather than the external business environment; aside from a need to be aware of the external environment, the international manager must also know the internal business environment – managers need to understand the strengths and weaknesses of their organizations. In the previous chapter we recognized the need for the organization to leverage its resources. In order to do this they must know what they are and how they contribute to value creation and goal attainment. There are several favoured ways to analyze the internal environment such as the resource or skills audit, value chain analysis and comparative methods such as competitor intelligence, benchmarking and internal comparisons. Strategy is accomplished through the allocation and utilization of resources. However, as we shall see later, there are two contrasting views about the starting point for strategy formulation; some start with the external while others the *internal* environment.

The internal environment is made up of the organization's resources, capabilities and competencies and reflects what the organization can do. Organizational resources include all assets, capabilities, organizational processes, firm attributes, information, knowledge, etc. controlled by an organization that enable it to conceive and implement strategies that improve its efficiency and effectiveness (Barney 1991).

Intangible resources are non-physical assets such as information, reputation and knowledge. Physical resources are the tangible resources owned by a company. Examples include land, buildings and plant. Physical resources are also known as tangible assets. Organizations also distinguish between transformed resources, i.e. the resources that are treated, transformed or converted in a process, usually a mixture of materials, information and customers and transforming resources that act upon the transformed resources, usually classified as facilities (the buildings, equipment and plant of an operation) and staff (the people who operate, maintain and manage the operation), Slack, Chambers, and Johnston (2007).

Capabilities refer to what the organization can do (Grant 2007), a company's distinctive competencies to do something well and efficiently (Dibb, Simkin, Pride, and Ferrell 2006).

Organizational resources all assets, capabilities, organizational processes, firm attributes, information, knowledge, etc. controlled by an organization that enable it to function and add value

Efficiency doing things right

Effectiveness doing right things

Capabilities what the organization can do

Competences are the activities and processes through which an organization deploys its resources effectively and a core competence refers to those capabilities fundamental to the organization's strategy and performance. Eustace (2003) discusses the internal resources used to add value and how the emphasis has shifted – from natural resources, machinery and financial capital, now regarded as commodities, to intangible resources as factors of competition (see Figure 2-11).

Figure 2-11

Assets which drive value (Adapted from Eustace (2003))

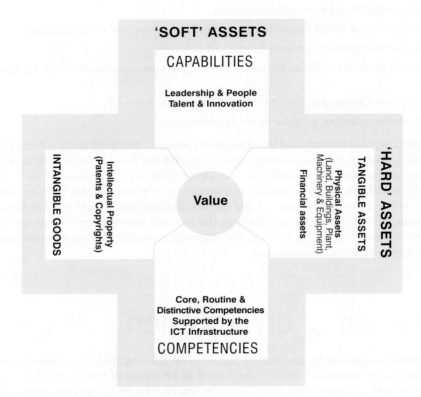

'SOFT' ASSETS

CAPABILITIES

Leadership & People
Talent & Innovation

INTANGIBLE GOODS

Intellectual Property
(Patents & Copyrights)

Value

Physical Assets
(Land, Buildings, Plant,
Machinery & Equipment)

Financial assets

'HARD' ASSETS TANGIBLE ASSETS

Core, Routine &
Distinctive Competencies
Supported by the
ICT Infrastructure

COMPETENCIES

When organization-specific assets are assembled in integrated clusters, spanning individuals and groups, so that they enable distinctive activities to be performed, these activities constitute organizational routines and processes (Teece, Pisano, and Shuen 1997). Routines are the organizationally specific 'ways we do things around here' which tend to persist over time and guide people's behaviour. The concept of 'organizational routine' helps us to understand capabilities. Organizational routines are regular and predictable patterns of activity which are made up of a sequence of coordinated actions by individuals (Grant 1991).

Organizational routines when resources come together in a way that enables distinctive activities to be performed, these activities constitute organizational routines

A capability is, in essence, a routine, or a number of interacting routines. The organization itself is a vast network of routines. These include the sequence of routines which govern the passage of raw material and components through the production process and top management routines which include routines for monitoring business unit performance for capital budgeting, and also for strategy formulation. The concept of organizational routines offers illuminating insights into the relationships between resources, capabilities and competitive advantage (discussed further in the next chapter).

Routines are to the organization what skills are to the individual. Just as the individual's skills are carried out semi-automatically, without conscious coordination, so organizational routines involve a large component of tacit knowledge, which implies limits on the extent to which the organization's capabilities can be expressed. Just as individual skills are acquired through practice over time, so the skills of an organization are developed and sustained only through experience. The advantage of an established organization over a newcomer is primarily in the organizational routines that it has perfected over time. The Boston Consulting Group's 'experience curve' represents an attempt to relate the experience of the organization to its performance. However, in industries where technological change is rapid, new organizations may possess an advantage over established ones through their potential for faster learning of new routines because they are less committed to old routines.

Key resources and capabilities are identified with reference to industry key success factors. If low-cost production determines why some organizations in an industry are more successful than others, then an advantage may be conferred by capabilities or access to raw materials which can reduce costs. The organization needs to identify the resources and capabilities most important in conferring sustainable competitive advantage. The organization must also evaluate the relative strength of its capabilities. To identify and appraise a company's capabilities, managers must look both inside and outside the organization.

Benchmarking may be used to compare organizational performance with that of competitors. Appraising relative strength and strategic importance allows the organization to highlight its strengths and weaknesses. Having identified resources and capabilities that are important and where the organization is strong relative to competitors, the key task is to formulate strategy to ensure that these resources are deployed to the greatest effect. The organization must identify how to exploit its strengths most effectively and must decide what to do about its key weaknesses, by either developing such areas or reducing vulnerabilities associated with them. Weaknesses may be converted into strengths though this is likely to be a long-term task. An alternative solution may be to outsource. When developing resources and capabilities, organizations typically conduct a *gap analysis* – identifying discrepancies between the current position and the desired future position. A key problem faced by the international organization concerns the *replication* of capabilities for internal use in different products and geographical markets.

In the previous chapter we discussed the benefit of having resources that are difficult to imitate by competitors. Such resources provide long-term strength for the organization. As we will find in subsequent chapters, resources and capabilities (especially intangible assets such as knowledge) may exist in some parts of the international organization but not others. They therefore face a key challenge of identifying and diffusing such resources and capabilities throughout the whole company. The globalization of markets has therefore made resources and capabilities more important to international organizations.

Throughout this chapter we have presented concepts and frameworks to help organizations better understand their environments as sources of opportunity and threat. We have also described the internal environment in terms of strengths and weaknesses when compared with industry competitors. Opportunities may be present in the organization's present strategic group, the value system, other strategic groups, in substitute industries, new market segments and for complementary products and services.

The organization's strengths and weaknesses, opportunities and threats (SWOT) are typically analyzed during the strategy formulation process (see Chapter 3). SWOT alongside PEST/PESTLE can be used as a basis for the analysis of business and environmental factors. A SWOT analysis summarizes the key issues from the business environment and the strategic capability of an organization both of which are most likely to impact upon strategy development, see Figure 2-12. It involves specifying the objective of the business venture or project and identifying the internal and external factors which are favourable and unfavourable to achieving that objective. The internal factors may be viewed as strengths or weaknesses depending upon their impact upon organizational objectives.

Opportunity favourable or advantageous circumstance that may shape or facilitate goals

Threat circumstances with the potential to cause loss or harm and may hinder goal achievement

SWOT analysis summarizes the key issues from the business environment and the strategic capability of an organization both of which are most likely to impact upon strategy development

Contingency and environmental perspectives

Having considered both the external (macro and micro) and internal business environment we now consider the relationship, drawing on contingency theory, between the two. International organizations study the environment to enable themselves to be more

Figure 2-12
SWOT analysis

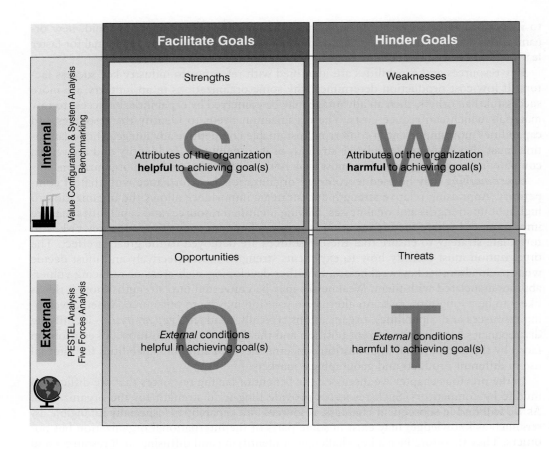

effective and efficient. There are many ways for organizations to organize themselves and many strategies to follow. However, there is no single best way of doing things and there is widespread acceptance that the best way to organize is based upon (contingent) the situation.

Strategic 'fit' is about matching the internal (resources, capabilities and activities) with the needs and demands of the external environment. If the external environment is constantly changing, then the internal environment needs to be flexible. Contingency theories have been applied to strategy, structure, culture, leadership, management styles and capabilities. Environmental determinism, discussed earlier, is a contingency perspective which claims that internal organizational responses are wholly or mainly shaped, influenced or determined by external environmental factors.

The work of Pugh (1973) and others (see the Aston programme) was instrumental in shaping theories about internal context (*internal environment*) and organizational form. Later, Nadler (1980) discussed different ways of thinking and the views held about organizations, starting with systems views where organizations are seen as 'composed of interdependent parts' where 'change in one element of the system will result in changes in other parts of the system'. With the aim of providing a 'usable tool for managers' Nadler introduces an approach called a 'congruence model of organizational behaviour'. The model (discussed further in Chapter 5) recognizes the environment as a major input to the system (a source of opportunity, threat and constraints), which becomes encoded in the strategy (a match of organizational resources to the environment). The inputs then enter a transformation process composed of four components:

■ task;

■ individual;

■ informal; and

■ formal organization.

The *task* is about the work to be done; individuals are the people performing the task; formal arrangements include processes, structures and systems; and informal arrangement refers to organizational culture, routines and actual practice. Finally the model outputs are organizational performance, with reference to the goals and strategy (inputs). 'Each component can be thought of as having a relationship with each other component. Between each pair, then, we think of a relative degree of consistency, congruence, or "fit"' (Nadler 1980) and 'the basic hypotheses of the model is therefore that organizations will be most effective when their major components are congruent with each other'. This approach to organization is thus a contingency approach. Nadler points out that 'often changes in the environment necessitate organizational change. For example, factors related to competition, technology, or regulation, shift and thus necessitate changes in organizational strategy.' Nadler argues that incongruent organizations are ineffective organizations.

The contingency approach to management (also called the situational approach) assumes there is no universal answer to many organizational problems because organizations, people, the environment and situations vary and change over time. Crossing borders through trade and investment brings the international organization into different environments that require various adaptations. Thus, the right thing to do depends on a complex variety of critical environmental and internal contingencies.

> **Contingency approach to management** the idea that there is no one best way to manage and to be effective, planning, organizing, leading, and controlling must be tailored to the particular circumstances faced by an organization

Positioning versus resource-based perspective

Thus far we have suggested that the organization must understand and analyze the global business environment (external and internal) when developing and implementing strategy. Organizations may either analyze the external environment and adapt to fit within it or develop hard to imitate capabilities and exploit them, seeking out and making opportunities that utilize them. Thus, there are two views (perspectives) on how to compete in global markets. One looks outward (the positioning perspective) and the other inwards (the resource-based perspective).

The positioning perspective (external orientation) describes organizations that focus on the (external) competitive environment and adapt strategy accordingly; the emphasis is on where the company chooses to compete, i.e. finding a favourable market environment. Such organizations are market driven and through an understanding of the five competitive forces, find and defend a favourable competitive position within an industry. Resources are important to exploit opportunity but they are not the starting point for developing strategy.

The resource-based perspective is a perspective that emphasizes the internal environment and unique capabilities as the starting point for strategy development; the emphasis is on how the company competes. This perspective stresses the uniqueness of the organization and uses this as a basis for sustainable competitive advantage.

> **Positioning perspective** a perspective that emphasizes the external environment and opportunity as the starting point for strategy development
>
> **Resource-based perspective** a perspective that emphasizes the internal environment and unique capabilities as the starting point for strategy development

We return to these two perspectives in the next chapter when we consider strategy formation. Given the two perspectives, scholars have attempted to determine which is most likely to lead to success. Studies conclude that both can lead to success and that organizations needn't choose one over the other; rather they may emphasize one over the other. The international organization must identify what it does best while focusing on the industry environment.

Summary of key learning points

This chapter focused on analyzing the environmental factors affecting international organizational performance. We began by recognizing that the international organization does not function in a vacuum but in the global business environment. The environment provides the context (situation and circumstances) for organizational action and activity. International organizations seek to attain goals which normally include profit maximization. First, they identify sources of opportunity (determined by the industry forces, threats and customer needs) and match them with organizational capabilities (the internal environment). Thus, understanding the global business environment and its economic, social and political influences is crucial to success in today's international business world. The external environment is complex and its future uncertain yet managers attempt to make sense of it if they are to identify opportunities and threats and respond appropriately. Similarly, through comparisons within the multinational organization and with competitors in the micro environment, the organization can identify its strengths and weaknesses. Through an understanding of such factors the organization can compete and fulfil customer needs more effectively and efficiently.

Various models exist to help managers make sense of their environment and were reviewed throughout this chapter. The PESTLE diagnostic framework was used to make sense of the general factors in the macro environment; Porter's five forces framework was presented to help in identifying the sources and forces of competition in an industry (the micro environment). The framework provides an approach for determining the financial performance of an industry, and thus its attractiveness for investors, at a specific point in time. However, recognizing the dynamic nature of environments we introduced the industry life cycle, used to describe change within an industry. Furthermore, we then focused upon the importance of intra-industry strategic groupings in understanding differences across firms within an industry.

Having considered the external environment, particularly in terms of opportunity and threat, we then suggested that managers need to also understand the strengths and weaknesses of their organizations. We therefore turned our attention to the internal environment. The internal environment is made up of organizational resources, capabilities and competencies and reflects what the organization can do. There are several favoured ways to analyze the internal environment such as the resource or skills audit, value chain analysis and comparative methods such as competitor intelligence, benchmarking and internal comparisons.

Finally, having considered both the external (macro and micro) and internal business environment we considered the relationship, between the two by drawing on contingency theory. We argued, through contingency and systems theory, a need for aspects of all environments to fit together; that organizations will be most effective when their major components are congruent with each other. Organizations may analyze the external environment, and adapt to fit within it, or develop hard to imitate capabilities and exploit them, seeking out and making opportunities that utilize them. Thus, there are two views (perspectives) on how to compete in global markets. One looks outward (the positioning perspective) and the other inwards (the resource-based perspective).

Review questions

Analysis of the environment

1 Conduct a PESTLE analysis for the airline industry, focusing on Europe.
2 Identify the opportunities and threats for airline companies wishing to operate in Europe.

Cultural impacts

By using data from Hofstede in the text, compare the national culture of two countries (A and B). Explain how differences might affect relationships in the following scenarios:

1 an employee of country A is to work on a project with an employee from country B – the work is to be undertaken in country B;

2 an employee of country A is to sell one of its products in country B to a customer; and

3 an employee of country A is to manage, on a temporary basis, staff in country B.

Discuss in groups whether or not you believe that culture can be measured and people from different countries compared with each other.

Economic impacts

Evaluate the consequences of greater economic integration from a multi-stakeholder perspective.

Technological impacts

Explain how technology has influenced

1 The airline industry.
2 The banking industry.
3 The education industry.

Critically evaluate the impact of technology on the work that employees do, commenting on job losses and job creation, de-skilling and up-skilling work.

Political and legal impacts

Critically discuss the proposition that integration of country legal frameworks (i.e. the development of global law) would benefit societies.

Ecological impacts

Consider the airline industry – in groups discuss whether or not you feel governments should intervene in order to regulate airline emissions or other environmentally unfriendly activities associated with the industry.

Would you expect culture to impact upon whether or not a government becomes involved in regulation? Explain your answer.

Analysis of the environment

Discuss how different levels or categories of environmental complexity, dynamism and uncertainty might influence international organizations. What are the implications of increased turbulence in the business environment?

References

Bain, P. and Taylor, P. (2008) 'No passage to India? Initial responses of UK trade unions to call centre offshoring', *Industrial Relations Journal* 39(1):5–23.

Barney, J. (1991) 'Firm Resources and Sustained Competitive Advantage', *Journal of Management* (March 1991) 17(1):99–120.

Boddewyn, J. and Brewer, T. L. (1994) 'International-Business Political Behavior: New Theoretical Directions', *Academy of Management Review* (January 1994) 19(1):119–143.

Child, J. (1997) 'Strategic choice in the analysis of action, structure, organizations and environment: Retrospect and prospect', *Organization Studies – Berlin* 18(1):43–76.

Christensen, C. M. (2001) 'The Past and Future of Competitive Advantage', *MIT Sloan Management Review* (Winter 2001) 42(2):105–109.

Clarke, G. (2005) 'International Marketing Environment Analysis', *Marketing Review* (Summer 2005) 5(2):159–173.

Dibb, S., Simkin, L., Pride, W. M. and Ferrell, O. C. (2006) *Marketing: Concepts and Strategies* (5 ed), Boston: Houghton Mifflin.

Duncan, R. (1972) 'Characteristics of Organizational Environments and Perceived Environmental Uncertainty', *Administrative Science Quarterly* 17(3):313–327.

Emery, F. E. and Trist, E. L. (1965) 'The Causal Texture of Organizational Environments', *Human Relations* (February 1965) 18(1):21–32.

Eustace, C. (2003) 'A new perspective on the knowledge value chain', *Journal of Intellectual Capital* 4(4):588–596.

Fitzpatrick, M. (1983) 'The Definition And Assessment Of Political Risk In International Business: A Review Of The Literature', *Academy of Management Review* (April 1983) 8(2):249–254.

Grant, R. (1991) 'The Resource-Based Theory of Competitive Advantage: Implications for Strategy Formulation', *California Management Review* (Spring 1991) 33(3):114–135.

Grant, R. (2007) *Contemporary Strategy Analysis* (6 ed), Oxford: Blackwell Publishing.

Hellriegel, D. and Slocum, J. W. (1973) 'Organizational design: A contingency approach A model for organic management design', *Business Horizons* (April 1973) 16(2):59–68.

Hofer, C. W. (1975) 'Toward a Contingency Theory of Business Strategy', *The Academy of Management Journal* (December 1975) 18(4):784–810.

Hofstede, G. (1984) *Cultures Consequences – abridged*, Newbury Park: Sage.

Hofstede, G. (1997) *Cultures and Organizations*, New York: McGraw-Hill.

Hofstede, G. (2006) 'What did GLOBE really measure? Researchers' minds versus respondents' minds', *Journal of International Business Studies* 37:882–896.

IJBE (2008) www.inderscience.com/browse/index.php?journalID=69 accessed 29 Jan 2008.

Javidan, M. and House, R. (2001) 'Cultural Acumen for the Global Manager: Lessons from Project GLOBE', *Organizational Dynamics* (Spring 2001) 29(4):289–305.

Kalakota, R. and Whinston, A. (1996) *Frontiers of Electronic Commerce*, Redwood City: Addison Wesley.

Kelly, P. (2005) *Information Systems Risk*, London: Witherbys.

Kobrin, S. (1979) 'Political Risk: A Review and Reconsideration', *Journal of International Business Studies* (Spring/Summer 1979) 10(1):67–80.

Lawrence, P. R. and Lorsch, J. W. (1967) 'Differentiation and Integration in Complex Organizations', *Administrative Science Quarterly* (June 1967) 12(1):1–47.

Luthans, F. and Stewart, T. (1977) 'A General Contingency Theory of Management', *Academy of Management Review* 2:181–195.

McGahan, A. (2000) 'How Industries Evolve', *Business Strategy Review* (Autumn 2000) 11(3):1–16.

McGee, J. and Thomas, H. (1986) 'Strategic Groups: Theory, Research and Taxonomy', *Strategic Management Journal* (March/April 1986) 7(2):141–160.

McKelvey, B. (1975) 'Guidelines for the Empirical Classification of Organizations', *Administrative Science Quarterly* (December 1975) 20(4):509–525.

Mullins, L. (2008) *Management and Organizational Behaviour* (8 ed), Harlow: FT Prentice Hall.

Nadler (1980) in Mabey, C. (1993) *Managing Change*, London: The Open University pp. 85–98.

O'Connell, J. and Zimmerman, J. (1979) 'Scanning the International Environment', *California Management Review* (Winter 1979) 22(2):15–24.

OECD. (2001) Corporate Responsibility: Results of a Fact-Finding Mission on Private Initiatives, OECD Working Papers on International Investment, 2001/2, OECD Publishing doi: 10.1787/701174424371.

Porter, M. E. (1979) 'How competitive forces shape strategy', *Harvard Business Review* (March/April 1979) 57(2):137–145.

Porter, M. E. (1986) 'Changing Patterns of International Competition', *California Management Review* (Winter 1986) 28(2):9–41.

Prahalad, C. and Hamel, G. (1990) 'The Core Competence of the Corporation', *Harvard Business Review* (May/June 1990) 68(3):79–91.

PricewaterhouseCoopers (2008) 'How managing political risk improves global business performance', www.pwc.com accessed 1 February 2008.

Pugh, D. S. (1973) 'Does Context Determine Form?', *Organizational Dynamics* (Spring) 19–34.

QAA (2008) 'Academic Standards Master's awards in business and management', www.qaa.ac.uk/academicinfrastructure/benchmark/masters/MBAintro.asp.

Scottish Trades Union Congress (2004) 'A Strategy to Sustain Call Centre Jobs in Scotland', www.stuc.org.uk/policy/economic-industrial-policy/a-strategy-to-sustain-call-centre-jobs-in-scotland.

Slack, N., Chambers, S. and Johnston, R. (2007) *Operations Management* (5 ed), Harlow: Financial Times Press.

Teece, D. J., Pisano, G. and Shuen, A. (1997) 'Dynamic Capabilities and Strategic Management', *Strategic Management Journal* (August 1997) 18(7):509–533.

Terreberry, S. (1968) 'The Evolution of Organizational Environments', *Administrative Science Quarterly* (March 1968) 12(4):590–613.

Valentin, E. K. (2001) 'Swot Analysis from A Resource-Based View', *Journal of Marketing Theory & Practice* (Spring 2001) 9(2):54–69.

Suggestions for further reading

Journals

International Journal of Business Environment (IJBE)

The IJBE fosters research on how firms behave under different types of environment and aims to examine the external influences on business organizations. This journal examines a wide variety of business decisions, processes and activities within the business environment. IJBE addresses managerial issues in the social, political, economic, competitive, and technological environments of business.

www.inderscience.com/browse/index.php?journalID=69.

Key articles

Scholars of this subject area have often read the following:

1 Porter, M. E. (1979) 'How competitive forces shape strategy', *Harvard Business Review* (March/April 1979) 57(2):137–145.

2 Vernon, R. (1966) 'International Investment and International Trade in the Product Cycle', *The Quarterly Journal of Economics* (May 1966) 80(2):190–207.

3 Duncan, R. (1972) 'Characteristics of Organizational Environments and Perceived Environmental Uncertainty', *Administrative Science Quarterly* 17(3):313–327.

4 McGee, J. and Thomas, H. (1986) 'Strategic Groups: Theory, Research and Taxonomy', *Strategic Management Journal* (March/April 1986) 7(2):141–160.

5 Lawrence, P. R. and Lorsch, J. W. (1967) 'Differentiation and Integration in Complex Organizations', *Administrative Science Quarterly* (June 1967) 12(1):1–47.

6 Terreberry, S. (1968) 'The Evolution of Organizational Environments', *Administrative Science Quarterly* (March 1968) 12(4):590–613.

7 Boddewyn, J. and Brewer, T. L. (1994) 'International-Business Political Behavior: New Theoretical Directions', *Academy of Management Review* (January 1994) 19(1):119–143.

8 McKelvey, B. (1975) 'Guidelines for the Empirical Classification of Organizations', *Administrative Science Quarterly* (December 1975) 20(4):509–525.

9 Kobrin, S. (1979) 'Political Risk: A Review And Reconsideration', *Journal of International Business Studies* (Spring/Summer 1979) 10(1):67–80.

10 Hellriegel, D. and Slocum, J. W. (1973) 'Organizational design: A contingency approach model for organic management design', *Business Horizons* (April 1973) 16(2):59–68.

Introduction

Purpose and strategy

Corporate strategic choices

Competing with business-level strategy

Strategy implementation

Key concepts

■ Value ■ Strategy (intended, realized and deliberate) ■ Mission ■ Vision ■ Strategic choices
■ Strategy development and implementation ■ Global and multidomestic strategy
■ Vertical integration ■ Geographic scope ■ Competitive strategies ■ Advantage ■ Synergy
■ Market-entry strategy ■ Corporate and business level strategy

By the end of this chapter you will be able to:

■ Explain what strategy is and how it is formed and implemented in the international organization

■ Explain the role of values, mission and vision in formulating and implementing strategy

■ Identify and describe the strategic importance of resources, competencies, core competencies and dynamic capabilities and evaluate how they may be used to confer a sustainable competitive advantage

■ Explain generic strategies and how managers may develop strategic capabilities within international organizations

■ Discuss the strategic choices and decisions according to the corporate, business and business unit or departmental level

Active learning case

Li & Fung

Mathews (2006) asks how do some firms challenge established positions in the global economy and displace incumbents, some of them highly advanced and fiercely competitive – especially when the challengers start small, lack key resources, and are distant from major markets. 'Dragon multinationals' are firms from the Asia-Pacific region that have successfully internationalized and in some cases become leading firms in many sectors. These are firms that start from behind, and overcome their deficiencies to emerge as industry leaders. In terms of the resource-based view, widely regarded in strategy, the dragon multinationals may be seen as evaluating resources strategically in ways very different from incumbents. The newcomers and latecomers see the world as full of resources to be tapped, provided the appropriate complementary strategies and organizational forms can be devised.

Li & Fung from Hong Kong, is a good example of the organizations which have pursued accelerated internationalization over the course of the past decade and acquired global reach in a fraction of the time taken by their predecessors. Li & Fung is a supply chain management company. It has globalized through the construction of vast supplier networks across several continents. Li & Fung accelerated its internationalization through the purchase of existing players, including Inchcape, and captures latecomer advantages through its low costs (producing mostly in developing economies) and its razor-thin profit margins. It is plausible to suppose newcomers and latecomers, like Li & Fung, form part of the vanguard of the emergent global economy precisely because they are equipped with a global outlook and because they are prepared to experiment with strategic and organizational innovations that place global considerations ahead of all others. In this case study we briefly trace their history from a strategic perspective.

Founded in Canton (1906), Li & Fung a traditional family-owned enterprise was one of the first companies financed solely by Chinese capital to engage directly in exports from China. Initially it traded largely in porcelain and silk before diversifying. At the outset, the company added value through their ability to speak English and Chinese. No one at Chinese factories spoke English, and American merchants spoke no Chinese. Li & Fung could therefore gain margin as a simple intermediary. Some years later the company moved to Hong Kong which served as the deep water port for South China (the river port in Guangzhou was too shallow for ocean-going clippers).

After Second World War, China became a Communist country and Li & Fung was cut off from its factory sources and needed to find a new way of doing business. Li & Fung was reinvented as an exporter of the labour-intensive consumer goods produced in Hong Kong during the post-war period. The company dealt in garments, toys, and electronics. Its primary customers were retailers in the United States. As Hong Kong's manufacturing economy grew, Li & Fung grew with it. Li & Fung was basically a broker, charging a fee to put buyers and sellers together. A wide range of products made Li & Fung one of Hong Kong's biggest exporters, in the 1970s, in dollar terms. But as an intermediary, the company was vulnerable and became squeezed between the growing power of the buyers and the factories. Nearby economies were developing enough manufacturing capacity to compete with Hong Kong. Meanwhile, buyers were more inclined to bypass the middleman (disintermediation) and deal directly with the manufacturer. This was a significant threat to

Founded in Guangzhou, the People's Republic of China in 1906, the Li & Fung Group is a multinational group of companies driving strong growth in three distinct core businesses – export sourcing through Li & Fung Limited, distribution through IDS and retailing through CRA and other non-listed entities. The Li & Fung Group has a total staff of over 25 000 across 40 countries worldwide, with total revenue of over US$10 billion in 2006.

The case examines the evolution of Hong Kong-based Li & Fung Limited from a traditional trading company into a global consumer goods export trading giant. It discusses in detail the company's efforts to evolve its business model constantly in response to the changes in the external environment and customer needs and preferences. The case examines Li & Fung's major strategies which contributed to the company's emergence as one of the world's leading consumer goods trading companies.

▶ ▶ ▶

Li & Fung as one of their roles was to connect buyers with factories in Hong Kong. Margins slipped and senior management recognized change was needed.

Li & Fung recognized a need to move from a manufacturing to a predominantly service company. In 1973 Li & Fung went public and was listed on the Hong Kong Stock Exchange. This allowed the company to better separate the roles of ownership and management. Next, Li & Fung developed a buying network throughout the region (Far East). The company embarked on a staged strategy. In the first stage, they acted as a regional sourcing agent and extended their geographic reach. Offices were established in various countries in order to diversify their manufacturing sources. By expanding geographically, Li & Fung acquired broader regional expertise and a more substantial base of manufacturing contacts, and thus was able to offer its clients a more valuable service. With expanded knowledge and resources, the company could expertly source large orders by putting together a package from the entire region. Throughout the 1970s a key strategic position was built around regional familiarity but their services remained basic, attracting only a low profit margin.

Opportunity was presented with the opening up of China in 1979; Hong Kong manufacturers relocated factories there. As manufacturing in Hong Kong became increasingly expensive, almost all labour-intensive work moved across the border to China, while design, packaging, and other technically advanced manufacturing techniques were still done in Hong Kong. The rapid industrialization of the relatively less developed Asian countries was also gathering pace at this time, widening supply source options. Eventually the whole East Asian region was pulled into the manufacturing process, depending on each country's particular industrial strengths. Li & Fung quickly appreciated the opportunities from these developments. In the 1980s they changed strategy to become more involved in the entire production planning process.

Further structural changes were also witnessed in the 1980s. The company refocused on its core trading business, selling off unrelated enterprises. By the late 1980s, Li & Fung was offering a broader range of services related to its trading business. Once a company had an idea of the product it needed, it would send design sketches to Li & Fung. Li & Fung would find the right type of material, create prototypes for the customer, set up contacts for each step of the supply process and develop a production schedule that covered the entire fashion season. Li & Fung was gradually making the transition from middleman to programme manager. The company began a period of exceptionally rapid growth in 1991. In this second strategic stage, they took the company's sourcing-agent strategy one step further becoming a manager and deliverer of manufacturing programmes. They decomposed and fragmented the value chain and optimized each step – globally. A garment labelled 'Made in Thailand' might contain Korean yarn that was woven and dyed in Taiwan, sewn at different factories in Thailand, and fitted with zippers made in China by a Japanese company. Breaking up the value chain (dispersed manufacturing) was a novel concept. Managing dispersed production was a real breakthrough; the company developed specific practices to reduce costs and lead times. They had developed a model of borderless manufacturing. Supply chain management is about buying the right things and shortening delivery cycles. It requires 'reaching into the suppliers' to ensure that certain things happen on time and at the right quality level. Li & Fung produce a truly global product by pulling apart the manufacturing value chain and optimizing each step.

Further growth was seen through acquisitions during the 1990s. In the following years Li & Fung continued to diversify geographically, moving into emerging centres of production in Africa. By 2000, the company was making an effort to move production closer to its North American and European end markets and began sourcing from factories in Central America, the Caribbean, and Turkey. Li & Fung was becoming a multinational company with a workforce based in over 40 economies. Li & Fung had made the transition from buying agent to supply chain manager, from the old economy to the new, from traditional Chinese family conglomerate to innovative public company. Li & Fung provide the convenience of a one-stop shop from product development, through production management, to customs clearance and delivery when required.

Websites and resources:

(1) www.icmr.icfai.org/casestudies/catalogue/Business%20Strategy2/BSTR149.htm.
(2) www.lifunggroup.com/ front.html.
(3) www.lifung.com.
(4) Mathews, J. (2006) 'Dragon multinationals: New players in 21st century globalization', *Asia Pacific Journal of Management* (March 2006) 23(1):5–27.
(5) Li & Fung, Ltd. *SWOT Analysis* (August 2007) 1–9.
(6) Magretta, J. (1998) 'Fast, Global, and Entrepreneurial: Supply Chain Management, Hong Kong Style. An Interview with Victor Fung', *Harvard Business Review* (September/October 1998) 76(5):102–114.

Introduction

In the introductory chapter we defined an organization as a social system consisting of subsystems of resource variables, interrelated by various management policies, practices and techniques which interact with variables in the environmental suprasystem to achieve a set of goals or objectives (Luthans and Stewart 1977) and an international organization is an organization that engages in business activity in more than one country, i.e. it crosses country borders to achieve its goals. When contemplating international organizations as systems it is often helpful to recognize that systems are nested. Typically, the smaller units comprising a system are called subsystems or components, and the larger unit enclosing a system is called a suprasystem or environment (discussed in the previous chapter). Like the domestic commercial organization the international organization must seek out opportunity and identify and exploit sources of profit (as was demonstrated by Li & Fung in the opening case). One of the basic questions faced by the profit-making organization is: 'how do we make money?' Put another way *how* can we create value? In order to do this they must determine *what* their business is and what they are trying to achieve.

Managing in conditions of rapid change and in the face of international competition requires the international organization to identify sources of superior business performance and then form and implement a strategy that exploits these sources of superior performance. Strategies need to be based on understanding customer needs, competition, and the internal strengths and weaknesses of organizations. Business is about creating value and the challenge for strategy is first to create value for customers and second to extract some of that value in the form of profit for the organization. Value may be created through production (physical transformation activities discussed in Chapter 15) or by commerce (trade – transferring products from individuals and places of where they are of less value to individuals and locations to where they are more valued).

There are a number of fundamental questions every international company must answer such as:

- What do we do?
- Why are we here?
- What kind of company are we?
- What kind of company do we want to be?
- What is our current strategy?
- What is happening in the environment?
- What are our goals?
- In which markets and in which geographic areas will we compete?
- What products and services will we offer and to whom?
- What technologies will we employ?
- What capabilities and capacities will we require?
- What will we make by ourselves and what will we buy (outsource) from others?
- Finally, how will we compete?

The answers to such questions may be provided through strategic problem solving activities. Strategy is concerned with *how* the international organization will achieve its aims and goals and is explored in this chapter. In this chapter we also outline the issues associated with defining organizational purpose, the '*what*' questions.

A brief history of strategy is presented by Collis and Montgomery (1995). The field of strategy has largely been shaped around a framework first conceived by Andrews in his classic book *The Concept of Corporate Strategy* (Irwin 1971). Andrews' defined strategy as the match between what a company can do (organizational strengths and weaknesses) within the universe of what it might do (environmental opportunities and threats). Although the power of Andrews' framework was recognized from the start, managers were given few insights into how to assess either side of the equation systematically. The first important breakthrough came in Porter's book *Competitive Strategy: Techniques for Analyzing Industries and Competitors*. Porter's work built on the structure-conduct-performance paradigm of industrial-organization economics. The essence of the model is that the structure of an industry determines the state of competition within that industry and sets the context for companies' conduct – that is, their, strategy. Most important, structural forces (which Porter called the five forces) determine the average profitability of the industry and have a correspondingly strong impact on the profitability of individual corporate strategies. This analysis put the spotlight on choosing the 'right industries' and, within them, the most attractive competitive positions.

Although the model did not ignore the characteristics of individual companies, the emphasis was clearly on phenomena at the industry level. With the appearance of the concepts of core competence and competing on capabilities, the pendulum swung dramatically in the other direction, moving from outside to inside the company. These approaches emphasized the importance both of the skills and collective learning embedded in an organization and of management's ability to marshal them. This view assumed that the roots of competitive advantage were inside the organization and that the adoption of new strategies was constrained by the current level of the company's resources. The external environment received little, if any, attention, and what we had learned about industries and competitive analysis seemed to disappear from our collective psyche.

The emerging resource-based view of the firm helps to bridge these, seemingly, disparate approaches and to fulfil the promise of Andrews' framework. Like the capabilities approaches, the resource-based view acknowledges the importance of company-specific resources and competencies, yet it does so in the context of the competitive environment. The resource-based view shares another important characteristic with industry analysis: It, too, relies on economic reasoning. It sees capabilities and resources as the heart of a company's competitive position, subject to the interplay of three fundamental market forces: demand (does it meet customers' needs, and is it competitively superior?), scarcity (is it imitable or substitutable, and is it durable?), and appropriability (who owns the profits?).

More recently, Grant (2007: 18) produced a similar brief history of business strategy, charting the evolution of strategic management dominant themes. From analysis of the past decade he considers the key themes defining strategy for the new economy and millennium. Since 2000 we have observed new business models, disruptive technologies and global strategies. Not only has there been a focus on innovation but also on CSR and business ethics; a topic we consider in the next chapter. There are many forces that might influence an organization's strategy. Aside from the impact of PESTEL and competitive forces on strategy, the organization must also consider ethical and cultural forces that will guide organizational goals and purpose and the way in which they are accomplished. In summary, strategy is concerned with what the organization should do (scope) and the development and channelling of resources to accomplish goals, see Figure 3-1.

To provide structure and aid learning this chapter is organized into four main sections:

- strategy and purpose;
- corporate strategic choices;
- competing with business level strategy;
- strategy implementation.

Throughout the chapter we tackle several contradictions or opposing views. For example, historically, certain scholars have emphasized strategy formulation as an analytical process while others suggest strategy may be formed in an incremental manner through strategic thinking and synthesis. Some argue a need to select industries first and then develop the organization accordingly, while others suggest analysis of core internal capabilities first and then market selection and development. Certain companies treat the world as a single market, others compete country by country. Regardless of conflicting views, organizations must make strategic decisions.

Figure 3-1

A dual approach to (profit) goal achievement

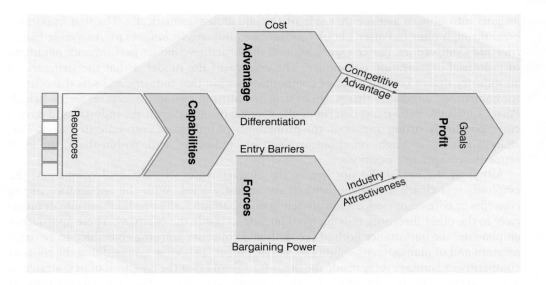

In the opening section we focus on what strategy is, organizational purpose, and sources of advantage. We then briefly explore generic strategies before considering strategy at two levels: corporate and business (subsidiary). The former determines organizational scope – the geographical areas of business and diversification and the latter focuses on competing within the boundaries set in the corporate strategy. Finally, we consider strategy implementation.

Purpose and strategy

Mintzberg (1978) commented on the much misunderstood process of strategy formation in organizations and asked, 'What are strategies and how are they formed in organizations? He summarized three popular views of strategy: (1) the *planning* mode, which depicts the process as a highly ordered, neatly integrated one, with strategies spelled out on schedule by a purposeful organization; planning theory postulates that the strategy-maker 'formulates' from on high while the subordinates 'implement' lower down. In sharp contrast, (2) the *adaptive* mode, depicts the process as one in which many decision-makers with conflicting goals bargain among themselves to produce a stream of incremental, disjointed decisions. In some of the literature the process is described in (3) the *entrepreneurial* mode, where a powerful leader takes bold, risky decisions toward his or her vision of the organization's future.

Intended strategy strategy formulated through a conscious process (planned)

Realized strategy the strategy actually implemented

In common terminology, he notes a strategy is a 'plan' (intended strategy). However, by defining a strategy as 'a pattern in a stream of decisions' (realized strategy), we are able to research strategy formation in a broad descriptive context. In other words, when a sequence of decisions in some area exhibits a consistency over time, a strategy will be considered to have formed. Mintzberg therefore believes we can study both strategies that were intended and those that were realized despite intentions. Defining strategy in this way enables us to consider both sides of the strategy formation coin: strategies as intended, as well as strategies as evolved. In other words, the strategy-maker may formulate a strategy through a conscious process before he or she makes specific decisions (formulation), or a strategy may form gradually, perhaps unintentionally, as he or she makes decisions one by one (strategy formation). In general terms, strategy formation in most organizations can be thought of as revolving around the interplay of three basic forces:

a an environment that changes continuously but irregularly;

b an organizational operating system, or bureaucracy, that above all seeks to stabilize its actions, despite the characteristics of the environment it serves; and c a leadership whose role is to mediate between these two forces, to maintain the stability of the organization's operating system while at the same time ensuring its adaptation to environmental change.

Intended and *realized* strategies can be combined in three ways:

1 intended strategies which are realized; these may be called deliberate strategies;

2 intended strategies that are not realized, perhaps because of unrealistic expectations, misjudgements about the environment, or changes in either during implementation; these may be called *unrealized* strategies; and

3 realized strategies that were never intended, perhaps because no strategy was intended at the outset or perhaps because, as in (2), intended strategies were displaced along the way; these may be called emergent strategies.

Deliberate strategy intended strategies which are realized

Emergent strategy realized strategies that were never intended

Despite presenting this trichotomy, Mintzberg noted that in practice other relationships exist – intended strategies that, as they are realized, change their form and become, in part at least, emergent; emergent strategies formalized as deliberate ones; and intended strategies which are, over-realized. Mintzberg concludes that the very word 'formulation' is misleading.

Typical of the planning view, Bourgeois (1980) considers strategy making to include:

1 environmental scanning;

2 objective setting (the formation of goals and targets);

3 distinctive competence selection or the choice of tools and competitive weapons with which to negotiate with the environment;

4 power distribution, or the determination of authority and influence relationships among organizational subunits;

5 resource allocation or the deployment of financial and physical resources to carry out a strategy; and

6 monitoring and control of outcomes, or the comparison of intended and manifested strategy contents.

There are three basic levels of strategy within the large organization: corporate (defining scope – where to compete, the activities to perform and products to sell), business (how to compete and add value) and departmental. In this case the term corporate refers to the whole company and business corresponds with the division, strategic business unit or subsidiary of the multinational corporation. The departmental strategy may be a functional strategy such as the IT or marketing strategy or may be a product or area-based strategy. Operational strategies are concerned with how specific parts of an organization deliver the corporate and business level strategies effectively in terms of resources, processes and people. The corporate strategy (see next section) considers industry attractiveness and the business strategy considers competitive advantage as sources of profitability. No matter what the level, strategy is about winning. It is the means (plans, actions and policies) by which organizations achieve their objectives.

Corporate strategy a whole company plan or pattern of decisions identifying where the company will compete (in terms of geography, product, and industry) and which resources will be used

Business strategy a subunit plan or pattern of decisions identifying how to compete and add value under the umbrella of the corporate strategy

Strategy may be confined to the minds of senior managers or may be articulated in the vision, mission (statement of purpose), business model (statement of approach to revenue generation) or strategic plan (goals and the required resources and approach to goal attainment). Strategy is a device that unifies, constrains, coordinates and motivates the members of an organization. Common elements in successful strategies include an understanding of the environment, internal resources and simple goals. Strategy is the link between the organization (strengths and weaknesses) and its external environment (opportunities and threats). The task of strategy is to determine how the organization will deploy resources within its environment in order to achieve goals. Strategy is essentially about making choices with regard to *where* and *how* to compete; there is therefore a critical need to establish competitive advantage.

Competitive advantage stems from the resources and capabilities of the organization which act as the basis for strategy formulation. Contemporary organizations set out to identify how they differ from their competitors and design strategies to exploit such differences – strategy is about being different. Strategy is the long-term direction and scope of an organization, aiming to achieve advantage in a changing environment through its configuration of resources and competencies with the goal of fulfilling stakeholder expectations. Strategic decisions typically bring about considerable organizational change and their implementation requires considerable planning, coordination, collaboration, communication and control.

Organizations are a consciously coordinated social unit, created by groups in society to achieve specific purposes, common aims and objectives by means of planned and co-ordinated activities. Organizational goals are something that the organization is striving to achieve, a future expectation, a desired future state and something towards which the activities of the organization are directed in an effort to attain. The *purpose* is shaped by leaders, stakeholders, the vision, and ethics and delivered through the activities guided by mission and more specific objectives. People expect businesses to have profit maximization as a purpose but they also expect businesses to take into account the interests of the wider community, behaving morally and responsibly, a matter we explore in the next chapter.

The determination of purpose is considered with the definition of organizational activities, the resources of an organization and a consideration of its customers. The environment will also play a role in determining purpose. The purpose of the organization is multidimensional and may include a consideration of survival, growth and profit maximization, the importance of value add and so on. When developing purpose, there is a need to develop a vision of the future. Leaders can have a profound influence on the company and vision, mission and objectives and we discuss leadership theory in Chapter 6. Statements of purpose will normally identify how the organization is adding value and will also tend to be linked with sustainable competitive advantage. Clarifying the organization's purpose is crucial to strategy development. Since the purpose identifies *what* the organization wants to achieve and the strategy identifies *how* this will be done. Consequently, the purpose of the organization is typically defined at the outset of strategy development.

When a company operates in many countries and seeks to respond to local needs (a differentiation strategy) the organization is a *multinational* and when the company treats the whole world as one market it is referred to as any *global* organization. Such distinctions are important because they have different strategic implications. It is important to both recognize the purpose and the organization can and probably will change over time. New developments, innovation, knowledge and technology may well change the purpose of the organization. The choice of activities of the organization will vary with time. Decisions about how value will be added and the sources of sustainable competitive advantage will also vary. Resources will change as the organization's purpose changes.

Organizations find it helpful to have some clear explicit statement of their purpose and the broad, long-term tasks that the organization wants to accomplish are outlined in the mission. The development of the mission statement is a useful starting point for strategy development. It can be circulated and discussed, provides a sense of direction and focus and draws the organization together. The purpose of the mission statement is to communicate what the company stands for and where it is heading. It needs to reflect the basic values and beliefs of the organization and the elements of sustainable competitive advantage, be realistic and attainable, specific and flexible enough to guide behaviour in a dynamic environment.

Mission a statement of the overriding direction and purpose of an organisation

A mission statement is a statement of the overriding direction and purpose of an organization. A mission statement answers the question, 'Why do we exist?' and articulates the company's purpose both for those in the organization and for the public; it identifies the reason for being and may define the organization's primary customers, the products and services they produce, and the geographical location in which they operate. The value of the mission statement is also sometimes thought to increase with the size of an organization. Effective mission statements generally have the following attributes and content:

- simple, declarative statements, easily articulated and remembered;
- realistic;

■ can define not only what a company's business goals are, but also the methodologies it chooses to get there.

While the mission refers to the overriding purpose and communicates the answer to the question, 'what business are we in?' the vision describes strategic intent, where the organization wants to be in the future.

A vision is an aspirational view of what the organization will be like in the future, (Grant 2007). The vision statement is a detailed description of how things will be when the organization eventually reaches its destination.

Vision a description of the business as you want it to be

In summary, the vision and mission of a company should be a driving force, setting the strategic direction of the business. General aims of the organization are communicated qualitatively in the organizational goals while objectives convey similar information in a more specific, measurable and often quantitative form.

Specific objectives then translate the mission into more specific commitments of what will be done and when, if the objectives are to be accomplished. While the mission, vision and goals focus on what will be done, the business model and specific strategies may communicate *how* the organization will add value and compete. In addition, the organization may make use of other mechanisms to guide organization actions and the behaviour of employees. Thus the explicit statements of purpose, values and mission statements serve to unify the members of an organization and the strength of this unification force will be, in part, governed by the way such statements were formed and are communicated.

Consider the following examples of vision and mission statements – can you match the statement to the right company?

1 Examples of vision statements:

   1 To be earth's most customer centric company; to build a place where people can come to find and discover anything they might want to buy online.

   2 A world where everyone can be connected.

   3 To create a better everyday life for the many people.

Nokia | Amazon | IKEA

1) Amazon 2) Nokia 3) IKEA

2 Examples of mission statements:

   A To organize the world's information and make it universally accessible and useful.

   B To be the most successful computer company in the world at delivering the best customer experience in markets they serve.

   C To create the world's leading e-commerce franchise.

   D To refresh the world – in mind, body and spirit; inspire moments of optimism – through our brands and actions, and create value and make a difference – everywhere they engage.

(1) Dell (2) eBay (3) Coca-Cola (4) Google

A) Google B) Dell C) eBay D) Coca-Cola

   3 Refer back to the previous chapter and then draft a mission statement for easyJet.

STOP & THINK

Your easyJet mission statement may have read something like, 'To provide our customers with safe, good value, point-to-point air services. To effect and to offer a consistent and reliable product and fares appealing to leisure and business markets on a range of European routes. To achieve this we will develop our people and establish lasting relationships with our suppliers.'

Goals of an organization set out in broad terms the purpose of the organization; something that the organization is striving to achieve, a future expectation, a desired future state and something towards which the activities of the organization are directed in an effort to attain.

Examples of international organizational goals

To achieve their mission, Coca-Cola have developed a set of goals, which they will work with their bottlers to deliver:

Profit: Maximizing return to shareowners while being mindful of our overall responsibilities.
People: Being a great place to work where people are inspired to be the best they can be.
Portfolio: Bringing to the world a portfolio of beverage brands that anticipate and satisfy people's desires and needs.
Partners: Nurturing a winning network of partners and building mutual loyalty.
Planet: Being a responsible global citizen that makes a difference.

Strategic management

Having explored and defined the purpose of the organization, it is now possible to develop the strategy. While there are many approaches to developing strategy it is common to identify two key processes: the prescriptive and the emergent. The prescriptive process is a set of related activities typically starting with analysis (environmental and internal scanning leading to problem structuring), the formulation of the vision mission and objectives followed by the development and selection of strategic options (choice of strategies that may achieve the organizational purpose such as cost leadership and differentiation) which are then implemented. This is envisaged as a continuous process though many companies treat it as a cycle to be performed every two, three or five years. The analysis activities focus on both the internal and external environment and are drawn together with a SWOT analysis. Strategic options may be generated based on an environment-based view or a resource-based view (discussed at the end of the previous chapter).

Michael Porter described three general types of strategies (options) that are commonly used by organizations. They are cost leadership, differentiation, and market segmentation (or focus). Generic strategies such as cost leadership, and differentiation and competitive scope are a means of generating basic options and will be discussed later. Earlier we identified strategy as the means by which the organization achieves its goals (purpose). Strategic management involves decisions concerning:

- what a company might do, given the opportunities in its environment;
- what it can do, given the resources at its disposal;
- what it wants to do, given the personal values and desires of key decision-makers; and
- what it should do, given the ethical and legal context in which it is operating.

Strategic management is more than managing the process of strategic decision-making and includes understanding the strategic position of an organization, strategic choices (process whereby power-holders within organizations decide upon courses of strategic action, Child 1997) and the means to turn strategy into action. The strategic position is determined by the external environment, organizational capabilities (resources and com-

Strategic position concerned with the impact on strategy of the external environment, an organization's strategic capability (resources and competences) and the expectations and influence of stakeholders

Strategic choices the process whereby power-holders within organizations decide upon courses of strategic action

petencies) and the expectations and influence of stakeholders. The environment, gives rise to opportunities for and threats to the organization and capabilities reflect strengths and weaknesses, and therefore constraints on strategic choices for the future. There are strategic choices concerning how the organization may compete at the business level, requiring the organization to identify sources of competitive advantage. At the corporate level, there are choices about the portfolio and the business scope. Finally, the challenges of ensuring strategies are translated into action is discussed at the end of the chapter.

The strategy is enabled in the way that resources (people, information, finance, physical assets and technology) are allocated and used. Managing strategy, typically involves change and the management of that change. One process of developing strategy is outlined in Figure 3-2 – we revisit this later.

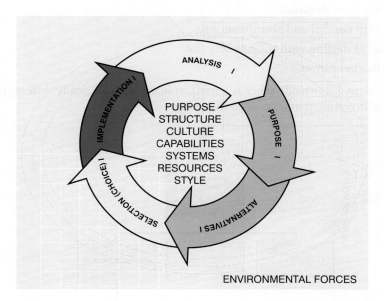

Figure 3-2

Strategy process

The process of strategy development may be complicated not only by the context (a turbulent environment rendering environmental analysis and subsequent assumptions invalid), but international considerations may also impact upon the process during every stage. Cultural differences may make certain approaches acceptable in one country and unworkable in another. In some countries, government involvement may be expected. In other countries obligations to society may outweigh those to shareholders. In yet other countries, shareholders are given the first consideration in developing strategy.

Values, attitudes, beliefs and expectations vary worldwide creating problems for international strategy development. Not only are strategic goals likely to vary from country to country but also attributes of the strategic process such as the extent of employee involvement. The essence of strategy formulation is to design a strategy that makes the most effective use of core resources and capabilities; to not only deploy existing resources, but also to develop the organization's resource base.

Corporate strategic choices

In the previous section we noted that, once the organization purpose and mission had been decided, the company must face choices about the markets to compete in and the means to do so. Strategic choices are concerned with decisions about the international organization's future. Such choices may be made at a variety of levels within the organization. The corporate strategy (also referred to as headquarter level strategy) identifies the industries (scope) within which the organization participates. The organization must make decisions about its product range (product scope); geographic spread (geographic scope) and the vertical range of activities it will perform for itself (vertical scope) – the *boundaries* of the international organization (see Figure 3-3). In relation to each dimension of scope, the basic issue is relative efficiency of the single organization compared with several specialist organizations – it is a matter of creating efficient and effective corporations. Scope decisions may bring benefits and costs. For example benefits of vertical integration may include:

- economies of combined operations;
- economies of internal control and coordination;
- assured supply or demand;
- better quality control and coordination;
- avoid costs of dealing with the market; and
- a gain in market power.

On the potential downside there is a need to manage strategically different businesses; higher capital investment and reduced flexibility.

Geographic scope choice of countries in which to do business

Vertical scope choice of activities to be performed by the organization

Figure 3-3

Multi-business organization

Vertical integration extension of the organization's activities into adjacent stages of production, i.e. those providing the organization's inputs or outputs

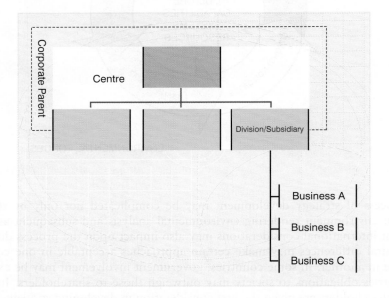

Vertical integration (both upwards and downwards) may reduce costs and may confer scale advantages

© Appler | Dreamstime.com

Vertical integration refers to the extent to which an organization owns vertically related activities either upstream (backward) or downstream (forward). BP is an example of a vertically-integrated company which performs activities to obtain its inputs (oil exploration), processes those inputs (refining) and then distributes and sells output products (petrol/gas station forecourts). The physical integration of processes throughout the value system may reduce costs such as energy and transportation and may confer scale advantages in the manner in which resources are utilized. There are different types of vertical relationship aside from direct ownership. Partnerships and long-term contracts may also be considered. Ultimately, at the corporate level, the organization must decide which parts of the value chain and system it will engage in and which to outsource. *Vertical strategies* are not simply make-or-buy choices. If a company is to sustain competitive advantage, it must restrict itself to those activities where it possesses the capabilities that are superior to those of other companies that perform those activities (see Figure 3-4).

Geographical scope describes the multinationality of the organization. Global strategies (see later) change the locations from where organizations may purchase inputs, sell outputs to, locate activities performed in the value chain and find intellectual capital. *Internationalization*, first introduced in the introductory chapter, is a significant force shaping the competitive environment of business. Internationalization occurs through trade and direct investment and has implications for strategy formulation or formation either in terms of opportunity to expand markets or through the threats posed by overseas competitors.

Internationalization the process by which a company enters a foreign market

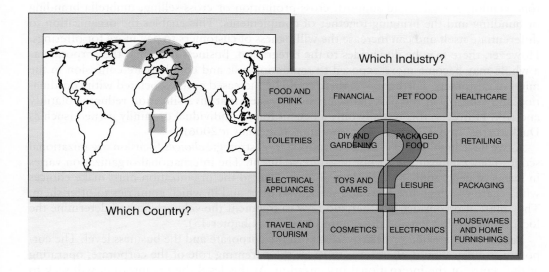

Figure 3-4

Choosing corporate scope

In considering the management of corporations, three models of corporate management can be envisaged. In the first type there may be relatively few business units with one or two at the core (dominant business corporation). In such cases there are many opportunities for resource sharing (logistics, operations, etc.) because the corporate infrastructure required by each business unit provides similar services, see for example Dell discussed in Chapter 10. Such organizations are narrow in horizontal scope. At the opposite end, the unrelated business corporation is the conglomerate (see for example the First Pacific case study in Chapter 17). The relations among business units of the conglomerate are low, consequently only generic resources may be shared. Conglomerates tend to emphasize tight financial control (as opposed to operating control) as a way of optimizing cash management, increasing liquidity and improving resource allocation. They tend to have small corporate offices and coordinate through skill transfer. In between the dominant business corporation and the conglomerate is the related business corporation which has more business units than dominant business corporations, but maintain threads to link their businesses (see Bosch discussed in Chapter 11).

Larger organizations may pursue horizontal scope either through ownership, joint-venture, alliance and other partnership approaches. In devising corporate strategy, managers should be aware of the impact on individual business units (where competition takes place). A successful corporate strategy will aid its business units, making them better able to compete in their specific industries. However, corporate strategy can result in failure, undermining business unit strategy and the ability to compete. Business units should only be combined (broadening scope) and their activities coordinated as a multiple business unit (corporate) if this results in the units' increased ability to create and capture more value than they could as independent, unassociated units. The corporate must add value.

Next the corporate manager should consider whether the set of business units needs to be jointly owned in order to maximize the amount of value created and captured. If coordinated action is valuable then the corporate manager must ask whether their company is particularly well-placed to act upon the opportunity identified before capitalizing on it. It should be borne in mind that there is a tendency towards overexpansion in the belief that bigger-is-better or in pursuit of a personal desire to build an empire and increase the resources under managerial control.

Similar questions may be used by the corporate manager considering divesting a unit in order to narrow scope. Scope expansion may be beneficial when it makes an industry more attractive, through changes to industry structure (for example, changing the nature of rivalry) and can improve a company's position within its industry. There may be beneficial cost effects (shared cost economies, activities and resources) facilitating a cost leadership strategy. Similarly, value may be created by enabling the corporate to offer a one-stop shop (one vendor) for sales and support, cross-promotion or cross-selling, umbrella branding or bundling and the bringing together of complements. This enables the organization to differentiate itself and can increase the willingness of customers to pay more for offerings. However, there may be downsides to the integration. Business units and the corporate as a whole may become more exposed to reputation risk and could create confusion in the mind of customers. Furthermore, there could be increased costs associated with coordination and control. In the past managers have argued that diversification reduces volatility and risk. However, this is really only a benefit for the individual or family owned (such as Duckworths' case, Chapter 11) corporation (Ghemawat 2006).

As we have highlighted thus far, corporate level strategic *choices* focus on organizational scope. They establish the corporate strategic intent. The international organization varies in terms of geographic and product diversity and so the organization must make choices with regard to which products and services to offer and in which countries to offer them. They must also consider whether and how to fragment the value chain and determine the location of production and distribution facilities (Chapter 15).

Value can be created or destroyed at both the corporate and the business level. The corporate strategy should, therefore, consider the parenting role of the corporate, operating at the centre of the international organization. At this level the organization will seek to manage its portfolio of interests. Whereas at the business level we are more likely to discuss benefits arising from economies of *scale* (producing more of the same) at the corporate level we will consider benefits arising from *economies of scope* – using existing resources and capabilities to deliver new products and services or enter into new markets. In many cases, scope benefits may be described as benefits of synergy. In the management literature, synergy has generally been used to mean an overall fit or congruence between units (see previous chapter). More recently, studies have examined the joint effects between activities rather than between entire business units. Ensign (1998) suggests corporate strategy must move beyond the idea that the primary way of creating synergy is the combination of related businesses (by buying and selling businesses). Corporate strategy must focus on creating value that is independent of business unit value. This means developing horizontal strategies that have the objective of coordinating activities and developing programmes that encourage the sharing of resources and skills. An understanding of the horizontal organization helps to emphasize that organizational structure and processes are significant in developing interrelationships with the potential to reach the goals of synergy and competitive advantage.

Synergy describes how – by sharing capabilities – each cooperating entity strengthens each of their competitive positions. Such efforts may be seen as 'co-managed strategies' which result in a 'systemic solution'. For example, within Hewlett-Packard, R&D strategies may be common to several business units. Such shared purpose serves to avoid costly duplication of efforts, i.e. redundant research or 'reinvention'. To facilitate exchange between business units, Hewlett-Packard utilizes a standardized infrastructure. Communication is enhanced through the use of technology. It is important to note that though a system may be flexible and ever-evolving, it must be consciously designed with procedures to promote collaboration (create value) between activities. Although synergy has been used as a justification for why the international organization chooses to diversify, the overall failure rate of diversifications seems to indicate that positive joint effects may not always be achieved.

Success in resource sharing depends upon two things: first, upon the selection of activities where resource sharing (interrelationships) will occur. This is important because the potential benefits from resource sharing can vary in different organizational contexts. Recognizing the costs and benefits to specific circumstances is important; knowing when not to pursue interdependencies may be as crucial as knowing when to seek them. Second,

Synergy the benefits that might be gained where activities or processes complement each other such that their combined effect is greater than the sum of the parts; cooperative action – either the working together of two or more things (combined action) or the shared use of a resource

the realization of potential opportunities depends upon how effectively linkages between activities are actually managed. That is, just because an opportunity exists does not mean that it may be possible to fully develop it or bring it to fruition. Four types of synergy are frequently discussed:

- *Sales* – when products use common sales administration, distribution channels, advertising, sales promotion, or reputation.
- *Operating* – results from higher utilization of facilities and personnel, spreading of overhead, advantages of common learning curves, or common inputs.
- *Investment* – results from the joint use of plant, carryover in research and development, common machinery, tooling, or raw materials.
- *Management* – carryover of managerial ability in strategic, organizational, and operating problems.

Corporate strategy is frequently intent on making the diversified international organization worth more than the sum of its parts. Consequently, it must organize and manage business units so that each can benefit from their links with the rest of the larger organization. Synergy must emanate from relationships between the skills and activities in the various business units. Synergy is not simply a phenomenon that occurs at the corporate level – between whole business units – but is best viewed as resulting from specific instances of resource or activity sharing between segments/portions of different business units.

In summary, we have discussed the role of headquarters (corporate) in defining scope and adding value to enable the subsidiaries or business units comprising the whole organization. The role and power of the headquarters or corporate is determined by whether the organization is in pursuit of a global or multidomestic strategy – discussed next.

Global and multidomestic strategies

International strategy is concerned with choices about where the organization offers its products and services and where it locates value adding activities. In the introductory chapter we identified a number of reasons why organizations pursue international strategies: homogenation of customer demand (globalization) leading to economies of scale, access to different markets for economies of scope and growth and to serve the needs of global customers. By internationalizing, the organization is able to broaden the size of its market. International strategy considers not only where to locate facilities and activities but also how to enter different markets, i.e. the appropriate entry mode (to be discussed in the next section). There are a number of benefits associated with such strategies.

Such a strategy should enable efficiency advantages. First there is opportunity to produce more, which may enable economies of scale through both experience and the ability to spread fixed costs over a greater number of units. Second there will be scale benefits in the ability to replicate knowledge and technology within the organization. Once created, knowledge can be reused at close to zero cost if it can be transferred. As has already been mentioned, efficiencies may also be gained from locating different activities in different places. Furthermore, organizations may make use of positive cash flows in one region to cross-subsidize and invest in another region. However, organizations have fundamentally different views of world markets and these are reflected in strategy. Two broad generic international strategies can be distinguished:

1 The global strategy – assumes a single market and offers a standard product(s) to meet customer needs wherever they are located. This is essentially a cost leadership strategy, exploiting economies of scale and other cost efficiencies.

2 The multidomestic strategy – assumes variance in customer needs according to their location and therefore issues a differentiation strategy, adapting products and services to make unique local requirements.

Global strategy assumes a single market and offers a standard product(s) to meet customer needs wherever they are located

Multidomestic strategy assumes variance in customer needs according to their location and therefore adopts a differentiation strategy, adapting products and services to make unique local requirements

The extent to which services may be standardized across national boundaries or need to be adapted to meet specific local requirements is often referred to as the global-local dilemma. In practice, organizations rarely pursue a pure and a single generic strategy and seek out a position between the two. Most large multinational organizations face the need to tailor their product or service to some extent. While there are many benefits to an international strategy such as economies of scale and scope, access to new markets for growth and the exploitation of location advantages, the organization becomes much more complex requiring more money and time to be spent on coordination, collaboration, communication, formalization and control (challenges we consider in the remainder of the book). Consequently not all organizations benefit from internationalization in the same way and some may not benefit at all.

As was noted, a *global strategy* is one that views the world as a single market. This means that customers are assumed to be similar across country boundaries and that there is therefore little or no need for differentiation at the country level; consequently, more decisions are likely to be made at the headquarters. However, as was noted in the previous chapter, laws and government regulations, variance in disposable income, national culture and country infrastructure may impact upon products and services and the means by which they are delivered to customers.

Global strategies are very much about *integration* while other international business strategies may focus on national *differentiation*. In the case of some products and services there are national differences in customer preferences and as a consequence the organization must consider customer needs in different locations. Products and services must then be designed or adapted to meet those needs. As we will see in Chapter 15, however, common basic designs and common components can reduce the cost of national differentiation. Flexible manufacturing systems, computer-aided design and manufacture with lean production processes help create customized products at a lower cost.

Reconciling conflicting forces for global efficiency and national differentiation represents one of the greatest strategic challenges facing the international or multinational corporation. Many organizations opt for a hybrid approach – one of global localization, i.e. 'glocal' (transnational). In such cases the organization will seek to standardize aspects of the product or service and primary activities where scale economies are substantial and will differentiate where national preferences are strongest. Whether or not the international organization pursues a global or a local strategy will impact upon the organizational structure and management systems. Business units such as IT, research and development and procurement can be more centralized or at least organized at a global level since it is likely that scale economies can be attained through sharing such resources across the whole organization.

The downstream and primary activities of marketing and customer service and the secondary activities associated with human resource management are more likely to reflect local differences. While manufacturing lies somewhere in between, it has strong globalization potential, being located near raw materials, low-cost or highly skilled labour. In Chapter 9 we recognize that the simultaneous pursuit of responsiveness to national markets and global coordination places particular requirements on structure and we introduce the concept of the transnational organization to guide and direct organizational design. Whether pursuing a global, multidomestic or global strategy, the international organization will establish operations, sales and other facilities in other countries and we therefore consider market entry strategies next.

Market entry strategies

How do international organizations enter new country markets?

Having decided *which* markets to enter, for the majority of organizations, the most significant decision they are likely to make next is *how* they should enter new markets. In this section we examine the different market entry options open to organizations to enable them to select the most appropriate method for their given situation. There are advantages and disadvantages with each market entry method and critical in the decision-making process is the organizational assessment of the costs and risk associated with each method. There is no ideal market entry strategy and different market entry methods might be adopted by different organizations entering the same market. There are a variety of ways in which organizations can enter foreign markets. The main ways are direct or indirect, marketing only or production in a foreign country (see Figure 3-5). Alternative market entry methods include:

- Products are supplied from the organization's domestic operations:
  - indirect exporting (the simplest and lowest cost method of market entry-products are sold overseas by other organizations);
  - direct exporting (the organization becomes directly involved in the presence of exporting).
- Products are supplied from the organization's overseas operations:
  - foreign manufacturing strategies without direct investments (contract manufacturer, franchising and licensing);
  - cooperative strategies (joint ventures and strategic alliances);
  - foreign manufacturing strategies with direct investment (wholly owned subsidiary, company acquisitions and mergers).

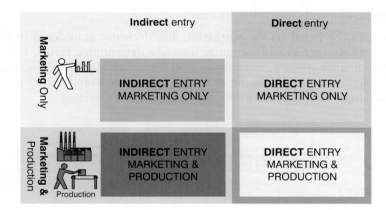

Figure 3-5

Market entry

There are many alternative ways (modes) to enter a new market. Many factors determine the market entry mode such as availability of resources, attitudes to risk, attributes of the served market, product considerations and environmental factors. The process by which a company enters a foreign market is termed internationalization (refer back to the introductory chapter). The internationalization process of the individual firm is most closely associated with the research of Johanson and Wiedersheim-Paul who distinguished four different modes of entering an international market, where the successive stages represent higher degrees of international involvement:

Stage 1: No regular export activities

Stage 2: Export via independent representatives (agents)

Stage 3: Establishment of an overseas sales subsidiary

Stage 4: Overseas production/manufacturing units.

Since their work there have been a variety of stage models proposed by various scholars representing internationalization. Market-entry modes can be classified according to whether they require indirect or direct involvement by the organization and whether they involve both marketing and production or simply marketing. As the organization becomes more involved in marketing and production, the risk and control of the organization increases. The mode of entry or extent of internationalization is a reflection of the value chain activities, i.e. which are insourced or outsourced, undertaken at the home or served country. With regard to marketing and sales, organizations may simply export from the home country or may establish a foreign sales office. With regard to production they can license, franchise or contract out production or invest in their own production facility in the target country market (direct foreign investment). There are many choices. Each market entry method reflects a different level of involvement by the organization in international operations. The level of involvement has significant implications in terms of levels of risk and control. When deciding on market entry strategy, the organization should ask questions such as:

- What level of control over international business is required?
- What level of risk are we willing to take?
- What cost can we afford?

Whereas we have focused on the entry strategy from an internationalization and value chain perspective, we can also consider entry strategies according to the organization's **competitive strategy**. Organizations may enter into new foreign markets and compete through:

1 technical innovation strategy – perceived and demonstrable superior products;
2 product adaptation strategy – modifications to existing products;
3 low price strategy – penetration price; and
4 total adaptation and conformity strategy.

Such strategies are based on the marketing mix decisions considered in Chapter 16. The market entry strategy should recognize time as a determining factor. The building of marketing information systems, operations, distribution channels and creating branding awareness through promotion take time, effort and money. Brand names do not appear overnight and large investments in promotion campaigns are needed.

Competitive strategies a firm can develop cost leadership, product differentiation, and business innovation strategies to confront its competitive forces

Pricing strategy is an important part of creating competitive advantage

© iStockphoto.com/LyaC

Competing with business-level strategy

The corporate or multinational is typically made up of several businesses. At the business (subsidiary) level the organization is concerned with how it might obtain and achieve sustainable competitive advantage either through generic or other strategies (cost leadership, differentiation or focus). The value chain will help identify competitive advantage. Focusing on the way the organization may use its resources may allow the organization to identify how it can be different and unique or where it can be more efficient. The organization may have unique technology, talented human resource, financial resources and special relationships within the value system. Since an international organization will typically comprise of more than one business, the organization should be decomposed into strategic business units (though this can present problems such as barriers to corporate synergy) with different strategies considered for each. A strategic business unit is part of an organization for which there is a distinct external market for goods or services that is different from another strategic business unit. The organization must consider how each unit or subsidiary will compete under the umbrella of the corporate scope.

As was discussed in the micro environmental analysis part of Chapter 2, when customers have a choice, the organization must compete for their business. With this in mind we might ask how companies compete. An organization can develop cost leadership, product differentiation, and business innovation strategies to confront its competitive forces. Competitive advantages exist in relation to rivals operating within an industry as factors that enable an organization to earn a higher rate of profit. Such advantages emerge from the actions of organizations (internal sources) or from changes in the external environment (external sources). With regard to external sources, an organization may be more capable or better equipped to exploit changes in customer demand, technology, political or economic factors. An external change may create opportunity for profit. Consequently, organizations must be able to identify and respond to opportunity. As markets become increasingly turbulent, so responsiveness to external change has become increasingly important as a source of competitive advantage.

There are two fundamental, internal sources of competitive advantage: cost and differentiation. An organization may compete by offering customers what they want at the lowest price/cost or may differentiate their products and services in such a way that the customer is prepared to pay a premium price for them. Cost leadership requires the organization to find and exploit sources of cost advantage, typically selling a standard, no-frills product or service while differentiation necessitates the organization providing something unique and valuable to buyers. They represent two fundamentally different approaches to business strategy and two of the three generic strategies referred to by Porter. A third source of competitive advantage is based on focus. Cost leadership and differentiation are industry-wide sources of competitive advantage while focus strategies seek out competitive advantages for particular market segments.

Cost leadership may be achieved in many ways such as through efficient manufacturing processes and tight cost controls while differentiation is dependent upon creativity and marketing abilities (see Chapters 15 and 16 in particular). Exploiting new technologies (discussed in Part IV) and business processes (Chapter 10) may improve production techniques and thus increase efficiency. Also in the domain of operations management is capacity utilization and a variety of techniques aimed at cost reduction are presented within Chapter 15. Cost advantages may also be obtained through a reduction in input costs. This may come from access to raw materials and location advantages (global sourcing). One form of location advantage may be a reduction in labour costs (an advantage exploited by companies such as Dyson see Chapter 15 and Burberry see Chapter 7).

Differentiation is about understanding customers and how the organization can meet their needs. The organization differentiates itself from competitors when it provides something unique and valuable to those customers; for example the product may perform better or be of higher quality. In return, customers are prepared to pay the organization a premium price. Differentiation may manifest itself in product or service features and in any of the possible interactions between the organization and the customer in selling, delivering and providing associated customer services in relation to the product or service offered. Differentiation is based much more on an understanding of customers and their needs, a challenge typically allocated to the marketing function, explored in Chapter 16. Establishing differentiation advantage requires creativity. As with cost advantages, the value chain provides a useful framework for analyzing opportunities to gain differentiation advantage. The value chain enables the organization to analyze how value is created for customers and focus on those activities that can be used to achieve differentiation. The essence of differentiation advantage is to increase the perceived value of offerings to customers. Differentiation is only effective if it is communicated to customers. Organizations will therefore engage in more extensive marketing and brand development when pursuing differentiation strategies. Differentiation advantages tend to be more sustainable than cost-based advantages. This is because cost-based advantages are much more vulnerable to change as a result of external forces. Advantages based on low labour costs, technology or business processes can quickly disappear.

While we have presented two core generic strategies, they are not presented as an either or choice and organizations tend not to consider differentiation strategy in isolation to cost-based strategies. All organizations must consider efficiency goals. Interestingly, however, differentiation adds costs. Differentiation costs include higher quality raw materials and other inputs, specialized production machinery and skilled employees. Organizations who differentiate are likely to spend more on packaging, marketing, and sales channels. In pursuit of differentiation strategies organizations will still seek out cost efficiencies as a prerequisite of profitability.

Differentiation can provide something unique and valuable to an organization's customers

As was noted earlier, organizations achieve competitive advantage by providing their customers with what they want, or need, better or more effectively than competitors. Customers choose from a variety of competitive offerings, based on perceived value for money. We can classify competitive strategy options based upon the relative emphasis a business unit places on *price* and *differentiation* and whether or not they focus on a particular market segment *(focus)*. For simplicity we might classify price in terms of low, medium (standard) and high (premium) and similarly might classify the differentiation strategy (customer benefits/value added) in terms of low (no-frills), medium (standard) and high. If we take this approach, we might distinguish nine different competitive strategy options, see Figure 3-6. In reality, infinite options exist on a continuous scale.

Considering competitive alternatives in this manner reveals some options will be less likely to succeed in some contexts rather than others. The first option (no-frills) is typified by the budget airlines (refer back to the opening case study of the previous chapter) – organizations adopting this competitive approach are likely to operate in a price sensitive market segment. Option two presents a standard offering low price and option three delivers the most value at the lowest price – such a business is both creative and cost efficient. Low-price strategies are typically associated with low margins and therefore lower reinvestment unless they can attract more sales and increased volume. Similarly there are three standard cost options: with low, medium and high (differentiation without the premium price) value. Finally there are three premium price options: with low, medium and high (differentiation with the premium price) value. The organization is also likely to consider a focused approach where it considers premium pricing and high degrees of differentiation. Strategies which seek to charge a premium price for a standard or no-frills product or service are unlikely to survive in most competitive international environments. Charging higher prices for poor quality/low value is only feasible in non-competitive (monopolistic) environments.

Figure 3-6

Competitive strategies

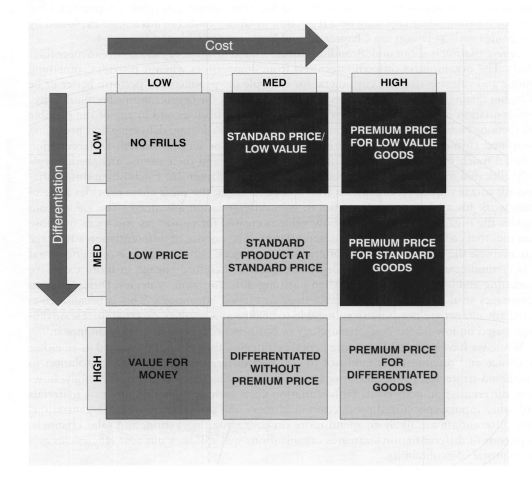

Companies that are more *responsive* may also have an advantage over their sluggish rivals. Responsiveness is enabled through resources (information) and capabilities (flexibility). Speed of response as a source of competitive advantage is termed time-based competition. This will be discussed at length in the chapters about operations management and marketing presented later. Technological improvements in communications (see for example Internet and mobile application technologies), and business process improvements, coupled with manufacturing technologies, have enabled organizations to be both flexible and responsive, reducing cycle times drastically.

The process of adaptation to the external environment and changing customer needs may necessitate new approaches to work the way business is conducted which depend upon entrepreneurial (innovation and creativity) capabilities. Alternative strategies and sources of advantage are based upon diversification. Diversification may be categorized as related (within the capabilities of the organization) or unrelated (beyond current capabilities, e.g. a conglomerate). There are also different forms of related diversification: backward integration refers to development into activities concerned with upstream activities (the organization's inputs) and forward integration refers to development into activities downstream such as closer contact with customers in terms of product repair and servicing or retail.

Development into activities which are complementary to present activities is referred to as horizontal integration, describing opportunities in other markets that may be exploited by the organization in strategic capabilities. Concentric diversification is a growth strategy in which a company seeks to develop by adding new, but related products to its existing product lines to attract new customers. This strategy is appropriate when:

- the industry is slow-growth or no-growth;
- complementary products enhance sales of current products;
- new complementary products can be offered at competitive prices; and
- current products are in the decline stage of life cycle.

Once established, competitive advantage is subject to erosion by competition. The durability of the advantage is related to the ability of competitors to either imitate or substitute factors leading to advantage. Imitation necessitates competitor identification and diagnosis of the source of competitive advantage and must be both able and motivated to acquire or develop the resources and capabilities necessary for imitating the advantage. Organizations seek out sustainable competitive advantages where barriers exist to imitation. For example they may secure exclusive access to key raw materials, develop proprietary standards, act in secrecy or take steps to persuade rivals that imitation will be unprofitable. In some cases there may be a first mover advantage whereby the initial occupant may gain access to resources and capabilities that a follower cannot match, for example through a patent or copyright.

The search for competitive advantage typically involves decomposing the organization into parts, however the strategist should recognize that competitive advantage also comes from the integrated whole. Competitive advantage comes from an integrated set of choices about activities and an organization whose choices do not fit together well is unlikely succeed. (Internal consistency) production decisions affect marketing choices, distribution choices need to fit with operations decisions. The organization should seek out mutually reinforcing choices. It should also recognize that there may be more than one internally consistent way to do business within the same industry. As far as the international organization is concerned, global presence by itself does not confer global competitive advantage. Global presence makes available to the firm's managers five value-creation opportunities:

1 to adapt to local market differences;
2 to exploit economies of global scale;
3 to exploit economies of global scope;
4 to tap optimal locations for activities and resources; and
5 to maximize knowledge transfer across locations.

(Gupta and Govindarajan 2001)

Earlier we discussed the resource-based view (RBV) – a perspective on strategy that stresses the importance of capabilities in determining sustainable competitive advantage, (Slack, Chambers, and Johnston 2007); the resource-based view of strategy assumes the competitive advantage of an organization is explained by the distinctiveness of its capabilities. Unique resources are those resources that critically underpin competitive advantage and that others cannot easily imitate or obtain.

If an organization is to achieve competitive advantage over others, it will do so because it has capabilities that the others do not have or have difficulty in getting. These capabilities could be the resources the organization has or the way resources are used or deployed (organization's competencies); the competitive advantage of an organization is explained by the uniqueness of its capabilities. Any organization competing in a particular industry must possess a set of basic capabilities to survive. Such capabilities do not confer competitive advantage. Advantages tend to come from unique capabilities that competitors do not have and cannot imitate.

Unique capabilities may themselves derive from unique resources of the manner in which resources are deployed and value-adding activities performed. Strategic capabilities are likely to deliver sustainable competitive advantages when they are based on competencies that are rare and difficult to transfer or when the organization has secured preferred access to customers, suppliers or resources. Competencies and capabilities are likely to be embedded as organizational routines associated with organizational culture, making them difficult to imitate. In many cases it may be difficult to understand exactly how the competence is derived, also making it difficult to imitate. When competitors find it difficult to identify the source of advantage, i.e. it may be difficult to identify cause and affect it is more likely that advantage will be sustainable. As a general rule, it is less likely that contemporary international organizations will achieve competitive advantage through their physical resources (though country specific advantages clearly exist) but more likely they will achieve such advantage from the way they do things and the experience they have accumulated. Consequently, knowledge about how to do things becomes the basis of strategic capability and can be a rare resource. Knowledge management strategies are therefore a key aspect of the international organizational strategy and we consider them in more detail in Chapter 12.

People are frequently at the heart of strategic capability in the international organization through the work activities they perform and the experience and know-how they accumulate. Human resource management and managers generally can therefore improve and develop capabilities by recruiting, training and developing people. Furthermore HR policies and practices, the subject of Chapter 7, are also used to develop particular competencies. Thus, there are many ways for the organization to sustain competitive advantage and we have already discussed the use of resources and creation of competencies and capabilities that are both rare and difficult to imitate. Organizations may also sustain advantage by locking customers and suppliers into their value system either by increasing their *switching costs* or by dominating the market. In many cases, a first mover may be able to do this. The organization's products or services may become the industry standard, see for example Microsoft. It is more difficult to sustain competitive advantage in highly volatile (*hypercompetitive*) markets. In such cases, the organization is likely to derive advantage from an ability to be responsive to such change.

Thus far we have discussed strategy at the corporate (scope) and business (value add and competitive) levels. Departments also consider strategic issues and a variety of functional strategies are considered throughout this book. We therefore offer this chapter as an introductory and general chapter on strategy and as an introduction to much of the book. Having discussed strategic choices and alternatives we now consider how strategies are implemented.

Strategy implementation

Chapter 2 focused on analysis and the preceding paragraphs of this chapter considered strategic design alternatives. In this final section we consider implementation of the choices made. Thus far we have highlighted strategy formation, using a variety of tools and techniques, leading to choices about scope and competitiveness. The alternative approaches selected must then be implemented – a matter we discuss next.

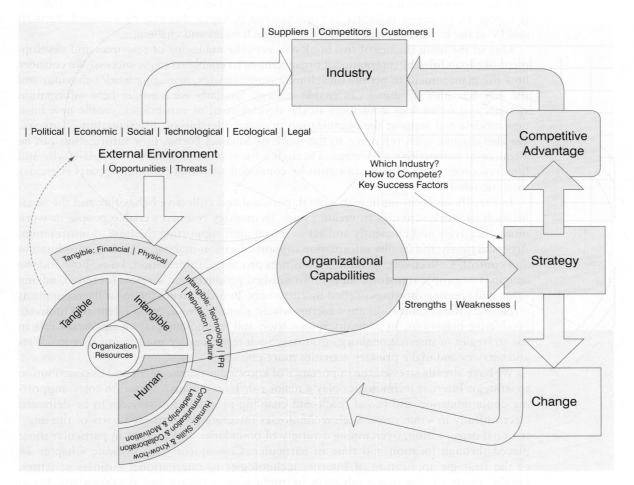

Figure 3-7

Chapter 3 model

The prime aim in implementing strategy is to deliver the mission and objectives of the organization. Strategy implementation usually involves change (Chapter 5). The basic implementation process takes strategy choice as inputs and then creates specific quantitative and qualitative objectives which are then used to formulate specific plans (tasks, deadlines and responsibilities) to which resources are allocated. Such plans are then subjected to monitoring and control procedures to ensure delivery. Implementation covers the activities required when an organization translates strategies into practice. However, this is a fairly simplistic view and many scholars now believe it is difficult to separate implementation from strategy formulation and that implementation may shape strategy.

Turning strategy into action is a significant challenge for the organization and a variety of helpful frameworks have been proposed; see for example the balanced scorecard – a framework for setting and monitoring business performance and strategy – metrics are structured according to customer issues, internal efficiency measures, financial measures and innovation. It is important to communicate a clear message of what is required and why, plus identify who will do what and when. It is important for people to be committed to the new strategy and commitment is typically higher when those responsible for implementation have some say in the choices of what must be done and why. When operating in a turbulent environment the organization needs to be flexible since it is often difficult to specify task objectives in detail. Strategies need resources allocated to them if they have to be implemented successfully. Organizations vary in their methods for resource allocation processes.

Strategy is typically turned into action through tactical or operational decision-making and choices, organizational structure, business processes, systems, the allocation of resources and mechanisms to ensure performance. In many cases significant, change to structure (Chapter 9), processes (Chapter 10) and systems (Chapter 13) may be required. Parts III and IV of the book focus more specifically on such issues and challenges.

One of the main themes of this book concerns the managing of resources and development of capabilities by international organizations to enable strategic success. We consider how the management of people (developing competencies, managing work behaviour and the way activities are done) can enable strategy. Similarly we consider how information systems and technology contribute to the development of capabilities, enable new business models and support the organization in cost leadership or differentiation strategies. We also discuss, with reference to the work of Michael Porter, how information can be a source of competitive advantage. Through a focus on capabilities, we explain why and how resources and competencies must be combined such that the sum of parts is greater than the whole.

In Part III we focus on human capital, personal and collective behaviour and the organization of work activities to create value. Technology resources enable people to work more effectively and efficiently and act as the conduit supporting the flow of information. Access to timely and quality information supports decision-making, planning, coordination and control. Collectively, technology, business processes, information, know-how and the activities of people transform inputs into finished products and services (outputs), adding value and creating offerings needed by customers. In order to get the most from people as a resource, the organization must recruit wisely, identify and develop talent and motivate productive behaviour. In addition, information and technology plays a significant role in the strategies of international organizations. Such resources are used to improve products and services and make primary activities more efficient.

We have already stressed the importance of knowledge management and its contribution to strategy. Internet technologies play a major role by reducing transaction costs, supporting communication and broad reach and enabling products and services to be delivered electronically in some cases. Such technologies integrate the dispersed parts of the international organization, overcoming a variety of boundaries and barriers in particular those placed through location and time in particular. Consequently we dedicate Chapter 14 to the strategic application of Internet technologies to international business activities. Finally, there are the major advances in application software and databases which can further integrate business activities, linking activities wherever they are located, through the free flow of information both in the value chain and system. Combined with Internet (networking) technologies, such applications, in the form of enterprise systems, not only deliver efficiency gains but also contribute to making the organization more responsive, thus allowing it to share explicit knowledge throughout business units. Such systems benefit

Balanced scorecard a framework for setting and monitoring business performance and strategy – metrics are structured according to customer issues, internal efficiency measures, financial measures and innovation

production, logistics, sales and marketing, finance and human resource management alike. In Chapter 13 we explore such systems in more detail.

In the final part of the book we not only consider operations and marketing strategy but also the management of financial resources as a key determinant of strategic success. While we have structured Parts II, III and IV of the book around specific resources and activities, in this chapter and in the chapter on leadership, we emphasize the need to integrate resources when creating competencies and capabilities. Resources, on their own, are less likely to be a source of sustainable competitive advantage. The international organization must be able to integrate resources both inside the organization and within the value system. Integration not only enables synergistic benefits but also enables agility, adaptability and the responsive organization to also be able to compete with time-based advantages. Furthermore, integrated resources are more difficult to understand and imitate, thus providing more sustainable advantage to the international organization.

Throughout this chapter we have discussed strategy as a plan, pattern of actions, competitive position and an overall perspective. In his book, *Levers of Control*, Simons (1995) proposes a control framework to assure organizational goals are correct and achieved (effectively and efficiently). His framework operates at the strategic level and is essentially about strategy assurance. The book seeks to provide guidance for implementing and controlling strategy. Monitoring and control procedures are an important aspect of implementation and help with resource allocation decisions, progress reporting, performance appraisal and feedback. Control systems typically utilize information about customer satisfaction, quality, market share and internal key performance indicators and other financial measures, allowing action to be taken where required. Control strategies are discussed in Chapter 8. For now we note the important role of belief systems (the mission and goals in particular) in assuring strategy is implemented through the appropriate behaviour of employees.

In this chapter we have explained how the organization develops strategy to ensure goals are achieved. Throughout Chapter 2 and this chapter, we discussed the purpose and actions of the organization and recognized a need for the organization to do the right thing and those strategic decisions necessitated knowledge of change management in order to implement decisions. In Chapter 4 we discuss corporate ethics and social responsibility which are further inputs into the strategy. In Chapter 5 we discuss change management, further adding to our understanding of implementation.

Summary of key learning points

In this chapter we focused on strategy: what the organization should do (purpose) and how it should be done. In determining the overall purpose and strategy (articulated in the vision, mission and goals) an organization relies on inputs such as an analysis of the internal and external environment (see previous chapters), the values of other stakeholders, corporate social responsibilities (considered in Chapter 4), the values, experience and predisposition of leaders (considered in Chapter 5), culture and the thoughts of employees. The purpose and strategy are seen as devices to unify, constrain, coordinate and motivate the organization. Strategy may result from a formal and planned process or may emerge from a collection of decisions and actions.

The overall strategy will be influenced by perspectives on the environment (internal or external) and convergence (global versus local). Once the overall direction and purpose has been agreed, the organization, typically through corporate level decision-making, must determine the scope for organizational activities. It must decide and make choices about where to compete (geographic scope), the product to sell (product scope) and the activities to perform (vertical scope). Such decisions determine the boundaries for action. Corporate headquarters must ensure these activities add value. This is achieved through synergy – by enabling resource sharing and mutual support. Having identified the countries in which to operate, the corporate must also devise market entry strategies. Subsidiaries and business units will then determine how to compete within this defined scope. A variety of strategies were discussed such as cost leadership, and differentiation (the two leading generic strategies), focus and time-based competitive advantage. The value chain is a useful concept and framework used to identify where the organization can apply resources to either differentiate itself or reduce costs through efficiency savings.

We recognized the problem of competitive advantage erosion and discussed the need to identify sustainable competitive advantages. These are more likely to come from differentiation strategies based on the use of internal resources through competences and capabilities. Finally, we considered the implementation of strategy, noting the remaining parts of the book would focus on this. Implementation concerns the allocation of resources typically through plans, the structure and budgets. Implementation results in change, considered in Chapter 5. Assuring the strategy is realized requires effective monitoring and control. However, it is erroneous to believe that this whole process of strategy occurs in an ordered sequence of steps or that the intended strategy is always realized.

Review questions

Strategy and purpose

1 In your own words explain what is meant by: vision, mission and goals.
2 Discuss their role on strategy formulation.
3 In your opinion, what should be the starting point for strategy formulation be?

International strategy

1 What is the difference between global and multidomestic strategy?
2 Identify five examples of each.

Value chain and value system

1 Explain how the concept/framework of the value chain and value system may help in the strategy formulation process.
2 With reference to the value chain, identify alternative strategies available to the international organization.

Generic strategy

1 Describe each of the generic strategies.
2 Identify and describe other strategies that may deliver a competitive advantage.

Strategy formulation

1 Identify and describe the different ways strategy may be formed within organizations.
2 Describe the key stages in a typical 'planning' approach to strategy formulation.
3 Critically evaluate, compare and contrast the planning and adaptive modes of strategy formulation.

Competitive advantage

1 In your own words explain what is meant by: resource, routine, capability and competence.

2 Discuss what is meant by competitive and sustainable competitive advantage.

3 Explain how organizational capabilities may confer a sustainable competitive advantage.

4 Evaluate why many scholars now identify knowledge management as a key source of sustainable competitive advantage.

5 In what contexts might organizational culture be

a a source of sustainable competitive advantage; or

b a source of disadvantage?

6 Why is it necessary for many contemporary organizations to develop dynamic capabilities?

Strategic choices

1 Identify the differences between corporate and business level strategy.

2 Evaluate how the corporate body can add or remove value from the activities of business units – you should discuss the concepts of synergy and diversification in your answer.

Discuss the concepts of internationalization, the fragmented value chain and strategies for entering foreign markets.

References

Barney, J. (1986) 'Organizational Culture: Can It Be A Source Of Sustained Competitive Advantage?', *The Academy of Management Review* (July 1986) 11(3):656–665.

Bourgeois, L. J. (1980) 'Strategy and Environment: A Conceptual Integration', *The Academy of Management Review* (January 1980) 5(1):25–39.

Child, J. (1997) 'Strategic Choice in The Analysis Of Action, Structure, Organizations and Environment: Retrospect and Prospect', *Organization Studies – Berlin* 18(1):43–76.

Christensen, C. M. (2001) 'The Past and Future Of Competitive Advantage', *MIT Sloan Management Review* (Winter 2001) 42(2):105–109.

Collis, D. and Montgomery, C. A. (1995) 'Competing On Resources: Strategy in the 1990s', *Harvard Business Review* 73(4):118–128.

Drucker, P. (1999) 'Managing Oneself', *Harvard Business Review* (March/April 1999) 77(2):65–74.

Dyer, J. H. and Singh, H. (1998) 'The Relational View: Cooperative Strategy And Sources Of Interorganizational Competitive Advantage', *The Academy of Management Review* 23(4):660–679

Ensign, P. C. (1998) 'Interrelationships and horizontal strategy to achieve synergy and competitive advantage in the diversified firm', *Management Decision* 36(10):657–668.

Ghemawat, P. (2006) *Strategy and the Business Landscape* (2 ed), Upper Saddle River, NJ: Pearson Prentice Hall.

Govindarajan, V. and Gupta, A. (2001) 'Building an Effective Global Business Team', *MIT Sloan Management Review* 42(4):63–71.

Grant, R. (1991) 'The Resource-Based Theory Of Competitive Advantage: Implications For Strategy Formulation', *California Management Review* (Spring 1991) 33(3):114–135.

Grant, R. (2007) *Contemporary Strategy Analysis* (6 ed), Oxford: Blackwell Publishing.

Hamel, G. and Prahalad, C. (1993) 'Strategy As Stretch And Leverage', *Harvard Business Review* (March/April 1993) 71(2):75–84.

Hitt, M. A., Hoskisson, R. E. and Kim, H. (1997) 'International Diversification: Effects on Innovation and Firm Performance In Product-Diversified Firms', *The Academy of Management Journal* (August 1997) 40(4):767–798.

Hofer, C. W. (1975) 'Toward A Contingency Theory of Business Strategy', *The Academy of Management Journal* (December 1975) 18(4):784–810.

Hrebiniak, L. G. and Joyce, W. F. (1985) 'Organizational Adaptation: Strategic Choice and Environmental Determinism', *Administrative Science Quarterly* (September 1985) 30(3):336–349.

Johnson, G., Scholes, K. and Whittington, R. (2006) *Exploring Corporate Strategy Enhanced Media Edition*, FT Prentice Hall.

Kaplan, R. S. and Norton, D. P. (1993) 'Putting the Balanced Scorecard To Work', *Harvard Business Review* (September/October 1993) 71(5):134–147.

Kaplan, R. S. and Norton, D. P. (1996) *The Balanced Scorecard*, Boston, Mass: HBS Press.

Kaplan, R. S. and Norton, D. P. (2007) 'Using the Balanced Scorecard As A Strategic Management System', *Harvard Business Review* (July/August 2007) 85(7/8):150–161.

Kim, C. and Mauborgne, R. (2004) 'Blue Ocean Strategy', *Harvard Business Review* (October 2004) 82(10):76–84.

Lieberman, M. B. and Montgomery, D. B. (1988) 'First-Mover Advantages', *Strategic Management Journal* (Summer 1988) 9:41–58.

Luthans, F. and Stewart, T. (1977) 'A General Contingency Theory of Management', *Academy of Management Review* 2:181–195.

Magretta, J. (2002) 'Why Business Models Matter', *Harvard Business Review* 80(5):86–92.

Mahoney, J. and Pandian, J. R. (1992) 'The Resource Based View Within The Conversation Of Strategic Management', *Strategic Management Journal* 13:363–380.

Mcgahan, A. and Porter, M. E. (1997) 'How Much Does Industry Matter, Really?', *Strategic Management Journal* (Summer Special Issue) 18:15–30.

McGee, J. and Thomas, H. (1986) 'Strategic Groups: Theory, Research and Taxonomy', *Strategic Management Journal* (March/April 1986) 7(2):141–160.

Mintzberg, H. (1978) 'Patterns In Strategy Formation', *Management Science* (May 1978) 24(9):934–948.

Mintzberg, H. (1987) 'Crafting Strategy', *Harvard Business Review* (July/August 1987) 65(4): 66–75.

Mintzberg, H. (1994) 'The Fall and Rise of Strategic Planning', *Harvard Business Review* (January/February 1994) 72(1):107–114.

Ouchi, W. G. (1980) 'Markets, Bureaucracies, and Clans', *Administrative Science Quarterly – Ithaca* 25(1):129–141.

Peteraf, M. A. (1993) 'The Cornerstones Of Competitive Advantage: A Resource-Based View', *Strategic Management Journal* (March 1993) 14(3):179–191.

Peters, T. (1984) 'Strategy Follows Structure: Developing Distinctive Skills', *California Management Review* (Spring 1984) 26(3):111–126.

Porter, M. E. (1979) 'How Competitive Forces Shape Strategy', *Harvard Business Review* (March/April 1979) 57(2):137–145.

Porter, M. E. (1986) 'Changing Patterns Of International Competition', *California Management Review* (Winter 1986) 28(2):9–41.

Porter, M. E. (1996) 'What Is Strategy?', *Harvard Business Review* 74(6):61–78.

Prahalad, C. and Hamel, G. (1990) 'The Core Competence of the Corporation', *Harvard Business Review* (May/June 1990) 68(3):79–91.

Schein, E. (1997) *Organizational Culture and Leadership* (2 ed), San Francisco: Jossey Bass.

Schein, E. (1999) *The Corporate Culture Survival Guide,* San Francisco: Jossey Bass.

Simon, H. A. (1955) 'A Behavioral Model Of Rational Choice', *The Quarterly Journal of Economics* (February 1955) 69(1):99–118.

Simons, R. (1995) *Levers of Control*, Boston, Mass: Harvard Business School Press.

Slack, N., Chambers, S. and Johnston, R. (2007) *Operations Management* (5 ed), Harlow: Financial Times Press.

Stalk, G. (1988) 'Time – The Next Source Of Competitive Advantage', *Harvard Business Review* (July/August 1988) 66(4):41–51.

Stalk, G., Evans, P. and Shulman, L. E. (1992) 'Competing On Capabilities: The New Rules of Corporate Strategy', *Harvard Business Review* (March/April 1992) 70(2):54–66.

Teece, D. J., Pisano, G. and Shuen, A. (1997) 'Dynamic Capabilities and Strategic Management', *Strategic Management Journal* (August 1997) 18(7):509–533.

Valentin, E. K. (2001) 'SWOT Analysis from A Resource-Based View', *Journal of Marketing Theory & Practice* (Spring 2001) 9(2):54–69.

Venkatraman, N. (1989) 'The Concept Of Fit In Strategy Research: Toward Verbal And Statistical Correspondence', *The Academy of Management Review* (July 1989) 14(3):423–444.

Vernon, R. (1966) 'International Investment and International Trade In The Product Cycle', *The Quarterly Journal of Economics* (May 1966) 80(2):190–207.

Suggestions for further reading

Journals

Strategic Management Journal (SMJ)

The *Strategic Management Journal* (SMJ) has since its inception in 1980, been the official journal of the Strategic Management Society. It is published in 13 issues per year by Wiley-Blackwell Publishing. The journal publishes original material concerned with all aspects of strategic management. It is devoted to the improvement and further development of the theory and practice of strategic management and it is designed to appeal to both practising managers and academics. See http://www3.interscience.wiley.com/journal/2144/home/ProductInformation.html.

California Management Review (CMR)

CMR emphasizes three areas of critical importance to both practising managers and academic researchers: Strategy and Organization, Global Competition and Competitiveness, and Business and Public Policy. CMR focuses on contemporary developments in the global economy, strategies for innovation, strategic planning, the management of technology, corporate culture, managing human resources, and business ethics. See http://cmr.berkeley.edu/about_cmr.html.

Business Strategy Review

Analyses and interprets contemporary research on strategic management and the wider business environment, publishing articles which combine disciplines and cross cultural boundaries (www.blackwellpublishing.com/journal.asp?ref=0955-6419).

Key articles

1 Mintzberg, H. (1978) 'Patterns in Strategy Formation', *Management Science* (May 1978) 24(9):934–948.
2 Mintzberg, H. (1994) 'The Fall and Rise of Strategic Planning', *Harvard Business Review* (January/February 1994) 72(1):107–114.
3 Mahoney, J. and Pandian, J. R. (1992) 'The Resource Based View within the Conversation of Strategic Management', *Strategic Management Journal* 13:363–380.
4 Dyer, J. H. and Singh, H. (1998) 'The Relational View: Cooperative Strategy and Sources of Interorganizational Competitive Advantage', *The Academy of Management Review* 23(4):660–679.
5 Teece, D. J., Pisano, G. and Shuen, A. (1997) 'Dynamic Capabilities and Strategic Management', *Strategic Management Journal* (August 1997) 18(7):509–533.
6 Porter, M. E. (1979) 'How competitive forces shape strategy', *Harvard Business Review* (March/April 1979) 57(2):137–145.
7 Peteraf, M. A. (1993) 'The Cornerstones of Competitive Advantage: A Resource-Based View', *Strategic Management Journal* (March 1993) 14(3):179–191.
8 Vernon, R. (1966) 'International Investment and International Trade in the Product Cycle', *The Quarterly Journal of Economics* (May 1966) 80(2):190–207.
9 Prahalad, C. and Hamel, G. (1990) 'The Core Competence of the Corporation', *Harvard Business Review* (May/June 1990) 68(3):79–91.
10 Stalk, G., Evans, P. and Shulman, L. E. (1992) 'Competing on capabilities: The new rules of corporate strategy', *Harvard Business Review* (March/April 1992) 70(2):54–68.

Chapter 4

Behaving responsibly around the world

Introduction

Business ethics

Stakeholder theory

Corporate social responsibility

CSR implementation

Key concepts

- Ethics ■ Business ethics ■ Morality ■ Moral ■ Integrity ■ Immoral ■ Amoral
- Ethical egoism ■ Utilitarianism ■ Code of ethics ■ Deontological ■ Teleological
- Existentialism ■ Contractarianism ■ Stakeholder management ■ Corporate social responsibility
- Corporate governance ■ Ethics programme ■ Ethical leader

By the end of this chapter you will be able to:

- Identify and explain ethical theories relevant to decision-making in international business
- Distinguish the behaviours seen as desirable in all international employees
- Discuss the important ethical issues and challenges facing the contemporary international organization
- Explain what is meant by stakeholder theory and its relevance to ethical management
- Explain what is meant by corporate social responsibility and the reason organizations pursue CSR strategies
- Critically evaluate methods used to implement CSR and create an ethical organization

Active learning case

Texas Instruments

'TI's reputation for integrity – for honesty, fairness, candour and respect in all business dealings – dates back to the founders of the company. That reputation is a priceless asset. It is vitally important that we communicate our ethical values and make sure everyone understands these values and knows what kind of behavior is expected at TI.' Jerry Junkins – Former Chairman, President and CEO, Texas Instruments – 1990.

Ethics

In 1961, TI published its first written code of ethics. TI believes maintaining the highest ethical standards requires a partnership between employees and employers; the employer proactively supports employees by communicating values and giving individual guidance, while empowered employees participate actively in problem-solving. In 1987, TI decided to support employees actively by establishing a TI Ethics Office and appointing a TI Ethics Director. The TI Ethics Office has three primary functions: to ensure business policies and practices continue to be aligned with ethical principles; to communicate clear ethical expectations; and to provide multiple channels for feedback through which people can ask questions, voice concerns and seek resolution to ethical issues.

Ethics Is the Cornerstone of TI: Know what's right. Value what's right. Do what's right.

TI believes that its reputation depends upon all the decisions they make and all the actions they take personally each day. Their values define how they will evaluate decisions and actions – and how they will conduct business.

'We are working in a difficult and demanding, ever-changing business environment. Together we are building a work environment on the foundation of Integrity, Innovation and Commitment. Our high standards have rewarded us with an enviable reputation in today's marketplace ... a reputation of integrity, honesty and trustworthiness. That strong ethical reputation is a vital asset ... and each of us shares a personal responsibility to protect, to preserve and to enhance it.'

By understanding and applying the values, each of us can say to ourselves and to others, 'TI is a good company, and one reason is that I am a part of it'.

■ We exercise the basic virtues of respect, dignity, kindness, courtesy and manners in all work relationships.

■ We recognize and avoid behaviours that others may find offensive, including the manner in which we speak and relate to one another and the materials we bring into the workplace, both printed and electronically.

■ We respect the right and obligation of every TIer to resolve concerns relating to ethics questions without retribution and retaliation.

■ We give all TIers the same opportunity to have their questions, issues and situations fairly considered while we understand that being treated fairly does not always mean that we will all be treated the same.

Texas Instruments Worldwide Headquarters, Dallas, Texas

Courtesy of Texas Instruments

Texas Instruments Incorporated engages in the design, manufacture, marketing, and sale of high-technology components in the United States and internationally. It operates in two segments, semiconductor and education technology. The company was founded in 1930 as Geophysical Service and changed its name to Texas Instruments Incorporated in 1951. TI is headquartered in Dallas, Texas, and has manufacturing, design or sales operations in more than 25 countries.

Revenue (2006): $14.2B

Employees (2006): 30 896

The TI Ethics Director ensures that all company guidelines remain aligned with ethical standards. The Director reports to the TI Ethics Committee, which reports to the Audit Committee of the Board of Directors. The TI Ethics Director is responsible for updating the TI Ethics Committee, the Audit Committee of the Board of Directors, and the president and CEO on a regular basis. The TI Ethics Committee was established in 1987 and oversees the activities of the TI Ethics Office, reviews and approves ethics-related policies, procedures and primary publications, monitors compliance to laws and regulations as well as ethical practices, reviews any major ethical issues that may arise from time to time and approves appropriate corrective actions.

■ We trust one another to use sound judgement in our use of TI business and information systems.

■ We understand that even though TI has the obligation to monitor its business information systems activity, we will respect privacy by prohibiting random searches of individual TIers' communications.

■ We recognize that conduct socially and professionally acceptable in one culture and country may be viewed differently in another.

Certain behaviours have been included in their Code of Business Conduct in recognition of the growing interest that investors have in the conduct of publicly-held companies, their employees and their directors. All TIers are expected to comply with the TI Values and Ethics Statement and the Code of Business Conduct.

Ethics in the global market

Increased competition, stricter government controls and emerging global markets have raised ethical questions. 'Ethical questions face business people every day, especially when a company is involved with worldwide markets', said Carl Skooglund, former Vice President and director of ethics. 'Finding the right answer isn't often easy.' TI is global in scope and culture with a tradition of conducting business in an ethical and legal manner. But, that is an increasingly difficult challenge fuelled by the changing times, relationships and situations facing companies today. TI's global vision is world leadership in digital solutions for the networked society. The company is competing to win at a global level – entering into strategic partnerships, alliances and joint ventures in every corner of the globe. The success of these relationships depends greatly upon the company's representatives understanding the ethical standards and expectations of others. The challenge in this dynamic environment, with its close calls and uncertainties, according to Skooglund:

'is to provide tools to our employees so that they can make the tough, quick decisions on the fly, on the firing line. And, make them correctly. There are two elements to making decisions and taking action on behalf of an organization: 1) a clear understanding of the organization's values, principles and ethical expectations and 2) sound personal judgment and appropriate choices.'

To meet these challenges, TI has adopted a three-level approach to ethical integrity on a global level. The first level simply asks: Are we complying with all legal requirements on a local level? The next level asks: Are there business practices or requirements at the local level which impact upon how we interact with co-workers in other parts of the world? A growing number of local regulations – rigid environmental regulations in some parts of Europe, for example – have a significant effect on products that we ship to and from those countries. The third level is: Do some of our practices need to be adapted, based on the local laws and customers of a specific locale? he concluded:

'What we think is perfectly proper in one country may not migrate well to another ... [Action] must be guided by a shared understanding of basic values and principles of integrity. And they must be supported by resources that will help people to recognize when the caution lights should come on and to know where they can seek expert advice quickly. TI's reputation is completely in our hands, to be enhanced or damaged by the nature of our actions.'

Source:
www.ti.com.

Introduction

In Chapter 3 we considered the *purpose* of the organization and the strategic choices made to attain that purpose. We placed emphasis on competing and attaining profit goals in order to satisfy investors. In this chapter we recognize that there are other stakeholders who must also be considered by the organization in its strategy and day-to-day business decisions and corporate behaviour. From the opening case study it was clear that Texas Instruments has committed significant resources to create an ethical infrastructure within the company. Unethical behaviour can cost a company its reputation its customers and therefore revenues and hard cash; it can also result in a loss of investors and may lead to a reduction in share price. Furthermore, employees do not like working for unethical companies and suppliers and other value-system players do not like to do business with such companies. If loss of revenue were not incentive enough, corporate wrong doings may be dealt with in the courts with directors, employees or the organization receiving punishment. It is no longer sufficient for organizations to simply follow a profit-only goal and recognize investors as the only stakeholders who matter.

In the ongoing public debate on globalization outlined in the first chapter, concerns have been expressed about the economic, social and environmental impacts of deepening international trade and investment ties and about the activities of the multinational enterprises. These concerns focus on a variety of issues, including labour relations, human rights, the environment, corruption, control of technology and consumer protection (OECD 2001). The high profile of this debate, coupled with governmental pressure, means that most multinational enterprises now pay close attention to public perceptions of their activities in the societies within which they operate.

Globalization has also brought with it additional management challenges for organizations in an area that has come to be called 'legal compliance'. Multinational enterprises are often present in dozens of jurisdictions covering many legal and regulatory areas. These companies need to keep themselves informed about the regulations affecting them and must take steps to ensure that they comply with law and regulation. Compliance can be quite complex, especially when the enterprise's operations straddle a variety of regions and business cultures. Thus, compliance with law and regulation is often not a straightforward task, especially for multinational enterprises. Organizations have attempted to respond to public concerns and to the growing challenge of 'legal compliance' in a globalizing business environment. New management techniques have emerged. However, mere compliance with the law is not enough, and companies must also comply with an array of ethical principles, identifying moral and social obligations.

Over 20 years ago, organizations began issuing policy statements (or codes of conduct) that set forth their commitments in various areas of business ethics and legal compliance. A second step was the development of management systems designed to help them comply with these commitments and the emergence of standardized management systems. A new management discipline has emerged involving professionals who specialize in regulatory, legal and ethical compliance. More recently, steps have been taken to formulate standards, providing guidance for business reporting on non-financial performance.

As the first decade of the new millennium quickly comes to an end, international organizations continue to address the ethical behaviour of their employees wherever they are working. The main aims of this chapter are to make the student aware of what is normally considered as unethical behaviour and to introduce the issues relating to corporate social responsibility and business ethics so that students will be better prepared for the ethical dilemmas and challenging decisions faced in the international business environment.

This chapter builds on the previous two chapters in several ways. We extend our consideration of the environment not just responding to environmental influences in the form of laws, regulations and public opinion but also consider how the organization might impact upon the environment; we also consider the organization's purpose in relation to a variety of stakeholders and consider a number of strategic decisions and the relationship between corporate social responsibility and competitive advantage. We will revisit the concept of the value chain and system and use it to explore and analyze where unethical behaviours are likely to be observed. Ethical issues in business are both global and domestic in nature and we integrate a global focus within this chapter. We start by identifying what ethics and ethical theories are and then distil key ethical issues faced by international organizations. We then discuss stakeholder theory as a foundation for applying ethical decision-making. Next we identify what is meant by corporate social responsibility (CSR) distinguishing the key components of CSR. Finally, we consider two approaches (compliance and values-based) to implement CSR programmes in international organizations.

Active learning case

Business ethics

Seroxat is an antidepressant. It was released in 1992 by the pharmaceutical company GlaxoSmithKline (GSK). In 2006 it was the fifth-most prescribed antidepressant in the United States retail market. It is also available in other countries such as the UK. Despite this, the drug later resulted in the GSK brand being significantly tarnished.

'Drug giant covered up safety fear on Seroxat' (*Daily Mail*) was just one of several UK headlines tarnishing GSK's reputation in 2007/8. In January 2007 the *Daily Mail* reported that GSK had covered up vital evidence about the safety of an antidepressant linked to a string of suicides … GSK revealed it had fears about the drug's safety years earlier. But GSK, which makes £1billion a year from Seroxat, continued to promote it for youngsters. British experts said the continued prescription of Seroxat led to young people's deaths. An investigation revealed three key documents among thousands released for a US court case brought by bereaved families. One from GSK's marketing department in 1999 refers to side-effects, adding: 'It seems incongruous that we state [the drug] is safe yet report so many serious adverse effects'. In 2001, the firm still claimed it was safe, telling sales staff it showed 'remarkable safety and efficacy in the treatment of adolescent depression'. And an e-mail from a PR executive admits research showed it did not work on teenage depression – 'not something we want to publicise'. Other allegations suggested the company was putting profit ahead of the safety of young people. Pam Armstrong, of the Council for Information on Tranquillisers and Anti-Depressants, said: 'I cannot understand that so many people in one company could feel it was okay to do nothing. When you are looking at the possibility of children being affected it is reprehensible.' It was not until 2004 that GSK published full details of studies from as early as 1993 showing children on Seroxat were twice as likely to feel suicidal as those on a dummy pill. Karen Barth Menzies, a lawyer in the US case, said: 'Even when they have negative studies that show Seroxat is going to harm some kids, they still spin that study as remarkably effective and safe for children.' Not only did the product and the way it was managed attract reputation-damaging publicity for GSK, it also led to legal action against the company. Not only were the company selling a drug that could have serious side-effects, there was also doubt as to whether it actually worked for teenagers. An investigation by the MHRA, published March 2008, found that the manufacturer withheld evidence that the antidepressant increased the risk of suicide among teenagers. According to the *Guardian* newspaper, nine clinical trials by GSK, conducted between 1994 and 2002, found the drug was not effective in treating depression in children. Apparently, GSK failed to notify the MHRA of this when in 2002 the firm indicated it was planning to apply for approval to use the drug to treat children. The *Daily Mail* revisited

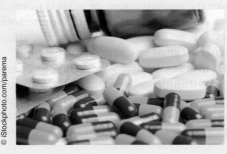

© iStockphoto.com/parema

the story following MHRA's investigation, stating 'Drug company bosses concealed information about the dangers of the anti-depressant Seroxat for five years while it was still being prescribed to children … Documents released yesterday as part of a four-year criminal investigation into GlaxoSmithKline show that the pharmaceutical giant had evidence that the drug didn't work in children as early as 1998. There were also suggestions the firm was aware of possible links to attempted suicides and suicidal thoughts. But Glaxo did not alert Britain's drugs watchdog to the problem until 2003, when the suicide link had become clear.' The Medicines and Healthcare Products Regulatory Agency hit out at Glaxo for withholding the information. Glaxo denied it had withheld data, saying it 'firmly believed' it had acted 'properly and responsibly' and safety of its medicines was 'paramount'.

Sources

1 www.dailymail.co.uk/pages/live/articles/health/healthmain.html?in_article_id=432217&in_page_id=1774 29 January 2007.
2 *The Sun* 'Drugs giant rap over "joy" pills' published 7 March 2008, www.thesun.co.uk/sol/homepage/news/article887022.ece.
3 Batty guardian.co.uk, Thursday March 6 2008 Q&A: Seroxat.
4 Brown, C. (2008), Drugs law to be tightened as Seroxat firm is rebuked', *The Independent* 7 March 2008 online at www.independent. co.uk/news/uk/politics/drugs-law-to-be-tightened-as-seroxat-firm-is-rebuked-792756.html.

Ethics and ethical theories

We will critically evaluate the opening TI and GSK cases later, having explored ethics theory first. You may have heard people talking about ethics, moral standards, business ethics, marketing ethics or a code of ethics – but what do they mean? Ethics is a branch of philosophy dealing with what is considered to be *right* and *wrong* and Business ethics concerns the accepted principles (beliefs and values) of right or wrong governing the conduct of business people. Ethics is the study of morality. Ethical principles can be used by individuals acting as free moral agents to make choices which guide their *behaviour*. In general terms, morality is concerned with individual character or personality and beliefs governing right and wrong.

In summary then, ethics can be defined as the values an individual uses to interpret whether any particular action or behaviour is considered unacceptable or appropriate. Business ethics concerns the collective values of a business organization that can be used to evaluate whether the behaviour of the collective members of the organization are considered appropriate and acceptable. It is generally accepted that most people think, then act and that their actions have consequences, see Figure 4-1 We will refer to aspects of this model throughout the chapter identifying what the common principles are and how organizations try to educate their employees about the organizations' principles and values, then seek to inculcate or assure such principles are followed. We will also consider why some people do not follow such principles and the resultant consequences for the organization. Moral lapses occur when individuals fail to grasp the ethical implications of the situation.

Earlier we identified business ethics as collective values and we therefore explore the relationship of culture, introduced in Chapter 2, with business ethics. National culture will influence a member's view of what is right and wrong and there are differences worldwide in such views. What is acceptable in one country may not be in another and vice versa – as was recognized by TI in the opening case. Aside from employees of the international organization being influenced by their home-country values, the organization will seek to establish values and principles of its own. In Chapter 2 we observed that culture was about sharing values and developing common ways of thinking and behaving. We revisit related issues later. Given the diversity in ethical views and practice worldwide it becomes important to ask, should international/multinational organizations treat the world as one, i.e. take a global and standard approach to business ethics, or should they take a multidomestic approach, treating every country as different? If they adopt the former, should they take an ethno- or

Ethics a branch of philosophy dealing with what is considered to be right and wrong

Business ethics the accepted principles (beliefs and values) of right or wrong governing the conduct of business people

Morality individual character or personality and beliefs governing right and wrong

polycentric approach to the formation of moral values? If they take the multidomestic approach, how should employees behave when in a different country? Is it a case of when in Rome, do as the Romans do? Some take the view that common moral values already exist and that these are shared throughout the world already – indeed TI 'define universal standards'. This has been reflected in a number of global instruments (see for example the OECD or the UN) stating principles of good conduct for whoever, operating wherever.

Figure 4-1

Thinking and behaving with principles

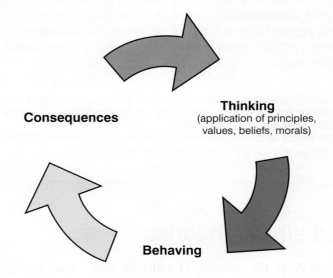

If we accept that the terms ethics and morality are essentially synonymous in the organizational context, we may speak of immoral, amoral, and moral management as descriptive categories of three different kinds of managers. In relation to Figure 4-1, we might apply the model in three ways, describing three types of person. People considering and applying accepted principles of right and wrong are described as moral. Those that consider but do not apply such principles may be described as immoral. In between are those people who simply do not consider, through ignorance, ethical and moral principles and we might describe such people as amoral. With regard to their stated principles, most international organizations seek to manage employee (to include managers) behaviour, preventing immoral and encouraging moral behaviour. The immoral manager does the wrong thing, focusing on their own goal; the amoral manager fails to contemplate ethical issues during decision-making and may therefore unintentionally commit unethical acts while moral managers are the decision-makers who understand the importance and relevance of considering ethical issues when they make decisions.

We have discussed principles of right and wrong but what are they? There are a number of views or theories on ethics and we now outline them. Some views, ethical egoism, allow for self-interests to play a role in the conduct of individuals, particularly if there are also positive benefits for others. In such situations, individuals may be *motivated* by selfish and unselfish factors together, i.e. a win-win situation. In some cases individuals will focus on the consequence of their actions (the output) and in other cases may focus on the motives or means (the process). Utilitarianism holds the belief that any action of an individual should be based on providing the greatest good for the greatest number of people; this may be described as benevolent (caring and generous) behaviour. Supporters of ethical egoism will focus more on self-interest, placing the needs and goals of the organization foremost, while utilitarianists are more likely to take a multiple stakeholder perspective, accepting government intervention as a way to protect the interests of the majority against the decisions of the minority within any given business. Utilitarianism and ethical egoism focus on whether the results are favourable or not (they are teleological frameworks).

An alternative approach (deontological frameworks) may focus on the duty (obligation) of the individual employee and organization – recall that 'duty' was at the centre of the GSK

Moral person someone who considers and applies accepted principles of right and wrong

Immoral person those that consider but do not apply accepted principles of right and wrong

Amoral person people who simply do not consider accepted principles of right and wrong

Ethical egoism holds we ought to pursue our own self-interest exclusively

Utilitarianism the belief that any action of an individual should be based on providing the greatest good for the greatest number of people

Teleological ethics in which the rightness or wrongness of an act is judged with reference to some end result that is regarded as good

Deontological an approach that says the nature of what is right and wrong does not depend on outcome but on certain principles of fundamental and objective rules

case study. Such approaches focus on the determination of right and wrong. Existentialism is based on the belief that only the person making the decision can determine what is right and wrong; individuals determine their own actions and are responsible for the consequences. Contractarianism advocates the principle of being fair and that as members of a society we have particular duties and responsibilities. Linked to this is the principle that an individual should act in a way in which one would expect everyone to act (see Kant's ethical view).

Over time, a variety of general principles have been proposed to describe what is meant by ethical behaviour. Individuals should:

- keep promises (*fidelity*);
- be fair (*justice*);
- not harm others;
- put right any wrong caused (*reparation*);
- show gratitude to others; and
- improve the lives of one's self and others (*beneficence*).

Other principles include:

- fiduciary obligations (not putting self-interest above the overall interests of the organization);
- reliability (fulfilling promises);
- transparency (open and honest);
- dignity (respect others);
- fairness (not taking bribes or colluding with others);
- citizenship (respecting the law and the environment);
- responsiveness; and
- respecting property.

When people and organizations adhere to a moral code, they are said to have *integrity*. As integrity is eroded, unethical and illegal behaviour follows. We have summarized desirable behaviours in Figure 4-2.

Existentialism the belief that only the person making the decision can determine what is right and wrong

Contractarianism the principle of being fair and that as members of a society we have particular duties and responsibilities

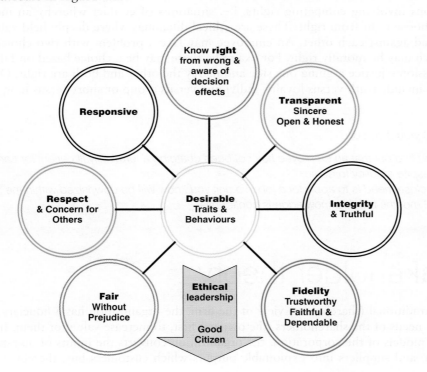

Figure 4-2

Desirable employee behaviours

Consider Figure 4-2 – make a list of categories of undesirable behaviour.

In the above task you may have considered corruption, bribery, extortion, embezzlement, theft, other dishonest acts, self-interest, waste, illegal acts, or anything that breaches human rights or harms the environment. In Figure 4-4 we map sources of unethical and undesirable behaviour against the organization's activities. We make use of the value chain concept introduced in the previous chapter as the analytical framework.

Ethical issues

At this point we might ask, why should the international organization worry about how business is conducted, ethics, integrity and doing the right thing? In recent times we have witnessed environmental issues gaining prominence, financial mismanagement, the use of child labour and exploitation of workers, unsafe work practices, excessive surveillance, breaches of privacy, intellectual property theft and many other events leading to the erosion of confidence in corporations. Whereas unethical behaviour may result in a loss of confidence, trust and business, ethical and responsible behaviour can enhance reputation and win business.

How then might individuals and organizations evaluate their integrity and the integrity of their actions? Several tests have been offered to help with this evaluation. The individual could consider how they would feel about their actions being publicly scrutinized, whether they would feel comfortable telling a friend or family member about their actions or whether they would like to be treated in the same way themselves. In developing personal integrity we can distinguish good from bad behaviour as well as evaluating behaviour with the aforementioned tests. People develop a sense of ethics through various ways. They can, for example, learn ethical values through socialization processes. They can also learn through reinforcement tactics associated with compliance frameworks. Ethical issues arise not only from a problem of identifying right from wrong but also in situations involving competing rights, i.e. situations of conflict whereby an individual must choose right from right. These are ethical dilemmas where deeply held values may be pitted against each other. An employee may face a problem with two choices, both of which may be morally right. For example, there may be a choice based on fairness or compassion – justice arguing one side and mercy the other and both are right. Other examples include truth versus loyalty, individual versus group or short versus long term.

What would you do?

1 *You find out that an employee has not been charging a terminally ill patient for care despite a policy to do so.*
2 *A close friend is to apply for a job in a unit you know will be downsized within the next 12 months but this knowledge is confidential.*

Stakeholder theory

In the traditional (shareholder) view of the firm, the organization has a fiduciary duty to put the needs of the shareholders (the owners) first, to increase value for them. In input–output models of the corporation, the organization converts the inputs of investors, employees, and suppliers into exploitable outputs which customers buy, thereby returning funds (benefit) to the organization. Through this model, organizations only attend to the needs and wishes of those four groups:

- investors;
- employees;
- suppliers; and
- customers.

Stakeholder theory argues there are other parties involved, including governmental bodies, trade associations, trade unions, communities, and the public, see Figure 4-3.

Stakeholder theory the role of the organization is to satisfy a wider set of stakeholders, not simply the owners

Figure 4-3
Stakeholder model

Over the past two decades we have seen a gradual rejection of the 'management serving the shareowners' model, and a greater acceptance of stakeholder theory based either on broad theories of philosophical ethics, such as utilitarianism, or on narrower 'middle-level' theories derived from the notion that a 'social contract' exists between corporations and society. Stakeholder theory suggests the role of the organization is to satisfy a wider set of stakeholders, not simply the owners. The theory is used to interpret the function of the corporation – how things should be, including the identification of moral or philosophical guidelines for the operation and management of corporations. Donaldson and Preston (1995) believe that the ultimate justification for the stakeholder theory is to be found in its normative base. The normative approach, is categorical; it says, in effect, 'Do (Don't do) this because it is the right (wrong) thing to do'.

The alternative to stakeholder theory (i.e., the 'management serving the shareowners' theory) is morally untenable. Stakeholder theory recommends attitudes, structures, and practices that, taken together, constitute **stakeholder management**. Stakeholder management requires, as its key attribute, simultaneous attention to the legitimate interests of all appropriate stakeholders, both in the establishment of organizational structures and general

Stakeholder management attitudes, structures, and practices, taken together to organize relationships with stakeholders

policies and in case-by-case decision-making. This requirement holds for anyone managing or affecting corporate policies, including not only professional managers, but shareowners, the government, and others. The theory does, however, not imply that all stakeholders (however they may be identified) should be equally involved in all processes and decisions.

The model represented in Figure 4-1 shows that there are consequences (effects of our actions), but who is affected and how? Organizations typically consider consequences in relation to stakeholders. Several definitions of stakeholder have been suggested. A **stakeholder** is a member of a group who has a vested interest in or whose support is necessary for the organization to exist. They include investors, employees, suppliers, customers, local communities, trade associations, the government and society as a whole, see Figure 4-3. Earlier we discussed three types of employee (moral, immoral and amoral). The three different managerial types represent three different management styles. The immoral manager gives minimum attention to shareholders, treats employees simply as a means of production, exploits customers and will generate revenue by any means possible. Moral managers will typically consider the interests of all stakeholders and will treat employees with dignity and respect and customers as equal partners, furthermore, they proactively engage with the local community. However a key challenge faced by the international organization is the determination of the relative importance of different stakeholders.

Stakeholders can impact upon the international organization by establishing expectations, or through experiences of the organization which they may then evaluate and act upon. Employees, as stakeholders, are important not only because their behaviours define organizational culture but also because a satisfied employee is likely to be loyal, committed, motivated and therefore engage in ethical behaviour. It is also important for the organization to consider suppliers as stakeholders and to ensure that the relationship between suppliers and the organization is based on ethical values. The supplier must be in strict compliance with the law and behave ethically. In the previous chapter, we discussed the fragmentation of the value chain, global sourcing and outsourcing. Organizations typically engage in such strategies in the pursuit of cost leadership or differentiation. They may locate in countries where working conditions are poor, workers are exploited, abused or are children. Customers, as stakeholders, may threaten the survival of the international organization. Figure 4-4 (the value chain) identifies critical areas where unethical relationships with customers and other stakeholders may exist.

Stakeholder any individual or group with a vested interest in the organization

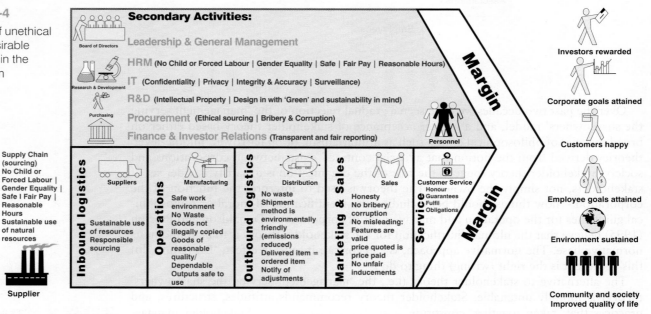

Figure 4-4

Sources of unethical and undesirable behaviour in the value chain

Look back
See chapter 3, p. 75

Previously we discussed Li & Fung and observed their ability to source globally. Indeed many of the companies featured in this text derive competitive advantage through global sourcing, outsourcing or fragmenting their value chains in some way. Companies routinely buy goods from emerging countries either to give better choice or to lower costs. However, while today's customers demand variety and low pricing they do not want companies to exploit resources and workers from overseas. Low prices often reflect low wages and poor working conditions in the supply chain. And while cost cutting is key to most strategies, see Chapter 3, global companies cannot afford to be ignorant of the ethics of their suppliers. We may describe these as ethical problems of procurement or outsourcing. Such problems have resulted in damaging publicity to a number of companies in recent times. This increases the range of ethical issues for the international organization to manage and they must take steps to protect their brand. They need to demonstrate that their supply chain management (SCM) supports and reinforces the values and behaviours associated with their brands. At the heart of ethical procurement management is accountability. In the final section we discuss the initiatives taken by organizations to overcome risks, safeguard against damaging accusations and trade ethically.

Stakeholder identification

Since Freeman (1984) published his landmark book, *Strategic Management: A Stakeholder Approach*, the concept of 'stakeholders' has become embedded in management scholarship and management thinking. He defined stakeholders as, 'any group or individual who can affect or is affected by the achievement of the organization's objectives'. Yet, as popular as the term has become and as richly descriptive as it is, there is no agreement on what Freeman (1994) calls 'The Principle of Who or What Really Counts'. That is, who (or what) are the stakeholders of the organization? And to whom (or what) do managers pay attention?

For more than a decade the stakeholder approach to understanding the organization in its environment has been a powerful heuristic device, intended to broaden management's vision of its roles and responsibilities beyond the profit maximization function, to include interests and claims of non-stockholding groups. Stakeholder theory attempts to articulate a fundamental question in a systematic way: which groups are stakeholders deserving or requiring management attention, and which are not? Management's challenge is to decide which stakeholders merit and receive consideration in the decision-making process. In any given instance, there may be numerous stakeholder groups (shareholders, consumers, employees, suppliers, community, social activist groups) clamouring for management's attention. How do managers sort out the urgency or importance of the various stakeholder claims? If we are to better manage stakeholders we need a method to categorize them. Narrowing the range of stakeholders requires applying some acceptable and justifiable sorting criteria to the field of possibilities.

Mitchell, Agle and Wood (1997) contribute to a theory of *stakeholder identification* and salience based on stakeholders possessing one or more of three relationship attributes: power, legitimacy and urgency. By combining these attributes, they generate a typology of stakeholder's propositions concerning their salience (making them stand out and be noticed) to managers of the organization. Their theory of stakeholder identification can explain how managers prioritize stakeholder relationships, i.e. determine organizational resource allocation in response to stakeholder claims. The model, summarized in Figure 4-5, can assist managers, improving effectiveness, in dealing with multiple stakeholders' interests.

Mitchell, Agle and Wood (1997) proposed that stakeholders possess some combination of three critical attributes: power, legitimacy, and urgency (identification typology) and predict that the salience of a particular stakeholder to the firm's management is low if only one attribute is present, moderate if two attributes are present, and high if all three attributes are present.

Dormant stakeholders have little or no interaction with the organization. However, because of their potential to acquire a second attribute, management should remain cognizant of such stakeholders, for the dynamic nature of the stakeholder–manager relationship suggests that dormant stakeholders will become more salient to managers if they acquire either urgency or legitimacy.

Figure 4-5

Stakeholder identification model (Adapted from Mitchell, Agle and Wood 1997)

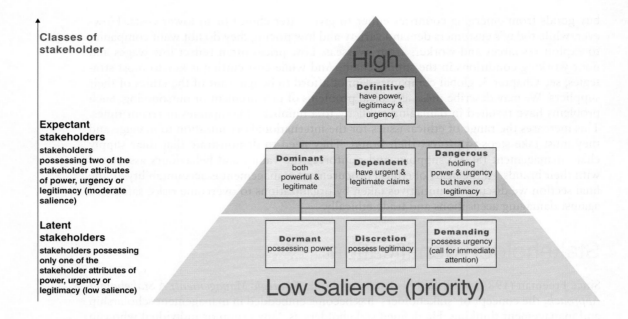

Discretionary stakeholders are most likely to be recipients of corporate philanthropy. The key point regarding discretionary stakeholders is that, absent power and urgent claims, there is absolutely no pressure on managers to engage in an active relationship with such a stakeholder, although managers can choose to do so. As more salient stakeholders, *dominant* stakeholders typically have some formal mechanism in place that acknowledges the importance of their relationship with the firm, e.g. an investor relations office to handle ongoing relationships with investors; a human resources department that acknowledges the importance of the firm–employee relationship; public affairs offices that are common in firms that depend on maintaining good relationships with government. In addition, corporations produce reports to legitimate, powerful stakeholders, including annual reports, proxy statements, and, increasingly, environmental and social responsibility reports. Dominant stakeholders expect and receive much of managers' attention.

We characterize stakeholders who lack power but who have urgent legitimate claims as '*dependent*' because these stakeholders depend upon others for the power necessary to carry out their will. Included in this category may be local residents, animals, and even the natural environment itself.

Dangerous stakeholders lack legitimacy, and may be coercive and possibly violent, making the stakeholder 'dangerous', to the organization (wildcat strikes, employee sabotage, and terrorism). 'Coercion' is suggested as a descriptor because the use of coercive power often accompanies illegitimate status.

Mitchell, Agle and Wood (1997) caution managers to never forget that stakeholders change in salience, requiring different degrees and types of attention depending on their attributed possession of power, legitimacy and or urgency, and that levels of these attributes (and thereby salience) can vary from issue to issue and from time to time.

The important functions of stakeholder management are to describe, understand, analyze, and finally, manage (Carroll 1991). Thus, five major questions might be posed to capture the essential ingredients we need for stakeholder management:

- Who are our stakeholders?
- What are their stakes?
- What opportunities and challenges are presented by our stakeholders?
- What corporate social responsibilities (economic, legal, ethical, and philanthropic) do we have to our stakeholders? and
- What strategies, actions, or decisions should we take to best deal with these responsibilities?

Stakeholder theory is not only of use to ethical decision-making, but, as we will see in the next and subsequent chapters, can also act as a foundation for change management initiatives. Stakeholder theory also acts as a foundation for ethical decision-making discussed next.

Ethical decision making

Managing the international organization ethically may mean following laws and regulations, ensuring equal opportunity or dealing with social responsibility issues. In many cases it is about ensuring ethical decision-making and resultant action. In order to do this, the organization must ensure employees understand ethical and moral values and can use this understanding to make sense of business problems. In considering options for action, the organization needs its employees to show good ethical judgement, being able to evaluate different options and determine which are more acceptable, based on the moral values and beliefs of the decision-makers and the organization as a whole. Ethical business decisions involve choosing between right and wrong.

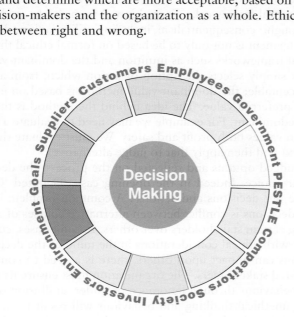

Figure 4-6

Decision-making considerations

In the opening case study, TI recognized the difficulties associated with ethical decision-making when they noted that clear choices do not always exist. Arriving at a moral judgement is not a straightforward or linear process. Instead it is a process in which the formulation of the moral problem, the formulation of possible 'solutions', and the ethical judging of these solutions go hand in hand (Poel and Royakkers 2007). Moral problems do not usually have one best solution, but a range of more or less acceptable solutions. This is due to the fact that no single criterion exists to order the possible solutions from best to worst. Identifying a moral problem needs a conception of what morality is. The different ethical theories are not only relevant in identifying and formulating moral problems but also in judging them. The diversity of theories also reveals a diversity of reasonable moral opinions among different people on moral issues. Moral problem-solving is thus a messy and complex process. This does, however, not preclude the possibility of a systematic approach to the identification, analysis and solution of moral problems. Poel and Royakkers (2007) describe such an approach: the *ethical cycle*.

Ethical theories may be instrumental in discovering the ethical aspects of a problem or situation. Different ethical theories stress different aspects of a situation; consequentialism for example draws attention to how consequences of actions may be morally relevant; deontological theories might draw attention to the moral importance of promises, rights and obligations and virtue ethics may remind us that certain character traits can be morally relevant. Ultimately, moral problem solving is directed at finding the morally best, or at least a morally acceptable action in a given situation in which a moral problem arises.

During the problem analysis phase, the relevant elements of the moral problem are described. Three important elements can be distinguished: the *stakeholders* and their interests, the moral values that are relevant in the situation and the relevant facts. Stakeholders are both the people who can influence the options for actions being chosen and the eventual consequences of this action as well as those people suffering or profiting from those consequences. After the analytic phase when the moral problem is formulated, a synthetic phase follows in which possible solutions for action are generated in the light of the formulated problem analysis. Often a moral problem is formulated in terms of whether it is acceptable to engage in a certain action or not; a range of possible actions may be considered. The fourth phase results in moral judgements about the various options for action. These judgements need not be the same because different frameworks can result in different preferred options for action in a given situation. In this phase, a judgement is made on the moral acceptability of the various options for action. This can be done on the basis of both formal and informal moral frameworks. Formal moral frameworks are based on the main theories of ethical thought: consequentialism, including utilitarianism, deontology and virtue ethics. Ethical judgement is not only to be based on formal ethical theories but also on more informal ethical frameworks such as intuition and the dominant-value method. The intuitivist framework simply selects the option or action which, from a personal view, is instinctively most acceptable; the dominant-value method is based on either an individually or a collectively preferred value. The idea behind the method is that in many actual cases, one value is predominant. For example we may need to evaluate a moral problem as a decision-maker who values both profit and safety. We must evaluate the dominant value in the problem context and then apply that to judge alternatives.

Having ethically judged options and reflected on the process, the decision-maker may then implement their choice. Indeed in the opening case, TI noted 'Our values define how we will evaluate our decisions and actions'. A common problem located within international business decisions is conflict between alternative courses of action, with some alternatives favouring certain stakeholders over others. In some cases, commercial considerations may conflict with ethical considerations in the mind of the decision-maker. Since such business decisions can impact upon others, there is a need to consider and balance the interests of all vested stakeholders. The organization must ensure its employees do not engage in unethical behaviour through ignorance or under an illusion of objectivity (bias free). In some cases, unethical thinking and behaviour will result from implicit forms of prejudice and in some cases the decision-maker may show a favourable bias to a particular group and in other cases themselves (conflict of interest). A bias occurs when there is a conflict of interest and the decision-maker favours a solution in which there would be a personal benefit. Consequently, decision-makers should be aware of the potential unconscious biases which can impact upon their decision-making.

Thus far we have outlined ethical, stakeholder and ethical decision-making theories. We have also put forward the argument that the traditional model of placing the investor first may, on occasions, be morally wrong since the organization has obligations to a broader mix of stakeholders. One of those stakeholders is society and in the next section we consider corporate responsibilities to society.

Corporate social responsibility

Corporate social responsibility a concept whereby organizations consider the interests of society by taking responsibility for the impact of their activities on all stakeholders, including the environment

Corporate social responsibility (CSR) is a concept whereby organizations consider the interests of society by taking responsibility for the impact of their activities on customers, suppliers, employees, shareholders, communities and the environment in every aspect of their operations and decision-making; it is about good business citizenship. Central to the CSR approach is that the organization should use resources responsibly (sustainable, no waste, to produce the goods and services for society in a profitable manner) and should comply with relevant laws and regulations. In addition to the moral issue, there are many arguments in favour of CSR. A CSR programme can be seen as an aid to recruitment and retention, particularly within the competitive graduate student market.

Reputations and brands that take time and resources to build up can be ruined in hours through unethical decisions manifest in incidents such as corruption scandals or environmental accidents. These events can also draw unwanted attention from regulators, courts, governments and media as was seen in the GSK case. Building an ethical culture of 'doing the right thing' can offset these risks. Furthermore, by taking voluntary action, organizations can persuade governments and the wider public that they are taking issues such as health and safety, employee relations or the environment seriously, and so avoid intervention. Since the late 1990s there have been several significant initiatives which seek to influence thinking about global corporate responsibility and bring improvement in international business conduct, see for example Figure 4-7.

The Body Shop – a company with a prominent CSR policy.

Caux Principles for Business: (issued in 1994) The Caux Principles are an aspirational (something that you hope to achieve) set of recommendations covering many areas of corporate behaviour. They "seek to express a world-wide standard for ethical and responsible corporate behaviour".

Global Reporting Initiative (GRI): (issued in 1999) The GRI is an international reporting standard for voluntary use by organisations, the GRI has sought to develop a list of specific indicators for reporting on social, environmental and economic performance.

Global Sullivan Principles: (issued in 1999) The Global Sullivan Principles are an aspirational standard developed with the input of several multinational corporations. The principles include eight broad directives on labour, business ethics and environmental practices of multinational companies and their business partners. Companies endorse the Principles by publicly pledging to integrate them into their operations.

OECD Guidelines for Multinational Enterprises: (revised in 2000) The Guidelines are recommendations covering nine areas of business conduct addressed by governments to multinational enterprises.

Principles for Global Corporate Responsibility – Benchmarks: (revised in 1998) The "Benchmarks" are designed to provide a "model framework" through which stakeholders can assess corporate codes of conduct, policies and practices related to corporate social responsibility expectations. The standard contains nearly 60 principles the sponsors consider "fundamental to a responsible company's actions".

Social Accountability 8000 (SA 8000): (issued in 1998) SA 8000 is a voluntary, factory-based monitoring and certification standard for assessing labour conditions in global manufacturing operations. SA 8000 is modelled after the quality and environmental auditing processes developed through the International Standards Oganisation in its ISO 9000 and ISO 14000 standards. SA 8000 relies on certified monitors to verify factory compliance with the standard. The sponsor of the standard is Social Accountability International.

United Nations Global Compact: (issued in 1999) The UN Global Compact was announced at the World Economic Forum in Davos, Switzerland in January 1999 and formally launched in September 2000. UN Secretary General Kofi Annan called on world business leaders to "embrace and enact" a set of nine principles in their individual corporate practices and by supporting complementary public policy initiatives. The standard includes specific practices that endorsing companies would commit to enact.

Figure 4-7

Global instruments for CSR

Organizations remain influenced by global as well as local government initiatives. For example, the 27 principles of the Rio Declaration define the rights and responsibilities of nations as they pursue human development and well-being. Negotiated in 1992, the Declaration is based on the notion of sustainable development and defines a number of basic principles (e.g. precautionary principle, polluter pays principle, the right to development). Such principles impact upon what is seen as appropriate behaviour from international organizations and will therefore be reflected in CSR views. For example:

Principle 1 of the Rio Declaration states that human beings are at the centre of concerns for sustainable development. They are entitled to a healthy and productive life, in harmony with nature.

Principle 4 (needs of present and future generations) states that in order to achieve sustainable development, environmental protection shall constitute an integral part of the development process and cannot be considered in isolation from it.

Principle 15 identifies the precautionary principle – in order to protect the environment, the precautionary approach shall be widely applied by

States according to their capabilities. Where there are threats of serious or irreversible damage, lack of full scientific certainty shall not be used as a reason for postponing cost-effective measures to prevent environmental degradation.

Principle 16 introduced the polluter pays principle where national authorities should endeavour to promote the internalization of environmental costs and the use of economic instruments, taking into account the approach that the polluter should, in principle, bear the cost of pollution, with due regard to the public interest and without distorting international trade and investment.

Thus far we have considered what CSR is and why organizations may seek to behave in the manner advocated by core CSR thinking. CSR is considered at all organizational levels, influencing strategic, tactical and operational decisions and activities. In the next section we identify and discuss the key CSR components before exploring CSR implementation in the final section.

Components of CSR

Carroll (1991) explored the nature of corporate social responsibility (CSR) with a view towards understanding its component parts. Carroll starts by asking what it means for a corporation to be socially responsible and the related question of how the organization can reconcile its economic orientation with its social orientation. He suggests that four kinds of social responsibilities constitute total CSR:

- economic;
- legal;
- ethical; and
- philanthropic.

'Stated in more pragmatic and managerial terms, the CSR firm should strive to make a profit, obey the law, be ethical, and be a good corporate citizen.' This contrasts with the classical economic argument that management has one responsibility: to maximize the profits of its owners or shareholders. With a performance perspective, it is clear that organizations must formulate and implement social goals and programmes as well as integrate ethical sensitivity into all decision-making, policies, and actions. Carroll (1991) argues that stakeholder theory presents an integrating framework for the four CSR components (see Figure 4-8). There is a natural fit between the idea of corporate social responsibility and an organization's stakeholders.

The concept of stakeholder personalizes social or societal responsibilities by delineating the specific groups or persons business should consider in its CSR orientation. Sometimes the stake might represent a legal claim, such as that which might be held by an owner, an employee, or a customer who has an explicit or implicit contract. Other times it might be represented by a moral claim, such as when these groups assert a right to be treated fairly or with due process, or to have their opinions taken into consideration in an important business decision. Carroll (1991) also considers what the organization ought to be doing in an economic, legal, ethical, and philanthropic sense with respect to its identified stakeholder groups. According to Carroll there are five major stakeholder groups that are recognized as priorities by most organizations:

- owners (shareholders);
- employees;
- customers;
- local communities; and
- society at large.

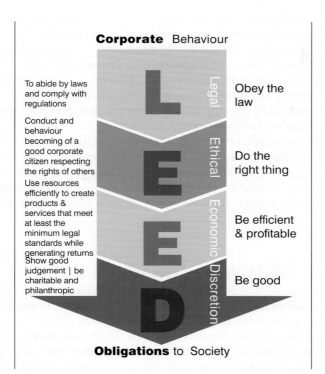

Figure 4-8
Components of CSR

Although the general ethical obligation to each of these groups is essentially identical (protect their rights, treat them with respect and fairness), specific behaviours and orientations arise because of the differing nature of the groups. Effective organizations will progress beyond stakeholder identification and question what opportunities and threats are posed by stakeholders; what economic, legal, ethical, and philanthropic responsibilities they have; and what strategies, actions or decisions should be pursued to address these responsibilities most effectively.

From a legal perspective, aside from country laws, corporate governance is the system used to control and direct a company's operations. It is more about the legal component of CSR, though in some countries corporate governance is assured through codes. The governance system ensures the needs of stakeholders (investors in particular) are satisfied. The system seeks to govern the behaviour of managers and employees within the organization, focusing on transparency, fairness and internal control. The board of directors are the stewards of the company, ensuring the interests of all stakeholders are met. They typically approve major plans and strategies, oversee risk management and insurance, coordinate internal units, make high level investment and expenditure decisions and issue stock and dividends. Some members of the board of directors may sit on the audit committee which is responsible for monitoring the internal operations of the organization and guaranteeing that financial statements are prepared accurately. In Chapter 17 we consider governance in more detail examining the UK's combined code and the USA's Sarbanes-Oxley Act. Both were established around the turn of the millennium, in direct response to corporate scandals and established in order to increase transparency, integrity and accountability. We also consider the issue of ethics and financial reporting in Chapter 17.

Environmental sustainability is the ability of an organization or a country to protect the use of future resources by properly maintaining and protecting the resources currently in use. Nobody owns the environment, we all do in common. Consequently, historically, there has been a lack of control over it. Companies have utilized resources such as the air,

Corporate governance the system used to control and direct a company's operations

Audit committee body formed by a company's board of directors to oversee audit operations

water, soil, forests and energy resources with little concern for the consequences. Many now consider the natural environment as a stakeholder represented by organizations such as Greenpeace and Friends of the Earth. Governments, to varying degrees, regulate and control the productive activities of organizations. Historically, such organizations have considered such controls as a production cost. However, more recently this has been turned into a competitive advantage by some organizations.

Adopting environmentally friendly or eco efficiency strategies may support differentiation of cost leadership initiatives discussed in Chapter 3. A positive corporate image is associated with such strategies, resulting in a strong reputation. Eco branding (see Chapter 16) allows potential customers to consider the natural environment when they are purchasing products and services. Customers may be willing to pay a premium for products that are eco friendly and marketing information may be used to differentiate such products and services. Having discussed CSR components we now consider how they are integrated with strategy.

Integrating CSR with strategy

Corporate responsibilities need to be integrated into the corporate and business strategies. The organization may consider structural alternatives – is there a need for a corporate social responsibility manager or department? – the implementation of standards such as ISO 14000 and social accountability 8000 certification; the creation of policies on equal opportunities, non-discrimination, fair trade, the protection of the environment and in the creation of committees, a code of ethics and educational programmes. Instead of focusing solely on financial performance, the triple bottom-line of people, planet and profit might be used to monitor the performance of the organization. Measuring such outcomes is more likely to reflect the interests of all stakeholders rather than just investors. How then can the organization integrate ethical issues into the strategy formulation process? Integrating social considerations more effectively into core business operations and strategy is about CSR. Four key arguments are posed to encourage organizations to act in a socially responsible manner:

- *moral obligation* – companies have a duty to be good citizens and to 'do the right thing'; they should achieve commercial success in ways that honour ethical values and respect people, communities, and the natural environment;
- *sustainability* – emphasizes the environment by meeting the needs of the present without compromising the ability of future generations to meet their own needs;
- *licence to operate* – every company needs tacit or explicit permission from governments, communities, and numerous other stakeholders to do business; and
- *reputation* – through this argument attempts are made to justify CSR initiatives on the grounds they will improve a company's image, strengthen its brand, boost morale, and even raise the value of its stock.

To convert these broad principles into practice, a company must integrate a social perspective into the core frameworks it already uses to understand competition and guide its business strategy. Companies need to be increasingly aware of the social impact of their activities (such as hiring practices, emissions, and waste disposal). Porter and Kramer (2006) make the link between *competitive advantage* (see previous chapter) and *corporate social responsibility* (discussed here). In recent years organizations have been heavily influenced by social responsibility when making strategic *choices*. Governments, activists, and the media have become adept at holding companies to account for the social consequences of their actions. In response, CSR has emerged as an inescapable priority for business leaders in every country. CSR can be much more than a cost, a constraint, or a charitable deed – it can be a powerful source of innovation and competitive advantage argues Porter and Kramer (2006).

Organizations may consider the quantity and quality of available business inputs (such as human resources or transportation infrastructure). Second, the rules and incentives that govern competition – such as policies that protect intellectual property, ensure transparency, safeguard against corruption, and encourage investment. Third, the size and sophistication of local demand, influenced by such things as standards for product quality and safety, consumer rights, and fairness in government purchasing. Fourth, the local availability of supporting industries, such as service providers and machinery producers. Any and all of these aspects of context can be opportunities for CSR initiatives. Strategy is always about making choices, and success in corporate social responsibility is no different. It is about choosing which social issues to focus upon.

Opportunity – emerging markets

In the previous paragraphs we discussed strategy and in Chapter 3, on strategy, considered the need for organizations to take advantage of opportunity. Many international organizations pursue business opportunity in emerging markets. The term emerging markets is commonly used to describe business and market activity in industrializing or emerging regions of the world. Countries such as China, India, Mexico, Brazil, Chile, much of Southeast Asia, South Asia, countries in Eastern Europe, the Middle East, parts of Africa and Latin America are considered to be in a transitional phase between developing and developed status. While there is a high potential for gains to the multinational doing business in such countries, there is also a great risk to company reputation if strategies, activities and decisions are not ethically managed. In some countries there is a high incidence of human rights abuses, corruption, a poor infrastructure and many locals may be antagonistic, believing that foreign companies plunder natural resources and wealth. Working conditions and business methods and practices are likely to be very different from the home country.

Mexico City, the centre of a transitional national economy

As was highlighted in Chapter 2, ignoring such risks is not an option and organizations must be seen to operate in an ethical manner. This normally means applying the same principles and standards as they would in developed countries. They should adhere to international principles and conventions on human rights, labour rights and the environment. Typical challenges for such organizations include dealing with repressive and/or corrupt regimes; benefiting from war economies; managing security arrangements; dealing with corruption and ensuring labour rights.

In the next section we build on previous sections by discussing how ethical, stakeholder and CSR theory may be implemented. We extend the list of CSR components, consider the use of generic standards and international principles of good behaviour and distinguish two fundamentally different approaches to implementation.

CSR implementation

There are many specific initiatives and approaches to make ethical management and CSR work, see Figure 4-9. Organizations may attempt to establish an ethical infrastructure to fulfil CSR by adopting a holistic and integrated, programme approach or may simply choose to focus on individual and specific programme elements (such as implementing a code of conduct or delivering ethical training). Weaver and Trevino (1999) used control theory to delineate two types of ethics programme, distinguishing compliance and values-based programmes. Such programmes are typically initiated either in response to external pressures or senior management's own commitment to ethics (executives can act both proactively and reactively). They represent efforts to manage employee ethical conduct. Control, a major responsibility of management, covers many types of behaviour in a company, including ethical conduct and compliance with the law. Control systems (discussed

Ethics programme a series of steps to be carried out in order to achieve ethics goals

Figure 4-9
CSR initiatives

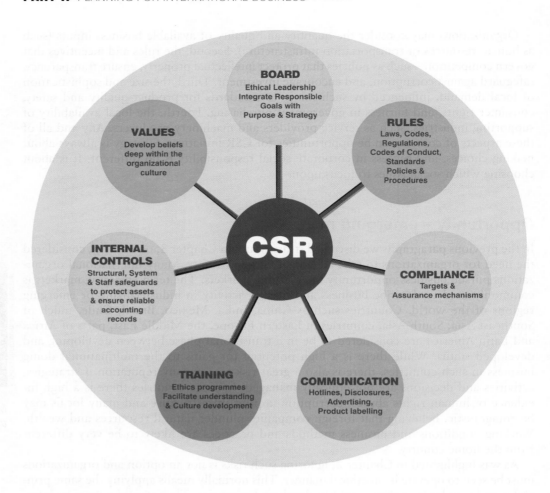

in Chapter 9) may be characterized by their control orientation – that is, the manner in which they standardize behaviour. Theorists distinguish between overtly coercive systems that rely on restraints like punishment to achieve behavioural compliance (formal or rule-based control) and systems that aim for member identification with and commitment to organizational goals and values.

Corporate ethics programmes similarly can differ in control orientation. Some ethics programmes embody a coercive orientation towards control that emphasizes adhering to rules, monitoring employee behaviour, and disciplining misconduct. We refer to such programmes as compliance-oriented. However, corporate ethics programmes may also aim to standardize behaviour by creating commitment to shared values and encouraging ethical aspirations. We refer to formal ethics programmes emphasizing support for employee ethical aspirations and the development of shared values as values-oriented. However, while two types of programme have been identified, compliance and values orientation, they need not be mutually exclusive. An organization's ethics programme may aim for both internalization of values and compliance with rules. Formal corporate ethics programmes typically include some or all of the following elements:

Compliance-oriented based on the establishment of formal rules and managers commanding the behaviour of employees

Values-oriented based on the establishment of broad principles and values intended to inform self-regulating behaviour

1 formal ethics codes, which articulate a firm's expectations regarding ethics;

2 ethics committees charged with developing ethics policies, evaluating company or employee actions, and/or investigating and adjudicating policy violations;

3 ethics communication systems (e.g. telephone lines) providing a means for employees to report abuses or obtain guidance;

4 ethics officers charged with coordinating policies, providing ethics education, or investigating allegations;

5 ethics training programmes, aimed at helping employees to recognize and respond to ethical issues; and

6 disciplinary processes to address unethical behaviour.

In the case of corporate ethics programmes, codes of conduct and other policy documents formalize company values and expectations for ethical behaviour. These policies are administered by occupants of specialized positions (e.g. corporate and divisional ethics officers, departmental ethics coordinators). Informal programmes on the other hand are characterized by initiatives to develop moral and ethical principles and means to share thinking among employees in a manner that leads to the establishment of an ethical culture. The scope of a corporation's ethics programme may be defined in terms of the number of different ethics programme elements and geographical coverage included in the ethics management effort. In some companies, ethics programmes are broad in scope, with multiple elements, including dedicated staff, supporting structures and policies, and extensive employee involvement. In other companies, the scope of ethics management is limited, with little, if any, staff and few supporting structures. The influence of senior management commitment is important in both types of ethics programme.

Jackson (1997) asks how the multinational company should design an *ethics program* to meet the challenges of the global business environment, noting that, despite the need to accommodate a certain measure of relativism, there is a substantial core of ethical norms for business that can be communicated and observed in multinational companies. Jackson suggests international organizations instil international business ethics standards into their corporate code of conduct. Codes of conduct should not remain parochial, that is, grounded only in national morals. Many ethical guidelines for international companies are framed in highly general terms, which make them operate more like principles than all-or-nothing rules, see Figure 4-10.

Next we discuss the two types of programme: compliance and value-based, before identifying the role of leaders in establishing and making such programmes work within the international organization. We conclude the chapter with a brief review of the recognition given to the most ethical companies.

CRT	OECD	UN	Figure 4-10
The responsibilities of business are beyond shareholders and are to all stakeholders.	Organizations must: Focus on sustainable development when contributing to economic, social, and environmental progress.	Businesses should: **Human rights** Make sure they are not associated with any human rights abuses.	Global ethical principles
The economic and social impact of business should be towards innovation, justice, and world community.	Respect human rights of all those individuals impacted by the organization.	**Labour standards** Allow the freedom of association and recognize collective bargaining of their employees.	
Business behaviour should be beyond the letter of the law towards a spirit of trust. Businesses need to respect the global rules.	Encourage local economic development through cooperation with the local community.	Eliminate all forms of forced and/or compulsory labour. Abolish all child labour. Eliminate all forms of discrimination in the workplace.	
Businesses need to support multilateral trade.	Not ask local or regional government for legal exemptions from legal requirements based on environmental, health/safety, labour, taxation, financial incentives, or any other legal issue.	**Environment** Support a precautionary approach to global environmental challenges.	
Businesses must respect the environment.	Support and uphold good corporate governance principles and apply good corporate governance practices.	Undertake all intiatives that promote a higher level of environmental responsibility.	
Businesses must avoid illicit operations.	Develop and apply effective self-regulatory practices and management systems.	Encourage the development and dissemination of environmentally-friendly technologies.	
Stakeholder principles: Businesses must treat all stakeholders with respect and dignity including customers, employees, owners/investors, suppliers, competitors, and communities.	Make all of their employees aware of all compliance and company policies that impact upon the behaviour of the employees.	**Anticorruption** Stop all forms of corruption including extortion and bribery.	
www.cauxroundtable.org	Not be involved in any discriminatory behaviour towards employees nor should they be unjust in the treatment of their employees. www.oecd.org	www.unglobalcompact.org	

Compliance oriented programmes

Compliance programmes are based on the establishment of formal rules and managers commanding the behaviour of employees. Central to compliance approaches are policies, rules and codes though the latter also has a place in the values-based programme as we will see later. The practice of issuing codes of business conduct started over 30 years ago. More recently, the OECD (2001) investigated private initiatives in the area of corporate responsibility, what companies do to promote legal and ethical compliance. They analyzed more than 250 codes of conduct. Codes of conduct are voluntary expressions of commitment that set forth standards and principles for business conduct. The codes address such issues as human rights, labour standards, environmental management, consumer protection, anticorruption, competition and information disclosure, see Figure 4-11. The most common issue areas addressed in the inventory are labour standards and environmental stewardship. Compliance with the law is a major concern in the codes and nearly all commitments to it apply to both home and host countries. Several types of code can be distinguished such as guidelines for suppliers, business partners or for employees.

Codes of conduct voluntary expressions of commitment that set forth standards and principles for business conduct

Figure 4-11

Issues addressed in codes of conduct

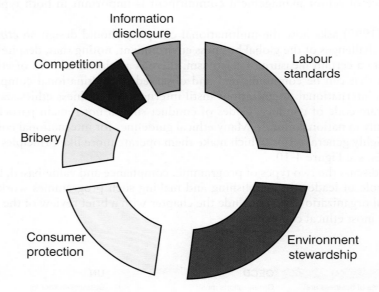

Establishing a code of ethics

The organization may create and adopt a number of statements to communicate the corporation's view on the subject of ethics. In Chapter 3 we mentioned value statements which act as guiding principles for the organization. Corporate credos state the company's beliefs and responsibilities to stakeholders. A *code of ethics* is a written document that explicitly states what acceptable and unacceptable behaviour is for all employees in the organization. When developing a code of ethics it is normal for the senior leadership team or CEO to write an introductory letter explaining the importance of ethics and compliance to each employee – see for example the TI chairman's comments at the beginning of the TI case study. The code may provide frameworks to assist with ethical decision-making and may list the resources available for obtaining guidance. Similarly the code may describe enforcement and implementation mechanisms and generic examples of what constitutes acceptable and unacceptable behaviour. The code should be distributed or made available to everyone and in some cases the organization may create a global code of ethics. This may be informed by the global ethical principles detailed in Figure 4-10.

The OECD guidelines, recommendations by governments to multinational enterprises (MNEs), help ensure that MNEs act in harmony with the policies of countries in which they operate and with societal expectations. They are a comprehensive, multilaterally endorsed code of conduct for MNEs. They establish non-binding principles and standards, covering a broad range of issues in business ethics. The basic premise of the guidelines is that internationally agreed principles can help to prevent misunderstandings and build an atmosphere of confidence and predictability among business, labour, governments and society as a whole. A 'global instrument' refers to a code or standard providing guidance to international business in relation to non-financial performance and practices.

The *OECD Guidelines for Multinational Enterprises* are one such instrument. Companies use these instruments as guidance – to understand their responsibilities and to formulate public commitments – codes of conduct – related to various aspects of business conduct. An OECD study of codes of conduct and related management and reporting systems notes that most large multinational enterprises have issued such codes. However, it also notes that while such practices are a global phenomenon, there is significant variation among companies in their commitments and management practices that cannot easily be explained by differences in their business environments. These findings suggested that global instruments may have a major impact on international business behaviour and play a prominent role in the public debate about the respective roles of companies, governments and individuals in ensuring that a broad cross-section of the world's people can enjoy improved economic, social and environmental welfare.

Gordon (2001) examines the similarities and differences between the guidelines and six other global instruments:

- Caux Principles for Business;
- Global Reporting Initiative;
- Global Sullivan Principles;
- Principles for Global Corporate Responsibility: Benchmarks;
- Social Accountability 8000 (SA 8000); and
- United Nations Global Compact.

Eight major issues in business ethics are identified:

- accountability (transparency and reporting);
- business conduct (compliance with the law, competitive conduct, corruption and bribery, conflicts of interest);
- community involvement (community economic development and employment of locals);
- corporate governance (investor rights);
- environment (policy, code of conduct and management systems to protect the environment);
- human rights (health and safety, child labour, forced labour, freedom of association, working hours, wages and benefits);
- consumer protection (marketing, product quality and safety, consumer privacy); and
- labour (workplace/employee) relations.

Some of the difficulties of seeking public endorsement from companies should be noted. These stem from the continuing large disagreements among various actors about what constitutes appropriate conduct for international business.

Implementing a corporate compliance programme can be a formidable task, requiring considerable managerial know-how. Normally all aspects of the firm's operations will be affected: structure of responsibilities, hiring, record keeping, incentive systems, external communications, training, production, legal services, emergency preparedness, etc. An important development in this area in recent years is the marked progress made in standardization of environmental management systems (EMS). Two main EMS standards are available, ISO14000 Series Environmental Management Systems and the European Union's Eco-Management and Audit Scheme (EMAS).

Often associated with codes and compliance programmes are ethics training programmes – to enhance the employee's knowledge of ethical issues, develop skills to support a strong ethical climate and ensure proper ethical decision-making by employees. As multinational corporations approach the issue of ethics training programmes, the level of complexity increases greatly due to the intricacies of doing business in a global environment. The more countries in which an organization does business, the more different cultural beliefs need to be addressed in global ethics training programmes. Such organizations have increased diversity in terms of ethics, culture and the legal environment. It is important to recognize employees in other parts of the world may interpret ethical information in different ways; they will see things through their cultural lens.

Values-oriented programmes

Organizational ethics means more than avoiding illegal practice and providing employees with a rule book. To foster a climate that encourages correct behaviour, corporations need a broad approach that goes beyond the often punitive legal compliance stance. Managers would be mistaken, however, to regard legal compliance as an adequate means for addressing the full range of ethical issues that arise every day. Conduct that is lawful may be highly problematic from an ethical point of view. While compliance is rooted in avoiding legal sanctions, organizational integrity is based on the concept of self-governance in accordance with a set of guiding principles. From the perspective of integrity, the task of ethics management is to define and give life to an organization's guiding values, to create an environment that supports ethically sound behaviour, and to inculcate a sense of shared accountability among employees.

The need to obey the law is viewed as a positive aspect of organizational life, rather than an unwelcome constraint imposed by external authorities. Many integrity initiatives have structural features common to compliance-based initiatives:

- a code of conduct;
- training in relevant areas of law;
- mechanisms for reporting and investigating potential misconduct; and
- audits and controls to insure that laws and company standards are being met.

But an integrity strategy is broader, deeper, and more demanding than a legal compliance initiative; broader in that it seeks to *enable* responsible conduct. Unlike a code of conduct, which articulates specific behavioural standards, the statement of vision, purposes, and beliefs lay out, in very simple terms, the company's central purpose and core values. Paine (1994) identifies features common to success:

- the guiding values and commitments make sense and are clearly communicated;
- company leaders are personally committed, credible, and willing to take action on the values they espouse;
- the espoused values are integrated into the normal channels of management decision-making and are reflected in the organization's critical activities;
- the company's systems and structures support and reinforce its values; and
- managers throughout the company have the decision-making skills, knowledge, and competencies needed to make ethically sound decisions on a day-to-day basis.

Weaver and Trevino (1999) added to the work of Paine, noting that whatever their orientation and goals, ethics programmes attempt to bring some degree of order and predictability to employee behaviour. Thus, it makes sense to characterize ethics programmes as organizational control systems argue Weaver and Trevino (1999); that is as systems which aim to create predictability in employee behaviour and correspondence between specific employee behaviours and more general organizational goals and expectations. Control systems have been distinguished according to whether they create order by coercing behavioral compliance or by generating employee identification with and commitment to collective organizational values. In the former case, a control system is seen as necessary to bring employee behaviour into conformity with organizational requirements – sometimes coercively. In the latter case, organizational goals are assumed to be such that employees can identify with them and thereby act according to them.

Ethics programmes can be characterized in similar terms. Some programmes are oriented toward rule – compliance and threats of punishment for non-compliance. Other programmes emphasize ethical values and the potential for employees to be committed to a set of ethical ideals embodied in the organization. Observers have suggested that these different approaches to ethics management will have different impacts on employee attitudes and behaviour. Paine, for example, suggested that compliance approaches will do little to generate commitment (Paine 1994), in part because they provide a kind of minimalist 'don't get caught' motivation. This suggests that these two types of programmes may influence different outcomes; a compliance orientation may generate behavioural conformity, while a values orientation may generate other outcomes, such as commitment to the organization.

If an ethics programme encourages a sense of shared values, and suggests that the programme exists to aid employees in doing their work and achieving their goals, the programme can influence employee role identity and can suggest to employees that they enjoy a high degree of organizational support. Widespread attention to shared values, through both formal and informal means, helps create expectations or norms for appropriate behaviour within an organization. Within business organizations, norms typically exist for profit-oriented, managerial behaviour, and for a corresponding role identity as a profit-seeking manager. However, in an organization with a well-developed, values-oriented ethics programme there will also be forms of social interaction which involve an expectation that employees will aspire to a set of shared ethical values, a perception that the organization supports employee goals and creates a sense of obligation by an employee to support the organization's goals in return.

Perceived organizational support has been found to be related positively to conscientiousness and commitment on the part of employees. A values-oriented ethics programme can be perceived as supporting employees. Instead of focusing solely on the detection and discipline of offences – suggesting perhaps that employees cannot be trusted, or are in some other way ethically incompetent – a values-oriented programme suggests that employees already are committed to ethical behaviour. The task of the programme is to encourage the development of meaningful, shared ethical values within the organization's particular context. In a values-oriented programme, emphasis is on activities that aid employees in decision-making, provide ethical advice and counselling, and support the development of a consensus about what constitutes good business ethics. Moreover, the focus on shared values in such programmes suggests that every organization member has the same status concerning ethics. A strong values orientation, then, supports employee aspirations, and suggests that the organization embodies a collective commitment which applies equally to all persons.

Values-oriented programmes make an employee's ethical role identity more salient, thus enabling employees to recognize and acknowledge more easily the ethical issues they face on the job. In organizations with values-oriented ethics programmes, we should find greater levels of employee awareness and open concern for ethical issues. The values orientation of an ethics programme, in effect, makes awareness of ethical issues an in-role behaviour, and should reduce tendencies towards 'moral muteness' in which employees keep silent about ethical issues at work (Weaver and Trevino 1999).

Value-driven approaches establish principles for employees to apply in their ethical thinking, particularly when there are no particular rules for a situation. It is about changing the attitudes and thinking of individuals so that collectively they share morals and ethics. The climate of integrity can be created through ethical leadership. More recently, Stansbury and Barry (2007) suggest many ethics managers have been moving their activities toward what have been called values-based or integrity-based approaches.

In summary, initial approaches to business ethics were more formal, reliant on rules, systems and compliance. However, as with formalization generally, people came to recognize the difficulties in using such approaches in dynamic environments. Situations arise for which there are no rules, rules become difficult to enforce and rely on communication. Rules are simply a manifestation of beliefs and so more people now see the benefit in values-based approaches. People sharing the same values are more likely to interpret ethical issues and make decisions in a similar, acceptable way. In many ways this is an issue of formal versus informal control over behaviour. However, most do not see this as an either/or problem, but see the two approaches working together in mutual support. However, values have little meaning unless they can be put to effect. In the final section we consider the role of leaders in making ethics programmes work.

Ethical leadership

While the board must play a key and leading role in the implementation of ethics programmes, all managers, as we shall see in Chapter 6, can also be leaders. Contemporary leaders must not only show skill in identifying and exploiting opportunity in pursuit of financial results, they must also act in a socially responsible manner. It has often been said that leadership by example is the most effective way to improve business ethics (Carroll 1991). Leaders must therefore be honest and trustworthy with high integrity. To be perceived as an *ethical leader*, it is not enough to just be an ethical person. An executive ethical leader must also find ways to focus the organization's attention on ethics and values and to infuse the organization with principles that will guide the actions of all employees. In return, ethical leaders can expect reduced legal problems and increased employee commitment, satisfaction, and employee ethical conduct. In their decision-making role, ethical leaders are thought to hold to a solid set of ethical values and principles. They aim to be objective and fair. They also have a perspective that goes beyond profit goals to include concerns about the broader society and community.

The executive's challenge is to make ethics and values stand out from a business landscape that is overloaded with messages about beating the competition and achieving quarterly goals and profits. Trevino, Hartman and Brown (2000) identified a number of ways moral managers can increase the salience of an ethics and values agenda and develop a reputation for ethical leadership. They serve as a role model for ethical conduct in a way that is visible to employees. They communicate regularly and persuasively with employees about ethical standards, principles, and values. Finally, they use the reward system consistently to hold all employees accountable to ethical standards.

Organizations now use a variety of initiatives to establish an ethical infrastructure; taken together, rules and values present complementary components of an ethical programme. We have summarized the basic steps in establishing such an infrastructure in Figure 4-12. The process starts with understanding where the organization is now, the current ethical climate, and the organization's goals and values. A senior manager may be appointed or identified to show senior commitment at the outset. Next the organization identifies what it will do to the necessary components such as codes-of-conduct or credo statement and then develops any instruments and implements them. Broad participation is encouraged during this stage. Next, the 'do's and don'ts' ethical decision making frameworks and organizational resources need to be communicated. This is typically done through a letter from the CEO, board or other high profile entity. Later, communication will include reporting efforts and progress to stakeholders. Employees should then receive training to clarify values and enhance ethical and moral awareness, discuss ethical decision-making and examine the ethical infrastructure as a support network.

During the earlier phase of component development the organization would also expand resources such as help lines to assist employees. The infrastructure will also include people systems, with committees being established and roles and responsibilities assigned. Next, the work of enforcing rules and measuring the effectiveness of systems and approaches becomes important. Finally, the organization must allow the ethical infrastructure to develop, evolve and be improved. The establishment of an ethical infrastructure should help the organization build and enhance its reputation.

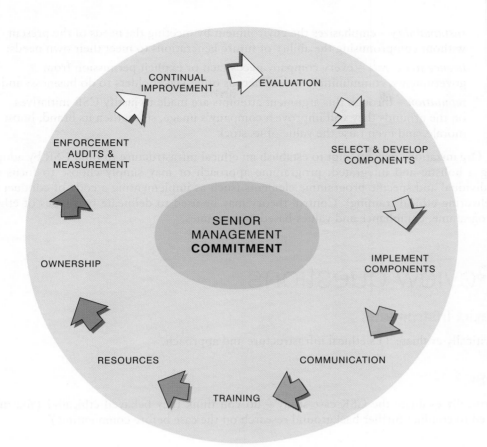

Figure 4-12
Establishing an ethical infrastructure

Summary of key learning points

Business ethics is concerned with the application of morals to the conduct of business people asking what is 'right' or 'wrong'. When people and organizations adhere to a moral code they are said to have integrity. As integrity is eroded, unethical and illegal behaviour follows. General principles have been proposed to describe what is meant by ethical behaviour. Individuals should keep promises (fidelity), be fair (justice), not harm others, put right any wrong caused (reparation), show gratitude to others, and improve the lives of one's self and others (beneficence). Other principles include fiduciary obligations (not putting self-interest above the overall interests of the organization), reliability (fulfilling promises), transparency (openness and honesty), dignity (respecting others), fairness (not taking bribes or colluding with others), citizenship (respecting the law and the environment), responsiveness and respecting property.

Corporate social responsibility (CSR) is a concept whereby organizations consider the interests of society by taking responsibility for the impact of their activities on customers, suppliers, employees, shareholders, communities and the environment in every aspect of their operations and decision-making. Stakeholder theory suggests the role of the organization is to satisfy a wider set of stakeholders, not simply the owners. The theory is used to interpret the function of the corporation – how things should be, including the identification of moral or philosophical guidelines for the operation and management of corporations. Central to the CSR approach is that the organization should use resources responsibly and comply with relevant laws and regulations. Four key arguments have been offered to encourage organizations to act in a socially responsible manner:

1 *moral obligation* – companies have a duty to be good citizens and to 'do the right thing'; they should achieve commercial success in ways that honour ethical values and respect people, communities, and the natural environment;

2 *sustainability* – emphasizes the environment by meeting the needs of the present without compromising the ability of future generations to meet their own needs;

3 *licence to operate* – every company needs tacit or explicit permission from governments, communities, and numerous other stakeholders to do business; and

4 *reputation* – through this argument attempts are made to justify CSR initiatives on the grounds they will improve a company's image, strengthen its brand, boost morale, and even raise the value of its stock.

Organizations may attempt to establish an ethical infrastructure to fulfil CSR by adopting a holistic and integrated, programme approach or may simply choose to focus on individual and specific programme elements (such as implementing a code of conduct or delivering ethical training). Control theory may be used to delineate two types of ethics programme, compliance and values-based programmes.

Review questions

Texas Instruments

Critically evaluate TI's ethical infrastructure and approach.

GSK

Critically evaluate the GSK case study – do you think they behaved ethically? (You may need to conduct further background research on the case before commenting.)

Traditional theory

Discuss why traditional theory – management serving stakeholders – is morally untenable in the contemporary business world.

Conceptual understanding

In your own words explain what is meant by:

1 Business ethics
2 Ethical egoism and utilitarianism
3 Code of ethics
4 Existentialism
5 Stakeholder management
6 Corporate social responsibility
7 Ethics programme.

References

Alexander, L. D. and Matthews, W. F. (1984) 'The Ten Commandments of Corporate Social Responsibility', *Business & Society Review* (Summer 1984) 50:62–66.

Carroll, A. B. (1979) 'A Three-Dimensional Conceptual Model of Corporate Performance', *Academy of Management Review* (October 1979) 4(4):497–505.

Carroll, A. B. (1991) 'The Pyramid of Corporate Social Responsibility: Toward the Moral Management of Organizational Stakeholders', *Business Horizons* (July/August 1991) 34(4):39–49.

Cochran, P. L. (2007) 'The Evolution of Corporate Social Responsibility', *Business Horizons* 50(6):449–454.

Donaldson, T. and Preston, L. E. (1995) 'The Stakeholder Theory of the Corporation: Concepts, Evidence, and Implications', *Academy of Management Review* (January 1995) 20(1):65–91.

Ethisphere (2007) www.ethisphere.com/2007-worlds-most-ethical-companies/ accessed 18 March 2008.

Friedman, A. L. and Miles, S. (2002) 'Developing Stakeholder Theory', *Journal of Management Studies* (January 2002) 39(1):1–21.

Freeman, R.E. (1984) *Strategic Management: A Stakeholder Approach* Boston: Pitman.

Gordon, K. (2001) 'The OECD Guidelines and Other Corporate Responsibility Instruments: A Comparison', OECD Publishing, doi:10.1787/302255465771.

Handy, C. B. (2002) 'What's A Business For?', *Harvard Business Review* (December 2002) 80(12):49–56.

Hart, S. L. (1997) 'Beyond Greening: Strategies for A Sustainable World', *Harvard Business Review* (January/February 1997) 75(1):66–76.

Hart, S. L. and Milstein, M. B. (1999) 'Global Sustainability and the Creative Destruction of Industries', *Sloan Management Review* (Fall 1999) 41(1):23–33.

Jackson, K. T. (1997) 'Globalizing Corporate Ethics Programs: Perils and Prospects', *Journal of Business Ethics* (September 1997) 16(12/13):1227–1235.

Kaptein, M. and Avelino, S. (2005) 'Measuring Corporate Integrity: A Survey-Based Approach', *Corporate Governance* 5(1):45–54.

Mitchell, R. K., Agle, B. R. and Wood, D. J. (1997) 'Toward A Theory of Stakeholder Identification and Salience: Defining the Principle of Who And What Really Counts', *Academy of Management Review* (October 1997) 22(4):853–886.

Murphy, P. E. (2005) 'Developing, Communicating and Promoting Corporate Ethics Statements: A Longitudinal Analysis', *Journal of Business Ethics* (December 2005) 62(2):183–189.

OECD (2001) Corporate Responsibility: Results Of A Fact-Finding Mission On Private Initiatives', OECD Working Papers on International Investment, 2001/2, OECD Publishing, doi:10.1787/701174424371.

Orsato, R. J. (2006) 'Competitive Environmental Strategies: When Does It Pay To Be Green?', *California Management Review* (Winter 2006) 48(2):127–143.

Paine, L. S. (1994) 'Managing for Organizational Integrity', *Harvard Business Review* (March/April 1994) 72(2):106–117.

Poel, I. and Royakkers, L. (2007) 'The Ethical Cycle', *Journal of Business Ethics* (March 2007) 71(1):1–13.

Porter, M. E. and Kramer, M. R. (2006) 'Strategy & Society: The Link between Competitive Advantage and Corporate Social Responsibility', *Harvard Business Review* 84(12):78–92.

Porter, M. E., and van der Linde, C. (1995) 'Green and Competitive: Ending the Stalemate', *Harvard Business Review* (September/October 1995) 73(5):120–134.

Robertson, C. J. and Crittenden, W. F. (2003) 'Mapping Moral Philosophies: Strategic Implications for Multinational Firms', *Strategic Management Journal* (April 2003) 24(4):358–393.

Schwartz, M. S., Dunfee, T. W. and Kline, M J. (2005) 'Tone at the Top: an Ethics Code for Directors?', *Journal of Business Ethics* (April 2005) 2:58(1–3):79–100.

Singh, J. B. (2006) 'A Comparison of the Contents of the Codes of Ethics of Canada's Largest Corporations in 1992 and 2003', *Journal of Business Ethics* (March 2006) 64(1):17–29.

Stansbury, J. and Barry, B. (2007) 'Ethics Programs and the Paradox Of Control', *Business Ethics Quarterly* (April 2007) 17(2):239–261.

Stanwick, P. and Stanwick, S. (2009) *Understanding Business Ethics*, Upper Saddle River, NJ: Prentice Hall.

Trevino, L. K., Weaver, G. R., Gibson, D. G. and Toffler, B. L. (1999) 'Managing Ethics and Legal Compliance: What Works and What Hurts', *California Management Review* (Winter 1999) 41(2):131–151.

Trevino, L. K., Hartman, L. P. and Brown, M. (2000) 'Moral Person and Moral Manager: How Executives Develop A Reputation for Ethical Leadership', *California Management Review* (Summer 2000) 42(4):128–142.

Weaver, G. R. and Trevino, L. K. (1999) 'Compliance and Values Oriented Ethics Programs: Influences on Employees' Attitudes and Behavior', *Business Ethics Quarterly* (April 1999) 9(2):315–335.

Suggestions for further reading

Journals

According to the Institute of Business Ethics, the four main journals in the field are the *Business Ethics Quarterly* (BEQ), the *Journal of Business Ethics* (JBE), *Business Ethics: A European Review* (BE:ER), and *Journal of Business Ethics Education* (JBEE). In addition, there are specialist journals such as the *Business and Society Review, Corporate Governance: An International Review, Corporate Governance:* the *International Journal of Business and Society* and *Philosophy of Management* that are also directly concerned with business ethics issues, as well as an increasing occurrence of business ethics related papers in mainstream or specialist management journals such as the *Academy of Management Review* and *Long Range Planning* (including special editions devoted to business ethics topics).

Business Ethics Quarterly

The Journal of the Society for Business Ethics: *Business Ethics Quarterly* is a peer-reviewed scholarly journal that publishes theoretical and empirical research relevant to the ethics of business. This interdisciplinary journal publishes articles and reviews on a broad range of topics, including the internal ethics of business organizations, the role of business organizations in larger social, political and cultural frameworks, and the ethical quality of market-based societies and market-based relationships. http://www.pdcnet.org/beq.html.

Journal of Business Ethics

The *Journal of Business Ethics* publishes original articles from a wide variety of methodological and disciplinary perspectives concerning ethical issues related to business. Contributors examine moral aspects of systems of production, consumption, marketing, advertising, social and economic accounting, labour relations, public relations and organizational behaviour. http://www.springerlink.com/content/100281/

Business Ethics: A European Review

Business Ethics: A European Review is a quarterly scholarly journal, which aims to advance knowledge and understanding at every level on all issues relating to ethics in business. Its focus is primarily, though not exclusively, European. http://www.blackwellpublishing.com/journal.asp?ref=0962-8770&site=1

Key articles

Scholars of this subject area have often read the following:

1 Mitchell, R. K., Agle, B. R. and Wood, D. J. (1997) 'Toward A Theory of Stakeholder Identification and Salience: Defining the Principle of Who and What Really Counts', *Academy of Management Review* (October 1997) 22(4):853–886.
2 Donaldson, T. and Preston, L. E. (1995) 'The Stakeholder Theory of the Corporation: Concepts, Evidence, and Implications', *Academy of Management Review* (January 1995) 20(1):65–91.
3 Carroll, A. B. (1979) 'A Three-Dimensional Conceptual Model of Corporate Performance', *Academy of Management Review* (October 1979) 4(4):497–505.
4 Carroll, A. B. (1991) 'The Pyramid of Corporate Social Responsibility: Toward the Moral Management of Organizational Stakeholders', *Business Horizons* (July/August 1991) 34(4):39–49.
5 Porter, M. E. and van der Linde, C. (1995) 'Green and Competitive: Ending the Stalemate', *Harvard Business Review* (September/October 1995) 73(5):120–134.
6 Paine, L. S. (1994) 'Managing for Organizational Integrity', *Harvard Business Review* (March/April 1994) 72(2):106–117.

Chapter 5

Managing change in the international organization

Introduction

Understanding change

Theories of change

Implementing and managing change

Key concepts

■ Organizational change ■ Gap analysis ■ Visioning ■ Resistance ■ Transformational change
■ Transactional change ■ Change agent ■ Open system (view) ■ Systems thinking
■ Change model ■ Organizational theory ■ 7-S model ■ Nadler and Tushman congruence model
■ Burke-Litwin model ■ Force-field analysis

By the end of this chapter you will be able to:

■ Describe the main theoretical foundations of change management

■ Critically evaluate the planned and the emergent approach to change

■ Identify and describe a selection of integrated change management models

■ Understand the situations in which the various approaches to change are most appropriately
used

■ Understand the role of leaders, managers and change agents in the change process

■ Understand resistance to change

Active learning case

The subject of this case study is the dominant 'monopolistic' telecomms company PLDT, one of the Philippines' most profitable companies (rich in assets and revenue), a large (approximately 14 000 employees) and mature (approximately 75 years old) organization spread throughout the Philippines.

Towards the end of the 20th century, the company was on the one hand pursuing growth, from 1.6 million to 2 million subscribers by 2000, while on the other hand seeking to reduce costs, particularly by downsizing and reducing overheads. The company offered a wide range of services and had strategic plans to expand and modernize (digitalize) its network.

In 1998 the company received approximately one billion dollars in revenue and in the annual report, recognized threats of declining market share and shrinking margins.

The Philippine Long Distance Telephone Co

In 1998 the largest company in the Philippines, PLDT – the dominant telecomms operator – was taken over and a new management team brought in, headed by Asia's highest paid CEO, to transform and turn the company around with help from a UK-based consultancy.

Context and situational factors

Throughout the 1990s the Philippines was committed to deregulation and privatization. In terms of opportunity, there are approximately 70 million Filipinos yet less than 5 in every 100 had fixed line telephony service and less than two in every hundred owned a mobile phone (mid-1990s). High growth was witnessed in the telecomms industry, 17.2 per cent in 1998 but as high as 30 to 40 per cent previously. As a result of the government's deregulation policy, telecomms investments rose from 81 billion pesos (approximately two billion US dollars) in 1983 to 245 billion pesos (approximately six billion US dollars) in 1997. Several significant global telecomms giants were attracted to invest in the Filipino telecomms market where they partnered local telecomms companies (local companies were typically backed by some of the richest families in the Philippines). Investors were attracted to this newly emerging open market, primarily because of the low penetration rates and consequent high growth opportunities and opportunity to compete with the dominant carrier (PLDT) accused of poor service.

Throughout the 1990s, both globally and locally, significant *technological* change was highly visible in the telecomms industry and was reflected in the product portfolio (equipment), the supporting network (see digitalization, value-add-services and mobility) and the organizational infrastructure (see customer billing and service systems). If telecomms had a 'big bang' in the 1990s, it was attributable to deregulation and technological innovation, primarily in the form of digitalization and then followed by significant advances in mobile telephony. Technology is used, through service differentiation, to win customers and stimulate network use; it can also provide cost benefits and efficiency gains.

©iStockphoto.com/Marcelo Wain

In November 1998 PLDT was taken over by Hong Kong's 'First Pacific', owners of the Philippines' dominant mobile operator Smart, headed by Asia's highest-paid executive Manny V. Pangilinan (MVP), himself a Filipino, who became President and CEO. Shortly after the new management team entered office they recognized the urgent need to instil greater control into the organization (culture) and prepare the company for greater competition post deregulation. Early in 1999, Kelly (a UK-based telecomms consultant) agreed to conduct a high level (scoping) review of the organization. The purpose of the *scoping exercise* was to diagnose high level problem areas and determine what

was in need of change. At the time, the new CFO described PLDT as having a 'monopolistic culture' and an environment of little company information, no regular reporting and no easy-to-follow procedures. Aside from the lack of information and visibility, there were reliability concerns with any data that was created. With the absence of information, it was difficult for him to ascertain the 'real' nature of the problems at PLDT.

The UK-based consultancy submitted a high level change-plan authorized by the sponsors of the project – the CEO and CFO. Locally, they appointed a PLDT manager to act as coordinator and facilitator. The external lead consultant and the PLDT manager worked together almost in the manner reported by Hofstede (1997: 200) who discusses the *Fachpromoter* (expert) and *Machtpromoter* (power-holder) when he discusses strategies for culture change.

The Change Project: a team of consultants and PLDT employees was formed to undertake the change project. A steering committee made up from the company's most senior managers (the Revenue Assurance Committee 'RAC') was formed as a multidisciplinary senior decision-making forum to promote and coordinate company-wide revenue issues and initiatives. The project goal was best described in the revenue assurance vision, developed collectively by the new team, adopted at the beginning of the change project, 'To ensure that all revenues for access to and use of the [PLDT telecomms] network are accurately billed, collected and grown'. This was communicated to and endorsed by the RAC at their inaugural meeting. In an introductory presentation to the Committee (attended by the President, CFO, and other group heads), the objectives of the Revenue Assurance Programme (RAP) were outlined. It was suggested that the programme be delivered in four phases over a six-month period from April 1999 to October 1999, starting with a detailed company [diagnostic] review phase.

The main roles of the external change consultants were to provide a company-wide *neutral 'interpretation of what is going on'* (Schein 1997: 71) and to help identify 'what is important, what needs attention' to *help people understand* what is at the 'root of the problem' (1997: 77) and to facilitate communication between PLDT internal groups. They also offered specialist advice on alternative problem solutions and delivered training, while directing the overall change programme.

Problem diagnosis: From the detail of the review process (phase 1 of 4), the change team identified company-wide issues and presented their findings to the RAC. They described findings as a 10–20 billion-peso problem of debt, fraud and poor billing processes and systems (unable to bill (missing data, etc.) and no person to bill); there were over 6000 customer disputes per month costing 180 million pesos; 1 in 20 subscribers disputed tolls and 1 in 5 customers complained. Furthermore, the bill-collection timeline was too long resulting in cash flow problems. In many cases problems were considered to be a consequence of the now dysfunctional culture, structure, systems and a lack of overall responsibility. Their findings were used as the structured and diagnosed problem definition for the subsequent stages of the project and were presented to the RAC in association with an outlook of the next steps in the programme.

Following a period of lobbying power holders and other activities to communicate the identified problems, five strategic initiatives were proposed:

1 reorganization;

2 new policy;

3 measurement and reporting;

4 specific control initiatives to reduce risk; and

5 improve coordination and culture change.

One of the main objectives was to introduce more control and improve the company's information systems. Control and responsive behaviour was to be achieved, in part, through information which would make problems visible to the whole organization in a timely manner. With regard to 'measurement and reporting', the consultants proposed to develop key performance indicators (KPIs) for visibility and to aid root-cause-analysis, focus and support decision-making. One of the major concerns of the review team was the propensity, throughout the company, to engage in *adaptive* as opposed to *corrective* action.

Change

A major reorganization occurred with a new structure and supporting processes. Established during implementation, the change team frequently communicated progress and early successes throughout the organization using face-to-face meetings, the intranet and the company's own internal newspaper; they also circulated detailed briefings each week of ongoing problems they had diagnosed. The consultants worked closely with the new divisions, developing people, technologies and capabilities, focusing especially on the role of *information-as-control* and the involvement of the whole organization in collective pursuits. Influenced by Andres, who suggests that the answer lies in communication, 'self-direction and self-control', the change team devised and implemented a diagnostic control system based upon the cybernetic hypothesis, the feedback loop as the fundamental building block for action.

Schein (1997: 65–67) discusses 'corrective processes' noting that 'self-corrective action often is taken because people now recognize problems about which they can do something'. Schein also notes that, 'the remedial or corrective strategies that an organization employs in response to the information it gathers about its performance represent an important area around which cultural assumptions form'. Locally, Andres (1997) discusses the need for *information*, 'the individual in organizations needs information and understanding of the company's goals, policies and procedures, rules and regulations. He is, most often than not, unaware of their gravity, hence his actions are uncaring and seemingly irresponsible.' As different parts of the organization addressed the problems diagnosed, they were encouraged to present their actions to the RAC which gave profile to their actions and support. Following the assignment, the CFO stated that the project led to '*significant operational efficiencies within the company*' and '*significant additional revenues for PLDT*'. One senior manager described the outcome of the assignment as, '*influencing a culture change in the company which is focused in making everyone revenue conscious*'. Estimated savings arising from the project were at least $100 million.

Attributed to the success was the 'assurance' model of operation; working closely with senior management, the specialists produce and share company problem information with the relevant organizational parts and the RAC – who are best placed to understand what the company needs to achieve – to define continuously and dynamically what is important and to ensure that problems do not become insurmountable. Organizations frequently respond to the challenges of a dynamic environment through the adoption of empowerment strategies believing this will make the organization more responsive. Yet people within the organization must know what they need to do and to what they are responding.

Viewing organizations as systems, a collection of interrelated parts, can help structure performance problems. Parts need to be coordinated and controlled and the whole system must have goals. In dynamic environments, senior managers must establish mechanisms (diagnostic controls and early warning systems) which inform the parts of the organization continuously of what is important and in need of attention. This must be done in a participatory way whereby the parts are empowered to act in a manner determined by them. Shared understanding of organizational problems coupled with direction from senior management can be used to develop the culture of the organization.

Sources:

Kelly, P. (2005) 'Building a Collaborative Culture with Managed Feedback Loops and Cybernetics Theory', *International Journal of Knowledge, Culture and Change Management* 5(7):1–12.

Andres, T. D. (1997) *Understanding Filipino Values – A Management Approach*, Quezon City: New Day Publishers.

Hofstede, G. (1984) 'Cultures Consequences – abridged', London: Sage.

Hofstede, G. (1997) *Cultures and Organizations,* London: McGraw-Hill.

Schein, E. (1997) *Organizational Culture and Leadership* (2 ed), San Francisco: Jossey Bass.

Introduction

Organizational change is essential to guarantee long-term success in an organization. Change has already been discussed in the three preceding chapters: change in the environment, strategic change and changes in the ethical thinking (and fundamental purpose) of international organizations. Change will also be discussed in subsequent chapters. Most contemporary management scholars and practitioners agree that the amount, pace, unpredictability and impact of change are greater than ever before. New products, processes and services have appeared at an ever increasing rate. Local markets have become global markets and, as was highlighted in the opening case study, industries have been opened up to competition. State owned companies have been privatized as more countries become ever more capitalist.

Significant change was witnessed throughout the 1990s in the build-up to the millennium. This was fuelled by globalization, deregulation, digital technologies including the Internet and improvements to transportation and communication generally. Overall, we entered the new millennium embracing change as persistent and normal. Within organizations we have observed restructuring, delayering, fragmentation, outsourcing, culture change programmes, business process reengineering, the implementation of enterprise systems, empowerment strategies, the development of competences and capabilities, new business models and the introduction of new products and services.

Yet perhaps the major organizational changes observed over the past 20 years may be better known for their failure than their success. TQM, BPR (discussed in Chapter 10) and enterprise resource planning (discussed in Chapter 13) change programmes in particular, have in many cases, been costly, ineffective and disruptive in many companies. The failure rate for new technology projects is often reported above 50 per cent; a higher rate reported for TQM. BPR and ERP projects have threatened the survival of and bankrupted many large companies. In many cases, such initiatives simply do not achieve or deliver what was promised. Changes can take longer to implement than planned (*time problems*); may not live up to expectations (*quality problems*) or may cost more to implement than was budgeted (*cost overrun problems*). Perhaps more worrying, is the fact that, in relation to the three aforementioned change initiatives, failures occurred despite there being a great deal of information, advice and assistance available.

There is little doubt then that managing change is very difficult and risky – why should this be so? Perhaps one reason is the absence of a universal change theory. Change management requires an interdisciplinary perspective and an understanding of organization, strategy, change, psychological and sociological theories. Before attempting to change something, managers must understand what it is they intend to change. They need to understand organizations, organizational behaviour, technology, operations, marketing and finance. Managers also need the ability to lead the organization, coordinate, motivate and control people and other resources. They must also be aware of intervention strategies, alternative solutions and how to overcome resistance to change. Furthermore, the international organization must understand such theories in the context of different country and organizational cultures and business environments.

In order to help manage change within the international organization, this chapter aims to provide an understanding of the theories and approaches to change and to indicate their usefulness and drawbacks. There are links between this chapter and each and every other chapter, especially chapters organized in this part of the book. To provide structure and aid learning, this chapter is organized into three main sections:

- understanding change;
- theories of change;
- implementing change.

We start by defining change and exploring what it is that can and usually is changed within organizations. Several change types are identified and the need for change discussed.

In recognition of the absence of a single universal change theory we explore a number of related theories used in change management. In particular we focus on *what* should be changed and *how* organizations may accomplish change. A variety of models are discussed to assist with both challenges. In the final section we consider the role of the change agent and the challenges associated with implementing change, particularly in the face of resistance and the context of complexities associated with international organizations.

Understanding change

Whenever a large organization gets into trouble – and especially if it has been successful for many years – people blame sluggishness, complacency, arrogance and mammoth bureaucracies. It is true that a successful organization's practices and behaviours that worked for decades can cease to be right. The realities (environment) that each organization actually faces change quite dramatically though assumptions about them may not. Whereas reality may change, the theory of the business (assumptions about the environment, the mission and the core competencies needed) may not changed with it – in some organizations. While some theories of the business may last for a long time, eventually they become outdated and then unsound.

The first reaction of an organization whose theory is becoming outdated is almost always a defensive one; to pretend that nothing is happening. The next reaction is an attempt to patch; but patching never works. Instead, when a theory shows the first signs of becoming obsolete, it is time to start thinking again, to ask again which assumptions about the environment, mission, and core competencies reflect reality most accurately. There is a need for each organization to adopt proactive measures, to systematically monitor and test the theory of the business, i.e. a need for early diagnosis. There is also a need to rethink a theory that is stagnating and to take effective action in order to change policies and practices, bringing the organization's behaviour in line with the new realities of its environment, with a new definition of its mission, and with new core competencies to be developed and acquired.

Drucker (1994) suggests each organization should frequently challenge every product, every service, every policy, every distribution channel with the question; if we were not in it already, would we be going into it now? Without this self-challenging approach, an organization will be overtaken by events. It will waste and misuse its resources on things it should never have been doing or should no longer do. Organizations change all the time, each and every day. However, not all organizational changes are the same. The change that occurs in organizations is, for the most part, unplanned and gradual. Planned organization change, especially on a large-scale (new mission, strategy, leadership, and culture), affecting the entire system, is less common. Most organizational change is evolutionary. From time-to-time, organizations are faced with the need to modify themselves. In this section we consider *what* is meant by change and *why* organizations pursue it. The following section addresses the problems of *what* to change and *how*.

What is change and what can be changed?

The basic tension that underlies many discussions of organizational change is that it would not be necessary if people had done their jobs right in the first place. Planned change is usually triggered by the failure of people to create continuously adaptive organizations. Thus, organizational change routinely occurs in the context of failure of some sort. Weick and Quinn (1999) suggest both that change starts with failure to adapt and that change never starts because it never stops. Organizational change concerns the alteration of organizational components (such as the mission, strategy, goals, structure, processes, systems, technology and people) to improve the effectiveness or efficiency of the organization.

Organizational change the alteration of organizational components (such as the mission, strategy, goals, structure, processes, systems, technology and people) to improve the effectiveness or efficiency of the organization

Change may take place in any part and at any level of the organization. When we think of organizational change, we may think of significant changes aimed at making the organization more effective such as:

- mergers;
- acquisitions;
- buyouts;
- downsizing;
- restructuring;
- the launch of new products; and
- the outsourcing of major organizational activities.

Effectiveness capacity to do the right thing

Examples of smaller (efficiency-based) changes include: departmental reorganizations, the implementation of new technologies and systems. The primary needs for change derive from the need for alignment between the organization's internal and external environments.

Efficiency doing the right thing well, without waste

First, we must begin with the external environment. The organization must constantly make attempts to understand customer needs and determine levels of satisfaction with products and services, relationships and other supply issues. The organization must also consider the views of other stakeholders such as investors, and their views of the organization. In analyzing the industry, the organization will want to know where it ranks in the industry compared with its competitors; it will also want to know whether it has the right technology, people or other resources necessary to meet customer needs. Having looked inside and outside the organization, it must ask if they are still in the right business and doing the right things or whether there is a need for change. If a need for change is identified the organization must also consider how ready it is for such change. This will mean examining culture and then determining whether they are locked into particular ways of doing things. There are many *types of change* distinguished according to a variety of variables:

- *Discontinuous versus continuous/revolutionary (second-order) versus evolutionary (first order)* – change may occur continuously in order to improve the organization by modifying existing systems or may take place in a more radical and fundamental way (revolutionary). The phrase *episodic change* is used to group together organizational changes that tend to be infrequent, discontinuous and intentional. Such changes arise as a result of the organization's inability to respond to external environmental changes adequately.
- *Planned versus unplanned* – planned change is a deliberate, conscious decision to improve the organization in some manner.
- *Organizational level: individual, group or total system* – at the individual level, the focus of attention is on activities such as recruitment, replacement and displacement, training and development, coaching and counselling. At the group level, the focus is on teambuilding and self-directed work units. At the total system level, the emphasis is on organizational purpose, mission, strategy, structure of culture.

As a first step toward understanding organizational change, we must identify types of organizational change (Nadler and Tushman 1989). They argue change can be considered in two dimensions. The first is the scope of the change – that is, subsystems of the organization versus the entire system. Changes which focus on individual components, with the goal of maintaining or regaining congruence, are incremental changes. For example, adapting reward systems to changing labour market conditions is an incremental change. Changes that address the whole organization, including strategy, are strategic changes. Incremental changes are made within the context, or frame, of the current set of organizational strategies and components. They do not address fundamental changes in the definition of the business, shifts of power, alterations in culture, and similar issues. Strategic changes alter that frame. The second dimension of change concerns the positioning of the change in relation to key external events. Some changes are clearly in response to an event

©iStockphoto.com/Cristina Almeida

Revolutionary change modifies existing systems in radical and fundamental ways

or series of events. These are called relative (reactive) changes. Other changes are initiated, not in response to events but in anticipation of external events that may occur. These are called anticipatory (proactive) changes. Four classes of change are the result:

- *Tuning* – proactive incremental change which seeks to increase *efficiency*.
- *Adaptation* – non-fundamental reactive incremental change made in response to external events such as the actions of a competitor, changes in market needs or new technology.
- *Reorientation* (frame-bending changes) – proactive strategic (fundamental) change – the emphasis on bringing about major change without a sharp break with the existing organization frame.
- *Recreation* (frame-breaking changes) – strategic change necessitated by external events, usually ones that threaten the very existence of the organization Such changes require a radical departure from the past and include shifts in senior leadership, values, strategy and culture.

Intensity relates to the severity of the change and, in particular, the degree of shock, upset, or discontinuity created throughout the organization. Strategic changes are obviously more intense than incremental changes, which can frequently be implemented without altering an organization's basic management processes. Reactive changes are more intense than anticipatory changes because of the necessity of identifying and implementing change in a short period of time without the opportunity to prepare people to deal with the interruption. There is also less room for mistake. Relative intensity is further affected by organizational complexity. Organizations become more difficult to change as they increase in complexity – complexity determined by:

1 size of the organization in terms of employees; and
2 the diversity of the organization in terms of the number of different businesses and geographic dispersion.

Smaller organizations, with a few highly related businesses are easier places in which to implement changes than are larger, highly diverse organizations. The least difficult changes are those that are low intensity and take place in fairly noncomplex settings. The most difficult changes are those that are high intensity (strategic) and take place in highly complex settings. Recreations are the most risky and traumatic form of change. The different types of organizational change require different approaches, tools and techniques if they are to be accomplished successfully. Many scholars and practitioners also distinguish between the content and process of organization change. Content has to do with purpose, mission, strategy, values and what the organization is all about – or should be about. Process has to do with *how* the change was planned, launched, more fully implemented, and, once into implementation, sustained. We revisit the concept of change-difficulty in the final section.

STOP & THINK

What do you think may cause organizational change to happen? In answering, you should draw on Chapter 2 in particular.

Gap analysis identification of discrepancies between the current position and the desired future position

Visioning mental process in which images of the desired future (goals, objectives, outcomes) are made explicit motivators for action

As has been noted already, much change starts with shifts in an organization's environment, see Figure 5-1. There may be changes in the social, cultural and demographic environment, new technologies may become available, and the external political landscape may change as might economic or environmental forces. In some cases an environmental change will have a significant and in other cases a minor impact upon the organization. Gap analysis and visioning are among the tools that help instigate change. Gap analysis is used by change leaders to frame the vision for the change. Change may be triggered by competitor actions, public complaints, or the fact that organizational members are no longer happy with how the organization is performing. Changes in the external environment cause organizations to consider what to change in their organization to meet new challenges and to survive as an organization. In some cases there will be a need for significant (transformational) and in other cases less significant (transactional) change.

Failure may arise when organizations merely conduct minor changes when more fundamental change is called for from the environment. Such problems are more likely in successful organizations which are likely to hold onto their assumptions for too long. Studies suggest that greater success typically leads to greater strategic resistance after a radical environmental change and such persistence results in a performance decline.

Transformational change a fundamental change impacting upon the whole organization (the leader, mission, strategy and culture)

Transactional change changes to components of the organization such as the structure, systems and processes

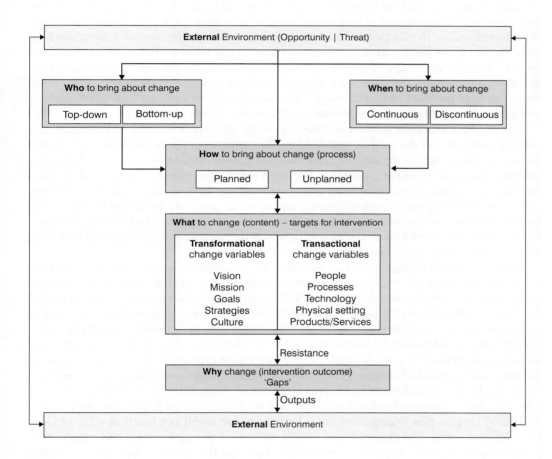

Figure 5-1
Generic change model

Figure 5-1 shows the environment as a driver for change – a source of opportunity and threat, mediated through individuals who then see a need to change aspects within the organization as a result of the external changes. In some cases the change initiators are the senior managers (top down change) and in other cases may be managers, professionals or employees from lower levels within the organization (bottom-up change). Change may also be initiated by external consultants or other employees employed by the MNC. Change may occur as a 'one-off' activity or may be viewed as a constant process of alignment and pursuit for efficiency. In some cases the change will be formally planned, typically using rational tools and techniques and in other cases will simply emerge from the day-to-day activities and decisions of the organizational members.

As we said earlier, there are many aspects of the organization that can be changed – some more fundamental than others. Change managers differentiate between major or transformational change or less major transactional change. Examples of transformational

Look back
See chapter 2, p. 46

and transactional targets for intervention are shown in Figure 5-1. Change is initiated for a reason – there is a need for the change. In some cases the need is more obvious than other cases. In the case of the model shown in Figure 5-1 we could have shown the 'Why change' box directly beneath the environment. We have shown it further down the model to emphasis a need to demonstrate the need for change in order to overcome resistance, particularly emanating from the recipients of change. We will consider each aspect of the model in the remainder of the chapter but for now focus on recognizing and building the need for change.

Building the need for change

In many cases, the need for change will derive from an evaluation of organizational outputs (products and services), where it operates, what it does (primary activities) and how it performs such activities (work). Some people may consider the current way of working to be *ineffective* or *inefficient* or may consider that such ways of working will become ineffective or inefficient in the future. The need for change is the pressure for change in the situation – sometimes the pressure is high (typically a problem of ineffectiveness), other times lower (a problem of inefficiency). This need can be viewed as a 'real need' demonstrated by data and facts or a 'perceived need' seen by change participants.

Look back
See chapter 4

The need for change will often be based upon the analysis of internal and external data or the perspectives of the various *stakeholders*, the concerns of senior managers and change leaders in particular. In the case of data analysis, it is important to note that alternative interpretations are frequently possible. The need for change may arise from a crisis, commanding a *reactive approach* or from *proactive* thinking. In some cases it will result from new opportunities to do things differently and in other cases will be driven by threat, the failures of some existing system or approach to work. It is important to make such distinctions as they will impact upon the ease with which the argument for change can be based; the need for change being clearer in the case of a crisis.

Once a need for change has been identified by a change initiator, it will then become important to direct the organization's attention to change (change awareness) and gain support for it. In many cases there is likely to be confusion and disagreement over the need for change, what needs changing, when and how to bring about change. It is important to recognize the different perspectives on change which will be dependent upon the stakeholder type considered and if this is an employee, where they sit within the organization. Change leaders need to consider multiple perspectives if they are to create a consensus on the need and method of change. Not only must they consider multiple perspectives, they must also be able to influence and persuade others of the problem and possible solutions, but must also be prepared to listen to others and modify their own thoughts in the process.

Inertia the tendency of an organization to remain as it is (the status quo), unless acted upon by a significant force

Sull (1999) argues that organizations may become unsuccessful as a result of inertia (doing more of the same), complacency and flawed analysis. Existing routines and capabilities, power structures, and entrenched perceptions regarding the nature of business are among the sources of inertia (Grant 2007: 279). Once the rigidities of the status quo are known, the organization can commence and guide change.

Having established the *need* for change, change initiators should then consider whether the organization is in fact ready for change. Creating awareness for the need for change can help make the organization ready. Creating awareness of the need for change is normally accomplished by presenting the evidence. There are, however, other ways of heightening awareness or establishing the need for change such as creating dissatisfaction with the status quo or creating a crisis, developing stretching goals or a vision that create dissatisfaction with the status quo or by bringing in a transformational leader who will build awareness of the need for change. One way of ensuring people recognize the need for change is to focus on the factors that may prevent such recognition or fuel resistance to change. Past success and the existing culture may well impede attempts to enhance awareness of the need for change. One of the ways to enhance the perceived need for change is to create a powerful vision for change.

Look back
See chapter 3

As was mentioned in Chapter 2, it is important for organizational members to personally identify with such a vision if they are to actively engage in bringing the change to fruition. Good change visions are:

- Clear;
- Unforgettable;
- Pragmatic;
- Inspiring; and
- Demanding
- (CUPID).

In addition, change leaders and agents will typically form partnerships in order to increase pressures for change (see coalition building). Other factors that may impede change include the existing structure and systems of the organization. Formal systems and structures significantly influence where, how and why decisions are made and what action ensues. They play important coordination, communication and control roles. It is important to understand how existing structures and systems are currently influencing outcomes and how they are likely to facilitate or impede the proposed change. In order to do this, we must be able to make sense of organizational structures and systems.

Parts III and IV of this book are presented to help the reader achieve this. Thus far, we have identified what we mean by organizational change and discussed how the organization identifies the *need* for change. In the next section we focus on the theoretical foundations of *what* to change and *how* to bring change about in the organization.

Coalition building the forming of partnerships to increase pressures for or against change

Theories of change

A theory is a logical explanation of something. Theories are constructed in order to explain, predict and master things. In many instances theories are contained within constructed models of reality. In the context of change management we expect theory to explain and make organizational change comprehensible. The theory and practice of change management draws on a number of social science disciplines and traditions.

The *individual* perspective school focus on behaviour resulting from an individual's interaction with their environment (both internally and externally). At the individual level, change approaches may consider motivation, expectancy and job satisfaction theory (see Maslow, Vroom and Lawler, Hertzberg and Hackman and Oldham).

The *group* dynamics school emphasizes bringing about organizational change through teams or workgroups rather than individuals arguing that individual behaviour is a function of the group in its environment. To bring about change, therefore it is useless to concentrate on changing the behaviour of individuals, according to the group dynamics school. The focus of change must be at the group level and should concentrate on influencing and changing group norms, roles and values.

Look forward
See chapter 6

The open *systems* school consider the organization in its entirety viewing organizations as composed of a number of interconnected subsystems. A change to one part of the system will have an impact upon other parts of the system. The emphazis is on achieving overall synergy rather than optimizing the performance of any individual part. The three aforementioned schools each contribute to change management theory. The appropriateness of each school of thinking will be dependent upon circumstances.

To understand organizational change, we must begin with some basics about organizations. An organization is a social arrangement for achieving controlled performance in pursuit of collective goals. Organization theory is the study of the structure, functioning and performance of organizations and the behaviour of groups and individuals within them. Any human organization is best understood as an open system. An organization is open because of its dependence on and continual interaction with the environment in which it operates. To consider organizational change, it is important to take a total system perspective.

Open system (view) considers the organisation's structures, systems, processes and external environment to be interrelated and able to affect one another

Systems are conceived as a set of interrelated parts that take inputs and transform them into outputs. In many cases it will be a part of the organization system that will be selected for change as a result of diagnosis. However, when some aspect of a system is changed, other aspects will eventually be affected, thus calling for a total system approach. A failure to consider other parts of a system during any change initiative is likely to result in a failure of the change initiative.

We will first discuss systems theory as an important foundation for several change theories. Then we consider a variety of change models put forward to help us understand *what* can be changed and *how*.

Systems theory

Whereas scientific method increases our knowledge and understanding by breaking things down into their constituent parts and exploring the properties of these parts, systems thinking explores the properties which exist once the parts have been combined into a whole. A system is a set of elements connected together which form a whole, thereby possessing properties of the whole rather than of its component parts. Systems are not chains of linear cause-and-effect relationships but complex networks of interrelationships. Senge (1996) argues that we must recognize that everything is interconnected. Systems theory is the study of the behaviour and interactions *within* and *between* systems. It is a theory that sees our world in terms of 'systems', where each system is a 'whole' that is more than the sum of its parts, but also itself a 'part' of larger systems; it is a framework by which one can analyze and/or describe any group of objects that work in concert to produce some result.

In a *systems approach* to a problem, one starts by realizing that there is no inherent end to a system. Using systems thinking, we can learn to handle complex tasks and cause more good things to happen in our organization (Senge 1996). The systems framework is fundamental to organizational theory as organizations are complex dynamic goal-oriented processes. In recent years, systems thinking has been developed to provide techniques for studying systems in holistic ways. The systems approach gives primacy to the interrelationships, not to the elements of the system.

In Chapter 1, we referenced Porter's value chain, a model that emphasized the linkages between the primary activities of organizations. In this chapter, starting with the work of Kurt Lewin, we note many of the change theories are based on systems thinking. Systems are described as closed or open. Closed systems are completely autonomous and independent of what is going on around them. *Open systems* exchange materials, energy and information with their environment. Figure 5-1 depicts change in an open system. The systems of interest in managing change can all be characterized as open systems.

Applied to change management, systems theory highlights the following:

■ a system is made up of related and interdependent parts, so that any system must be viewed as a whole;

■ a system cannot be considered in isolation from its environment and the actors within a system have a view of that system's function and purpose;

■ actors' views may be very different from each other.

Systems thinking is also used widely in management information systems theory (see for example the work of Peter Checkland) and will be considered in Chapter 11. Next we introduce various change theories and models to explain how we determine *what* to change and *how* to bring about change. Many of the theories incorporate systems theory and in some cases adopt an open systems perspective as will be seen in the following sections.

Organizational change models

A model is a representation to show the construction or appearance of or explain something. An organizational model can be useful in a number of ways. It can help to categorize,

Systems thinking a holistic approach to analysis that focuses on the way a system's constituent parts interrelate and how systems work over time and within the context of larger systems

System a set of elements connected together which form a whole, thereby possessing properties of the whole rather than of its component parts

Systems theory the study of the behaviour and interactions within and between systems

Organizational theory the study of the structure, functioning and performance of organizations and the behaviour of groups and individuals within them

Look back
See p. 143

Model a representation to show the construction or appearance of or explain something aid understanding and focus attention. An organizational model can also help to diagnose problems and guide action for change, identifying targets for change and the sequence of priorities, enabling the organization to create a roadmap and implementation strategy. However, the use of models can also restrict thinking and may result in a lack of attention to certain components and blinkered vision. We have discussed different *models* in each of the chapters presented thus far. In this section we focus on a particular type – the change model. Managers must decide *what* and where to change, *how* to change and, they should also consider *why* and when change may be required. Such matters were outlined in the Figure 5-1. In this section we consider *what* and *how* to change, using a range of theories.

The change process begins with an assessment of why change is needed. Following the recognition of the need for change, change leaders are faced with the task of defining and describing the desired future state in contrast to the organization now in existence. This allows leaders to identify the *gap* between where we are now and where we want to go. The vision, contrasted against the present, allows change leaders to address how they propose to close the gap. There are many models used to help with organizational change. Models are comprised of components and it is those components that present potential targets for intervention. Typical components include people, technology, organizing arrangements (such as goals, strategies, structure and systems), social factors such as culture and physical work settings such as location and interior design.

Many models indicate how organizations operate and what the key elements are in that operation. Models can be used to help us understand the organization (see for example the value chain), to help us understand what to change and how to intervene or to help us understand change itself. If the required change is discontinuous, then we need to concentrate on the organization's interface with its external environment (mission, and goals, strategy and culture) as targets for change. In the case of continuous change our focus may be on different targets in the organization such as technology, processes or management practices. How we think about an organization will determine what we think needs changing.

Analysis may focus on different parts or levels of the organization and may be presented from a variety of perspectives such as the economist, psychologist or technologist. A variety of models exist to help managers develop a sense of what needs to change in their organization; such models enable the organization to be analyzed and consider the organization's strategy, how it fits with the changing environment and how the various components of the organization also fit with the strategy and the environment. We develop an appreciation of *what* to change, through the use of models of organizational analysis such as the McKinsey 7-S model, the Nadler and Tushman congruence framework and the Burke-Litwin model. In this chapter, we also consider Sterman's systems dynamic model and Greiner's model of organizational growth. Such models help us structure our thinking.

One way of thinking about organizational components and their alignment with the environment can be found in the McKinsey 7-S model – explained by Peters and Waterman (1982: 10). The components of this model include: strategy, structure, systems, style, staff, shared values and skills. The underlying thesis of the model is that organizational effectiveness is a function of the degree of 'fit' achieved among these factors and the environment. When organizations experience change, the degree of 'fit' is affected, and the challenge of change management is to make changes so that high levels of 'fit' among the seven elements can be achieved. Changes to one of the components can affect all the other components.

The organizational system model proposed by Leavitt (1965) is made of four major components:

- task (the organization's purpose);
- people (those who carry out the task);
- technology (tools and computers, etc.); and
- structure.

Change model an abstract representation describing the content or process of changes

McKinsey 7-S model a model for organizational analysis and dynamics including components: strategy, structure, systems, style, staff, shared values and skills

Nadler and Tushman congruence model view of organizations as a set of internal, transformational, components that must be congruent with each other and the organization's strategy and environment

Burke-Litwin model a causal model of transformational and transactional organizational variables represented in an open system

Sterman's systems dynamic model a representation describing organizations as interactive, dynamic and non-linear

Greiner's model of organizational growth a generalized representation of change associated with organizational growth phases

Table 5.1

McKinsey 7-S model

The Hard Ss	
Strategy	Actions a company plans in response to or in anticipation of changes in its external environment.
Structure	Basis for specialization and coordination influenced primarily by strategy and by organization size and diversity.
Systems	Formal and informal procedures which support the strategy and structure.
The Soft Ss	
Style/Culture	The culture of the organization, consisting of two sub-components: Organizational culture: the dominant values and beliefs, and norms which develop over time and become relatively enduring features of organizational life. Management style.
Staff	The people/human resource management – processes used to develop employees, recruitment and socialization processes.
Skills	The distinctive competences – what the company does best, ways of developing competences.
Shared Values/ Goals	Guiding concepts, fundamental ideas around which a business is built.

Figure 5-2

The organizational system model

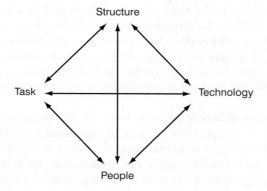

The components are interdependent of one another and a change in any one of the components will result in change among the other three, he argues. This model, see Figure 5-2, is grounded in systems thinking but is not based on open system theory, i.e. forces in the external environment are not modelled.

A decade later, Nadler and Tushman developed their *congruence* model for diagnosing organizational behaviour, see Figure 5-3. Recognizing the organization is influenced by its environment, their model took account of both systems and open system theory. Nadler and Tushman (1989) divided their model into inputs, process and outputs. Their (transformation or internal) process contained similar components to the model proposed by Leavitt. Inputs came from the environment including organizational history and current strategy which help define how people in the organization behave. Nadler and Tushman also argued a need for the transformational process components to be congruent or 'fit' with each other. Nadler and Tushman (1989) did however recognize that such congruence may present advantages and disadvantages. In the short term, a system with high congruence is an effective and performing system, however such a system may be resistant to change. Their model suggests there is no one best way to organize. Rather, the most effective way of organizing is determined by the nature of the strategy as well as the work, the individuals who are members of the organization, and the informal processes and structures (including culture) which have emerged over time.

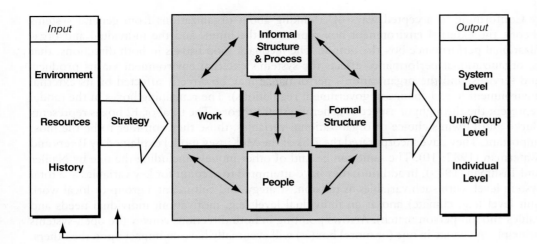

Figure 5-3
Organization model (Source:
Nadler and Tushman (1989))

Critically evaluate the three models presented in the preceding text.

STOP & THINK

Thus far we have reviewed the 7-S, Leavitt and Nadler and Tushman models. Each of which has inherent strengths and weaknesses. The strengths of the 7-S model are its description of organizational variables which convey obvious importance – strategy, structure, systems, etc. – and its recognition of the importance of the interrelationships among all of these seven variables, or dimensions. The 7-S model, on the other hand, does not contain any external environment or performance variables. The model is a description of these seven important elements and shows that they interact to create organizational patterns but there is no explication of how these seven dimensions are affected by the external environment. Nor do we know how each dimension affects the other or what specific performance indices may be involved. The Leavitt model adopts a systems theory perspective but does not incorporate open systems theory, i.e. takes no account of the external environment. Finally, the Nadler and Tushman model overcomes many of the aforementioned shortfalls, however, one criticism of this model is that a system which is highly congruent, may in fact be resistant to change as it develops ways of insulating itself from outside influences.

More recently Burke and Litwin (1992) presented a more complex model of organizational performance and change. Their model has its roots in the organizational climate studies previously conducted by Litwin and his colleagues. The model, see Figure 5-4, conforms to the open system way of thinking, with the external environment represented as an input. The authors go beyond description and suggest causal linkages that hypothesize how performance is affected and how effective change occurs. Change is depicted in terms of both process and content, with particular emphasis on transformational compared with transactional factors. Transformational change occurs as a response to the external environment and directly affects organizational mission and strategy, the organization's leadership, and culture. In turn, the transactional factors are affected – structure systems, management practices, and climate. These transformational and transactional factors together affect motivation, which, in turn, affects performance. Through their model, Burke and Litwin attempt to provide a causal framework that encompasses both the what and the how – what organizational dimensions are key to successful change and how these dimensions should be linked causally to achieve the change goals. Burke and Litwin incorporated dimensions from earlier models, in one form or another, their model. Interestingly, both the 7-S and the Burke and Litwin models were informed by consulting practice.

Organizational climate the prevailing atmosphere surrounding the organization – the level of morale and strength of feelings or belonging, care and goodwill among members. Organizational climate is based on the perceptions of members towards the organization

Conforming to accepted ways of' thinking about organizations from general systems theory, the external environment box represents the input, and the individual and organizational performance box the output. The feedback loop travels in both directions: that is, organizational performance affects the system's external environment via its products and services, and the organization's performance may be directly affected by its external environment (e.g. a change in government regulations). The remaining boxes in the model represent the throughput aspect of general systems theory. The total of 12 boxes represents Burke and Litwin's choice of organizational variables, those they consider to be the most important. They have incorporated the 7-Ss of the McKinsey model explained by Peters and Waterman (1982: 10). The same can be said of other models, including the one by Nadler and Tushman (1989). In addition, they have attempted to account for key variables at a total system level, with such variables as mission, strategy, and culture, at a group or local work unit level (e.g. climate) and at an individual level (e.g. motivation, individual needs and values and job-person match). Arrows pointing in both directions convey the open-systems principle. A change in one (or more) box(es) will eventually have an impact upon the others. The transformational-transactional way of thinking about organizations that Burke and Litwin use for the model, comes from leadership theory to be discussed in the next chapter.

With regard to the model, and in keeping with the leader (transformational)-manager (transactional) distinctions, transformational change is therefore associated more with leadership, whereas transactional change is more within the purview of management. For major organizational change to occur, the top transformational boxes represent the primary and significant levers for that change. For organizations where the problems are more of a fine tuning, improving process; the second layer of the model serves as the point of concentration.

Figure 5-4

A model of organizational performance and change (Source: Burke and Litwin (1992))

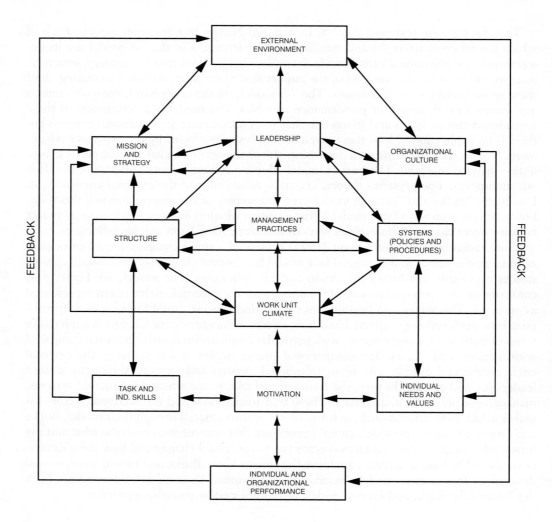

Whichever model is used, we must not allow it to determine exclusively what we diagnose or how we handle organization change. We cannot afford to allow the model to become ideology, as Morgan (1986) has warned, and that our 'way of seeing is a way of not seeing' (Morgan 1986: 73). The models described thus far focus on organizational components and the way such components 'fit' together and in some cases, the way they 'fit' with the external environment. Some theorists have attempted to explain organizational change over *time*. Greiner (1972) describes evolution and revolutions as organizations grow, presenting a five-phased model of organizational growth (see the related models of the industry and product life cycle). He suggests that organizations pass through five generic phases as the organization increases in both *size* and *age*. Each stage is associated with both evolutionary and revolutionary change. Over time, incremental changes in how we think about and how we operate the business become less effective; increasingly, the internal and external environments become less congruent, i.e. aspects of the organization become increasingly asynchronous with the environment. Eventually the pressure builds up to drive a more radical and transformational change.

The small and young organization grows through creativity, eventually facing a crisis of leadership and change ensues. With better leadership and direction, further growth is attained and the organization grows larger and more mature. With increased size comes the problem of too much work being centralized and eventually a crisis of autonomy resulting in change that seeks to empower employees, resulting in growth through delegation. However, this then creates a problem of control and changes are made to improve coordination. In some cases the organization may become overly bureaucratic, resulting in changes such as delayering and deformalizing the organization. This is then followed by growth enabled through collaboration. The model presented by Greiner (1972) is a simplistic one that can explain change associated with organizational growth and transition. However, it should be noted that not all organizations follow the pattern suggested and organizations need not develop as Greiner claims.

In this section we have briefly described several change models to help the organization diagnose what (and in some cases how) to change. In the next section we consider a range of models which influence the thinking of change managers on *how* to bring change about.

How to change

As was the case in Chapter 3 (Strategy), two main approaches to change management have been suggested in the literature: a *planned* and an *emergent* approach. The former tends to see change management as a formal, top-down, rational and pre-planned process while the latter sees change management as a disordered, bottom-up, less rational and ongoing emergent process. Like strategy formation we will observe that, up until the 1980s, the *planned* approach dominated change management thinking. However, researchers observed the difficulties in applying such approaches in ever increasing dynamic and turbulent environments (typical of the 1990s and of the present day). In such environments, many scholars argue *emergent* approaches and continuous transformation models of change to be more appropriate. As with strategy, the emergent approach has not replaced but competes with or complements the planned approach in different organizational contexts.

Look back
See chapter 3, p. 81

In the 1940s and 1950s, Kurt Lewin concluded that to be successful, the change process needs to follow a three-step procedure:

- unfreezing;
- moving; and
- refreezing.

His theories were later expanded by Schein who described the three stages as:

1 *unfreezing* – creating motivation and readiness to change by demonstrating a need and vision for change in a manner that would not result in the blame being associated with the managers who had let the organization deteriorate;

2 *changing* – organizational members identify with a new model or way of doing things; and

3 *refreezing* – refreezing must occur at the individual level with employees accepting new behaviours and also at the interpersonal and interdepartmental levels ensuring new behaviours fit well with the rest of the organization.

Since Lewin volunteered his model, several scholars have developed adaptations. Lewin's three stages of change – unfreeze, change, and refreeze – continue to be a generic recipe for organizational development.

Figure 5-5

Three-staged change process

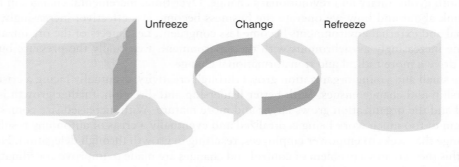

Unfreeze   Change   Refreeze

Look back
See p. 113

Force-field analysis a process of identifying and analyzing the driving and restraining forces associated with a change

Resistance to change the desire not to pursue change

Many change agents use force-field analysis as an analytical tool to understand the *dynamics* of change. It is used in conjunction with stakeholder analysis. For any organization that wants to implement a change, there are a number of forces operating within the organization and environment that make such change desirable. Opposed to the forces for change are the forces resisting change, representing forces in favour of maintaining the status quo. Changes seen as a threat to individuals will lead to resistance.

Forces opposing change can take a number of forms and may also come from within or outside the organization. Some of the most common pressures to maintain the status quo are prior commitments to other businesses, obligations to consumers, and government regulations. One of the most likely internal reasons given for why a change cannot be implemented is limited organizational resources. Such limitations of resources may be valid and may restrict the range of alternatives that can be realistically considered; labour relations in unionized organizations represent another potentially powerful force resisting change. Furthermore, the extent of resistance is determined by the type of change pursued. Movement from the present to a future desirable state requires that forces for the change exceed forces resisting the change. Movement can be achieved by:

1 increasing the forces for the change; or

2 reducing the forces opposing the change.

Increasing one set of forces without decreasing the other set of forces will likely increase tension and the degree of conflict. Thus, reducing forces against change is usually seen as preferable to applying greater pressure for change. Development of a 'felt' need for change may enable an organization to 'unfreeze' or reduce forces resisting change. There are many strategies to overcome resistance. When those people affected and those who are pushing for the change feel that they are members of the same group, opposition to change is reduced. Participation and collaboration are commonly used techniques to make employees feel that they are part of the group *proposing* the change. Coercion may also be used to bring about change. As was discussed earlier, overpowering resistance tends to increase resisting forces and may result in conflict and tension. Sometimes changes must be implemented quickly to avoid highly undesirable events. However, caution should be applied when considering the use of financial rewards to encourage change as this may result in unethical behaviour (refer to Chapter 4). Finally, the change manager should remain

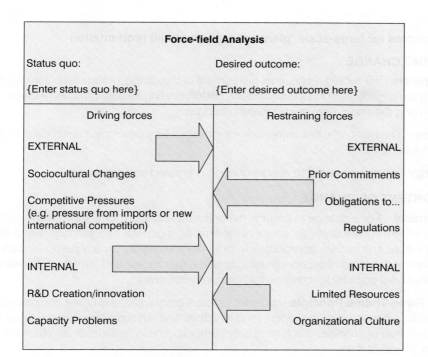

Figure 5-6
Force-field analysis

alert to the fact that some counter-resistance tactics may simply force change through in the short term only for old ways to return later.

Building on participative and consensus building approaches, stakeholder analysis, in this context, is the identification of those who can affect the change or those who are affected by the change. It enables the change agent to identify those people to focus or concentrate on. This integrative perspective assumes that an effective change requires consensus from a plurality of key stakeholders about what it should be doing and how these things should be done. The change agent (discussed in more detail later) may want to identify who has the authority to say 'yes' or 'no' to the change, which departments are likely to be affected and who manages those departments, who must change their behaviour in order to make the change successful and who can help make the change a success. *Stakeholder management* is the explicit influence of critical participants in the change process. The power to do things in organizations is critical to achieving change and change agents need to understand and influence the reactions and actions of others. In short, power is required to make things happen. There are many methods to influence and persuade others and sources of power available to individuals within the organization and we consider them in the next chapter.

Change agent any person seeking to promote, further, support, sponsor, initiate, implement or help to deliver change within the organization

Planned and emergent change approaches

Thus far we have discussed what is meant by change and distinguished types of change such as radical (transformational, discontinuous or frame bending/replacing) and less major change (continuous improvement, transactional). Generally, change scholars and practitioners associate 'planned' approaches with the former and 'emergent' approaches with the latter. Planned approaches are more likely to make use of the change models, tools and techniques discussed thus far. Nadler and Tushman (1989) provide advice, through ten principles, and guidance for large-scale, long-term organizational reorientation – effective organizational frame bending (reorientation) – see inset (next page).

Ten principles for large-scale 'planned' organizational reorientation

INITIATING CHANGE

P1 Diagnosis (The 'what') – concerns the content of the change: diagnostic thinking involves analyzing the organization in its environment, understanding its strengths and weaknesses, and analyzing the implication of anticipated changes.

P2 Vision – The most effective reorientations include a fully developed description of the desired future state.

P3 Energy – Must be created to ensure change is initiated and executed.

THE CONTENT OF CHANGE

P4 Centrality – For a change to engage the entire organization, it must be clearly and obviously linked to the core strategic issues of the firm. As a general rule, managers of a change can only initiate and sustain approximately three key themes during any particular period of time. Employees are bombarded with programmes, messages, and directives. In many situations, individuals cope by ignoring certain company initiatives.

P5 The Three-Theme Principle – In order to focus employees and better communicate changes, as a general rule, managers tend to initiate and sustain approximately three key themes (the hub of changes) such as quality competitiveness, or innovation, etc., during any particular period of time.

LEADING CHANGE

P6 Magic Leader – Large-scale organizational change requires active and visible leadership to help articulate the change and to capture and mobilize the hearts and minds of the people in the organization. Such leaders are enablers – helping to create the processes, resources, or structures that enable employees to do the things they have been motivated to do.

P7 Leadership-Is-Not-Enough – Success depends on a broader base of support built with other individuals who act first as followers, second as helpers, and finally as co-owners of the change.

ACHIEVING and SUSTAINING CHANGE

P8 Planning-and-Opportunism – Successful reorientations involve a mix of planning and unplanned opportunistic action.

P9 Many-Bullets – Effective reorientations make use of as many different devices as possible to change behaviour (changes in strategy, the definition of work, structure, informal process, and individual skills – along with attitudes and perceptions. Rewards and incentives; Standards and measure of performance; Planning processes; Budgeting and resource allocation methods and Information systems).

P10 Investment-and-Return – Large-scale, significant organizational change requires significant investment of time, effort, and cash.

NADLER AND TUSHMAN (1989)

We have summarized a 'planned' approach to change in Figure 5-7. Models of planned organization change depict the process in a linear, step-by-step fashion. However, what actually occurs in reality is anything but linear. The implementation process is disordered: things do not proceed exactly as planned and people will do things in their own way and not in accordance with the plan. Episodic change is driven by inertia and the inability of organizations to keep up, while *continuous change* is driven by alertness and the inability of organizations to remain stable (Weick and Quinn 1999). Lewin's change model, with its assumptions of inertia, linearity, progressive development, goal seeking, disequilibrium as motivator, and outsider intervention, is relevant when it is necessary to create change. However, when change is continuous, the problem is not one of unfreezing. The problem is one of redirecting what is already under way. In the face of inertia, it makes sense to

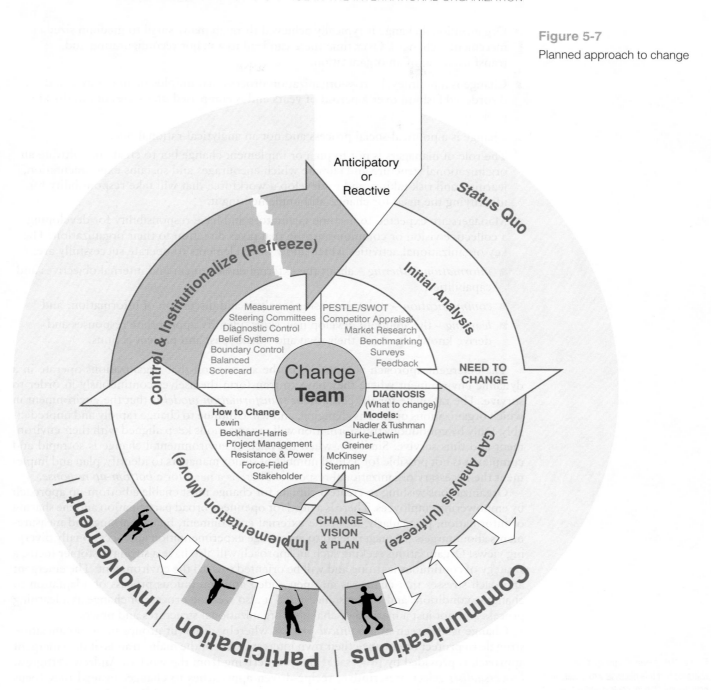

Figure 5-7
Planned approach to change

view a change intervention as a sequence of unfreeze, transition, refreeze. However in the face of continuous change, applying unfreeze, transition, refreeze will be inappropriate and ineffective.

There are a number of different labels for more recent perspectives on change such as the continuous transformation models. Collectively they are often referred to as emergent approaches. Supporters of emergent change tend to be united more by their disbelief in planned change than by a commonly agreed alternative. Nevertheless, there does seem to be some agreement regarding the main view of what constitutes emergent (evolving) change:

■ Organizational change is a continuous process of experimentation and adaptation, aimed at matching an organization's capabilities to the demands of a dynamic and uncertain environment.

Emergent change a view that organizational change is a continuous process of experimentation and adaptation achieved through many small to medium sized incremental changes

- Organizational change is typically achieved through many small to medium sized incremental changes. Over time these can lead to a major reconfiguration and transformation of an organization.

- Change is a multilevel, cross-organization process that unfolds in an iterative and disordered fashion over a period of years and is comprised of a series of interlocking projects.

- Change is a political-social process and not an analytical-rational one.

- The role of managers is not to plan or implement change but to create or cultivate an organizational structure and climate which encourages and sustains experimentation, learning and risk taking, and to develop a workforce that will take responsibility for identifying the need for change and implementing it.

- Managers are expected to become facilitators and have responsibility for developing a collective vision or common purpose that gives direction to their organization. The key organizational activities which allow these elements to operate successfully are:

  - *information gathering* – about the external environment and internal objectives and capabilities;

  - *communication* – the transmission, analysis and discussion of information; and

  - *learning* – the ability to develop new skills, identify appropriate responses and derive knowledge from their own and others' past and present actions.

The emergent approach is founded on the assumption that organizations operate in a dynamic environment where they have to transform themselves continuously in order to survive. The rationale for the *continuous transformation model* is that the environment in which organizations operate is changing, and will continue to change rapidly and unpredictably. Only by continuous transformation will organizations keep aligned with their environment and thus survive. Similarly, when the pace of environmental change is so rapid and complex it is not possible for a small number of senior managers to identify, plan and implement the necessary organizational response. There is a need for a *bottom-up response*.

Organizations wishing to create a climate for change must enable a bottom-up approach by empowering employees. There is a need for openness, broad participation and the sharing of information, particularly about the external environment, benchmarking and measurements about targets. Managers need to encourage experimentation and occasionally diverging views. Organizations seeking such an approach will also have a strong customer focus, a strategy of continuous learning and will be oriented toward the environment. The emergent approach stresses that change is an open ended and continuous process of adaptation to changing conditions and circumstances; and it also sees the process of change as a learning process and not just a method of changing organizational structures and practices.

Change is also seen as a *political* process whereby different groups in an organization struggle to protect or enhance their own interests. One of the main strands of the emergent approach is provided by processual analysts deriving from the work of Andrew Pettigrew. *Processualists* reject prescriptive, recipe-driven approaches to change. Instead they focus on the interrelatedness of individuals, groups, organizations and the wider environment. For Pettigrew, change cuts across functions, and hierarchical divisions, and has no neat starting or finishing point. Instead it is a complex analytical, political and cultural process of challenging and changing the core beliefs, structure and strategy of the organization.

The organizational structure, culture, learning, managerial behaviour, power and politics can all be used to drive or hinder the change process. Dynamic and chaotic environments require organizations to adopt more flexible structures. Many would argue that an organization with more delegation, i.e. a flat hierarchy, is in a better position to manoeuvre. Organizations need to be flexible to allow new organizational structures to emerge. Learning plays a key role in preparing people for and allowing them to cope with change. Information, particularly in the form of measurements and performance indicators can be used to identify problem areas and act as a motivator for change (refer back to the opening case study). The affective organization is one which encourages and supports learning

Processual theory a perspective claiming that it is necessary to understand how the substance, context and process of organizational change interact to generate the observed outcomes from change. This means that an open management style, encouraging initiative and risk, is needed. Instead of directing change from the top, managers are expected to operate as facilitators and coaches, able to bring together and empower teams and groups to identify the need for, and achieve, change in the emergent model.

Under the emergent approach, managers need leadership skills to give direction and build support, motivating people to attain goals. To be effective in this new role, managers require knowledge of strategy formulation, human resources, operations, marketing and finance. They must operate in boundary spanning roles and must be tolerant of ambiguity. An organization's ability to gather, disseminate, analyze and discuss information is crucial for successful change, from the perspective of the emergent approach. Power plays a key role in the emergent approach but it tends to be built up by coalition, by winning support from multiple stakeholders. A variety of political skills can be used to manage change and a variety of power sources can be used to influence others. The ability to utilize resources, authority, and information and to negotiate are more important and are matters we consider in the next chapter.

Implementing and managing change

Having analyzed and diagnosed the present (as-is) and the desirable future situation (vision), established and communicated the need for change and overcome prechange problems, the organization must then execute the things that will bring about the change. Change agents should organize a project, to ascertain who does what, when and how and may manage planned change through the use of project management tools and techniques. Successful change managers build a change team, develop detailed communication plans and understand how to manage the change *transition*. There is a need to mobilize commitment to change (through joint diagnosis and the development of a shared vision and fostering consensus), reduce resistance, communicate and manage the change.

We have previously mentioned the need to educate and communicate with others so that they can see the need and logic for the change. There is also a need to get others involved and participating and to allocate resources, training or time to support the change. Implementing the change involves translating the change vision into specific actions undertaken by employees. The plan outlines, targets and dates and considers contingencies. Measures are critical components of the control system which guide the change and integrate the initiatives and efforts of various parties. There are many ways to control projects, change and employee behaviour and care must be taken in selecting the methods of control and the variables to measure; noting the belief that what gets measured gets managed.

As has been identified, change presents itself in a wide variety of shapes and sizes. Consequently there are many approaches to managing change. Some forms of change are more difficult to manage than other forms, see Figure 5-8. Change difficulty is determined by change type, complexity and resistance. The more difficult the change the more time and resources required. A number of circumstances may trigger change such as performance problems and new opportunity or threat – competition will drive organizations and individuals to innovate and change. Such triggers will create *forces* for change. The forces act upon the status quo, however, there will also be forces for stability. Consequently, change agents attempt to create willingness for change by making people aware of the pressures for change. Performance feedback is used to identify areas in need of attention. Aside from considering the forces for change, the organization will seek to understand people's fears and concerns that may bring about resistance to change.

Openness helps people to understand the need for change. There is a need to gain support from people and as a consequence, many organizations develop an involvement strategy. Communication and involvement are essential to gain people's understanding of

Project an undertaking with a beginning and end, carried out to meet established goals within cost, schedule and quality objectives

Project management the combination of systems, techniques, and people used to control and monitor activities undertaken within the project – project management coordinates the resources necessary to complete the project successfully

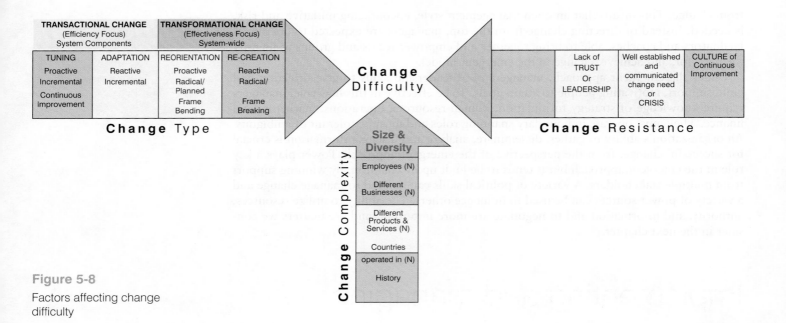

TRANSACTIONAL CHANGE (Efficiency Focus) System Components		TRANSFORMATIONAL CHANGE (Effectiveness Focus) System-wide	
TUNING	ADAPTATION	REORIENTATION	RE-CREATION
Proactive Incremental Continuous Improvement	Reactive Incremental	Proactive Radical/ Planned Frame Bending	Reactive Radical/ Frame Breaking

Change Type

Change Difficulty

	Lack of TRUST Or LEADERSHIP	Well established and communicated change need or CRISIS	CULTURE of Continuous Improvement

Change Resistance

Change Complexity

Size & Diversity

Employees (N)

Different Businesses (N)

Different Products & Services (N)

Countries operated in (N)

History

Figure 5-8

Factors affecting change difficulty

the need for change and to develop their commitment to such change. Successful change requires attention to many areas. However, Kotter and others (see Kotter (2007) Eight Steps to Transforming Your Organization) generally thought there is a need to:

- establish a sense of urgency;
- create a guiding coalition;
- develop a vision and strategy;
- communicate this with others;
- empower action;
- generate short-term wins;
- consolidate gains; and
- produce more change and anchor new approaches in the culture.

In judging the applicability of approaches to managing change, we need to assess whether they apply to individual and group or system-wide change.

Change is about replacement – one system for another, one process for another, one strategy or mission for another. There are several methods presenting options for the diffusion of changes – particularly technological changes. Parallel adoption is a method for transferring between an old to a new system in an organization. In order to reduce risk, the old and new system run simultaneously for some period of time after which, if the criteria for the new system are met, the old system is decommissioned. The process requires careful planning and control and a significant investment of resources.

There are three other diffusion or adoption methods: 'big-bang', phased, or pilot. A big-bang approach involves transferring the entire organization from the old system to the new system in an instant changeover. In phased approaches, the organization gradually changes to a new system in different phases, per module or sub-system. Finally, the pilot approach is used for large organizations that have multiple locations or large independent departments. Changes are introduced in one of the locations or departments and extended to other locations or departments over time. Each approach involves some trade-off between costs and risk.

In the remainder of this section and chapter we turn our attention to the key people involved in organizational change and consider the roles and *behaviour* of change leaders, managers, agents and recipients. The person(s) who identifies the need and vision for

In many cases, a change agent will take responsibility for ensuring that change takes place

©iStockphoto.com/Jacob Wackerhausen

change and champions the change is known as the change initiator (see also change agent or change leader); the people responsible for making change happen are change implementers; the change recipient is the person affected by the change and the change facilitators assist the three aforementioned change roles.

Change leaders and agents

Change requires decision-making and resource allocation and is therefore dependent on the will of the organization's power holders. Leaders must monitor the environment, identify and establish the need for change and provide clear direction, be persuasive and political and overcome resistance. Not only must they establish a need for change they must also communicate that need and initiate activities. Managers can identify opportunities, promote ethical behaviour, and develop capabilities within the organization in order to keep it aligned with its environment. On the other hand, they can prevent change and hold back the organization. In short they can either inhibit or facilitate change.

Typically, a change *champion* will fight for the change and senior executives will act as *sponsors*, fostering commitment to the change and helping to make it happen. In larger change initiatives, it is common to establish a steering and a design and implementation team (refer back to the opening active learning case). The steering team provide advice to the champion regarding the direction of the change in light of other events and priorities in the organization. It plays an advisory and navigational function for the change project and is the major policy determining group. The design and implementation team focuses on the tasks that must be accomplished and will deal with the stakeholders who have primary responsibility for implementation. Typically, the design and implementation team will often have a change project manager who tracks the change efforts and the team's progress towards change targets.

> What qualities and attributes do you believe typical of a good change agent? How might they differ for the internal versus the external change agent?

STOP & THINK

In many cases, more so with planned change, some person or group (change agent) will take responsibility for ensuring that change takes place. The change *agent* is any one seeking to encourage, advance, support, sponsor, implement or help to deliver change. Buchanan and Boddy (1992) list competencies of effective change agents as clarity of specifying goals, team building activities, communication skills, negotiation skills and 'influencing skills' to gain commitment to goals. However, under the emergent approach, change is not seen as a specialist activity driven by an expert but an important part of every manager's role.

Among the skills and competencies seen by some as necessary to achieve successful change are: diagnostic, communication and negotiation skills. The argument of many in the emergent school is that the complexity and multilevel nature of change mean that it cannot be left to a few experts or a few managers, but is the responsibility of everyone in the organization. Consequently there are several models of change agents:

■ leadership models emphasize the role of senior managers as change agents;
■ management models emphasize middle management;
■ consultancy models utilize consultants as change agents and team models where change agents are seen as teams who operate at various levels in the organization.

Change agents may come from within or outside the organization and may become involved at different stages of the entire change process from initial diagnosis to

Change initiator the person(s) who identifies the need and vision for and champions the change

Change implementers the person(s) who puts the change plan into practice and takes steps to assure the change vision is realized – make change happen

Change recipient individual on the receiving end of a change initiative implementation. The change agent must be able to understand the situation and in some cases will lead by creating or facilitate integration of the change vision and in other cases will ensure management of the change process. The role of the change agent shifts depending upon the type of change pursued. In some cases they will need to be persuasive, possibly drawing upon strong analytical skills. In other cases they need to be creative and with strong formal planning skills. The change leader develops the need for change and the change manager creates change by working with others, overcoming resistance and problem-solving situations. There are differences between internal and external change agents.

The internal change manager is more likely to be a facilitator capable of teambuilding, negotiation and influence. The internal change manager is more likely to focus on process management skills and act as the catalyst for change, resource linker and solution giver.

Often organizations use external change agents or consultants to promote change, as they can bring technical change management expertise to the change team. Consultants can provide a more objective external perspective on the change and provide subject matter expertise, giving credibility to the project. However, on the downside, they often come with pre-packaged solutions, insensitive to the organization's culture or needs and can be used by line managers to avoid decision-making and problem ownership.

In larger initiatives, a change team will be formed. Such a team will be knowledgeable about the business and enthusiastic about the change. They should have excellent communication skills and be both open-minded and respected.

Thus far we have considered change from the perspective of those orchestrating it and we now, in the final section, consider change from the recipient perspective.

The recipients of change

Earlier we identified the change recipient as the person affected by the change. Change recipients may be concerned about how the change will impact upon their relationships with others (the people they currently work with), their ability to do what is being asked of them and their future needs. Such concerns will result in mixed feelings about the change. How they conceive the changes will depend on their assessment of the situation. Thus, in some cases the change will be *supported* and in other cases *resisted*. Understanding resistance to change is an important part of the change process.

Resistance to change is a desire not to pursue the change and can stem from differences in the perception for the need to change. Rather than adopt a top-down approach and make attempts to impose change, change leaders should make attempts to understand the reasons for resistance. In such cases, change should be seen as a process of persuasion. Resistance is normal and may occur because the proposed change may result in a loss of something valuable or could be harmful to the *recipient*. Resistance is also likely when there are low degrees of trust between the recipient and those representing change (possibly caused by previous experiences where employees may have been 'tricked' in to change) or where employees have a different perspective as a result of their location or level in the organization. Furthermore, either as a result of skill or personality, some employees have a greater need for stability and may not be ready for change.

Some individuals may welcome change early on in the process (innovators and early adopters) while others may move with the majority and yet others wait even longer (laggards, late or non-adopters). It is thought best to encourage the public voicing of concerns in an organized manner so that they can be addressed. Change, at the organizational and individual level, is more likely to be adopted when the benefits outweigh the costs. Consequently, change leaders should not merely focus on organizational benefits but should also consider matters from the individual perspective. They should not assume automatic support simply because the organization will benefit, i.e. they must think of the impact on individuals. Strong support for change is more likely when there are positive consequences for both the organization and the individual. Individual positive consequences might include more rewarding work; improved work conditions, stability or other rewards. In many cases, recipients experience a range of emotions from opposition and resistance eventually through to support for the proposed change.

Possible coping responses may be undesirable such as absenteeism, sabotage or departure from the company. We all vary in our tolerance of ambiguity and uncertainty and in many cases this may disrupt work during a transitional period. Uncertainty creates discomfort which may be dealt with in a number of ways, including denial and a need to hold on to established ways of working. *Involving* change recipients can allow concerns to be addressed. Managing change should include efforts to facilitate recipient sense-making processes. Negative reactions occur because the recipient feels imposed upon, unprepared, negatively affected, confused or can see problems or shortcomings with the proposed change initiatives. The proposed change may affect the psychological contract between the recipient and the organization with the change recipients perceiving arrangements to be unfair. Changes which threaten an employee's sense of security and control will produce a loss of trust, fear, resentment and possibly anger.

Reaction to change begins in advance of the actual change as individuals worry (pre-change anxiety) about what will happen and their personal consequences. Following the anticipation and anxiety phase, during the change, possible reactions include shock, anger, denial, depression and guilt. Many of these reactions may be fuelled by rumours and uncertainty. During this phase the recipient may engage in bargaining behaviours in order to balance the costs and benefits associated with the change and the consequences for themselves as individuals. Finally, after the change (acceptance phase) people resign themselves to the fact that change is or has happened and become ready to adapt themselves to new requirements.

Alternative *models of change reactions* have been presented by a number of scholars seeking to explain change recipient behaviour. Personality and prior experience with change can affect recipients' views of change. Similarly, change leaders can influence how recipients view the change. Recipients who trust their leaders are likely to respond more positively to leaders' suggestions for change. In other cases the recipient may experience positive feelings about the change, possibly seeing an opportunity for personal growth and promotion, new challenges and work variety.

In summary, this chapter has discussed what is meant by change, what can be changed and why and who may bring about change and how. We believe that a prerequisite for change is a thorough understanding of *how* organizations *function*. The remainder of this book seeks to impart such an understanding. Through the remaining chapters we present alternatives and business approaches and solutions that may make more effective and efficient those organizations dependent upon context and their 'frame'. Throughout the forthcoming chapters we frequently refer to and build upon how organizations function.

Coping responses a human emotional response to distress caused by change, suggesting that individuals typically experience first denial, then anger, bargaining, depression and finally acceptance

Summary of key learning points

Organizational change concerns the alteration of organizational components (such as the mission, strategy, goals, structure, processes, systems, technology and people) to improve the effectiveness or efficiency of the organization. Change may take place in any part and at any level of the organization. When we think of organizational change, we may think of significant changes aimed at making the organization more effective or smaller (efficiency-based) changes such as departmental reorganizations, the implementation of new technologies and systems. The primary needs for change derive from the need for alignment between the organizations' internal and external environments.

There are many types of change distinguished according to a number of variables: discontinuous versus continuous; planned versus unplanned; and organizational level: individual, group or total system. Some changes are clearly in response to an event or series of events. These are called relative (reactive) changes. Other changes are initiated, not in response to events but in anticipation of external events that may occur. These are called anticipatory (proactive) changes. Intensity relates to the severity of the change and, in particular, the degree of shock, upset, or discontinuity created throughout the organization. Strategic changes are obviously more intense than incremental changes.

Diagnosis (through models such as the McKinsey 7-S model, the Nadler and Tushman congruence framework and the Burke-Litwin model), problem information, gap analysis and visioning are used to motivate and determine what to change. Having established the need for change, change initiators then consider whether the organization is in fact ready for change.

Lewin concluded that the change process needs to follow a three-step procedure: unfreezing, moving and refreezing. Many change agents use force-field analysis as an analytical tool to understand the dynamics of change. It is used in conjunction with stakeholder analysis. Various people are responsible for making change happen; leaders need to be persuasive and political and overcome resistance. They must monitor the environment, identify and establish the need for change and provide clear direction for organizational change effort. They must also communicate that need and initiate activities. Managers can identify opportunities, promote ethical behaviour, and develop capabilities within the organization in order to keep it aligned with its environment. The success of implementing change is associated with those who facilitate the change process. Change leaders need to understand why people react to change as they do – they should consider those on the receiving end. Change recipients may be concerned about how the change will impact upon their relationships with others (the people they currently work with), their ability to do what is being asked of them and their future needs. Such concerns will result in mixed feelings about the change. Possible coping responses may be undesirable such as absenteeism, sabotage or departure from the company.

Review questions

What is change and what can be changed

Review the opening active learning case:

1 How would you classify the changes taking place in PLDT: transformational or transactional? You should explain your choice.

2 Do you believe that culture can be changed according to some plan? Discuss your answer with reference to Chapter 1 national culture and your knowledge of organizational culture (a matter we revisit in Chapter 7).

3 Why do you think *information* plays such an important role in change management?

4 Critically evaluate, considering advantages and disadvantages, the use of external consultants on such a project.

5 Imagine you are a UK consultant – how might you have prepared for this assignment?

Investigate, through self-directed learning, the concept of single and double-loop learning. How can these concepts be applied to the PLDT case?

How sustainable do you believe the changes made were? How long might it take PLDT to refreeze? What are the chances of the organization reverting to old ways once the consultants completed their assignment?

Discuss the difficulties in bringing about change at PLDT.

Transformational and transactional change

Critically evaluate the following statement: 'Transformational change is about being effective and transactional change is about being efficient'.

Create a model that shows different types of change. The model should identify all of the different types of change (such as transactional, radical, emergent, planned, continuous, etc.) and cluster related terms according to some common attribute.

Theoretical foundations

Describe the main theoretical foundations of change management.

Planned and the emergent approach

Critically evaluate the planned and the emergent approach to change.

Change management models

Identify and describe a selection of integrated change management models.

Resistance to change

Explain, with examples, what is meant by resistance to change.

References

Audia, P. G., Locke, E. A. and Smith, K. G. (2000) 'The Paradox of Success: An Archival and a Laboratory Study of Strategic Persistence Following Radical Environmental Change', *Academy of Management Journal* (October 2000) 43(5):837–853.

Bamford, D. (2006) 'A case-study into change influences within a large British multinational', *Journal of Change Management* 6(2):181–191.

Barkema, H. and Bauer, J. M. (2002) 'Management Challenges in a New Time', *Academy of Management Journal* (October 2002) 45(5):916–930.

Bridges, W. (1986) 'Managing Organizational Transitions', *Organizational Dynamics* (Summer 1986) 15(1):24–33.

Buchanan, D. A. and Badham, R. (1999) 'Politics and organizational change: the lived experience', *Human Relations* 52(5):609–629.

Buchanan, D. A. and Boddy, D. (1992) *The Expertise of the Change Agent*, London: Prentice-Hall.

Burke, W. and Litwin, G. H. (1992) 'A Causal Model of Organizational Performance and Change', *Journal of Management* (September 1992) 18(3):523–545.

Burke, W. (2008) *Organization Change – Theory and Practice* (2 ed), Thousand Oaks, Cal: Sage.

Burnes, B. (2004) *Managing Change* (4 ed), Harlow: FT Prentice Hall.

Cawsey, T. and Deszca, G. (2007) *Toolkit for Organizational Change,* Thousand Oaks, Cal: Sage Publications.

Clark, L. (2006) 'Sandvik seeks standard business processes with global ERP roll-out', *Computer Weekly* (28 November 2006) p. 18.

Cross, R. and Prusak, L. (2002) 'The People Who Make Organizations Go – or Stop', *Harvard Business Review* (June 2002) 80(6):104–111.

Dent, E. B. and Goldberg, S. G. (1999) 'Challenging Resistance to Change', *Journal of Applied Behavioral Science* (March 1999) 35(1):25–41.

Dowling, P. J., Festing, M. and Engle, A. D. (2008) *International Human Resource Management* (5 ed), London: Cengage Learning.

Drucker, P. (1994) 'The Theory of the Business', *Harvard Business Review* (September/October 1994) 72(5):95–104.

Furnham, A. (2001) 'Vocational Preference and P-O Fit: Reflections on Holland's Theory of Vocational Choice', *Applied Psychology: An International Review* (January 2001) 50(1): 5–25.

Geppert, M., Matten, D. and Williams, K. (2002) 'Change Management in MNC: How Global Convergence Intertwines With National Diversities', *Academy of Management Proceedings* pp. 1–6.

Giangreco, A. and Peccei, R. (2005) 'The Nature and antecedents of middle manager resistance to change: evidence from an Italian context', *International Journal of Human Resource Management* 16(10):1812–1829.

Graen, G. and Hui, G. (1996) 'Managing Changes in globalizing business: how to manage cross-cultural business partners', *Journal of Organizational Change Management* 9(3):62–73.

Granered, E. (2006) 'Managing Change across cultures', *Multilingual* 17(8):69–72.

Grant, R. (2007) *Contemporary Strategy Analysis* (6 ed), Oxford: Blackwell Publishing.

Greiner, L. E. (1972) 'Evolution and Revolution as organizations grow', *Harvard Business Review* 50(4):37–46.

Hendry, C. (1996) 'Understanding and Creating Whole Organizational Change Through Learning Theory', *Human Relations* (May 1996) 49(5):621–642.

James, M. and Ward, K. (2001) 'Leading a multinational team of change agents at Glaxo Welcome (now Glaxo SmithKline)', *Journal of Change Management* 2(2):148–160.

Kotter, J. (2007) 'Leading Change', *Harvard Business Review* (January 2007) 85(1):96–103.

Leavitt, H. J. (1965) 'Applied organizational change in industry: structural, technological and humanistic approaches', in: *Handbook of Organizations* J. G. March (ed), Chicago: Rand McNally.

Lewin K. (1951) *Field Theory in Social Science*, New York: Harper & Row.

Lipton, M. (1996) 'Demystifying the Development of an Organizational Vision', *Sloan Management Review* 37(4):83–92.

Martin, G. and Beaumont, P. (2001) 'Transforming multinational enterprises: Towards a process model of strategic Human Resource Management change', *International Journal of Human Resource Management* 12(8):1234–1250.

Meteer, J., Hummel, L., Wicks, F. and Nolan, T. (2004) 'Global Improvement Initiatives', *Multinational Business Review* 12(1):111–120.

Morgan, G. (1986) *Images of Organization* Beverly, Hills, CA: Sage.

Nadler, D. A. and Tushman, M. (1989) 'Organizational Frame Bending: Principles for Managing Reorientation', *Academy of Management Executive* (August 1989) 3(3):194–204.

Peters, T. and Waterman, R. (1982) *In Search of Excellence*, London: Harper Collins Business.

Rajagopalan, N. and Spreitzer, G. M. (1997) 'Toward a Theory of Strategic Change: A Multi-lens Perspective and Integrative Framework', *The Academy of Management Review* (January 1997) 22(1):48–79.

Saka, A. (2003) 'Internal Change agents' view of the management of change problem', *Journal of Organizational Change Management* 16(5):480–496.

Savage, G. T., Nix, T. W., Whitehead, C. J. and Blair, J. D. (1991) 'Strategies for assessing and managing organizational stakeholders', *Academy of Management Executive* (May 1991) 5(2):61–75.

Senge, P. M. (1996) 'Systems thinking', *Executive Excellence* 13(1):15.

Sterman, J. D. (2001) 'System Dynamics Modeling: Tools for learning in a complex world', *California Management Review* (Summer 2001) 43(4):8–25.

Sull, D. N. (1999) 'Why Good Companies Go Bad', *Harvard Business Review* (July/August 1999) 77(4):42–50.

Thomas, J. (1985) 'Force field analysis: A new way to evaluate your strategy', *Long Range Planning* (December 1985) 18(6):54–59.

Thornberry, N. (1997) 'A View about "vision"', *European Management Journal* (February 1997) 15(1):28–35.

Van de Ven, A. H. and Poole, M. S. (1995) 'Explaining Development and Change in Organizations', *The Academy of Management Review* (July 1995) 20(3):510–540.

Weick, K. E. and Quinn, R. E. (1999) 'Organizational Change and Development', *Annual Review of Psychology* 50(1):361–386.

Withey, M. J., Cooper, W. H. (1989) 'Predicting Exit, Voice, Loyalty, and Neglect', *Administrative Science Quarterly* (December 1989) 34(4):521–539.

Suggestions for further reading

Journals

Journal of Change Management (Published By: Routledge) – Given the additional pressures of new technology, global competition and changing markets, companies are increasingly encountering the need for strategic level transformation. This transformation encompasses all parts of a business, its structure, processes, resources, technology and culture. Success goes to those who can visualize how markets are changing, identify new configurations of service or delivery and 'change the rules of the game'. The *Journal of Change Management* provides an international, peer-reviewed forum to explore all the strategic and tactical factors affecting and effecting change in organizations today. http://www.tandf.co.uk/journals/titles/14697017.asp.

Journal of Organizational Change Management (JOCM) – The goal of the journal is to provide alternative philosophies for organizational change and development.

The International Journal of Knowledge, Culture and Change Management – The focus of the journal is those intangible drivers which determine not only the livability of organizations for insiders, and their credibility and attraction to outsiders; but also their tangible results in the form of efficiency, effectiveness and productivity. The intangibles of knowledge, culture and change management do not appear on balance sheets, but ultimately do have an enormous impact on 'bottom lines'. The journal attempts to address dynamics of knowledge, culture and change as they manifest themselves in organizations. http://ijm .cgpublisher.com/about.html.

Key articles

Scholars of this subject area have often read the following:

1 Van de Ven, A. H. and Poole, M. S. (1995) 'Explaining Development and Change in Organizations', *The Academy of Management Review* (July 1995) 20(3):510–540.
2 Rajagopalan, N. and Spreitzer, G. M. (1997) 'Toward a Theory of Strategic Change: A Multi-lens Perspective and Integrative Framework', *The Academy of Management Review* (January 1997) 22(1):48–79.
3 Weick, K. E. and Quinn, R. E. (1999) 'Organizational Change and Development', *Annual Review of Psychology* 50(1):361–386.
4 Drucker, P. (1994) 'The Theory of the Business', *Harvard Business Review* (September/October 1994) 72(5):95–104.
5 Greiner, L. E. (1972) 'Evolution and revolution as organizations grow', *Harvard Business Review* 50(4):37–46.
6 Burke, W. and Litwin, G. H. (1992) 'A Causal Model of Organizational Performance and Change', *Journal of Management* (September 1992) 18(3):523–545.
7 Nadler, D. A. and Tushman, M. (1989) 'Organizational Frame Bending: Principles for Managing Reorientation', *Academy of Management Executive* (August 1989) 3(3):194–204.

Chapter 6

International leadership and management

Introduction
Leadership and management
Power and influence
Leadership theories
International leadership

Key concepts

- Motivation ■ Power ■ Referent power ■ Expert power ■ Information power
- Reward power ■ Legitimate power ■ Coercive power ■ Authority
- Compliance ■ Internalization ■ Personal identification
- Contingency theory of leadership ■ Participative leadership ■ Delegation
- Empowerment ■ Transactional leadership ■ Transformational leadership

By the end of this chapter you will be able to:

- Explain the apparent differences between the concepts of leadership and management

- Evaluate how situation and organizational context impact upon leadership style

- Understand the potential benefits and risks of shared and delegated leadership

- Understand how position and personal attributes can be a source of power for leaders

- Understand various psychological processes which explain how leaders influence people

- Discuss how leadership styles and behaviour may need to be adapted when working in other cultures

Active learning case

Infosys Technologies

www.infosys.com

Organizations need talented people ... of the many powerful forces driving companies to develop leaders more effectively, the most important is the world economy's long-term shift from dependence on financial capital towards human capital. Fortune[1] asked the top ten companies to share their best practices for developing leaders in a global economy. Infosys Technologies, Bangalore, India was voted one of those companies.

'Empower Young Employees. At Indian information-technology powerhouse Infosys, the average age of an employee is 26. But senior executives, who were looking to young up-and-comers for feedback and new ideas, grew frustrated when they realized that many of those recruits were keeping their opinions to themselves. In response, top management inaugurated a program called Voice of Youth, which gathers together a group of top-performing twentysomethings and gives them a seat on the company's management council. There's no holding back at that point: Members of all ages are expected to "debate, discuss, and critique" any and all aspects of the business.'

The company vision is, 'to be a globally respected corporation that provides best-of-breed business solutions, leveraging technology, delivered by best-in-class people'. In their 25 years, they have contributed to India's emergence as the global destination for software services talent. The values include leadership by example: 'to set standards in our business and transactions and be an exemplar for the industry and ourselves'. Interestingly, Infosys and PLDT (refer to the opening case study for Chapter 5) collaborate in offering call centre solutions. Infosys regained the No. 1 position as the best employer in India (2005), according to the study on 'The Best Companies to Work for in India 2005' based on research by three partners: *Business Today*, a leading Indian business publication; Mercer Human Resource Consulting, an international HR consulting firm; and the Indian arm of international market research major TNS. Furthermore, Mr N. R. Narayana Murthy, Chairman and CEO, was named among the '25 most influential global executives' by TIME/CNN[4]. A former socialist who in the 1970s gave away all his money, Murthy, 55, is now among India's richest men. 'One of his country's most admired men, he is vigilant about his employees' well-being – granting stock options, building exercise facilities and spreading values as much as wealth.' Mr Murthy articulated, designed and implemented the Global Delivery Model, which has become the foundation for the success of IT services outsourcing from India. He has also led key corporate governance initiatives in India. In 2005 *The Economist* ranked him 8th on its list of 15 most admired global leaders. He was ranked 28th among the world's most respected business leaders by *The Financial Times* in 2005. In 2004, *TIME magazine* identified him as one of ten global leaders helping shape the future of technology. He was featured in *Business Week*'s 'The Stars of Asia' consecutively from 1998 to 2000. Voted the 'World Entrepreneur of the Year' by Ernst & Young in 2003 he was also declared by the *Economic Times* as India's most powerful CEO for three consecutive years (2004 to 2006). Mr Murthy received the Ernst Weber Engineering Leadership medal from The Institute of Electrical and Electronics Engineers in 2007 for his pioneering role in the globalization of IT services.

Infosys believes the success of economies depends upon how adept they are at attracting, nurturing and retaining talent. In the knowledge economy, countries must focus on education to develop a skilled labour force. Infosys believes that world-class talent

Infosys Technologies Ltd. (NASDAQ: INFY) commenced trading in 1981 and is now a global leader in the 'next generation' of IT and consulting with revenues of over US$ 3 billion. Infosys define, design and deliver technology-enabled business solutions to help Global 2000 companies. Infosys' service offerings span business and technology consulting, application services, systems integration, product engineering, custom software development, maintenance, re-engineering, independent testing and validation services, IT infrastructure services and business process outsourcing.

Infosys has a global footprint, with offices in 23 countries and development centres in India, China, Australia, the UK, Canada and Japan. Employing 80 500 people, Infosys has workforce coverage across 66 nationalities.

The Infosys board brings together a team of technology, business and social visionaries who provide direction to Infosys' executive management in a dynamic economic and business environment.

The Bangalore Pyramid on Infosys' main campus

© Fredrik Renander / Alamy

knows no geographical boundaries. We are tapping into the global pool of talent to empower talent and realize its potential. Infosys is a proud partner of the Forum of Young Global Leaders, a newly formed, unique, multi-stakeholder community of exceptional young leaders who share a commitment to shaping the global future. The Forum brings together young leaders who are currently internationally prominent and those who are destined for future greatness. Each year, the World Economic Forum identifies 200–300 exceptional individuals, drawn from every region in the world and many disciplines and sectors. Together, they form a powerful international community which can affect the global future dramatically.

Websites:
(1) http://money.cnn.com/magazines/fortune/leadership/2007/index.html
(2) http://www.infosys.com/
(3) http://www.thehindubusinessline.com/2007/04/20/stories/2007042002410400.htm
(4) http://www.time.com/time/2001/influentials/ybmurthi.html
(5) http://www.younggloballeaders.org/

Introduction

Influencing the behaviour of others

In Chapter 1 we discussed the attainment of organizational goals and superior performance. In particular, we explored effectiveness (performance in activities that support the mission) and efficiency (the use of resources). We also recognized organizational performance to be a broad concept that includes productivity, customer and employee satisfaction. We noted that superior performance is dependent on sustainable competitive advantage and that one of the main tasks of managers was to create, renew and maintain such advantages and devise strategies that utilize them. Organizational effectiveness and strategy are seen as essential determinants and superior performance. Advantages emanate from activities and the manager must decide where activities take place, who will perform them and what resources will be allocated.

Efficiency is about how the organization uses is resources to undertake activities and we noted that-some companies are able to get more out of their resources than others. In the case of human resources, this is achieved through motivation. Later, we discussed strategy and the need to give direction, purpose, a mission and goals. We also identified general perspectives such as positioning and the resource-based view. Choosing a unique position, improving operational effectiveness, leveraging resources, making sense of the environment (Chapter 2), formulating strategy (Chapter 3), making strategic choices, ensuring the organization behaves responsibly (Chapter 4), developing visions, mobilizing commitments and articulating the need for change (Chapter 5) and enabling the organizational parts to work together (integration) are all associated with leadership and management. Management is about getting things done with the aid of people and other resources or more specifically it is the process of leading and directing all or part of an organization, through the deployment and manipulation of resources (people, technological, financial, material, intellectual or intangible). It concerns the effective utilization and coordination of resources to achieve defined objectives with maximum efficiency.

This chapter explores the concepts of leadership and management and will focus on the leaders' use of power to influence and persuade followers to act in ways that help the organization attain its goals. To provide structure and aid learning this chapter is organized into four sections:

- leadership and management;
- power and influence;
- leadership theories;
- international leadership.

Leadership and management

This chapter commences with a discussion regarding what is meant by the terms leaders and managers and what it is they are required to do. Leadership has been defined in terms of traits, behaviours, influence, interaction patterns, role relationships, and occupation of organizational positions. Most definitions of leadership infer a process whereby one-person influences another. In the case of organizational leadership, people are influenced to do what is ethical and beneficial for the organization. Yukl (2006) defines leadership as the process of influencing others to understand and agree about what needs to be done and how to do it, and the process of facilitating individual and collective efforts to accomplish shared objectives. Typically associated with the concept of influence is motivation; leadership may be considered as the ability of an individual to influence, *motivate* and enable others to contribute towards the effectiveness and success of the organization.

Leadership the process of influencing others to understand and agree about what needs to be done and how to do it, and the process of facilitating individual and collective efforts to accomplish shared objectives

Yukl (2006) notes that a person can be a leader without being a manager and a person can be a manager without leading. He notes a continuing controversy about the difference between leadership and management with some writers treating them as different to the point of being mutually exclusive, i.e. that management and leadership cannot occur in the same person. Other scholars view leading and managing as distinct *processes* that do not assume leaders and managers are different types of people. Both processes are necessary for the success of an organization. The relative importance of the two processes and the best way to integrate them depends upon the situation at the time. In the next section we briefly consider what leaders and managers are and what they do.

Managers and leaders

Can a manager be a leader – are leaders born to lead?

Historically, scholars have argued the leader and manager as different roles while others have deemed them synonymous. While there can be evidence for both arguments, dependent upon how management and leadership is defined, we take the view that leadership is one aspect of the management role. The terms leader and manager are used interchangeably in this chapter to indicate people occupying positions in which they are expected to perform a leadership role. Leadership is essentially an influencing process; the process is ultimately aimed at goal achievement. The function of the leader is to ensure the organization does the right thing (effectiveness) while the manager ensures things are done right (efficiency); the leader is concerned with establishing direction, the vision and organizational goals and influencing followers to obtain commitment. Consequently, the leader must be a good communicator and able to influence others – motivating and inspiring. The manager ensures goals are attained through plans, budgets, resource allocation, organization and problem-solving, see Figure 6-1. Similar functions were described by Mintzberg (1975) who distinguished interpersonal, informational and decisional roles for managers. Many scholars argue the distinction between leadership and management is blurred in practice and the effective manager requires some leadership qualities.

Figure 6-1

Leadership versus management roles and functions

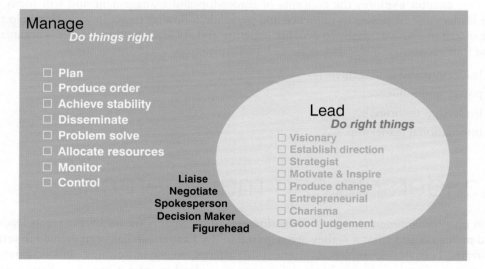

Leadership is an important role requirement for managers. There are many ways to measure leadership effectiveness such as performance, follower satisfaction and commitment and the extent to which tasks are completed and goals are attained. Three key concepts exist in most leadership theories:

- the leader (who may be a manager/boss);
- the follower (who may be a subordinate); and
- the relationship between them (see Figure 6-2)

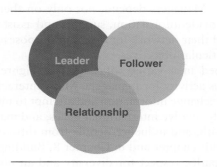

Figure 6-2

Leader – follower relationship

Most definitions of leadership and theories about effective leadership focus on behaviours used to directly influence followers. Influence may be direct, i.e. on immediate subordinates, or indirect, influencing colleagues, other employees, senior managers, clients and customers alike. Consequently, some differentiate between direct and indirect leadership. Leadership can be both a specialized role and a social influence process. We have described leadership as an influence process. Leaders can influence many things such as the choice of objectives and goals to follow; the organization and coordination of work activities and allocation of resources to such activities; the design of formal structure, programmes and systems and the shared beliefs and values of members (culture). They can also motivate and develop others, build trust and win support.

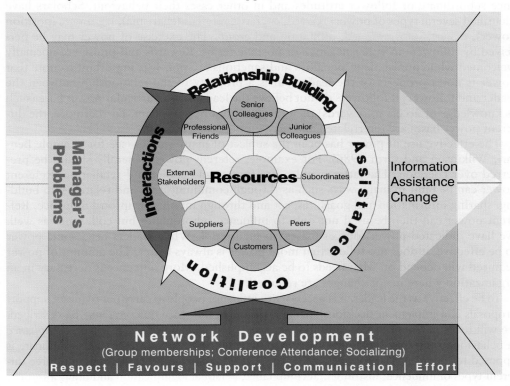

Figure 6-3

Network development, interactions and resources

Managerial activity can be described in terms of several general processes:

- relationship management;
- information management;
- decision-making; and
- influencing people.

To carry out their responsibilities, managers need to obtain recent, relevant information which often exists only in the heads of people who are widely scattered within and outside the organization; they need to make decisions based on information that is both overwhelming and incomplete; and they need cooperation from people over whom they have no formal authority. Managers depend, not only on their subordinates but a large network of contacts to provide information, support and assistance, see Figure 6-3. Managers use different parts of their network for different purposes and extend the network as needed to accomplish particular objectives.

Networks are developed in a variety of ways (see Figure 6-3) and the process of *networking* is a continuous activity for managers. Many interactions involve oral communication which is used to exchange information and attempt to influence people. Managerial responsibilities increasingly involve international issues, and managers must be able to understand, communicate with, and influence people from different cultures, a challenge to which we return later in this chapter and in Chapter 8. Building cooperative relationships requires considerable empathy, respect for diversity and an understanding of the values, beliefs, and attitudes of people from different cultures.

Power and influence

Effectiveness is influenced by the leader's power. Influence is the essence of leadership.

Leadership is about influencing the behaviour of others (followers). Power describes the ability to influence others, to get them to do things. In some cases the leader may influence subordinate or follower attitudes and in other cases their behaviour. Scholars have identified several types of power: reward, coercive, referent (charisma), legitimate (position power), expert, informational, affiliation and *group*. The exercise of power may be perceived by followers in either negative or positive terms. Rewards and praise are normally welcomed while punishment, penalties and sanctions are not. It is important to note that power is not a property of the leader but is a property of the relationship between the leader and follower; if followers do not believe the leader has a particular power base (such as knowledge or access to rewards) then they may not be compliant. Furthermore, the different power bases are interrelated and may support each other.

The effective use of power has been the subject of many studies (see for example Benfari, Wilkinson and Orth 1986). For example, referent power generally should be preferred over coercion. The latter may lead to long-term conflict and retaliation. Referent power can be built in many ways such as through communication and relationship building, sharing information and goals, respect and through inviting reciprocal influence. Referent power can then be used not only to influence subordinates but colleagues as well. We have indicated power sources (bases) in Figure 6-4. While leaders need some power to be effective, it does not follow that more power is always better. The amount of power required will depend on what needs to be accomplished. More influence is necessary in an organization where major changes are required.

To be effective as the leader, it is necessary to influence people to carry out requests, support proposals and implement decisions. While a variety of influence outcome may be described, we will focus on *commitment* (attitudes are influenced and agreement reached), *compliance* (a behavioural response, willing to make a minimal effort) and *resistance* (the subordinate is opposed to the proposal or request). Kelman (1958) outlined a process identifying three different types of influence: instrumental compliance, personal identification and internalization. The type of behaviour used intentionally to influence the attitudes and behaviour of another person is usually called an *influence tactic*. Impression management tactics are intended to influence people to like the leader; political tactics involve attempts to influence the degree of importance of the decisions made and who makes them and *proactive influence tactics* include:

- *rational persuasion* – the use of explanations, logical arguments and factual evidence to show that a request for proposal is feasible and relevant for attaining task objectives;
- *pressure* – the leader persistently reminds the subordinate to carry out a request;
- *legitimating* – the leader establishes authority by referring to rules, policies or a contract;
- *apprising* – the leader explains how the subordinate will benefit personally as a result of carrying out the request or supporting a proposal;

Authority typically associated with a particular position, gives the leader the right to make particular decisions and to exercise control over resources

Power is the ability of individuals or groups to persuade, induce or coerce others into following certain courses of action

Reward power the ability of a leader to exert influence based on the belief of followers that the leader has access to valued rewards which will be handed out in return for compliance (see also remunerative power)

Coercive power the perceived ability to bestow negative influences onto employees

Referent power influence over others, acquired from being well liked or respected by them (see charisma)

Legitimate power a right, perceived by the follower, to exercise influence because of the leader's role or position in the organization (see also, position power)

Expert power an individual's power deriving from the skills or expertise of the person and the organization's needs for those skills and expertise

Information power the ability to get scarce but needed information

Affiliation power stems from close association with other powerful figures on whose authority the power holder is able to act

Conflict a disagreement through which the parties involved perceive a threat to their needs, interests or concerns

Instrumental compliance the motivation for the behaviour is purely instrumental, i.e. the only reason for compliance is to obtain reward or avoid punishment

Personal identification the motivation for the subordinate relates to their need for acceptance and esteem and a desire for leader approval. Subordinates therefore imitate the leader's behaviour or adopt similar attitudes because they want to be like the leader

Internalization the follower or subordinate is committed to the leader's request or decision because it is congruent with their personal values and beliefs

- *consultation* – encouraging involvement at an early stage;
- *ingratiation* – the leader uses praise and flattery or may express confidence in the subordinate's ability to undertake a particular task;
- *personal appeal* – the leader asks the subordinate for a personal favour;
- *exchange* – the leader offers something specifically in return for the subordinate's help; and
- *coalition* – the leader gets others to persuade the subordinate to do something.

Figure 6-4

Power and influence

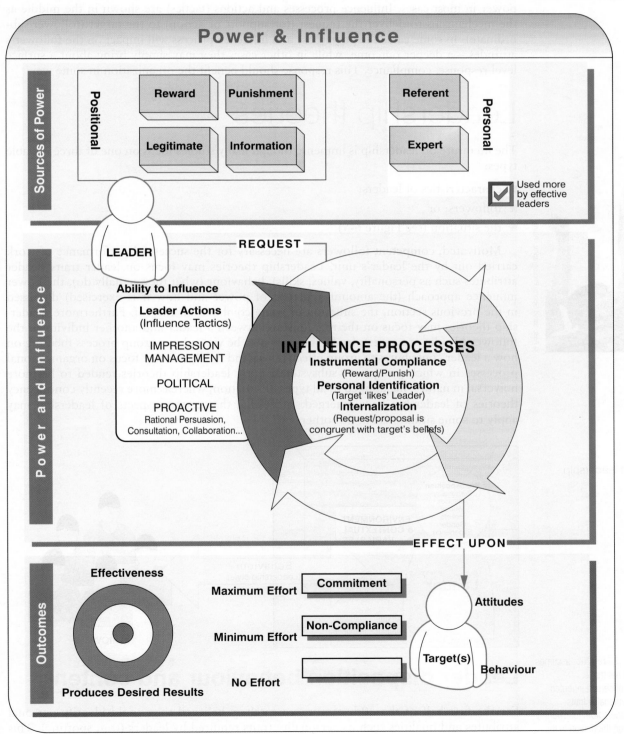

STOP & THINK

Consider the last time you tried to influence someone to do something – review the list of proactive influence tactics – did you use one of the listed tactics? Think of each tactic and recall an occasion when you may have used such an approach.

The power and influence figure summarizes the different sources of power and categorizes them as positional or personal. Personal power should be used in preference to positional power in most cases. Influence processes and actions (tactics) are shown in the middle as the mechanisms to deliver the request (for support or action) to the target (follower/subordinate). In some cases the powerbase and influence process will impact on the follower's attitudes – a deeper outcome, while in other cases they may simply bring about a surface level response, compliance. This response should benefit the organization in some way.

Leadership theories

The literature on leadership is immense though many studies focus on one of three variable types:

- characteristics of leaders;
- followers; or
- the situation (see Figure 6-5).

Motivated, competent followers are necessary for the successful performance of work carried out by the leader's unit. Leadership theories may focus on leader traits (leader attributes such as personality, values, skills), behaviour (what they actually do), the power influence approach (the amount and type of power and how it is exercised) discussed in the previous section, the situation or some combination thereof. Furthermore, leadership theories may focus on the relationship between a leader and another individual, the follower (dyadic processes); leadership may also be viewed as a group process focusing on how a leader contributes to group effectiveness and finally we may focus on organizational processes in which groups are subsystems. Early leadership theories tended to be more universal in nature, i.e. applied to all types of situation, whereas more recently contingency theories of leadership have emerged, suggesting that certain aspects of leadership may apply to some situations but not others.

Figure 6-5

The evolution of leadership theories

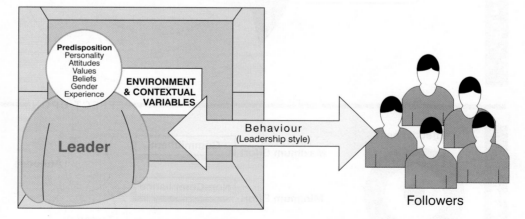

Traits approach to leadership assumes leaders are born and not made. Leadership consists of certain inherited characteristics, or personality traits, which distinguish leaders from followers. Attention is focused on the person in the job and not the job itself

Leader disposition behaviour and content

For the first half of the 20th century, researchers believed they could identify personal attributes and qualities such as personality traits required by leaders (**trait** spotting). This would make it possible to identify, select and promote such individuals into leadership positions. While the authors of numerous studies have proposed a range of leadership traits and qualities, many of them are vague and of limited value in trying to identify leaders. While leaders may score high on ability, sociability and motivation so too do many followers. While researchers concluded that a person's predispositions can help predict behaviour, they then shifted their attention from trait identification to the study of leadership behaviour patterns and later, the identification of appropriate behaviours for different contexts. Personality traits likely to be found in effective leaders include:

- high energy levels and stress tolerance;
- self-confidence;
- high internal locus of control;
- emotional stability and maturity;
- personal integrity.

Leaders must cope with demanding work, requiring high levels of energy and a tolerance of stress. The introduction of change often requires a self-confident individual to take the initiative with regard to oral problem solving. However, over self-confidence may be dysfunctional. People differ in their beliefs about what causes events to happen: their actions or chance. Leaders typically have a high internal locus of control believing their actions cause events to happen. Consequently they are more likely to plan to accomplish goals. Leaders must interact with others, communicate and network. Emotionally mature people understand their strengths and weaknesses and are less moody, therefore more likely to maintain cooperative relationships with others.

Finally, we have noted how a leader must build trust, loyalty, cooperation and support; it is less likely that people will be influenced by a leader with low personal integrity, i.e. dishonest, unethical or trustworthy. Aside from such traits, to be a successful leader, managers are likely to need a variety of:

- *cognitive* (memory of detail and analytical ability);
- *interpersonal* (persuasive and good communicators); and
- *technical* skills.

Predispositions, traits, skills and abilities may all be used to select and develop people for managerial positions. We return to leadership development later in this chapter.

For some time now, scholars have searched for the types of leadership behaviour most likely to influence subordinate satisfaction and performance. In the second half of the 20th century, leadership and management styles (behaviour patterns) became a major focus for research. Types of leadership behaviour are summarized in Figure 6-6. Based on research, *leadership behaviours* tend to be grouped into those focusing on work (task oriented behaviour) and those considering the follower (subordinate in many cases). Consideration behaviours are based on relationship building (relations oriented behaviour), supporting, developing, recognizing and helping others. Specific task behaviours include planning work activities, clarifying roles and objectives and monitoring operations and performance – how things get done. The two key orientations (task and relationship building) reflect a concern for people and a concern for production, both of which are important for effective leadership.

A person-oriented behaviour may result in higher job satisfaction; build trust, respect and loyalty and organizational commitment while the task orientation may result in better coordination and the more efficient utilization of resources. Together, both are important for the overall performance of the organization. Consequently, both types of behaviour need to be embraced by an effective leader. A person (manager or leader) can emphasize one or both. Studies suggest that people (followers) preferred their leaders to be both considerate and performance oriented as well. Subsequent research added a third orientation, behavioural set, based on approaches to change. Change-oriented behaviour is concerned with understanding the environment, finding innovative ways to adapt to it, and implementing major changes in strategies, products, or processes. Leaders use impression management tactics (demonstrated dedication, ingratiation – providing praise and appreciation, self-promotion – informing people about their skills and knowledge and intimidation) in an effort to appear more decisive, competent, powerful and trustworthy.

Impression management the process of influencing how others perceive you and behaviours used for this purpose

Figure 6-6

Leadership behaviour and its consequences for followers

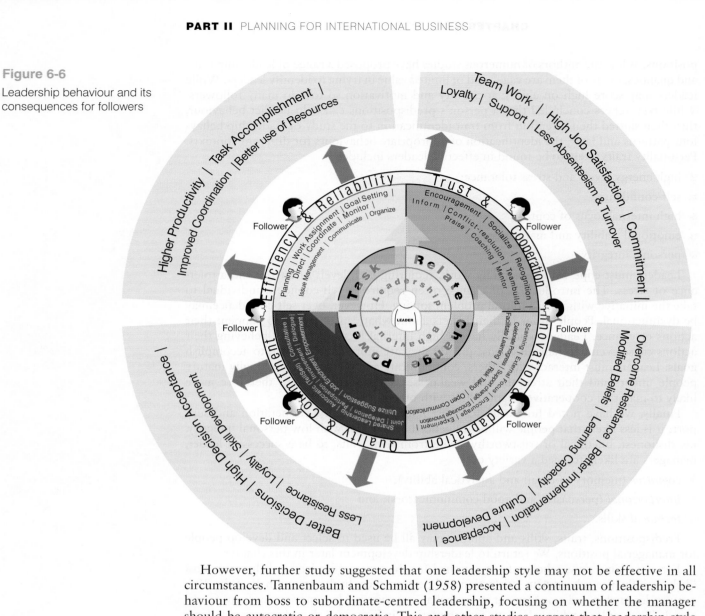

However, further study suggested that one leadership style may not be effective in all circumstances. Tannenbaum and Schmidt (1958) presented a continuum of leadership behaviour from boss to subordinate-centred leadership, focusing on whether the manager should be autocratic or democratic. This and other studies suggest that leadership style (behaviour) is dependent (contingent) on a variety of factors such as those contained in the situation, followers and the leader themselves. Leadership style is dependent on the organizational culture, size, task, managerial role, unit size, organizational life cycle, uncertainty, subordinate need for independence and expectations of involvement, leader confidence in subordinates and the leader predispositions.

The **contingency theory of leadership** is a perspective which suggests that leaders must adjust their style in a manner consistent with aspects of the context, i.e. there is no one ideal leadership style. Contingency theory argues that leaders must either change their style to fit the context or the context to fit their style. Adapting style to meet the demands of the context is referred to as **situational leadership**; it can also refer to instances where the person who is best suited to lead in a particular situation takes on the role of leader. The importance of the situation is the focus and the person who is seen as the most suitable leader is appointed by the group. However, many scholars emphasize the difficulties for leaders in diagnosing the context within which they are operating. Furthermore, the extent to which a leader can adapt their style is questionable.

Numerous studies have attempted to categorize leadership styles (see for example Goleman 2000). Leaders who expect followers to do as they are told adopt a coercive style, leaders who seek followers' views and input are more democratic or **participative,** whereas leaders seeking to develop people may suggest 'try this', i.e. a coaching style. The situational

Contingency theory of leadership a view which argues that leaders must alter their style in a manner consistent with aspects of the context

Situational leadership an approach to determining the most effective style of influencing

Participative leadership involves consulting with subordinates (followers) and the evaluation of their opinions and suggestions before the manager makes the decision

or contextual determinants of leadership behaviour are shown in Figure 6-7. Leaders vary their behaviour with regard to how they may or may not share leadership (see participative leadership). So far we have discussed three types of behaviour: task, relationship and change (see the inner circle of Figure 6-6). We have shown the different behaviours relating to power-sharing in the fourth quadrant.

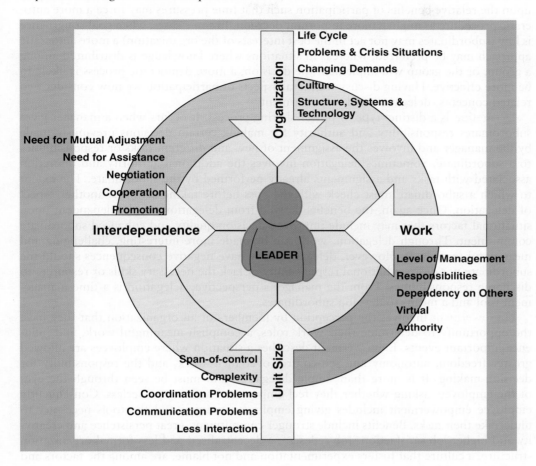

Figure 6-7

Determinants of leader behaviour

Consider the factors shown in Figure 6-7 – how might you expect them to impact upon leadership style?

STOP & THINK

Participative leadership

In this section we consider participative leadership, delegation and empowerment. Participative leadership (consultation, joint decision-making, power-sharing, decentralization, empowerment and democratic management) involves effort by a leader to encourage and facilitate participation by others in making important decisions. Participative leadership, delegation and empowerment are concepts linking the power and behaviour approaches to leadership. Participative leadership can take many forms. With regard to decision-making, a manager:

- may make the decision alone (autocratic – 'tell' style);
- may consider inputs from others before making the decision alone (consultation – 'sell' style);
- may discuss the problem and make the decision with others (joint decision); or
- may give an individual or group the authority and responsibility for making a decision themselves (delegation).

In reality, decision procedures may be plotted on a continuum between 'no' and 'high' influence by others. Participation and involvement in the decision process can enhance understanding of the problem and generate the optimum solution thus resulting in benefits such as better decision quality and acceptance along with higher satisfaction from followers/subordinates who become more developed in the process. Situation variables impact upon the relative benefits of participation such that time pressures may force a more autocratic procedure as might a more important decision. In some cases, when goal congruence is low (subordinates may not act in the best interests of the organization) a more autocratic approach may be preferred, whereas in situations where knowledge is distributed among a group, or the group will implement the decision, a more democratic process is likely to be more effective. Having discussed general aspects of participation we now consider two related concepts: delegation and empowerment.

Delegation is a distinct type of power-sharing process. It occurs when a manager gives subordinates responsibility and authority for making certain decisions previously made by the manager and involves the assignment of new and different tasks or responsibilities to a subordinate. Sometimes delegation involves the additional authority and discretion associated with tasks and assignments already performed by the subordinate. The extent to which a subordinate must check with the boss before taking action is another aspect of delegation. Once again, the benefits derived from delegation will be dependent upon situational factors that may include improved decision quality and enhanced subordinate commitment. Through delegation, work can be made more interesting, challenging and meaningful (enriched). However, delegation may have negative consequences should the subordinate not desire additional responsibility or lack the necessary skills or resources to discharge responsibilities. From the manager's perspective, delegation is a time management tool and a means to develop subordinates.

Empowerment involves the perception by members of an organization that they have the opportunity to determine their work roles, accomplish meaningful work, and influence important events. Empowerment describes a situation where employees are allowed greater freedom, autonomy and self-control over their work, and the responsibility for decision-making. It is more than simple delegation and must be seen through the eyes of the employee, asking whether they feel empowered and not powerless. Consequently employee empowerment includes giving employees training and the tools necessary to undertake their tasks. Benefits include stronger commitment, great persistence and creativity and higher job satisfaction. Job redesign, a decentralized and less formal organization structure, a culture that fosters experimentation and not blame, are among the factors and conditions enabling empowerment in organizations.

In this section we have discussed power sharing and its benefits. In the next section we consider specific aspects of leadership in a one-to-one and a one-to-many context before considering leadership in the international context.

Dyadic (special) relationships

Leaders vary their behaviour toward subordinates, i.e. dyadic relationships are not identical. Theories such as the leader – member exchange (LMX) theory describe how a leader develops a relationship with each subordinate over time and how the two parties influence each other (see Graen and Uhl-Bien (1995)). The leader – subordinate relationship may be described as one of *high* or *low* exchange. Leaders typically surround themselves with a small number of trusted subordinates (assistants, deputies and advisers) with whom they maintain a high-exchange (special) relationship.

A favourable exchange relationship is more likely when a subordinate is perceived competent, reliable and similar to the leader in values and attitudes. In such relationships, the leader has control over the outcomes that are desirable to a subordinate: delegated responsibility, high participation, special benefits, more interesting work and career enhancement. In return for greater status, influence and benefits such subordinates are expected to work harder, be more committed and loyal and may take on some of the leaders' responsibilities.

Delegation a distinct type of power sharing process that occurs when a manager gives subordinates the responsibility and authority for making certain decisions previously made by the manager

Empowerment the perception by members of an organization that they have the opportunity to determine their work roles, accomplish meaningful work and influence important events

In the case of a *low-exchange* relationship, low level of mutual influence, the subordinate merely complies with formal duties in return for the standard job benefits. High exchange relationship takes time to develop. While such relationships are commonplace in the work environment, leaders should recognize the potential dangers in having low exchange relationships with some employees/subordinates. Leaders tend to be biased, i.e. less critical in evaluating the performance of subordinates with whom they are established a high exchange relationship.

Leading teams

In this section we turn our attention to how leaders can influence team processes with the aim of improving performance. For our purposes we will not differentiate between the concept of a team and a group and will use the terms interchangeably (refer to Chapter 7). There are many types of group within the organization such as the functional, cross functional, self-managed, task force, virtual and executive team. They vary in size and degrees and interdependence and consequently their need for communication, coordination, control and leadership. Each can vary in relation to degrees of autonomy, authority, diversity of membership, stability of membership and the duration of existence. Groups are unified through shared goals. Whereas groups can outperform individual effort, it takes time for them to develop the necessary structure to perform.

Group-structure variables such as stage-of-development and cohesiveness may be seen as preconditions for group performance. According to Levine and Moreland (1990), group performance is the process and outcome of members' joint efforts to achieve a collective goal or the collective pursuit of a particular end. Group performance depends, at least in part, on the abilities and personalities of group members and the size and cohesiveness of the group.

Discussing the group process, Houldsworth and Mathews (2000) noted many factors become involved in the newly created social system of a group, not least being the developing reciprocal influences. This implies that individuals' cognitive processes affect, and become affected by, the other team members. Communication among the team members is the means by which the gradually growing interdependence of cognition and behaviour develops, such that efforts (or effort avoidance) become coordinated and shared.

Cohesion is about group solidarity and sense of community. Members of cohesive groups are more likely to talk and collaborate. Cohesion may be measured in many ways, for example, by asking people to describe their personal feelings about a group and its members. How is cohesion produced in small groups? Several factors may be important. First, simply assembling people into a group is enough to induce some cohesion and the more time people spend together, the stronger their cohesion becomes. Second, cohesion is stronger in groups whose members like one another. Third, groups that people find more rewarding tend to have stronger cohesion. The group can be rewarding because people enjoy its activities, approve of its goals, and/or believe that membership will be useful to them in another context. Cohesion can have many effects on a group and its members. Members of cohesive groups are more likely than others to participate in group activities, staying in the group themselves. Many studies suggest that cohesion affects group performance.

High interdependency, the extent to which members depend upon each other and exchange information and resources to accomplish their respective tasks, necessitates organization, cooperation and trust. Essential leadership processes include:

- building commitment and loyalty;
- organizing activities;
- clarifying roles;
- building trust and cooperation;
- managing resources;
- motivating members;

Self-managed team members determine, plan, and manage their day-to-day activities and duties

Virtual teams where the primary interaction among members is by some electronic information and communication process

Executive team are the group ultimately responsible for the administration of a business

- sharing information; and
- acting as the spokesperson or figurehead for the group.

In some cases there may be a formal leader, in others no obvious leader will be evident. In most cases of group work leadership roles will be shared. Group effectiveness is determined, in part, by the quality of leadership. As has been previously discussed, leadership functions may be divided into those that focus on the task and those that focus on relationships, i.e. group maintenance in this case.

Leading change

Effective leadership is needed to give new life to an organization and facilitate adaptation to the changing environment. Change leaders must understand the current and desired organizational situation and the mechanisms to move the organization from one state to another. They must also understand resistance to change and redirect this energy to drive change forward. People resist change due to a lack of trust, fear of what may go wrong or a lack of understanding. Effective leaders can use a variety of influence tactics to overcome such resistance.

A key change activity enabled by leaders is the development and communication of a shared vision (refer to Chapter 3) for a better future. When leading change, managers need to persuade people to support and commit to the vision and associated changes. Change leaders typically build coalitions. In the early stages of change it is important for key people to demonstrate their commitment. The change leader(s) must both support and motivate people (people-oriented actions) through and beyond the transition period. Support is obtained through explanations of why change is necessary; explaining current and future problems. Enthusiasm and continued support, commitment and motivation will be enhanced with demonstrated progress and the change leader should identify and communicate early successes – providing evidence of progress to boost confidence. Followers must perceive a leader's continued commitment to see the change programme through to a successful conclusion. Finally, commitment will be strengthened when employees feel a part of change. This means empowering them and delegating authority, where possible.

In the 1970s, James MacGregor Burns identified two types of leadership:

- transactional; and
- transformational.

Transactional leadership involves giving employees something in return for their compliance and acceptance of authority, usually in the form of incentives such as pay raises or an increase in status

Transformational leadership style of leadership in which the leader identifies the needed change, creates a vision to guide the change through inspiration, and accomplishes the change with the commitment of the followers

Transactional leadership occurs when one person takes the initiative in making contact with others for the purpose of an exchange of something valued; that is, 'leaders approach followers with an eye toward exchanging' (p. 4); it is based on legitimate authority within the bureaucratic structure of the organization.

Transformational leadership (charismatic) is based on more than the compliance of followers; it involves shifts in the beliefs, the needs, and the values of followers. Bass (1985 cited in Kuhnert and Lewis (1987)) applied Burns' ideas to organizational management. He argued that transactional leaders 'mostly consider how to marginally improve and maintain the quantity and quality of performance, how to substitute one goal for another, how to reduce resistance to particular actions, and how to implement decisions' (p. 27). In contrast, transformational leaders attempt and succeed in raising colleagues, subordinates, followers, clients, or constituencies to a greater awareness about the issues of consequence. Such leaders make followers more aware of the importance and value of the work and convince followers to put the organization goals first, ahead of self-interest. This heightening of awareness requires a leader with vision, self-confidence, and inner strength to argue successfully for what he or she sees is right or good, not for what is popular or is acceptable according to established wisdom. In many ways, we might consider the transactional style to equate with management and the transformational style with leadership.

Developing leaders

Managers need to develop their own and the leadership skills of others, especially their subordinates. Many have argued that the turbulence environment increases the need for leadership and a number of ways exist to develop leaders. In some cases people develop themselves and in other cases may participate in formal training or on the job development. Development can take place at work through coaching and mentoring while undertaking certain assignments. Formal training programmes may use lectures, case studies and exercises, discussions and business gains, but much of the skill essential for effective leadership is learned from experience.

Individuals may be given a particular assignment as an opportunity to develop and a mentor or coach can be used to help individuals make sense of their experience. People also learn by copying and emulating behaviours of other leaders at work. It is important for individuals to obtain feedback about their behaviour and its consequences if they are to learn from such experiences. Such feedback may come from the individual's manager, coach or mentor or they may receive multisource (360 degree) feedback. They may be rated by peers, subordinates, outsiders and their managers. In some cases feedback may come from a standard questionnaire filled out by such people and in other cases feedback may be presented verbally. Leadership development is contingent upon the learning climate at the organization.

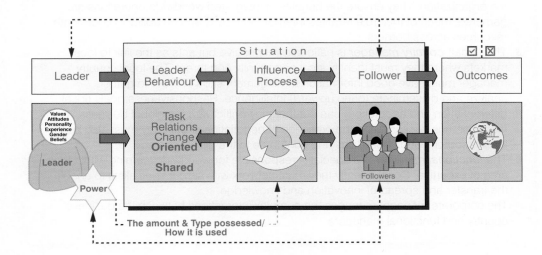

Figure 6-8
Leadership processes

The key leadership concepts, theories and processes are highlighted in Figure 6-8. This diagram acts as a summary for the chapter presented thus far and will be used to identify aspects of leading within the international organization, to be discussed next.

International leadership

Organizational leadership the ability of an individual to influence, motivate, and enable others to contribute toward the effectiveness and success of the organizations of which they are members

Organizational leadership is the ability of an individual to influence, motivate and enable others to contribute toward the effectiveness and success of the organizations of which they are members (House *et al.* 1999). Having explored key leadership theories, roles, functions and processes we must now consider their application in the international organization. In particular we consider how to motivate and influence others in different cultures. We must ask whether the leadership theories are relevant or appropriate in different parts of the world and whether the local culture and environmental forces define situations that warrant *specific* leadership approaches, styles and behaviours. Throughout this section we recognize that other contextual factors may also determine leadership style such as managerial position (senior/high or junior/low) the internal organizational context and specific responsibilities.

Aside from the hierarchical management structure, in 'What Is a Global Manager?' (first published in September/October 1992), Bartlett and Ghoshal outline a management structure model that balances the local, regional, and global demands placed on companies operating across the world's many borders. In the turbulent world of the international organization, they claim there is no such thing as a 'universal' global manager. Rather, there are three groups of specialists: business, country and functional managers, additionally there are the senior (corporate) managers at headquarters who manage the complex interactions between the three; this latter group identify and develop the talented executives required by a successful transnational. This kind of organizational structure characterizes a transnational rather than a multinational, international, or global company. Transnationals integrate assets, resources, and diverse people in operating units around the world. Through a flexible management process, in which business, country, and functional managers form a triad of different perspectives that balance one another, transnational companies can build three strategic capabilities: global-scale efficiency and competitiveness; national-level responsiveness and flexibility; and cross-market capacity to leverage learning on a worldwide basis (Bartlett and Ghoshal 1992).

Management roles in the transnational

- The *(global) business manager* is globally competitive, identifying opportunity across borders and boundaries and linking the capabilities that exist throughout the organization. They ensure the benefits of integrated worldwide operations are garnered. Much of their role requires interpersonal skills and an ability to coordinate resources across borders.
- The (local) *country manager* is nationally responsive but acts as the link to local markets where they must identify local opportunity and threat. The local country manager must have good information management skills in order to gather, analyze and disseminate (often upward) intelligence. Responsiveness goals (local differentiation and adaptation) can put them in conflict with the global business manager thus necessitating the presence of negotiation skills. They must also build local resources and capabilities and contribute to the global strategy.
- The *functional manager* is a specialist responsible for worldwide learning within their area of expertise. Consequently they must network with similar specialists to enable the transfer and spread of innovation and knowledge.
  The corporate manager manages the complex interactions between the business, country and functional managers.

Each of the transnational management roles described above will include leadership functions to build consensus, commitment, trust and cooperation, organize, coordinate resource, develop and empower people to varying degrees. Each of the above roles will vary in the volume and type of relationships they have with others in their organization world wide. We start this section with a discussion on the challenge of motivating subordinates and other followers wherever they are located, and close the chapter with a critical discussion on leading in other cultures.

Motivating others

Earlier we identified *motivating others* as a leadership function and explore this in more detail here. The word 'motivation' is often used to describe certain sorts of behaviour. This section is mainly concerned with the basic management and leadership problem of, *how do we motivate or persuade others to do what we want them to do?* Motivation can be defined as a concept used to describe the factors within an individual which stir up, maintain and channel behaviour towards a *goal* (the purpose toward which an endeavour is directed; an objective). Motivation is goal-directed behaviour. Since it is part of a manager's job to get their work done through others, managers need to understand why people do things (that is, what motivates them) so they can influence others to work towards the goals of the organization.

Motivation can be considered to comprise an individual's *effort* (how hard a person is trying), persistence (how long a person keeps trying) and the *direction* (what a person is trying to do) of that behaviour. Motivation theories focusing on the goals we seek are known as *content theories*, theories that focus on how we make choices with respect to desired goals are known as *process theories*. There are many motivation theories which will be outlined here before considering cross-cultural research on motivation. One of the early well known theories was developed by Abraham Maslow. We start with a focus on content theories and then move on to discuss process theories.

Motivation the driving force within individuals by which they attempt to achieve some goal in order to fulfil some need or expectation

Content theories

Content theories of motivation focus on the satisfaction of needs, see for example:

- Maslow's hierarchy of needs: lower needs must be met first.
- McClelland's acquired needs theory is also a three-need model.
- Herzberg's motivation-hygiene theory.

Maslow's hierarchy of needs is a psychology theory. There are five main sets of goals, which we may call basic needs (Maslow 1943). Maslow argues that we are motivated by the desire to achieve or maintain the various conditions upon which these basic satisfactions rest and by certain more intellectual desires. Maslow's hierarchy of needs is often illustrated as a pyramid consisting of five levels, see Figure 6-9: the four lower levels are grouped together as being associated with physiological (deficiency) needs, while the top level is termed growth needs (associated with psychological needs). According to this theory, deficiency needs must be met first – the individual does not feel anything if deficiency needs are met, but feels anxious if they are not met. Once these are met, seeking to satisfy growth needs drives personal growth – enduring motivations or *drivers* of behaviour. Self-actualization is the instinctual need of people to make the most of their abilities and to strive to be the best they can. In short, self-actualization is reaching one's fullest potential. The higher needs in this hierarchy only come into focus when the lower needs in the pyramid are satisfied. Once an individual has moved upwards, to the next level, needs in the lower level will no longer take precedence. If a lower set of needs is no longer being met, the individual will temporarily re-prioritize those needs by focusing attention on the unfulfilled needs, but will not permanently revert to the lower level. No claim is made by Maslow that his theory is ultimate or universal for all cultures.

Hierarchy of needs a theory of motivation developed by Maslow which states that people's behaviour is determined by their desire to satisfy a progression of physiological, social and psychological needs

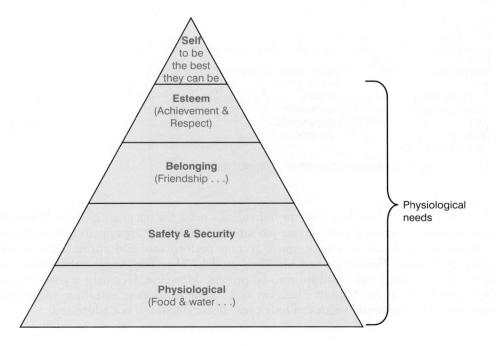

Figure 6-9
Maslow's hierarchy of needs

Another influential scholar was David McClelland who pioneered *workplace* motivational thinking, developing achievement-based motivational theory and models. David McClelland is most noted for describing three types of motivational need, which he identified as:

■ *Achievement motivation* – The 'achievement motivated' person seeks achievement, attainment of realistic but challenging goals, and advancement in the job.

■ *Authority/power motivation* – The 'authority motivated' person has a need to be influential, effective and to make an impact. There is a strong need to lead and for their ideas to win through.

■ *Affiliation motivation* – The 'affiliation motivated' person has a need for friendly relationships and is motivated towards interaction with other people. The affiliation driver produces motivation and a need to be liked and held in popular regard. These people are team players.

Individuals develop an emphasis towards one of three needs – achievement, affiliation or power (see McClelland's achievement needs theory). McClelland said that most people possess and exhibit a combination of these characteristics. Some people exhibit a strong bias to a particular motivational need and this motivational or needs 'mix' consequently affects their behaviour and working/managing style.

McClelland's ideas relate closely to the theory of Frederick Herzberg. According to Herzberg, man has two sets of needs:

■ first as an animal to avoid pain; and

■ second as a human being to grow psychologically.

He is most noted for his famous 'hygiene' and motivational factors theory. He and others like him did not develop their theories to be used as 'motivational tools'. They were intended purely as a means to improve organizational performance. They sought primarily to explain how to manage people properly. Herzberg's research proved that people will strive to achieve 'hygiene' needs because they are unhappy without them, but once satisfied the effect soon wears off – satisfaction is short term. People are not 'motivated' by addressing 'hygiene' needs. People are only truly motivated when able to reach for and satisfy the factors that Herzberg identified as real motivators, such as personal growth, development, etc. which represent a far deeper level of meaning and fulfilment. Thus, Herzberg proposed a two factor theory of motivation.

Hygiene factors aspects of work which remove dissatisfaction but do not contribute to motivation and performance, including pay, company policy, supervision, status, security and working conditions are known as hygiene or context factors

Table 6-1

Hygiene factors	Motivator factors
(organizational context)	(job content) achievement
pay	advancement
company policy	growth
supervisory style	recognition
status	responsibility
security	the work itself
working conditions	

Motivator factors aspects of work which lead to high levels of job satisfaction, motivation and performance, and include achievement, recognition, responsibility, advancement, growth and the work itself are known as motivator or content factors

Motivator factors are based on an individual's need for personal growth. When they exist, motivator factors actively create job satisfaction. If they are effective, then they can motivate an individual to achieve above-average performance and effort. There is some similarity between Herzberg's and Maslow's models. They both suggest that needs must be satisfied for employee motivation to be present. However, Herzberg argues that only the higher levels of the Maslow hierarchy (e.g. self-actualization, esteem needs) act as a motivator. The remaining needs can only cause dissatisfaction if not addressed.

You may have identified breakdowns in employee communication and relationships, low productivity or poor service quality. According to Herzberg, management should focus on reorganizing work so that motivator factors can take effect. He suggested three ways in which this could be done: job enlargement, job rotation and job enrichment. *Job enrichment* is the addition of tasks to a job thus increasing the amount of employee control or responsibility. It is a vertical expansion of the job as opposed to the horizontal expansion of a job, which is called *job enlargement* (the addition of tasks at the same level of skill and responsibility). Organizations use job enrichment to make work more challenging and rewarding for their employees. The job characteristics model (JCM) proposed by Richard Hackman and Greg Oldham in 1976 is a model of job enrichment which attempts to address how a core set of job characteristics affect a number of psychological states, leading to specific related outcomes in the work environment. The model was developed to complement Herzberg's two factor theory, creating high intrinsic motivation. At the heart of the model is the idea that jobs can be analyzed in terms of five core dimensions:

- Skill variety – the extent to which a job makes use of different skills and abilities.
- Task identity – the extent to which a job involves a 'whole' or meaningful piece of work.
- Task significance – the extent to which a job affects the work of others.
- Autonomy – the extent to which a job provides independence and discretion.
- Feedback – the extent to which performance information is related back to the individual.

According to Hackman and Oldham's model, skill variety, task significance and task identity are used in the work environment to stimulate meaningfulness and the presence of autonomy and feedback leads to the psychological state of felt responsibility for outcomes, resulting in high job satisfaction.

Process theories

Having considered *content* theories in the previous section we now consider the *process* theories of motivation. Process theories of motivation focus upon what people are thinking when they decide whether or not to place *effort* into a particular activity. Process theories of motivation define in terms of a rational cognitive process; see for example:

- Adams' equity theory: balanced give and take.
- Locke's goal theory.
- Vroom's expectancy theory: we expect what we predict.

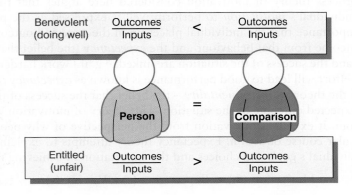

Figure 6-10
Equity theory

Equity theory is a process theory of motivation which argues that the perception of unfairness in an organizational setting leads to tension, which drives the individual to act to resolve that unfairness (Adams 1963). The theory proposes that individuals who perceive themselves as either under-rewarded or over-rewarded will experience distress, and that this distress leads to efforts to restore equity within the relationship, see Figure 6-10. The theory argues that the motivation of individuals can not be considered in isolation and that the rewards and treatments of others influence an individual's level of satisfaction. People are motivated by what they consider a fair/equitable return for their efforts. Outcomes are the perceived benefits from work, including material benefits, social status, and intrinsic rewards, and inputs are the perceived contributions such as work effort. In terms of the theory, inequity is felt as uncomfortable and tends to generate behaviour aimed at restoring equity, such as altering inputs or outcomes or cognitively distorting them, leaving the organization, attempting to distort the other person's perceptions of inputs or outcomes, or changing the person used as a point of comparison. Equity theory speculates that if the person perceives that there is inequality, where either their output/input ratio is less than or greater than what they perceive as the output/input ratio of the other person in the relationship, then the person is likely to be distressed. The basic idea behind the Equity Theory is that workers attempt to balance what they put in to their jobs and what they get from them.

Goal setting is a powerful way of motivating people. Goal-setting theory states that goals can be a major motivational source at work. Goals, when accepted, lead to higher performance levels. *Goal theory* (see Latham and Locke 1984 and Locke 1968) proposes that both motivation and performance will be high if individuals are set specific goals which are challenging, but accepted and where feedback is given on performance. According to Locke, employees are motivated by clear goals and appropriate feedback. Locke went on to say that working towards a goal provided a major source of motivation to actually reach the goal – which, in turn, improved performance. Goal setting is a process theory of motivation and a motivational technique, based on the argument that work performance can be explained with reference to characteristics of the objectives being pursued, such as goal difficulty, goal specificity and knowledge of results.

The value of goal setting is well recognized (see for example management by objectives). Goal setting theory is generally accepted as among the most valid and useful motivation theories in organizational behaviour. Locke's research showed that there was a relationship between how difficult and specific a goal was and people's performance of a task. He found that specific and difficult goals led to better task performance than vague or easy goals. To motivate, goals must be:

- clear (you know what's expected);
- challenging (the goal is possible but stretching);
- have commitment (goals must be understood and agreed upon if they are to be effective); and
- workers must receive feedback.

The final process theory of motivation considered here argues that the strength or 'force' of an individual's *motivation* to perform well is expressed as the product of the *valence* (the importance that the individual places upon the expected outcome of a situation) of the outcome from that behaviour and the *expectancy* (the belief that output from the individual and the success of the situation are linked, e.g. if I work harder then this will be better) that effort will lead to good performance is known as *expectancy theory*. A third key variable in the theory is *instrumentality* – the belief that the success of the situation is linked to the expected outcome of the situation. This theory of motivation was pioneered by Victor Vroom. It examines motivation from the perspective of why people choose to follow a particular course of action. Expectancy theory attempts to explain behaviour in terms of an individual's goals and choices and the expectation of achieving the objectives.

Motivation (m) = Expectation (e) × Valence (v).

In short, this theory suggest that employee motivation depends upon whether the employee wants the reward on offer for doing a good job and whether they believe more effort will lead to that reward. Therefore, in order to motivate people we must show them something desirable, indicate how straightforward it is to obtain it, and then support their self-belief that they can complete the task and achieve the reward.

In this section we have considered the problem. How do we motivate or persuade others to do what we want them to do? Motivation theories are important to managers and others seeking to be effective leaders. While there is no all-encompassing explanation, the aforementioned theories are helpful in understanding motivation. But how useful are they to the international manager? Are theories of motivation universal or culture dependent?

Cross-cultural motivation

Cross-cultural research has as its goal both a description of human diversity and a search for universals (general, worldwide theories). As was mentioned in the previous section, if an organization is to accomplish its objectives, leaders and managers must encourage people to perform their jobs efficiently and effectively through a variety of motivational techniques. In this section we consider whether the motivational techniques discussed so far can be used to equal effect in any given country, i.e. we need to establish whether motivational techniques are universal or culture-based.

Consider the aforementioned theories of motivation and the cultural dimensions offered by Hofstede (see Chapter 2). Would you expect the various motivational techniques to work in the same way in any given country? How would you expect people to be motivated (what may be used as motivators) according to their national culture?

STOP & THINK

Employees and workers from countries with a high uncertainty avoidance may value and be motivated by job security. Workers from collectivist cultures (low individualism) are more likely to be motivated through group goals as opposed to individual reward. Employees of certain cultures do not like to openly compete with each other. Hofstede (1980: 255) made reference to culture and motivation. He notes that high individualism implies a 'calculative involvement' of the Americans in organizations. He suggests this explains the popularity in the United States of 'expectancy' theories of motivation. Similarly, the combination of high individualism, low uncertainty avoidance and masculinity in the United States explains the popularity of Maslow's hierarchy of human needs – Maslow's supreme need, self-actualization, is a highly individualistic motive. Hofstede suggests that Maslow's hierarchy and Hertzberg's two factor theory are culturally determined. He also argues for a motivational 'map of the world' and against a universal order of needs. Whereas countries such as the USA and UK may be motivated by individual success in the form of wealth, recognition and self-actualization; other countries may determine success in terms of the collective and in the quality of human relationships. The implication is that no one motivational technique will achieve the same outcome in any given country.

The importance of *context* to motivation has been recognized much more in recent years than in the past (Latham and Pinder 2005). Significant advances have been made in understanding how national culture, characteristics of the job itself, and the fit between the person and the organization influence motivation and in understanding cross-cultural differences in work motivation. Mediating mechanisms explain why motivational strategies vary in effectiveness in different countries. For example, they cite the work of Erez and Earley (1993) who developed a model of 'cultural self-representation' to guide individual behaviour and managerial practices in cross-cultural settings. Their model is based on two dimensions frequently used to characterize national cultures: collectivism versus individualism, and power distance. Three principles are advanced to assist the design and interpretation of motivation and reward systems:

a identify the cultural characteristics of a country regarding collectivism/individualism and power distance;

b understand yourself and the cultural values you represent; and

c understand the meaning of various managerial practices (such as differential versus flat salary reward distribution and top-down versus two-way communication styles) in each country.

Projecting values onto people from other cultures that differ on the above two dimensions (individualism and power distance) can create dysfunctional consequences in terms of employee motivation, interpersonal communication, and overall performance. Researchers have also suggested motivational strategies by managers have more effect on subordinates in cultures with high levels of power distance than in cultures low in power distance (see involvement in goal setting and performance management theory).

Sue-Chan and Ong (2002) investigated the effect of goal assignment on goal commitment, self-efficacy, and performance of people from ten different countries. Self-efficacy (self-confidence) mediated the effect of goal assignment on performance for those low in value for power distance. The results of this study support Hofstede's (1994) and Erez's (2000) contention that management theories, concepts and practices cannot be applied universally without regard to individual difference characteristics that have a cultural basis. The results suggest the motivational effects of participation for low power distance individuals are large; for high power distance individuals, they may be non-existent.

Corporations that employ people who differ on the power distance value dimension would be well advised to involve their low power distance employees in determining their performance goals due to the clear motivational benefits of such participation (option 3 in Figure 6-11 (see below)). Such individuals, for example, could be expected to have even lower commitment, self-efficacy and performance when assigned a goal through the 'tell' method relative to the 'tell and sell' method used in the Sue-Chan and Ong (2002) study. No such involvement is required when dealing with high power distance individuals who do not appear to derive any additional motivational and subsequent performance benefits from participation in goal setting. For such individuals, goal assignment through 'tell', 'tell and sell' and participation are likely to have the same consequences in terms of goal commitment, self-efficacy, and performance. The results of the study suggest that, when compared with a situation in which goals are assigned by an authority figure, participation in goal setting is beneficial only to low power distance individuals and is neither beneficial nor harmful to high power distance individuals. This finding corroborates those of other researchers.

Performance management
Performance management involves enabling people to perform their work to the best of their ability, meeting and perhaps exceeding targets and standards

Figure 6-11

The role of power distance in goal theory

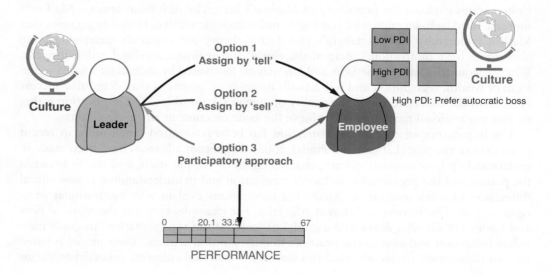

If we are to get people, from any country or culture, to do what we want them to do, in the best interest of the organization, we must understand their needs and goals in order to motivate them. This necessitates an understanding of their values, attitude and beliefs and in particular those in relation to work. Work attitudes vary from country to country. Employees in certain countries expect to work longer hours, take shorter holidays and earn less money. Snir and Harpaz (2006) examined the 'workaholism' phenomenon (the individual's steady and considerable allocation of time to work). They examined workaholism from a cross-national perspective through representative samples of the labour force in Belgium, Israel, Japan, The Netherlands, and the USA. They found that the Japanese worked more hours per week than all other nationalities (the total weekly work hours differences were considerable, and ranged from 4.50 to 8.23 hours).

Respondents with a high level of work centrality worked more hours per week than did those with a low level of work centrality. The conceptualization of working long hours as a nation-level phenomenon is encountered in the literature mainly in regard to the Japanese and the Americans, as opposed to Western Europeans, who are 'known to enjoy the pleasures of the good life'. The emphasis placed on leisure by Western Europeans from the 1970s until recently results in a reduction of work hours per employee. The reasons for working long hours in Japan are not just economic but also socio-cultural. To the Japanese, work is an end in itself – what one does if one is human. It is the process of carrying out obligations owed to society and to oneself as a social being. White-collar managers and skilled workers are like the samurai of old, who worked on behalf of their lords without question or complaint. In the Japanese culture, time logged at one's desk or workstation is often a symbolic statement of submission to managerial power and loyalty to the organization.

Work centrality is defined as the degree of general importance that working has in one's life at any given time. The work centrality concept is rooted in Weber's Protestant work ethic theory. In general, work is found to be of higher importance than other areas of life. It is usually deemed more important than leisure, community, and religion, and in several studies ranked second only to family. Research findings show work centrality to be positively related to important organizational variables such as job satisfaction, participation in decision-making, and job tenure, and negatively related to the leisure ethic. Even nowadays, the dictum that work is a virtue and play is a sin still pervades in several industrial societies. The work ethic encourages people to work hard and put in long hours. The finding that the Japanese work more hours per week than any other nationality is in accord with the fact that work centrality was found to be higher in Japan than in the other nations. Some workers in Japan are often asked to volunteer for overtime or work considerable unpaid extra time; such a request would not be well received in some European cultures. However, the typical number of hours worked per week in any given culture is not a static measure. While the overall trend in Japan during the 1990s was towards shorter working hours, in Western Europe the opposite is true due to economic stagnation and competition from low-wage countries in the enlarged European Union and Asia.

Work hours are, however, not always positively related to productivity. Moreover, there is a growing body of research on the negative effects of long work hours and overtime work on health and health-related behaviour. Hattrup, Mueller, Joens (2007) made comparisons of value importance across nations and organizations and indicated substantial similarity. Studies have discriminated societal norms according to the degree that they emphasize work as a right to which everyone is entitled versus a duty or obligation that everyone owes to society. Work values refer to the goals or rewards people seek through their work. They are expressions of more general human values in the context of the work setting. The international manager should take account of work centrality and other attitudes to work when seeking to encourage people to perform their jobs efficiently and effectively through a variety of motivational techniques.

Aside from reported differences in the meaning of work, worker needs and goals, research has also highlighted similarities and differences in how individuals benefit from work and the relative importance of different benefits such as pay, status and providing opportunity to serve society or engage in an interesting and satisfying pursuit. In certain countries, certain factors are relatively more important than others. We have highlighted

Work centrality the degree of general importance that working has in one's life at any given time

The reasons for working long hours in Japan are not just economic but also socio-cultural

Figure 6-12
Motivating workers

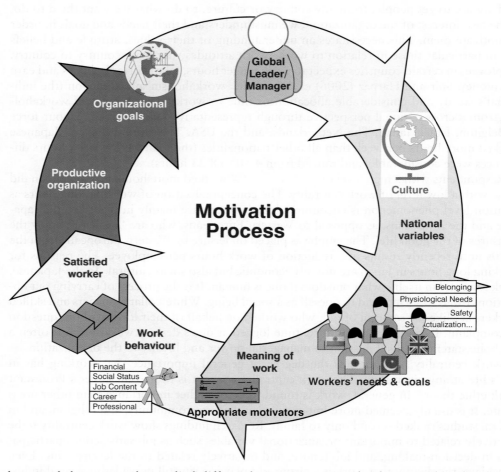

how goal theory may be applied differently in some national cultures. Other theories of motivation must similarly be applied differently in certain countries.

Earlier we noted Hofstede's suggestion that Maslow's hierarchy and Hertzberg's two factor theory are culturally determined. While studies have found the needs to be of universal application, other studies have questioned their order on a hierarchy. The hierarchy reflects the Western culture where Maslow conducted his study. However, it is now known that Eastern cultures focus on the needs of society more than the needs of individuals. Nevis (1983) provides information on a study that compared and contrasted major cultural characteristics of the United States (US) and China in terms of economic productivity. Differences were reported between US and China in terms of the hierarchy of needs.

Given that we cannot assume the universal applicability of motivational theories, how then should the international manager set about the task of motivating people from a culture different from themselves? The motivation process depicted in Figure 6-12 suggests a need to understand the context and the difference between the leaders and employees values, attitudes, beliefs and goals. Once the needs of the worker have been determined, appropriate motivators can be designed and implemented. International managers must make use of their cultural knowledge to infer the best means of motivating in that context. As has been advocated throughout this text, they should avoid an ethnocentric attitude in which they assume another person's goals, motivation and work attitudes will be the same as their own. Through an understanding of what work means to the individual, the manager/leader may design culturally appropriate motivation systems.

Hofstede (1997: 200) discusses managing in relation with organizational culture. In some cases, more success may be attained through the actions of two parties working closely together (a power holder and an expert). The expert (fachpromotor) knows what must be done and the power holder (machpromotor) knows how best to achieve it. For example, when undertaking an overseas assignment, the expert may pair-up with a 'local' thus pairing two important knowledge bases: technical expert and local culture. In such cases, two heads may indeed be better than one. In other cases, the leader may first consider the motivational techniques in use in the target country but should not simply assume them to be similar to back home. At the beginning of this section we outlined organizational leadership as including more than motivating others and we explore next further aspects of leading in other cultures.

Leading in other cultures

To what extent is leadership culturally contingent?

Organizational leadership is the ability of an individual to influence, motivate, and enable others to contribute toward the effectiveness and success of the organizations of which they are members (House *et al.* 1999). In this final section we ask how leadership *styles* and *practices* vary around the world. Leaders in the international organization must be capable of identifying global opportunities and have a good appreciation of company strengths and weaknesses and the resources and capabilities to seize such opportunities.

As with the domestic leader, the international leader must inspire and influence people anywhere in the world. Leadership is required within every organization around the world, however culture must be considered when contemplating the different theories of leadership. We have already identified situational determinants of leadership and concluded that no single leadership style worked well in all situations. Certain leadership traits and behaviours seem to be generally accepted (such as being trustworthy), however certain styles and behaviours have been found to be culturally contingent. In discussing motivation theory we identified a relationship between culture and participation and similar relationships exist with other aspects of participation in leadership processes.

Being a participative leader is more important in some countries as opposed to others. Once again, Hofstede's cultural dimensions provide a useful framework or model to study leader – subordinate relationships. Subordinates from high power distance countries are more likely to favour autocratic leadership while employees of lower power distance countries are more likely to prefer a consultative or participatory leadership style. An inappropriate style can be counterproductive in certain cultures.

A variety of studies have investigated cultural differences and similarities in leadership traits; the largest study thus far was project GLOBE, the Global Leadership and Organizational Behaviour Effectiveness Research Program. The combined results of the major GLOBE study and the follow-up study demonstrate that several attributes reflecting charismatic/transformational leadership are universally endorsed as contributing to outstanding leadership (Den Hartog, Hanges and Dorfman 1999). Attributes include:

- motive arouser;
- foresight;
- encouraging;
- communicative;
- trustworthy;
- dynamic;
- positive;
- confidence builder; and
- motivational.

Several other charismatic attributes are perceived as culturally contingent. These include:

- enthusiastic;
- risk taking;
- ambitious;
- self-effacing;

- unique;
- self-sacrificial;
- sincere;
- sensitive;
- compassionate; and
- wilful.

GLOBE, as well as a substantial amount of other empirical research has demonstrated that what is expected of leaders, what leaders may and may not do, and the status and influence bestowed on leaders vary considerably as a result of the cultural forces in the countries or regions in which the leaders function.

Figure 6-13

Leading in other cultures

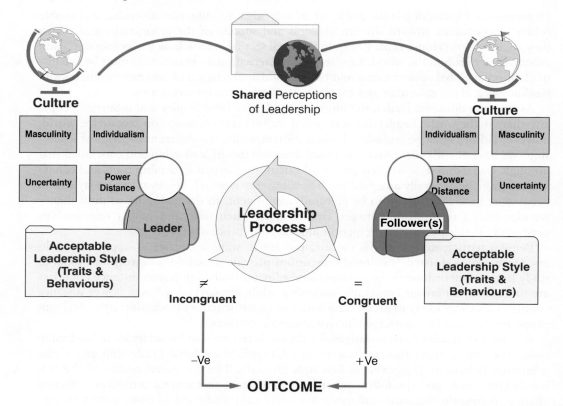

Leaders who are required to interact with a diverse set of followers, or who work in a foreign environment, need to recognize that notions of what constitutes ideal leadership may vary culturally, see Figure 6-13. For instance, in cultures that value decisiveness and hierarchy, leaders might prefer to be autocratic, and subordinates might prefer to be loyal and obedient. Conversely, in cultures that value egalitarianism, leaders might prefer to be consultative, and subordinates might prefer to be challenging and outspoken. Since followers act on perceptions of leadership, such perceptions can impact upon the outcomes of the leadership process. Furthermore, it is important for leaders to be aware of followers' expectations given the reciprocity of influence in the leader – follower relationship. Leader acceptance and effectiveness may depend upon leader attributes and behaviours being congruent with the legitimate implicit leadership expectations of followers.

Followers who categorize a manager as a typical leader are likely to allow him or her to exert leadership influence on them. If leadership concepts differ as a function of cultural differences, they can constrain the influence of foreign managers: in other words, the more leadership concepts differ between managers and subordinates or colleagues, the less influence will be exerted. Furthermore, certain characteristics of a culture may render specific leadership characteristics and styles more acceptable and effective. For example, a

Egalitarianism the moral doctrine that equality ought to prevail among some groups

leader who adopts an autocratic style may be more accepted and effective in a high power distance culture than in a low power distance culture.

An important determinant of being perceived as an effective leader is the congruence between the follower's pre-existing notions of the ideal characteristics of an effective leader and his or her perceptions of the leader's *actual* characteristics. The better the match between ideal and actual characteristics, the more likely it is that the leader will receive credit for favourable work outcomes and therefore attain the social power essential for effective leadership. The perceptual processes of followers are shaped to a large extent, by their cultural background and influence their perceptions of leadership (Hofstede 1980). Culture can be regarded as 'software of the mind' (Hofstede 1980) in that it provides members of a collective with shared cognitive structures that reflect shared ideologies and values and influence interpretations of specific behaviours. Consequently, the acceptability of a particular leadership style is likely to depend largely upon the cultural background of the followers.

Look forward
See chapter 8, p. 248

There is evidence of cross-cultural differences and similarities in leadership, some traits are universally endorsed as typical of effective leaders, whereas the endorsement of other traits may be culturally contingent. Studies have found leadership traits to be strongly related to Hofstede's (1980) cultural dimensions. The findings of Project GLOBE suggest that some traits (e.g. visionary, intelligent, trustworthy, and decisive) are endorsed universally as positive attributes for a leader to possess, whereas the endorsement of other traits is more culturally contingent (e.g. compassionate, domineering, orderly, and risk taker). Brodbeck *et al.* (2000) found that leadership differed systematically with the general cultural values held by managers and employees in different regions of Europe. Some traits (e.g. integrity, performance-oriented, team integrator, and visionary), however, were seen as facilitating outstanding leadership in all of the regions (e.g. integrity and visionary), with the exception of France.

In this section we have recognized two key variables culture and management/leadership style. There are many different cultures and many ways to lead or manage. We explored the interrelationship between societal cultural diversity and the diversity in management style and concluded there to be some universal aspects of leadership or managerial style that were unlikely to, at worse, have dysfunctional outcomes in any given culture. We also concluded that followers in certain cultures had preconceived ideas as to how leaders should lead and that an incongruent leader may not gain the power needed to lead in such cultures. Consequently, leaders and managers of international organizations, dependent on their role, managerial level and context may need to adapt their styles and behaviours dependent upon where and with whom they are working. An understanding of culturally endorsed differences in leadership concepts can be used by international managers to adjust their leadership behaviour to that required in a host country. Knowledge about particular cultural variations in leadership can help such managers more accurately anticipate potential problems in cross-cultural interactions within business.

Summary of key learning points

Management is about getting things done with the aid of people and other resources or more specifically it is the process of leading and directing all or part of an organization, through the deployment and manipulation of resources (people, technological, financial, material, intellectual or intangible). It concerns the effective utilization and coordination of resources to achieve defined objectives with maximum efficiency. Leadership appears to be a critical determinant of organizational effectiveness – much of leadership is about influencing the behaviour of others.

The function of the leader is to ensure the organization does the right thing (effectiveness) while the manager ensures things are done right (efficiency); the leader is concerned with establishing direction, the vision and organizational goals and influencing followers to obtain commitment. Consequently, the leader must be a good communicator and able to influence others – motivating and inspiring. Many scholars argue the distinction between leadership and management is blurred in practice and the effective manager requires some leadership qualities. Leadership is an important role requirement for managers. There are many ways to measure leadership effectiveness such as performance, follower satisfaction and commitment and the extent to which tasks are completed and goals are attained.

Power describes the ability to influence others, to get them to do things. In some cases the leader may influence subordinate or follower attitudes and in other cases their behaviour. Scholars have identified several types of power: reward, coercive, referent (charisma), legitimate (position power), expert, informational, affiliation and group. The exercise of power may be perceived by followers in either negative or positive terms. The type of behaviour used intentionally to influence the attitudes and behaviour of another person is usually called an *influence tactic*. Participative leadership (consultation, joint decision-making, power-sharing, decentralization, empowerment and democratic management) involves effort by a leader to encourage and facilitate participation by others in making important decisions. Participative leadership, delegation and empowerment are concepts linking the power and behaviour approaches to leadership. Participative leadership can take many forms.

Leadership behaviours tend to be grouped into those focusing on work (task oriented behaviour) and those considering the follower (subordinate in many cases). Consideration behaviours are based on relationship building (relations oriented behaviour), supporting, developing, recognizing and helping others. Specific task behaviours include planning work activities, clarifying roles and objectives and monitoring operations and performance – how things get done. The two key orientations (task and relationship building) reflect a concern for people and a concern for production, both of which are important for effective leadership. Subsequent research added a third orientation, behavioural set, based on approaches to change. Change-oriented behaviour is concerned with understanding the environment, finding innovative ways to adapt to it, and implementing major changes in strategies, products, or processes. The contingency theory of leadership is a perspective which suggests that leaders must adjust their style in a manner consistent with aspects of the context, i.e. there is no one ideal leadership style.

Organizational leadership is the ability of an individual to influence, motivate, and enable others to contribute toward the effectiveness and success of the organizations of which they are members. If we are to ensure people, from any country or culture, do what we want them to do, in the best interest of the organization, we must understand their needs and goals in order to motivate them. This necessitates an understanding of their values, attitude and beliefs and in particular those in relation to work. Work attitudes vary from country to country. The international manager should take account of work centrality and other attitudes to work when seeking to encourage people to perform their jobs efficiently and effectively through a variety of motivational techniques. Leaders who are required to interact with a diverse set of followers, or who work in a foreign environment, need to recognize that notions of what constitutes ideal leadership may vary from culture to culture. Leaders and managers of international organizations, dependent on their role, managerial level and context may need to adapt their styles and behaviours according to where and with whom they are working. An understanding of culturally endorsed differences in leadership concepts can be used by international managers to adjust their leadership behaviour to that required in a host country. Knowledge about particular cultural variations in leadership can help such managers more accurately anticipate potential problems in cross-cultural interactions within business.

Review questions

Cross-cultural leadership theory

Consider the Indian-based Infosys discussed in the opening case study. Imagine a young Indian leader, presently working in an Infosys India office is to be developed through an international assignment at an Infosys overseas office in the UK, China, Japan or Australia. The manager is allowed to choose which country the assignment will take place.

1　In which country is the manager most likely to need to adapt their leadership style and in which country will they least need to adapt their leadership style? Explain your answer, identifying what adaptations may be required in each country.

2　Assume the manager is preparing for the assignment but has not yet been advised of the country of assignment. With reference to concepts such as work centrality, culture and motivation, evaluate and comment on preferred motivational strategies best suited to each country if the manager is to both satisfy and get the best performance out of his subordinates and other 'followers' associated with the unit's goals.

3　Critically evaluate methods to develop the manager as a leader.

4　What challenges and difficulties might you expect the young manager to experience when seated on the management council, given the role spans all aspects of the business? Your answer should make reference to leadership traits, perceptions of leadership, power and high and low level leadership.

Teaching leadership

Schatz (1997) makes the point that, unlike other MBA subjects which 'only involve learning theory', and can thereby be taught, leadership involves an activity and thereby requires training; attempts to teach leadership through classroom learning alone may be doomed to failure.

1　Critically discuss the argument put forward by Schatz.

2　Imagine you have been asked to advise on a new MBA course design. Discuss what aspects of leadership theory and practice you would include in the new course and identify how different elements would be taught. You should first design a course for MBA students generally and then for a specialized international MBA.

Analysis by Mellahi (2000) revealed that leadership curricula on MBA programmes is broadly conceived in the US corpus and assumes universality. The research argued that there is a need for western management schools to adopt a more eclectic view of leadership teaching and to cast their perspective beyond western idiosyncrasies and include non-western business perspectives. However, the author does acknowledge the ethnocentric approach to the teaching of leadership is due, to a large extent, to the unavailability of alternative theories and published empirical evidence outside the USA.

1　Compare and contrast leadership theories published since 1995. At least half should be sourced from non-US writers/researchers.

2　What are the Western and non-Western perspectives? How do they differ? In comparing leadership in the East with the West are we comparing like concepts, i.e. apples with apples or apples with oranges?

3　Mellahi (2000) claims that the body of management knowledge primarily originates in the West. Based on the literature review conducted by yourself when answering (1) above, do you feel that more work is being conducted in the East than was previously the case?

Mellahi asks whether we are giving non-Western students appropriate skills. Research argues that managerial and leadership attitudes, values, and behaviour differ across national cultures and, thus, effective leadership styles are culture bound. Discuss this issue in a group comprising Eastern and Western members. First, split the group into East and West. In sub-groups, brainstorm your perception of a good leader and identify leadership theories with which the sub-group is familiar. Next, bring the sub-groups together and compare findings.

References

Adams, J. S. (1963) 'Towards an Understanding of Unequity', *The Journal of Abnormal and Social Psychology* (November 1963) 67(5):422–436.

Alimo-Metcalfe, B. and Alban-Metcalfe, J. (2003) 'Under the Influence', *People Management* 9(5):32–36.

Alimo-Metcalfe, B., Alban-Metcalfe, J. and Pickard, J. (2002) 'The Great and the Good', *People Management* 8(1):32–35.

Astley, W. G. and Sachdeva, P. S. (1984) 'Structural Sources of Intraorganizational Power: A Theoretical Synthesis', *Academy of Management Review* 9(1):104–113.

Badaracco, J. L. (2001) 'We Don't Need another Hero', *Harvard Business Review* (September 2001) 79(8):120–126.

Bartlett, C. and Ghoshal, S. (1992) 'What Is a Global Manager?', *Harvard Business Review* (September–October 1992) 124–132.

Benfari, R., Wilkinson, H. and Orth, C. (1986) 'The Effective Use of Power', *Business Horizons* 29(3):12–17.

Brodbeck, F. C. *et al.* (2000) 'Cultural variation of leadership prototypes across 22 European countries', *Journal of Occupational & Organizational Psychology* (March 2000) 73(1):1–29.

Buchner, T. W. (2007) 'Performance management theory: A look from the performer's perspective with implications for HRD', *Human Resource Development International* (March 2007) 10(1):59–73.

Cacioppe, R. (1997) 'Leadership Moment by Moment!', *Leadership & Organization Development Journal* 18(7):335–345.

Casimir, G. and Waidman, D. A. (2007) 'A Cross Cultural Comparison of the Importance of Leadership Traits for Effective Low-level and High-level Leaders: Australia and China', *International Journal of Cross Cultural Management* 7(1):47–60.

Den Hartog, D. N., Hanges, P. and Dorfman, P. (1999) 'Culture specific and cross-culturally generalizable implicit leadership theories. Are attributes of charismatic/transformational leadership universally endorsed?', *The Leadership Quarterly* (Summer 1999) 10(2):219–256.

Erez, M. (2000) 'Make practice fit national culture', in Locke, E. A. (ed.), *The Blackwell Handbook of Principles of Organizational Behaviour* Oxford: Blackwell.

Goleman, D. (2000) 'Leadership That Gets Results', *Harvard Business Review* (March/April 2000) 78(2):78–90.

Graen, G. B. and Uhl-Bien, M. (1995) 'Relationship-based approach to leadership: Development of leader-member exchange (LMX) theory of leadership over 25 years: Applying a multi-level multi-domain perspective', *The Leadership Quarterly* (Summer 1995) 6(2):219–247.

Gronn, P. (2002) 'Distributed Leadership as a Unit of Analysis', *The Leadership Quarterly* (August 2002) 13(4):423–451.

Hackman, J. R. and Oldham, G. R. (1976) 'Motivation through the Design of Work: Test of a Theory', *Organizational Behavior & Human Performance* (August 1976) 16(2):250–279.

Hattrup, K., Mueller, K. and Joens, I. (2007) 'The Effects of Nations and Organizations on Work Value Importance: A Cross-Cultural Investigation', *Applied Psychology: An International Review* (July 2007) 56(3):479–499.

Hickie, S. (2003) 'How Can we Make Sense of Leadership in the 21st Century?', *Leadership & Organization Development Journal* 24(5):273–284.

Hofstede, G (1980) 'Motivation, leadership, and organization – Do American theories apply abroad?', *Organizational Dynamics* 9(1):42–63.

Hofstede, G. (1984) *Culture's Consequences: International Differences in Work-Related Values* (abridged) Newbury Park, CA: Sage.

Hofstede, G (1997) *Cultures and Organizations*, New York: McGraw-Hill.

Houldsworth, C. and Mathews, B. P. (2000) 'Group composition, performance and educational attainment', *Education + Training* 42(1):40–53.

House, R., Hanges, P., Ruiz-Quintanilla, S. A. and Dorfman, P. (1999) 'Cultural influences on leadership and organizations: Project GLOBE', *Advances in Global Leadership* 1:171–233.

Javidan, M. and House, R. (2001) 'Cultural Acumen for the Global Manager: Lessons from Project GLOBE', *Organizational Dynamics* (Spring 2001) 29(4):289–305.

Kelman, H. (1958) 'Compliance, identification, and internalization three processes of attitude change', *Journal of Conflict Resolution* 2(1):51–60.

Kotter, J. (1995) 'Leading Change: Why Transformation Efforts Fail', *Harvard Business Review* (March/April 1995) 73(2):59–67.

Kotter, J. (1999) 'What Effective General Managers Really Do', *Harvard Business Review* (March/April 1999) 77(2):145–159.

Kotter, J. (2001) 'What Leaders Really Do', *Harvard Business Review* (December 2001) 79(11): 85–96.

Kotter, J. (2007) 'Leading Change', *Harvard Business Review* (January 2007) 85(1):96–103.

Kuhnert, K. W. and Lewis, P. (1987) 'Transactional and Transformational Leadership: A Constructive/ Developmental Analysis', *The Academy of Management Review* (October 1987) 12(4):648–657.

Laitin, D. and Lustick, I. (1974) 'Leadership: A Comparative Perspective', *International Organization* (Winter 1974) 28(1):89–118.

Locke, F. A. and Latham, G. P. (1984) *Goal Setting: A Motivational Technique that Works* Englewood Cliffs, NJ: Prentice Hall.

Latham, G. P. and Pinder, C. (2005) 'Work Motivation Theory and Research at the Dawn of the Twenty-First Century', *Annual Review of Psychology* 56(1):485–516.

Levine, J. M. and Moreland, R. L. (1990) 'Progress in small group research', *Annual Review of Psychology* 41(1):585–634.

Locke, E. (1968) 'Toward a theory of task motivation and incentives', *Organizational Behavior and Human Performance* 3(2):157–189.

Maslow, A. H. (1943) 'A Theory of Human Motivation', *Psychological Review* (July 1943) 50(4): 370–396.

Mellahi, K. (2000) 'The Teaching of Leadership on UK MBA programmes – A critical analysis from an international perspective', *Journal of Management Development* 19(4):297–308.

Mintzberg, H. (1975) 'The Manager's Job: Folklore And Fact', *Harvard Business Review* (July/August 1975) 53(4):49–61.

Mintzberg, H. (2004) 'Enough Leadership', *Harvard Business Review* (November 2004) 82(11):22.

Nevis, E. C. (1983) 'Cultural Assumptions and Productivity: The United States and China', *Sloan Management Review* (Spring 1983) 24(3):17–30.

Palmer, B., Walls, M., Burgess, Z. and Stough, C. (2001) 'Emotional Intelligence and Effective Leadership', *Leadership & Organization Development Journal* 22(1):5–10.

Pfeffer, J. (1977) 'The Ambiguity of Leadership', *The Academy of Management Review* (January 1997) 2(1):104–112.

Politis, J. D. (2001) 'The Relationship of Various Leadership Styles to Knowledge Management', *Leadership & Organization Development Journal* 22(8):354–364.

Sarros, J. C. and Santora, J. C. (2001) 'The Transformational-Transactional Leadership Model In Practice', *Leadership & Organization Development Journal* 22(8):383–394.

Schatz, M. (1997) 'Why we don't teach leadership in our MBA programmes', *Journal of Management Development* 16(9):677–679.

Schein, E. (1997) 'Organizational Culture and Leadership' (2 ed), San Francisco: Jossey Bass.

Senge, P. M. (1999) 'Sharing Knowledge', *Executive Excellence* 16(9):6–7.

Shaw, J. B. (1990) 'A Cognitive Categorization Model for the Study of Intercultural Management', *The Academy of Management Review* (October 1990) 15(4):626–645.

Smith, M. E. (2003) 'Changing An Organization's Culture: Correlates of Success and Failure', *Leadership & Organization Development Journal* 24(5):249–261.

Snir, R. and Harpaz, I. (2006) 'The Workaholism Phenomenon: a cross-national perspective', *Career Development International* 11(5):374–393.

Sue-Chan, C. and Ong, M. (2002) 'Goal assignment and performance: Assessing the mediating roles of goal commitment and self-efficacy and the moderating role of power distance', *Organizational Behavior and Human Decision Processes* (November 2002) 89(2):1140–1161.

Tannenbaum, R. and Schmidt, W. H. (1958) 'How To Choose A Leadership Pattern', *Harvard Business Review* (March/April 1958) 36(2):95–101.

Uhl-Bien, M., Marion, R. and McKelvey, B. (2007) 'Complexity Leadership Theory: Shifting leadership from the industrial age to the knowledge era', *The Leadership Quarterly* 18(4):298–318.

Van de Vliert, E. (2006) 'Autocratic Leadership Around the Globe', *Journal of Cross-Cultural Psychology* 37(1):42–59.

Yukl, G. (2006) 'Leadership In Organizations' (6 ed), Upper Saddle River, NJ: Prentice Hall.

Zagorsek, H., Jaklic, M. and Stough, S. (2004) 'Comparing Leadership Practices Between The United States, Nigeria, and Slovenia: Does Culture Matter?', *Cross Cultural Management: An International Journal* 11(2):16–34.

Suggestions for further reading

Journals

The Leadership Quarterly

An international journal of political, social and behavioral science published in affiliation with the International Leadership Association – www.elsevier.com/.

Leadership & Organization Development Journal

The *Leadership & Organization Development Journal* explores behavioural and managerial issues relating to all aspects of leadership. It also looks at individual and organization development, from a global perspective. www.emeraldinsight.com/info/journals/lodj/lodj.jsp.

Strategy & Leadership

Strategy & Leadership is a journal containing articles concerning leadership and corporate strategy and strategic management. http://www.emeraldinsight.com/info/journals/sl/sl.jsp.

Leadership

Leadership is an international journal designed to provide an ongoing forum for academic researchers to exchange information, insights and knowledge, based on both theoretical development and empirical research on leadership. *Leadership* is available electronically on Sage Journals Online at http://lea.sagepub.com.

International Journal of Cross Cultural Management

The *International Journal of Cross Cultural Management* provides a specialized academic medium and main reference for the encouragement and dissemination of research on cross cultural aspects of management, work and organization. It aims to improve understanding and improvement of international management practice – online at http://ccm.sagepub.com/.

Key articles

Scholars of this subject area have often read the following:

1. Mintzberg, H. (1975) 'The manager's job: folklore and fact', *Harvard Business Review* (July/August 1975) 53(4):49–61.
2. Graen, G. B. and Uhl-Bien, M. (1995) 'Relationship-based approach to leadership: Development of leader-member exchange (LMX) theory of leadership over 25 years: Applying a multi-level multi-domain perspective', *The Leadership Quarterly* (Summer 1995) 6(2): 219–247.
3. Goleman, D. (2000) 'Leadership That Gets Results', *Harvard Business Review* (March/April 2000) 78(2):78–90.
4. Tannenbaum, R. and Schmidt, W. H. (1958) 'How to Choose A Leadership Pattern', *Harvard Business Review* (March/April 1958) 36(2):95–101.
5. Pfeffer, J. (1977) 'The Ambiguity of Leadership', *The Academy of Management Review* (January 1997) 2(1):104–112.
6. Badaracco, J. L. (2001) 'We Don't Need Another Hero', *Harvard Business Review* (September 2001) 79(8):120–126.
7. Kotter, J. (2001) 'What Leaders Really Do', *Harvard Business Review* (December 2001) 79(11):85–96.
8. Kotter, J. (1995) 'Leading Change: Why Transformation Efforts Fail', *Harvard Business Review* (March/April 1995) 73(2):59–67.
9. Astley, W. G. and Sachdeva, P. S. (1984) 'Structural Sources of Intraorganizational Power: A Theoretical Synthesis', *Academy of Management Review* 9(1):104–113.
10. Smith, M. E. (2003) 'Changing an organisation's culture: correlates of success and failure', *Leadership & Organization Development Journal* 24(5):249–261.

Part II Summary

Learning case

We started out by analyzing the internal and external environment which provided the context for international organizational activity. The environment is a source of opportunity, threat, strength and weakness. Through an understanding of such factors the international organization can compete and fulfil customer needs more effectively and efficiently. Two perspectives were discussed – an emphasis on the external environment (the positioning perspective) and internal environment (resource-based view) both of which were developed in the strategy chapter. We focused on what the international organization should do and how it should do it. Strategies are used to unify, constrain, coordinate and motivate the organization. They specify how resources will be allocated to develop sustainable competitive advantage – and the scope of the organization – where it will compete. We then considered the need for organizational members to behave responsibly in all their business activities – wherever they are conducted. In the introductory chapter we discussed performance and in Chapter 5 discussed organizational change which concerns the alteration of organizational components (such as the mission, strategy, goals, structure, processes, systems, technology and people) to improve the effectiveness or efficiency of the organization. The key role of leaders and managers was recognized, particularly in setting direction and allocating, developing and motivating resources to ensure goals are obtained.

Part III

Managing human resources

This part identifies ways in which the performance of the international organization may be improved through usage of human resources and the effective management of people. After completing studies in this section of the book you should be able to: explain how the management of human resources may lead to sustainable completive advantage; analyze and synthesize designs and structures for the international company; discuss the need for cultural competence and benefits of diversity management in international companies; critically evaluate alternative mechanisms for control and coordination in international companies and explain how global business processes may be modelled and the approaches used plus reasons for striving to continuously improve them. This part of the book has four related chapters:

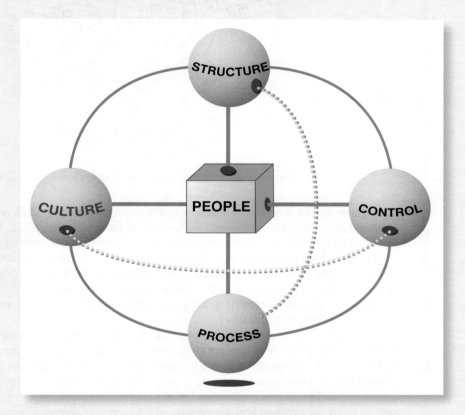

In Part III we focus on the attainment of organizational goals, the strategy and sustainable competitive advantage through people resources. When people are motivated, satisfied, committed, loyal, able, skilled, knowledgeable and competent they become capable of performing organizational goals efficiently, while delivering value, quality and innovation. As components of the transformational process discussed in Chapter 5, when aligned with other resources such as management and information systems and technology they form a bundle of resources which are difficult to imitate and therefore a source of sustainable competitive advantage. Chapter 7 focuses on the worldwide management of human resources – how to make the most efficient use of human resources in the international context. The role of the HR specialist is considered alongside the components of the HR system: philosophy, HR policies and practices. We investigate challenges associated with the application of such a system worldwide, particularly in terms of their universal application. The tension associated with a need for integration and differentiation is considered in terms of the diffusion of HR practices throughout worldwide operations.

Chapter 8 focuses on managing difference and assuring people are able to work productively with one another regardless of these differences. In particular, we focus on working with other cultures, across borders. We argue the business case for diversity, explaining how the multicultural

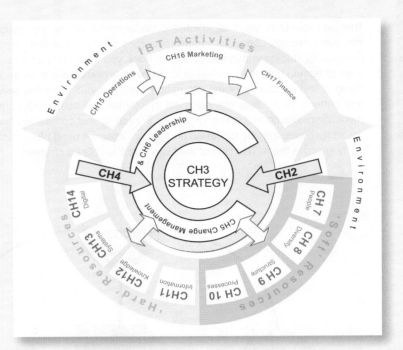

organization can be a source of sustainable competitive advantage. Multicultural group work is explained along with the associated positive and negative work outcomes. This is an essential precursor for the final chapter, process organizations, which are dependent on teamwork.

In Chapter 9 we identify the organizational mechanisms used to control and coordinate worldwide operations. We explain the need to divide and allocate work and the different philosophies, systems and designs used for such division and allocation. Ultimately the aim will be to design an international organization which is globally competitive, flexible, adaptable and able to share and develop resources and capabilities.

In Chapter 10 we focus more on how work gets done within the international organization. Building on the value chain concept discussed in Chapter 3, we decompose the primary and secondary value adding activities into business processes, sub-processes and tasks. The link is made between work, people, structure, processes, culture, information systems and technology and an alignment model presented. In this chapter, the problems of traditional work design and structure are explored and the benefits of a horizontal orientation discussed. We highlight how resources may be used through a horizontal focus to best add value and deliver customer requirements in an optimum way. This final chapter paves the way for the following part of the book which discusses information resources and technology.

Chapter 7

Managing human resources worldwide

Introduction

Strategic use of human resources

The IHRM function and global practices

IHRM practices and procedures

Performance management

··

Key concepts

■ Human capital management ■ HRM ■ HR planning ■ IHRM ■ Behavioural science
■ HRM process ■ Resourcing ■ HRM strategy ■ Succession planning ■ Motivation ■ RBV
■ Staffing policy ■ Recruitment and selection ■ Training and development
■ Performance management ■ Compensation ■ Employee relations ■ International assignments
■ HR (IT) systems

By the end of this chapter you will be able to:

■ Identify HRM issues and problems arising from the internationalization of organizations

■ Explain how human capital can be a source of sustainable competitive advantage

■ Identify and describe the core HR practices

■ Explain the role of the IHRM function

■ Discuss factors which may impact upon HR policy and practice design

Burberry

'A British company? Widely recognized as a British brand around the world …
Burberry is a luxury brand with a distinctive British sensibility, strong international recognition and differentiating brand values that resonate across a multi-generational and dual-gender audience. The Company designs and sources apparel and accessories distributing through a diversified network of retail, wholesale and licensing channels worldwide. Since its founding in England in 1856, Burberry has been synonymous with quality, innovation and style' [1] Burberry web site 2007.

Company background

This public company was established in 1856 and celebrated 150 years of history as it announced the closure of its Welsh factory. At the time of the closure, company revenues were approximately £0.75 billion. Through its operations, the group designs, sources, markets, licenses and distributes apparel (clothing in general), accessories and other lifestyle products for women, men and children. Burberry products are sold worldwide through a network of 260 directly operated stores and concessions, 71 third-party operated retail locations and a network of wholesale customers, which include leading prestige retailers in each market. In the financial year to 31 March 2006, the group generated total revenue of £743m. Approximately one-third of sales were made in Europe; one-third in Japan and almost one-third in North America and Asia.

In their Annual Report and Accounts for 2005/06 they discuss initiatives to redesign their supply chain (project Atlas). The company launched a major infrastructure redesign (five year) programme to enhance efficiency and effectiveness. The programme's goals included both cost reduction and sales growth. For the past five years the company has continued to grow from revenues of below £0.5 to £0.75b. The company is dependent upon the strength of its brand, trademarks and other intellectual property – 'We believe that our trademarks and other proprietary rights are fundamentally important to our success and competitive position.' Amongst other risks, acknowledged in their annual report, are manufacturing problems in the supply chain and the related Atlas project. 'Burberry continues to evolve its sourcing strategy, refining its selection of suppliers to maintain and enhance product quality whilst improving sourcing efficiency … this process may adversely affect relationships with existing suppliers during the transition period.'

Employment and related policies

The company is committed to a policy of equal opportunity as stated in the annual report 2005/06. The group aims to recruit the most capable job applicants and develop competent employees. All employees should receive fair and equal treatment irrespective of nationality. With regard to employee involvement, Burberry believes that employee communication is important in building strong relationships with and in motivating employees. With regard to remuneration, the company aims to provide competitive salaries. Burberry has a Corporate Social Responsibility (CSR) committee which, in 2005 considered items which included the supply chain – maintaining acceptable labour, environmental and social practices in the group's supply chain. They recognized that 'good workplace standards, health and safety, fair pay and fair employment conditions together with care for the environment are all elements

Alex Segre/Alamy

of a successful and professionally run business'. Commenting on their approach to the working environment they declare that they are committed to providing a working environment that encourages everyone employed by Burberry to contribute both to their own and the company's success. Within this environment, employees are rewarded in accordance with their contribution. Human resource issues are managed by the head office HR team under the direction of the human resources director. Regional divisions also have similar HR functions and some of these regions have 'significant' local autonomy.

Redundancy and closure (2006–07)

In September 2006, Burberry announced the proposed closure of its factory at Ynyswen, Treorchy in the Rhondda (Wales – UK). Closure plans affected 310 workers there – roughly one-third of Burberry's manufacturing jobs in the UK. Through this factory there has been an association with the clothing industry for 70 years. The loss posed a major blow to the community [3]. 'Burberry has a corporate social responsibility policy, committing itself amongst other things to fair employment practices and acceptable employment practices in its supply chain. But now it plans to export jobs from Britain to countries with much lower wages and worse working conditions' [3]. Janet Street-Porter commented in the Independent, 'last week when it emerged that one of our most iconic brands, Burberry, is planning to close its factory in the Rhondda Valley, in South Wales, because it costs about £12 to make one of their polo shirts in the UK and about £4 in the Far East. To many, Burberry is just as British as the Union Jack – it's up there with Marmite, bulldogs, beefeaters and jellied eels' *The Independent* (2006). Since the closure announcement a major campaign has been run by the unions, principally the GMB but also Amicus, involving local politicians and local people [3]. The *Sunday Times* (26 November 2006 – 'Charles joins rebellion over Burberry move to China') suggested that Prince Charles intervened in the row over plans by Burberry to shut down its Welsh factory with the loss of 300 jobs. 'He is understood to have contacted government ministers to ask if there is anything he can do' [5].

Burberry managers were 'feeling the heat' of a campaign to save a factory, First Minister Rhodri Morgan said (30 January 2007). The high-profile campaign to save the jobs of 300 people attracted the support of a string of celebrity backers including actor Ioan Gruffudd and singer Tom Jones. 'The fact that everybody knows now that they are contemplating moving production to China is doing reputational and therefore market damage and therefore we should be keeping the heat up' [6]. Early in 2007, the *Sunday Telegraph* ran with the headline …. the battle to check Burberry goes global – 'The GMB union, which is organizing the campaign to save the Treorchy jobs, has chosen St Valentine's Day to launch simultaneous protests outside Burberry stores in Las Vegas, Paris, New York and San Francisco …' A Burberry spokesman said: 'The factory in Treocrchy is just one of many polo shirt factories around the globe. It is an issue of costings. It costs twice as much to make a shirt in Treorchy as it does elsewhere' [7]. Pressure on Burberry continued as, 'Workers fighting to keep Burberry's south Wales factory open have taken their campaign to the House of Commons. Before meeting MPs, the workers ceremonially cut a Burberry tie with a pair of scissors to claim how the brand is 'cutting ties' with its UK roots. The firm, which is marking its 150th anniversary this year, has reported an 11 per cent rise in half-year sales with pre-tax profits of more than £70m … Burberry has said the factory is not 'commercially viable' [8].

picture courtesy Leighton Andrews AM

Burberry workers from Treorchy in the Rhondda protest about the closure of their factory outside Burberry's flagship New Bond Street store in London in November 2006

Union campaign

A trade union is a membership-based organization with the primary aim to protect workers' rights. According to their website [8] GMB (Britain's general union) is a strong, modern, dynamic trade union focused on one thing – protecting its members in the workplace. GMB is a general union – which means that membership is open to all adults rather than employees working in a specific commercial sector. They claim to have over 600 000 members working in every part of the UK economy. One in every 32 people at work in the UK is a member of GMB. They state that their fundamental approach is that 'together we can achieve more than we can do on our own … Whether you're looking for better pay, improved childcare, realistic work-life balance, a change to long working hours, the elimination of poor health and safety or simply a desire for respect from your employer; together our voices are much more powerful than one voice alone.' The GMB's stated purpose is to improve the quality of life for all its members.

The GMB was successful in delaying the closure date of the Burberry factory and warehouse in Treorchy from 4 January 2007 until 31 March 2007. GMB Senior Organizer Mervyn Burnett, along with local Rhondda MP Christ Bryant, also lobbied members of the Welsh Assembly to help bring the company to the table. On Thursday 7 September (2006) a mass meeting of GMB members employed at the factory was held. The Company has a legal obligation to consult with the workers' recognized trade union about any serious proposal involving redundancies.

Sources:

(1) http://www.burberry.com
(2) http://news.bbc.co.uk/1/hi/wales/6222983.stm accessed 9 Feb 2007
(3) www.keepburberrybritish.com/
(4) *The Independent* (2006), http://comment.independent.co.uk/columnists_m_z/janet_street_porter/article1963421.ece accessed 9 Feb 2007
(5) www.timesonline.co.uk/tol/news/uk/article650365.ece
(6) http://icwales.icnetwork.co.uk/0300business/0100news/tm_headline=keep-up-the-heat-on-burberry—morgan&method=full&objectid=18552248&siteid=50082-name_page.html
(7) www.telegraph.co.uk/news/main.jhtml?xml=/news/2007/01/28/nburb28.xml
(8) www.gmb.org.uk/ accessed 9 February 2007

Introduction

Since the early 1990s there has been a growing interest in international HRM (IHRM), reflecting the growing recognition that the effective management of human resources internationally is a major determinant of success or failure in international business argue Scullion and Starkey (2000). In this introductory section, we establish the scope of IHRM, define key terms in international human resource management (IHRM) and outline the differences between domestic and international human resources. We also consider the context for IHRM recognizing that the human resource (HR) function and systems do not operate in a vacuum, and that HR activities are determined by, and influence, internal, organizational, and external factors. Ultimately throughout this chapter, we aim is to establish the role of HRM in sustaining international business operations and growth.

Wernerfelt (1984) first explored the usefulness of analyzing organizations from a resource perspective. Human capital (HC) resources include the training, experience, judgement, intelligence, relationships, and insight of individual managers and workers in an organization. Organizational capital resources include a company's formal reporting structure (see Chapter 9), its formal and informal planning, controlling, and coordinating systems, as well as informal relations among groups within a firm and between a firm and those in its environment.

In the previous chapter we noted the general role of leadership and management including, developing and getting the most from HC. In order to maximize the return on investment from the organization's HC larger firms establish a *human resources* function. Human resource management (HRM) aims to improve the *productive* contribution of individuals – it is about *people* and their ability to be economically productive, to enhance organizational performance. The goal of HRM is to help an organization meet strategic goals by attracting, and retaining, employees and also to manage them effectively. HRM is therefore concerned with the strategic management of human resources to achieve a competitive advantage. A variety of activities may be associated with HRM: strategic HR management, equal employment opportunity (EEO), resourcing (Staffing), training and development, reward and recognition, health, safety, and security, and employee (labour) relations. HRM is all about managing people, human capital and culture (see Chapter 8) for business success.

The field of IHRM may be subdivided with one (centralized) area focusing on *the management of employees operating in different countries* (expatriates, consultants and other employees on assignment) and the other area concerned with approaches to HRM in other countries (the MNC with multiple HR groups across the globe). IHRM is characterized by several broad approaches: cross-cultural management, HRM systems in various countries and international HRM within the international context.

Drawing on the work of Schuler *et al.* (1993), Schuler, Budhwar and Florkowski (2002) describe three major components of IHRM: issues, functions and policies and practices, see Figure 7-1. International organizations must decide how to be sensitive to the unique local demands without inhibiting their ability to coordinate and control such units in pursuit of global strategies (*issues*). The resources devoted to and the location of IHRM operations vary considerably and are described under the *HRM function*. Finally, the general guidelines on how individuals will be managed are encapsulated in IHRM *policies and practices*. We explore each IHRM component in detail throughout the remainder of this chapter.

In the introductory chapter we introduced the global-local (glocal) issue which impacts upon international HRM. For example, can and how do MNEs link their globally dispersed units through HR policies and practices? Can and how do MNEs facilitate a multidomestic response that is simultaneously consistent with the need for global coordination and the transfer of learning and innovation across units through human resource policies and practices? Schuler, Dowling and De Cieri (1993) discuss two major strategic components of MNEs that give rise to and influence strategic IHRM. These are the *interunit* linkages and *internal* operations. Multinational enterprises are concerned with operating effectively in several different countries. Consequently, MNEs are continually discussing how to manage

IHRM international human resource management (IHRM) is about the worldwide management of human resources

Look back
See chapters 1 and 3

Training any intervention aimed at increasing an individual's knowledge or skills

Organizational capital knowledge embedded in the organization's systems and processes

Look back
See chapter 2

Training and development the design and delivery of workplace learning to improve performance

Reward and recognition providing competitive salary and benefits to attract and retain the best people

Human capital management the measurement and value of employees (human capital) to the organization and as a key indicator of a company's success

Strategic international human resource management (SIHRM) human resource management issues, functions and policies and practices that result from the strategic activities of multinational enterprises and that impact upon the international concerns and goals of those enterprises

Figure 7-1

IHRM components

their various operating units. In particular, they are interested in how these units are to be differentiated and then how they are to be integrated, controlled and coordinated.

The key objective in interunit linkages appears to be balancing the needs of variety (diversity), coordination and control for purposes of global competitiveness, flexibility and organizational learning. MNEs are also concerned about strategic issues other than those dealing with the linkage of the units. They are concerned about the internal operations of those units. In addition to working together, each unit has to work within the confines of its local environment, its laws, politics, culture, economy and society. Each unit also has to be operated as effectively as possible relative to the competitive strategy of the MNE and the unit itself. As an MNE it needs to be aware of how much autonomy it can and needs to grant to local units. It needs to decide how much to control and how to coordinate those units. The IHRM approach should be contingent upon firm characteristics (international strategy, structure, organizational culture, etc.), home and host country factors.

In a multidomestic industry, the role of the HR department will most likely be more domestic in structure and orientation. At times, there may be considerable demand for international services from the HR department (e.g. when a new plant or office is established in a foreign location and the need for expatriate employees arises), but these activities would not be pivotal – indeed, many of these services may be provided by consultants and/or temporary employees. The main role for the HR function would be to support the primary activities of the organization in each domestic market to achieve competitive advantage through either cost/efficiency or differentiation (value added to products or services). If, however, the organization is in a global industry, the 'imperative for coordination' described by Porter would require a HR function structured to deliver the international support required by primary activities of the firm.

In order to build, maintain, and develop their corporate identity, multinational organizations need to strive for consistency in their ways of managing people on a worldwide basis. Yet, and in order to be effective locally, they also need to adapt those ways to the specific cultural requirements of different societies. While the global nature of the business may call for increased consistency, the nature of cultural environments may be calling for differentiation (Laurent 1986: 97).

We have structured this chapter, with Figure 7-1 in mind, into three main sections:

- *Issues* are dealt with in the first section where we present an overview of human resource management in the international organization and discuss competing with HC.

- Next we focus on the central and strategic issues of integrating and coordinating the organization operating internationally and the role of the HRM function.

- We then finish the chapter with a review of core HR practices (operational HR).

Orientation introducing a new employee to his or her job and the organization

You should reflect on the opening case study and make links with other chapters of the book while reading this chapter. Our main goal throughout the chapter is to explore two key challenges: to acquire and develop skilled and knowledgeable human resources and to motivate human resources to engage in productive behaviours.

Strategic use of human resources

Within this section we first consider the scope and importance of IHRM before evaluating human capital (HC) as a source of *competitive advantage*. *HRM goals* specify how to make best use of the people resource of an organization and IHRM is about the worldwide management of human resources suggest Schuler, Budhwar and Florkowski (2002). The IHRM goal is, to assist organizations to make the most effective use of their human resources in the international context (Shen 2005). The purpose of IHRM is to enable the MNE to be a global success (*see* also Schuler, Budhwar and Florkowski (2002)). This entails being:

a competitive throughout the world;

b efficient;

c locally responsive;

d flexible and adaptable within the shortest of time periods; and

e capable of transferring knowledge and learning across their globally dispersed units.

Kidger (1991) suggested that HRM thinking should consider the integration of HRM with business strategy (refer back to Chapter 3); the development of distinctive corporate culture and the creation of a skilled, flexible and committed workforce which is adaptive to changing circumstances. Integrated market-related strategies, a unifying corporate culture and a committed workforce can all be argued as necessary responses to forces of competition. An international company may pursue different strategies in different countries and may either decide that HRM policy should follow local strategy or seek to determine some overall HRM principles that may create some commonality. Any manager considering whether to introduce what is apparently a successful idea from another country has to consider whether account should be taken of national culture differences (a matter explored in Chapter 2).

Kidger (1991) asks whether management practices are culture-bound or culture-free – 'can management policy developed within the culture of the multinational's home country be transferred elsewhere'? A problem we discuss later in this chapter. However, Kidger (1991) notes there to be differences between organizations arising out of their differing sizes, technologies, histories, organizational cultures and competitive positions. These differences exist within and across national boundaries – national culture is an important part of the external context. A full picture of international HRM must include both the *common* and the *different*. International HRM will not consist of identical practices since HRM is not identical within a single industry in one country, let alone on a worldwide stage. Rather it will be about choices which managers must make to meet objectives within given contexts.

As was highlighted in Chapter 3, sustainable competitive advantage is something that:

1 distinguishes a company from its competitors;

2 provides positive economic benefits; and

3 is not readily duplicated.

While scholars proclaim the importance of employees as a critical resource for competitive advantage, it is important to note that not all employees possess skills that are equally unique and/or valuable to a particular organization. It may be the case that some organizations manage all employees the same way or may use multiple modes for different groups

IHRM goal to assist organizations to make the most effective use of their human resources in the international context

IHRM purpose the purpose of IHRM is to enable the MNE to be a global success. This entails being: (a) competitive throughout the world; (b) efficient; (c) locally responsive; (d) flexible and adaptable within the shortest of time periods; and (e) capable of transferring knowledge and learning across their globally dispersed units of *human capital*. To date, most strategic HRM researchers have tended to take a holistic view of employment and human capital, focusing on the extent to which a set of practices is used across all employees of an organization as well as the consistency of these practices across organizations (Lepak and Snell 1999).

A selection of organizations may act in the belief that there may be a universally best set of HR practices for every organization, others argue that there may actually be no one best set of practices for every employee within an organization. Organizations seek to identify which forms of HC have the potential to be a source of competitive advantage today and in the future, as well as those that do not. If that potential is identified, developed, and deployed strategically, organizations may well be able to gain a competitive advantage. Lepak and Snell (1999) argue that HR systems are not likely to be appropriate in all conditions but, rather, depend upon the value and uniqueness of human capital. Certain forms of human capital are more valuable to organizations and more available in the open labour market than others.

Becker and Gerhart (1996) ask whether HR decisions create value, or just reduce costs. Those holding the resource-based view of the firm suggest that resources are valuable when they enable a firm to enact strategies that improve efficiency and effectiveness, exploit market opportunities, and/or neutralize potential threats (Barney 1991). Accordingly, the value of HC is inherently dependent upon its potential to contribute to the competitive advantage or core competence of the organization. Like other organizational assets, employee skills can be classified as core or peripheral assets: core assets, in particular, are vital to the competitive advantage of an organization and often require continual internal development.

The value of human capital can be influenced by a multitude of sources, such as an organization's strategy and technologies. Employees can add value if they can help organizations offer lower costs or provide increased benefits to customers. Because value has a direct impact upon the performance of organizations (Barney 1991), we expect it to influence employment decisions. Thus, advocates of transaction cost economics and resource theory have argued convincingly that idiosyncratic resources are essential. If an asset or skill cannot be duplicated or imitated by another organization, it provides a potential source of competitive advantage to the organization (Barney 1991).

STOP & THINK

Consider the opening case study organization (Burberry). Within which parts of the organization do you think HC will be highly valued and in which parts less so? In which parts might HC be more unique and firm specific? How do you think the organization is using HC as a source of competitive advantage – is this sustainable?

The effective management of international HR is increasingly seen as a key source of competitive advantage in international business and the quality of management seems to be even more critical in international than in domestic operations (Dowling *et al*. 1999). Although some resources are more susceptible to imitation than others, every organization's competitive advantage is continually threatened (for example it may be imitated or substituted). As Barney notes, 'Although a firm's resources and capabilities have added value in the past, changes in customer tastes, industry structure, or technology can render them less valuable in the future' (1995: 51). If we assume that competitive situations change, we must also assume that value and uniqueness of human capital change and evolve. As the organization's environment changes and the nature of competition increases or shifts, barriers to imitation face greater threats, and the organization's existing stock of knowledge and skills may become obsolete.

Given enough effort, competitors can often nurture and develop the same or functionally equivalent skills to mimic an organization's competitive advantage or develop new skills that render existing advantages obsolete, i.e. human capital shifts from high levels of value and uniqueness toward more generic and less valuable forms. Time and competition tend to erode the strategic positioning of human capital (the decay of human capital). However, organizations may try to sustain their competitive position by offering competitors a 'moving target' that is difficult to emulate by reinvesting in the skills and competencies that provide a source of advantage. To make the deployment and value of human capital more organization specific, managers may try to enhance the degree of uniqueness of human capital by customizing or adjusting skills (see the training and development section later in this chapter). Those experiences that increase employee tacit knowledge (rather than explicit knowledge that can be transferred to competitors) are likely to increase the organization specificity of human capital. Employee training not only averts human capital decay (by continuously enhancing employee skills) but may also increase the uniqueness of human capital (Lepak and Snell 1999). Given the problems of environmental change, decay and imitation organizations must integrate flexibility into their HR architectures and systems to adapt to dynamic changes while maintaining congruence among the individual components to meet their existing needs, i.e. organizations must simultaneously develop and utilize both current as well as future forms of human capital simultaneously for competitive advantage (Lepak and Snell 1999).

It has been argued that certain business strategies demand a unique set of behaviours and attitudes from employees and that HR policies and practices may produce the desired responses (behaviour) from employees. Some have argued that HR practices constitute a source of sustainable competitive advantage while others have argued that any individual HR practice could easily be copied by competitors. Consequently, others have argued that it is the workforce itself (when highly skilled and motivated) that constitutes a source of sustainable competitive advantage. HR practices when viewed collectively as a system (see people management or HR system) can be unique and difficult to replicate and may therefore be a source of sustainable competitive advantage. An organization not only needs skilled people, they must also be well managed. While any given employee may be talented they may not necessarily apply that talent to perform (see discretionary behaviour). In short, competitive advantage is also dependent upon the employee choosing to engage in behaviour that will benefit the organization.

There are many practices that seek to influence behaviour. Huselid (1995) revealed a relationship between HR practice and performance (return on assets); Koch and McGrath (1996) found that HR practices (recruitment and staffing) were related to productivity and Wright *et al.* (1999) linked appraisal and training practices with skill development and compensation practice with motivation. Sustainable competitive advantage is not just a function of isolated components but rather a combination of skills, behaviour and the supporting people management or HR system. HR activities are thought to lead to the development of a skilled workforce and one that engages in functional behaviour for the organization; this results in higher operating performance, which translates into increased profitability, see Figure 7-2.

According to Bartlett and Ghoshal (2002) *skilled* and *motivated* people are central to the operations of any company that wishes to flourish in the new age – 'In short, people are the key strategic resource, and strategy must be built on a human-resource foundation'. It is widely accepted that in order to compete in a rapidly changing environment

Look forward
See chapter 12

HR policies and practices those HR tools used to manage the human capital pool

Recruitment locating, identifying, and attracting capable applicants

Staffing how a company staffs its offices

Look forward
See chapter 10

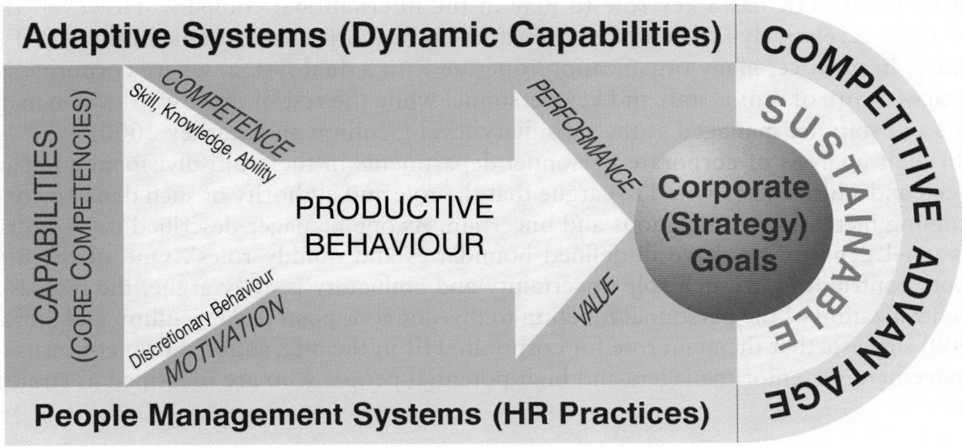

Figure 7-2

HC and competitive advantage (Adapted from Wright, Dunford and Snell 2001)

companies must continually improve their performance by reducing costs, innovating products and processes, and improving quality, productivity and speed to market (Becker and Gerhart 1996). HR systems represent a largely untapped opportunity to improve company performance.

As has been previously noted, in order to provide extraordinary returns over time, any source of competitive advantage must be difficult to imitate. Traditional sources of success – product and process technology, protected or regulated markets, access to financial resources, and economies of scale – can still provide competitive leverage argues Pfeffer (1994: 11) but to a lesser degree now than in the past, leaving organizational culture (*see* Chapter 8) and capabilities, derived from how people are managed, as comparatively more vital. As other sources of competitive success have become less important, what remains as a crucial, differentiating factor is the organization, its employees, and how they work. Culture, how people are managed (the 'soft' side of business) and practices may be difficult to understand (particularly as they exist as a wider system – set of interrelated components) and therefore difficult to copy.

Within this section we have identified the importance of HC and established a need to manage it from two key perspectives:

1 the unique and valued skills; and
2 to encourage employees to engage in productive behaviour (motivation).

In the previous chapter we noted that every manager plays a role in assuring that we attract, develop, retain and motivate HC. In this role, they may be supported by HR professionals and HR systems. We have also considered the context for HR. The convergence-divergences debate (glocal) – forces for standardization are mainly internal to the multinational driven by the need for control and to sustain competitive advantage. Forces for adaptation come from external constraints. In the next section we consider the specialized role of the HR professional within the international organization before reviewing specific HR practices and procedures.

The IHRM function and global practices

Having considered the need for talented employees and outlined the IHRM concept we now turn our attention to the role played by the corporate HR function in managing people in a multinational context. The question addressed here is: *what is the role of the corporate HR function in the international firm?* In answering this question we might also ask, what is it that the corporate HQ can do that cannot be done by the business units? In essence this is about the role of the corporate centre. Scullion and Starkey (2000) argue that corporate HR has a key role to play in the international company. However, they note there is relatively little empirical research on the corporate HR role in the HRM literature. In practice, many organizations operate with a dual system where corporate HR manages a core of senior staff and key personnel while the rest of the lower-level management and staff are managed at the subsidiary level (Scullion and Starkey 2000).

In their analysis of corporate personnel departments in the multi-divisional company, Purcell and Ahlstrand (1994: 113) argue that the role and authority of such departments is becoming increasingly ambiguous and uncertain. As one manager described it, 'corporate personnel departments have ill-defined boundaries and muddy roles'. One of the main factors contributing to such role uncertainty and ambiguity is, they argue, the increasing decentralization of the personnel function to divisional or plant level. Scullion and Starkey (2000) suggests that the main role for corporate HR in the international firm concerns the management of senior managers and high-potential people who are identified as strategic human resources and seen as vital to the company's future and survival. The work of Scullion and Starkey (2000) supports the argument that the process of globalization not only brings the HR function closer to the strategic core of the business but also changes the scope and content of HRM.

Much of the IHRM literature is focused on whom to place in control of foreign operations and activities. Additionally, we must identify HR matters in need of central (specialist) control and those that may be delegated to subsidiary HR managers. In this section we focus on the actions and activities assigned to or required or expected of the IHR group; 'the duties of the job' and the service they provide to the rest of the organization. We also consider strategic and structural issues. For a discussion on the evolving role of the personnel, now HR function, starting around the beginning of the 20th century, see Miles and Snow (1984) summarized in Figure 7-3.

The contemporary HRM function may undertake a variety of activities, such as determining staffing needs and whether to use temporary staff or hire employees to fill these needs, recruiting and training the best employees, ensuring they are high performers, dealing with performance issues, and ensuring HR practices conform to various regulations. Activities also include managing employee benefits and compensation, employee records and personnel policies. Bartlett and Ghoshal (2002) discuss the evolving (leading strategic) role of HR and the implications for HR professionals. In the 1980s their function was typically supportive and administrative. The role of HR staff was to ensure that recruitment, training, benefits administration and the like supported the well-defined strategic and operational agenda.

When strategic priorities became more organizationally focused in the 1990s, human-resources managers were increasingly included in the strategic conversation, often to help define and develop the company's core competencies – and almost always to align the organizational design and management skills to support those strategic assets (2002: 37). Now, as companies move into the war for talent and as individuals with specialized knowledge, skills and expertise are recognized as the scarce strategic resource, HR professionals must become key players in the design, development and delivery of a company's strategy. The key HR activity in the evolving role of human resources suggested by Bartlett and Ghoshal (2002: 37) is building human capital as a core source of competitive advantage. This presents a central role for HR in strategy. Bartlett and Ghoshal (2002) outline three major strategic tasks that align the HR function with the strategic challenge of developing the company's HC for sustainable competitive advantage:

- **building** – (HR systems, processes and culture);
- **linking** – (developing social networks – vital to knowledge management);
- **bonding** – (creating a sense of identity and belonging).

1900	1925	1950	1975	2000
People managed by the owners & line Personnel departments starting to appear in functional organizations Admin role	Principles of Scientific Management place emphasis on specialists and a role for personnel to recruit and develop them Emphasis on standardization encourages the development of personnel practices Towards centralization of people management practices	Basic (supportive) role of personnel established Role includes: HR planning Recruitment & selection Homogenous 'one-size fits all' approach Centralized	HR profession established Greater strategic role/ internal consultant approach Broader HR practices and policies Emphasis shifts from HRM → (Strategic) SHRM De-layering and downsizing influences decentralization in some organizations	Increased internationalization/ globalization Focus on people as a source of sustainable competitive advantage (value and uniqueness) Emphasis on competencies and capabilities HR focus on building, linking and bonding Heterogeneous approaches
Industrial Age	**Scientific management**		**Information age → knowledge economy**	**Intangible economy**

Figure 7.3

Managing human capital – the evolving HR role

Social networks (of senior managers) the systems of relationships senior managers have with employees and others outside of their organization

The building task includes identifying opportunities to gain competitive advantage through hiring decisions (locating, attracting, developing, rewarding and retaining the best people). In the linking role, HR professionals take the lead in developing the social networks that are vital to the capture and transfer of knowledge (discussed in Chapter 12); they break down bureaucracy and unlock core competencies. Finally, HR must help management develop the engaging, motivating and bonding culture necessary to attract and keep talented employees.

There is variation in the roles of the corporate HR department between different types of companies. Research by Sisson and Scullion (1985) revealed that some corporations had large corporate personnel departments undertaking a wide range of activities, while others had a small team of corporate personnel executives or a single executive, and one corporation had no corporate personnel department at all. The researchers suggested that some international organizations were essentially run as a single business. In these businesses, managers at the centre are not only responsible for developing business strategy but are also involved in a number of critical functions of operating management. Personnel is one of these critical functions, because of the need for a standard approach without which the corporation would find difficulty in meeting its overall business objectives. Within multi-divisional companies, they suggested that, other things being equal, the more diversified the activities of the corporation, the less likely it is to have an influential corporate HR function (Scullion and Starkey 2000: 1066).

Dowling (1988) cited in Schuler, Budhwar and Florkowski (2002) documented several types of *IHRM structures*. They include: totally centralized; centralized HR policy development/regional input in implementation; corporate group and divisional HR units. More recently, Andolšek and Štebe (2005) studied the shift of HRM tasks from central HRM departments to managers themselves, a phenomenon known as *devolution* – a business model of HRM, where line managers are seen as the key decision-makers in HR issues. Poole and Jenkins (1997), cited in Andolšek and Štebe (2005), listed several reasons why the decentralization of responsibility to the line has been viewed as a key characteristic of the modern form of HRM. First is the effective implementation of HR strategy only through the line and second is the supposition that line management is critical for the high commitment and motivation of the employees (see previous chapter).

Purcell and Ahlstrand (1994) argued that the overall shift to decentralization of key activities has meant that corporate HR managers are playing more of a monitoring and control function, with the emphasis on the coordination of divisional and plant personnel around a more broadly defined group policy or objective, and they suggest that the need for a corporate HR department is less than it appeared a decade ago. With a trend to devolve HR management activities to line managers the role of corporate human resource management is reduced to the management of key international assignments in some MNCs.

Three distinctive groups of international firms emerged from the analysis by Scullion and Starkey (2000): *centralized HR companies, decentralized HR companies and transition HR companies.*

HR planning ensuring the organization has the appropriate number of suitably skilled people in the right places and at the right times

- *Centralized (large) HR* – (companies with comprehensive and sophisticated international HR planning systems) had large, well-resourced corporate HR departments which were responsible for a wide range of functions; the key role for the corporate HR function in these firms was to establish and maintain control over all high-grade management positions worldwide. In the global and centralized companies strategic staffing was under central control and corporate HR played a key role in the allocation of strategic human resources, including expatriate appointments, worldwide. Expatriates were often used to control local operations and international assignments increasingly became central to the organizational and career development process. In the global companies centralized control was reinforced through corporate HR control over the design and management of the rewards system.

- *Decentralized (small) HR* – (a declining role for the corporate HR but increased influence of corporate HR over senior employees and senior expatriates) the trend towards decentralization (and downsizing) in the late 1980s and early 1990s had resulted in the overall reduction in the size of corporate offices in many organizations, i.e. small HR departments. These companies tended to have only one or two corporate HR executives who undertook a more limited range of activities. The corporate HR function in the decentralized businesses faced problems which were different in nature and, arguably, more challenging than their counterparts in the global/centralized group of companies. Scullion and Starkey (2000) found the problem of shortages of international managers was more acute in the decentralized companies. They also found that training and preparation of managers for international assignments in the decentralized companies were much more limited and ad hoc than in the global/centralized companies.

■ *Transition (medium sized) HR* – all of the companies in this group had medium-sized corporate HR departments staffed by a relatively small group of corporate HR executives. Corporate HR managers sometimes find it difficult to persuade senior divisional managers to release their best people for developmental-type international assignments or to employ expatriates who worked abroad for other divisions.

It would seem then that there is a link between the strategy and structure of the company and the roles of the HR function and that the three distinctive approaches come with different advantages and disadvantages. Research by Scullion and Starkey (2000) has highlighted a considerable variation in the roles of the corporate HR function in different types of international firms. Companies may also consider HR *outsourcing* an important part of maximizing their performance – see the example below. Outsourcing can be defined as the delegation of one or more HR business processes to an external provider who then owns, manages and administers the selected HR processes, based on defined and measurable performance metrics.

Example

'One Unilever'

Unilever and Accenture worked together to transform the manufacturer's HR function across 100 countries and 200 000 employees. The seven-year contract covers services from recruitment to payroll processing and performance management.
Source: Personnel Today; 11/14/2006, p8-8

What do you think are the advantages and disadvantages of outsourcing the HR function?

What actions and decisions must be taken when selecting a suitable outsourcing partner?

For some answers, see Table 7-1.

STOP & THINK

Advantages of outsourcing the HR function	Disadvantages of outsourcing
• Reduced costs/increased efficiency • Improved HR IT systems • Improved HR metrics • Access to HR expertise (not available internally) • Increased flexibility • Reduced risk • Frees up HR resources from 'factory tasks' allowing them to operate more strategically	• Contracts tend to be long (5-10 years) • Loss of local processes and knowledge • Detachment from employees – no upward feedback • Standardization of processes in line with provider preferences not organizational preferences (cultural misfit)

Table 7.1

Advantages and disadvantages of outsourcing the HR function

A directory of companies that offer services related to personnel management is presented in *Workforce Management* (2006).

What actions and decisions must be taken when selecting a suitable outsourcing partner?

- Understand existing HR position – costs, responsibilities, levels of service.
- Vision of HR requirements for future.
- Speak with other organizations serviced by the outsource provider.
- Consider cultural and geographical factors.
- Develop clear metrics within a service level agreement (SLA).

HR policies and practice

Previously we highlighted the need to build HR systems, policies and practices. In this section we explore how the HR function may accomplish this task before discussing specific practices in more detail. The issues, challenges and propositions associated with MNEs are different from those of domestic firms (Sundaram and Black 1992 cited in Schuler, Dowling and De Cieri 1993).This applies to all functional areas of managing an MNE, particularly HRM. MNEs confront many international HRM issues and challenges and can devote considerable time, energy and financial resources towards managing HR.

International organizations exert control of dispersed international operations through the use of HR philosophy and congruent policies. In some cases the headquartered HR function may develop HR practices for subsidiary use. In other cases subsidiaries will be autonomous, developing their own practices but in line with the overarching philosophy/policy framework. Policies and procedures constitute elements of the formal HR system and are used to influence HR related decisions throughout the organization. Statements of human resource philosophy, while general, have the ability to prescribe limits on the actual treatment of individuals regardless of location, (Schuler, Dowling and De Cieri 1993). This is done through their top-down impact upon HR policies and practices.

With an HR philosophy, MNEs are able to define further how employees are to be treated: HR policies help to specify the meaning of the philosophy. From these policies come more specific IHRM practices can be implemented at the unit level, see Figure 7-4. These are the HRM activities that have a direct impact on employees, e.g. types of compensation, staffing methods, appraisal methods and forms of training and development. There are many choices among the array of possible IHRM practices. And because they, as do the other IHRM activities, influence the behaviours of individuals, they need to be selected systematically to be aligned with the other IHRM activities. Developing policies to be used as umbrellas for the practices within units then facilitates the attainment of the main objective of *interunit linkage*. Policies can help ensure units develop their practices systematically and link them with common human resource policies.

Philosophy a theory or attitude held by a person or organization that acts as a guiding principle for behaviour

Figure 7.4

Approach to IHRM policy and practice

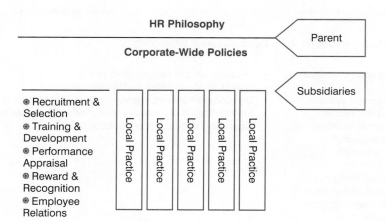

Balancing the needs and demands of coordination, control and autonomy is a fundamental objective for MNEs. Units may need to be given the autonomy to make the best decisions for the local conditions and autonomy is required to enhance motivation. However, the headquarters of the MNE may wish to utilize more global, company-wide criteria – such relationships and the tensions influence HR policies and practices. Units strive for autonomy and are often resistant to policies, or, at most, accepting of some general guidelines that allow for local discretion. General HR policies (guidelines), however, can enable the balance to be achieved. For example, an MNE might have an HR policy indicating that performance will be rewarded. Given that this is a rather general statement, each MNE unit could be free to develop specific practices that are both consistent with local conditions and with the general policy. For example, under the above policy, one local unit might develop an individual incentive plan for the general manager tied to the sales of the local operation while another unit might develop a group incentive plan for the entire senior management team, linked with sales of the local operation (Schuler, Dowling and De Cieri 1993).

IHRM policies and practices that are most relevant to the strategic needs of MNEs include those related to staffing, appraising, rewarding and training and developing people (see also labour-management relations, employee rights and safety and health practices). The IHRM policies and practices that appear to be most directly associated with interunit linkages include:

a determining and maintaining staffing levels that are an appropriate mix and flow of parent-country nationals (PCNs), third-country nationals (TCNs) and host-country or local nationals (HCNs) (increasingly these three groups are being labelled 'international assignees', but we use the three groups for purposes of distinguishing staffing sources);

b developing HR policies and practices that link units but also allow local adaptation; and

c using management development to create shared visions and mindsets to cohere interunit linkages.

Policy a guiding principle designed to influence decisions, actions, etc.

Practice an accepted method or standardized activity

Figure 7-5

Factors affecting IHRM policies and practices – a contingency model

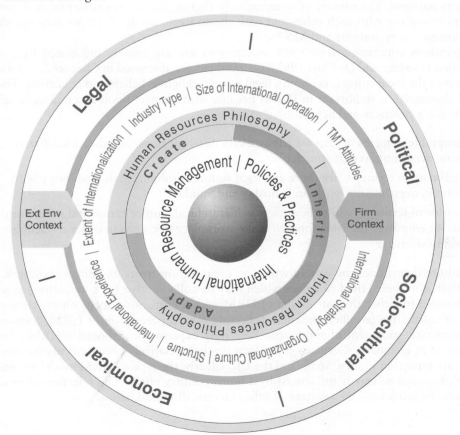

The transfer of HR practices in MNCs

The glocal theme will affect the choice of appropriate HR practices, whether to inherit them from the parent company, adapt or create them locally. Transferring practices (diffusion) enables the beneficial transfer of knowledge and expertise (competencies and capabilities) across parts of the multinational company. Practices originate and become established in a given legal, institutional, political and cultural context, see Figure 7-5. To some extent, they are dependent on this context and cannot operate in a different environment. The extent of this dependence varies from one area of HRM to another; in other words the diffusion ability of some practices is higher than that of others.

Managers at the headquarters of the multinational may seek to operate a practice in a number of countries that might be prevented from doing so by the legal, institutional and cultural constraints of the country to which the practice is directed. The country of origin, the way the multinational is structured, the way in which it established its foreign subsidiaries and the nature of production, integration or either may constrain or facilitate the transfer of practices across borders. Transfer may not be restricted to a top-down approach. The way in which multinational companies transfer practices developed in their foreign subsidiaries to their domestic operations has been referred to as reverse diffusion.

Beyond fitting in with the local environment and with the MNE, the local HR unit needs to fit in with its competitive strategy. That is, the local unit needs to develop HR practices that are not only consistent with the policies of the MNE, but also fit the competitive strategy of the unit. The local unit needs to fit the local HR practices to aspects beyond the local culture in order to be effective and yet still retain some responsiveness. The major objective of IHRM regarding internal operations is: being responsive to and effective in the local environment, yet willing and ready to act in a coordinated fashion with the rest of the MNE units (Schuler, Dowling and De Cieri 1993: 734). To facilitate local adaptation and fit, the subsidiary or local unit may staff the HR function with host-country nationals. In fact, this is one of the positions that MNEs seem to insist upon filling with a host-country national. The process of systematically aligning human resource practices, policies and philosophies with each other and with the strategic needs of the business are similar for domestic corporations and MNEs.

Questions concerning *which HR practices to use* are heavily influenced by culture, (Schuler, Dowling and De Cieri 1993). Cultural factors, discussed in Chapter 2, can include aspects of the local culture, economy, legal system, religious beliefs and education. The cultural imperative is important in IHRM because of its impact upon acceptable, legitimate and feasible practices and behaviours:

- **acceptable** in terms of 'can we pay workers different rates, and thereby differentiate them, according to performance?';
- **legitimate** in terms of 'are there any legal statutes prohibiting us from not paying workers overtime for work on Saturday and Sunday?';
- **feasible** in terms of 'while the society is hierarchical, authoritarian and paternalistic, can we empower the workforce to make workplace decisions in order to facilitate our quality strategy?'

Culture determines the way in which an organization treats its human resources. This is reflected in their HRM practices which may be collaborative (or cooperative) practices emphasized in either the soft model of HRM with a humanistic focus on the determination or calculative (conflict) practices reflecting a hard perception of HRM, focusing on the autocratic treatment of employees. Relatively expensive collaborative HRM practices dominate in Denmark, Germany and Norway; their relatively cheap calculative counterparts are typical in France, Spain and the UK. Clearly, the type of HRM model adopted by a multinational is heavily influenced by a home country effect. The selection of practices will also be influenced by a variety of other factors, discussed below.

The attitudes, values (see orientations) and overseas experiences of senior management at headquarters are likely to be significant influences on strategic IHRM. Three orientations (refer back to Chapter 1 and Perlmutter) can be described (each orientation is likely to influence strategic IHRM in a relatively specific way). The ethnocentric approach may manifest as little autonomy in subsidiaries, strategic decisions are made at headquarters and key jobs at both domestic and foreign operations are held by headquarters management personnel. In the case of a polycentric approach, the MNE treats each subsidiary as a distinct national entity with more decision-making autonomy. Subsidiaries are usually managed by local nationals who are seldom promoted to positions at headquarters. This leads to considerable autonomy with regard to HR decisions and activities in local operations.

Finally a geocentric approach is characterized by a focus on ability. A study by Dowling (1989), which surveyed international HR directors, found that the length of time which firms had been involved in international operations was positively correlated with the structure of their international HR operations. Firms with more years of overseas experience had a more diverse set of HR practices than those with fewer years' experience. One interpretation of this finding is that the longer firms operate internationally, the more likely they are to change their HR practices to accommodate local or regional demands if the situation deems it appropriate. The results reported by Dowling (1989) also suggest that the MNE with limited international experience will assume that one set of HR practices can work everywhere; thus it will have a predominantly ethnocentric IHR orientation.

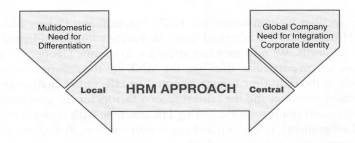

Figure 7.6

Determining the right HRM approach

In this section we discussed variance in how international organizations approach HRM. The international organization faces many choices such as whether to use local or central (parent) HR resources (people, policies and practices), to allow headquarters or local operations to make HR decisions and so on. Figure 7-6 identifies determinants of the HRM approach and indicates whether a central or local approach is contingent on such factors. According to Monks, Scullion and Creaner (2001) it has been argued that the fundamental strategic problem for senior managers in international firms is balancing the economic need for integration with the social, cultural and political pressures for local responsiveness (Bartlett and Ghoshal 1989).

The underlying challenge is that, while the nature of global business calls for consistency in the management of people, cultural diversity requires adaptation and differentiation (Laurent 1986) and this involves a balance between centralized control of HRM strategy and responsiveness to local circumstances. Contingency theory suggests that a *HRM system* that 'fits' with the factors highlighted in Figure 7-5, should be more effective than one that does not. Other factors which may impact upon the effectiveness of the HRM system are shown in Figure 7-7. The effective international organization should be able to include representatives and ideas from many cultures in its planning and decision-making processes and should have a well-balanced senior management team.

Look back
See Figure 7-5, p. 217

Figure 7.7

Characteristics of an effective
transnational HR system

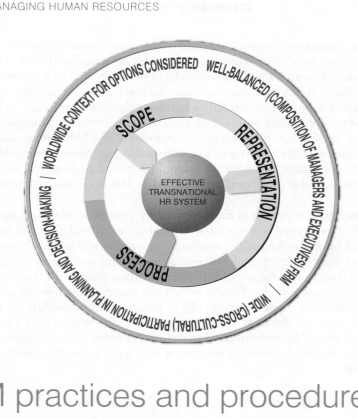

IHRM practices and procedures

In the previous sections we considered the HRM function and factors which may determine whether HR practices are inherited from the parent company, adapted or created to meet specific local needs. We now turn our attention to specific HR practices; focusing on several key areas, see, in particular. Ensuring the MNE has the appropriate people in place around the world at the right time is just one aspect of HR. Other challenges include identifying management potential and the critical success factors for the international manager, providing development opportunities; linking HR planning with business strategy, providing meaningful assignments, relocation and expat management, managing cultural/orientation training, remuneration and payroll administration. The remainder of this section is organized with Figure 7-8 in mind. Each major area of practice will be discussed further.

Figure 7.8

HRM process

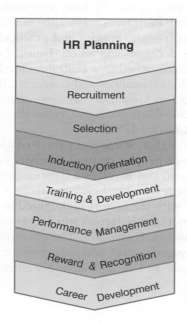

Resourcing: planning, recruitment and selection

Resourcing includes the activities responsible for filling positions within the organization (staffing, recruitment and selection). Recruitment represents investment in HC. By recruiting a merely average individual, the company loses the opportunity to gain competitive advantage through a hiring decision, according to Bartlett and Ghoshal (2002). They recognized that people are the key strategic resource, and strategy must be built on a human-resource foundation. However, as more and more companies come to that conclusion, competition for scarce human resources intensifies. In companies that function in a global environment, there is a need to distinguish between different types of employees – as mentioned earlier in this chapter. Traditionally, they are classified as one of three types:

- Parent country national (PCN)
  The employee's nationality is the same as the organization's.
- Host country national (HCN)
  The employee's nationality is the same as the location of the subsidiary.
- Third country national (TCN)
  The employee's nationality is neither that of the organization nor that of the location of the subsidiary.

In many organizations an employee's classification is tied to remuneration as well as benefits and opportunities for promotion.

Staffing is a major IHR practice that MNEs have used to help coordinate and control their far-flung global operations. Traditionally MNEs have sent PCNs or expatriates abroad to ensure that the policies and procedures of the home office were being carried out to the letter in foreign operations. As costs became prohibitive and career issues made these assignments less attractive, MNEs turned to TCNs and HCNs to satisfy international staffing needs, (Schuler, Dowling and De Cieri 1993: 730). While this approach solved the staffing need, it raised the concern about its ability to help with the needs for coordination and control. An organization's reaction (to the need for coordination and control) could be classified by:

a establishing rules and procedures for HCNs or TCNs to carry out; or

b socializing the HCNs or TCNs to think and behave like expatriates.

A MNE faces several options when considering its IHRM approach, Shen (2005) discusses IHRM orientations, see Figure 7-9. Approaches not only concern how a company resources (staff) its overseas and domestic offices but includes the approach to the entire HRM system which may be transferred (exported to and inherited by the host country) the ethnocentric approach or adapted or created locally, the polycentric approach. The role of the IHR manager will vary dependent upon the international orientation of the organization. It is, therefore, critical that managers working in this field are able to interpret international organizational strategy and develop IHR policies and practices which support that focus.

Host country nationals local people hired by a multinational

Ethnocentric staffing individuals from the home country manage operations abroad

Polycentric staffing individuals from the host country manage operations abroad

Strategy/ Approach	Advantage	Disadvantage
Ethnocentric staffing	Familiarity with parent company (goals, policies etc.) Unified culture Knowledge transfer Access to key skills and competencies Closer control and coordination of international subsidiaries	Host country resentment leading to motivation and morale problems Cost Difficult to adapt to the local environment
Polycentric staffing Local approach	Low cost Familiar with the host country environment Demonstrates trust Increased acceptance of the company by the local community Ensures local considerations are factored into the decision-making process	Limits mobility Isolates headquarters Less control over the subsidiary Recruitment of qualified people may be difficult
Geocentric staffing Worldwide approach	Efficient Networking	Cost

Figure 7.9
International staffing strategies

STOP & THINK

What factors should be considered when the MNE determines the most appropriate approach: ethnocentric, polycentric or geocentric?

Selection screening job applicants to ensure the most appropriate candidates are hired

Approaches to recruitment vary worldwide. Variance may be determined by culture, law, government policy and other factors. Such factors may require a specific approach. In some cases a country may require an organization to recruit locally, requiring permission to hire PCNs or TCNs. In choosing the right candidate, a balance between internal corporate consistency and sensitivity to local labour practices is a goal (Treven 2006). Different cultures emphasize different attributes in the selection process, dependent upon whether they use achievement or ascriptive criteria. When determining a hiring decision, people in an achievement oriented country consider skills, knowledge, and talents. In an ascriptive culture, age, gender, and family background are important. An organization selects someone whose personal characteristics fit the job. Good recruitment practices ensure the best candidates are identified for the job, resulting in decreased staff turnover and costs. Steps in the recruitment process include: writing a job description and person specification, choosing selection methods, preparing the job advertisement, shortlisting candidates, interviewing, checking references and making a job offer, see Figure 7-10.

Figure 7.10
Recruitment procedure

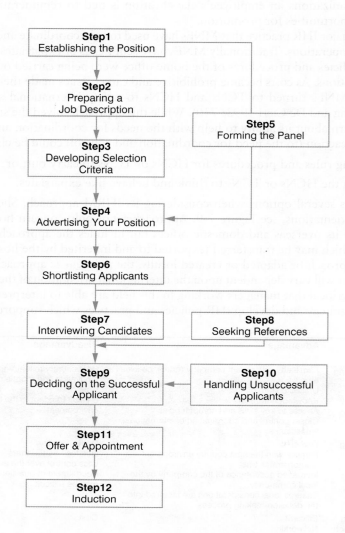

Given pressures for both efficiency and flexibility, firms are exploring the use of different employment modes to allocate work. In addition to the use of internal full-time employees, many firms are depending increasingly on external workers, such as temporary employees, contract labourers, and the like (Lepak and Snell 1999). Pfeffer (1994: 22) discusses the 'externalization' of employment. He finds it ironic that organizations may use temporary help, part-time employees and contract workers in core activities in industries where competitive success is achieved through people. Pfeffer (1994: 25) states that the appropriate use of a contingent workforce involves first understanding the real source of success in one's business and then ensuring the key activities are performed by people with enough connection to the organization to encourage them to do a good job and to receive the necessary training and skill development. We consider the practice of training and development next.

Training and development

Earlier in this chapter, when discussing sustainable competitive advantage through HC, we noted that advantage could be eroded, decay or be substituted. We concluded a need to develop employee skills *continuously*. Training aims to improve employees' current work skills and behaviour, whereas development aims to increase abilities in relation to some future position or job. If competitive success is achieved through people, then the skills of those people are critical argues Pfeffer (1994: 18). After a company has acquired top talent, the HR function must lead company efforts in constantly developing those talented individuals (Bartlett and Ghoshal 2002: 38). That requires more than is provided by traditional training programmes.

Today development must be embedded in the company's bloodstream; with all managers responsible for giving their team members ongoing feedback and coaching. Companies that invest in employee development can outperform the market (Bassi and McMurrer 2004). Managers are always claiming that people are our most important asset, but deep down they can't shake the feeling that employees are costs – big costs and they treat them that way. Pfeffer (1994) suggests several reasons why many organizations provide less training than is optimal:

Look back
See chapter 6

1   a lack of public policy designed to encourage training; and

2   training costs are clear and immediate while benefits are often long term and may in fact benefit other organizations; consequently, training, particularly in the United States is often the first thing to be cut.

There are several roles for the training function: supporting expatriate *adjustment*, international managers working overseas and on-assignment performance generally. At the international level, HR development professionals may be responsible for:

Expatriates overseas personnel – an employee relocated from one country to work in another country. The stay is temporary – they do not intend to stay permanently in the host culture

1   training and development of employees located in subsidiaries around the world;

2   specialized training to prepare expatriates for assignments abroad; and

3   development of a special group of globally minded managers (Treven 2006).

Since prolonged international business travel is increasingly important in today's global market, the need to develop successful training programmes is also critical (Zakaria 2000). Creation and transfer of international human resource development programmes may be carried out in two ways: centralized and decentralized. With a centralized approach, training originates at headquarters and corporate trainers travel to subsidiaries, often adapting to local situations. This fits the ethnocentric model. A geocentric approach is also centralized, but the training develops through input from both headquarters and subsidiary staff. Trainers could be sent from various positions in either the headquarters or subsidiaries to any other location in the company. In a decentralized approach, training is on a local basis, following a polycentric model. When training is decentralized, the cultural backgrounds of the trainers and trainees are usually similar.

Geocentric staffing the best-qualified individuals, regardless of nationality, manage operations abroad

Look forward
See chapter 8

Cultural factors may have a strong impact upon training practices in different parts of the world (Johnson 1991). In a theoretical paper Rodrigues, Bu and Min (2000) argue the relationship between national culture and learning preference – learners from certain countries are more likely to favour teacher-centred-learning (low student control, e.g. lecturing) while others favour hands-on (student-centric) learning (such as experiential-learning and individual problem solving projects where there is high student control). Given the forces of globalization, employees and trainers are now more mobile. Organizations may either:

1 send trainers to foreign countries (alternate cultures) to train in the host country; or

2 employees from foreign countries may go to other countries to be trained.

In the case of option (1) (foreign trainer) the class will essentially be homogenous i.e. from a single national culture but may be diverse in terms of other factors. In the case of option (2) (foreign employee) trainers may encounter a heterogeneous student population, i.e. class members may come from a variety of countries and national cultures. Consequently, trainers may experience different challenges in each of the above scenarios. It is suggested that students from high power distant countries rely on superiors for direction and structure and have not been encouraged to make decisions on their own. Consequently, they prefer to learn through a teacher-centred approach. The opposite is true for students nurtured in a low-power-distant country. Collectivist societies tend to measure high on power-distance hence may prefer a teacher-centred approach.

Within individualistic societies the individual is responsible for his or her own development. Individuals who feel uneasy in situations of uncertainty and ambiguity prefer structure and direction. Such individuals are likely to prefer a teacher-centred training approach. Finally, learners from countries whose culture is based on the Confucian philosophy probably also prefer a teacher-centred training approach. Learner-centred (hands-on) teaching methods commonly used in Western business education, such as case studies and projects are not well received in many Asian countries. According to Rodrigues (2005: 609), tutors will be ineffective if they fail to take account of students' preferred teaching technique (as influenced by their home country upbringing). In a nutshell, he believes we should consider whether the student's home country favours structure and leaves decisions to superiors (typical of the East) and if so modify teaching methods accordingly (i.e. adopt more passive methods such as lecturing); for a more recent discussion see Kelly (2008).

International assignment preparation

Preparing managers for work overseas remains a critical feature of international HRM. Typically the literature discusses expatriates as overseas workers though consideration is also given to the 'international manager' as a manager who is sent on an international assignment which may vary in length, and the *transpatriates* – individuals who operate globally rather than in specific local cultures. Expatriates need an understanding of the host culture and require skills that will enable them to choose the 'right' combination of verbal and non-verbal behaviours to achieve a smooth and harmonious relationship with their hosts in the foreign culture. Typically they require skills, such as adaptation, cross-cultural communication, and partnership, work transition, stress-management, relationship building, and negotiation techniques (see Chapter 8).

The management of international assignments is a vast and complex subject, covering many different topics. It is therefore impossible within the scope of this section to do more than outline the important points to be considered. The main elements of international assignments include:

- resourcing;
- preparation;
- terms and conditions;
- remuneration;

International assignment an international assignment is a temporary overseas task/work duty that may be short or long term. Long-term assignments tend to last between two and five years and involve moving the worker and family to the host country. The worker is expected to return 'home' after the assignment is completed. Short-term assignments can last from a few months to one year and involve moving only the worker abroad, not the family. Duties requiring a stay of less than 31 days' duration per single visit are typically referred to as business trips

- dual career problems; and
- repatriation.

International assignments incur substantial direct costs for the employer related to the relocation of the employee (and family), the provision of remuneration packages while abroad, repatriation costs and the recruitment and relocation of a replacement if required. The costs of failure are also high and include damage done to relations with subsidiary staff, customers, suppliers, and the local community. Some of the important implications of inadequate adjustment to international assignments are costly for both the organizations and individuals in terms of absenteeism; early return to the home country; and lower performance.

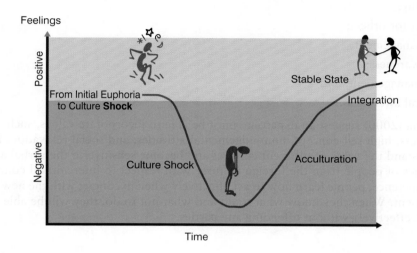

Figure 7-11

The acculturation curve (Adapted from Hofstede (1997: 210))

Research by Bassi and McMurrer (2004) shows that 'treating employees like the assets they are – by investing in their development – boosts returns over the long term'. Despite this, many companies still do not train managers for an international assignment suggests Scott (2005). Lack of preparation generally has been associated with a higher expatriate failure rate (Schuler, Budhwar and Florkowski 2002: 51). One of the most challenging tasks for any company operating internationally is to manage its expatriates. The statistics showing their efficiency on that matter are not encouraging (Treven 2006). Typical problems include culture shock/conflict, using international assignments as a means to shift problem employees and family problems. The need to select and train employees for overseas assignments has long been recognized, see for example Tung (1981) cited in Treven (2006).

Hofstede (1997: 207) discusses intercultural encounters – a matter we focus on in the next chapter. He suggests that the simplest form of intercultural encounter is between one foreign individual and a new cultural environment – 'The foreigner usually experiences some form of culture shock'. People on temporary assignment to a foreign cultural environment often report an acculturation curve, see Figure 7-11. Acculturation refers to the changes that occur as a result of first-hand contact between individuals of differing cultural origins. It is a process whereby an individual is socialized into an unfamiliar or new culture. The greater the acculturation, the more the language, customs, identity, attitudes and behaviours of the predominant culture are adopted. However, many expatriates experience difficulty in fully acculturating; only adopting the values and behaviours they find appropriate and acceptable to their existing cultures. It is a question of willingness and readiness (Zakaria 2000).

Expatriates typically experience a new culture which is unfamiliar and strange. In the initial stage of confrontation with the new culture, the user experiences a culture shock. Then full or partial acculturation takes place, depending on factors such as former

Look forward See chapter 8

Culture shock psychological process affecting people living and working abroad that may affect their work performance

Acculturation refers to the changes that occur as a result of first-hand contact between individuals of differing cultural origins. It is a process whereby an individual is socialized into an unfamiliar or new culture

Cultural change a transition between one's own culture and a new culture

experience, length of stay, cultural distance between home and new culture, training and language competency among other factors. The greater the users' ability to acculturate, the less the impact of culture shock on them. The ability to acculturate and reduce the impact of the culture shock can be developed through an appropriate and effective cross-cultural training. Apart from that, training can also help the users to develop intercultural communication competence, which is needed to adapt better and perform well in the new environment (Zakaria 2000).

Couzins (2004) identifies several key areas to explore when selecting and preparing expatriates for assignment:

- adaptiveness;
- listening skills;
- empathy;
- respect for others;
- self-management;
- self-awareness;
- time management; and
- political awareness.

Zakaria (2000) suggest an expatriate must be able to incorporate values, such as open-mindedness, high self-concept, non-judgemental attitudes, and social relaxation, in order to understand the value of different cultures and become sensitive to the verbal and non-verbal cues of people from the foreign culture. With respect to intercultural communication competence, people learn how to act effectively when in contact with the new cultural environment. When they know what to do and what not to do, they will be able to communicate effectively without offending any parties.

Table 7.2

Selection	Training
• Technical competence	• Cultural sensitivity
• Personal traits	• Languages
• Family situation	
• International experience	

Cross-cultural training any procedure used to increase an individual's ability to cope with and work in a foreign environment

Cross-cultural training is fast becoming a recognizably important component in the world of international business (Zakaria 2000). As the world gets 'smaller', more and more people are spending time living and working away from their home country, giving rise to greater face-to-face contact among people from very different cultural backgrounds. Globalization not only requires the adoption of a cross-cultural perspective in order to accomplish goals successfully in the context of global economy; but also needs a new and higher standard of selection, training, and motivation of people. Numerous benefits can be achieved by giving expatriates *cross-cultural training*. It is seen as:

- a distinct advantage for organizations;
- a means for conscious switching from an automatic, home-culture international a management mode to a culturally appropriate, adaptable and acceptable one;
- a means of reducing the uncertainty of interactions with foreign nationals;
- a means of enhancing expatriates' coping ability by reducing stress and disorientation; and
- an aid to improve coping with unexpected events or culture shock in a new culture.

Repatriation the process of returning home at the end of an overseas assignment

Once the assignment is complete the employee returns home. The process of returning home at the end of an overseas assignment is termed repatriation. It is important to manage the repatriation process well if the experience is to benefit the employee and employer. Various studies found that employees who have completed an overseas assignment leave their company (often to join a competitor) soon after their return. This high rate of turnover impacts negatively on corporate effectiveness and efficiency by costing organizations in terms of losing a manager with valuable overseas experiences. This problem is exacerbated when both senior and high performing employees are specially selected for such assignments. Causes of employee turnover upon return from international assignments include:

- financial shock;
- psychological shock;
- lack of repatriation training;
- lack of career development;
- lack of positive corporate values related to the importance of an overseas assignment in the organization; and
- perceived impact of corporate turbulence on being able to place repatriates.

Employees on international assignment often have greater autonomy and authority than similar domestic positions; they enjoy greater rewards and enjoy a high quality of life in the international assignment. Various surveys have revealed that many employees felt the return to the home office was not handled well and the repatriation process could have been handled much better. Repatriation training can help the person to set expectations about social and cultural readjustment challenges and thus reduced the re-entry culture shock. Organizations should consider progression and career planning with the repatriated employee, finding ways to utilize their knowledge and expertise upon their return. Not only does this make sense for the employer but will motivate the employee, raising esteem through recognition for the assignment.

In the international human resource management (IHRM) literature, staff movements tend to refer to those employees assigned to foreign operations for an extended period of time. Recently, there has been an observed trend towards increased use of non-standard (short term) international assignments. Changes are partly due to cost containment initiatives, as expatriates can be prohibitively expensive to support. In addition, multinational firms confront an increase in staff immobility, due to the rise in the number of dual-career couples, and other constraints, such as aged parents and single-parent families, along with changing work arrangements and shifting priorities that impact upon career choices. This forces companies to consider alternatives, with many using 'business trips' as a way of dealing with this issue. At any point in time, companies engaged in foreign activities will have numerous staff travelling from one country location to another.

The observed trend to reduce the use of expatriates has added to the ranks of the international traveller (Welch, Welch and Worm 2007). An important category of international operator is the international business traveller (IBT), also known popularly as globetrotter or frequent flier. IBTs are often a neglected resource, particularly in terms of skills and knowledge transfer. The international business traveller plays an important role in furthering the objectives of the internationalizing firm in areas such as sales, knowledge transfer, performance monitoring and control. During their frequent visits, IBTs are acquiring, collecting, assimilating, recording and transferring information and knowledge about foreign markets and operations. They are agents or carriers of articulated and tacit knowledge. Why then do employees travel when we have email? Davenport (1994) argues that most important information is not on computers, and that people prefer to get information from people. The Internet facilitates the rapid exchange of knowledge, but does not easily identify the relevant knowledge and who has it.' According to Welch, Welch and Worm (2007), 'People need to make personal visits to international destinations for a variety of reasons, involving a wide range of activities'.

© iStockphoto.com/Alexander Hafemann

Look forward
See chapter 12

International business travellers (IBTs) IBTs are persons for whom a part – generally a major part – of their role involves international visits to foreign markets, units, projects and the like

On the internal side, as companies become more geographically dispersed and foreign units more integrated into global activities, organizational pressures and requirements appear to increase the need for international movement. 'Management-by-flying-about' is one-way of describing how international travel has become an essential component of business life. Group and regional meetings, staff briefing sessions, joint training sessions, product development meetings and cross-border project work, opening or closing factories, and solving technical problems are just some of the activities that involve international travel between MNC units and affiliates.

On the external side, staff frequently undertake activities related to stakeholders in various international markets: to negotiate and close important deals, raise finance, sell products and services, and maintain and extend the important relationships with global stakeholders that are essential to smooth international operations. International sales representatives attend trade fairs, visit foreign agents and distributors, demonstrate new products to potential clients, and negotiate sales contracts.

Developing globally minded managers

Bartlett and Ghoshal (2002) saw of the development of a cadre of managers with a global mindset is the only way in which organizations working across borders can create a common culture and deal effectively with the complexity inherent in international business. International assignments are used to develop such a mindset. Scullion and Starkey (2000) found an emerging agenda for corporate HR in international firms which focuses on senior management development, succession planning and developing a cadre of international managers. Multinational corporations are still heavily influenced by the characteristics of their home country. However, as global competition increases, it is increasingly important for successful companies to have a group of managers with a global perspective argues Treven (2006).

Companies must identify managers with global potential and provide them various training and development opportunities. For example, having one or more international assignments, working on cross-national teams and projects, and learning other languages and cultures contribute to making a manager more globally minded. In addition, an organization should include not only parent country nationals but also host country nationals and third country nationals in this group. A broader concept is international management development (IMD) which involves more than simple training and development and also comprises succession planning and performance management. We focus on the latter point next.

Managers must develop a global perspective whilst being culturally sensitive

© Kineticimagery | Dreamstime.com

Performance management the process of creating a work environment or setting in which people are enabled to perform to the best of their abilities

Performance management

Performance management is a process which contributes to the effective management of individuals and teams in order to achieve high levels of organizational performance. In explaining the significance of human resources to organizational performance, the majority of work in strategic HRM has adopted the 'resource-based' view of the firm. According to Katou and Budhwar (2006) *organizational performance* is usually indicated by indices such as: effectiveness, efficiency, development, satisfaction, innovation and quality. The ability to gain and retain competitive advantage is crucial to an organization's growth and prosperity. There is a general consensus that *HR practices* mediated through the development of HRM outcomes, contribute to organizational performance. The general consensus developed among researchers is that HR practices and HRM systems do not lead directly to business performance. Rather they influence firm resources, such as the human capital, or employee behaviours, and it is these resources and behaviours that ultimately lead to performance. It has been argued that HR practices influence company performance by creating a workforce that is skilled, motivated, satisfied, committed and empowered. Others have suggested that the social context and organizational climate represent additional intervening factors.

In Chapters 1 and 3 we noted that it is 'bundles' of resources that create capabilities and that these are more difficult to imitate by competitors and therefore provide a more sustainable advantage to the organization. The organizational performance of an organization depends to a large extent on human resources, processes and technology (Curtis et al. 1995, cited in Katou and Budhwar (2006)). For human resources to be effective with processes and technology, the human resources in an organization must be present at the 'right number and competent' enough with the required knowledge, skills and abilities, motivated, satisfied, committed and cooperated, within the organization and present. Competence is an important factor that affects organizational effectiveness, thus when employees are competent they are more likely to help the organization to perform well.

Considering that the synergy between competent individuals is a necessary requirement for organizational effectiveness, cooperation among employees is more likely to help the organization to perform well. In order to bring lasting and better results and to contribute significantly to the success of their organization, employees must be motivated, satisfied and committed. Furthermore, turnover and absenteeism may have a negative impact on organizational effectiveness. Unless the organization is able to retain its employees, it can not capitalize on the human assets developed within the organization. Generally, if employees have good attitudes and behaviours they are more likely to work for the benefit of the organization, thereby positively affecting company performance, Katou and Budhwar (2006).

For simplicity, HRM policies can be grouped into two HRM systems:

1 resourcing and development, the systems aiming at 'attracting' human resources (which includes the HRM policies of recruitment; selection; separation; flexible work arrangements; individual and team training and development; monitoring training and development; careers; work design; performance appraisal); and

2 rewards and relations, aiming at retaining and motivating human resources (which includes the policies of job evaluation; compensation; promotion arrangements; incentive schemes; benefits; employee participation; employee involvement; communications; and health and safety).

Huselid (1995) highlights two HRM systems: 'employee skills and organizational structures' and 'employee motivation'. Core competencies among employees are developed through selection, training and design of work (first HRM system) and are subsequently reinforced through employee motivation (second HRM system). From the literature, Katou and Budhwar (2006) suggest that the HRM systems to attract and retain human resources have both a direct and indirect influence on organizational performance by creating a workforce that is competent and cooperated, motivated, committed and satisfied and being present and staying within the organization. In other words, the HRM outcomes of skills (competent, cooperation), attitudes (motivation, commitment, satisfaction) and behaviours (turnover, absenteeism) mediate HRM systems and organizational performance. The relationship between HRM systems and organizational performance is outlined in Figure 7-12.

Summary of key learning points

This chapter focused on worldwide human capital and its management in the international organization. In particular we focused on the role of the specialist central and local HRM function in acquiring, developing and motivating HC in order to improve (productive)

Figure 7.12

HRM systems and performance (Adapted from Katou & Budhwar (2006))

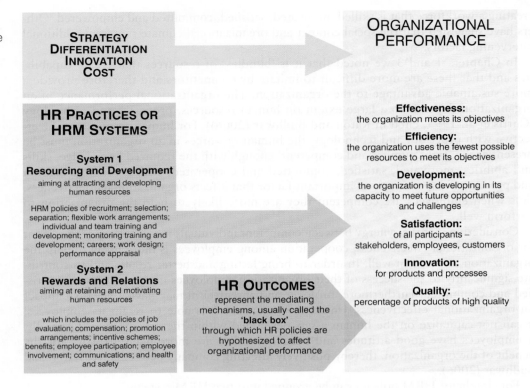

performance and develop a sustainable competitive advantage. HC (or Human Resources) are seen as strategically important due to attributes which are difficult to imitate thus ensuring any derived competitive advantage is sustainable. Specific mention of the RBV was made.

The IHRM role can be both strategic and operational. It is strategic in that the continued availability of HC must be assured in order for the strategy to be met. However, it must also be operational via the administration of certain HR practices such as resourcing, training and development and performance management. The IHRM function develops and implements HR systems comprising the HR philosophy, policies and practices. In some cases practices may not be adopted by subsidiaries due to local cultural and legal forces. However, practices may be adapted for local use or developed under the influence of overarching philosophies and policies. This ensures a certain level of control and interunit linkage for integration benefits while allowing for local differentiation.

Whereas the global MNC will seek to diffuse centrally developed HR practices and maintain a larger more powerful HR function, the multidomestic subsidiary is more likely to create its own practices or adapt those of the parent company and will maintain a much smaller IHRM function in the headquarters.

Resourcing strategies were discussed and three employee types identified: the parent, local or third country nationals. These were discussed in relation to ethnocentric, polycentric and geocentric strategies. We noted the heavy reliance on expatriates and travelling managers and that corporate HR functions had several roles associated with their management. Managers need to be prepared for overseas assignments which are described as intercultural encounters. We discussed how they can be prepared and supported for such roles and the dangers of inadequate support. The next chapter considers the issues in more detail under the umbrella concept of managing diversity.

Review questions and exercises

Burberry case questions

1 'Obviously Burberry has thought long and hard about its decision', suggests Janet Street-Porter. List all the qualitative and quantitative advantages and disadvantages of the factory move for Burberry.

2 Discuss the marketing issues associated with this decision. Imagine you are the corporate communications manager for Burberry. Draft a briefing to (1) Burberry managers around the globe, (2) Burberry managers at the affected factory, (3) the affected factory employees and (4) the press.

'Burberry's image is still centred on its Britishness. Behind the scenes, however, the focus of the company has been shifting to Asia, where the label is growing in popularity.'

In a GMB press item (GMB Calls On Welsh Assembly To Support Burberry Workers – 11 September 2006) 'GMB members also expressed their anger and rage at the way the Company conducted itself during their closure announcement. For a long serving, hard working and dedicated workforce to be treated in this cavalier fashion is nothing more than downright disrespectful and un-professional and we would have expected far more from a Company with such high standards of quality and corporate image. It was evident that this was sadly lacking and our members were treated with total disregard and some disdain.'

3 Imagine you were the Burberry HR Director and were called to a strategic meeting before the closure announcement. At the meeting the Operations Director informs you of the 'intention' to move production from Wales to China – a compelling argument for the action is put forward.

   a What HR issues and challenges would you advise the Board of in relation to the plan?

   b Draft a high level action plan of what you, as HR Director, would want to do to manage the people aspects of this problem both in Wales and China. You should indicate the order of the tasks and activities.

4. HR practice

   Write an HR practice for Burberry UK. Discuss whether the practice could be easily transferred or adapted for use in China.

5. SHRM, human capital and sustainable competitive advantage

   Explain what is meant by sustainable competitive advantage and then discuss how HR capital at Burberry may be used to create such advantages. What employment modes might you expect at the company?

References

Andolšek, D. and Štebe, J. (2005) 'Devolution or (de)centralization of HRM function in European organizations', *International Journal of Human Resource Management* (March 2005) 16(3):311–329.

Barney, J. (1991) 'Firm Resources and Sustained Competitive Advantage', *Journal of Management* (March 1991) 17(1):99–120.

Barney, J. (1995) 'Looking Inside for Competitive Advantage?', *The Academy of Management Executive [AME]* 9(4): 49–61.

Barney, J. (1996) 'The Resource-based Theory of the Firm', *Organization Science* (September/October 1996) 7(5):469.

Bartlett, C. and Ghoshal, S. (2002) *Managing across Borders: The Transnational Solution* (2 ed), Boston, MA: Harvard Business School Press.

Bartlett, C. and Ghoshal, S. (2002) 'Building Competitive Advantage through People', *MIT Sloan Management Review* (Winter 2002) 43(2):34–41.

Bassi, L. and McMurrer, D. (2004) 'How's Your Return on People?', *Harvard Business Review* (March 2004) 82(3):18–19.

Becker, B. and Gerhart, B. (1996) 'The impact of human resource management on organizational performance: Progress and prospects', *Academy of Management Journal* (August 1996) 39(4):779–801.

Becker, B. and Huselid, M. (2006) 'Strategic Human Resources Management: Where Do We Go From Here?', *Journal of Management* (December 2006) 32(6):898–925.

Brewster, C. and Scullion, H. (1997) 'Expatriate HRM: a review and an agenda', *Human Resource Management Journal* 7(3):32–41.

Broderick, R. and Boudreau, J. W. (1992) 'Human resource management, information technology and the competitive edge', *Academy of Management Executive* 6(2):7–17.

Caligiuri, P. (1999) 'The ranking of scholarly journals in international human resource management', *International Journal of Human Resource Management* (June 1999) 10(3):515–519.

Collins, C. and Clark, K. (2003) 'Strategic Human Resource Practices, Top Management Team Social Networks, and Firm Performance: The Role of Human Resource Practices In Creating Organizational Competitive Advantage', *Academy of Management Journal* (December 2003) 46(6):740–751.

Considine, J. and Cowen, L. (2002) 'Contemporary Employment Relations Issues', *Businessdate* (August 2002) 10(4):5–8.

Couzins, M. (2004) 'Expert's View: Susan Bloch on Preparing for an Overseas Assignment', *Personnel Today* (11 May 2004) p. 29.

Davenport, T. (1994) 'Managing in the New World of Process', *Public Productivity & Management Review* (Winter 1994) 18(2):133–147.

Dowling, P. J., Festing, and Engle, A. (2008) *International Human Resource Management* (5 ed), London: Cengage Learning.

Dowling, P. J. 'Completing the Puzzle: Issues in the development of the field of international human resource management', *Management International Review* 39, special issue 3: 27–43.

Dowling, P. J. 'Hot Issues Overseas', *Personnel Administrator* 34, 1: 66–72.

Gratton, L. and Ghoshal, S. (2003) 'Managing Personal Human Capital: New Ethos for the "Volunteer" Employee', *European Management Journal* 21(1):1–10.

Green, K., Wu, C., Whitten, D. and Medlin, B. (2006) 'The impact of strategic human resource management on firm performance and HR professional' work attitude and work performance', *International Journal of Human Resource Management* (April 2006) 17(4):559–579.

Hendrickson, A. (2003) 'Human Resource Information Systems: Backbone Technology of Contemporary Human Resources', *Journal of Labour Research* (Summer 2003) 24(3):381–394.

Hofstede, G. (1984) *Cultures Consequences – abridged*, Newbury Park: Sage.

Hofstede, G. (1997) *Cultures and Organizations*, New York: McGraw-Hill.

Huselid, M. A. (1995) 'The impact of human resource management practices on turnover, productivity, and corporate financial performance', *Academy of Management Journal* 38(3):635–672.

Johnson, H. (1991) 'Cross-cultural Differences: Implications for Management Education and Training', *Journal of European Industrial Training* 15(6):13–16.

Katou, A. and Budhwar, P. (2006) 'Human resource management systems and organizational performance: a test of a mediating model in the Greek manufacturing context', *International Journal of Human Resource Management* (July 2006) 17(7):1223–1253.

Kelly, P. P. (2008) 'Achieving desirable group-work outcomes through the group allocation process', *Team Performance Management,* 14(1/2):22–38.

Kidger, P. (1991) 'The emergence of international human resource management', *International Journal of Human Resource Management* (September 1991) 2(2):149–163.

Koch M. J. and McGraith R. G. (1996) 'Improving labour productivity: Human resource management policies do matter', *Strategic Management Journal* 17:335–354.

Laurent, A. (1986) 'The cross-cultural puzzle of international human management', *Human Resource Management* 25(1):91–103.

Lepak, D. and Snell, S. (1999) 'The Human Resource Architecture: Toward a Theory of Human Capital Allocation and Development', *Academy of Management Review* 24(1):31–48.

Lepak, D. P. and Snell, S. A. (2002) 'Examining the Human Resource Architecture: The Relationships among Human Capital, Employment and Human Resource Configurations', *Journal of Management* 28(4):517–43.

McGregor, J. (2006) 'The Struggle To Measure Performance', *Business Week* (9 January 2006) 3966:26–28.

Miles, R. and Snow, C. C. (1984) 'Designing strategic human resource systems', *Organizational Dynamics* 13:36–52.

Monks, K., Scullion, H. and Creaner, J. (2001) 'HRM in international firms', *Personnel Review* 30(5):536–553.

Paauwe, J. and Farndale, E. (2004) 'Best practice template for global HR', *European Business Forum* (Autumn 2004) 19:72.

Porath, C. (1999) 'Examining human resource options: Does investment in employees pay off?', *Academy of Management Executive* (February 1999) 13(1):110–111.

Porter, M. E. and Millar, V. E. (1985) 'How information gives you a competitive advantage', *Harvard Business Review* (July–August 1963) 149–174.

Pfeffer, P. (1994) 'Competitive advantage through people', *California Management Review* (Winter 1994) 36(2):9–29.

Purcell, J. and Ahlstrand, B. (1994) *Human Resource Management in the Multi-Divisional Company*, Oxford: Oxford University Press.

Rees, C. and Edwards, T. (2006) *International Human Resource Management*, Harlow: FT Prentice Hall.

Robbins, S. and Coulter, M. (2007) *Management* (9 ed), New Jersey: Pearson – Prentice Hall.

Rodrigues, C., Bu, N. and Min, B. (2000) 'Learners training approach preference: national culture as a determinant', *Cross Cultural Management: An International Journal* 7(1):23–32.

Rodrigues, C. (2004) 'The importance level of ten teaching/learning techniques as rated by university business students and instructors', *Journal of Management Development* 23(2):169–182.

Rodrigues, C. (2005) 'Culture as a determinant of the importance level business students place on ten teaching/learning techniques', *Journal of Management Development* 24(7):608–621.

Schuler, R., Dowling, P. J. and De Cieri, H. (1993) 'An integrative framework of strategic international human resource management', *International Journal of Human Resource Management* (December 1993) 4(4):717–764.

Schuler, R., Budhwar, P. and Florkowski, G. (2002) 'International Human Resource Management: Review and Critique', *International Journal of Management Reviews* (March 2002) 4(1):41–71.

Scott, B. (2005) 'How to ... prepare for an overseas assignment', *Contract Journal 00107859* (23 February 2005) 427(6513).

Scullion, H. (1994) 'Staffing policies and strategic control in British multinationals', *International Studies of Management and Organization* 3(4):86–104.

Scullion, H. and Starkey, K. (2000) 'In search of the changing role of the corporate human resource function in the international firm', *International Journal of Human Resource Management* (December 2000) 11(6):1061–1081.

Shen, J. (2005) 'Towards a generic international human resource management (IHRM) model', *Journal of Organizational Transformation & Social Change* 2(2):83–102.

Sisson, K. and Scullion, H. (1985) 'Putting the Corporate Personnel Department in its Place', *Personnel Management* (December) 36–39.

Treven, S. (2006) 'Human Resources Management in the Global Environment', *Journal of American Academy of Business* (March 2006) 8(1):120–125.

Tüselmann, H., McDonald, F. and Thorpe, R. (2006) 'The emerging approach to employee relations in German overseas affiliates: A role model for international operation?', *Journal of World Business* (February 2006) 41(1):66–80.

Welch, D., Welch, L. and Worm, V. (2007) 'The international business traveller: a neglected but strategic human resource', *International Journal of Human Resource Management* (February 2007) 18(2):173–183.

Wernerfelt, B. (1984) 'A Resource-based View of the Firm', *Strategic Management Journal* (April–June 1984) 5(2):171–180.

Workforce Management (2006) 'GLOBAL HR', *Workforce Management* 85(24):22–23.

Wright, P., McCormick, B., Sherman W. S. and McMahan G. C. (1999) 'The role of human resources practices in petro-chemical refinery performance', *The International Journal of Human Resource Management* 10:551–571.

Wright, P., Dunford, B. and Snell, S. (2001) 'Human resources and the resource based view of the firm.' *Journal of Management* 27(6):701–721.

Youndt M. A, and Snell S. A. (2001) 'Human resource management, intellectual capital, and organizational performance'. *Working paper*, Skidmore College.

Zakaria, N. (2000) 'The effects of cross-cultural training on the acculturation process of the global workforce', *International Journal of Manpower* 21(6):492–495.

Suggestions for further reading

Journals

IHRM has its roots in the academic field of management. A study by Caligiuri (1999) was intended to provide IHRM scholars with guidance regarding the most appropriate and most prestigious journal outlets for their research. Given the rapid increase of globalization in today's economy, research addressing the management of the human capital across national borders is becoming more critical for the success of multinational enterprises. IHRM scholars examine meaningful topics, such as cross-national comparative human resources, expatriate management, cross-cultural diversity within multinational enterprises, and the like. IHRM gained momentum throughout the 1990s and established itself as a subfield of both HRM and IM.

Based on the opinions of experts in the field of international human resource management (IHRM), scholarly journals were nominated and ranked (Caligiuri (1999)). Each respondent nominated five journals he or she would reference when writing a manuscript or researching a topic in international human resource management. The same journals were also ranked. Based on both the nominations and rankings, strong agreement was found for the top journals in IHRM. These included both mainstream management journals (e.g., *Academy of Management Journal*) and sub-field journals (e.g., *International Journal of Human Resource Management*). According to Caligiuri (1999: 517) the top five journal outlets for the sub-field of IHRM are:

1 *Journal of International Business Studies;*
2 *International Journal of Human Resource Management;*
3 *Academy of Management Journal;*
4 *Academy of Management Review; and*
5 *Human Resource Management.*

The *Journal of International Business Studies* (JIBS) solicits and welcomes research across the entire range of topics encompassing the domain of international business studies. The journal's scope includes research on multinational and transnational business activities, strategies and managerial processes that cross national boundaries, joint ventures, strategic alliances, mergers and acquisitions interactions of such firms with their economic, political and cultural environments, as well as cross national research involving innovation entrepreneurship, knowledge-based competition, judgement and decision-making, bargaining, leadership, corporate governance and new organizational forms (see http://www.jibs.net/).

The *International Journal of Human Resource Management* is the forum for HRM scholars and professionals worldwide. Concerned with the expanding role of strategic human resource management in a fast-changing global environment, the journal focuses on future trends in HRM, drawing on empirical research in the areas of strategic management, international business, organizational, personnel management and industrial relations (http://www.tandf.co.uk/journals/routledge/09585192.html).

Key articles

Scholars of this subject area have often read the following:
1 Barney, J. (1996) 'The Resource-based Theory of the Firm', *Organization Science* (September/October 1996) 7(5):469.
2 Barney, J. (1991) 'Firm Resources and Sustained Competitive Advantage', *Journal of Management* (March 1991) 17(1):99–120.
3 Bartlett, C. and Ghoshal, S. (1992) 'What Is a Global Manager?', *Harvard Business Review* (September–October 1992) 124–132.
4 Broderick, R. and Bounreau, J. (1992) 'Human resource management, information technology, and the competitive edge', *Academy of Management Executive* (May 1992) 6(2):7–17.

5 Kidger, P. (1991) 'The emergence of international human resource management', *International Journal of Human Resource Management* (September 1991) 2(2):149–163.

6 Lepak, D. and Snell, S. (2002) 'Examining the Human Resource Architecture: The Relationships Among Human Capital, Employment, and Human Resource Configurations', *Journal of Management* 28(4):517–543.

7 Lepak, D. and Snell, S. (1999) 'The Human Resource Architecture: Toward A Theory of Human Capital Allocation and Development', *Academy of Management Review* 24(1): 31–48.

8 Miles, R. E. and Snow, C. C. (1984) 'Designing Strategic Human Resources Systems', *Organizational Dynamics* (Summer 1984) 13(1):36–52.

9 Schuler, R., Budhwar, P. and Florkowski, G. (2002) 'International Human Resource Management: Review and Critique', *International Journal of Management Reviews* (March 2002) 4(1):41–71.

10 Scullion, H. and Starkey, K. (2000) 'In search of the changing role of the corporate human resource function in the international firm', *International Journal of Human Resource Management* (December 2000) 11(6):1061–1081.

Chapter 8

Managing difference – culture

Introduction

The contemporary workplace

Diversity

Working with other cultures

Building cross-cultural competence

Diverse and multicultural groups

Key concepts

- Diversity ■ Multicultural organization ■ Stereotypes ■ Ethnocentric
- Culture ■ Values ■ Cultural adaptation ■ Cultural assimilation
- Social identity ■ Social influence ■ Social group ■ Perception ■ Prejudice
- Cultural literacy ■ Cultural intelligence ■ Multicultural and diverse groups

By the end of this chapter you will be able to:

- Evaluate diversity and multiculturalism as source of sustainable competitive advantage

- Explain, with reference to social identity theory, stereotyping, generalizing, perception and attribution theory why some employees of the international organization may be treated differently from others

- Discuss the organization consequences of discriminatory behaviours

- Evaluate why it is important to understand culture and inter-cultural communication in the contemporary workplace of the international organization

- Critically evaluate methods for building cross-cultural competence and discuss the cultural challenges both working with and managing people from different cultures

- Critically evaluate the performance of multicultural groups working within the international organization

Active learning case

Diversity in broadcasting

At a meeting called in 1996, the MD at Carlton TV expressed concern about the lack of minority ethnic employees working for his TV Company (in 1996 fewer than 5 per cent of staff in Carlton newsrooms were from minority ethnic backgrounds), and the loss of minority ethnic viewers from his channel. In one of Greg Dyke's early speeches as Director-General of the BBC he identified changing the ethnic diversity of his workforce as a key organizational priority for his time in office[1]. A little later he was interviewed by a BBC programme and asked if he thought broadcasting in Britain was 'hideously white' – he replied he thought the BBC was. His comments made the front page of several newspapers: 'Director-general admits BBC is "hideously white"'[2] – 'Mr Dyke did not say the corporation was racist but acknowledged that, in common with the Metropolitan Police, it had a problem with race relations. He admitted that the management structure at the BBC was more than 98 per cent white, and said that the organization was unable to retain staff from ethnic minorities.' The figures we have at the moment suggest that quite a lot of people from different ethnic backgrounds that we do attract to the BBC leave.

Later, in May 2002[3], he gave a speech about diversity in public service broadcasting at the Commonwealth Broadcasting Association (CBA) conference in Manchester. He began with the statement, 'diversity is an issue no broadcaster – public or commercial – can afford to ignore'. He went on to say,

'We live in a fascinating, fast changing world in which the traditional institutions – in both the commercial and public sectors – are struggling to keep up with the enormous pace of change. Change, which is driven by a number of factors, which we all know well – technological, economic, cultural, societal.

One consequence of this speed of change is that all our audiences are more diverse in every sense of the word. The old idea of a homogeneous mass audience who turn onto a particular channel and stayed with you for an evening is long gone. In a world of hundreds of channels any audience loyalty has to be earned. In this context one of the great dangers for any broadcaster is not to notice as your audience grows away from you in ideas and attitudes. Ethnic diversity is one of the central defining characteristics of modern Britain – particularly among the young. For young people in this country today multiculturalism is not about political correctness, it is simply a part of the furniture of their everyday lives … Our aim at the BBC must be to actively reflect that.'

This illustration first appeared in the Sept–Oct 2006 issue of Catalyst *magazine, which was published by the Commission for Racial Equality*

www.catalystmagazine.org

Much of the case study concerns the BBC. The BBC exists to enrich people's lives with great programmes and services that inform, educate and entertain. Its vision is to be the most creative, trusted organization in the world.

■ The BBC provides a wide range of distinctive programmes and services for everyone, free of commercial interests and political bias. They include television, radio, national, local, children's educational, language and other services for key interest groups.

■ BBC popular services are used by over 90 per cent of the UK population each week. Financed by a TV licence paid by households (the BBC received over £2.65 billion in licence fees for the financial year 2002–2003). Not needing to serve the interests of advertisers, or produce a return for shareholders. The BBC can concentrate on providing high quality programmes and services for everyone, many of which would not otherwise be supported by subscription or advertising.

The BBC promotes these values:

Trust is the foundation of the BBC: we are independent, impartial and honest
Audiences are at the heart of everything we do
We take pride in delivering quality and value for money
Creativity is the lifeblood of our organization
We respect each other and celebrate our diversity so that everyone can give their best
We are one BBC: great things happen when we work together.

www.bbc.co.uk/info/purpose

Dyke (2002) discussed opportunities and challenges – 'The growing multi-cultural nature of 21st century Britain is a fundamental challenge for the BBC, which has implications for everything we do: how we are organized – for example whom we employ; the services we choose to operate; the content we run on those channels, networks and on-line sites'. In a question and answer session at 'A New Future for Public Broadcasting' Conference[5] Greg Dyke (then Chair of the cultural diversity network), was asked how he saw increasing demands for public television to reflect ethnic diversity. Dyke replied: 'We've actually made big strides in our programming, in the last couple of years. Our workforce [has] just about 10 per cent from ethnic minority backgrounds, compared with 8 per cent four years ago. But that's been a lot of hard work.' He went on to comment about recent BBC research regarding ethnic minority programming among ethnic minorities. 'What was interesting is, the thing that came back quite strongly is, we as a disproportionately white, Anglo-Saxon organization have a perception of life as ethnic minorities which [was different from ethnic minorities' perceptions]. And we've got to come to terms with that and change our view.'

As time moved on, diversity issues were seen not simply as a domestic problem. One headline[6] read – BBC correspondents abroad 'too white' – the Corporation's new diversity tsar wants to establish 'cultural accuracy' among staff. The BBC's team of foreign correspondents should come from the same ethnic background as the country they are reporting from, according to the corporation's new diversity tsar. Speaking in her first interview in the newly created role, BBC 'editorial executive of diversity', the tsar said the 'cultural accuracy' among reporting staff was on her hit list. She said there were too many white reporters reporting from non-white nations, particularly in Africa. Her comments are in line with those of Trevor Phillips, chairman of the Commission for Racial Equality, who said last May:

'Newsrooms which are monocultural are in danger of being like comedy that isn't funny … Without cultural knowledge – you don't ask the right questions … I get tired of repeatedly seeing programmes where [the situation is] "here we are in Africa and here's a white person, saying well, look at these people". I would prefer to see somebody who understands that culture, understands what's going on and can say "look with me, because I am a part of this". It feels more authoritative and more involved.'

Fitzpatrick said that the same rule on ethnicity and reporting should be applied in the corporation's domestic coverage, and that the broadcaster should recruit more reporters who could 'confidently speak' to non-white Britons.

Despite the comments of Dyke in 2001 and the appointment of a diversity tsar, in 2007, Nick Pollard[7] asked whether the BBC had indeed changed – 'Why is it so difficult to bring diversity into the newsroom?' Discussing the question of the ethnic make-up of our newsrooms he notes that it is an uncomfortable fact that they are still, in Greg Dyke's memorable phrase, 'hideously white'. That goes for pretty much every facet of operations – presenters, reporters, producers, camera crews and certainly for newsroom executives. Pollard asks why is it still so hard to find, recruit and develop non-white talent. He suggests that all executives are on the lookout for it and take every chance to open doors when someone good comes along, but the awkward truth is that it often seems in short supply. All news broadcasters see the sense in trying to widen the base of their staff but the truth is that it's proving much harder than we thought and change still seems to be a long, slow process. The extent of change was also considered. 2007's MediaGuardian 100 was exclusively white[8], it is rare to find a black or Asian face in MediaGuardian's annual list of the most 100 powerful people in the British media. The scope of diversity issues went beyond race and class to include gender and age equality at the BBC.

Questions:

Why might the BBC and similar organizations find it difficult to retain staff from ethnic minorities?

Why is it difficult to change monocultural into multicultural organizations?

How do diversity challenges manifest themselves as specific organizational problems?

Should there be a 'fair' representation of Britain's ethnic population on screen and behind the camera?

Explain your answer with reference to commercial and ethical arguments – for and against.

Why should members of different cultural groups hold different world-views/perceptions of the world?

What are the implications, if any, for business?

How important is it for broadcasters such as the BBC to have correspondents that come from the same ethnic background as (1) the country they are reporting from and (2) the people they are reporting to?

Explain your answer. We all differ in many ways. In some cases those differences are clearly visible (age, gender, colour) but in other cases difference is not so obvious (sexuality, values, religion, culture).

How might this impact upon the way organizations see and manage diversity challenges?

Why might an overall workforce, be representative but continue to have too few minorities represented at senior and board levels?

Sources:

(1) www.bbc.co.uk/pressoffice/speeches/stories/dyke_cba.shtml
(2) See Telegraph.co.uk by Paul Hunter (2001)
(3) www.bbc.co.uk/pressoffice/speeches/stories/dyke_cba.shtml
(4) www.cdnetwork.org.uk/index.html
(5) www.newfuture.govt.nz/speech/greg-dyke-QA.html (20/11/03)
(6) www.guardian.co.uk/race/story/0,,1843714,00.html – *The Observer*, Sunday 13 August 2006
(7) *The Independent*, published: 12 February 2007
(8) Minority report, *The Guardian* Monday 2 April 2007 www.guardian.co.uk/race/story/0,,2047801,00.html
(9) Jane Thynne, published: 8 April 2007 news.independent.co.uk/media/article2432334.ece

Introduction

In this chapter we build in particular on the theories presented in Chapters 3, 6 and 7 and continue with the theme of how best to use *human resources* to meet organizational goals through high levels of performance (motivated, effective and efficient workers) and compete in the global marketplace. We build on the arguments presented earlier, in the RBV, and further argue that a *diverse and multicultural workforce* can deliver sustainable competitive advantage because it is difficult to imitate, is creative and mirrors the marketplace; therefore able to better understand customer needs worldwide. Not only are there economic arguments for the development of a multicultural organization but social arguments suggest that it is the right and responsible way to manage the international organization – in compliance with the CSR principles and doctrine considered within Chapter 4. However, we will also argue that a multicultural organization is both difficult and costly to manage and has the potential for negative outcomes. It is therefore important for international organizations to understand how people from different social and cultural groups behave, interact and perceive the world.

Employees of the international organization and its affiliates must learn to work together productively; furthermore, employees must understand how to do business with entities located throughout their supply chain; the international organization must understand the role of cultural variables in determining how work is carried out in different countries and how their outputs (products and services) may need to be adapted for differing customer tastes worldwide. In short, the international organization and its human resource must learn how to manage difference.

With globalization comes increased mobility for workers and organizations. As a consequence, many international organizations and their subsidiaries or operating units have become increasingly diverse. To capitalize on diversity benefits and comply with diversity laws while minimizing the potential costs, leaders are advised to create multicultural organizations. Many of the associated challenges can be presented as *integration* and communication problems. In our day to day business lives we must learn how to act and interact in different circumstances. In the contemporary international organization there are likely to be people from all over the world within the workforce, in the marketplace and among the organization's suppliers and business partners. When they come together to work and conduct business they bring with them different values, attitudes, beliefs, experiences, assumptions and expectations that will be reflected in their worldviews, perceptions, ways of communicating and approach to work activities. Learning how to *motivate*, *communicate*, and work *productively* with co-workers and customers who may differ in significant ways is a necessary workplace skill.

We begin this chapter by exploring the changing nature of the workplace as a result of globalization; managing in the contemporary international business environment necessitates employee interaction with the same and different cultures. A model for this chapter is presented in Figure 8-1. We will explore what is meant by diversity and consider the role of social identity theory and then cultural theory to explain differences, how they come about and how they can be categorized and analyzed. Next we consider the consequences of diversity (difference), how people think and act differently and the implications (outcomes) of this for international business. The content of the chapter is both strategic and operational and of relevance to the specialist HR function discussed in the previous chapter and every manager working within the international organization.

Multicultural organization an organization that contains many different cultural groups and values diversity

The contemporary workplace

Immigration, changing demographics, globalization, increased international business and technology impact upon today's workforce which is older, more racially diverse, more female, and more varied. Consequently Harvey and Allard (2009) describe the 21st century workplace as having a diverse (heterogeneous) workforce. Where there is a need

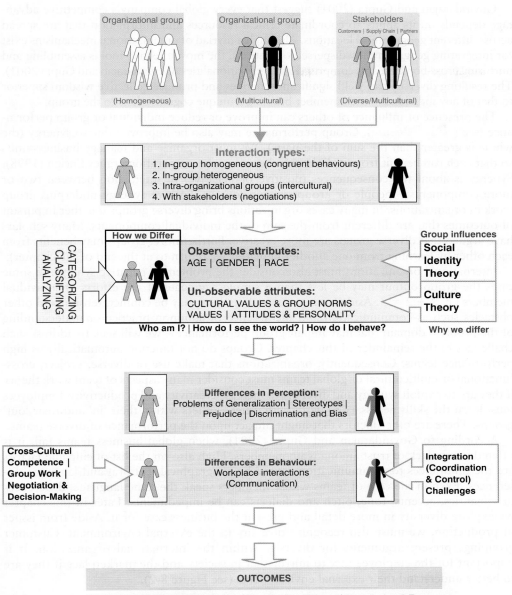

Figure 8-1

Model for Chapter 8 content

to motivate, communicate and work productively, this necessitates an understanding of workers as people. Within such environments the management aim remains to maximize benefits and minimize costs and to enable all workers to achieve their full potential. There are many challenges associated with the way people interact and communicate to conduct business in the international and multicultural or diverse contemporary organization. Several key business challenges relate to the fact that culture unifies while globalization diversifies. Such challenges are explored throughout this chapter.

The contemporary workplace is composed of individuals and groups of individuals. There are many reasons to focus on groups and the productivity challenge within international organizations. As was highlighted in the previous two chapters, international organizational goals may include exploiting economies of global scale and scope, maximizing the transfer of knowledge or cultivating a global mind-set and ensuring a productive workforce. Managers may become dependent upon the output of a group and will thus take steps to make the group more efficient and effective. Groups can learn from each other (no need to reinvent the wheel – see knowledge sharing in Chapter 12) and may attain synergistic benefits from collaboration and working together in teams.

Govindarajan and Gupta (2001) suggest that every global company's competitive advantage depends on its ability to coordinate critical resources and information that are spread across different geographical locations. Although a myriad of organizational mechanisms exist for integrating geographically dispersed operations, the most effective tool is assembling and nurturing cross-border teams comprised of many nationalities (Govindarajan and Gupta 2001). The resulting diversity can yield significant synergies and produce collective wisdom superior to that of any individual – each member bringing a unique cognitive lens to the group.

Social influence the process where attitudes and behaviour are influenced by the real or implied presence of others

The presence or influence of others can improve or reduce individual or group performance (see social influence). Group performance may also be improved due to synergy (the whole is greater than the sum of the parts). We must organize and manage business units so that each can benefit from its link with the rest of the corporation argues Ensign (1998). Synergy is about the consequences (positive or negative) of interaction between two or more components – people or groups in our context. Positive synergy underpins group work in organizations. In many cases organizations bring diverse groups together in pursuit of outcomes that are different from the sum of the individual components. Many scholars have argued that diverse groups are more creative. Furthermore, groups may benefits from each other by learning from one another (a matter we return to at the end of the chapter).

Social loafing the inclination for individuals to apply less effort when working as part of a group, i.e. to let others do the work

International organizations must also consider the problem of negative synergy. In some cases the group output may be less than a simple aggregate of the efforts of individual members i.e. $2 + 2 = 3$. Aside from social loafing there may be conflict, tension and other obstacles such as communication and the absence of common practice or understanding of the problem domain that may impair group performance – we will seek to address such challenges in the remainder of this chapter. Groups do not function automatically as high performance teams. Consequently, organizations that make use of diverse, project, cross-functional or multicultural or global teams must consider many aspects of team work theory if they are to exploit synergy and diversity to increase creativity and productivity. Employees must learn the skills necessary to work with others; others within their 'in' and their 'out' groups. There are other factors that might impact upon the performance of diverse teams.

According to Govindarajan and Gupta (2001), when global business teams fail, it is often due to a lack of trust among team members. High also on the list of culpable factors are the hindrances to communication caused by geographical, cultural and language differences. Even in the case of teams whose members speak the same language, differences in semantics, accents, tone, pitch and dialects can be impediments. Later in this chapter we explore diversity in more detail and present the business case for it. Aside from issues of production, we must also recognize diversity in the external environment. Customer groupings present arguments for diversity within the international organization. It is important for the employee mix to mirror that in society and the marketplace if they are to better understand their external environments (see Figure 8-2).

Diversity

Diversity all the ways in which we differ

There is no question that today's workforce is more diverse. As with any social construct there are many definitions for diversity. It has been described as the heterogeneity of attitudes, perspectives and backgrounds among group members; valuing, respecting, and appreciating the differences (such as age, culture, education, ethnicity, experience, gender, race, religion, and sexual orientation, among others) that make people unique or more simply as all the ways in which we differ. When a person from one group encounters people from another different group they often use their own values to judge that other group. When a person or group believes their culture to be superior to the other culture, they adopt an ethnocentric approach. This may prove problematic as ethnocentric attitudes are more likely to result in a disregard for the beneficial characteristics of other cultures; similarly, organizations adopting an ethnocentric approach may find problematic their attempts to impose home country practices, products and services – thus meeting resistance and failure.

Ethnocentric using one's own set of standards and customs to judge all people, often unconsciously

About the BBC

Policies, Guidelines and Reports

Policies
Diversity and the BBC

Diversity is a creative opportunity for the BBC to reflect the totality of the UK audience.

As a public service broadcaster the BBC is committed to reflecting the diversity of the UK audience in its workforce, as well as in its output on TV, on radio and online.

The aim is to be inclusive of the differences that make up the reality of modern Britain, including gender, age, ethnicity and cultural diversity, people with disabilities, different faiths and social backgrounds, and different sexual orientations.

The BBC has set targets for ensuring that diversity happens on and off air, supported by a number of initiatives aimed at promoting diversity in the workforce and in output and content. The Corporation has met and is now reviewing its targets for the portrayal of black and minority ethnic and disabled people on screen. There are also workforce targets to be met by December 2007 of:

- 12.5% for black and minority ethnic staff overall in the BBC workforce
- 7% for SMs (senior manager grades)
- 4% for staff with a disability

Figure 8-2

Diversity and the BBC

(Source: www.bbc.co.uk/info/policies/diversity.shtml)

International organizations cannot engage in ethnocentric thinking if they are to be effective and efficient. Within this section we explore what is meant by diversity, drawing on social identity to explain how we come to label groups and how people identify with them. We then consider how people from diverse groups perceive themselves and others and the implications of such thinking on their behaviour towards each other. Drawing on people perception theories, we discuss problems in generalization and stereotyping. We consider the business case for diversity and briefly consider initiatives employed to encourage diversity within organizations.

Definitions and perceptions of workforce diversity vary. Two general approaches to defining workforce diversity seem to dominate: the first, the narrow view, defines workforce diversity only as a term related to equal employment opportunity; the second argues that workforce diversity is a broader concept that includes all the ways in which people can be different. The narrow view typically adopts categories of race, colour, religion, sex and national origin while a broader definition makes use of additional categories such as teaching, education, sexual orientation and differences in values, abilities, organizational function, tenure and personality. It is argued that a narrow focus fails to deal with the root causes of prejudices and inequality and does little to develop the full potential of every man and woman in the company. Furthermore, it is argued that a narrow view (solely in terms of gender and race discrimination) can lead to employee anger with consequences for morale, turnover and performance (Carrell, Mann and Sigler 2006: 6). Modern definitions of workforce diversity focus on the ways that people differ that can affect a task or relationship within an organization (Carrell, Mann and Sigler 2006). They argue that this broader definition allows all employees to embrace a culture that supports diversity.

Taking a broader view, diversity management initiatives attempt to maximize the potential of all employees in direct benefit to the organization. Consequently, the best employees are recruited resulting in greater profits and job security. Such outcomes are understood by employees who therefore support the organization's efforts at managing diversity. According to Carrell, Mann and Sigler (2006: 7), increased diversity in the workplace converges with increased use of teams in the workplace. Team composition has implications for diversity management. Drawing upon the work of Thomas and Ely, the authors describe three paradigms for managing diversity:

1 discrimination and fairness – a focus on assimilation and ignoring differences;

2 access and legitimacy – which focuses on differentiation and placing people in jobs based on the ways they are different; and

3 learning and effectiveness – the integration of the differences that people bring to work, promoting equal opportunity and valuing difference.

We have already defined diversity as all the ways in which we differ. In the next section we discuss social identity theory which distinguishes groups and group membership according to difference. Having determined how people come to define themselves through group membership we then consider the consequences. The importance of groups has already been identified in this chapter. But what is it about groups that we must understand? Is a level of diversity a necessary evil that must be curbed or a source of strength that should be cultivated?

Social identity theory (SIT)

Belonging to *groups* (both socially and at work) affects the way we think about and see ourselves (whom we are) and the way others think about us and see us. Such thinking impacts upon behaviour, the way we behave and the way others behave in relation to ourselves and the groups to which we may belong. The way we view ourselves (self-concept) is determined in part by the groups to which we belong (*social identity*). Thus, social identity defines the person and appropriate behaviours for them. This typically happens through social comparison – individuals not only compare themselves with other individuals with whom they interact, but they also compare their own group with similar, but distinct, outgroups. We all see ourselves as members of various social groupings, which are distinguishable and hence different from other social groupings.

According to SIT, people tend to classify themselves and others into various social categories, such as organizational membership, religious affiliation, gender, and age cohort. As these examples suggest, people may be classified in various categories, and different individuals may utilize different categorization schemas. Categories are defined by typical characteristics abstracted from the members (Ashforth and Mael 1989). According to Huczynski and Buchanan (2007), 'the consequence is that by identifying with certain groupings but not others, we come to see the world in terms of us and them'. While group membership may have its benefits (self-esteem, privilege) it can also be a source of conflict and may, through generalizations and stereotypes determine inappropriate behavioural responses. The group can impact upon:

1 perceptions of individual members (see social representation theory, the process of socialization and shared frame of reference);

2 individual performance (see social influence and synergy);

3 individual behaviour (see group norms, and obedience and conformity theory); and

4 individual attitudes.

Social classification serves two functions. First, it segments cognitively and orders the social environment, providing the individual with a systematic means of defining (labelling)

others. A person is assigned the typical characteristics of the category to which he or she is classified. As suggested by the literature on stereotypes, however, such assignments are not necessarily reliable. Second, social classification enables the individual to locate or define themselves in the social environment. According to SIT, the self-concept is comprised of a personal identity encompassing idiosyncratic characteristics (e.g., bodily attributes, abilities, psychological traits, interests) and a social identity encompassing salient group classifications.

Social identification, therefore, is the perception of oneness with or belongingness to some human aggregate (note that Ashforth and Mael use social and group identification interchangeably). For example, a woman may define herself in terms of the group(s) with which she classifies herself (I am a German; I am a woman, etc.). Social identification provides a partial answer to the question, who am I? The extent to which the individual identifies with each category is clearly a matter of degree. Once a person has identified who they are they may then define appropriate behaviours, mimicking like people.

Stets and Burke (2000) discuss the concept of identity – in social identity theory and identity theory, the self is a product of social categories or classifications (self-categorization). Through the process of self-categorization or identification, an *identity* is formed. In social identity theory, a social identity is a person's knowledge that he or she belongs to a social category or group. A social group is a set of individuals who hold a common social identification or view themselves as members of the same social category. Through a social comparison process, persons who are similar to themselves are categorized with the self and are labelled the in-group; persons who differ from them are categorized as the out-group. The two important processes involved in social identity formation, namely self-categorization and social comparison, produce different consequences. The consequence of self-categorization is an emphasis of the perceived similarities between the self and other in-group members. This accentuation occurs for all the attitudes, beliefs and values, affective reactions, behavioural norms, styles of speech, and other properties that are believed to be correlated with the relevant intergroup categorization.

Social group two or more people who identify with one another

The consequence of the social comparison process is the selective application of the accentuation effect, primarily to those dimensions that will result in self-enhancing outcomes for the self. As Hogg and Abrams (1988), cited in Stets and Burke (2000), make clear, the social categories in which individuals place themselves are parts of a structured society and exist only in relation to other contrasting categories (for example, black vs. white); each has more or less power, prestige, status, and so on. Much of social identity theory deals with intergroup relations – that is, how people come to see themselves as members of one group/category (the in-group) in comparison with another (the out-group), and the consequences of this categorization, such as ethnocentrism and prejudice.

The individual's work organization may provide one answer to the question, 'Who am I'? Hence, Ashforth and Mael (1989) argue that *organizational identification* is a specific form of social identification. The organization, as a social category, is seen to embody characteristics perceived as typical of its members, and may well define who a particular individual is, i.e. contributes to their identity. At the very least, SIT maintains that the individual identifies with social categories partly to enhance self-esteem. The individual's social identity may be derived not only from the organization, but also from his or her work group, department, union, lunch group, age cohort, fast-track group, and so on. Consequently, individuals often retain multiple identities. Factors traditionally associated with group formation (interpersonal interaction, similarity, liking, proximity, shared goals or threat, common history, and so forth) may affect the extent to which individuals identify with a group, although SIT suggests that they are not necessary for identification to occur. It should be noted, however, that although these factors facilitate group formation, they may also directly cue the psychological grouping of individuals since they can be used as bases for categorization (Ashforth and Mael 1989).

The explanatory utility of SIT to organizations can be illustrated by applications to organizational *socialization*, role *conflict*, and intergroup *relations*. The SIT literature suggests several consequences of relevance to organizations. Individuals tend to support the institutions embodying identities with which they associate. Thus, it is likely that identification with an organization enhances support for and commitment to it. SIT suggests that much intergroup conflict stems from the very fact that groups exist, thus providing a fairly pessimistic view of intergroup harmony (Ashforth and Mael 1989). More specifically, in SIT it is argued that:

a given the relational and comparative nature of social identifications, social identities are maintained primarily by intergroup comparisons; and

b given the desire to enhance self-esteem; groups seek positive differences between themselves and reference groups.

This suggests groups have a vested interest in perceiving or even provoking greater differentiation than exists and disapproving of the reference (out) group on this basis. Difference can determine the ability of people from around the world to work effectively and efficiently together in pursuit of common goals.

Cultural racial diversity

Increasing cultural diversity in the workforce poses one of the most challenging HR and organizational issues of our time. However, cultural diversity does in fact add value and, within the proper context, contributes to competitive advantage argues Orlando (2000). Cultural diversity is taken to mean the representation, in one social system, of people with different group affiliations of cultural significance. The term 'cultural diversity' is used interchangeably with *racial diversity*. Because race has been cited as the most frequently picked component of diversity by human resource (HR) managers and CEOs, and because past findings validate race as a dimension of cultural diversity, few would argue that it is not a major dimension of diversity.

Proponents of diversity maintain that different opinions provided by culturally diverse groups make for better-quality decisions. Heterogeneity in decision-making and problem-solving styles produces better decisions through the operation of a wider range of perspectives and a more thorough critical analysis of issues. Studies have provided support for the

Cultural diversity the representation, in one social system, of people with different group affiliations of cultural significance

The mission statement of the UK's Equality & Human Rights Commission

---

Vision, mission and priorities

Gweledigaeth, cenhadaeth a blaenoriaethau

Our vision

A society built on fairness and respect. People confident in all aspects of their diversity.

Our mission

The independent advocate for equality and human rights in Britain, the Equality and Human Rights Commission aims to reduce inequality, eliminate discrimination, strengthen good relations between people, and promote and protect human rights.

The Commission challenges prejudice and disadvantage, and promotes the importance of human rights.

The Commission enforces equality legislation on age, disability, gender reassignment, race, religion or belief, and sexual orientation and encourages compliance with the Human Rights Act.

In order to bring about effective change, the Commission uses influence and authority to ensure that equality and human rights remain at the top of agendas for government and employers, media and society. We will campaign for social change and justice.

Acting directly and by fostering partnerships at local, regional and national levels, the Commission stimulates debate on equality and human rights.

www.equalityhumanrights.com

idea that racial diversity benefits decision-making; for example, Watson, Kumar, and Michaelsen (1993) studied for 17 weeks the interaction and performance of culturally homogeneous and culturally diverse groups. They reported that homogeneous groups initially scored higher on both process and performance effectiveness. Over time, both types of groups showed improvement on process and performance, and the between-groups differences lessened. By week 17, there were no differences in process or overall performance, but the heterogeneous groups scored higher on two task measures (range of perspectives and alternatives generated). More recently, results from a controlled experimental brainstorming study (McLeod et al. 1996) showed that the ideas produced by ethnically diverse groups were judged to be of higher quality than the ideas produced by homogeneous groups. In general, these few studies indicate the value obtained from cultural diversity, Orlando (2000).

In the previous chapter we noted SHRM is a means of gaining competitive advantage through one of a company's most important assets: its people. As other sources of competitive advantage, such as technological and physical resources (discussed later in the book), have become easier to emulate, the crucial differentiating factor between organizations can be how human resources work within an organization (Pfeffer 1994). Cultural diversity in human capital serves as a source of sustained competitive advantage because it creates value that is both difficult to imitate and rare. Human resources, particularly diverse resources, are protected by knowledge barriers and appear socially complex because they involve a mix of talents that are elusive and hard to understand. As was discussed in the previous chapter, a strategic asset must be rare in order to offer sustained competitive advantage.

Orlando (2000) examined the *performance* impact that *cultural diversity* has on organizations; benefits include skills transfer and insight and cultural sensitivity pertinent to reaching different market segments as companies enter new markets. Furthermore, cultural diversity can provide organizations with diverse experience and knowledge. However, research has shown that although diversity in human resources may contribute to the quality of ideas, it also creates additional costs stemming from increased coordination and control. Based on his survey findings, Orlando (2000) believes that organizations should promote cultural diversity – not only for the sake of corporate social performance (see Chapter 4), but also in the interests of corporate financial performance (see Chapter 17). Recognizing that group membership impacts upon how people see the world we now consider perception and the associated business challenges.

Perception a mental process used to manage sensory data

Perception

How can people look at a particular situation and see or not see things other may or may not have seen? None of us sees the events in our lives in a totally objective way. Our views of reality are determined by our own personal attitudes, values, beliefs and expectations. We then filter everything through this lens that makes up our individual 'world view' and assign meaning to the people, things, and events in our lives based on our *personal* interpretation.

If English is your first language you probably missed two or three of the 'F's' out – why should this be so?

International business practitioners (and all business practitioners) should study *perception* because of its influence on behaviour: human behaviour is a function of the way in which we perceive the world around us. This includes how we perceive other people – a focus of this chapter. In order to understand one another's behaviour we need to be able to understand one another's perceptions and why we perceive things differently. When we meet or consider other people we tend to make judgements about them (see the halo effect) and may consign them to a particular category or group (stereotype). This enables us to predict how best to relate to them. While such approaches can be beneficial we can however, make errors in the way we perceive and categorize others. Such errors may lead to inappropriate behaviour such as *discrimination*. Within this section we consider the perceptual process (selective attention and perceptual organization); why we see things differently, causes

STOP & THINK

Read the following sentence:
'Finished files are the result of years of scientific study combined with the experience of years.'
How many letter 'Fs' are there in the sentence?

of discrimination and outline how we can avoid errors in and the consequences of our perceptions.

Two people can observe the same thing but perceive it in quite different ways – why should this be so? Perhaps the first thing to consider are the elements of the perception process, see Figure 8-3. Through our senses (especially sight) the brain receives incoming raw data from the outside world (stimuli). We are not able to pay attention to everything so we filter out less relevant or important information through *perceptual filters*; this allows us to focus on what we see is important (**selective attention**); we concentrate on the matters of particular interest and importance to us. Individual predispositions (personality, learning

Selective attention focusing on particular aspects of individual's environment

Figure 8-3
The process of perception

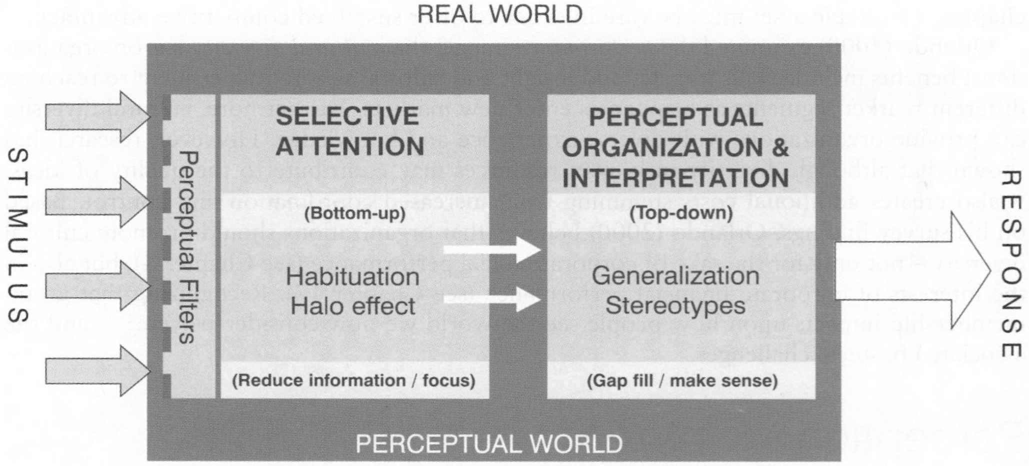

STOP & THINK

Have you ever lived by a busy urban road and considered why you do not hear the traffic in the same way a farmer might?

and motivation, see **perceptual set**) control what we see. What we have described so far are activities in a bottom-up process; errors can be introduced at this stage of the perceptual process (see the halo effect and **habituation** to be discussed later).

Following selective attention, we organize the filtered incoming stimuli in systematic and meaningful ways (**perceptual organization**); we classify or group similar stimuli together. During this activity (top-down processing) we may fill in the gaps of incomplete or ambiguous information (see the principle of closure). We make sense of a situation and then respond through our actions; our perceptions (the meanings we attach to incoming information) shape our actions. Such activities are also susceptible to problems (see stereotyping to be discussed later). Classification or categorization helps us make sense of the world; for example, we categorize people as male or female, black or white – such categories are social constructs (see previous sections) which we learn and what we learn

Perceptual set an individual's predisposition to respond to aspects of the environment in a particular manner

Habituation the filtering out of familiar stimuli

Perceptual organization the process through which incoming stimuli are organized or pattern in systematic and meaningful ways is often culture bound. We classify people that resemble each other (the similarity principle); for example the person(s) may be of a similar ethnic origin. A related concept is the proximity principle where we assume people are similar just because they are near to each other – possibly living or working in the same location.

One of the problems with 'closure' is that we may take incomplete information about someone or event and then draw inferences from it (see the problem of generalization). For example, we might only know a person's country of origin but may then assign traits to them based on our learned knowledge of people from that country, i.e. once we know or assume a person's apparent group membership (categorization) we may then attribute a range of qualities to them based on stereotypes and generalizations. In some cases such generalizations may prove convenient in other cases they could be wrong.

We refer to an individual's personal internal picture of their environment as their **perceptual world** as shown in Figure 8-4. Successful interpersonal relationships are dependent upon perceptual world's and an understanding that we may see things differently. Indeed a failure to appreciate the importance of differences in individual perception creates many organizational problems, particularly with communication (discussed later in this chapter). Given that perception shapes action (behaviour) in order to understand an individual's behaviour we need to know something about their perceptions and how they might have

Figure 8-4

'World views'

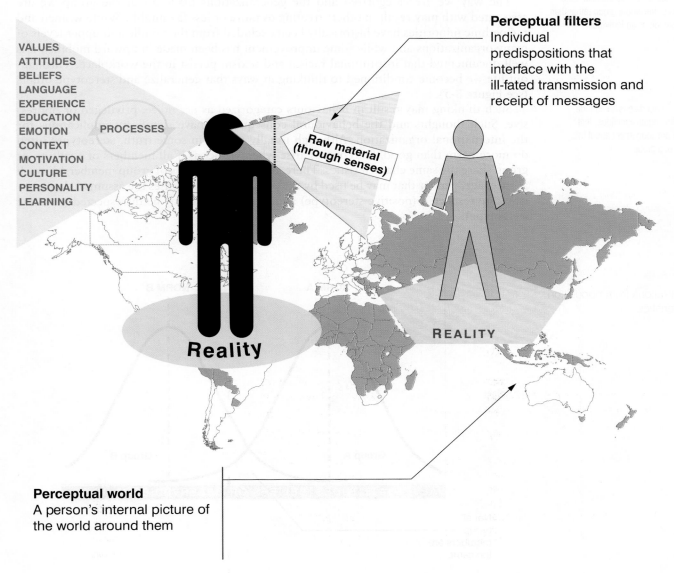

VALUES
ATTITUDES
BELIEFS
LANGUAGE
EXPERIENCE
EDUCATION
EMOTION
CONTEXT
MOTIVATION
CULTURE
PERSONALITY
LEARNING

PROCESSES

Raw material (through senses)

Perceptual filters
Individual predispositions that interface with the ill-fated transmission and receipt of messages

Reality

REALITY

Perceptual world
A person's internal picture of the world around them

been caused. Following on from this, if we can manipulate perceptions we may be able to influence workplace behaviour.

Throughout our social and working lives we frequently encounter and form perceptions about other people. We typically make judgements about what kind of person they are and often arrive at such judgements using limited information. Judgements are made to guide our behaviour in relation to them: Will we like them or not? How should I respond? etc. It has been shown that first impressions of another person are important. We often rely on a single striking characteristic such as their nationality, how they dress, and their posture to make judgements about them (the halo effect). If this judgement is favourable we allocate a halo if not, horns.

The halo effect is an error at the selective attention stage and may cause us to filter out later information which is not consistent with our earlier judgement. We tend to give *more favourable* judgement to people who have characteristics in common with us. The halo effect can be used to describe problems in many business situations but is particularly important in staff selection and promotion, negotiations, customer service and work team formation. Bias in person perception may also take place during perceptual organization when we group together people who seem to us to share a similar characteristics–stereotyping. Stereotypes are over-generalizations which enable us to shortcut the evaluation process and make predictions about an individual's behaviour.

The way we are categorized and the generalizations made about the group we are associated with may result in others treating us more or less favourably. White women and racioethnic minorities have historically been excluded from the middle and upper levels of many organizations and while some improvement has been made in upward mobility, it is well documented that institutional racism and sexism persist in the workplace. Throughout life we become conditioned to thinking in ways that generalize and stereotype others (see Figure 8-5).

Such thinking may result in behaviours categorized as prejudice, privileged or oppressive. Such thoughts and the behavioural consequences have significant implications for the international organization. Although usually rooted in some truth, stereotypes often do more harm than good. Stereotypes arise when we act as if all members of a culture or group share the same characteristics. There are many indicators of group membership such as race, age, gender that may be used by the observer. In some cases the assumed characteristics are respected (positive stereotype) and in other cases may be disrespected (negative stereotype).

Halo effect a judgement based on a single striking characteristic

Stereotypes stereotypes are formed when we ascribe generalizations to people based on their group identities and the tendencies of the whole group rather than seeing a person as an individual

Prejudice prejudice is an attitude, usually with negative feelings, that involves a pre-judgement about the members of a group

Figure 8-5

Generalizations from population characteristics

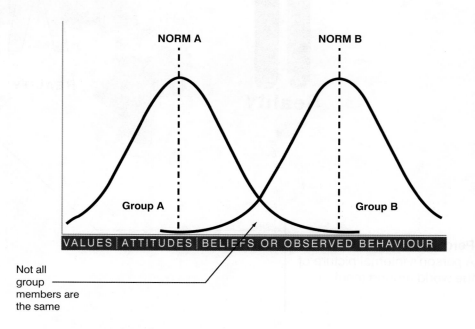

NORM A   NORM B

Group A   Group B

VALUES | ATTITUDES | BELIEFS OR OBSERVED BEHAVIOUR

Not all group members are the same

As we have discussed, the perceptual process concerns making sense of our external environment. Frequently we observe the actions and behaviour of ourselves and others and the consequences of the behaviour. We then often attempt to determine the cause of such actions and interpret our experience. Typically we are concerned with why something happened in the way it did: why did something work and why did something else not work? If we understand the causes of particular outcomes we may be able to adjust our behaviour accordingly.

Attribution is the process of attaching *causes* or reasons to the actions and events we see. An attribution is a belief about what causes certain things to happen. In some cases we determine ourselves or the person to be the cause (internal causality), i.e. things happened as a result of our capabilities or lack of them and in other cases we attribute an aspect of the environment (external causality) as the cause. Typically when things go right for us we believe it to be a result of our capabilities but when things go wrong we blame the circumstances. This is known as projection. We project blame onto external causes that are beyond our control. However, when considering the behaviour of others we tend to attribute cause to their disposition, i.e. lack of ability rather than blame an external issue.

Attribution theory is used to explain aspects of discrimination within the organization. Attribution research suggests that discrimination is based on our perceptions of causal links. Why is it that your appearance may have an impact upon your pay and career progression? Furthermore, our attributions are related to our stereotypes. We seem to attribute explanations of people's behaviour to aspects of their appearance. Discrimination against particular groups and individuals, on the basis of sex, sexual orientation, age or ethnic background, is now widely recognized. We make attribution errors by jumping quickly and unconsciously to judgements when we have little information about the other person on which to base a more careful assessment. Huczynski and Buchanan (2007: 29) discuss the main sources of errors in person perception. Errors include:

- not collecting enough information about other people;
- making judgements on irrelevant or insignificant information;
- only seeing what we want or expect to see;
- accepting stereotypes uncritically; and
- basing attributions on poor evidence.

We can avoid such errors if we take more time in making our judgements about others, collecting more information about them and recognizing sources of bias.

Social identity theory, stereotyping, generalizing, perception and attribution theory explain why some people may be treated differently (discriminatory behaviour) from others. In some cases certain groups may be discriminated against. Prejudice and other discriminatory behaviours have consequences in the organization. If people feel that they are not being treated fairly their *motivation* and performance are likely to be affected; people may leave the organization or be absent from work. This will impact upon productivity. Throughout this chapter we have made reference to the consequences of diversity within the organization; we summarize arguments for and against diversity in the next section.

Attribution the process by which we make sense of our environment through our perceptions of causality

The business case for diversity

In the previous section we outlined the organizational consequences of diversity. Within this section we focus in more detail on the arguments (pragmatic and ethical) for and against diversity in business. Within today's workforce we can observe the extensive use of cross-functional, heterogeneous teams designed to produce creative solutions to business problems, and the increased reliance on non-traditional workforce talent. This clearly demonstrates that diversity management has become a critical aspect of operating business. Diversity integration requires a long-term commitment and the payback is often not as tangible or predictable as say investing in new product development. However, a competitive edge can be gained by optimizing the people resource of the organization.

A critical challenge for senior management today is to turn cultural diversity into a differentiating advantage in an increasingly competitive global marketplace. Human resource executives must create a clear, compelling business case for diversity linked to the company's strategic business objectives. This section outlines, describes and updates the competitive and business reasons for managing diversity. Business reasons for managing diversity include:

- *Cost savings* Higher turnover costs (dissatisfied employees leaving the company), higher absenteeism rates and possible lawsuits on sexual, race and age discrimination.
- *Winning the competition for talent* Companies must attract, retain and promote excellent employees from different demographic groups. Companies cited as the best places to work for women and minorities have reported an increased inflow of applications.
- *Improved marketplace* Understanding your workforce should reflect your consumer base.
- *Enhanced creativity and increased quality of team problem-solving* Research shows that heterogeneous teams produce more innovative solutions to problems.

Look back
See chapter 3

McNett cited in Harvey and Allard (2009) questions the ethical underpinnings of diversity aside from the rational, pragmatic reasons. McNett considers the economic arguments for diversity: the market driven arguments, increased creativity and access to talented human capital. She suggests that such arguments rest on the RBV way of thinking about business. A diverse workforce with established customer relationships is an example of such a difficult to imitate resource. Aside from the pragmatic arguments for diversity, McNett suggests several ethical arguments. Thus far we have introduced compelling arguments to support diversity initiatives. There are, however, a number of counterarguments that may be presented. Diverse groups require more effort to integrate, coordinate and control. Minority members of groups may feel alienated and pushed out. We will explore more of the problems associated with diversity towards the end of the chapter when we focus on multicultural groups. Having considered the arguments for diversity we now turn our attention to the initiatives used to encourage diversity.

Thus far we have considered what is meant by diversity and explored the business consequences. In this section we seek answers to questions such as what diversity initiatives are there, how difficult is it to make diversity initiatives (see Figure 8-6) work within organizational contexts and how is diversity implemented?

Harvey and Allard (2009) argue that effective diversity management is a complex issue. They believe that both individuals and organizations need to begin the process by becoming more knowledgeable about their values and beliefs as well as those of people who may be different in their salient social identities. Increased awareness and heightened understanding become the foundation upon which individual and organizational changes can build. Superficial diversity efforts, like unexamined thinking, often produce superficial results. Diversity efforts involve both individual and organizational development. As companies become more culturally diverse, they can socialize newcomers through diversity initiatives to identify with positive, distinctive, and enduring characteristics of an organization or organizational subunit.

Figure 8-6

Integration of identity groups

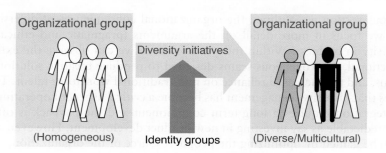

Identification enables new employees to develop loyalty to an organization and support it. Cox (1991) suggested that firms, particularly multicultural organizations, need new employee diversity orientation programmes that create a two-way socialization process, ensuring that:

1 bias is reduced; and

2 minority perspectives influence organizational norms and values.

Human resource practitioners can add value not only through the implementation of particular HRM practices, but also by generating a cultural mix in the human resource base, Orlando (2000).

Working with other cultures

We discussed national culture in Chapter 2 and at the beginning of this chapter we noted the benefits of synergy for organizational performance. However, as Prof. Geert Hofstede, Maastricht University states, *'Culture is more often a source of conflict than of synergy. Cultural differences are a nuisance at best and often a disaster.'*

Globalization opens many opportunities for business, but it also creates major challenges. An important challenge is the understanding and appreciating of cultural values, practices, and subtleties in different parts of the world argue Javidan and House (2001). To be successful in dealing with people from other cultures, managers need knowledge about cultural differences and similarities among countries. They also need to understand the implications of the differences and the skills required to act and decide appropriately and in a culturally sensitive way. Cultures evolve over time as societies try to adapt to their environments and find ways of managing their internal relationships. People in some societies and in some selected natural environmental conditions have learned that their survival depends upon strong cooperation. If they do not help each other, very few may survive. To the extent that different communities face different types of survival challenges, their collective learning in the form of culture may be different. This is the process that leads to cultural differences. In many ways culture (uniformity) can mean the opposite of diversity. A strong (homogeneous) culture is a workforce of like-minded individuals.

Back in the 1980s, Peters and Waterman (1982: 75) proposed that 'the stronger the culture and the more it was directed toward the marketplace, the less need was there for policy manuals, organization charts, or detailed procedures and rules. In these companies people way down the line know what they are supposed to do in most situations…. While there may be much truth in their proposition, later researchers considered the role of culture in the context of the organization's environment; many now believe that a homogeneous culture offers advantages in predictable environments where the direction of the company can be determined and all need to go in the same direction; this offers efficiency benefits.

However, in dynamic environments, the danger with a strong culture is that everyone heads in the wrong direction. A weak culture (heterogeneous) has less like-minded people and may, therefore, be more creative and adaptive. A key theme running through this section concerns cultural sensitivity and competence which we believe can help individuals and organizations to:

■ adapt and develop;

■ interact; and

■ manage (AIM) to attain their goals.

In the introduction to the chapter we outlined a range of situations where employees of international organizations may need to interact and work with people from other cultures. In some cases this will mean working with other cultures while in their home country; in other cases this may mean visiting other countries. However, the challenge of working with other cultures is not restricted to matters of national difference and a broad view of culture is considered here. First we consider the traditional challenges of developing cross-cultural competence and doing business in other countries. We then consider negotiation challenges before concluding with a discussion on work in multicultural groups.

Building cross-cultural competence

In Chapter 3 we discussed the strategic importance of certain organizational capabilities and competencies (work related knowledge, skill or ability – the way organizational resources are used). One such competence concerns the ability to understand, work and communicate with people from different countries and cultures. Thus in this section we discuss the *ability* of the international organization to work in different cultural environments. Cross-cultural understanding (cultural literacy) refers to the basic ability of people within business to recognize, interpret and correctly react to people, incidences or situations that are open to misunderstanding due to cultural differences. The fundamental intention of cross-cultural training is to equip the learner(s) with the appropriate skills to attain cross-cultural understanding.

People typically develop 'cross-cultural knowledge and awareness' becoming familiar with cultural characteristics such as values, beliefs and behaviours. This may lead to an ability to read into situations, contexts and behaviours that are culturally rooted and be able to react to them appropriately (sensitivity). 'Cross-cultural competence' is and should be the aim of all those dealing with multicultural clients, customers or colleagues. 'Competence' refers to an ability to work effectively across cultures. Cultural competence has been defined as a set of skills and attitudes that allow individuals to effectively and appropriately communicate with people who are different from themselves.

In this section we will therefore explore working in other countries, doing business in different cultures and intercultural communications. Many international business failures have been ascribed to a lack of cross-cultural competence (CC) on the part of business practitioners argue Johnson, Lenartowicz and Apud (2006). The authors propose a definition of CC as it applies to international business and develop a model for understanding how CC is nurtured in individuals, linking our definition to the concept of cultural intelligence.

Many international business failures have been ascribed to a lack of *cross-cultural competence* (the ability of individuals to function effectively in another culture) on the part of business practitioners. A globally competent manager must learn about many foreign cultures, be skilful in working with people from, and be able to adapt to living in, different cultures. Cross-cultural competence in international business is an individual's effectiveness in drawing on a set of knowledge, skills and personal attributes (*see* Figure 8-7) in order to work successfully with people from different national cultural backgrounds at home or abroad. Cultural knowledge is an important determinant of one's ability to minimize misunderstandings with someone from another culture. Cultural knowledge has a positive effect on other (cross-cultural competence) attributes and maximizes intercultural competency.

There are two different types of cultural knowledge: culture general (awareness and knowledge of cultural differences, components of culture, how cultural values are learned, and frameworks for understanding and comparing/contrasting different cultures) and culture specific (specific knowledge about another culture such as information about geography, economic, politics, law, history, customs, what to do and what not to do etc.) Culture specific knowledge is both explicit and tacit. Consequently, culture specific knowledge is sometimes imparted through training in the classroom and in other cases through a process of socialization (such as through visits overseas) whereby awareness of behaviour is developed. Cross-cultural training enables the individual to learn both content and skills that will facilitate effective cross-cultural interaction by reducing misunderstandings and inappropriate behaviours.

Cultural literacy knowledge about a culture that enables a person to function effectively within it

Cross-cultural competence an individual's effectiveness in drawing on a set of knowledge, skills and personal attributes in order to work successfully with people from different national cultural backgrounds at home or abroad

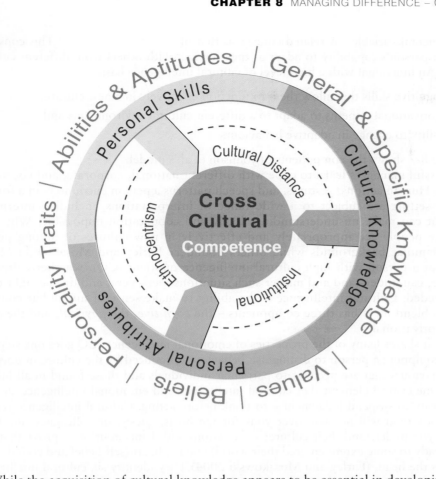

Figure 8-7
An IB model of cross-cultural
competence

While the acquisition of cultural knowledge appears to be essential in developing cross-cultural competence, the culturally competent manager must not only acquire cultural knowledge (learning) they must also apply the knowledge (doing and performing). It is generally thought that certain components of cultural competence cannot easily be taught, and that certain individuals may have an aptitude for developing cultural competence where others do not. Openness to new ideas and tolerance for ambiguity are examples of attributes that facilitate the learning of cross-cultural knowledge and skills. Consequently, organizations may attempt to screen applicants (see methodologies of cross-cultural assessment) for certain international business positions (Johnson, Lenartowicz and Apud 2006).

In their model of cross-cultural competence in international business, Johnson, Lenartowicz and Apud (2006) discuss three dimensions or antecedents of cultural competence:

1 personal attributes such as values, beliefs and personality traits;

2 personal skills; and

3 cultural knowledge.

The authors also introduce and discuss two environmental factors whose presence can impede cross-cultural competence in the international business context: institutional ethnocentrism and cultural distance. Ethnocentrism in a multinational business corporation is defined as imposing on affiliates abroad the ways of working at the headquarters in the home culture, i.e. institutional ethnocentrism promotes the home culture's way of doing things. Johnson *et al.* (2006) suggest we should expect *institutional ethnocentrism* to have a negative effect on an individual's ability to respond appropriately to cultural differences in the workplace.

Cultural distance aims to capture the overall difference in national culture between the home country and affiliates overseas. As the cultural distance increases, the difficulties facing business processes overseas also increase. A large cultural distance not only reflects a difference in cultural values, but also in many cases reflects a significant difference in other

Cultural distance cultural distance aims to capture the overall difference in national culture between the home country and affiliates overseas. As the cultural distance increases, the difficulties facing business processes overseas also increase

environmental variables. A related concept is that of cultural intelligence. This construct reflects a person's capability to adapt as they interact with others from different cultural regions. An individual with a high level of cultural intelligence has:

- the cognitive skills that allow them to function effectively in a new culture;
- the motivational impetus to adapt to a different cultural environment; and
- the ability to engage in adaptive behaviours.

Figure 8-7 shows the components of Johnson et al.'s model.

Successful managers learn to cope with different national, corporate, and vocational cultures. Human actions, gestures, and speech patterns a person encounters in a foreign business setting are subject to a wide range of interpretations, including interpretations that can make misunderstandings likely and cooperation impossible. Why then can some people act appropriately and effectively in new cultures or among people with unfamiliar backgrounds while others flounder? Earley and Mosakowski (2004) argue that a person with high cultural intelligence quotient (CQ), whether cultivated or innate, can understand and master such situations, persevere, and do the right thing when needed. Cultural intelligence is the ability to make sense of unfamiliar contexts and then blend in. It has three components – the *cognitive*, the *physical*, and the *emotional*/motivational.

While it shares many of the properties of emotional intelligence, CQ goes one step further by equipping a person to distinguish behaviours produced by the culture in question from behaviours that are peculiar to particular individuals and those found in all human beings. One critical element that cultural intelligence and emotional intelligence share is a propensity to suspend judgement – to think before acting. Cultural intelligence resides in the body (you will not win over your foreign hosts, guests, or colleagues simply by showing you understand their culture; your actions and demeanour must prove that you have already to some extent entered their world) and the heart (self-belief and confidence), as well as the head, (Earley and Mosakowski 2004).They identify six cultural intelligence profiles:

- **The** '*provincial*' is effective when working with people of similar background but runs into trouble when venturing farther afield.
- The '*analyst*' methodically deciphers a foreign culture's rules and expectations by resorting to a variety of elaborate learning strategies.
- The '*natural*' relies entirely on intuition rather than on a systematic learning style.
- The '*ambassador*', like many political appointees, may not know much about the culture just entered, but communicates convincingly that they belong there.
- The '*mimic*' has a high degree of control over their actions and behaviour, if not a great deal of insight into the significance of the cultural cues they pick up.
- The '*chameleon*' possesses high levels of all three CQ components and is a very uncommon managerial type.

Earley and Mosakowski (2004) believe cultural intelligence (see Figure 8-8) can be developed. In order to do this, the individual first examines their CQ strengths and weaknesses in order to establish a starting point for subsequent development efforts. Next, the person selects and applies training that focuses on their weaknesses. Finally they enter the cultural setting they need to master.

Harris and Kumra (2000) discuss cross-cultural training (international manager development) in highly diverse environments. They argue the international assignments conducted between the 1960s and 1980s were quite different from those conducted today. Previously, employees would stay two or three years in a foreign subsidiary, predominantly in the Third World. In such circumstances there was a power differential between the headquarters and the subsidiary which led to an inevitable ethnocentric outlook. For the most part, expatriates were sent for purposes of command and control over local nationals.

	1: Strongly Disagree	2: Disagree	3: Neutral	4: Agree	5: Strongly Agree
1. Before I interact with people from a new culture, I ask myself what I hope to achieve					
2. If I encounter something unexpected while working in a new culture, I use this experience to figure out new ways to approach other cultures in the future					
3. I plan how I'm going to relate to people from a different culture before I meet them					
4. When I come into a new cultural situation, I can immediately sense whether something is going well or something is wrong					
Cognitive CQ (ΣQ1:Q4)/4					
5. It's easy for me to change my body language (for example, eye contact or posture) to suit people from a different culture					
6. I can alter my expression when a cultural encounter requires it					
7. I modify my speech style (for example, accent or tone) to suit people from a different culture					
8. I easily change the way I act when a cross-cultural encounter seems to require it					
Physical CQ (ΣQ5:Q8)/4					
9. I have confidence that I can deal well with people from a different culture					
10. I am certain that I can befriend people whose cultural backgrounds are different from mine					
11. I can adapt to the lifestyle of a different culture with relative ease					
12. I am confident that I can deal with a cultural situation that's unfamiliar					
Emotional/motivational CQ (ΣQ9:Q12)/4					

Figure 8-8

Diagnosing your cultural intelligence

Harris and Kumra (2000) argue that, in such cases, the expatriate did not need a detailed understanding of local cultures nor did they need to adapt.

Throughout the 1990s we witnessed rapid globalization, more internationalization of organizations, changing economic conditions (resulting in the cost effectiveness of expatriates to be questioned) and an increase in the need for assignments in the developed countries also. Harris and Kumra (2000) further discuss the changing nature of international assignees themselves; no longer the exclusive domain of the privileged male but extended to well-educated managers of more diverse origin. Harris and Kumra (2000) also recognized many new forms of international working such as short-term assignments, commuter assignments and other roles that require extensive international travel as part of their home-based role. Consequently, international management competences are now recognized to be of critical importance for many organizations.

In the remaining culture-based sections we consider challenges such as how to conduct business in different countries, intercultural encounters and specific communication issues and intercultural negotiations before concluding the chapter with further discussion on multicultural group work.

Conducting business in different cultures

Many business practitioners and scholars argue that when doing business in another culture, it is important to understand their customs and manners (ways of behaving). A lack of understanding may result in embarrassing mistakes or offence. Such a knowledge (business etiquette) may help with negotiations (covered later in this chapter), marketing and operations management (see Chapter 15). Examples of good business etiquette include giving and receiving business cards carefully; not being too familiar too soon and using humour cautiously. Behaviour also manifests itself in customs (ways of behaving in specific circumstances). In some countries it is customary to give gifts. This may be done at the start of, during or end of a business relationship. However, giving gifts is not without problem. In some cultures is may be considered a bribe and in others, the gift itself or the way it is wrapped signifies things (a knife may signify the severing of a relationship in some cultures). Tendering favours and giving gifts can break down boundaries to some extent. Confucianism stresses hard work, thrift and perseverance. In such cultures, who you know is more important than what you know (connections – Guangxi, Kankeit and Kwankye) kinship, locality and relationships are based on shared experiences and form the basis of guangxi. Non-Chinese people can use other Chinese (respected businessman) people as intermediaries. It is important to cultivate personal relationships and trust in China – this means getting to know people, delivering what you promise and not cheating.

In the next section we focus on communication and intercultural interaction before specifically turning our attention to negotiations and decision-making where intercultural knowledge may be put into practice.

There is no question that one of the most important features of a global manager's job is to communicate effectively with people from other parts of the world (Javidan and House 2001). People, and managers in particular, spend a great deal of their time communicating with others either verbally, in writing or through some electronically mediated channel. The ability to communicate across cultural boundaries will influence the success of international business transactions and the performance of a culturally diverse workforce. While communication has many purposes, its primary function is to coordinate, control, motivate and disseminate information to workers.

Effective communication requires the ability to listen, to frame the message in a way that is understandable to the receiver, and to accept and use feedback. When a member of one culture sends a message to another, intercultural communication takes place. Effective cross-cultural communication involves finding integrated solutions, or at least compromises, that allow decisions to be implemented by members of diverse cultures.

© Freddie Jones / Alamy

STOP & THINK

Compare Hofstede scores; see Table 2-2 Scores of cultural dimensions (by country) for the UK and Philippines – how should a British consultant prepare for an assignment in the Philippines?

Discuss the cultural distance between the two countries.

Look back
See chapter 2, p. 54

Now re-read the case study.

Look back
See p. 136

Consider the culture-general and culture-specific knowledge available to the consultants based on the work of Hofstede and Andre.

How might you expect the similarities and differences between the two countries and their cultures to impact upon how the consultancy team communicated with Filipinos and the transfer of practices and management style from the UK to the Philippines?

STOP & THINK

While this sounds simple, it can be quite complicated in cross-cultural situations. In countries with high levels of power distance, communication is almost always one way, top to bottom (see for example the PLDT active learning case discussed in Chapter 5). The manager is always expected to know more than the subordinates. Input or feedback from subordinates is seldom solicited and in fact may be seen as impolite and disloyal. In collectivist cultures, the process and content of communication is expected to help group cohesion and harmony. The language tends to be soft and indirect. Any form of communication that could lead to discomfort and conflict is avoided. The language tends to be general, and the process is highly involved, with a great deal of discussion.

In contrast, in individualistic countries people are much less concerned about group cohesion and more concerned about individual response. The process tends to be simpler, with less involvement and participation. Finally, in countries high on humane orientation, the nature of communication is more focused on avoiding conflict and being caring and paternalistic. The process of communication may be more focused on being supportive than leading to any output results. In fact, the process itself may be the end result because it helps build cohesion. Cultural dimensions and profiles provide managers with an interesting starting point for the preparation of cross-cultural communication and resolution of cross-cultural conflict.

Look back
See chapter 5, p. 136

Knowing that a society is high on uncertainty avoidance, for example, helps a manager to know what to expect and do with respect to scheduling meetings, enforcing punctuality, preparing agendas, and formalizing decisions made during meetings. However, there is much more to uncertainty avoidance than formalized rules and procedures. In high uncertainty-avoidance societies, accounting systems are more explicit and detailed. There are undoubtedly a host of other managerial and informal practices that reflect high uncertainty-avoidance tendencies on the part of members of such societies. Knowing a society is high on uncertainty avoidance provides the starting point when investigating what to expect with respect to all of the management practices associated with the various functions of organizations such as marketing, production, finance, purchasing, accounting, and human resource management.

Inter-cultural negotiations

Negotiation is a process of communication involving the exchange of information on parties' interests, positions, and needs. Negotiations and decision-making are both intertwined and culture bound. Cross-cultural negotiations may be a one-off occurrence (a sale) or a frequent occurrence (in alliances and joint ventures). They may have an external or internal focus involving a variety of stakeholders. Management may negotiate with trade unions and other employee groups or external influence groups. In any event, it is widely agreed that while the negotiations and decision-making processes are more a general and universal matter, the behaviour of participants is somewhat more specific and culture bound.

Organizations, through their representatives, must engage frequently in negotiations with other entities throughout the world when establishing business relationships, procuring raw materials (see Chapter 15), goods and services or selling to others (see Chapter 16). A *negotiation* is a discussion intended to produce an agreement and possibly resolve a conflict; it is a form of social interaction and the process by which two or more parties try to resolve an issue. There are essentially two types of negotiation: transactional and conflict. Transactional negotiation involves buyers and sellers negotiating terms; conflict (dispute) resolution negotiations involve parties that seek to overcome something that is blocking goal attainment.

In order to understand the effect of culture on negotiation it is useful to have a model of negotiation. Negotiation is an exchange activity which promotes the possibility of mutually beneficial outcomes. While there is no uni-cultural approach to negotiation, typical stages within the negotiation process include preparation, relationship building, information exchange, persuasion, concession and agreement. *Cooperative and competitive behaviours* may be observed at each stage. Negotiation is essentially about bargaining, persuading and influencing others and reaching agreements. Negotiations present situations where people of different cultural backgrounds interact with one another. On occasions, employees of international organizations will be asked to negotiate with a party from a different culture.

Cross-national mergers, acquisitions, joint ventures, sales, licensing agreements and distribution service contracts are examples of transactions almost always initiated through some form of a face-to-face negotiation. In addition, companies must manage sources of internal conflict, possibly negotiating with trade unions and other employee representatives. Given that there are many differences in the way cultures approach negotiation and the importance of those negotiations it is important for such employees to develop an ability to negotiate successfully. This requires an understanding of the negotiation process, cultural differences in negotiation and an understanding of cultural differences in decision-making processes. The failure to negotiate productively may result in lost business and increased costs.

Salacuse (2005) lists ten of the top ways that culture can affect negotiation. Cultural differences between negotiators can create barriers that impede the negotiating process. However, Salacuse (2005) notes that the great diversity of the world's cultures prevents any negotiator from fully understanding them all. Through the ten key elements of intercultural negotiation he suggests an overarching framework to help identify cultural differences that might arise during the negotiations process. He argues that through application of the framework we can better understand our counterpart and avoid misunderstandings. The following negotiation factors are presented:

- *Goal* – Negotiators from different cultures may tend to view the purpose of a negotiation differently with some oriented toward the contract and others the relationship. Consequently, they may expect different things from the negotiation. As a relationship is more long term, they may want to spend more time getting to know one another.

- *Attitudes* – Win/win negotiators see deal making as a collaborative problem-solving process whereas the win/lose negotiator adopts a more confrontational/competitive approach.

- *Personal styles* – Culture strongly influences the personal style of any negotiator (how they talk to and interact with others, etc.). Informal negotiators may initiate discussions on a first name basis; such an act may be disrespectful and therefore bad in other cultures (see Japanese for example). Negotiators in foreign cultures must respect appropriate formalities.

- *Communications* – Methods of communication vary among cultures with some more direct than others.

- *Time sensitivity (high:low)* – Consideration should be given to differences in cultural attitudes towards time. Some cultures negotiate more slowly than others, some try to make a quick deal. Whereas some cultures may try to get down to business quickly, others will want to create a relationship first.

- *Emotionalism* – Some countries show more emotions than others.

- *Agreement form* – The negotiating transaction is typically encapsulated in some form of written agreement (contract). However, while very detailed contracts attempting to anticipate all possible circumstances may be desired in some cultures, others prefer simple contracts in the form of the general principles rather than detailed rules.

- *Agreement building* – In some cases negotiating may start with general principles proceeding to detailed (a deductive process) while in other cultures it may start with specific (an inductive process). Different cultures tend to emphasize one approach over the other.

- *Team organization* – In any organization, it is important to know how the other side is organized, who has the authority to make commitments, and how decisions are made. Some cultures emphasize the individual while others stress the group. In some cases it may be difficult to identify who the leader is and who has the authority to commit. In some cases the negotiating team may be very small and in other cases large.

- *Risk taking* – Certain cultures are more risk averse than others. Faced with a risk-averse counterpart Salacuse (2005) advises that you do not rush the negotiation process; devote attention to risk reduction mechanisms; provide information; build relationships and consider restructuring the deal so that it proceeds step by step in an incremental manner.

Several national culture dimensions are thought to influence negotiation behaviour. For example, individualists pursue personal goals as opposed to group goals. Individualists are more likely to pursue competitive rather than cooperative behaviours. The competitor seeks to maximize the difference between his own and others' outcomes (Brett 2000). To preserve collective harmony, collectivist cultures are less likely to take a dominating or coercive stance toward negotiation, but instead seek a middle ground between conflicting positions; such cultures tend to see the confrontational aspect of problem solving as potentially destructive and opt for moderate positions that partially satisfy both parties. By contrast, individualistic cultures consider problem solving as an integrative approach because they are oriented toward fact-based solutions within negotiations.

The egalitarian culture supports direct, face-to-face negotiations to resolve conflict; others favour the use of intermediaries – third parties to help with conflict resolution (Brett 2000). Throughout this chapter we have identified a need to understand how negotiators think and behave and have identified cultural variables as determinants of such thinking and behaviour. However, East/West distinctions at the level of cultural values grossly oversimplify more fine-grained cultural differences in negotiation and norms. Brett (2000) cautions us – not all members of a cultural group with a distinct value profile behave and act consistently with the cultural norms (i.e. we should be careful how we rely upon generalizations and stereotypes). Cultural information and knowledge may be harmful if it stimulates biased perceptions and inappropriate adjustments of negotiation strategy.

Diverse and multicultural groups

As organizations globalize their operations, it is likely that the frequency with which employees will interact with people from different countries will increase. Further, domestic populations are becoming more diverse, suggesting that domestic organizations will also need to learn how to manage more heterogeneous workgroups than they have managed previously. In addition, the trend toward using teams to coordinate and manage work in organizations is increasing the amount of time that employees spend with people outside their particular functional or product groups, thereby bringing them into contact with people who may have very different training, skills, functional background, and even values. In this last section we consolidate previous work on diversity, perception, culture and

© Yuri_arcurs / Dreamstime.com

working with others and turn our attention to specific problems associated with making diverse and multicultural groups work within the international organization.

The international organization needs groups that perform, are motivated and productive, creative, dynamic and a source of sustainable competitive advantage. Milliken and Martins (1996) review the effects of different types of diversity in group composition and argue that diversity in the composition of organizational groups affects outcomes such as employee turnover and performance through its impact on affective, cognitive, and communication processes. Research on heterogeneity in groups suggests that diversity offers both a great opportunity for organizations as well as an enormous challenge. Diversity appears to be a double-edged sword, increasing the opportunity for creativity as well as the likelihood that group members will be dissatisfied and fail to identify with the group. A group that is diverse could be expected to have members who may have had significantly different experiences and, therefore, significantly different perspectives on key issues or problems. However, such differences can create serious coordination and communication difficulties for groups.

The largest organizational group is the organization itself and findings suggest that individuals who are different in racial or ethnic background tend to be less psychologically committed to their organizations, less inclined to stay with the organization, and more likely to be absent. Further, research on racial differences in performance ratings by supervisors indicated that black people were generally rated lower than white people by supervisors. Studies have also found that black people were assessed as having lower potential for promotion and were more likely to have plateaued in their careers. One study found evidence that new black recruits tended to be assigned to black supervisors more frequently than to white supervisors. Lefkowitz (1994) also found evidence that this segregation grew over time in that, when reassignments occurred, the likelihood of blacks ending up with black supervisors became even higher. He labelled this phenomenon ethnic drift.

McLeod and Lobel (1992) found that groups that were heterogeneous with respect to the ethnic backgrounds of their members produced higher quality ideas in a brainstorming task than more homogeneous groups did, although they did not necessarily produce more ideas or a greater number of unique ideas. Watson and colleagues (1993) found that group diversity in nationality/ethnic background had differing impacts upon group process and performance at different time points in their experiment. Homogeneous groups reported significantly more effective processes than diverse groups initially, but the two types of groups were equal after a number of weeks working together. Initially, the homogeneous groups scored higher than diverse groups on all performance measures, but later, diverse groups scored higher on two aspects of performance (range of perspectives and alternatives generated), and overall performance was the same for both types of groups.

The results of this research suggest that diversity in ethnic background may have negative effects on individual and group outcomes early in a group's life, presumably because it takes some time for group members to get over their interpersonal differences on observable dimensions that tend to be associated with lower levels of initial attraction and social integration. However, after this stage, once a certain level of behavioural integration has been achieved, groups may be able to obtain benefits from the greater variety of perspectives inherent within a diverse group.

For a more recent study into the performance of multicultural MBA groups, see Kelly (2008). Research on the effects of gender diversity in groups points to a similar set of processes and results as those found in the case of racial diversity. Similar to groups that are diverse in race or gender, groups that have more diversity in terms of ages represented tend to have higher turnover rates. Not surprisingly, the people who are different from their group members in terms of age are more likely to leave. In summary, studies into directly observable attributes appear to be fairly consistent. In general, the more diverse a group is with respect to gender, race, or age, the higher its turnover rate and the more likely it is that dissimilar individuals will leave the organization and be absent.

It has been suggested that diversity may lead to discomfort for all members of a group, leading to lower integration within the group and a higher likelihood of turnover. There is also some evidence of negative affective reactions to observable differences on the part of supervisors – in that supervisors tend to perceive dissimilar subordinates less positively and tend to give them lower performance ratings. The turnover of dissimilar members of groups suggests that organizational groups may not be fully capitalizing on the potential cognitive benefits of diversity. Further, prior to departing, it is likely that individuals who feel that they are distant from other group members may feel alienated and withhold contributions to the group.

Milliken and Martins (1996) identified common patterns in the processes by which diversity affected individual, group, and organizational outcomes. They discuss four types of mediating variables that seem to affect the long-term outcomes (e.g., turnover, performance) of diverse groups. According to Milliken and Martins, diversity in observable attributes has consistently been found to have negative effects on *affective* outcomes (e.g., identification with the group, satisfaction) at both the individual and group levels of analysis. Further, greater negative effects have been found for diversity on race and gender than for diversity on age, suggesting the possibility that the deep-seated prejudices some people hold against people who are different from themselves on race and gender may be adding to the difficulty of interaction for these groups.

There is also clear evidence that groups with skill-based diversity seem to have greater coordination costs than groups composed of people with more homogeneous skills or backgrounds. In addition, diversity in organizational and group tenure also appears to be associated with lower social integration and higher turnover for the group as well as greater turnover for individuals who are different from the group. Further, supervisors appear to prefer subordinates who have similar organizational tenure and give them higher performance ratings. These findings are consistent with the idea that the more similar people are in background variables such as socioeconomic status or attitudes, the more attracted they are likely to be to each other, at least initially, a phenomenon that when observed in friendship patterns is called *homophily bias*. One reason for this phenomenon is that people who are similar in backgrounds may have similar values and share common life-experiences; they therefore, find the experience of interacting with each

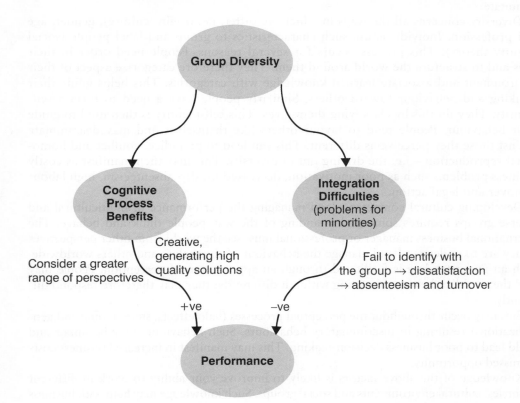

Figure 8-9

Consequences of group diversity

other positively reinforcing. Even similarity on a variable such as time of entry into an organization may be important in affecting interaction frequency and attraction between people. Group heterogeneity, thus, may have a negative impact on individual feelings of satisfaction through decreasing individuals' sense of identification or social integration within the group. The cognitive consequences of diversity refer to the effects diversity might have on the group's ability to process information, perceive and interpret stimuli, and make decisions.

Thus, research repeatedly suggests the presence of a systemic problem, namely, that groups and organizations will act systematically to push out individuals who are different from the majority, unless this tendency to drive out diversity is managed (Schneider, 1987). This finding is a manifestation of the tendency of people to identify with particular groups and then define these groups as the in-group and all other groups as out-groups, and it is the outcome of natural social processes (see SIT theory). In the context of organizations, such processes will tend to create what Kanter (1977), cited in Milliken and Martins (1996), referred to as homosocial reproduction; resulting in the creation of very homogeneous groups that are not representative. This tendency to drive out diversity is an extremely serious and systematic force that organizations that value diversity will have to develop mechanisms to counteract (Schneider, 1987). It is clear that there are many benefits associated with diversity; however, diversity also leads to serious affective costs.

Look back
See p. 244

Summary of key learning points

Globalization and internationalization create internal and external challenges for the organization. Economic and social arguments (creativity, improved marketplace understanding, stakeholder approval and winning talent) are devised to manage the international organization as a diverse and multicultural entity. Strategic arguments are also created for such an entity through RBV theory – a diverse and multicultural organization is difficult to imitate.

Diversity concerns all the ways in which we differ, i.e. origin (culture), gender, age and profession. Individuals use such characteristics to group and label people (social identity theory). This process occurs for several reasons. People need order in their lives and to structure the world around them. They therefore categorize aspect of their environment and associate learned knowledge with categories. This helps guide their thinking and behaviour toward others. Similarly people have a need to form a self-identity. They do this by classifying themselves. This self-identity is then used to guide their behaviour. People tend to favour others like themselves and may discriminate against those they perceive as different. This can lead to prejudice, conflict and homosocial reproduction – i.e. the driving out of diversity. This may then manifest as costly business problems such as poor motivation, decreased loyalty, absenteeism, high labour turnover and legal action.

Developing cultural competence and managing the performance of multicultural and diverse groups requires some understanding of the way people think and behave. The international business manager or professional must see the world from other perspectives if they are to understand and manage the behaviour of themselves and others worldwide. Such an understanding is facilitated through an appreciation of perception. People may 'see' the world and events occurring within it differently; they may therefore respond differently.

Bias may occur throughout the perceptual processes (halo effects, stereotyping and generalizations) resulting in discriminatory behaviours. Such behaviours may be unfair and could lead to poor business decision-making. This may manifest in increased business costs or missed opportunity.

Knowledge of the above factors is likely to improve your ability to work in different countries, cultural environments and social groups. Such knowledge may help with business negotiations, communication, decision-making, coordination and control, managing and motivating others. When such knowledge is routinely practised at the organizational level, competitive advantages associated with the diverse and multicultural organization are more likely to take hold. Organizations must strive continuously to attain such advantages, constantly facing the forces of homosocial reproduction and the natural drive towards the creation of homogeneous organizations.

Review questions

Activity: Group formation

You have been asked to form a group (with students on your course or colleagues in the workplace) – consider how you might form a work group. Next, based on the group composition, consider what the potential of the group. Do you envisage any issues, challenges or problems that might emerge in the group processes? If so, how might you overcome such problems? Consider your answers in relation to the stages of group formation.

Group activity: Cultural competence

Discuss the extent to which people are born culturally competent.

Group activity: Working in other countries

Select a country and research inhabitants behaviours (consider Hofstede's measurements for the country and matters that might impact upon the way business is done in that country).
Team up with a classmate who chose a different country in the exercise above.

1 Each person should brief the other on findings.
2 Consider the factors that might affect relationships between managers of the two countries – what may prevent/help them work together?

Activity: Planning for negotiation (1)

Refer back to the Burberry active learning case in Chapter 7.
Your role: Burberry production manager – Far East.
Negotiator Company: Polo Shirt Manufacture by ABC Holdings Ltd.
Negotiation: identify potential supply chain alternatives that include manufacturing in lower cost locations like China.
Brief: The Burberry group has asked you to contract out polo shirt production and generate cost savings in the supply chain. Presently, in the UK, it costs the company around £12 to make a polo shirt.

Task 1: How would you classify this type of negotiation?

Task 2: Consider the negotiation process and lay out the next steps for negotiation with the potential supplier: ABC Holdings Ltd, China.

Task 3: Review the pros and cons of the different operating alternatives in China, including the use of an independent supplier, developing a joint venture and even incorporating as a Wholly Foreign Owned Enterprise (WFOE). Consider the advantages and disadvantages of shifting production to China. Does it make sense to move production overseas?

Task 4: What is your goal and what is the other party's goal? What are your needs/interests (in priority order) and what are the other party's needs/interests? Consider pricing, quality, risk and other issues.

Look back
See chapter 7, p. 204

Task 5: Develop a culture profile for China and consider the communications context. Which cultural factors do you expect to have greatest impact upon the negotiation process and why? What strategy (type and approach to negotiation) will you use? Consider how you will use power and information throughout the process. How important will relationship commitment, trust and relationship building be and what measures will you use to achieve the required relationship? What problems might you encounter?

Note: This task can be made more interesting with two or more parties taking part. In which case the exercise may be turned into a role play activity with some group members allocated to the 'UK' team and some to the ABC Holdings Ltd, China team. Teams may prepare for negotiation and then compare notes or role play the negotiation. It may be necessary to conduct several rounds of negotiation to simulate a real world event.

References

Adair, W. (2003) 'Integrative Sequences And Negotiation Outcome In Same- And Mixed-Culture Negotiations', *International Journal of Conflict Management* 2003 14(3/4):273–296.

Adair, W. and Brett, J. (2005) 'The Negotiation Dance: Time, Culture, and Behavioural Sequences in Negotiation', *Organization Science* (January/February 2005) 16(1):33–51.

Arnold, J., Cooper, C. and Robertson, I. (1998) *Work Psychology – Understanding Human Behaviour in the Work Place* (3 ed), London: Financial Times/Prentice Hall.

Ashforth, B. and Mael, F. (1989) 'Identity Theory and the Organization', *Academy of Management Review* 14(1):20–39.

Bantel, K. A. and Jackson, S. E. (1989) 'Top management and innovations in banking: Does the composition of the top team make a difference?', *Strategic Management Journal* 10:107–124.

Brett, J. (2000) 'Culture and Negotiation', *International Journal of Psychology* (April 2000) 35(2): 97–104.

Carrell, M. and Mann, E. (1995) 'Defining workforce diversity in public sector organizations', *Public Personnel Management* (Spring 1995) 24(1):99–112.

Carrell, M., Mann, E. and Sigler, T. (2006) 'Defining Workforce Diversity Programs and Practices in Organizations: A Longitudinal Study', *Labour Law Journal* (Spring 2006) 57(1):5–12.

Cox, T. (1991) 'The multicultural organization', *Academy of Management Executive* (May 1991) 5(2):34–47.

Cox, T. (1994) *Cultural Diversity in Organizations: Theory, research, and practice*, San Francisco: Berrett Koehler.

Barkema, H., Shenkar, O., Vermeulen, F. and Bell, J. (1997) 'Working abroad, working with others: How firms learn to operate international joint ventures', *Academy of Management Journal* (April 1997) 40(2):426–442.

Eagly, A. H. and Chaiken, S. (1993) *The Psychology of Attitudes*, Orlando FI: Ted Buchholz.

Earley, P. and Mosakowski, E. (2004) 'Cultural Intelligence', *Harvard Business Review* (October 2004) 82(10):139–146.

Ely, R. J. (1994) 'The effects of organizational demographics and social identity on relationships among professional women'. *Administrative Science Quarterly*, 39:203–238.

Ensign, P. C. (1998) 'Interrelationships and horizontal strategy to achieve synergy and competitive advantage in the diversified firm', *Management Decision* 36(10):657–668.

Ghauri, P. (1986) 'Guidelines for international business negotiations', *International Marketing Review* (Autumn 1986) 3(3):72–83.

Govindarajan, V. and Gupta, A. (2001) 'Building an Effective Global Business Team', *MIT Sloan Management Review* 42(4):63–71.

Hampden-Turner, C. M. and Trompenaars, F. (2000) *Building Cross-Cultural Competence – How to create wealth from conflicting values*, Chichester: Wiley.

Harris, H. and Kumra, S. (2000) 'International manager development – Cross-cultural training in highly diverse environments', *Journal of Management Development* 19(7):602–614.

Harvey, C. and Allard, M. (2009) *Understanding and Managing Diversity* (4 ed), Upper Saddle River, NJ: Pearson Education.

Hofstede, G. (1997) *Cultures and Organizations*, New York: McGraw-Hill.

Hofstede, G. (1984) *Cultures Consequences – abridged*, Newbury Park: Sage.

Hofstede, G. (1995) *The cultural relativity and organizational practices and theories*, London and New York: Routledge.

Hofstede, G. (1991) 'Management in a multicultural society', *Malaysian Management Review* (April) 26(1):3–12.

Hofstede, G. (1985) 'The Interaction Between National and Organizational Value Systems', *The Journal of Management Studies* 22(4):347.

Hofstede, G. (1989) 'Organizing for cultural diversity', *European Management Journal* 7:390–397.

Hofstede, G. (1998) 'Attitudes, values and organizational culture: Disentangling the concepts', *Organization Studies* 19(3):477–492.

Hofstede, G. (2006) 'What did GLOBE really measure? Researchers' minds versus respondents' minds', *Journal of International Business Studies* 37:882–896.

Huczynski, A. and Buchanan, D. (2007) *Organizational Behaviour* (6 ed), Harlow: FT Prentice Hall.

Javidan, M. and House, R. (2001) 'Cultural Acumen for the Global Manager: Lessons from Project GLOBE', *Organizational Dynamics* (Spring 2001) 29(4):289–305.

Johnson, J., Lenartowicz, T. and Apud, S. (2006) 'Cross-cultural competence in international business: toward a definition and a model', *Journal of International Business Studies* (July 2006) 37(4):525–543.

Kelly, P. (2008) 'Achieving desirable group-work outcomes through the group allocation process', *Team Performance Management* 14(1/2):22–38.

Kossek, E. and Zonia, S. (1993) 'Assessing diversity climate: A field study of reactions to employer efforts to promote diversity', *Journal of Organizational Behavior* 14:61–81.

Lefkowitz, 1. (1994) 'Race as a factor in job placement: Serendipitous findings of ethnic drift', *Personnel Psychology* 47:497–513.

Lin, X. and Miller, S. (2003) 'Negotiation approaches: direct and indirect effect of national culture', *International Marketing Review* 20(3):286–303.

Luostarinen, R. (1980) 'Internationalization of the firm', Helsinki: Helsinki School of Economics cited in Barkema *et al.* (1997).

McLeod, P. L. Lobel, S.A. and Cox, T. H., Jr. (1996) 'Ethnic diversity and creativity in small groups', *Small Group Research* 27:246–264.

McLeod, P. L. and Lobel, S. A. (1992) 'The effects of ethnic diversity on idea generation in small groups', *Academy of Management Best Paper Proceedings* 227–231.

Milliken, F. and Martins, L. (1996) 'Searching For Common Threads: Understanding the Multiple Effects of Diversity in Organizational Groups', *Academy of Management Review* 21(2):402–433.

Mullins, L. (2005) *Management and Organizational Behaviour*, Harlow: FT Prentice Hall.

Mumford, E. and Beekman, G. J. (1994) *Tools For Change & Progress*, Leiden, Netherlands: CSG Publications.

Orlando, R. (2000) 'Racial Diversity, Business Strategy, and Firm Performance: A Resource-Based View', *Academy of Management Journal* 43(2):164–177.

Ouchi, W. G. (1980) 'Markets, Bureaucracies, and Clans', *Administrative Science Quarterly – Ithaca* 25(1):129–141.

Ouchi, W. G. and Wilkins, A. L. (1983) 'Efficient Cultures: Exploring the relationship between culture and organizational performance', *Administrative Science Quarterly* 28(3):468–481.

Peters, T. and Waterman, R. (1982) *In Search of Excellence*, London: Harper Collins Business.

Pfeffer, I. (1994) *Competitive advantage through people*, Boston: Harvard Business School Press.

Robinson, G. and Dechant, K. (1997) 'Building a business case for diversity', *Academy of Management Executive* (August 1997) 11(3):21–31.

Sackett, P. H., DuBois, C. L. Z. and Noe, A. W. (1991) 'Tokenism in performance evaluation: The effects of work group representation on male-female and white-black differences in performance ratings', *Journal of Applied Psychology* 76:263–267.

Salacuse, J. (2005) 'Negotiating: The top ten ways that culture can affect your negotiation', *Ivey Business Journal* (March/April 2005) 69(4):1–6.

Schein, E. (1999) *The Corporate Culture Survival Guide*, San-Francisco: Jossey Bass.

Schein, E. (1997) *Organizational Culture and Leadership* (2 ed), San Francisco: Jossey Bass.

Schein, E. (1999) 'Empowerment, coercive persuasion and organizational learning: do they connect?', *The Learning Organization* 6(4):163.

Schein, E. (1996) 'Culture: The missing concept in organization studies', *Administrative Science Quarterly* 41(2):229.

Schein, E. (1996) 'Three cultures of management: The key to organizational learning', *Sloan Management Review* 38(1):9.

Schneider, B. (1987) 'The people make the place', *Personnel Psychology* 40:437–453.

Schuster, C. and Copeland, M. (2005) *Global Business Practices: Adapting for Success*, Mason, Ohio: Thomson.

Stets, J. and Burke, P. (2000) 'Identity Theory and Social Identity Theory', *Social Psychology Quarterly* 63(3):224–237.

Tannen, D. (1995) 'The Power of Talk: Who Gets Heard and Why', *Harvard Business Review* (September/October 1995) 73(5):138–148.

Trice, H. M. and Beyer, J. M. (1993) *The cultures of work organizations*, Upper Saddle River NJ: Prentice Hall.

Tsui, A. S., Egan, T. D. and O'Reilly, C. A. (1992) 'Being different: Relational demography and organizational attachment', *Administrative Science Quarterly* 37:549–579.

Tsui, A. S. and O'Reilly, C. A. (1989) 'Beyond simple demographic effects: The importance of relational demography in superior-subordinate dyads', *Academy of Management Journal* 32: 402–423.

Watson, W. E., Kumar, K. and Michaelsen, L. K. (1993) 'Cultural diversity's impact on interaction process and performance: Comparing homogeneous and diverse task groups', *Academy of Management Journal* 36:590–602.

Wiersema, M. F. and Bantel, K. A. (1993) 'Top management team turnover as an adaptation mechanism: The role of the environment', *Strategic Management Journal* 14:485–504.

Suggestions for further reading

Journals

The Academy of Management publishes several scholarly journals such as the AMR and AME:

The Academy of Management Review (AMR)
The mission of the *Academy of Management Review* (AMR) is to publish new theoretical insights that advance our understanding of management and organizations.

Academy of Management Executive (AME)
The Academy of Management Executive has changed its name to the Academy of Management Perspectives. Prior issues of the Academy of Management Executive (AME) provide practising executives with relevant management tools and information based on advances in management theory and research. Articles enhance knowledge about the process of managing an organization, as well as techniques, trends, and issues growing out of management research of significance.

http://www.aomonline.org

Organizational Dynamics

Organizational Dynamics domain is primarily organizational behaviour and development and secondarily, HRM and strategic management. The objective is to link leading-edge thought and research with management practice. *Organizational Dynamics* publishes articles that embody both theoretical and practical content, showing how research findings can help deal more effectively with the dynamics of organizational life.

http://www.elsevier.com

Journal of Organizational Behavior

The *Journal of Organizational Behavior* aims to report and review the growing research in the industrial/organizational psychology and organizational behaviour fields throughout the world. The journal will focus on research and theory in all the topics associated with occupational/organizational behaviour including: motivation, work performance, equal

opportunities at work, job design, career processes, occupational stress, quality of work life, job satisfaction, personnel selection, training and organizational change.
http://www3.interscience.wiley.com

Key articles

Scholars of this subject area have often read the following:

1 Ashforth, B. and Mael, F. (1989) 'Identity Theory and the Organization', *Academy of Management Review* 14(1):20–39.
2 Cox, T. (1991) 'The multicultural organization', *Academy of Management Executive* (May 1991) 5(2):34–47.
3 Barney, J. (1986) 'Organizational Culture: Can it be a Source of Sustained Competitive Advantage?', *The Academy of Management Review* (July 1986) 11(3):656–665.
4 Hofstede, G. (1980) 'Motivation, leadership and organization: do American theories apply abroad?', *Organizational Dynamics* (Summer) 42–63.
5 Milliken, F. and Martins, L. (1996) 'Searching For Common Threads: Understanding the Multiple Effects of Diversity in Organizational Groups', *Academy of Management Review* 21(2):402–433.
6 Robinson, G. and Dechant, K. (1997) 'Building a business case for diversity', *Academy of Management Executive* (August 1997) 11(3):21–31.

Chapter 9

International organization design and structure

Introduction
Elements of structure
Organization designs
Designs for international organizations
Integration: coordination and control

Key concepts

- Organization design ■ Contingency theory ■ Control ■ Dependency theory
- Environmental–determinism ■ Formalization ■ Centralization
- Specialization ■ Informal organization ■ Structure types ■ Coordination
- Divisional structure

By the end of this chapter you will be able to:

- Define and discuss the nature of international organization design
- Explain factors likely to determine the design of international organizations
- Identify and describe common forms of international organization design
- Describe how international firms coordinate activities
- Explain the general purpose and methods of control in international business

Active learning case

BP

www.bp.com

www.bp.com

BP plc is the third largest oil company in the world. The company is integrated, with operations in three main segments. The first, exploration and production, operates in 29 countries and produces 1.93 million barrels of crude oil and 7.6 billion cubic feet of natural gas each day. BP's second segment consists of 'downstream' businesses such as refining, marketing, supply, and transportation. In this segment, the company operates oil refineries, with total daily throughput of 3.2 million barrels, and approximately 25 000 service stations around the world. BP's third major segment is the production of petrochemicals – substances obtained from petroleum. BP is now one of the world's largest energy companies, providing its customers with fuel for transportation, energy for heat and light, retail services and petrochemicals products. BP has transformed, growing from a local oil company into a global energy group; employing almost 100 000 people and operating in over 100 countries worldwide.

There is no doubt that in an industry where change is the norm, setting objectives to meet all these criteria is not easy. One enduring characteristic of the oil industry has been change. As a company with a long history in oil and natural gas, petrochemicals and more recently in renewable energy technologies, BP has learned to be responsive to change and indeed to be at the forefront of the change process. BP's strategic priorities are enduring: to build production in some of the world's largest oil and gas fields; to focus on advantaged refineries and retail markets; to capture world-scale gas market positions; and to participate in fast-growing markets for gas and low-carbon power. BP believes that people are the most valuable resource for any organization. The BP organization is well suited to a modern, global, learning corporation. It enables BP to remain responsive and flexible, to spread success across the company and to ensure core values and objectives are embedded everywhere within the organization. In 2007, BP was organized into three business segments, operating across four geographic regions and supported by a number of key corporate functions:

1 exploration and production;

2 refining and marketing; and

3 gas, power and renewables.

This is a factual, problem oriented case exploring organizational design problems in a true business setting. The target organization is a large sized international company. Issues of design, coordination and control are presented for students to engage with the variety of problems presented.

BP at a glance

BP is one of the world's largest energy companies, providing its customers with fuel for transportation, energy for heat and light, retail services and petrochemicals products.

Turnover	$284 billion (year 2007)
Number of employees	97 600 (at Dec 2007)
Service stations	24 000
Exploration	Active in 29 countries
Refineries	17

The data above is taken from the 2006 and 2007 Annual Report and Accounts. BP is one of the largest integrated oil companies in the world, with an estimated global market share of around 3 per cent of oil and gas production and 4 per cent of refining capacity in the major global markets in which they operate.

Business segments reflect externally recognized and reported business activities. BP's businesses are organized to deliver the energy products and services required by people around the world right now. Each business segment is made up of a number of business units (BUs), grouped together to form strategic performance units (SPUs). The allocation of resources to group assets is focused at the SPU level. The three business segments are:

- *Exploration and production* – assets and operational activities relating to the discovery and production of hydrocarbons.
- *Gas, power and renewables* – assets and operational activities relating to the marketing of gas and gas-based products and to the development of a renewable energy business.
- *Refining and marketing* – assets and operational activities relating to the refining and marketing of oil products. Also includes aromatics and acetyls businesses.

Activities are divided into four regions, each comprising a group of countries or territories. Each region has an organization structure that enables integration and coordination of activities and represents the group to external parties. The four regions are:

- Europe (including the UK);
- The Americas (including the Caribbean);
- Africa, Middle East, Russia and the Caspian; and
- Asia, the Indian sub-continent and Australasia.

Corporate activities and capabilities are organized into functions. Each function is defined by its skill base and operates in either a centralized or de-centralized manner. Functions include:

- diversity and inclusion (D&I);
- global property management and services (GPM&S);
- health, safety, security and the environment (HSSE);
- human resources management (HRM);
- marketing;
- planning;
- procurement;
- technology;
- finance; and
- tax and accounts.

Each of the three business segments – exploration and production, gas, power and renewables and refining and marketing – has an executive committee (ExCo), headed up by the chief executive of the segment. Together with the heads of the functions, the deputy group chief executive and the group general counsel, they comprise the group chief executive's meeting – under the leadership of the group chief executive. Performance 'contracts', agreed between the executive committee of each of the businesses and its BUs, are the means which enable BU leaders to operate with considerable independence while providing a direct link to the delivery of group objectives and standards. Towards the end of 2007 consultants were called in to help make BP's structure more efficient. On 11 October BP announced their intention to simplify the organizational structure. From 1 January 2008, there are only two business segments – exploration and production and refining and marketing, i.e. the gas, power and renewables segment ceased to report separately. A separate business, 'Alternative Energy', now handles BP's low-carbon businesses and future growth options outside oil and gas. This includes solar, wind, gas-fired power, hydrogen, biofuels and coal conversion.

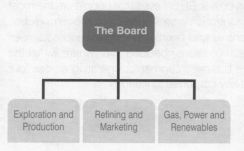

Introduction

BP has around 100 000 employees representing a significant human resource. Not all perform the same work activities, nor should they if efficiency gains are to be made from specialization. There are many work tasks to be done in such a large organization and consequently the work must be divided up and allocated. In this chapter we determine how we should set about this enormous challenge and ask how we can make efficient and effective use of human resources in order to attain goals and derive a sustainable competitive advantage. In organizing its human resources, the international organization must identify *who* will do *what* and *where*; in some cases they may also specify the *how*, *why* and *when* (matters also addressed in the next chapter). Such international organizational problems were first considered by Clee and Di Scipio (1959) and Clee and Sachtjien (1964). Since their work, the environment and organizational theories have evolved. Clee and Di Scipio (1959) and Clee and Sachtjien (1964) were among the first to claim the need for a global structure – within any international organization there is a need to divide, allocate, coordinate and control activities so that goals and organizational aims are achieved.

In addressing such challenges we may pose three related questions:

1 What is the organization trying to do?
2 How is it trying to do it? and
3 Why do it in that way?

The first question is concerned with strategy (see Chapter 3) and the second with structure (considered in this chapter). The overall pattern of structural components and configurations used to manage the total organization is termed the *organization design*. A number of fundamental questions for design may be proposed for managers of international organizations:

- Should jobs be broken down into narrow areas of work (specialization) or do we, for flexibility, require generalists?
- Should there be a tall or flat hierarchy (spans of control), i.e. how many levels of management do we need?
- How should jobs and therefore people be grouped together (by function/geography, etc.)?
- How should employee groups be differentiated and integrated? and
- How should the organization be controlled?

Hierarchy the number of levels of authority

Within this chapter we seek answers to such questions and consider aspects of organizational design and structure, noting Duncan (1972) who suggested that organizational structure is more than boxes on a chart; it is a pattern of interactions and coordination linking technology, tasks and human components of the organization to ensure the organization accomplishes its purpose.

Perhaps the first major design challenge – typically considered by senior managers supported by HR professionals – concerns the manner in which employees are grouped together (by area, function/specialism, product or process worked on). Arguments for the alternative grouping approaches typically consider the type of knowledge that is most important when adding value and undertaking the organization's primary activities – is it more important to know about the area worked in or the product created? Arguments may also be made in relation to organizational strategy and the source of sustainable competitive advantage. Once the grouping problem has been addressed the next challenge is to determine where to locate organizational groups (a matter we revisit in Chapter 15). Having decomposed and dispersed the organization's human resources (differentiation) the organizational designers must confront several consequential challenges.

With differentiation is the associated problem of integration. Groups are typically given goals and their behaviour may work against the attainment of the organization's goals (necessitating control) and parts of the organization may depend upon each other. They

Integration the required level to which units in an organization are linked together, and their respective degree of independence (integrative mechanisms include rules and procedures and direct managerial control)

will therefore need to be coordinated and will rely on communication and information to unify the parts (refer back to systems theory). Furthermore there is a need to ensure resources are shared (see synergy) to capitalize upon benefits of scale. Thus there are problems necessitating coordination, communication and control. Some of the problems are addressed using technological solutions described in the next part of the book. Others may use management systems, policies, procedures, practices, informal systems and the organizational structure itself. Like the space shuttle, the way the parts are connected will impact significantly upon performance.

The search for a good design is continual. An appropriate design might yield benefits such as efficiency and scale, the ability to access specialized and location-embedded resources, enhanced innovation through operations across markets, and the creation of operational flexibility with which to respond to factors outside a firm's control. The design can impact upon performance through employee motivation, commitment and loyalty and has the ability to link interdependent activities. The design may also impact upon the sharing of resources, including information and knowledge. In Chapters 3 and 5 we advocated the need to ensure the structure 'fits' the strategy and therefore, an appropriate design might enable the achievement of strategies such as cost leadership, differentiation and focus.

Design (structure) purpose the primary purposes of design are to divide and allocate work and then coordinate and control that work so that goals are met

The *purpose* of design is to divide up organizational activities, allocate resources, tasks and goals and to coordinate and control activities so that goals can be achieved. Organization theory, according to Pugh (1997) is the study of the structure, functioning and performance of organizations and the behaviour of groups and individuals within them. Within this chapter we continue several themes discussed in the previous two chapters. For example, we continue to focus on sources of competitive advantage, this time through design, control and coordination.

This chapter is organized into four main sections, which to some degree mirror the chapter learning outcomes. We start, in the first section, with a description of the elements of structure (the 'tools' or 'parts'), identifying what is meant by organizational structure and design. The basic parts of an organization and traditional design approaches (bureaucracy) are considered. After reading the first section you will recognize that many organizational designs, structures, patterns and configurations are possible – that organizations may be more or less hierarchical, formal, centralized or specialized.

In the next section we review a collection of designs for international organizations commenting on the associated strengths and weaknesses and control and coordination needs. We also explain how international organizational designs have evolved with reference to changes in the world environment. As with the challenge of designing or building any complex structure we then discuss the factors that might determine the specific structure for any given organization. Factors in the internal and external environment, strategy and decision-maker preferences are considered with contingency theory and the notion of 'best fit' in explaining how designs are instigated and evolve. This section provides us with arguments as to why organizational parts should be configured in particular ways.

Finally, we turn our attention to the associated and consequential challenges of coordination and control – a recognized source of competitive advantage in international organizations. The organizational design typically breaks up the workforce into parts that must work together – parts are dependent upon each other (see systems theory – the organization is a set of interrelated components working toward a common goal) and consequently must be coordinated if goals are to be attained in an efficient manner. The concept of dependence is investigated and we identify means to overcome dependence problems, i.e. via coordination mechanisms. Structure, coordination and control are not exclusive concepts, they overlap. Generally, throughout this chapter, we are concerned with their integrative properties.

Elements of structure

Organization a group of people who work together to achieve shared goals

An *organization* is a group of people who work together. The group share a unifying purpose, i.e. they have common goals. As companies (organizations) grow they need to arrange and cluster workers together according to the business-related activities they undertake. One of the most challenging tasks of a business may be organizing the people who perform its work. A business may start small but as the business grows, the amount and type of work performed increases, and more people are needed to perform various tasks. In order to avoid duplication and ensure all necessary work is undertaken, companies typically allocate work to individuals and group the individuals who perform similar work. Through this division of work, individuals can become specialists at a particular job (and therefore more efficient). However, no one person will typically transform all of the raw materials into the finished product or create and deliver the complete service to the customer. Consequently, the outputs of one person's work may form the inputs of another, i.e. different individuals and parts of the organization become dependent upon each other.

Because there are many people – often in different locations – working towards a common objective, there must be a plan showing how the work will be organized. Work must also be coordinated and controlled if efficiency gains are to be made and goals attained. The plan for the systematic arrangement of work is the formal organization structure. Organization structure (also termed design) is comprised of functions, relationships, responsibilities, authorities, and communications of individuals within each part of the company. In this section we explore the dimensions, tools and elements of organizational structure before considering how such dimensions and elements may be configured in overall organizational designs.

The formal organization is the collection of work groups that has been consciously designed by senior management to maximize efficiency and achieve organizational goals as opposed to the informal organization – the network of relationships that establish themselves spontaneously between members of an organization on the basis of their common interests and friendships. The formal organization is the planners' conception of how the intended consequences of the organization may best be achieved (Argyris 1957). However, the organization is a social arrangement for achieving controlled performance in pursuit of collective goals. The tools used to add structure include:

> **Informal organization** the network of relationships between members of an organization that form of their own accord on the basis of common interests and companionship

- *Organizational chart* – a diagram of formal relations which the company intends should prevail within it.
- *Job definitions* – the task requirements of a particular job in the organization.
- *Span of control* – the number of subordinates who report directly to a single manager or supervisor. The principle of span of control states that administrative efficiency is increased by limiting the span of control of a leader to no more than five or six subordinates whose work interlocks.
- *Authority* – the right to guide or direct the actions of others.
- *Responsibility* – an obligation placed on a person, who occupies a certain position in the organization structure, to perform a task, function or assignment.
- *Accountability* – responsibility for some activity.

When establishing the structure, designers typically start by defining larger groups and then decompose them into smaller units. *Departmentalization* is a process of grouping together employees who share a common supervisor and resources, who are jointly responsible for performance and who tend to identify and collaborate with each other. The organizational chart usually shows the departments within an organization. The chart also shows relationships between departmental staff in the organization which can be line (direct relationship between superior and subordinate); lateral (relationship between different departments on the same hierarchical level), staff and functional.

> **Staff relationship** a link between workers in advisory positions and line employees – staff employees use their specialized expertise to support the efforts of line employees who may choose to act on the advice given

At a high level, designers distinguish between different categories of employee. For example, staff employees are workers who are in advisory positions and who use their specialized expertise to support the efforts of line employees. Employees may be related to one another in a variety of ways:

> **Line relationship** the links, as shown on an organizational chart, that exist between managers and staff whom they oversee directly

- a line relationship is a formal relationship between individual positions within an organization where authority flows vertically down through the structure;

Functional relationship a situation where specialists have the authority to insist that line employees implement their instructions concerning a particular issue

■ a functional relationship is where staff department specialists have the authority to insist that line managers implement their instructions concerning a particular issue; and

■ a lateral relationship is a formal relationship which exist between individuals in different departments or sections, especially between individuals on the same level.

In many large companies the organization chart can be large and incredibly complicated and is therefore sometimes broken down into smaller charts for each individual department within the organization. There are several limitations with organizational charts. First, they only show 'formal relationships'. Second, they do not show anything about the managerial style adopted (e.g. autocratic or democratic). The types of relationships are shown on Figure 9-1.

Figure 9-1

Organizational relationship types

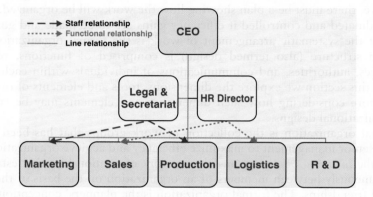

Aside from considering the aforementioned elements of structure there are other constructs that may be utilized during the design process. Mintzberg, at the strategic level, identified five basic parts of an organizational structure:

■ *Strategic apex* – the people who direct the organization (senior management).

■ *Middle line* – managers who ensure policies are followed and goals are attained.

■ *Operating core* – the people directly involved in adding value through the transformation of inputs to create outputs.

■ *Technostructure* (technical support) – design systems, processes and procedures, provide information services.

■ *Support staff* – provide administrative and clerical support: includes HRM; security, facilities management, etc.

Parts may be assembled and designs represented in many ways. Traditionally, designs were shown in a pyramid form, depicting vertical and horizontal dimensions, see Figure 9-2. The broad base indicates that the majority of employees are at the bottom. The number of people occupying the bottom, middle and top layers will vary from organization to organization as will the levels of management (see span of control). Tall structures have more

Figure 9-2

Pyramid form – organizational structure

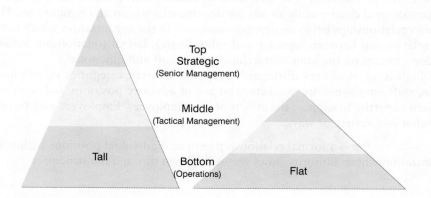

levels of management than flatter structures. As we will see later, the 1990s, witnessed organizations embarking upon restructuring programmes to delayer tall structures with a view to becoming flatter and more responsive.

With reference to national culture, which structure (tall or flat) might be prevalent within an organization whose parent company is located in the 'East' and which may be more typical of the 'West'? Which structure might be most fitting for a predictable environment and which may be more suited to a dynamic or turbulent environment? Explain your answer.

STOP & THINK

Traditional design

In the previous section we identified tools and concepts used in organizational design. Organizations vary in many ways. Pugh, Hickson and Turner (1968) investigated and measured structural differences systematically across a large number of diverse work organizations. From an examination of the literature of organization theory, six primary dimensions (variables) of organization structure were postulated: specialization (the division of labour within the organization given responsibility for a specific activity or task), standardization (established methods, processes, or practices governing how work tasks are accomplished), formalization (the extent to which rules, procedures, instructions, and communications are written), centralization (the locus of authority – the extent to which power is consolidated under a central control), **configuration** (the arrangement of the parts), and flexibility.

In the early 20th century there was a focus on productivity (mass production) and efficiency – a best machine and a best working method for each task (see scientific management). Twentieth-century organizations were heavily influenced by scientific management theories and administrative principles, i.e. the bureaucratic model, with the work of Taylor, Fayol and Weber frequently cited. Bureaucracy refers to a form of organizational structure that is characterized by a specialization of labour, a specific authority hierarchy, a formal set of rules, and rigid promotion and selection criteria. Child (2001) argues that: 'Bureaucracies have been with humanity since ancient times ... and they continue to represent the dominant form for major institutions.'

However, as was noted in Chapter 2, the external environment changed considerably in the last quarter of the 20th century. Boundaries were removed and markets opened, driving competition and change. As a consequence, bureaucracy acquired negative meaning in the 1980s and 1990s when associated with 'red-tape' and 'obstructive' organizations. Later others argued it to have dysfunctional properties in dynamic environments. Pugh (1997) argues that 'traditional authoritarian bureaucracies respond too slowly to survive' and Schein (1999) argues 'the traditional bureaucratic norms of command and control systems are believed to discourage individual creativity'. A number of scholars have presented arguments for and against two key structural dimensions of bureaucracy in particular:

■ centralization might give the decision-maker the ability to plan, coordinate, and control all activities but can slow down decision-making time;

■ formalization is thought to lead to greater efficiency because the predefined rules and procedures serve to routinize repetitive activities and transactions but can stifle creativity and risk taking.

Additionally, bureaucracy (centralization in particular) through the loss of individual autonomy has been shown to decrease the satisfaction and motivation of employees resulting in less commitment to the implementation of corporate strategies. More fundamentally, when lower level employees are removed from organizational planning and control processes, they have less knowledge of the details and purposes of organizational strategies.

Specialization the degree to which an organization's activities are divided into specialist roles

Standardization the degree to which an organization lays down standard rules and procedures

Formalization the degree to which instructions, procedures, etc. are written down

Centralization the degree to which the authority to make certain decisions is located at the top of the management hierarchy

Bureaucracy a form of organization structure (found more in larger organizations) which is characterized by a specialization of labour, hierarchy of authority, and a formal set of rules – decision-making may be centralized or decentralized though the former was more typical

Organizations vary in the amount of formal rules and structuring present – in some organizations this is more evident

If organizational members do not understand corporate goals and strategies, they may be unwilling or unable to take actions to implement them. Bureaucracy is now, therefore, characterized as slow to adapt when change is necessary.

It is important to recognize that organizations may be bureaucratic in any number of ways and there is no dichotomy, i.e. bureaucratic or not. Bureaucracy should be treated as a continuum with organizations lying somewhere between decentral (employees are autonomous and empowered) and central; less and more formal; highly specialized or more general; little or greater amounts of standardization. Centralization and decentralization are strongly linked to the problems of integration and differentiation. Within centralized organizations, headquarters staff can make decisions with the best interests of the whole organization in mind yet such decisions may not be best for some local aspects of the organization where there may be a need for different approaches. However, in situations where the organization must be locally responsive, a decentralized approach might be favoured. In any case (differentiation or integration) consideration should be given to the motivational benefits of empowerment approaches and other arguments. The international organization might centralize upstream operations (such as research and development and manufacturing), to take advantage of economies of scale and scope, and decentralize downstream operations (like marketing and sales), to respond to differences in national market requirements.

Empowerment a climate whereby employees are allowed greater freedom, autonomy and self-control over their work, and the responsibility for decision-making

Organization designs

In the preceding sections we have identified the formal and informal organization, organization parts, and dimensions of bureaucracy, departmentalization and organizational relationships. Organization designers make use of such concepts and variables when structuring the organization. The organizational design or organizational structure must be a solution to many problems. When grouping activities and people the designer must consider how much to take account of specialization (how narrow the work will be); whether the organization should be tall or flat (see span of control) and how to group people (by specialism, product or area). Degrees of control must also be determined along with centralization and formalization and the mechanisms to be used for integration. Design decisions have many consequences, as was noted in the introduction. In this section we first consider simple and then more complex designs for international organizations, i.e. examples of how parts may be defined, grouped and put together.

Organizational structure the way in which the interrelated groups of an organization are constructed

Simple designs

The *overall* design of organization structure indicates the needed work activities, reporting relationships and departmental groupings. Departments are created to perform tasks that are important to the company. Several basic options exist for groupings and are presented next. Simple options for departmental grouping include functional, product (also referred to as divisional grouping) and area. Functional and divisional grouping represent the two most common approaches to structural design.

Functional

Functional structure the organization is structured according to functional areas such as finance, marketing and HR

An organization with a functional structure groups people into functional departments such as purchasing, accounts, production, sales, marketing. These departments normally have functional heads called managers or directors where the function is represented at board level. A functional structure suits organizations with a single dominant core products because each subunit is adept at performing its particular portion of the process.

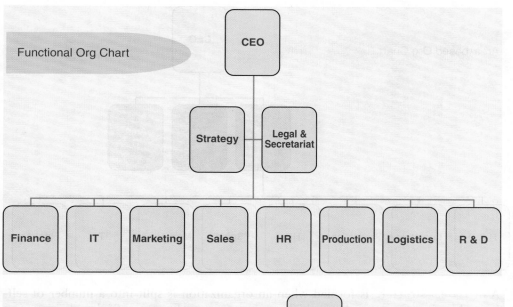

Figure 9-3
Functional organization chart

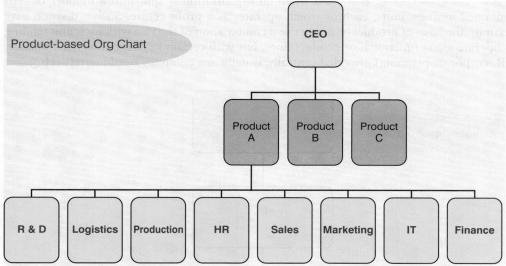

Figure 9-4
Product-based organization chart

Product

Here the organization is divided up according to the product or the service (product design). People focus on a particular product or set of related products and gain knowledge and expertise about them. While this may drive efficiency gains and innovation, there can be expensive duplication as each product group needs its own functional area skills such as sales, marketing, IT, etc. Product-based structure enables global economies of scale.

Area

Aside from area knowledge arguments (to be discussed later) the area structure may offer cost efficiencies when goods and service need to be close to the customer. Delivery, repair and maintenance costs may be lower with the area structure. The area (geographic) structure keeps knowledge close to the needs of individual countries.

Product-based structure the organization is structured according to related products or services

Area structure the organization is structured according to geographical areas

Search the Internet and find examples of the above structures in domestic organizations. Discuss your examples in class.

STOP & THINK

Figure 9-5

Area-based organization chart

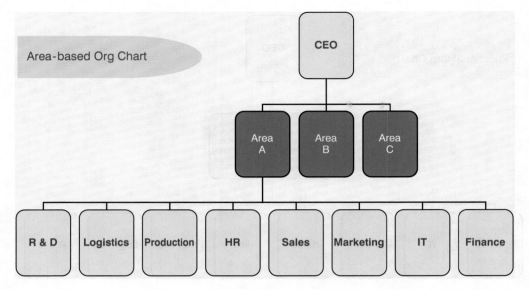

Divisional structure a design whereby an organization is split into a number of self-contained business units, each of which operates as a profit centre

A divisional structure is formed when an organization is split into a number of self-contained business units, each of which operates as a profit centre. Such a division may occur on the basis of product or market or a combination of the two with each unit tending to operate along functional or product lines, but with certain key functions (e.g., finance, HR, corporate planning) provided centrally, usually at a company headquarters (HQ).

Figure 9-6

Customer-based organization chart

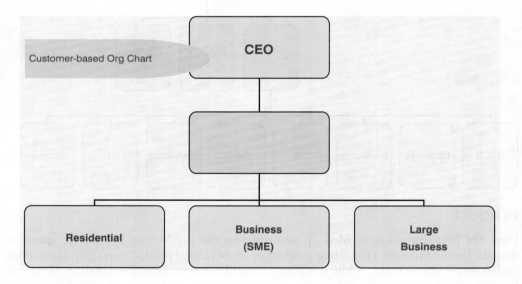

Customer

A firm that serves different customer groups may prefer a *customer design*. Organizations may group workers according to the customer group they serve; for example, many organizations differentiate between business and residential customers. This design is useful when the customer groups are different and require distinct approaches. Problems with this design include duplication and coordination costs.

Process

The vertical/functional hierarchy (see previous designs) has been at the core of business since the industrial revolution. There are, however, many associated problems: the vertical design fosters fragmented tasks, overspecialization, empires, and turf wars, delays in decision-making and other negatives that inhibit responsiveness. There is general agreement that vertical structures are too rigid and slow. An excessive level of authority reduces communication and coordination of activities (Hodge 1999). An alternative way of grouping individuals and their activities is based on business processes (see Chapter 10) which cut horizontally across traditional functional areas, i.e. horizontal grouping. There is real performance leverage in moving towards a flatter, more horizontal mode of organization, in which cross-functional, end-to-end workflows link internal processes with the needs and capabilities of both suppliers and customers (Ostroff and Smith 1992).

> **Processes** sets of logically related tasks performed to achieve a defined business outcome

Whereas functional groupings may be task centred the process groupings are more customer-oriented. The primary focus for functional groupings is on the 'what' whereas process groupings focus on 'how'. Functional organizations value specialists whereas process organizations value generalists. The functional organization may have a parochial perspective whereas the process organization has a more holistic perspective. Workers involved with a particular process are grouped together to facilitate communication and coordination through mutual adjustment. However, for most organizations it is not an either/or choice of vertical/functional versus horizontal/process and each company must seek its own unique balance between the features needed to deliver performance. Ostroff and Smith (1992) distil the key design principles on which a horizontal organization depends:

- organizing around process not task;
- flattening hierarchy by minimizing the subdivision of work flows and non-value-added activities;
- assigning ownership of processes and process performance; and
- linking performance objectives and evaluation to customer satisfaction.

Such organizations also make teams, not individuals, the basis of organizational design and performance.

Hybrid and matrix designs

In order to overcome duplication, coordination and communication problems and develop a more flexible organization, some firms decide on a matrix design; the matrix-structure overlays two organizational forms in order to benefit from both. A matrix structure exists where there is a two-way flow of authority and responsibility within an organization due to the vertical flow of authority and responsibility from the functional departments and the horizontal flow of authority and responsibility from project, product or area teams. It is a type of organization design that combines two different, traditional types of structure resulting in an employee being part of both a functional department and another, and as a consequence, having two reporting relationships. This design helps bring together functional, product and area expertise. There may, however, be delays in decision-making. Some global corporations adopt a matrix structure that combines geographical with product divisions. The organization structures considered thus far are summarized in Figure 9-7.

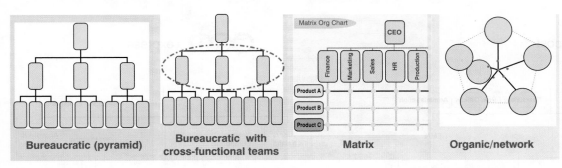

Bureaucratic (pyramid) **Bureaucratic with cross-functional teams** **Matrix** **Organic/network**

Figure 9-7

Types of organization structure

Design for international organizations

In 1946, Ken Thomas started his own Australian company – Thomas Nationwide Transport – with a fleet consisting of a single truck. In less than half a century, his company grew into a global enterprise, even operating its own fleet of aircraft. Much of the growth came from take-overs and interests acquired in other companies. Independently,

group.tnt.com

in Holland, Dutch post ceased to be a state enterprise in 1989. It became a private company called PTT Nederland NV. The change gave the company greater scope to respond to developments in a fast-changing market. Privatization was the launch pad for the strong position that PTT Post had built up in the international marketplace. In 1994 PTT became known as KPN. Two years later KPN took over TNT. Together, TNT and PTT Post embarked on a new era. Important steps were taken toward the integration of the business activities of TNT and PTT Post. TNT activities outside its core business (mail, express and logistics) were sold off. In October 1998, a new international road hub and national depot began operating in Duiven, the Netherlands. In December 1998, TPG acquired the express company Jet Services SA in France. TPG bought 100 per cent of the shares from Financière Jet Services SA founded in 1973; jet services provides express services in France, Germany, Belgium, the Netherlands, Great Britain, Hungary and Switzerland. Over the past few years TNT has grown as a result of take-overs, expansion and strategic partnerships.

As a holding company, TNT sets the agenda for the group as a whole as well as for the individual divisions. TNT provides an extended range of services around the world: collecting, sorting, transporting and distributing a wide variety of items (letters, parcels, freight) within specific timeframes. The company also provide all related data services. Delivery and network management are their stated core competencies. Whether it concerns a letter to a friend, business parcels to the other side of the world, component parts to car dealers, or line or container shipments across the globe, people and companies around the world depend on TNT for reliable delivery.

TNT serves more than 200 countries and employs around 139 000 people. Over 2006, TNT reported €10.1 billion in revenues and an operating income of €1276 million. The company strategy reflects their ambition of being a leading global network services company; TNT plans to focus on providing delivery services by expertly managing delivery networks. Its mission is to exceed customers' expectations in the transfer of their goods and documents around the world. TNT distinguishes between the following corporate divisions:

- express business which provides demand door-to-door express delivery services for customers sending documents, parcels and freight; and the
- mail business which provides services for collecting, sorting, transporting and distributing domestic and international mail.

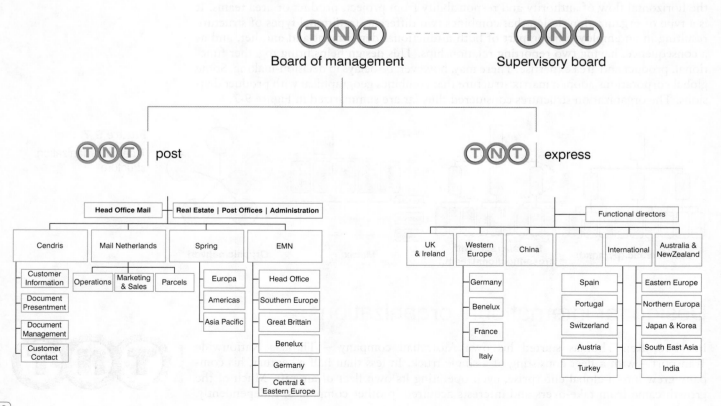

TNT's activities are therefore divided between two operational divisions: the combination of mail and express networks has several strategic advantages. TNT believe the combination of business-to-business and business-to-consumer deliveries, for which TNT have unique expertise in their express and mail divisions respectively, becomes increasingly relevant in an era where e-related deliveries are growing exponentially and mega cities which require complex high density citizen services will emerge. TNT also believes that over time certain operational and strategic synergies can be achieved across their portfolio, for example in linehaul activities. Having both mail and express in its portfolio gives TNT unique cross-selling opportunities. And finally, the fact that mail and express require comparable management capabilities, such as network design, execution and planning, customer focus, market segmentation and brand awareness, allows TNT to optimize management and competence development over the group.

*TNT Head Office, Hoofddorp,
the Netherlands*

According to the CEO

'People are the heart of our company – TNT's success, growth and leadership position in our industry depends largely on the energy and efforts of all our employees, serving our customers in all corners of the world. They are the people who make TNT a great company. In all their various capacities, throughout TNT's two divisions: Mail and Express, our people are the heart of our company. They always will be, because whether we're delivering the mail or working in a sorting centre for Royal TNT Post in the Netherlands, flying a TNT aircraft with urgent business documents, there's something fundamental that unites us in a common cause: every one of us is working in a service business. That means our people are the key determinant of our continuing success. TNT operates in 63 countries, all of which reflect a multitude of cultures, nationalities, religions, expertise and ideas. We have an extremely diverse customer base and, in order to achieve the highest levels of customer satisfaction, we need to reflect diversity within our organization. We focus on building an inclusive culture. We have networks in place to support employees with different backgrounds and beliefs and we work in partnership with local organizations to support people with fewer opportunities but greater skills. At TNT, we value and embrace difference and that is why our diversity and inclusion initiatives serve to make us the employer of choice. The commitment and creativity of all our people has enabled TNT to consistently reach and exceed our profit and value targets, even in years when growth has been hard to find. And because we continue to grow, we're continually on the look-out for excellent new people at every level who'd like to share the passion and pride of the around 128 000 people in 63 countries around the world already serving TNT's customers.'

TNT CEO (2007)

> Critically review the TNT case study presented above. How do the structures of the post and express divisions differ – why should this be so? Read the CEO's statement and review the comments with consideration to the previous chapter.

STOP & THINK

The design of international organizations was first considered in the mid 20th century when Clee and Di Scipio discussed creating a world enterprise and Clee and Sachtjien commented on organizing a worldwide business. Clee and Sachtjien (1964) argued that three basic organizational structures evolved; these basic organizational patterns are:

1 The traditional *international division structure*.

2 The *geographic structure*, replacing the international division with line managers at the senior management level who bear full operating responsibility for subsidiaries in assigned geographic areas.

3 The *product structure*, replacing the international division with executives at the senior-management level who bear worldwide responsibility for development of individual product groups.

Figure 9-8

Domestic and subsidiaries chart

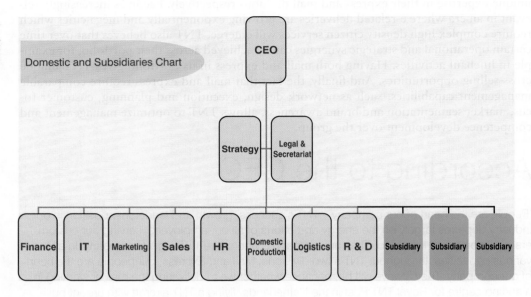

Domestic and Subsidiaries Chart

Eventually, international activities become too much for the domestic design to manage and the organization starts to place employees in overseas offices, subsidiaries and production facilities, Figure 9-8. With this comes added complexity, new coordination and control demands, new resource and task allocation problems and consequently a requirement for a new design and way of organizing. Not only must the organizational design fit the demand of the environment, it must also accommodate the organization's evolving internationalization process, i.e. it must fit with the strategy. Consequently, structural changes may become commonplace in dynamic and growing organizations. Typically, organizations start with a domestic structure and may add an export department. From here, with continued growth in exports, a foreign subsidiary may be added, followed by an international division (organized along functional, product or area lines) before moving to a global structure as shown below. Once groups are formed and given an international scope they must compete for resources with the rest of the organization.

Earlier in the chapter we outlined the domestic product, area and function design. When considered as global designs they have further associated advantages and disadvantages. Efficient production is associated with the global product design as factories can be set up wherever costs are lowest and a skilled workforce is available. However, each product group must develop local knowledge to adapt to the different markets in which they operate – each having different political, economic and socio-cultural factors to consider. The global area design is most likely to be used by a firm whose products are not readily transferable across regions. It allows the firm to differentiate – to quickly respond to local needs. Coordination is difficult and less efficiency gains are made.

Common forms of organization design are represented below. In addition to global product, area and functional designs, the international organization may choose a customer or matrix design. Each of the three main designs emphasise a particular type of knowledge, i.e. knowledge of the area, product or function and this knowledge will vary in importance to different organizations. There are a number of advantages and disadvantages associated with integrated global structures:

■ *Global functional* – more appropriate for companies offering similar products, using similar technology, with few products or customers. Managers can maintain highly centralized control over functional operations.

- *Global product* – each product is represented by a separate division and has its own functional departments, i.e. finance, production, sales and marketing specialists.
- *Global area* – probably the most common form of structure in larger international organizations. Area knowledge/needs are more important than product expertise or functional specialist knowledge. Local differences drive a focus on marketing and product adaptation.

Which of the structures shown in Figure 9.9 below best describes BP as discussed in the opening case study?

STOP & THINK

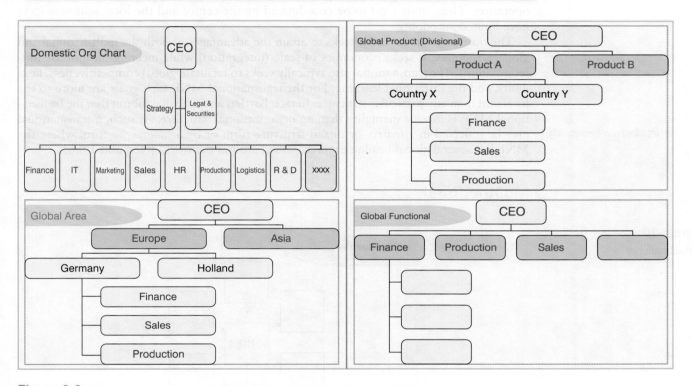

Figure 9-9

Consider BP and then place area, product and functional knowledge in order of importance to the organization. Explain your answer.

STOP & THINK

The globalization of business is making it more important than ever to understand how multinational enterprises (MNEs) can operate more effectively. Global companies must be more than just a gathering of overseas subsidiaries with executive decisions made at the corporate centre. As Hedlund (1986) notes, multinational corporations are evolving towards more complex structures and strategies. These are characterized by a heterarchy of many different kinds of centres where subsidiaries take strategic responsibility for the whole MNC, there are coalitions with other firms, and strategies are aimed at seeking and creating new competitive advantages rather than exploiting old ones. Companies must simultaneously capture global-scale efficiency, respond to national markets, and cultivate a worldwide learning capability for driving continuous innovation across borders.

Within the global form of organization there are several structural alternatives. These include the multinational, global, international and the transnational structure (see below).

MNC organizational mechanisms used to control and coordinate worldwide operations

In the multinational structure the MNE is basically organized by geographical location and is to a great extent, decentralized. This structure has the ability to respond to local market needs, although possibly at the loss of efficiency and economies of scale.

Two similar structures of MNEs described by Bartlett and Ghoshal are the 'global' and the 'international'. They differ mainly in the degree of centralization of decision-making and the global scale of production. Whereas the global structure operates on a global scale (to achieve economies of scale) and to spread development costs, the international MNE develops the ideas for operation and establishes local units, where needed, to implement them. In both cases, the foremost strategic decisions are made at the corporate headquarters, and the local units implement them. Whereas the multinational structure adapts well to local market needs (differentiation), the global structure, driven by global economies of scale, reflects a global agenda (integration); the MNE is effectively operated as one global operation. Thus, units tend to be coordinated by the centre and the local unit managers have limited autonomy.

The *transnational* structure seeks to attain the advantages of both the multinational and global structures; it seeks economies of scale (integration) while meeting local needs (differentiation). The transnational also typically seeks to facilitate global competitiveness, flexibility, and organizational learning. For the transnational MNE such goals are more to the forefront than any particular structure. In fact, Bartlett and Ghoshal submit that the transnational MNE is more a mentality than an organizational structure. As such, a transnational may be reflected in a matrix or mixed-structure form or by a heterarchy form where the MNE has several global headquarters dispersed around the world (Hedlund 1986).

Heterarchy organized non-hierarchically

Mulitnational

Figure 9-10

The multinational

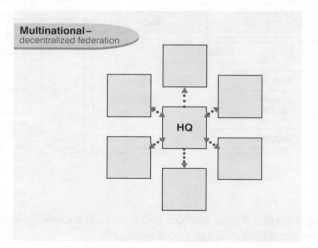

The multinational (multidomestic), see Figure 9.10, is a collection of national companies that manage their businesses with *minimal direction from headquarters*. This structure results from pressures for local differentiation.

Essentially polycentric/highly decentralized – good for national responsiveness. Production is localized, with little knowledge sharing.

Multinational the multinational (multidomestic) is a collection of national companies that manage their businesses with minimal direction from headquarters – decentralization is emphasized to achieve differentiation and a local response

Global form a form of international organizational design where foreign subsidiaries are modelled on the parent companies' domestic approach (replication) – standardization and centralization are emphasized in order to achieve integration

Global

In the global form, see Figure 9.11, there is a replication of the home country approach; greater use of expats and practices from the parent organization. This form typically involves tight control, standardized products and practices and a high degree of centralization. Efficiency gains are attained through global integration. It is premised on the assumption that all national markets are similar, i.e. there is little need for differentiation.

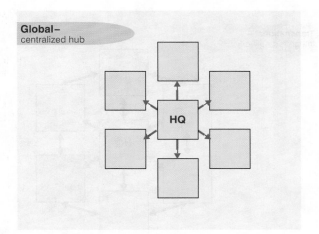

Figure 9-11
The global form

International

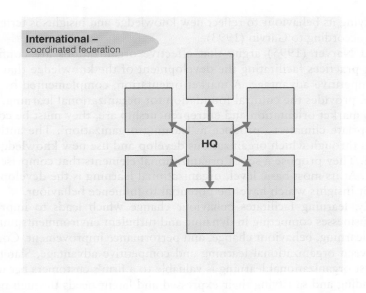

Figure 9-12
The international form

The international form, see Figure 9.12, is designed to transfer parent company knowledge and expertise to foreign markets but is less centralized than the global form as local adaptation is permitted.

A hybrid of the polycentric and ethnocentric form.

Transnational

The transnational form, see Figure 9.13, is an integrated geocentric network of sites, each with a distinct role. Sites are typically differentiated and take on a specialized role within the whole organization. The network integrates the parts, thus allowing efficiencies to be realized and knowledge to be shared. Network organizations are characterized by decentralized decision-making, delayering and less formalization.

Over the past decade or more, organizations have been shifting to flexible decentralized structures that emphasize horizontal collaboration. Today, organizations encourage and facilitate the learning and development of people at all levels (see the learning organization). They value outcomes, such as innovation, efficiency, environmental alignment and competitive advantage. An organization skilled at creating, acquiring, and transferring knowledge

International form the international form is designed to transfer parent company knowledge and expertise to foreign markets but is less centralized than the global form as local adaptation is permitted

Transnational form an organization design that seeks to be globally competitive through multinational flexibility and worldwide learning capabilities – organizational characteristics include (1) being dispersed, interdependent, and specialized, (2) having differentiated contributions by national units to integrated worldwide operations, and (3) developing knowledge jointly and sharing it worldwide

Learning organization an organization skilled at creating, acquiring, and transferring knowledge, and at modifying its behaviour to reflect new knowledge and insights

Figure 9-13

The transnational form

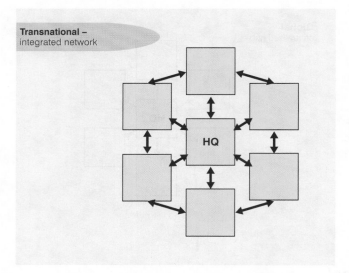

and at modifying its behaviour to reflect new knowledge and insights is termed a learning organization according to Garvin (1993).

Slater and Narver (1995) argue that effective organizations are configurations of management practices facilitating the development of the knowledge that becomes the basis for competitive advantage. A market orientation, complemented by an entrepreneurial drive, provides the cultural foundation for organizational learning. However, as important as market orientation and entrepreneurship are, they must be complemented by an appropriate climate to produce a 'learning organization'. The authors describe the processes through which organizations develop and use new knowledge to improve performance. They propose a set of organizational elements that comprise the learning organization. At its most basic level, organizational learning is the development of new knowledge or insights which have the potential to influence behaviour.

Presumably, learning facilitates behaviour change which leads to improved performance. All businesses competing in dynamic and turbulent environments must pursue the processes of learning, behaviour change, and performance improvement. Commenting on the link between organizational learning and competitive advantage, Slater and Narver (1995) suggest organizational learning is valuable to a firm's customers because it focuses on understanding and satisfying their expressed and latent needs through new products, services, and ways of doing business. This should lead to superior outcomes, such as greater new product success, superior customer retention, higher customer-defined quality, and, ultimately, superior growth and/or profitability.

Burns and Stalker (1961) were the first to suggest that high performing firms, competing in complex and dynamic industries, adopt an 'organic form' namely, an organizational architecture that is decentralized, with fluid and ambiguous job responsibilities and extensive lateral communication processes. Members of these organizations, both internal and external, recognize their interdependence and are willing to cooperate and share information to sustain the effectiveness of the organization (Miles and Snow 1992). The necessity of effective information sharing in the learning organization demands that systematic or structural constraints on information flows be dismantled (Woodman, Sawyer, and Griffin 1993). Gupta and Govindarajan (1991) conclude that high environmental uncertainty requires high frequency and informality in communication patterns among organizational units for effective diffusion of knowledge.

Mintzberg favours grouping experts in functional units for housekeeping purposes but deploying them in project teams for specific tasks, as well as relying on teams, task forces, and integrating managers to encourage mutual adjustment within and between the teams. Under these conditions, information is shared and decisions are made flexibly and informally to promote innovation and creativity. As standardization and bureaucratic routines are precluded as coordinating mechanisms, coordination becomes the responsibility of experts rather than individuals with hierarchical power. Consequently, the organization must make use of an extensive set of liaison devices, such as cross-unit committees, integrator roles, shared data bases, and matrix structures (Gupta and Govindarajan 1991) to encourage informal information sharing and discussion, Slater and Narver (1995).

Making continual learning a way of organizational life can only be achieved by breaking with the traditional authoritarian, command and control hierarchy to merge thinking and acting at all levels, Senge (1992). There are 'hard' (formal) and 'soft' (Informal) structural aspects of the learning organization. Senge (1995) discusses the learning infrastructure which can be thought of in terms of redesigning core processes (a matter we turn to in the next chapter). He suggests the real advantage for organizational learning may lie in informal networks. However, the power of informal networks can be difficult to harness. Organizational learning is a three stage process that includes information acquisition, information dissemination, and shared interpretation. In the next part of this textbook we focus on information and knowledge resources and return to the concept of the learning organization in Chapter 12.

Determinants of design

Organizational design provides a source of competitive advantage to all companies, domestic or international. Designing the organization involves configuring necessary structures, processes, practices and policies and allocating resources to achieve a desired business strategy. In the previous sections we outlined the components of an organization's structure and identified the many common ways such components may be configured, but have yet to consider *why* they may be configured in different ways. Thus far we have identified a variety of design types but how do organizations chose the most appropriate one?

'There is not one best organization design, or style of management, or method of working. Rather, different patterns of organization and management will be most appropriate in different situations.'

NADLER (1980)

Those responsible for organizational design focus on creating structures that are responsive to the environment and marketplace changes, oriented toward customer needs, and have empowered employees who are loyal, motivated, committed and able to act responsively to the challenges presented. Nadler points out that:

'Often changes in the environment necessitate organizational change [see Chapter 5]. For example, factors related to competition, technology, or regulation, shift and thus necessitate changes in organizational strategy.'

There are many questions and challenges to be considered when seeking the *best* design for the organization. In this section we consider factors in the external and internal environment that might present challenges or a context necessitating a particular design. Such factors may have a direct influence upon design choice or may be mediated through the organization's strategy or decision-maker's preferences and perceptions. Throughout this section we argue the design and structure must 'fit' the strategy and that the strategy must 'fit' the environment. Consequently we refer back to Chapter 2, the environment and Chapter 3, strategy, building on previous work and contingency theory. In summary, this section seeks to distil 'design-rules' or factors that guide structuring activities.

Contingency theory

Contingency theory was introduced in Chapter 3 and research has clearly demonstrated the correlation between structure and the environment and central to the contingency approach is the basic notion that organizational performance depends upon taking management actions consistent with the situation. It is now widely accepted that there is no single best way to organize, structure or manage the firm. Contingency theory, in the context of organization structure, argues that an organization, to be effective, must adjust its design/structure in a manner consistent with its environment, technology and other contextual factors.

The contingency approach is defined as identifying and developing functional relationships between environmental variables, management variables and *performance variables,* Luthans and Stewart (1977), see Figure 9-14. A distinction is made between external and internal environmental factors. Specific environmental variables have a direct and significant effect upon the organization, while general environmental variables have only an indirect influence on the organization and provide a context for the more directly relevant specific factors. General environmental variables include factors such as:

- cultural;
- social;
- technological;
- educational;
- legal;
- political;
- economic;
- ecological; and
- demographic.

Specific environmental variables might include customers/clients, suppliers (including labour), competitors, technology and socio-political factors. Environmental variables may impact upon any of a range of management variables. Finally, the achievement of organizational goals (performance) is seen to be contingent (dependent) on the management variables.

Environmental variables factors that affect the organization, but are beyond the direct or positive control of the organization. A distinction is made between external and internal environmental factors

Management variables those concepts and techniques expressed in policies, practices and procedures used by the manager to operate on available resource variables in defining and accomplishing objectives

Figure 9-14

The contingency approach

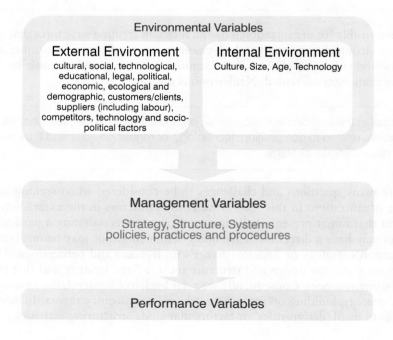

For almost a century scholars have been writing about the environment and its impact upon business; environmental determinism theory states that: 'internal organizational responses are wholly or mainly shaped, influenced or determined by external environmental factors. Externally, the contemporary turbulent environment calls for flexible, adaptable and responsive structures; historically, a more predictable environment favoured the bureaucratic approach.'

Pugh (1973) concluded that internal context (size, ownership, location and technology) was the overall determining factor of organizational structure (degree of specialization, centralization, standardization, formalization and configuration) along with the attitudes of the senior management. Further scholars, following Pugh have concluded that there are many internal factors influencing the firm's design. Factors include:

Look back
See chapter 2

- size;
- strategy;
- technology;
- environment;
- culture;
- degree of internationalization;
- product knowledge dependency;
- area knowledge dependency;
- need for efficiency (production, cost, coordination, control);
- need for autonomy;
- need for cross-group learning;
- local needs;
- customer needs;
- need for agility;
- corporate goal versus local goal achievement.

Organizations are formed with particular objectives in mind, and their structures mirror these objectives. The majority of experts on formal organization agree that no organizational structure will be ideal.

ARGYRIS (1957)

Chandler (1962) famously argued that 'structure-follows-strategy'. A firm that competes internationally must decide how to spread the activities in the value chain among countries. Discussing the value chain, Porter notes that downstream activities (sales and service) are more related to the buyer and therefore such activities tend to be found at the buyer location. If a firm is going to sell in one country, for example, it must usually provide service in that country and it must have salespeople stationed there. In some industries it is possible to have a single sales force that travels to the buyer's country and back again. Upstream activities (inbound logistics and operations) and support activities do not always have to be located near the buyer. Consequently, downstream activities create competitive advantages that are largely country specific (reputation, brand-name, service network) while competitive advantage in upstream and support activities often grows more out of the entire system of countries in which a firm competes. An implication of this is that downstream activities tend to be more multidomestic while in upstream activities global competition is more common.

Downstream activities the primary value chain activities such as outbound logistics, sales and service

Upstream activities the primary value chain activities such as inbound logistics and operations

Porter discusses the configuration of a firm's activities worldwide, i.e. where in the world each activity in the value chain is performed and coordination, which refers to how like activities performed in different countries are coordinated with each other. Understanding the competitive advantages of a global strategy requires specifying the conditions in which concentrating activities globally and coordinating dispersed activities leads to either cost advantage or differentiation. Activities may be concentrated in one or a few locations if economies of scale can be attained or if coordination advantages of co-locating linked activities (such as R&D and production) exist.

A comparative advantage may also be attained according to where the activity is performed. There are issues as to how many sites and where those sites are located; there may be some locations in the world that are better places than others to perform certain activities. Location may help with responsiveness and demonstrate local commitment to buyers. Transport, communication and storage costs may make it inefficient to concentrate the activity in one location. International coordination involves long distances, language problems and cultural barriers to communication. The organizational design is one important way to organize resources and assure the strategy is achieved. The structure must also be future proof; able to adapt and respond to environmental changes, i.e. it must be adaptive and flexible. Thus far we have commented on structure being determined by environmental variables mediated through the strategy. However, we must not forget that it is people that determine organizational designs and they may or may not operate rationally.

Considering the dimensions of bureaucracy as continuums, refer back to earlier discussions, suggests that organizations may choose a desired position. Child (1997) discusses 'strategic choice' – a process whereby power-holders within organizations decide upon courses of strategic action (in this case, structure). The decisions of such managers are coloured by their values, attitudes and beliefs; the sources of which include culture (e.g. professional, corporate or national membership), experience and training. Values, attitudes and beliefs impact upon evaluations, cognitions, mental process and actions. Attention is directed to the ways in which the leaders of organizations, whether private or public, are able in practice to influence organizational forms to suit their own preferences. Strategic choice analysis, with its focus on organizational actors, views the evolution of organizations as a product of actors' decisions and not just as a passive environmental selection process. Key actors are seen to play a particularly important role in initiating, shaping and directing strategic reorientations towards the environment. Thus, people within organizations, typically guided by HR professionals with strategy and their environment in mind, select what they believe to be the most appropriate (fitting) design.

How then should an international organization determine the most appropriate form? According to Devinney, Midgley and Venaik (2000) the global integration-local responsiveness framework has been one of the more enduring approaches to thinking about international business strategy and the organizational structure of global firms, see Figure 9-15. They consider this to be the most popular framework for studying international strategy in multinational firms and the best current approach for explaining international strategic orientation.

Strategic choice the process whereby power-holders within organizations decide upon courses of strategic action

Figure 9-15

The integration-responsiveness framework (Source: Devinney, Midgley and Venaik (2000))

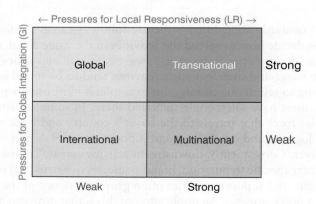

According to Prahalad and Doz (1987, p. 15), the managerial demands in a diversified multinational business fall into three categories – the need for global integration of ongoing activities, the need for global coordination of firm strategy, and the need for local responsiveness. Because the needs for integration and strategic coordination are often related, they 'recognized two essential demands' – global integration (GI) and local responsiveness (LR) – and assumed 'that the extent of strategic coordination is related to the need for integration' (1987, p. 16). A focus on such demands resulted in the IR grid, see Figure 9-15.

Integration pressures include the importance of multinational customers, the presence of multinational competitors, investment intensity, technology intensity, pressures for cost reduction, universal needs and access to raw materials and energy. Local responsiveness pressures embrace differences in customer needs, differences in distribution channels, availability of substitutes and the need to adapt, market structure, and host government demands. Although this framework provides an excellent aid to structural decisions, as was mentioned earlier in this chapter, other factors also need to be considered such as decision-maker preferences. Once a design has been chosen or created, there is a need to implement mechanisms to coordinate the parts that have been created and control the people and workflows operating within and between the parts.

Integration: coordination and control

Different structures of international operation create different requirements for coordination. For any large complex organization a central and continuing concern is the problem of ensuring that its constituent parts act in accordance with overall policy, purpose and goals. The specialization of subunits, which allows the organization to undertake complicated tasks, requires an equally developed system of integration to bind them into an operational whole. The issue of integration of multinational corporations is of interest not only to managers within the firm but also to policy makers in home and host countries.

Cray (1984) discusses integration processes – coordination and control. The integration of subunits into large organizations depends mainly on the manipulation of the two processes. His study seeks to illuminate the relationship between control and coordination as two components of the integration process. The purpose of control is to minimize idiosyncratic behaviour and to hold individuals or groups to articulated policy, thus making performance predictable. Control is seen as a process which brings about adherence to a goal or target through the exercise of power or authority. Coordination, on the other hand, is seen more as an enabling process which provides the appropriate linkage between different task units within the organization.

The two integration processes described provide very different solutions for the problem of binding subunits into the larger organization. Control is a more direct intervention into the operations of the subsidiary. The division of labour (the design process discussed in previous sections) creates *dependencies*, see Figure 9-16. Dependency concerns the extent to which an individual or unit's outcomes are controlled directly by or are contingent upon, the actions of another individual or unit (Victor and Blackburn 1987). Dependencies typically cause problems that are overcome through coordination mechanisms.

Control ensuring plans are properly executed; assuring the organization functions as planned

Coordination the process of linking and integrating functions and activities of different groups (assuring resources work well together towards the common goal)

Dependency the extent to which an individual or unit's outcomes are controlled directly by or are contingent upon the actions of another individual or unit

Figure 9-16

Dependencies in an organization

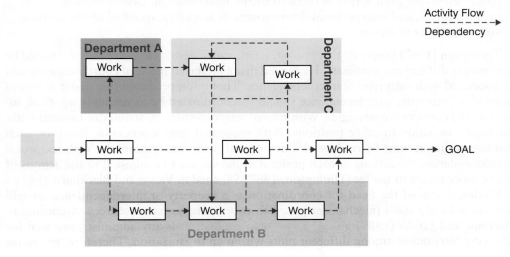

Commanding directing and motivating

Henri Fayol, an early 20th-century business practitioner credited with 'inventing' management and distinguishing its constituent elements, identified organizing, commanding, coordinating and controlling as key managerial activities. Included also was planning and forecasting. Managers need to coordinate even more closely operations that tend to be farther apart. How and why should we coordinate the increasing number of dispersed and yet *interdependent* international activities? The need for coordination is dependent upon the extent of interdependence among the organization's groups. A given group may rely on mutual assistance, support, cooperation, or interaction among constituent members within its group, between other groups in the organization or with various partner organizations. In some cases they simply cannot exist or survive without each other (interdependent).

Interdependence drives a need for cooperation and communication within and between the parts of the organization or within the organization's value system. Coordination is the process of linking and integrating the functions and activities of different groups, units or divisions; it is about assuring that segments of the organization are operating in compatible ways, i.e. one of the roles of management is to bring organizational parts together and cause them to work together efficiently.

Dependency example – telecommunications

When a new customer applies for a mobile telephone account, the sales department (new provisions) may process the order but the customer account will not be activated until the finance department have performed a credit check and the network group have populated various authentication databases throughout the mobile network. Similarly, the accounts department can only bill the customer when they have the customer details and details of the customer's billable network usage.

Groups and individuals may be dependent upon one another in differing ways (Victor and Blackburn 1987). Group tasks may be additive (task accomplishment depends on the sum of all group members' efforts), conjunctive or disjunctive. Tasks may be worked on jointly and simultaneously rather than being passed back and forth. Interdependency may range from *independent* to *sequential* to *reciprocal* to team. As dependency increases, the amount of coordination increases and as conflict increases the chosen coordination strategies become increasingly formal, controlling and centralized.

Interdependence theory proposes that the relationship between one work unit and another work unit(s) can be described in terms of three requirements for action:

Pooled interdependence represents an absence of work flow between units, each unit uses independent inputs and makes independent contributions to the organization

Serial interdependence represents a unidirectional exchange pattern where each unit's inputs are the outputs from another unit and similarly, each unit's outputs are another unit's inputs

Reciprocal interdependence represents a contingent pattern in the work flow where each unit's inputs are its own outputs recycled through other units

Coordination mechanism a coordination mechanism is any administrative tool for achieving integration among different units within an organization. The terms 'mechanisms of coordination' or 'mechanisms of integration' are often used as synonyms

- requirements for one's own actions;

- requirements for the actions of others; and

- requirements for joint action as dictated by the technological, environmental, organizational, and interpersonal determinants of workflow specified by the division and assignment of labour.

Thompson (1967) proposed that pooled, serial, and reciprocal interdependence would be increasingly difficult to coordinate. He argued that a preferred mode of coordination should be associated with each type of interdependence. Thompson predicted that under norms of rationality, increasing interdependence should be coordinated by increasingly informal, localized, and cooperative strategies. With pooled interdependence, action can proceed without regard to action in other positions. With sequential interdependence, however, each position in the set must be readjusted if any one of them acts improperly. With reciprocal interdependence, the actions of each position in the set must be adjusted to the actions of one or more others in the set (Thompson, 1967: 58, cited in Victor and Blackburn 1987).

Having discussed the need for coordination as a property of interdependence we will now consider the tools (mechanisms) used to coordinate human resources. According to Martinez and Jarillo (1989) a mechanism of coordination is any administrative tool for achieving integration among different units within an organization. Therefore, the terms 'mechanisms of coordination' or 'mechanisms of integration' will be used as synonyms. Broadly speaking, two categories of coordination or control mechanism are distinguished. Mechanisms may be formal or *informal*. Organizations can employ a range of coordination mechanisms dependent upon the firm's culture and needs. Typical mechanisms (to coordinate work and workflow) include:

Look back
See chapter 8

- *Departmentalization* – or grouping of organizational units, shaping the formal structure.
- *Centralization* – or decentralization of decision-making through the hierarchy of formal authority.
- *Formalization* – formal control and coordination is achieved through written policies, practices, rules, procedures, instructions, job descriptions and communications.
- *Mutual adjustment* – simple tasks are easily coordinated by mutual adjustment. This mechanism is based on the simple process of informal communication.
- *Liaison, line and staff roles* – through meetings, visits and supervision, performance and other behaviours can be directly influenced by a range of people within the organization such as head-office or local. In specific cases, collaborating groups may designate a specific person to a liaison role. In such cases they act as the communication pipe or conduit between the interdependent parts. Direct or vertical supervision achieves coordination by having one person take responsibility for the work of others, issuing instructions and monitoring their actions.
- *Lateral or cross-departmental relations* – temporary or permanent teams, task forces, committees, integrators, and integrative departments. A task force is a temporary organizational unit responsible for accomplishment of a specific mission. Often the members will come together from a variety of organization groups if the solution to a multidisciplinary or cross-functional problem is sought.
- *Informal networks* – employees may be connected in a variety of formal and informal ways. Informal networks can short-cut bureaucracy and may help get things done faster. They also allow individuals to use and influence resources elsewhere in their own or another organization.
- *Standardization* – another important mechanism of coordination is standardization (note that some scholars consider this to be an aspect of formalization, see for example Martinez and Jarillo (1989)). Here, the coordination is achieved 'on the drawing board'. Coordination is pre-programmed in one of three ways: *work processes* (see formalization above); *outputs* can be standardized, i.e. there are specifications which the product or work output must meet, but aside from that the workers are free to do as they wish and *worker skills* can be standardized. Professionals may learn to complete activities in the same way.
- *Workflow systems* – systems that use group support software for scheduling, routing, and monitoring specific tasks throughout an organization. Workflow systems are defined as systems that help organizations to specify, execute, monitor, and coordinate the flow of work cases within a distributed office environment.
- *Output and behaviour control.*
- *Socialization* – building an organizational culture.
- *Data management mechanisms* – (information systems, measurement systems, resources allocation procedures, strategic planning, budgeting process).
- *Manager's management mechanisms* – (choice of key managers, career paths, reward and punishment systems, management development, patterns of socialization).
- *Conflict resolution mechanisms* – (responsibility, integrators, business teams, coordination committees, task forces, issue resolution processes).

Bartlett and Ghoshal, in their analysis of the *'transnational'* firm', emphasized the need to simultaneously be responsive to different strategic requirements in order to remain competitive in today's economic and political environment. To do so, however, an MNC must develop an extremely sophisticated set of coordination mechanisms, avoiding the simplistic centralization–decentralization dichotomy. All informal mechanisms (developing informal networks of communication, stressing a corporate culture) must be used if the firm is to have enough flexibility to remain responsive to local differences and, at the same time, have enough consistency to take advantage of global opportunities, especially of learning and exploiting local expertise at a world level, Martinez and Jarillo (1989). The *multidomestic* strategic approach, calls for very little coordination. Among the few mechanisms employed are the structural ones, especially departmentalization arrangements.

Some MNCs use an international division to coordinate their foreign branches, while others prefer the direct personal reporting of subsidiary managers to the president or CEO of the MNC. Centralization of authority was rarely used as a coordination device, as subsidiaries enjoyed a considerable degree of autonomy, historically. In addition to the formal structure as a coordinating device, headquarters used a minimum of output control, asking for periodical financial reports, and behaviour control through the use of expatriate executives appointed in charge of those subsidiaries. Besides being a formal mechanism of coordination and control, the use of home nationals allowed headquarters to maintain informal linkages with subsidiaries by means of a corporate culture transmitted to these executives through a long training process while working at home. This mechanism enabled headquarters to ensure loyalty and identification of these expatriates with corporate values, and to preserve the company's management style even in remote regions of the world.

The subsequent pursuit of a global strategy witnessed the first serious organizational challenge to MNCs. Coordination mechanisms were much more required than in the former period, and took the form of structural and formal tools. Among the first, international divisions, worldwide product, area, and regional arrangements were the most common types of departmentalization adopted by headquarters to coordinate foreign subsidiaries.

Decision-making was highly centralized at headquarters to ensure an integrated response to global competition. MNCs exhibited a rather high level of formalization in processes such as planning and budgeting, and standardized programmes in functional areas such as marketing and manufacturing, while R&D was centrally performed. Tight, but simple output control, and frequent reports of almost all subsidiary functions were also used as coordination devices. In addition, some multinationals used expatriates as behaviour or personal control. This was especially the case with Japanese global multinationals, which combined personal control with control by socialization, thus creating 'cultural control', as opposed to 'bureaucratic control'.

In the latter part of the 20th century, with its contradicting requests on global strategies (integration) and national responsiveness (differentiation), traditional approaches to coordination based upon structural and formal mechanisms were considered inadequate. New cross-departmental, informal and subtle mechanisms had to be added to – not substituted for – the existing structural and formal managerial devices to cope with complex environmental conditions. Hence, MNCs adopting the integrated network strategy include new coordination tools in addition to earlier mechanisms (centralized decision-making, highly formalized processes and systems, tight controls, and highly frequent reports). These new coordination mechanisms are rather informal and more subtle than the existing ones. Among them are:

- micro structural arrangements (lateral relations) that cut across the formal lines of the macro structure, such as teams, task forces, committees, individual integrators and integrative departments.
- informal communication channels; and
- organizational culture.

STOP & THINK

With reference to Chapter 8, consider culture and discuss how it might be used as a coordination and control mechanism.

In summary, coordination is seen as a response to problems caused by dependencies. As we have noted, communication and information is integral to all of the coordination mechanisms discussed.

Control

Assuring organizational parts work together productively is a matter of coordination; *control systems*, on the other hand, seek to assure organizational goals are attained; to proactively keep problems away and reactively drive corrective and adaptive responses, keeping the organization on course. Don Hellriegel and John Slocum (1973) describe six management control strategies to exercise control over individuals on the basis of power:

(control through:)

- organization structure;
- policies and rules;
- recruitment and training;
- rewards and punishment;
- budgets and machinery.

In 'levers of control', Simons (1995) proposes a control framework to assure organizational goals are correct and achieved (effectively and efficiently). For Simons, *control* is about getting people to do what you want them to do in the way you want them to do it and minimizing the risk of them doing something that you do not want them to do. There are five control types (levers) proposed by Simons:

- *Belief systems* – inspire and direct the search for new opportunities: values, vision, mission, and purpose.
- *Boundary systems* – set the limits for opportunity-seeking behaviour: formal rules, proscriptions, codes of conduct and operational guidelines.
- *Diagnostic control systems* – motivate, monitor and reward achievement of specific goals: critical performance variables used to monitor, coordinate, correct and motivate.
- *Interactive systems* – stimulate learning: knowledge and information management throughout the organization to enable adaptation, renewal and change.
- *Internal control systems* – safeguards for assets and accounting information.

As with the argument previously posed, structure must fit strategy, so too must organizations ensure their control framework fits with the organizations control needs, which in turn is dependent upon the organization's environment – see Figure 9-17. Ouchi suggests

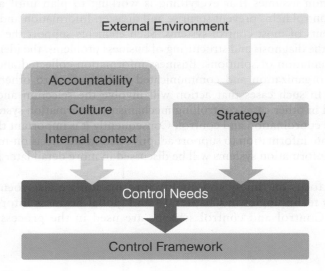

Figure 9-17

Establishing a control framework

the control approach will be determined by the environment. Likewise, Pugh noted that internal context will determine aspects of control; company size in particular.

Like coordination mechanisms, control may be formal (such as bureaucratic controls) or informal such as culture-as-control (clan control) and the processes of socialization. Bureaucracy controls employee behaviour through standardization, formalization, specialization and centralization (see earlier discussions in this chapter). Ouchi (1977) discusses control in organizations. As an organization increases in size, it increases in differentiation, which creates a control problem of integrating the differentiated subunits. In the literature on organizations, control and structure are not clearly distinguished from each other. Control may be related to structure, indeed, it shall be argued that it is; but it is not the same thing as structure.

The control system of an organization consists essentially of a process of monitoring, evaluating, and rewarding, and the data which is processed by this system may consist of measures of behaviour and of outputs. There is a distinction between the structure of an organization and its control mechanism. The structure consists of familiar variables such as vertical and horizontal differentiation, centralization, and formalization. The control system consists of two parts:

1 a set of conditions which govern the form of control to be used; and

2 the control system itself.

The control system itself consists primarily of a process for monitoring and evaluating performance; the process of control is basically a process of monitoring something. In controlling the work of people and of technologies, there are only two phenomena which can be observed, monitored, and counted: behaviour and the outputs which result from behaviour. Thus, many control systems can be regarded as based essentially on the monitoring and evaluation of one or the other, and these will be referred to as being behaviour control and output control – remembering that even in the case of output control, real control comes about only through changing the worker's behaviour, although the means is by selectively rewarding certain worker outputs. Controls may also be applied to inputs – see recruitment, selections, induction and socialization.

Several studies on Japanese MNCs dealt with informal mechanisms, see Ouchi and others. Subsequent studies on those firms found that Japanese MNCs employed a kind of 'cultural control' (behaviour control plus control by socialization) rather than a 'bureaucratic control'. This cultural control was based on the use of expatriates, a high frequency of visits, a policy of transfer of managers, and a strong socialization process, and as such allowed a more decentralized decision-making process. We explore monitoring/diagnostic control systems in more detail next.

Look forward
See chapter 11

The organization assumes that everything is working to plan until a disaster arises. Information-as-control helps prevent surprise and disaster. Information and communication are critical elements of most control systems. Such elements support the decision-making process enabling the diagnosis and structuring of business problems, the identification, selection and implementation of solutions. Business information collected and analyzed from one part of the organization and communicated and reported to others may drive responsive action. In such cases that action will involve the selection and application of coordination and in other cases controlling mechanisms. Information systems also play an important role in coordination and control. Consequently it is important that they provide timely and accurate information to support adaptive action and decision-making. Information quality and information systems will be discussed in more detail later in this book (see Chapter 11).

Aside from a focus on timely and quality information we also focus on communication (internet) technologies in Chapter 14 and global business information systems in Chapter 13. Control and control systems are used in the process of monitoring ongoing performance and making necessary changes to keep the organization moving towards its performance goals. According to the cybernetic hypothesis, the *feedback loop* is the fundamental building block for action. Inputs or outputs are analyzed and tested against a standard; if the comparison reveals a discrepancy, an error signal is generated, and the system takes some action via the effector to reduce the discrepancy. Human control systems are more complex – utilizing feedback to ensure the attainment of goals. When framed as a theory of behaviour, control theory has two primary elements: one cognitive, the other affective – the cognitive component is the 'recognition' of discrepancy and the 'affective' element is the desire to resolve the discrepancy. A key issue concerns what to measure – given the cliché what get's measured gets managed. Earlier in the chapter we introduced the concept of the learning organization. Feedback loops are also used in organizations to enable adaptive responses and continuous improvement, see single and double loop learning to be covered in Chapter 12.

Communication processes help to provide a sense of unity and purpose within the organization; the communication climate of the organization plays a crucial role in getting employees involved in the organization's activities. Organizations which are structured such that employees have easy access to management through an open and supportive communication climate tend to outperform those with more closed communication climates. The implication is that management needs to provide mechanisms for ensuring that there is a continual, free exchange of information between managers and employees. Employees must feel that they have access to management and that their opinions and thoughts will be taken seriously, without fear of negative repercussions.

Thus far we have focused on coordination and control mechanisms. We have noted that such mechanisms are selected and applied to 'fit' with the structure, strategy and environment. As with structural choices generally, control mechanisms may also be selected according to decision-maker preferences. An issue we consider next before ending the chapter.

Attitudes to control

The amount and type of control adopted within international organizations varies considerably. One explanation for this finding is given by Pugh (1997) who discusses the 'organizers' and 'behaviouralists', with the former believing in greater and the latter in less control within organizations. Pugh (1997: xii) asks the question 'how much organization and control of behaviour is necessary for efficient functioning?' He discusses the control of organizational behaviour believing there are, broadly speaking two types of people, the organizers and behaviouralists. Organizers believe 'more and better control is necessary for efficiency' while behaviouralists believe that 'the continuing attempt to increase control over behaviour is self-defeating', that 'increased efficiency does not necessarily occur with increased control'. Pugh indicates that behaviouralists' beliefs are aligned with environmental turbulence and the organizers are more prevalent in predictable environments where bureaucracy is favoured.

Managers vary in their attitude towards human resources. Managers may consider people (employees) generally to be responsible (Theory Y) or not to be trusted (Theory X); McGregor (1960) created the labels. People who subscribe to theory X believe that individuals will pursue their own goals, unless controlled, and that their goals will be incongruent with the organizational goals. Subscribers to theory Y, on the other hand, treat people as responsible beings who 'if treated as such will strive for the good of their work organization'.

Ouchi and Wilkins (1983) also considered the problem of how to control employees, suggesting two organizational control strategies (aside from market controls):

traditional/*formal* (bureaucratic) and *informal* ('clan' or 'cultural') control. They propose a general theory of clan control based on goal congruence – the idea is that if both the employee and employer are pursuing common goals or at least not mutually exclusive goals, the employee will naturally act in the best interest of the organization, thus removing the costly requirement for 'close monitoring' typical of bureaucracy. Under clan control, the employee is committed to the organization and this becomes a source of motivation to cooperate. Ouchi and Wilkins (1983) discuss a variety of determinants and consequences of control mechanism. Clan control is argued to be more adaptive, processing information rapidly and requiring less supervision. They argue that clan control should be preferred when goal congruence and uncertainty is high, see Figure 9-18. In contrast, they describe bureaucratic control, legitimate authority, rules and close monitoring argued to make organizations more efficient in stable environments where goals may be incongruent.

Figure 9-18

Fitting formal and informal controls with environmental needs

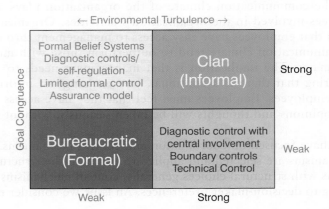

Organizations may thus vary in the degree of control they seek to assert (organizers pushing for more control) and the way they seek to control – formally or informally. They may also vary according to who is controlling (specialists, the management team, supervisors, clan-control or self-regulation) and how control is achieved at the formal level (instructions, physical and technical controls). Formal arrangements include belief systems, boundary controls such as conduct codes, process and technical controls. They may be applied to general conduct, task behaviour or assets and if linked to a process may be applied to inputs, the process or outputs.

Formal input controls may include vetting employees while informal input controls may focus on indoctrination, and socialization. Output controls (diagnostics) typically use feedback loops to distribute information as a force that might be used to influence behaviour, correct deficiency or renegotiate targets. It is important to treat output control as a variable according to the feedback recipient, which may be management (command and control regimes) or the employee (self-regulation, learning organization). Formal process controls include the elements typically associated with bureaucracy. In the absence of process control there is a heavy dependence on goals as a coordinating mechanism and goal congruence as a force to point the arrows, with motivation, provided by autonomy, the organizations mission and objectives. Aside from goal congruence, clan control (peer pressure) may be a force at work to channel the direction of individual behaviour.

In this chapter we have considered how to structure, coordinate and control human resources in the international organization; the key learning points are summarized next. Chapter 10, presented next, also considers structural problems focusing on the organization of work activities through business processes. We also return to structural issues in subsequent chapters.

Summary of key learning points

This chapter focused on how to make efficient and effective use of human resources in order to attain goals and derive a sustainable competitive advantage through design structure, coordination and control. We commenced by identifying the purpose of design – to divide up organizational activities, allocate resources, tasks and goals and to coordinate and control activities so that goals can be achieved. An appropriate design might yield benefits such as efficiency and scale, access to specialized and location-embedded resources, enhanced innovation and the creation of operational flexibility; the design can impact upon performance through employee motivation, commitment and loyalty and has the ability to link interdependent activities.

The tools used to structure organizations include: organizational charts, job definitions, span of control, authority, responsibility and accountability descriptions. Departmentalization is a process of grouping together employees. Such employees can then have line, functional or lateral relationships with one another. Employees are often grouped together by area, function/specialism, product, customer group or process. Mintzberg identified five basic parts of an organizational structure: strategic apex, middle line, operating core, technostructure and support staff. Organization theory identifies six primary dimensions (variables) of organization structure: specialization, standardization, formalization, centralization, configuration and flexibility. These variables were used to define traditional designs but remain useful today as dimensions of contemporary international organization structure.

A divisional structure is formed when an organization is split into a number of self-contained business units, each of which operates as a profit centre. In addition to global product, area and functional designs, the international organization may choose a customer or matrix design. Each of the main designs emphasize a particular type of knowledge. Companies must capture simultaneously a global-scale efficiency, respond to national markets, and cultivate a worldwide learning capability for driving continuous innovation across borders. Within the global form of organization there are several structural alternatives: the multinational, global, international and the transnational structure.

Arguments stating why organizational parts should be configured in particular ways were presented through contingency theory. Design determinants may be found in the external and internal environment and the predispositions of decision-makers. The integration-responsiveness framework was presented as a tool to identify a preferred international organizational form.

The organization design typically breaks up the workforce into parts that must work together. The concept of dependence was investigated and we identified the possible means to overcome dependence problems via coordination mechanisms. Assuring organizational parts work together productively is a matter of coordination. Control systems, on the other hand, seek to assure organizational goals are attained. A variety of management control strategies, formal (bureaucratic) and informal ('clan' or 'cultural') control, were discussed. Clan control is argued to be more adaptive and preferred when goal congruence and uncertainty is high. In contrast, bureaucratic controls make organizations more efficient in stable environments where goals may be incongruent. The amount and type of control adopted varies according to decision-maker predispositions: see the 'organizers' and 'behaviouralists'.

Review questions

Case study questions

1 BP aims to be responsive to change. How can organizations structure themselves to be more responsive to their environments? Are there any attributes of structure or an organization that might hinder or impair the company's ability to respond or be an agile competitor?

2 How might strategy impact upon the structure at BP? Would you expect BP to compete more on price (cost) or quality (differentiation)? How might structure help an organization and BP in particular, gain a competitive advantage?

3 The company has structured itself along product and then area lines; what advantages might this offer and what alternative structures might be considered?

4 BP operates in over 100 countries worldwide. What factors might be considered when grouping countries into regions?

5 The current organization is a collection of business units. Consider the mechanisms BP may use in order to assure groups are working towards the organization's goals rather than pursuing parochial interests.

6 How might structure impact upon knowledge sharing within BP?

7 Consider each of the listed corporate functions (HR, marketing etc.). Discuss the advantages and disadvantages of centralizing such functions. In what ways might such central functions influence the activities of operational workers in business units?

8 What would you expect the primary role of the executive committees to be?

Activity: organization design

In groups, discuss whether managers of international firms need to approach organization design differently from their counterparts in domestic firms.

Activity: organizational chart

Consider any of the case studies presented throughout this book and create an organizational chart for the company in focus. You should consider a range of options and explain your preferred choice. There are a number of software products that can be used to create organizational charts. Microsoft Visio and PowerPoint are common tools. Most often, a rectangle represents a person, position, or department on a chart. In a hierarchical organizational chart, the chief officer or president is represented by the top rectangle. The level underneath the chief officer contains senior managers or executives, and each succeeding level includes the subordinates of the line above.

Essay: design, coordination or control mechanisms

With regard to formal structure and design, coordination or control mechanisms critically discuss whether managers of international firms need approach challenges of integration and goal attainment differently from their counterparts in domestic firms – explain your answer.

Essay: bureaucratic model

Why do you think bureaucratic management remains a major factor in the structure, coordination and control of contemporary international organizations despite the attacks (dysfunctional) upon it toward the end of the 20th century?

Activity: organizational design

Select three large MNCs. Consider their products and services, environment, strategy and goals – would you expect the company to emphasize integration or differentiation? How might this be reflected in the location of the activities in their value configuration?

References

Argyris, C. (1957) 'The Individual and Organization: Some Problems of Mutual Adjustment', *Administrative Science Quarterly* (June 1957) 2(1):1–24.

Arnold, J., Cooper, C. and Robertson, I. (1998) *Work Psychology – Understanding Human Behaviour in the Work Place* (3 ed), London: *Financial Times* – Pitman Publishing.

Baliga, B. R. and Jaeger, A. M. (1984) 'Multinational Corporations: Control Systems and Delegation Issues', *Journal of International Business Studies* (Special Issue Autumn 1984) 15(2):25–40.

Bozeman, B. (1998) 'Risk Culture in Public and Private Organizations', *American Society for Public Administration* (March/April 1998) 58(2):109–118.

Burns, T. and Stalker, G. M. (1961) *The management of innovation*, London: Tavistock.

Caruana, A., Morris, M. H. and Vella, A. J. (1998) 'The effect of centralization and formalization on entrepreneurship in export firms', *Journal of Small Business Management – Milwaukee* 36(1):16–29.

Chandler, A. A. (1962) *Strategy and Structure: Chapters in the History of the Industrial Enterprise*, Cambridge, MA: MIT Press.

Child, J. (1972) 'Organization Structure and Strategies of Control: A replication of the Aston Study', *Administrative Science Quarterly* 17(2):163–177.

Child, J. (1973) 'Strategies of Control and Organizational Behaviour', *Administrative Science Quarterly* 18(1):1–17.

Child, J. (1997) 'Strategic choice in the analysis of action, structure, organizations and environment: Retrospect and prospect', *Organization Studies – Berlin* 18(1):43–76.

Child, J. (2001) 'Organizations unfettered: Organizational form in an information-intensive economy', *Academy of Management Journal – Briarcliff Manor* 44(6):1135–1148.

Clee, G. and Di Scipio, A. (1959) 'Creating a World Enterprise', *Harvard Business Review* (November/December 1959) 37(6):77–89.

Clee, G. and Sachtjien, W. (1964) 'Organizing a Worldwide Business', *Harvard Business Review* (November/December 1964) 42(6):55–67.

Cray, D. (1984) 'Control and Coordination in Multinational Corporations', *Journal of International Business Studies* (Autumn 1984) 15(2):85–98.

Daft, R. L. (2007) *Organization Theory and Design* (9 ed), Cincinnati, Ohio: Cengage Learning.

Devinney, T., Midgley, D. and Venaik, S. (2000) 'The Optimal Performance of the Global Firm: Formalizing and Extending the Integration-Responsiveness Framework', *Organization Science* (November/December 2000) 11(6):674–695.

Duncan, R. (1972) 'Characteristics of Organizational Environments and Perceived Environmental Uncertainty', *Administrative Science Quarterly* 17(3):313–327.

Edström, A. and Galbraith, J. (1977) 'Transfer of Managers as a Coordination and Control Strategy in Multinational Organizations', *Administrative Science Quarterly* (June 1977) 22(2):248–263.

Egelhoff, W. (1984) 'Patterns of Control in U.S., UK, and European Multinational Corporations', *Journal of International Business Studies* (Autumn 1984) 15(2):73–83.

Egelhoff, W. (1988) 'Strategy and Structure in Multinational Corporations: A Revision of the Stopford and Wells Model', *Strategic Management Journal* (January–February 1988) 9(1):1–14.

Emery, F. E. and Trist, E. L. (1965) 'The Causal Texture of Organizational Environments', *Human Relations* (February 1965) 18(1):21–32.

Fouraker, L. and Stopford, J. (1968) 'Organizational Structure and the Multinational Strategy', *Administrative Science Quarterly* (June 1968) 13(1):47–64.

Garvin, D. (1993) 'Building a Learning Organization', *Harvard Business Review* (July–August 1993):78–91.

Ghoshal, S. and Bartlett, C. (1990) 'The Multinational Corporation as an Interorganizational Network', *The Academy of Management Review* (October 1990) 15(4):603–625.

Gottschalk, P. (2006) 'Information systems in value configurations', *Industrial Management & Data Systems* 106(7):1060–1070.

Gupta, A. and Govindarajan, V. (1991) 'Knowledge Flows and the Structure of Control within Multinational Corporations', *The Academy of Management Review* (October 1991) 16(4):768–792.

Hall, R. (1968) 'Review of: Organization and Environment: Managing Differentiation and Integration, by Paul R. Lawrence and Jay W. Lorsch', *Administrative Science Quarterly* (June 1968) 13(1):180–186.

Hedlund, G. (1986) 'The Hypermodern MNC: A Heterarchy?', *Human Resource Management* (Spring 1986) 25(1):9–35.

Hellriegel, D. and Slocum, J. W. (1973) 'Organizational design: A contingency approach A model for organic management design', *Business Horizons* (April 1973) 16(2):59–68.

Herbert, T. (1984) 'Strategy and Multinational Organization Structure: An Interorganizational Relationships Perspective', *The Academy of Management Review* (April 1984) 9(2):259–270.

Hinings, C. R., Thibault, L., Slack, T. and Kikulis, L. M. (1996) 'Values and organizational structure', *Human Relations* 49(7):885.

Hodge, J. (1999) 'Creating the Horizontal Organization of the Future', *HR Magazine* (November 1999) 44(11):106–108.

Huczynski, A. and Buchanan, D. (2007) *Organizational Behaviour An Introductory Text* (6 ed), Harlow: Financial Times Prentice Hall.

Klein, H. J. (1989) 'An Integrated Control Theory of Work Motivation', *Academy of Management Review* 14(2):150–172.

Longenecker, J. and Pringle, C. (1978) 'The Illusion of Contingency Theory as a General Theory', *Academy of Management Review* (July 1978) 3(3):679–683.

Luthans, F. and Stewart, T. (1977) 'A General Contingency Theory of Management', *Academy of Management Review* 2:181–195.

Luthans, F. and Stewart, T. (1978) 'The Reality or Illusion of a General Contingency Theory of Management: A Response to the Longenecker and Pringle Critique', *Academy of Management Review* (July 1978) 3(3):683–687.

Malnight, T. (2001) 'Emerging Structural Patterns within Multinational Corporations: Toward Process-Based Structures', *The Academy of Management Journal* (December 2001) 44(6): 1187–1210.

Martinez, J. and Jarillo, J. (1989) 'The Evolution of Research on Coordination Mechanisms in Multinational Corporations', *Journal of International Business Studies* (Autumn 1989) 20(3):489–514.

McGregor, D. M. (1960) *The Human Side of Enterprise*, New York: McGraw-Hill.

Miles, R. E. and Snow, C. C. (1992) 'Causes of Failure in Network Organizations', *California Management Review* (Summer 1992) 34:53–72.

Nadler (1980) in Mabey, C. and Mayon-White, B. (1993) *Managing Change*, London: The Open University.

Ostroff, F. and Smith, D. (1992) 'The horizontal organization', *McKinsey Quarterly* 1:148–168.

Ouchi, W. G. (1977) 'The Relationship Between Organizational Structure and Organizational Control', *Administrative Science Quarterly* (March 1977) 22(1):95–113.

Ouchi, W. G. (1980) 'Markets, Bureaucracies, and Clans', *Administrative Science Quarterly – Ithaca* 25(1):129–141.

Ouchi, W. G. and Wilkins, A. L. (1983) 'Efficient Cultures: Exploring the relationship between culture and organizational performance', *Administrative Science Quarterly* 28(3):468–481.

Perlmutter, H. (1969) 'The Tortuous Evolution of the Multinational Corporation', *Columbia Journal of World Business* (January/February 1969) 4(1):9–19.

Peters, T. and Waterman, R. (1982) *In Search of Excellence*, London: Harper Collins Business.

Porter, M. E. and Millar, V. E. (1985) 'How information gives you a competitive advantage', *Harvard Business Review* (July–August 1963):149–174.

Porter, M. E. (1986) 'Changing Patterns of International Competition', *California Management Review* (Winter 1986) 28(2):9–41.

Prahalad and Doz (1987, p. 15) cited in Devinney, T., Midgley, D. and Venaik, S. (2000) 'The Optimal Performance of the Global Firm: Formalizing and Extending the Integration-Responsiveness Framework', *Organization Science* (November/December 2000) 11(6):674–695.

Pugh, D. S., Hickson, D. J. and Turner, C. (1968) 'Dimensions of Organization Structure', *Administrative Science Quarterly* 13(1):65–105.

Pugh, D. S. (1973) 'Does Context Determine Form?', *Organizational Dynamics* (Spring):19–34.

Pugh, D. S. (1997) *Organization Theory* (4 ed), Harmondsworth: Penguin.

Rapert, M. I. and Wren, B. M. (1998) 'Reconsidering organizational structure: A dual perspective of frameworks and processes', *Journal of Managerial Issues – Pittsburgh* 10(3):287–302.

Schein, E. (1999) 'Empowerment, coercive persuasion and organizational learning: do they connect?', *The Learning Organization* 6(4):163.

Senge, P. M. (1992) 'Building Learning Organizations', *The Journal for Quality and Participation* 15(2):30.

Senge, P. M. (1995) 'Learning infrastructures', *Executive Excellence* 12(2):7.

Simons, R. (1995) *Levers of Control*, Boston, Mass: Harvard Business School Press.

Sinkula, J. M. (1994) 'Market Information Processing and Organizational Learning', *Journal of Marketing* (January 1994) 58:35–45.

Slater, S. and Narver, J. (1995) 'Market Orientation and the Learning Organization', *Journal of Marketing* (July 1995) 59(3):63–74.

Stewart, T. and Jacoby, R. (1992) 'The Search for the Organization of Tomorrow', *Fortune* 125(10):92–98.

Tolman, E. C. and Brunswik, E. (1935) 'The organizm and the causal texture of the environment', *Psychol. Rev* 42:43–77.

Victor, B. and Blackburn, R. S. (1987) 'Interdependence: An alternative conceptualization'. *Academy of Management Review* 12(3):486–498.

Wollnik, M. and Kubicek, H. (1981) 'Determinants of Coordination in Business Organizations', *International Studies of Management and Organization – White Plains* (Spring 1981) 11(1):75.

Woodman, R. W., Sawyer J. E. and Griffin R. W. (1993) 'Toward a Theory of Organizational Creativity', *Academy of Management Review* 18(2):293–321.

Suggestions for further reading

Journals

Administrative Science Quarterly (ASQ) – ASQ has been at the cutting edge of organizational studies since the field began. ASQ publishes organizational theory papers from a number of disciplines, including organizational behaviour and theory, sociology, psychology and social psychology, strategic management, economics, public administration, and industrial relations.

Journal homepage: http://www.johnson.cornell.edu/publications/asq/

Organization Science is a top journal in management, widely recognized in the fields of strategy, management, and organization theory. *Organization Science* provides one umbrella for the publication of research from all over the world in fields such as organization theory, strategic management, sociology, economics, political science, history, information science, communication theory, and psychology.

Journal homepage: http://www.informs.org/site/Organization_Science/index.php?c=1&kat=Home

See also the *Academy of Management Review* identified as suggested further reading in the previous chapter.

Key articles

Scholars of this subject area have often read the following:

1. Ghoshal, S. and Bartlett, C. (1990) 'The Multinational Corporation as an Interorganizational Network', *The Academy of Management Review* (October 1990) 15(4):603–625.
2. Gupta, A. and Govindarajan, V. (1991) 'Knowledge Flows and the Structure of Control within Multinational Corporations', *The Academy of Management Review* (October 1991) 16(4):768–792.
3. Ouchi, W. G. (1980) 'Markets, Bureaucracies, and Clans', *Administrative Science Quarterly – Ithaca* 25(1):129–141.

4 Child, J. (1997) 'Strategic choice in the analysis of action, structure, organizations and environment: Retrospect and prospect', *Organization Studies – Berlin* 18(1):43–76.

5 Ouchi, W. G. (1977) 'The Relationship Between Organizational Structure and Organizational Control', *Administrative Science Quarterly* (March 1977) 22(1):95–113.

6 Argyris, C. (1957) 'The Individual and Organization: Some Problems of Mutual Adjustment', *Administrative Science Quarterly* (June 1957) 2(1):1–24.

7 Klein, H. J. (1989) 'An Integrated Control Theory of Work Motivation', *Academy of Management Review* 14(2):150–172.

Chapter 10

Global business processes

Introduction
The process view
A process view of organization
Global business processes (GBP)
Strategies for improving GBP
Business process management
Methods tools and techniques

Key concepts

- Process ■ Process enterprise ■ Process mapping ■ Total quality management
- Business process re-engineering ■ Business process management ■ Benchmarking
- Productivity ■ Parochialism ■ Continuous improvement ■ Process owner
- Business process improvement ■ Process enablers ■ Enterprise capabilities
- Process alignment

By the end of this chapter you will be able to:

- Define what is meant by a business process and explain how processes are designed and managed

- Explain how processes may be used in organization design and structuring

- Explain how the process view of organizations may provide the international organization with a source of sustainable competitive advantage and enable the attainment of strategic goals

- Compare and contrast the process view with traditional views on organizational design and structure

Dell is a large sized international company. Issues of managing processes are presented for students to engage with the variety of problems presented.

Founded in 1984 by Michael Dell, Dell is a leading computer systems company – designing, building and customizing products and services to satisfy a range of customer requirements (from the server storage and professional service needs of the largest global corporations, to those of consumers at home). Dell deals directly with customers, i.e. there are no intermediaries. They attribute much of their success to a strong customer focus – working hard to meet the needs of each customer 'with carefully tailored standards-based computing solutions'. Dell has a broad product portfolio and range of services and seeks to offer choice, support and value to customers. Uniquely enabled by its direct business model, Dell sells more systems globally than any computer company, placing it No. 25 on the Fortune 500. Dell's climb to market leadership is the result of a persistent focus on delivering the best possible customer experience by directly selling standards-based computing products and services. Annual revenues exceed $50 billion and the company employs approximately 78 700 team members around the globe.

Dell Inc.

By 1993 Dell was one of the top-five computer system makers worldwide. Dell is organized around serving the customer and strives to provide products directly to the end user with a much better level of service and support, Dell (1994). They make the customer the most important person in the business, and have embedded within their corporate culture, the concept of pleasing customers. The customer-focused culture has grown within the company from its early stages. Intent on customer satisfaction, Dell empowers employees to do special things for customers. Having a group of passionate employees who understand the company's agenda and are energized about helping customers is a huge competitive advantage, argues Dell (1994).

Additionally, he argues, feedback is critical to success. Every Friday morning at 7.30, he holds a customer advocate meeting, in which a large group of people throughout the business meet as a team to review the key statistics concerning customer responsiveness. They talk about the key processes within the company that enable them to advance their customer satisfaction capability. The Dell organization structure enables the company to customize hardware, software, peripherals and services and provide them directly to the customer. Dell has taken the approach that one size does not fit all – one size fits one. Their mass customization system allows them to make computers configured to meet customer needs, one at a time. They have also established a strategy of mass customization to enable them to tailor products and services to specific customers. For Dell, the key-to-success has been to continue to change their business model and make adjustments based on what they understand from their customers. Dell approach service as a product, and focus on continuously improving everything within the business. Instilling a continuous improvement culture within the business has been central to their success, argues Dell (1994). By 2001, Dell was ranked No. 1 in global market share and by 2006 Dell was shipping more than 10 million systems in a single quarter.

Dell's global strategy is to be the lead provider of products and services customers require to build their information – technology and internet infrastructures. With manufacturing facilities and sales offices throughout North America, Europe, Asia and South America, they are close to their customers wherever they are. The company is based on a simple concept: by selling computer systems directly to customers, Dell could best understand their needs and provide the most efficient and effective computing solutions to meet those needs. This direct business model eliminates retailers that add unnecessary time and cost, or can diminish Dell's understanding of customer expectations. The direct model allows the company to build every system to order and offer customers powerful, richly configured systems at competitive prices. Dell also introduces the latest relevant technology

Courtesy of Dell Inc

much more quickly than companies with slow-moving, indirect distribution channels, turning over inventory in just five days on average. Dell's direct model starts and ends with customers. Dell sells all its products both to end-user consumers and to corporate customers, using a direct-sales model via the Internet and the telephone network. Payment is received for products before Dell need pay for materials. Dell practices just-in-time (JIT) inventory management – an approach which utilizes the 'pull' system (to avoid overproduction by building computers only after customers place orders and by requesting materials from suppliers as needed). With a highly efficient supply chain and manufacturing organization and a dedication to reducing costs through business process improvements, Dell consistently seek to provide their customers with superior value.

Courtesy of Dell Inc

Building PCs to order requires Dell to have the parts and components on hand to build a wide array of possible configurations with little advance notice. In order to fill orders quickly, Dell must have excellent manufacturing and logistics capabilities supported by information systems. The company manufactures its computer systems in several locations worldwide and has a general policy of manufacturing its products close to its customers but there are exceptions. Dell coordinates a global production network to manufacture its products – final assembly is typically conducted as an in-house activity while outside suppliers (components and peripherals) and contract manufacturers (printed circuit board assemblies and some final products, e.g. notebook PCs) are used for other production tasks. Its PCs can be bundled with standard software such as Microsoft Office or with specialized software requested by corporate customers. Dell relies on outside partners for services such as system integration, installation, on-site repairs and consulting. Most sourcing is global, and done by procurement at headquarters. This allows Dell to strengthen its buying power and obtain better deals from suppliers. While sourcing of materials for PCs is done centrally, sourcing of other items may be local (box and shipping material, printing of manuals, etc.). Many materials are procured from low cost suppliers in Asia, but some sourcing is from local manufacturers. Suppliers are required to maintain inventory near or in Dell plants to support Dell's build-to-order production. They can produce elsewhere and ship to supply hubs, or they can set up production nearby. On the outbound side, Dell has distribution hubs to take advantage of location close to major markets, transportation networks and logistics expertise. A different logistics partner operates each hub.

Discussing the execution of strategy, Michael Dell stated that the company has metrics and agreed-to goals and objectives. Focusing on customer experience and efficiency, time-to-market and service levels, he explained business process improvement (BPI), in which any employee can be involved – 'If five workers on the production line see something that isn't working, instead of complaining about it, they have BPI. They form a team, they go solve it and it becomes a BPI project in a global database. We're saving $1.8 billion with this kind of process', Southwick (2003). Early in 2000 Dell started a corporate initiative called Business Process Improvement. Nearly five years later the programme, which includes Six Sigma, Lean, and Hoshin Planning, is still growing strong, becoming yet another model mimicked by other companies. According to Marie Moynihan, Human Resources Director, Dell, EMEA – BPI is a set of tools and skills used to understand, investigate and improve business processes. The BPI Mission is as follows: To empower employees with the knowledge, skill and tools in order to make Dell more efficient through reduced cycle time, improved quality or lower costs. Marx (2005) asked why Dell made BPI a priority. Listed BPI benefits included: quality/cost savings of more than $1.55 billion during the financial year 2004 and better customer experience through cost, quality and cycle time improvements. Decker (2004) a Marketing Executive at Dell argues that Six Sigma – or Business Process Improvement (BPI) as it's defined at Dell – can be a tool to change or enforce a culture. In the case of Dell, BPI enforces an established culture with a foundation of metrics and continuous improvement. However, because Six Sigma is an established practice and methodology, it can be a catalyst for change in the right hands, Decker (2004).

Sources:

Key facts from http://www.dell.com accessed 2007 with text adapted from a working paper by Kenneth L. Kraemer and Jason Dedrick entitled 'Dell Computer: Organization of a Global Production Network', Irvine, CA: Sloan Foundation Personal Computing Industry Center, 2002. http://pcic.merage.uci.edu/papers.asp

Introduction

Here, we build upon the previous chapter, considering not just the 'who', but the 'what' – i.e. who does what task, in what location and in what sequence in order to create value in products and services. The emphasis of this chapter is the *work* embedded in the organizational structure and how that work, like the people resources, is organized and designed. Work may be described in terms of labour, activities and tasks. Such terms are often used interchangeably. We first introduced work activities through the concept of the value chain discussed in Chapter 2 and build on this concept here. We also build on the transformational activity models presented in Chapter 4. Work is activity (a collection of tasks or specific types of work) directed at making or doing something. In the case of the international organization, work activities transform inputs into outputs (products and services) for the benefit of customers, adding value along the way.

In the previous chapter we commented on the interrelatedness of tasks (dependency); a collection of related work tasks and activities is typically labelled as a business process. Such processes may be operational, management or supportive. Well-designed processes are both effective and efficient and contribute to organizational capabilities. Business processes are often cross-functional, spanning the boxes of the organizational charts described in the previous chapter. Such processes share a number of common characteristics: they cannot exist alone and are embedded within the organizational structure; they exist as a defined set of tasks completed in a particular order (sequence), add value and have a particular customer and owner.

Look back
See chapter 5

The major focus of organizational analysis is the *transformation process* (Nadler 1993). One of the main components of the transformation process is the *task* – the work to be done (other components include *people* resources used to perform the task, and *structure* – how they are organized). We have already commented on the structural component; other formal organizational arrangements include *processes* and *systems* designed to facilitate individuals in the performance of organizational tasks. All of the components exist within the broader organizational system, as Nadler points out, the transformational process components are related to one another. For example, a particular individual or group (people) will do a particular type of work. Some work types may be facilitated through the use of technology which may enable or replace human resources in task accomplishment.

In the previous chapter we identified how work was decomposed into many tasks which are spread around the organization. We noted then that some organizational parts (possibly in different functional areas or groups) may be dependent upon others to complete their task. Work therefore needs to be coordinated and this may be accomplished, in part, through a process approach.

Look back
See chapter 5, p. 149

In Chapter 5 we presented various organizational models (see Figure 5-2 The organizational system model, Figure 5-3 Organization model and Figure 5-4 A model of organizational performance and change). Common to each model is a relationship between *structure* (considered in the previous chapter), human resources – *people* (considered in Chapters 7 and 8) and *work* – considered in this chapter. The Leavitt model also included *technology*, dealt with in the next chapter. Both the Nadler and Tushman and the Burke and Litwin models relate internal components to outputs and organizational performance – one of the main reasons for devoting this chapter to the topic. In the case of the latter model, this is mediated through motivation and in both models a causal link with the environment and the organization's strategy is present. Therefore, having considered all of the aforementioned components with the exception of work and technology we turn to each in this and in the next chapter. In this chapter we focus on work design.

In the previous chapter we considered organization and design and introduced the concept of the horizontal organization and an orientation towards business processes. In this chapter we explore business processes in more detail. In the opening active learning case we noted that Dell attributed much of its success to a strong customer focus and business process improvement. In this chapter we identify what is meant by BPI and present arguments for the means to develop a strong customer focus and customer-oriented culture. We will also consider the main arguments for a process approach to work in the international organization. The process approach:

1 presents an opportunity to improve effectiveness and efficiency thus adding value, differentiating products and services and reducing cost;

2 may lead to the enrichment of work by empowering people and enabling them to take a holistic perspective thereby seeing the value of their contribution;

3 may make better use of enterprise-wide information systems and technologies which can make the organization more responsive, enable time compression and further motivate people through the removal of mundane tasks which become automated.

Within this chapter we will first consider the *process view* of organizations. The structural problems associated with traditional designs (briefly considered in the previous chapter) will be highlighted as a driver for the process organization. After considering the structural and design issues associated with a process view of organizations, the next section explores processes in more detail. In the final section of the chapter we identify and discuss strategies for improving business processes. Three key approaches are discussed. The first considers *continuous improvement* and considers the contribution of total quality management (TQM) approaches. Next we consider radical changes through business process re-engineering (BPR) – vogue in the 1990s. We conclude by discussing business process management (BPM) as a strategy for improving processes either continuously or radically. Within this section we also identify a range of methods, tools and techniques used to improve business processes.

The process view

In the previous chapter we identified elements, dimensions and configurations of structure – organization designs. At the outset of the 1990s, Hammer challenged what he termed the 'centuries-old' notions about work. He argued that for many organizations, their job designs, work flows, control mechanisms, and organizational structures came of age in a different competitive environment and before the advent of the computer. Such organizations were geared toward efficiency and control. According to Hammer, commenting on 20th-century organizations, rules of work design are based on assumptions about technology, people, and organizational goals that no longer hold. He suggested that business processes and structures were outmoded and obsolete and had not kept pace with the changes in technology and business objectives. Companies had typically organized work as a sequence of separate tasks and employed complex mechanisms to track its progress.

This arrangement can be traced to the Industrial Revolution, when specialization of labour and economies of scale promised to overcome the inefficiencies of cottage industries. Businesses separated work into narrowly defined tasks, grouped the people performing those tasks into departments, and appointed managers to administer them. Such patterns of organizing work became so ingrained that, despite their serious drawbacks, managers and workers alike found it hard to conceive of work being accomplished any other way. Conventional process structures were fragmented and piecemeal, and they lacked the integration necessary to maintain quality and service. They were breeding grounds for tunnel vision, as people tended to substitute the narrow goals of their particular department for the larger goals of the process as a whole (see parochialism). When work is handed off from person to person and unit to unit, delays and errors are inevitable.

Organization designs like this make it difficult for workers to take a holistic perspective and see the big picture. Consequently, action and response may be too slow and inappropriate (Hammer 1990). Many organizations group the activities of its employees by their function. Organizations that group activities by function are known as 'silo' organizations because each functional area is distinct and isolated from all other functional areas. People

Cottage industries where the creation of products and services is home-based, rather than factory-based (i.e. not mass-produced)

Parochialism emphasis on narrow local concerns without any regard for more general or wider issues in silo organizations tend to focus on their individual task rather than the whole process delivered as a team. A serious problem with silo organizations is their limited built-in mechanism for coordinating process flows that cross boundaries from one functional area to another.

Functional organizations have an extra need for coordination and control from above, which tends to result in a more formalized bureaucratic hierarchical structure. However, it has been recently argued that organizing around processes, as opposed to functions, permits greater self-management and allows companies to dismantle unneeded supervisory structures. Consequently, we discuss the process view of organizations next.

A process view of organization

Process enterprise an organization whose design and supporting management systems are strongly oriented to horizontal work flows

One of the most promising ways for organizations to reinvent themselves is to focus on processes rather than functions (Sandoe, Corbitt and Boykin 2001). A process enterprise is the organizational form for a world in constant change, argues Hammer and Stanton (1999) in an article which describes how companies such as IBM and Texas Instruments are benefiting from redesigning their organizations around their core processes. The process enterprise is seen as flexible groupings of intertwined work and information flows which cut horizontally across the business, ending at points of contact with customers. Many companies have integrated their core processes, combining related activities and cutting out ones that do not add value. Shifting from a traditional business to a process enterprise is doubtlessly a significant challenge; however, Hammer and Stanton (1999) state there is really no alternative for most companies.

There are many reasons why traditional organizations implement large scale reengineering (change) programmes. Reengineering has helped companies to: operate faster and more efficiently; use information technology more productively and improve the jobs of employees, giving them more authority and a clearer view of how their work fits into the operations of the enterprise as a whole. Many problems may be encountered during the transformation. A significant consequence of partial change is that the horizontal processes pull people in one direction; the traditional vertical management systems pull them in another. Confusion and conflict ensue, undermining performance. It is impossible to overlay an integrated process on a fragmented (traditional silo) organization.

Hammer and Stanton discusses this problem with reference to changes at IBM, Texas Instruments and others. Observing that its large corporate customers were increasingly operating on a global basis, IBM decided it would have to standardize its operations worldwide. It would have to institute a set of common processes for order fulfilment, product development, and so forth to take the place of the diverse processes that were then being used in different parts of the world and in different product groups. Yet creating a process enterprise is an enormously complex undertaking. Traditional organizational units are naturally unreceptive to integrated processes, seeing them as threats to their power, therefore organizational and management structures have to be changed in fundamental ways. However, that does not mean existing vertical units such as functional, regional, or product groups are simply disbanded – in even the most process-focused business, vertical units continue to play essential roles, Hammer and Stanton (1999). Rather, it means that horizontal and vertical management structures have to coexist, not just in peace but in partnership. Not only does a company have to redistribute management responsibility, it has to change its basic management systems, and even its culture, to support a new balance of power.

The most visible difference between a process enterprise and a traditional organization is the existence of process owners – senior managers with end-to-end responsibility for individual processes. To succeed, a process owner must have real responsibility for and authority over designing the process, measuring performance and training the front-line workers who perform such processes. Traditionally, a geographical or functional manager

Look back
See chapter 6

oversees both the work and the people who do it. In a process enterprise, the process owner has responsibility for the design of the process, but the various people who perform the process typically report to the unit heads. However, becoming a process enterprise is more than a matter of establishing new management posts and reconfiguring responsibilities. As lines of authority become less precise, the way managers interact with one another and with workers also has to change.

Style is as important as structure (Hammer and Stanton 1999). Traditional styles of management have no place in a process enterprise. Managers can not command and control; they have to negotiate and collaborate – the coordinator coaches rather than controls the people who perform the process. They can not wield authority; they have to exert influence. Any company hoping to turn itself into a process enterprise needs to understand the associated changes in managerial style and their implications for staffing and training.

International companies composed of many different business units located around the world, face an important strategic question as they make the shift to a process enterprise: should all units do things the same way, or should they be allowed to tailor their processes to their own needs? In a process enterprise, the key structural issue is no longer centralization *versus* decentralization – it is process standardization *versus* process diversity. There is no one right answer. Process standardization offers many benefits, the arguments for standardization are:

- *Cost reduction* (one way of doing things requires fewer manuals, less to design, administer, etc.) standardizing procurement processes offers economies of scale – the company may aggregate its purchases and gain much more leverage over suppliers and standardization enables the company to present one face to its suppliers and customers, reducing transaction costs both for them and for itself (see Dell case study as example).

- *Organizational flexibility* When all business units are performing a process the same way, a company can easily reassign people from one unit to another, responding to shifts in demand. Its organizational structure becomes much more 'plastic'.

However, on the other hand, process diversity offers one big advantage: it allows different kinds of customers to be served in different ways. Consequently, some companies have decided to standardize certain processes but not others. Hammer and Stanton (1999) believe that companies should standardize their processes as much as possible without interfering with their ability to meet diverse customer needs.

Making the shift to a process enterprise involves much more than just redrawing an organizational chart. The changes proposed by Hammer and Stanton (1999) are fundamental ones, representing new ways of managing and working, and they are not easy to make. They require the full attention and commitment of the organization. Because the changes involved in becoming a process enterprise are so great, companies can expect to encounter considerable organizational resistance and a range of strategies are required to overcome it (refer back to Chapter 5). In the next section we explore types of process, what they are, how they are designed and managed.

Global business processes (GBP)

The challenges of the global external environment, through strategies, drive organizations to search out ways to reduce costs, deliver the products and services customers need and when they need them. This forces a focus on efficiency and effectiveness. In this section we focus on how work is organized and performed in the international organization. Our focus on how work is performed will be illuminated through an exploration of business processes. We identify what business processes are and how they are designed and managed. The success of any organization depends upon the performance of each of the three elements which comprise the organization: its products and services, i.e. its deliverables;

Efficiency relationship between the result achieved and the resources used

business processes and the fabric which supports them, and people, i.e. its employees and suppliers (Jones 1994). Processes are the essential link between customer or client requirements and the delivery of products or services. They are the *means* whereby the organization and its employees fulfil their purpose or 'mission'.

What is a process?

Commenting on the 1990s, Davenport suggests the contemporary business world is abound with references to the concept of process – a noun denoting how work is done (Davenport 1994). He starts by asking what a process is, defining it as a structured set of activities designed to produce a specified output for a particular customer or market. It has a beginning, an end, and clearly identified inputs and outputs. A process is therefore a structure for action, for how work is done. Processes also have performance dimensions – cost, time, output quality, and customer satisfaction – that can be measured and improved. Davenport argues that because the definition of process necessarily involves a customer receiving an output, taking a process approach implies adopting the customer's point of view. Processes are therefore the structure by which an organization does what is necessary to produce value for its customers. Process management is not strategy; it is a means of executing strategy – a tool for operational management, not strategic management (Davenport 1994: 145). A specified way to carry out an activity or a process is termed a procedure (see Figure 10-1).

Process a structured set of activities designed to produce a specified output for a particular customer or market

Procedure specified way to carry out an activity or a process

Figure 10-1
Procedural diagram

Products and services ultimately define the outputs, i.e. what is done; processes are about *how* it is done. People use *processes* and *technology* to produce products and services. Any activity or set of activities that uses resources to transform inputs to outputs can be considered as a process. For organizations to function effectively, they must identify and manage numerous interrelated and interacting processes. Often, the output from one process will form the direct input to the next process (see systems thinking). The systematic identification and management of the processes employed within an organization and particularly the interactions between such processes is referred to as the 'process approach'. International Standards such as ISO 9000 encourage the adoption of the process approach to manage an organization (see later).

Processes

Business process a specific ordering of work activities across time and place, with a beginning, an end, and clearly identified inputs and output

At its core, business process (see Figure 10.2) is all about how work gets done. A process is a group of business activities undertaken by an organization in pursuit of a common goal. Typical business processes include product development, receiving orders, marketing services, selling products, delivering services, distributing products, invoicing for services and accounting for money received. A more comprehensive list of processes may be seen

Figure 10.2
Process diagram. Concepts relating to processes (Adapted from ISO9000:2005)

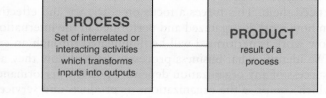

in Figure 10-3. A business process is usually dependent upon several business functions for support, e.g. IT, personnel, and facilities and rarely operates in isolation, i.e. other business processes will depend upon it and it will depend upon other processes. Processes are used to manage the flow of goods, products and services, information and money. They organize work as flows of related activities.

	Primary	Secondary	Development
Individual & Vertical	Billing/Invoicing Accounts Payable Accounts Receivable Credit Approval Order Fulfilment Outbound Logistics	Customer Acquisition Procurement Purchase Order Processing Customer Service Supplier Evaluation HR: Recruitment Inventory Mgt Marketing	Training
Horizontal (Cross-functional)	Inbound Logistics Production Planning Manufacture Sales Order Processing Customer Relationship Mgt	Investment Management Plant & Equipment Maintenance Construction and Project Management Planning & Resource Allocation Information Management	New Product Devt Continuous Improvement Performance Appraisal
Interorganizational	Supply Chain Management	Supplier Collaboration	Supplier Standards

Figure 10.3
Business processes

Note that in certain organizations the above processes may be classified differently.

Consider the processes identified in Figure 10-3. Select a company and identify which processes will be relevant or not for the company. Can you think of any additional processes not listed in the table? If so, list and categorize them.

STOP & THINK

Processes may be categorized in several ways. For example some companies choose to divide all business processes into four core types:

- product design processes;
- sales and marketing processes;
- supply chain processes; and
- enabling processes.

Alternatively we may distinguish:

1 management processes – the processes that govern the operation (corporate governance and strategic management);

2 operational processes – primary activities that create value, they are part of the core business (purchasing, manufacturing, marketing, and sales); and

3 Supporting processes – these support the core processes, examples include accounting, recruitment, and IT support.

Other scholars advocate a development process type – a process that seeks to improve the performance of other processes. In agreement with Porter's (1985) value chain model, Jones (1994) suggests two classes of business process: 'delivery', the customer facing processes and 'support', those required to sustain the delivery functions. Jones identifies three delivery processes:

Development process a process that seeks to improve the performance of other processes

1 *Product (service) development process* – the development of new product offerings from concept through research, development, introduction, update to withdrawal from the market.

2 *Customer order process* – the fulfilment of customer requirements for products or services from customer enquiry through invitation to tender, proposal, contract, production, distribution, installation, invoicing to debt collection.

3 *Product (service) maintenance process* – the provision of after-sales service and support from support plan development through inventory provision, service/support call management, service/support provision, invoicing to debt collection.

The provision and maintenance of the organization's personnel from HR planning through skills profiling, recruitment, induction, training and development, succession planning, motivation, appraisal, disciplinary action, termination and retirement to pension administration is encapsulated within the human resource acquisition process (refer back to Chapter 7). The provision of working capital to the business is managed in the cash acquisition process and the process of managing the business operation is the business management process. Having identified types of process we will now consider attributed and the structure of processes in more detail.

Process structure

Although there is not widespread consensus on the constructs that collectively form the essential basis of a process model, the following list includes many of those most frequently mentioned:

- Agent – an actor (human or machine) who performs a process element.
- Role – a coherent set of process elements to be assigned to an agent as a unit of functional responsibility (the capability of an agent – e.g. head of department, director, clerk).
- Artefact – a product created, modified or used by the enactment of a process element (documents used in processes include applications, approvals, contracts, reminders, receipts, tickets, notes, etc.) Curtis, Kellner and Over (1992).

A single agent can perform multiple roles, and a single role may be performed by multiple agents. A process can now be further elaborated as one or more agents acting in defined roles to enact the process steps that collectively accomplish the goals for which the process was designed. Typically, process steps either manipulate an artefact or coordinate tasks (Curtis, Kellner and Over 1992). Many forms of information must be integrated to adequately describe processes. Among the form of information that people want to extract from a process model are what is going to be done, who is going to do it, when and where will it be done, how and why will it be done, and who is dependent on its being done. Four of the most commonly represented perspectives are as shown in Figure 10-4 and the bulleted list below:

Process model an abstract description of an actual or proposed process representing selected process elements that are considered important to the purpose of the model and can be enacted by a human or machine

Agent an actor (human or machine) who performs a process element

Process element any component of a process substructure

Capability ability of an organization, system or process to realize a product that will fulfil the requirements for that product

Artefact a product created or modified by the enactment of a process element

Process steps an atomic action of a process that has no externally visible substructure

Figure 10.4

Perspectives (aspects) of process models

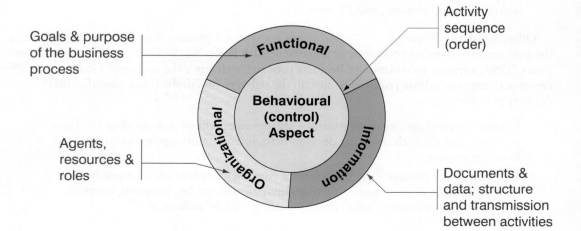

Goals & purpose of the business process

Agents, resources & roles

Activity sequence (order)

Documents & data; structure and transmission between activities

- Functional represents the process elements being performed, and the flows of informational entities (e.g. data, artefacts, products), relevant to these process elements.

- Behavioural represents when process elements are performed (e.g., sequencing), as well as aspects of how they are performed through feedback loops, iteration, complex decision-making conditions, entry and exit criteria, and so forth.

- Organizational represents where and by whom (which agents) in the organization process elements are performed, the physical communication mechanisms used for transfer of entities, and the physical media and locations used for storing entities.

- Informational represents the informational entities produced or manipulated by a process; these entities include data, artefacts, products (intermediate and end), and objects; this perspective includes both the structure of informational entities and the relationships among them.

These perspectives underlie separate yet interrelated representations for analyzing and presenting process information. When combined, these perspectives will produce an integrated, consistent, and complete model of the process analyzed (see Figure 10.5).

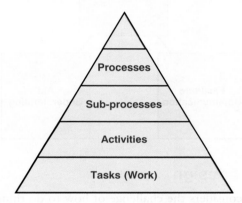

Figure 10.5
Process hierarchy

The goal of a process is usually the transformation of a set of inputs into a set of outputs. Within a process, there are a 'series of actions' which can be broken down into two types:

a   a *simple action*, where something is done, and subsequent action is always the same;

b   a *decision*, where nothing is done other than to decide on the subsequent action.

Processes are systematic, i.e. actions are not performed randomly, but in a predefined sequence. Each process may itself contain other processes, which in turn may contain further processes. The most common tool to show this sequence is a flowchart (see below), which uses different symbols to distinguish the different types of action. The operation of an entire company may be considered as a single process. This may then be broken down into the major sub-processes, such as purchasing and manufacturing, each of which can be iteratively decomposed to an appropriate level (typically to individual roles). This can then be used in the analysis of company, department or personal processes, investigating how well processes interact and contribute to real customer needs (see Figure 10-6). Processes define the way in which all the resources of an organization are used in a reliable, repeatable and consistent way to achieve its goals.

Zairi (1997) lists four key features to any process. A process must have:

- predictable and definable inputs;
- a linear, logical sequence or flow;
- a set of clearly definable tasks or activities; and
- a predictable and desired outcome or result.

As was discussed previously, processes may be categorized in several ways. They may be individual (carried out by separate individuals), functional (contained within a functional

Flowchart a pictorial summary that shows, with symbols and words, the steps, sequence, and relationship of the various operations involved in the performance of a process

Cross-functional processes processes that span multiple functional areas of the enterprise in a purely sequential fashion or involving reciprocal or simultaneous interactions between two or more functional areas

Figure 10-6
Process modelling benefits

department such as HR or finance) or may be cross-functional processes – a (horizontal) process that spans multiple functional areas of the enterprise in a purely sequential fashion or involving reciprocal or simultaneous interactions between two or more functional areas. Processes may also be interorganizational, i.e. include activities performed in other organizations.

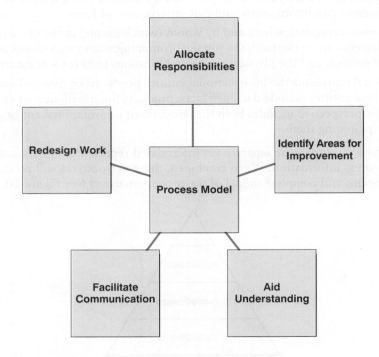

Business process design

Business process design considers the challenge of how to do things in the best way – effectively and efficiently, i.e. do the right things right. A process map identifies the specific activities that make up the flow of a process. Process *flow charts* are typically used to show how a process works. The flow chart is one common way of depicting a process and we identify how such charts are created in the points below.

- *A flow chart* is a diagram that uses symbols to depict the nature and flow of the steps in a process. A selection of the symbols can be used. Ovals indicate both the starting point and the ending point of the process steps; a box represents an individual step or activity in the process; a diamond shows a decision point, such as yes/no; other symbols show where documents may be created or delays experienced. Two other common symbols are the circle which indicates that a particular step is connected to another page or part of the flow chart and the triangle which shows where an in-process measurement occurs. flow charts may be created for different users and consequently vary in the level of detail shown. Senior managers may only need to see the bigger picture while those responsible for making improvements or following the process may require more detail.

- *Boundaries* are the starting and ending points for the flow chart. The boundaries determine the activities to be considered and the people involved in the process, both functionally and cross-functionally.

- Many experts suggest starting with the big picture – drawing a macro-level flow chart first. This should depict how things are done presently, i.e. the 'as-is' state. A good way to start flow charting a process is to walk through the current process, observing it in actual operation. Record the process steps on index cards or 'Post-it' notes – colour coding each individual or group involved. Arrange the sequence of steps and draw the flow chart using the symbols described above. After the big picture of the process has been depicted, the diagrams can be developed with increased levels of detail. We can then consider where improvements may be made and design a desired flow.

A flow chart assists with the understanding of a process and uncovers ways to improve that process only when used to analyze what is happening.

Draft a procurement process for company ABC.

In ABC managers are allocated budgets and corporate credit cards for purchases under €1000. Approval is required for purchases exceeding this amount or for any purchase whereby the buyer has no allocated budget. Approved purchases are made using a purchase order (with unique identifying number) which is completed and sent to procurement who then place the order with the supplier and notify the accounts department that an order has been placed.

An example of a procurement process flow chart is shown in Figure 10-7. We also present an example of a simple cross-functional process in Figure 10-8.

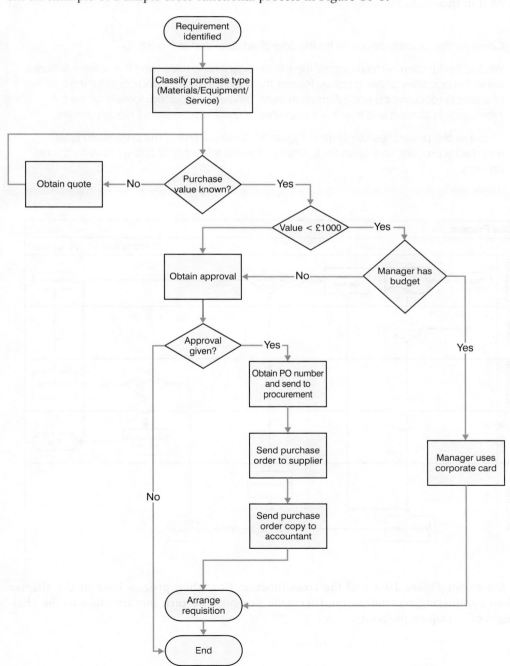

Figure 10-7

Process/decision flow (procurement) example

A flow chart describing a process, in which a number of different people, departments, or functional areas are involved, is termed a cross-functional flow chart. A simple example is shown in Figure 10-7.

Cross-functional flow charts

Companies use cross-functional flowcharts to show the relationship between a business process and the functional units (such as departments) responsible for that process. The cross-functional process can be presented either vertically or horizontally. A vertical layout places slightly more emphasis on the functional units while a horizontal layout emphasizes the process. Bands represent the functional units. Symbols representing steps in the process are placed in bands that correspond to the functional units responsible for those steps.

Divide the flowchart into rows or columns. Head up each row/column with the name of the person or function involved in the process, and each time they carry out an action show it in their column.

STOP & THINK

Consider the *process structure* for the flow chart depicted in Figure 10-7.

What is the function of the process? Identify the agents and roles (who is involved) featured within the boundary of this process. Review the activity sequence and consider the types of artefacts (documents) and information used, created or modified. Identify where the information is created and how it is transmitted or used in subsequent steps/activities.

Consider the processes identified in Figure 10-3. Select one of the processes listed and draft a process flow chart for it. Attempt this for a functional and a cross-functional process.

Figure 10-8

A cross-functional (sales) process

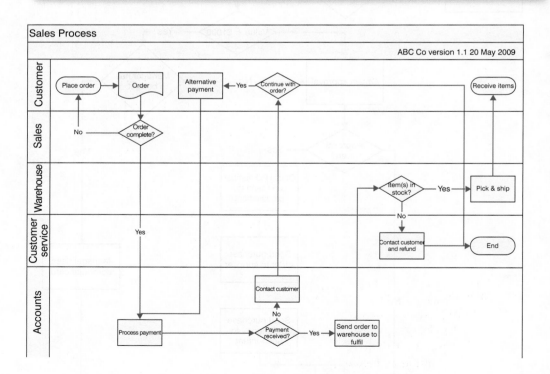

We revisit Figure 10-8 and the cross-function flow chart/process later in the chapter when considering continuous improvement. For now we turn our attention to the challenges of managing processes.

Managing processes

Managing processes involves establishing ownership, defining boundaries, documenting the processes, identifying control points and measurements and monitoring and taking corrective action where necessary. Prior to managing or improving business processes they must be understood and documented. A basic requirement for good process management is the identification and mapping of specific processes (Davenport 1994). For every process within the organization, the company should know its start and end points, key inputs and outputs, the key customers and suppliers of the process, and, for broad processes, a high-level flow of activities.

Process mapping identification of location and responsibilities for processes within an organization

An example of a process flow is shown in Figure 10-8. The process shows the task and decision sequence employees must follow when procuring goods and services on behalf of the company. An important aspect of process management is integration into the organizational structure. Process management *responsibilities* must be reconciled with other structural dimensions within the organization (functions and geographies, for example). For some organizations, it may make sense to assign responsibility for day-to-day execution of work to process owners, and the maintenance and development of functional skills to functional managers. An alternative is to give process managers responsibility for the redesign of processes, leaving daily work execution to functional, product, or geography managers.

Process owner the person who coordinates the various functions and work activities at all levels of a process. This person has the authority or ability to make changes in the process as required, and manages the entire process cycle to ensure performance effectiveness

Finally, in product or project-oriented organizations, it may be desirable to put end-to-end responsibility for product and project processes within these groups, and to leave infrastructural processes in the hands of functional executives (Davenport 1994). An emphasis on processes does not normally replace other dimensions of organizational structure claims Davenport (1994). The contemporary large organization actually has many dimensions of organizational structure. Divisions, products, distribution channels, and geographies – not just functions – form the basis for organizational structure. The need for these structural factors is not eliminated when an organization adopts process management. There is still a need for specialized functional skills, be they marketing, engineering, sales, or manufacturing. There is also a need for strong product management, business unit structures (in large organizations), and a focus on the specific needs of geographic markets; processes must be added to these other dimensions of structure.

Almost all large organizations already have some form of multidimensional structure. Just as firms have needed to balance product and functional orientations, organizations must now do this in the context of managing process performance. Organizational structures will emphasize processes, but not exclusively. Process management represents a major shift in organizational structure and culture Davenport (1994: 147).

Process infrastructure

Companies making the shift to a process enterprise must examine the basic elements of their organizational infrastructure. Traditional ways to measure performance, determine compensation, provide training, and even organize facilities are tailored to vertical units, not processes, and to individuals, not teams. Process owners not only use metrics to follow the status of a process and guide improvement efforts, they also circulate them throughout the organization to reinforce people's awareness of the process and to focus them on its performance. Since the same process measures are used to gauge the performance of everyone involved in the process, the measurements also help to reinforce teamwork. Measurements may also be used to reward teams and individuals and should be based at least in part on how well the processes perform. In many cases it is important to have team members together so that mutual adjustment and informal coordination and control may take place. Therefore, facilities should be made available enabling process workers to work as a team. In addition, for a process team to succeed, all the members must understand the whole process and how their individual efforts contribute towards it.

Process infrastructure system of facilities, equipment and services needed for the implementation of a process approach

Workers will often need to be trained to take on their broadened roles. To make new processes work, companies must redefine jobs more broadly, increase training to support those jobs and enable decision-making by frontline workers, and focusing reward systems on processes as well as outcomes. Enterprises also have to reshape organizational cultures to emphasize teamwork, personal accountability and the importance of the customer; redefining roles and responsibilities so that managers oversee processes instead of activities and develop people rather than supervise them. Information systems must be realigned so they help cross-functional processes work smoothly rather than simply support departments.

Recognizing the challenges and problems organizations face Hammer (2007) introduces a new framework to help companies plan and execute process-based transformations; the process and enterprise maturity model (PEMM) (see Table 10-1). He claims the model helps executives comprehend, formulate, and assess process-based transformation efforts. Hammer identifies two distinct groups of characteristics needed for business processes to perform exceptionally well over a long period of time: process enablers which affect individual processes and determine how well a process is able to function. They are mutually interdependent – if any are missing, the others will be ineffective. A company must also possess or establish organizational capabilities that allow the business to offer a supportive environment. Together, the enablers and the capabilities provide an effective way for companies to plan and evaluate process-based transformations. Process enablers and enterprise capabilities create a comprehensive framework that allows companies to evaluate the maturity of their business processes and the receptiveness of their organizations to process-based change. Companies can use their evaluations of the enablers and capabilities, in tandem, to plan and assess the progress of process-based transformations.

Table 10-1

The process and enterprise maturity model

Process enablers	
	■ **Design:** The comprehensiveness of the specification of how the process is to be executed.
	■ **Performers:** The people who execute the process, particularly in terms of skills and knowledge.
	■ **Owner:** A senior executive with responsibility for the process and its results.
	■ **Infrastructure:** Information and management systems supporting the process.
	■ **Metrics:** Measures used to track process performance.
Enterprise capabilities	
	■ **Leadership:** Senior executives who support the creation of processes.
	■ **Culture:** The values of customer focus, teamwork, personal accountability, and a willingness to change.
	■ **Expertise:** Skills in, and methodology for, process redesign.
	■ **Governance:** Mechanisms for managing complex projects and change initiatives.

Source: Hammer (2007)

Strategies for improving GBP

In 2002, the Dell president and COO Kevin Rollins, devised a new initiative called 'The Soul of Dell', designed to examine the company's culture and to find ways for Dell to be more than 'just the world's most efficient, relentless, and competitive machine'. Rollins identified a need for responsibility and introduced business process improvement. Dell targeted potential cost savings by doing things better. 'But it's a grassroots program' argues Rollins. On the business-improvement side, anybody can say, 'I'm going to gather the appropriate people, learn the process, follow through, and see savings'. From the factory floor to the boardroom, Dell employees are being put on notice that the success of the company lies in their own hands. If something is broken, it's an employee's responsibility to fix it – or to alert somebody who can, Tischler (2002).

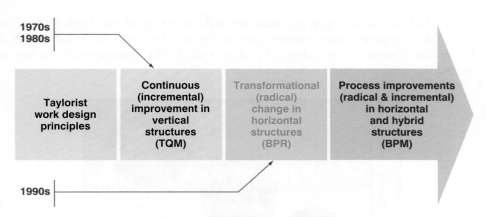

Figure 10-9
Strategy timeline

At this stage we might ask how we go about improving processes. Quality improvement has been defined as actions taken throughout the organization to increase the effectiveness and efficiency of activities and processes, resulting in added benefits to both the organization and its customers. Quality improvement is achieved by improving processes. The continual improvement of the organization is considered within a number of quality standards. To aid in ensuring the future of the organization and the satisfaction of interested parties, management should create a culture which involves people actively seeking opportunities for improvement of performance in processes, activities and products. In order to involve people, senior management should empower people. Such people may then identify opportunities where the organization can improve its performance. Ideally, senior management should define and implement a process for continual improvement.

Organizations should seek continuously to improve business processes in order to enhance the organization's performance and benefit its interested parties. There are two fundamental ways to conduct continual process improvement:

a breakthrough projects which either lead to revision and improvement of *existing* processes or the implementation of *new* processes; these are usually carried out by cross-functional teams outside routine operations; and

b small-step ongoing improvement activities conducted within existing processes by people.

Breakthrough projects usually involve significant redesign of existing processes. People in the organization are the best source of ideas for small-step or ongoing process improvement and often participate as work groups. Continuous improvement by either of the methods identified should involve the following:

a *Reason for improvement*: a process problem should be identified and an area for improvement selected, noting the reason for working on it.

b *Current situation*: the effectiveness and efficiency of the existing process should be evaluated and an objective for improvement set.

c *Analysis*: the root causes of the problem should be identified and verified.

d *Identification of possible solutions*: alternative solutions should be explored. The best solution should be selected and implemented, i.e. the one that will eliminate root causes of the problem and prevent the problem from recurring.

e *Evaluation of effects*: it should then be confirmed that the problem and its root causes have been eliminated or their effects decreased, that the solution has worked, and the objective for improvement has been met.

f *Implementation and standardization of the new solution*: the old process should be replaced with the improved process, thereby preventing the problem and its root causes from recurring.

g *Evaluation of the effectiveness and efficiency of the process with the improvement action completed*: the effectiveness and efficiency of the improvement project should be evaluated and consideration given for using its solution elsewhere in the organization.

Both methods of improvement are discussed in the next part of the chapter. We discuss small step or incremental improvement first as this was the focus of TQM during the 1980s. We then discuss radical change, the focus of the 1990s before considering business process management as a more recent concept.

Figure 10-10

Approaches to BPI
(Adapted from Ashaver *et al.*
(1998))

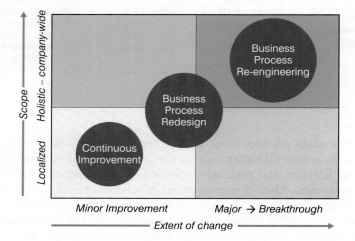

In order to restructure and improve processes in all functional areas in a corporation, three alternative approaches are suggested in the literature (see Figure 10-10):

- *Continuous process improvement.* This reduces variation in the quality of output products and services and results in incremental improvements to the flow of work within a functional activity.
- *Business process redesign.* This removes non-value added activities from processes, improves our cycle-time response capability, and lowers process costs.
- *Business process re-engineering (BPR).* This fundamentally or radically redesigns processes (through the application of enabling technology) to gain drastic improvements in critical contemporary measures of performance, inspired from a new mission, such as cost, process efficiency, effectiveness, productivity, and quality.

Davenport describes two approaches: the incremental/continuous process improvement (see TQM, etc.) and the more radical approach (process innovation, redesign, or re-engineering (see Table 10-2.)). In the 1970s and 1980s, organizations generally turned to continuous process improvement programmes while, later, in the 1990s, the same organizations turned to more radical process change approaches. Davenport (1994) compares and contrasts the two approaches:

Total quality management (TQM) a quality approach that emphasizes a continuous process of improvement, through the involvement of people

Table 10-2

Continuous improvement and process innovation programmes

Continuous improvement programmes	■ are considered successful if as little as 10 per cent improvement per year is achieved;
	■ start from the current state of the process and chip away at it;
	■ are highly participative; and
	■ stress the rigour of statistical process control to minimize unexplained variation in a process.
Process innovation or re-engineering programmes	■ strive for radical, as much as tenfold levels of improvement in the cost, time, or quality of a process;
	■ begin with a relatively clean slate;
	■ are more top-down in terms of how the new work design is created; and
	■ attempt to identify technological or organizational process enablers to maximize variation.

Each process should be evaluated with respect to its current performance (particularly in terms of cost and time), its relevance to overall strategy or mission, and its potential for successful change (Davenport 1994). Business people now need to roll up their sleeves to make their businesses perform better than ever before says Hammer (2001b). Business process improvement (BPI) concerns the optimizing of existing processes typically coupled with enhancements in information technology. A similar concept, business process management is an approach to increase process efficiency by improving information flows between people as they perform business tasks. Business process re-engineering is the fundamental rethinking and radical redesign of business processes to achieve dramatic improvements in cost, quality, speed, and service; it is about the identification of radical, new ways of carrying out business operations, often enabled by new IT capabilities.

Continuous improvement

Continuous improvement is a term used to describe a recurring activity to increase the ability to fulfil requirements. An individual or team tasked with continuous improvement may start by critically reviewing existing ('as is') process maps, models and flow charts. They may start by examining each delay and will then establish the cause of delay and how to reduce it; they may consider each activity and determine whether or not it is necessary, its value and how to prevent errors and for each decision they may ascertain whether or not a person is required to make the decision or whether it can be automated or eliminated.

Continuous improvement recurring activity to increase the ability to fulfil requirements

> Consider the flow chart shown in Figure 10-8.
>
> How might you improve the depicted process?

STOP & THINK

You may have generated ideas such as:

1. *Technology* – to capture orders and payments (e-commerce); to display and check stock availability automatically and databases for shipping information and pick lists.

2. *Additional sub-processes* – to offer credit arrangements there may be a need to refer credit risk assessment to the finance department or through an online tool; you may also have considered a sub-process that gains information from manufacturing to identify when out-of-stock items may become available-for-promise.

Every organization, regardless of size and sector, strives to provide a quality culture that will permeate every level of their organization. Establishing optimal working practices, which can enhance profit as well as customer satisfaction does not happen by accident.

Practices activities that are actually routinely performed (regardless of whether they are formally specified)

Example: Quality management principles

The ISO 9000 family is among ISO's most widely known standards. ISO 9000 standards are implemented by approximately one million organizations in 150 countries. ISO 9000 has become an international reference for quality management requirements in business-to-business dealings. The ISO 9000 family is primarily concerned with 'quality management'. This means what the organization does to fulfil:

■ the customer's quality requirements; and

■ applicable regulatory requirements; while aiming to

■ enhance customer satisfaction; and

■ achieve continuous improvement of its performance in pursuit of these objectives.

Continuous improvement is synonymous with TQM. TQM is an integrated management philosophy and set of practices that emphasizes, among other things, continuous improvement, meeting customers' requirements, reducing rework, long-range thinking, increased employee involvement and teamwork, process redesign, competitive benchmarking, team-based problem-solving, constant measurement of results, and closer relationships with suppliers ((Ross 1993), cited in Powell (1995)). TQM's origins can be traced to Japanese scientists devoted to improving Japanese productivity. TQM produced managerial innovations such as quality circles, equity circles, supplier partnerships, cellular manufacturing, just-in-time production, and hoshin planning (discussed later in Chapter 15). American firms began to take serious notice of TQM around 1980, when some US policy observers argued that Japanese manufacturing quality had equalled or exceeded US standards, and warned that Japanese productivity would soon surpass that of American firms. TQM may produce value, through a variety of benefits such as:

Productivity economic measure of efficiency that summarizes the value of outputs relative to the value of inputs used to create them

- the improved understanding of customers' needs;
- improved customer satisfaction;
- improved internal communication;
- better problem-solving;
- greater employee commitment and motivation;
- stronger relationships with suppliers;
- fewer errors; and
- reduced waste.

Despite TQM and related philosophies emerging in the 1980s the tools and techniques remain useful for contemporary organizations. An outline of the associated methodologies, tools and techniques will be presented later in the chapter but first we review approaches to radical change.

Radical change

At the beginning of the chapter we introduced BPR as vogue in the 1990s. In this section we review BPR in more detail and argue that while it may be out of favour as a one-off activity, the need for transformational change may present itself to companies throughout their existence. With process re-engineering any actual process is compared with the ideal process and on this basis unwanted activities are eliminated and improvements made. In order to operate successfully in a global business environment, processes must be restructured such that products and services can be standardized and in the meantime they should be flexible enough to meet the customer requirements in different market segments. In other words, worldwide operating companies need to render 'global processes, but for local customers' (Johansson *et al.* 1993), cited in Ashayeri *et al.* (1998). This way, a global business can take the advantage of synergy, while the feeling for local customers remains intact. The biggest benefit of synergy-effects in a global business can only be obtained when all different (sub)systems within the business are viewed as a system. BPR, in such situations, considers the worldwide activities as primary processes, while the other activities at local level are considered as secondary processes or supporting processes.

Primary processes processes that deal with the primary value and activities of the organization

Secondary processes processes that support the primary value and activities of the organization

Business re-engineering implementation can be characterized as the implementation of deliberate and *fundamental change* in business processes to achieve breakthrough improvements in performance (Grover and Jeong 1995). Fundamentally, BPR is about establishing and defining customer requirements and then aligning horizontal processes, that is, across departments and/or functions, to meet those needs (McKay and Radnor 1998). This has the potential to remove all wasted effort in the form of duplicated tasks, repeated information, etc. thus allowing clear roles and responsibilities to be defined. The result is an optimized, in some sense, process as well as an improved understanding. All this allows an environment of continuous improvement through a dedicated and empowered workforce.

Hammer (1990) outlined the essence of process re-engineering – whereas businesses traditionally focused on cost, growth, and control, Hammer argued a shift in focus to innovation and speed, service and quality as companies approached the new millennium. Hammer (1990) argued that re-engineering enabled companies to break away from the old rules about how they organize and conduct business.

Re-engineering requires looking at the fundamental processes of the business from a cross-functional perspective. At the heart of reengineering is the notion of discontinuous thinking – of recognizing and breaking away from the outdated roles and fundamental assumptions that underlie operations. Companies cannot achieve breakthroughs in performance by 'cutting fat' or automating existing processes. Rather, they must challenge old assumptions and shed the old rules that made the business under-perform in the first place. Creating new rules tailored to the modern environment ultimately requires a new conceptualization of the business process. Re-engineering need not be haphazard and Hammer (1990) suggested several guiding principles (see Figure 10-11).

Innovation creating value out of new ideas, new products, new services or new ways of doing things

---

🌐 Organize around outcomes, not tasks.
  Aim to have one person perform all the steps in a process. Design jobs around outcomes not tasks.

🌐 Have those who use the output of the process perform the process.
  When the people closest to the process perform it, there is little need for the overhead associated with managing it. Interfaces and liaisons can be eliminated, as can the mechanisms used to coordinate those who perform the process with those who use it.

🌐 Subsume information-processing work into the real work that produces the information.

🌐 Treat geographically dispersed resources as though they were centralized.
  Decentralizing a resource (whether people, equipment, or inventory) gives better service to those who use it, but at the cost of redundancy, bureaucracy, and missed economies of scale. Companies no longer have to make such trade-offs. They can use databases, telecommunications networks, and standardized processing systems to get the benefits of scale and coordination whilst maintaining the benefits of flexibility and service.

🌐 Link parallel activities instead of integrating their results.
  Forge links between parallel functions in order to coordinate them whilst their activities are in process rather than after they are completed. Communications networks, shared databases, and teleconferencing can bring the independent groups together so that coordination is ongoing.

🌐 Put the decision point where the work is performed, and build control into the process.
  In most organizations, those who do the work are distinguished from those who monitor the work and make decisions about it - the people who do the work should make the decisions and the process itself can have built-in controls. Pyramidal management layers can therefore be compressed and the organization flattened.

🌐 Capture information once and at the source.

Figure 10-11

Principles of re-engineering (Source: Hammer (1990))

Business strategy is the primary driver of BPR initiatives. The organization dimension reflects the structural elements of the company, such as hierarchical levels, the composition of organizational units, and the distribution of work between them. Information technology (IT) plays an important role in the reengineering concept. It is considered a major enabler for new forms of working and collaborating within an organization and across organizational borders. The people/human resources dimension deals with aspects such as education, training, motivation and reward systems. BPR is not limited to internal processes.

Hammer (2001) believed that companies have done a great job streamlining their internal process, but argued that their shared process – those that involved interactions with other companies – were largely a mess. He argues that streamlining cross-company processes is the next great frontier for reducing cost and enhancing quality. Successful organizations will be those companies that are able to take a new approach to business, working closely with partners' design and manage processes that extend across traditional corporate boundaries. A company, its suppliers, and even its customers will begin to share information and activities to speed the design of a product and raise the odds of its success in the market, Hammer (2001).

While there are many examples of companies having achieved dramatic performance improvements by moving toward a more horizontal structure, there are also failures.

Research conducted by Stalk and Black (1994) found that much of what people label the 'horizontal organization' or 'organizing around processes' is not. What really happens is the modification of traditional structures to make process management easier. Stalk and Black (1994) also found that different processes have fundamentally different characteristics – and they thrive in different structures and that 'one size does not fit all'. Critics claim that BPR dehumanizes the workplace, increases managerial control, and is or has been used to justify downsizing.

The most frequent critique against BPR concerned the strict focus on efficiency and technology and the disregard for people within organizations subject to re-engineering initiatives. Re-engineering treated the people inside companies as if they were just interchangeable parts to be re-engineered. But no one wants to be 're-engineered'. Other criticisms and problems associated with BPR include: implementation of generic (best-practice) processes that did not fit specific company needs and that many organizations simply perform BPR as a one-off project with limited strategy alignment and long-term perspective. The goal of process management is not to replace vertical structures with horizontal ones. Rather, it is to intertwine and reinforce the best aspects of both – strong functional expertise and flexible, responsive processes. The new organization must deliver both and more (Stalk and Black 1994).

Business process management

Business process management (BPM) can be considered as a successor to the BPR wave of the 1990s. BPM is intended to align business processes with strategic objectives and customers' needs but also requires a change in a company's emphasis from functional to process orientation. Elzinga *et al.* (1995) offer the following definition of BPM: a systematic, structured approach to analyze, improve, control, and manage processes with the aim of improving the quality of products and services. BPM differs from business process re-engineering in that it does not aim at one-off revolutionary changes to business processes, but at their continuous evolution. The activities which constitute business process management can be grouped into three categories: design, execution and monitoring. Whereas TQM emphasized continuous improvement in a traditional (vertical) structure and BPR advocated transformational change within the horizontal organization, BPM embraces both types of change but within a more horizontal design.

The roots of business process management can be traced back to the 1980s and that of TQM philosophy, and in the 1990s of business process re-engineering (BPR). The primary aim of BPM is to improve business processes and so ensure the critical activities affecting customer satisfaction are executed in the most efficient and effective manner. It may involve small steps of improvement; and ongoing learning from best practices, resulting in a radical redesign of business processes to achieve superior performance (Hammer 1996; Zairi and Sinclair 1995) cited in Hung (2006). The term business process management as a field of study is still in its infancy, yet the interest in BPM has grown steadily over recent years, Hung (2006); principles of business process management include:

Business process management (BPM) an approach dependent upon strategic and operational elements, use of modern tools and techniques, people involvement and on a horizontal focus to best suit and deliver customer requirements in an optimum and satisfactory way

- a holistic view (BPM addresses the interdependence of strategy, people, processes and technology in achieving business objectives);
- strategic imperative;
- enabled by information technology;
- corporate-wide impact, BPM affects every aspect of an organization, from its structure (organized around processes) to its management (process leaders versus functional heads); and
- emphasizes cross-functional process management.

In addition, McKay and Radnor (1998) indicate that many organizations develop their own approach to managing business process, and that the important concepts of business process management should include:

a process alignment; and

b people involvement.

We describe each concept next.

Process alignment

Process alignment is the concept which captures how well an organization manages the fit between its processes and its institutional elements. Process alignment can be interpreted as the organizational effort needed *to make processes the platform for organizational structure*, for strategic planning, and for information technology (Hammer 1996). The aim of process alignment is to arrange the various parts of the company to work in harmony in pursuit of common organization goals, in order to improve performance and sustain competitive advantage (Weiser 2000).

Organizational theory sees organizations as requiring their structures and systems to align the contingencies of environment, strategy, technology, and so on for survival and success (see previous chapter). Weiser (2000) posits that in order to link all areas of the organization and serve as an informational lifeline throughout the change and alignment process, the organizational structure needs to be redesigned to accommodate cross-functional requirements. Hall (2002) argues that alignment requires continual focus on customers and their constantly changing requirements and should also focus on strategic direction. An alignment model is presented in Figure 10-12.

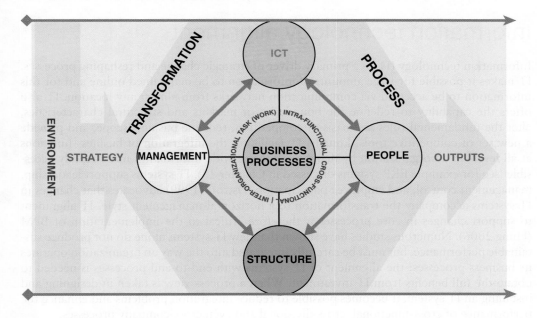

Figure 10-12

Transformation process congruence model (Adapted from Nadler (1979) in Mabey, C. (1993) and Kettinger *et al.* (1997))

Strategic alignment

In strategic theory (refer to Chapter 3), the external-internal alignment model is widely employed (Snow and Miles 1983). Organizational strategies should fit with the various parts of work in an organization. In companies that practice BPM, strategies are first developed for core processes such as customer acquisition or supply chain management. From these, functional strategies (marketing, sales, distribution and operations) are developed so that each business unit knows its contribution to the core process objectives. The aim is to achieve

Look back
See chapter 3

greater alignment between functional actions and organizational goals. Strategies for end-to-end processes which sit above and cascade into functional strategies are a defining feature of the guiding principles of business process management. Sustainable world-class performance will not occur if there is a misalignment between a firm's strategic objectives and actual market requirements (Hung 2006). In order for a firm to compete successfully through its strategic objectives, alignment must exist between the firm's strategies, actions and performance measures (Keen 1997). An effective strategy makes improvements and then so too do the capability of core and support processes. Understanding the strategic context of a BPM programme is essential to maximizing the value from process improvement.

Horizontal structural alignment

Daft (2007) acknowledges that organizational structure must accomplish two things for the organization. It must provide a framework of responsibilities, reporting relationships, and groupings, and it must provide a template for linking and coordinating organizational elements into a coherent whole. Early organization theorists stressed the vertical design of organizational charts (see the discussion at the beginning of this chapter) and relied on vertical structures. In recent years, some scholars have argued that organizations should depart from any form of vertical structure to a pure horizontal structure (Spector 1999). Many companies have started to move from a relatively functional and hierarchical structure to one with a focus on cross-functional teams and flattened organizational structures (Ostroff 1999). A horizontal management style should structure around core processes and increase the interaction of employees from different departments cultivating close working relationships and better communication (Ostroff 1999; Spector 1999). However, some of these structural changes have been successful while others have not (Hung 2006). Alignment (congruence or contingency) theory may be used to explain the importance of structure alignment in BPM.

Information technology alignment

Information technology (IT) is a primary driver of strategic change and reshaping processes. IT makes it possible for large amounts of information to be maintained online and for this information to be accessed via communication networks from almost any location. IT also offers the capability to redefine the boundaries of markets and structural characteristics, alter the fundamental rules and basis of competition, redefine business scope, and provide a new set of competitive tools. Equally, IT facilitates the integration of business functions at all levels in an organization by making corporate-wide information more readily accessible (see for example ERP systems discussed in Chapter 13). IT systems support leadership, management control, and employee participation. Ostroff (1999) advocates that changes in IT systems accompany the transformation to a horizontal management style. IT alignment to support changes in core processes is therefore critical to the implementation of BPM (Hung 2006). Numerous studies have shown that new IT systems alone do not produce sustainable performance, but must be carefully integrated into the way an organization operates its business processes; the alignment of IT systems with end-to-end processes is needed to obtain the full benefits from IT investment. When a process view is taken in designing and installing an IT system, it becomes possible to reduce integration problems and enhance the performance of cross-functional, cross-divisional and even cross-company processes.

People involvement

People involvement concerns executive commitment and employee *empowerment*. How well an organization involves people at all levels in the management of its processes has been discussed as a critical factor in organizational success. People involvement is about the extent of active participation of all members of an organization in decision-making and problem solving. It consists of sponsorship and support from senior management and the realignment of power, knowledge, and information to lower levels in the organization (Hung 2006). Organizations may encourage employee involvement to help with the achievement of performance improvement goals through: training, defining responsibilities and authorities, establishing individual and team objectives, managing process performance and evaluating results, facilitating involvement in objective setting, empowerment, reward and recognition, promoting an open communications climate, creating conditions to encourage innovation and ensuring effective teamwork.

Recognizing the importance of people in process management was one of the drivers for locating this chapter within the people part of the book. Two of the most important aspects of people involvement concern executive commitment and employee empowerment. Business process management, as one form of organization change, needs senior management support. Executive commitment has always played an important role in organizational change activity and the necessary commitment of senior managers in supporting change programmes has been extensively treated in the literature (refer to Chapter 5). Employee empowerment is thought to improve employee motivation – the willingness to exert high levels of effort toward organizational goals in order to satisfy individual need. Hung 2006 argues that motivation is translated into improved performance when people have the necessary skills and knowledge to perform well and when the technology and work situation allow people to have a significant effect on performance.

Methods, tools and techniques

In this final section, we outline a selection of methodologies, techniques, and tools (MTTs) for conducting business process change projects. There are numerous methodologies, techniques, and tools for conducting business process change projects. BPR projects typically include attempts to transform the organizational subsystems of management (style, values, and measures), people (jobs, skills, and culture), information technology, and organizational structures, including team and coordination mechanisms. Changes to these subsystems are viewed through the analytic lens of the business process (intrafunctional, cross-functional, and interorganizational). A BPR project is a set of coordinated efforts to modify various organizational subsystems through business process change. Methodologies generally focus on cross-functional and interorganizational processes. They take the customer view and leverage IT's coordination and processing capabilities. A six-staged BPR framework shown as Figure 10-13 (see Kettinger *et al.* (1997)) outlining project stages and activities, is considered next.

The first (envision) stage, in Figure 10-13, typically involves a BPR project champion obtaining the support of senior management. Next, a business case is submitted for re-engineering via benchmarking, identifying external customer needs, and cost benefit analysis (initiation stage) and 'buy-in' sought. A project is established and team formed. As with all rational problem solving approaches the next stage involves understanding the current situation (diagnosis). Current processes are documented in terms of process attributes such as activities, resources, communication, roles, IT, and cost. Next a solution is sought through the redesign stage. In this stage a new process design is developed. This is accomplished by devising process design alternatives through brainstorming and creativity techniques. The new design should meet strategic objectives and fit with the human resource and IT architectures. Documentation and prototyping of the new process is typically conducted, and a design completed of new information systems to support the new process. The new design must be implemented through change (reconstruct stage). Change management techniques are utilized to ensure a smooth passage to new process responsibilities and human resource roles. During this stage, the IT platform and systems are implemented, and the users go through training and transition. In the last stage (evaluate) of a BPR methodology the new process is monitored and evaluated to determine if it met its goals (Kettinger *et al.* 1997).

Methodologies a collection of problem-solving methods governed by a set of principles and a common philosophy for solving targeted problems

Techniques a set of specific steps for accomplishing a desired outcome

Tools instruments or certain tangible aids used when performing a task or to support one or more techniques

Benchmarking a process of systematically comparing your own organizational structure, processes and performance against those of best practice organizations, to achieve sustainable business excellence

Figure 10-13

BPR framework (Adapted from
Kettinger (1997))

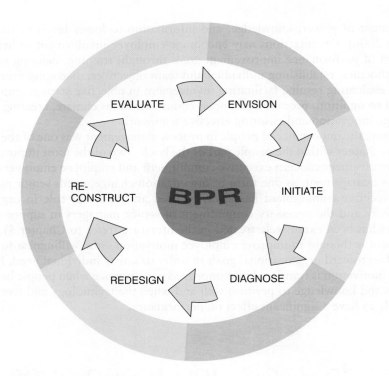

Tools and techniques

Research conducted by Kettinger *et al.* (1997) indicated that at least 72 techniques are used
to accomplish activities associated with TQM/BPR or BPM projects and a set of 102 tools
were identified. For example, techniques used in the diagnostic stage include process mapping to assist project teams in 'documenting the existing processes'. Consultants sometimes
use simple depiction techniques such as process flow charts or more structured techniques.
Techniques used in the reconstruct (implementation) stage include force field analysis.
Tools may be used in order to design and develop process models and other documentation; to initiate improvement projects; to investigate problem causes or establish cause-
and-effect relationships. Tools may make use of numerical or non-numerical data and all
members of the organization should receive training in the application of improvement
tools. A sample of appropriate tools and techniques is shown in Figure 10-14.

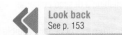

Look back
See p. 153

In this chapter we have explained the process view of organizations and identified different approaches to manage processes embedded within the organizational structure. We
finish this chapter with comments from Stewart and Jacoby (1992) who argue the 21st-
century organization arises at the joining together of three streams. One is described by
the term 'high-involvement workplace', meaning operations with self-managing teams and
other devices for empowering employees; a second is a new emphasis on managing business processes and third is the evolution of information technology to the point where
knowledge, accountability, and results can be distributed rapidly anywhere in the organization. The trick is to put them together into a coherent, practical design.

This part of the book has focused on human resources and the next section considers
information and IT resources. This chapter is located between the two parts. In short, we
have organized reading around the three streams suggested by Stewart and Jacoby (1992).
Collectively, human, process and information resources are central to resource-based views
of the firm and the attainment of sustainable competitive advantage from the way resources
are managed and configured. We believe it is important to take a multidisciplinary view of
business problems and challenges and that solutions are rarely subject area specific and
more a tangle of congruent themes and components, configured for the context they are
presented within. Figure 10-12, highlights the interaction of people, processes, information
and IT resources, management and structure when seeking to attain strategic goals – themselves a reflection of the environment. In discussing, the environment, strategy and change
we suggest this chapter plays a pivotal role in binding together other chapters of the book.

Figure 10-14

Tools and techniques for improvement

Tool / Technique	Description & Application
Flow chart 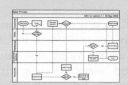	To describe an existing or design a new process. A flow chart illustrates the steps in a process. By visualizing the process, a flow chart can quickly help identify bottlenecks or inefficiencies where the process can be streamlined or improved.
Cause-and-effect diagram 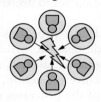	To facilitate problem solving from symptom to cause to solution. The cause-and-effect diagram (fish bone diagram) is a tool used for thinking through and displaying relationships between a given effect and its potential causes. Cause and effect analysis helps think through causes of a problem thoroughly. The major benefit is they encourage consideration of all possible causes of the problem, rather than just the obvious.
Brainstorming 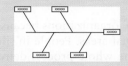	To identify possible solutions to problems and potential opportunities for quality improvement. Brainstorming is a technique for tapping the creative thinking of a team and generating a list of ideas, problems or issues.
Benchmarking	To compare a process against those processes of recognized leaders to identify opportunities for quality improvement. Competitive benchmarking involves analysis of available information about a competing company. This data is then used as a goal for your own improvement efforts. Many companies benchmark against those recognized as 'best in industry'.
Data-collection form	To gather data systematically to obtain a clear picture of the facts. A form used to collect data in a consistent manner.
Histogram 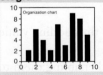	To display the pattern of variation of data and then support decision-making about where to focus improvement efforts. Data is displayed as a series of rectangles of equal width but varying height. A graphical representation of a frequency distribution.
Pareto diagram 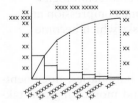	To display, in order of importance, the contribution of each item to the total effect. A simple graphical technique for ranking items. A chart used to graphically summarize and display the relative importance of the differences between groups of data.
Scatter diagram 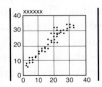	To discover and confirm relationships between two associated sets of data. A chart that plots the relationship of one numeric variable with another on a horizontal and vertical axis, and determines the degree of dependency or interdependency.

Summary of key learning points

Work is the emphasis of this chapter – how, like the people resources, it is organized and designed. In the case of the international organization, work activities transform inputs into outputs (products and services) for the benefit of customers, adding value along the way. We compared and contrasted the traditional (bureaucratic and 'vertical') view with process (horizontal) views on organizational design and structure. Traditional (bureaucratic) organizations typically adopt a hierarchical and functional perspective on structure, emphasizing command and control and organize work into specialist areas managed vertically by similar specialists (functions).

Organizations grouping activities by function are known as 'silo' organizations because each functional area is distinct and isolated from all other functional areas. People in silo organizations tend to focus on their individual task rather than the whole process delivered as a cross-functional team. It has been argued that organizing around processes, as opposed to functions, permits greater self-management and allows companies to dismantle unneeded supervisory structures.

We defined what is meant by a business process and explained how processes are designed and managed. A process is a structured set of activities designed to produce a specified output for a particular customer or market. It has a beginning, an end, and clearly identified inputs and outputs. A process is therefore a structure for action, for how work is done. The systematic identification and management of the processes employed within an organization and particularly the interactions between such processes is referred to as the 'process approach'. The most visible difference between a process enterprise and a traditional organization is the existence of process owners – senior managers with end-to-end responsibility for individual processes. However, companies making the shift to a process enterprise must examine the basic elements of their organizational infrastructure, particularly in terms of culture, teamwork, information and reward systems.

Traditional ways to measure performance, determine compensation, provide training, and even organize facilities are tailored to vertical units, not processes, and to individuals, not teams. We explained how the process view of organizations may provide the international organization with a source of sustainable competitive advantage and enable the attainment of strategic goals. The process approach:

1 presents an opportunity to improve effectiveness and efficiency thus adding value, differentiating products and services and reducing cost;

2 may lead to the enrichment of work by empowering people and enabling them to take a holistic perspective thereby seeing the value of their contribution;

3 may make better use of enterprise-wide information systems and technologies which can make the organization more responsive, enable time compression and further motivate people through the removal of mundane tasks which become automated.

Managing processes involves establishing ownership, defining boundaries, documenting the processes, identifying control points and measurements and monitoring and taking corrective action where necessary. Business process management (BPM) is intended to align business processes with strategic objectives and customers' needs but also requires a change in a company's emphasis from functional to process orientation. The primary aim of BPM is to improve business processes and so ensure the critical activities affecting customer satisfaction are executed in the most efficient and effective manner. Process alignment is the concept which captures how well an organization manages the fit between its processes and its institutional elements. It can be interpreted as the organizational effort needed to make processes the platform for organizational structure, for strategic planning, and for information technology.

Review questions

Opening case study

1 Discuss why 'feedback' should be critical to Dell's success.

2 Imagine visiting Dell, observing activities and meetings – what might you expect to see as evidence of a continuous improvement culture?

3 What benefits might arise from holding meetings which are attended by all divisions in the company – manufacturing, sales, finance, human resources, accounts receivable, product organization? How might 'key statistics' help them? You should make use of the structural, coordination and control concepts introduced in the previous chapter.

4 Dell's PCs are built to customer specifications upon receipt of an order. What advantages might this give Dell? Are there any disadvantages?

5 According to Dell (1994) 'many of our competitors are beginning to attempt to duplicate some of our strategic advantages. However … there are a number of aspects of our business which are not easily duplicated.' Critically review the Dell business model and then discuss, in groups, why it might be difficult to copy Dell's approach. You should revisit and discuss the concept of sustainable competitive advantage discussed earlier in the book. You should also consider culture and practice in particular.

6 Discuss key processes that might enable Dell to improve customer satisfaction.

7 Review Dell's business model. What design and structural configuration might best support the way it does business? You should draw on the theories presented in the previous chapter to help you frame an answer.

8 Discuss the information requirements at Dell. What information is communicated between customers and Dell and between Dell and its partners: contract manufacturers, component suppliers, other suppliers, logistic and distribution companies, systems integrators and repair companies? How important to Dell are business processes both within and between companies? To what extent will processes at Dell be standard and global as opposed to differentiated and local?

BPR

Write an essay arguing that BPR is more than a 1990s 'fad'.

Process view

List and describe the infrastructure elements needed to support the process view.

Structure

Explain why 'silo' organizations may be less effective or efficient as contemporary international organizational designs.

Process management

Describe the elements of a business process and discuss what is involved in the management of processes.

Empowerment

Critically discuss why empowerment is a central concept to the process enterprise.

Group activity

Identify five MNCs. Allocate one or more to each group member. Next, individually, research the web and recent annual reports for your allotted company. Investigate the company and identify references to 'quality', 'continuous improvement' and 'quality standards' in the material considered. Discuss each company as a group. For each company, discuss whether you felt their process or quality orientation was appropriate, over or understated.

References

Ackermann, F., Wall, S., van der Meer, R. and Borman, M. (1999) 'Taking a strategic view of BPR to develop a multidisciplinary framework', *Journal of the Operational Research Society* 50:195–204.

Armistead, C. (1996) 'Principles of business process management', *Managing Service Quality* 6(6):48–52.

Ashayeri, J., Keij, R. and Bröker, A. (1998) 'Global business process re-engineering: a system dynamics-based approach', *International Journal of Operations & Production Management* 18(9/10):817–831.

Bozarth, C. and Handfield, R. (2006) *Introduction to Operations and Supply Chain Management with Advanced Decision Support Tools*, Englewood Cliffs: Prentice Hall.

CEN Management Centre (2005) 'Quality management systems – Fundamentals and vocabulary BS EN ISO 9000:2005', European committee for standardization (CEN).

CEN Management Centre (2000) 'Quality management systems – Guidelines for performance improvements BS EN ISO 9004:2000', European committee for standardization (CEN).

Curtis, B., Kellner, M. and Over, J. (1992) 'Process Modeling', *Association for Computing Machinery communications of the ACM* (September 1992) 35(9):75–90.

Daft, R. L. (2007) *Organization Theory and Design* (9 ed), Cincinnati, Ohio: Cengage Learning.

Davenport, T. H. (1993) 'Need radical innovation and continuous improvement? Integrate process reengineering and TQM', *Planning Review* 21(3):6–12.

Davenport, T. (1994) 'Managing in the New World of Process', *Public Productivity & Management Review* (Winter 1994) 18(2):133–147.

Davenport, T. (1996) 'The Fad That Forgot People', *Fast Company, Premiere issue* 70–74.

Davenport, T. and Stoddard, D. (1994b) 'Reengineering: Business Change of Mythic Proportions?', *MIS Quarterly* (June 1994):121–127.

Decker, S. (2004) 7 Tips for 'Getting' Six Sigma Marketing (October 02, 2004) http://decker.typepad.com/welcome/2004/10/7_tips_for_gett.html.

Dell, M. (1994) 'Making the Right Choices for the New Consumer', *Managing Service Quality* 4(2):22–25.

DeToro, I. and McCabe, T. (1997) 'How to stay flexible and elude fads', *Quality Progress* 30(3):55–60.

Elzinga, D. J., Horak, T., Lee, C.-Y. and Bruner, C. (1995) 'Business Process Management: Survey and Methodology. *IEEE Transactions on Engineering Management* 42(2):119–28.

Grover, V. and Jeong, S. (1995) 'The implementation of business process reengineering', *Journal of Management Information Systems* (Summer 1995) 12(1):109–144.

Hall, M. J. (2002) 'Aligning the organization to increase performance results', *Public Manager* 31(2):7–10.

Hammer, M. (1990) 'Reengineering Work: Don't Automate, Obliterate', *Harvard Business Review* (July/August 1990) 68(4):104–112.

Hammer, M. (2001a) 'The Super efficient Company', *Harvard Business Review* (September 2001) 79(8):82–91.

Hammer, M. (2001b) 'The new business agenda', *Strategy & Leadership* 29(6) – Idea file.

Hammer, M. (2007) 'The Process Audit', *Harvard Business Review* (April 2007) 85(4):111–123.

Hammer, M. and Stanton, S. (1999) 'How Process Enterprises Really Work', *Harvard Business Review* (November/December 1999) 77(6):108–118.

Handfield, R. and Nichols, E. (2002) *Supply Chain Redesign: Transforming Supply Chains into Integrated Value Systems*, Upper Saddle River, NJ: Financial Times Press.

Harkness, W. L., Kettinger, W. J. and Segars, A. H. (1996) 'Sustaining Process Improvement and Innovation in the Information Systems Function: Lessons learned at the Bose Corporation', *MIS Quarterly* (September 1996) (20:3):349–368.

Holland, C., Shaw, D. and Kawalek, P. (2005) 'BP's multi-enterprise asset management system', *Information and Software Technology* 47:999–1007.

Hung, R. (2006) 'Business Process Management as Competitive Advantage: a Review and Empirical Study', *Total Quality Management* 17(1):21–40.

Jones, C. (1994) 'Improving Your Key Business Processes', *The TQM Magazine* 6(2):25–29.

Keen, P. (1997) *The Process Edge: Creating Value Where It Counts*, Boston, MA: Harvard Business School Press.

Kettinger, W., Teng, J. and Guha, S. (1997) 'Business Process Change: A Study of Methodologies, Techniques, and Tools', *MIS Quarterly* (March 1997):55–80.

Laguna, M. and Marklund, J. (2005) *Business Process Modeling, Simulation and Design*, Upper Saddle River, NJ: Prentice Hall.

Lee, R. and Dale, B. (1998) 'Business process management: a review and evaluation', *Business Process Management Journal* 4(3):214–225.

Mabey, C. (1993) *Managing Change*, London:The Open University.

Marx, M. (2005) Dell Inc. – Six Sigma, the Enabler 23 February 2005 accessed at 2005http://www .sixsigmacompanies.com/archive/dell_inc_six_sigma_the_enabler.html on May 14th 2007.

McAdam, R. (1996) 'An integrated business improvement methodology to refocus business improvement efforts', *Journal of Business Process Reengineering and Management* 2(1):63–71.

McKay, A. and Radnor, Z. (1998) A characterization of a business process, *International Journal of Operational and Production Management* 18(9/10):924–936.

(Nadler 1993) in Mabey, C. and Mayon-White, B. (1993) *Managing Change*, London: The Open University.

Ostroff, F. (1999) *The Horizontal Organization*, New York: Oxford University Press.

Pickering, J. W. and Matson, R. E. (1992) 'Why executive development programs (alone) don't work', *Training and Development* 46(5):91–95.

Porter, M. E. and Millar, V. E. (1985) 'How information gives you a competitive advantage', *Harvard Business Review* (July–August 1963):149–174.

Powell, T. (1995) 'Total Quality Management as Competitive Advantage: A Review and Empirical Study', *Strategic Management Journal* 16:15–37.

Plsek, P. E. (1997) *Creativity, Innovation and Quality*, Milwaukee, Wisconsin: ASQC Quality Press.

Sandoe, K., Corbitt, G. and Boykin, R. (2001) *Enterprise Integration*, New York: Wiley.

Shaw, D., Holland, C., Kawalek, P. and Snowdon, D. (2007) 'Elements of a business process management system: theory and practice', *Business Process Management Journal* 13(1):91–107.

Snow, C. C. and Miles, R. E. (1983) 'The role of strategy in the development of a general theory of organizations', *Advances in Strategic Management* 2:231–259.

Spector, B. A. (1999) 'The horizontal organization: what the organization of the future actually looks like and how it delivers value to customers', *Academy of Management Executive* 13(2):97–98.

Stalk, G. and Black, J. (1994) 'The myth of the horizontal organization', *Canadian Business Review* (Winter 1994) 21(4):26–30.

Stewart, T. and Jacoby, R. (1992) 'The Search For The Organization Of Tomorrow', *Fortune* 125(10):92–98.

Stoddard, D. and Jarvenpaa, S. (1995) 'Business Process Reengineering: Tactics for Managing Radical Change', *Journal of Management Information Systems* (Summer 1995) 12(1): 81–108.

Southwick, K. (2003) The pragmatic radical CEO Michael Dell is about to apply his tried-and-true business formula far beyond the PC, Published: 21 November 2003, CNET news.com.com/ The+pragmatic+radical/2008-1001_3-5110303.html.

Tischler, L. (2002) Can Kevin Rollins Find the Soul of Dell?, Fast Company Issue 64, October 2002, Page 110, available at http://www.fastcompany.com/magazine/64/rollins.html.

Weiser, J. R. (2000) Organizational alignment: are we heading in the same direction?, *The Kansas Banker* 90(1):11–15.

Zairi, M. and Sinclair, D. (1995) 'BPR and process management: a survey of current practice and future trends in integrated management', *Business Process Re-engineering and Management Journal* 1(1):8–29.

Zairi, M. (1997) 'Business process management: a boundaryless approach to modern competitiveness', *Business Process Management Journal* 3(1):64–80.

Zucchi, F. and Edwards, J. (1999) 'Human resource management aspects of business process reengineering: a survey', *Business Process Management Journal* 5(4):325–344.

Suggestions for further reading

Journals

Business Process Management Journal – This journal examines how a variety of business processes intrinsic to organizational efficiency and effectiveness are integrated and managed for competitive success. This journal provides insights into best practice management of key processes. The journal will help to build a deep appreciation of how to manage business processes effectively by disseminating best practice, and enhances your learning through a critical evaluation of the experience of others. Journal Home Page: http://info.emeraldinsight.com/products/journals/journals.htm?PHPSESSID=tqv5fdr5jkjsl e4urq38ruh613&id=bpmj.

See also various management information system or quality management journals.

Key articles

Scholars of this subject area have often read the following:

1 Hammer, M. (1990) 'Reengineering Work: Don't Automate, Obliterate', *Harvard Business Review* (July/August 1990) 68(4):104–112.
2 Powell, T. (1995) 'Total Quality Management As Competitive Advantage: A Review and Empirical Study', *Strategic Management Journal* 16:15–37.
3 Kettinger, W., Teng, J. and Guha, S. (1997) 'Business Process Change: A Study of Methodologies, Techniques, and Tools', *MIS Quarterly* (March 1997):55–80.
4 Davenport, T. and Stoddard, D. (1994) 'Reengineering: Business Change of Mythic Proportions?', *MIS Quarterly* (June 1994):121–127.
5 Hammer, M. and Stanton, S. (1999) 'How Process Enterprises Really Work', *Harvard Business Review* (November/December 1999) 77(6):108–118.
6 Grover, V. and Jeong, S. (1995) 'The implementation of business process reengineering', *Journal of Management Information Systems* (Summer 1995) 12(1):109–144.

Part III Summary

Part III was delivered in four related chapters: Managing human resources; Managing difference – culture; International organization design and structure and Global business processes. Our aim was to identify ways in which the performance of the international organization may be improved through the better use of human resources and the effective management of people.

In Chapter 7 we focused on worldwide human capital and its management in the international organization. In particular we focused on the role of the specialist HRM function both centrally and locally in acquiring, developing and motivating HC in order to improve (productive) performance and develop a sustainable competitive advantage. HC (or human resources) are seen as strategically important due to their difficult to imitate attributes which ensure any derived competitive advantage is sustainable.

Economic and social arguments (creativity, improved marketplace understanding, stakeholder approval and winning talent) were proposed in Chapter 8 to manage the international organization as a diverse and multicultural entity. Strategic arguments were also offered for such an entity through RBV theory – a diverse and multicultural organization is difficult to imitate. However, we also recognized the propensity for the driving out of diversity from organizations. This may then manifest as costly business problems such as poor motivation, decreased loyalty, absenteeism, high labour turnover and legal action. Developing cultural competence and managing the performance of multicultural and diverse groups requires some understanding of the way people think and behave. The international business manager or professional must learn to see the world from other perspectives if they are to understand and manage the behaviour of themselves and others worldwide. Such an understanding is facilitated through an appreciation of perception. People may 'see' the world and events occurring within it differently; they may therefore respond differently.

Chapter 9 focused on how to make efficient and effective use of human resources in order to attain goals and derive a sustainable competitive advantage through design structure, coordination and control. We commenced by identifying the purpose of design – to divide up organizational activities, allocate resources, tasks and goals and to coordinate and control activities so that goals can be achieved. An appropriate design might yield benefits such as efficiency and scale, access to specialized and location-embedded resources, enhanced innovation and the creation of operational flexibility. Design can impact upon performance through employee motivation, commitment and loyalty and has the ability to link interdependent activities. Arguments as to why organizational parts should be configured in particular ways were presented through contingency theory. The organization design typically breaks up the workforce into parts that must work together. The concept of dependence was investigated and the possible means to overcome dependence problems, i.e. coordination mechanisms. Assuring organizational parts work together productively is a matter of coordination. Control systems, on the other hand, seek to assure organizational goals are attained. A variety of management control strategies, formal (bureaucratic) and informal ('clan' or 'cultural') control, were discussed.

Finally, Chapter 10 emphasized work and how, like the people resources, it is organized and designed. We compared and contrasted the traditional (bureaucratic and 'vertical') view with process (horizontal) views on organizational design and structure. We explained how the process view of organizations may provide the international organization with a source of sustainable competitive advantage and enable the attainment of strategic goals. The process approach:

1 presents an opportunity to improve effectiveness and efficiency thus adding value, differentiating products and services and reducing cost;

2 may lead to the enrichment of work by empowering people and enabling them to take a holistic perspective thereby seeing the value of their contribution;

3 may make better use of enterprise-wide information systems and technologies which can make the organization more responsive, enable time compression and further motivate people through the removal of mundane tasks which become automated.

Drawing on process theories, towards the end of Part III, we introduced a further diagram that helps summarize how such transformational resources interact in the work environment. We discussed the need to create a 'high-involvement workplace' (operations with self-managing teams and other devices for empowering employees – people, management and structure); a new emphasis on managing business processes and apply and align information technology to the point where knowledge, accountability, and results can be distributed rapidly anywhere in the organization. The international organization must put all together into a coherent, practical design. In the next part of the book we consider ICT in more detail.

PART IV

Managing information
and technological resources

Part IV

Managing information and technological resources

At the beginning of the book we noted that organizations seek to meet their goals through superior performance. We suggested there were many ways by which the international organization can achieve this, such as through the possession of sustainable competitive advantages. We argued that operational effectiveness (performing similar activities better than rivals perform them – being effective and efficient) and strategy are essential for superior performance. A company can outperform rivals in the long run, only if it can establish a difference that it can preserve. Such differences often require constant work to develop and maintain. The international organization must deliver greater value or greater comparable value at a lower cost or both. Differences between companies in cost, price, product or service derive from the hundreds of activities undertaken by the organization and its partners. Cost is incurred performing activities through the use of resources (input or transformational). Organizations are therefore consistently in pursuit of operational improvements in productivity, quality and the time taken to complete tasks. They must get more out of resources, employ more advanced technology, motivate and enable human resources better. They must also seek out differences in the way they do things to create unique and valuable positions. In the introductory chapter we emphasized the need to leverage resources and capabilities.

In the previous part (Chapters 7 to 10) we focused on people resources, the role of human resource specialists, the need for structure, coordination and control, the need to design work and motivate people to complete work tasks and to manage diversity. We noted that people could be enabled by technology-machines replacing manual tasks and information systems helping with thinking activities. Communications technologies support coordination and control and, with information flow, tie or unite organizational parts so that the organizational system can attain its goals through synergy and holism. We have adopted a resource-based approach to this and the previous part of the book. The fundamental principle of the RBV is that the basis for competitive advantage lies primarily in the application of bundles of valuable resources which, when integrated, create capabilities and organizational competence.

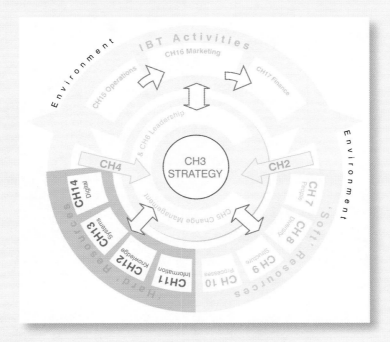

While we focused on human resources in the previous part, people are arguably components of information systems also. In this part of the book we focus on information system resources which include hardware, software, communication technologies and data. Systems theory is used to unite such resources. In this part we consider knowledge as an information resource. In some cases that knowledge is embedded in people (human capital) and in other cases is embedded in culture or organizational systems. We also consider the hardware, software and processes and communication technologies that enable its capture, transfer and use in transformational activities. Various IT resources considered in this part of the book enable the free flow of information (enterprise systems) throughout the organization in support of commerce, planning, decision-making, control and coordination. Finally we consider the role of Internet technologies as the 'glue' and 'conduit' for bundling resources together, making them available for work and value adding activities. We will argue that information system resources are strategically important resources, enabling and informing strategy, creating capabilities and competences when bundled with other resources. Collectively, this and the previous part of the book can be used to explain the organizational system proposed by Leavitt (1965), see Figure 5-2 and when coupled with the strategy part provide a detailed understanding of Nadler and Tushman's organizational model shown in Figure 5-3. They define what the organization is and how it competes in the global marketplace and provide a strong foundation for the final part of the book which makes use of this organizational system in the primary international business and trade activities of production, marketing and sales.

This part is structured into four chapters: information resources (foundation concepts); knowledge resources; enterprise systems; and digital (net) technologies.

Look back
See chapter 5, p. 148

Chapter 11

Managing information resources to add value and compete internationally

Introduction

Information resources: data, information and knowledge

Supporting international business

Decision-making flows

Competing with information resources

Enterprise and global information needs

Key concepts

■ Data ■ Information ■ Knowledge ■ Wisdom ■ Technology ■ Databases ■ MIS ■ DSS
■ Decision-making ■ Planning ■ Coordination ■ Control ■ Value ■ Value chain
■ Value system ■ Competitive advantage

By the end of this chapter you will be able to:

■ Differentiate between the concepts of data, information, knowledge and wisdom resources

■ Identify the role of information resources within the international organization

■ Explain how decisions are made within international organizations and the role of information in improving decision-making

■ Discuss how information resources can be used to deliver value and help the international organization compete

Active learning case

The Duckworth Group

'It was not the first time the issue of *information* and *knowledge management* had arisen at a Duckworth management meeting. "Sending my staff to China, India and South Africa to transfer knowledge is expensive in time and money but it lets us export our core competencies and share our intellectual property (borne out of central R&D efforts)" proclaimed the Technical Director. The Marketing Director faced similar problems. His central business groups could manage their MNC clients but there was still a need to coordinate the subsidiaries that catered for local taste and needs. Centralized procurement benefited from supplier discounts due to bulk purchasing but many materials needed to be sourced locally by subsidiaries. Finally, the Finance Director required visibility of expenditure and receivables throughout the group in order to compile financial reports and furnish other managers with data and information required for planning, control and decision making. A lack of systems integration, incompatible technologies and data structures made this a resource-hungry and time-consuming process. Aside from ongoing problems, the group was constantly seeking out new opportunities and was in constant need of market data and intelligence to meet new opportunities and counter threats.'

Duckworth operate within the food sector. According to Livingstone Guarantee (M&A specialists) by value, the food and beverage-processing industry remains the UK's single largest manufacturing sector. Around a fifth of consumer expenditure is spent on food and beverage. Industry exports of food and beverage products from the UK are significant. The industry is made up of the chilled food, beverages and confectionery sectors. Among the key trends in the industry is consolidation (through M&A) and the movement of production to cheaper countries (off-shoring). In order to compete, companies need to be innovative and cost conscious. In order to maintain a customer and product focus Duckworth created alcoholic beverages, confectionery, dairy, savoury and soft drinks business groups (responsible for product marketing). These headquartered staff gained understanding of requirements in key international markets by frequently visiting overseas subsidiaries and partners. Aside from the business groups receiving market intelligence, they also made such visits to develop the knowledge and expertise of all staff representing the Duckworth Group worldwide, a process they called '*exporting our core competency*'. These activities, plus conferences and headquarters-delivered training, were all aimed at sharing with the regions, headquarters skill and knowledge base to assist in local growth. Such coaching and mentoring aimed to develop local regional staff making them more self-sufficient and thus allowing the Duckworth export sales team to focus more time and effort on developing new regions. Duckworth believed their domestic market (UK) would always be the key to their success. However, they also appreciated they must understand markets and consumer trends on a global basis and fulfil home-country customers' requirements and meet supply challenges for international brands. They believed that by developing the skills of their staff in the international arena they would be prepared for the challenges of operating an increasingly global business.

Headquartered in Old Trafford, Manchester, England, this medium sized international organization had subsidiaries in China, South Africa (Cape Town), and India (Bangalore) with a technical centre in Lebanon. Marketing, R&D, Finance, HR and other key functional departments were located at the headquarters. Due to expansion, manufacture was moved to a new purpose built production facility in Runcorn (UK). Each of the subsidiaries had production capabilities. A highly specialized purchasing team audited suppliers and screened products from around the world to ensure only the finest ingredients available were procured. The sales teams were renowned for building lasting and professional relationships with their global client base. An experienced and knowledgeable shipping and distribution made sure products arrived at their destination on time – every time. A distribution fleet ensured efficient service was maintained – right up to the moment of delivery. As well as

The Duckworth Group has long been regarded as one of the world's leading suppliers of flavours to the soft drinks industry. They also offer a wide range of flavourings for alcoholic drinks, confectionery and bakery products and ice cream. For over a century, the group has been at the forefront of flavour research and development and has a reputation for innovation and quality, which once made it Britain's largest privately owned producer of flavourings and fruit compounds. As far back as the 1920s the company began exporting from the UK, building a network of business associates in some 25 locations worldwide allowing them to develop a presence in overseas markets. These relationships, coupled with the group's regional centres gave Duckworth a robust distribution network, allowing them to reach out to key customers globally. The group more than quadrupled in size throughout the 1990s and into the new millennium. Acquisitions, organic growth and a major investment programme all prepared the business to meet the current and future demands of the food and beverage industries in which they operate. New process facilities, world-class logistics, major technical advances, and extensive R&D programmes helped the group anticipate customer requirements and continue to grow market share.

investing in people, the Duckworth Group (post millennium) embarked upon a programme of substantial investments in its IT infrastructure, embracing both international telecommunications and corporate computing. As evidence of this commitment, the company completed a transition to SAP R/3 (Enterprise Resource Planning software). The Duckworth Group considered product development to be a key element in the future growth of their company. That is why they expanded their laboratory facilities, and more than doubled their dedicated development resource. As a direct result of this growing leading-edge resource, their teams of flavourists were able to work in environments offering optimum scope for creativity in flavour development – drawing on the latest international market and product data as well as over 110 years of creative flavouring knowledge.

Websites:

(1) www.livguarantee.com/image_uploads/LG%20Food%20survey%2005.pdf
(2) www.foodnavigator.com/news/ng.asp?id=47598-cargill-muscles-in
(3) www.ukbusinesspark.co.uk/bpfood04.htm (4)www.cee-foodindustry.com/news/ng.asp?id=52493-duckworth-aims-for

Introduction

One of the primary goals of today's global organization is to ensure the free flow of quality data and information within its value system and to use such resources to operate, add value and compete.

As could be seen from the opening case study, the international organization faces many challenges associated with the management of information resources. The required information may be generated from within or outside the organization and may be needed by parts of the organization that did not generate it – i.e. it needs to be shared. Not only must information resources be shared within the organization, but, in some cases, with suppliers, customers and other stakeholders working in the value system. Furthermore, information resources must exhibit the required quality attributes of accuracy, integrity, be complete and available when and where required. Technology is used to enable the sharing of information resources by providing collection, storage and dissemination capabilities.

Technology and information represent 'hard' and 'soft' resources available to the international organization. Collectively, information systems (IS) and associated technology (IT) can be a source of sustainable competitive advantage (refer to the resource-based view); help with positioning strategies and may counter industry forces enabling the organization to better compete in the global marketplace. Such resources can reduce uncertainty and improve the quality of managerial activities such as decision-making, planning, coordination, control and communication and support both transformational work activities and the linkages between them within the value chain and the value system. As a resource, information may be created, manipulated and shared. Unlike most resources that deplete when used, information and knowledge can be shared, and actually grow through application. Within this foundation chapter and the next chapter we focus on information resources and their role in international business and managing the international organization. Chapters 13 and 14 focus more on information technology.

Within this chapter we focus on three related information resources: data, information and knowledge. Information *came of age* in the 1970s and 1980s after the industrial age and before the 'knowledge economy'. The information age refers to a time when information was a scarce resource and its capture and distribution generated competitive advantage. When information ceased being scarce, the knowledge economy (the use of knowledge to produce economic benefits) was born. In the knowledge economy wealth is created through the economic exploitation of understanding. Within such a society, information technology plays a central role in production and information resources are considered productive assets. Peter Drucker set the foundation for the knowledge economy in a book The Effective Executive where he described the difference between the manual worker and the knowledge worker. A manual worker works with hands whereas a knowledge worker works with the head to produce ideas, knowledge, and information. Adopting a business perspective, Eustace (2003) asks how the modern knowledge economy differs from what preceded it. He suggests that it is now widely accepted that winning strategies are more often grounded in the accumulation and creative exploitation of intangibles that are more difficult to replicate.

According to Eustace (2003), we have witnessed a fundamental shift in the corporate value system, away from physical and financial assets (now commoditized) towards the creative exploitation of a nexus of intangible assets and competences – mainly in the form of distinctive capabilities derived from knowledge intangibles. In the present era, the 'intangible economy', key factors of production include: knowledge assets (what people know and put into use), collaboration assets (who people interact with to create value), engagement assets (commitment and motivation), and time (how quickly value is created). These are the four key resources from which economic activity and competitive advantage are primarily derived and delivered.

The international organization faces several key challenges: how to use information resources for competitive advantage; how to safeguard information resources; how

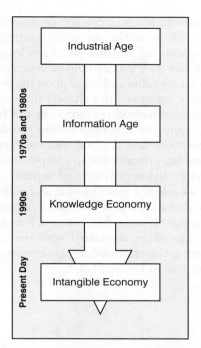

Figure 11-1

Information and the economy:
a timeline

to share information resources globally throughout the international organization, its partners, suppliers and customers and how to determine the extent with which to harmonize its IS and IT strategy worldwide, i.e. whether or not to adopt a global or multi-domestic perspective. The challenges are far from simple. For example, whereas in the information age, information systems were a source of competitive advantage, the move to open source and off-the-shelf systems has eroded benefits, making imitation much easier. Information resources must be safeguarded not only from legitimate competitors but also from those intent on stealing and copying intellectual property. While Internet and related technologies may support the sharing of information resources over borders; culture, language and legal systems may act as barriers, inhibiting information flow worldwide. Many (global) companies recognize the benefits of a homogeneous and integrated IS and IT system yet many international organizations grow by acquisition, inheriting disparate and legacy systems that may not easily fit with existing systems, thus fragmenting the organizations' information architecture and flows (see The Bosch Group case study described later.) We will consider such challenges, and more, throughout this part of the book. From a strategic perspective we consider both external (supporting positioning strategies) and internal (supporting the RBV) information resources available to the organization.

Look forward
See p. 371

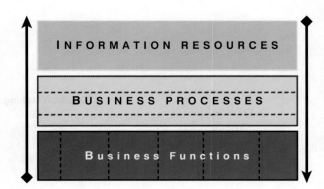

Figure 11-2

Business information resource perspectives

In many textbooks, information resources are considered from the perspective of discrete business functions such as marketing or accounting. This can result in a lack of integration and problems with information and knowledge flow within and between organizations. In this chapter we take a more holistic perspective (see Figure 11-2) of the use of information assets to create value and build upon the previous human resource and work design chapters. We have organized this chapter into four key sections. We start by identifying and defining key information resources. In the following sections we focus on the use of such resources and the way information resources support business functions and processes, i.e. operations and decision making. Next we investigate how such resources enable the international organization to compete locally and globally. Their role in shaping products and services, industry forces and improving value chain and system activities is discussed. Finally, we adopt a more holistic and global perspective by evaluating the information needs of the global enterprise. Problems of dispersed value chain activities, coordination and control are highlighted – this section acts as a foundation for Chapters 13 and 14. Finally we discuss key issues associated with the management of information resources. A diagram indicating the relationship between the information resources and key business activities can be seen in Figure 11-3.

Figure 11-3

The application of information resources: concept map

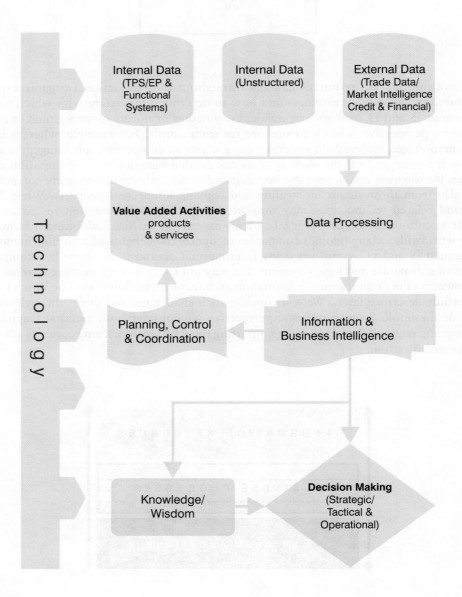

Information resources: data, information and knowledge

In previous chapters we discussed how organizations, operating in dynamic environments, often pursue *empowerment* strategies. They have flat organizations and autonomous workers. This creates a flexible and adaptive organization. Yet autonomous employees need access to the organization's information resources if they are to make timely, quality-decisions. Their activities must be controlled and coordinated – both tasks supported through information resources and ICT. A goal of today's organization is having 'the right information, in the right place, in the right format, at the right time – at the right cost'. Additionally, exploiting an organization's proprietary information as a strategic asset remains a significant contemporary challenge. Information resources management (IRM) is an emerging discipline that helps managers assess and exploit their information assets for business development. Organizations use information resources for many purposes, such as to: assess opportunity, understand customer needs, add value and create products and services, solve problems and improve decision-making, manage the organization, collaborate, buy and sell.

Organizations must identify information resources and establish responsibility for their maintenance. In today's competitive business environment every activity carried out in an organization comes under scrutiny to make sure it pays its way for the business (Skyrme 1994). Therefore, the cost and value of information resource needs to be ascertained. Such resources (assets) must be exploited and continually developed where appropriate. Within this section we explore information resources, focusing on data, information, knowledge and wisdom (DIKW). The subtle differences between data, information, knowledge and wisdom have given fundamentalist commentators in this area many hours of pedantic fun (Pantzar 2000). Discussing the DIKW hierarchy Pantzar suggests Wisdom is at the pinnacle and that wisdom = knowledge + accumulated experience. Knowledge may be derived from information which in turn may derive from data. We will explore the concepts and importance of the DIKW hierarchy in the following sections before exploring the application of such concepts in international business.

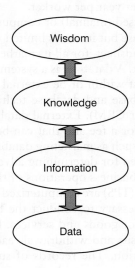

Figure 11-4

The DIKW hierarchy

Data

Data can be regarded as raw facts representing events occurring in organizations (such as business transactions) or the physical environment – objective measurements of the attributes (characteristics) of entities, such as people, places, things, and events. The price of

Data raw facts

Estimates suggest that more than 85 per cent of all business information exists as unstructured (or semi-structured) data

a product or service, the date of a customer order, contact details or an employee's date of birth are all examples of data. Data may be generated during business or may be collected from external sources. Sometimes the data refers to attributes of a person. In such cases the company may be obligated to protect it according to various privacy or financial operating laws.

The World Bank is a source of high quality national and international statistics (data). They argue that statistics form the foundation upon which sound policy is built. Good data is needed to set baselines, identify effective public and private actions, set goals and targets, monitor progress and evaluate impacts (World Bank 2006). We can classify data in a number of ways, for example, data may be structured or unstructured. People use both types of data every day. Examples of 'unstructured data' may include audio, video and unstructured text such as the body of an email or word processor document. Data that resides in fixed fields within a record or file (relational databases and spreadsheets) are examples of structured data. Structured data is managed by technology that allows for querying and reporting against predetermined data types and understood relationships. Data structure is a way of storing data in a computer so that it can be used efficiently. The management of unstructured data is recognized as one of the major problems in the information technology (IT) industry.

Tools and techniques used to transform structured data into business intelligence and actionable information simply do not work when it comes to unstructured data (Blumberg and Atre 2003). The management of unstructured data is a very large problem. According to projections from Gartner, white-collar workers will spend anywhere from 30 to 40 per cent of their time this year managing documents, up from 20 per cent of their time in 1997. Similarly, Merrill Lynch estimates that more than 85 per cent of all business information exists as unstructured (or semi-structured) data – commonly appearing in e-mails, memos, notes from call centres and support operations, news, user groups, chats, reports, letters, surveys, white papers, marketing material, research, presentations and web pages. There is a continuum between structured and unstructured data with semi-structured data lying between the two. Given the volumes of unstructured and semi-structured data, Blumberg and Atre (2003) review the need for better searches. Commenting on analysis of employee work they suggest that we now spend around 25 per cent of our time searching, gathering and analyzing information – with most of that time spent on the Internet. That equates to an average cost of over £10 000 per year per worker.

Data may be stored in paper-based (manual) or computer-based systems. A spreadsheet may be considered a simple database but its use is limited when considering many business problems. In many ways, the spreadsheet, for all its mathematical processing functionality, is little more than an electronic list. A database is a system or program in which structured data is stored. Databases may exist within or be external to the organization. In Chapter 13 we will observe that the database and database technologies are at the heart of the enterprise systems (such as ERP or CRM). External databases are commercially operated databases providing information for a fee and that can be accessed through the Internet. There are many types of database such as marketing databases – large databases containing marketing-related data and are used for determining advertisement and marketing strategies; databases support the major business operations of the organization.

Database a system or program in which structured data is stored

Transaction processing systems (TPS) (TPS) are computerized systems that perform and record the daily routine transactions necessary to conduct the business (basic business transactions include purchasing, orders for goods and services, billing, and payroll – banks, for example, handle millions of deposits and withdrawals each day); these systems serve the operational level of the organization. The records of such systems are typically stored within relational databases. Organizations make use of many databases and sometimes benefit from amalgamating them. A central source of data that has been extracted from various organizational databases and standardized and integrated for use throughout an organization is termed a *data warehouse*. Typically, data warehouses are large database systems (often measured in gigabytes or terabytes) containing detailed company data on sales transactions which are analyzed to assist in improving the marketing and financial performance of companies.

Transaction processing systems (TPS) computerized systems that perform and record the daily routine transactions necessary to conduct business

You may have considered the content of employee records (start date, age, date of birth, employee number); stock data (total amount in stock, supply or retail price, item code, location code); a purchase order (date of purchase, quantity of items ordered) or budget data (budgeted spend and actual spend). Thus far we have explained what data is. In many cases it is the building block for information resources, considered next.

Information

Total sales of a product in a particular location during a particular time period or a strategic summary of strengths and weaknesses represents examples of information. The words information and data, are used interchangeably in many contexts. This may lead to confusion, however, since they are not synonyms. Information is the summarization of data. Data that has been processed (sorted, summarized, manipulated or filtered) so that it is meaningful to people is normally considered to be information. Information may be used to reduce uncertainty and may therefore be used to improve decision-making. Information may be communicated by formal (structured) or informal (e.g. casual conversation) means. As you will see later in this chapter, information can add value to products and services and improved information flows can improve the quality of decision-making, collaboration, planning, coordination and control and internal operations (the management activities identified in Chapter 6).

Information data that has been processed (sorted, summarized, manipulated, filtered) so that it is meaningful to people

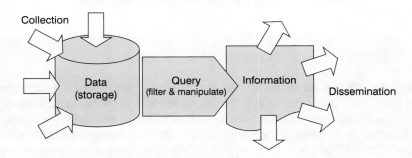

Figure 11-5

Data collection, storage, processing and output

The importance of information has been brought into sharp focus by advances in information and communication technology, especially the explosion in the use of the Internet, which has opened new windows of opportunity for accessing and disseminating information. The international trade center (ITC) discuss two categories of information. Trade information which consists of any business-related information that is required by exporters and importers to conclude successful international trade transactions and business information which is a broader concept and includes information needed to carry out any type of business transaction, not just exporting or importing. As was identified in the previous section, data may be stored within a database and may be collected through manual or electronic means. For example, data can be captured using a keyboard, mouse, scanner, optical character or voice recognition. Once stored (see Figure 11-5), queries and other programmes may be used to access or edit the data. Information reports are then generated through queries gathering and manipulating the data required to create the report. Reports may then be communicated and disseminated in many ways.

One reason to differentiate data from information concerns the application of technology. Data is highly structured and typically stored in a database. Information on the other hand is often created from the manipulation of data using queries, expressions or the efforts of knowledge workers. Information (the output) is created (the process) from data (the input) when it is required. In many cases, therefore, there is no need to store information. Whereas data is typically the focus of the transaction processing system (TPS), information is at the heart of the management information system (MIS). The TPS serves the needs of operations (primary activities in the value chain) and stakeholders in the supply chain whereas the MIS serves the needs of managers, typically involved in tactical decision-making.

Management information systems (MISs) are systems designed to provide past, present, and future routine information appropriate for planning, organizing, and controlling the operations functional areas in an organization. These systems provide feedback on organizational activities and help to support managerial decision-making. As a resource, the value of information may be enhanced, see Figure 11-6. Information is of more value when it is available to the right people, in the right form and at the time they need it. The quality of information can be increased and improved thus improving decision-making, products, services and work activities.

Management information systems (MISs) systems designed to provide past, present, and future routine information appropriate for planning, organizing, and controlling the operations functional areas in an organization

Figure 11-6

Aspects that add value to information (Skyrme 1994)

TIMELINESS	Currency – information should be up-to-date
ACCESSIBILITY	Easy to find and retrieve
USABILITY	Ease of use; user can manipulate to suit application
UTILITY	Is suited and usable for multiple applications
QUALITY	Accurate, reliable, credible, validated
MEDIUM	Appropriate for portability and ongoing use
REPACKAGING	Reformatted to match onward use
FLEXIBILITY	Easy to process; can be used in different ways

Example – Data mining

Throughout the 1990s, data mining spread from one industry to the next, enabling companies to know more about customers' needs and to focus in on the characteristics that distinguish the customers they want from those they do not. A credit-card company using a system designed by Teradata, a division of NCR, found that customers who fill out applications in pencil rather than pen are more likely to default. A major hotel chain discovered that guests who opted for X-rated films spent more money and were less likely to make demands on the hotel staff, according to privacy consultant Larry Ponemon. These low-maintenance customers were rewarded with special frequent-traveller promotions. Victoria Secrets stopped uniformly stocking its stores once MicroStrategy showed the chain sold 20 times as many size-32 bras in New York City as in other cities and that in Miami ivory was 10 times as popular as black. Aspect Communications, based in San Jose, Calif., sells a program that identifies callers by purchase history. The bigger the spender, the quicker the call gets answered. So if you think your call is being considered in the order in which it was received, think again.

Source: Data Miners – New software instantly connects key bits of data that once eluded teams of researchers By D. Franklin/Washington, Dec. 23, 2002 issue of TIME magazine www.time.com/time/globalbusiness/article/0,9171,1101021223-400017,00.html

Data mining searching organizational databases in order to uncover hidden patterns through statistical tools

Data mining is the term used for searching organizational databases in order to uncover hidden patterns or relationships in groups of data through the use of advanced statistical tools. The powerful capabilities of data mining help companies to be more profitable and efficient (Gates 1999). Data mining software attempts to represent information in new ways (to discover key business trends) so that previously unseen patterns or trends can be identified. The technology (data warehousing and data mining) is used to support decision-making and is present in decision support systems and business intelligence systems, discussed later in this chapter.

Communication and the dissemination of information

In Figure 11-5 we not only revealed the relationship between data and information but also indentified information as an *output* of the information system. This output must be disseminated if managers and workers are to improve decision-making, planning, control and coordination. The transmission (exchange or sharing) of information between people and systems defines the communication process, see Figure 11-7. The transmitter and receiver are entities (people, electronic devices) and the message may be communicated verbally or non-verbally through a variety of channels such as face-to-face, telephone, email, text, or video conference. Feedback is used to detect how the message has been received. Communications may be formal or informal, verbal or non-verbal, written, electronic, synchronous or asynchronous. Furthermore, communication may be enabled by technology. Technology (such as computing hardware and software and telecommunications) may be used to enhance the speed and the efficiency of the transfer of information. The information age continues to this day, and technological advances such as mobile phones, high speed connections, Voice-Over-IP have changed lifestyles around the world and spawned new industries around controlling and providing information. We consider communication technologies in Chapter 14.

Communication process the transmission of information between entities

Asynchronous communication the sending and receiving of messages in which there is a time delay between the sending and receiving; as opposed to synchronous communication

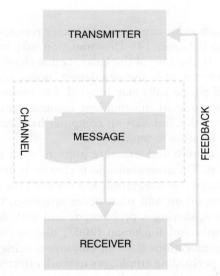

Figure 11-7
Communications process

> How might differences in time, location, language and culture impact upon this process?

STOP & THINK

Having collected and processed data, the organization must also make the information available. 'Dissemination' means the transmission of information, whether orally, in writing or by electronic means. The purpose of a dissemination activity is to assure that information/knowledge is useful in reaching decisions, making changes, or taking specific action and is available to those who can most benefit from it. Traditionally, managers would receive information in the form of reports generated by the MIS. Reports may be generated and disseminated *periodically* (such as monthly budget reports), by *exception* (when targets were met or not met), on *demand* i.e. ad hoc reports for specific one-off decisions and *push* reports (reports sent to recipients who may not have requested them), see Figure 11-8.

The problem with the periodic report is information overload; however, exception reports can help reduce such problems. Technology also affects the traditional ways of delivering information (the salesman, the mailshot, the advertising boarding) – i.e. there is a separation between information and its carrier. Traditionally there was a trade-off between the richness of information (amount, quality and interactivity) and the reach (number of people involved in the information exchange): typically, the richer the information the smaller the reach. New technologies mean that information exchange is open and virtually cost-free.

Figure 11-8

MIS information dissemination

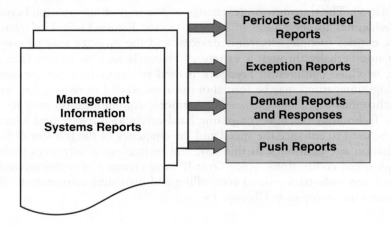

As information outputs, in many organizations, paper reports have all but disappeared with the advent of the web (Chapter 14). Dissemination may be achieved through traditional or electronic means. In the case of the latter, verbal channels such as presentations, meetings, the management chain, in-house newsletters, notice boards, seminars, employee reports, team briefings and phone calls may be used. Communications technologies support the electronic dissemination of information; communications technology refers to physical devices and software that link various computer hardware components and transfer data from one physical location to another.

Aside from technology, culture and structure impacts upon the free flow of information within the organization. The communications climate is one dimension of organizational culture. Schein comments on integration and the need for communication. We need to communicate what is important and what needs attention. Communication is highly important because without it, sharing is problematic and without sharing there is no collective experience. Huczynski and Buchanan (2007) discuss top-down communication, where organizational communications is about employees being made aware of management plans, goals, etc. and persuading employees to work effectively in the interests of the organization as a whole. The authors also discuss the communication climate, the prevailing atmosphere in which ideas and information are exchanged (an open climate promotes collaborative working). 'In closed communication climates, information tends to be withheld unless it is to the advantage of the sender, and the atmosphere of recrimination, secrecy and distrust can make working life very unpleasant.' Communication is a motivator and 'breeds' commitment. If people know what is going on and understand why, then they will be more likely to agree to management requests – consensus and compliance. Hofstede (1997) also identified communications climate as a dimension of organizational culture, describing closed communication climates as secretive and relating it to the time taken for new employees to feel at home in the organization. Communications climate is one of the few organizational culture dimensions associated with nationality according to Hofstede.

There are many barriers to communication. Aside from culture, there are also geographical and time barriers, language and technology barriers, legal constraints and power distances. All may impair communications and the sharing of information resources. In

Chapter 9 we discussed collaboration to describe the mutual efforts by two or more individuals or groups who perform activities in order to accomplish certain tasks. Enterprise collaboration systems help us to work together more efficiently and effectively as members of the many process and project teams and workgroups that make up many organizations today. Collaboration technologies help us to share information with each other (communication), coordinate our work efforts and resources with each other (coordination), and work together cooperatively on joint assignments (collaboration). The use of groupware tools and the Internet, intranets, extranets, and other computer networks are used to support and enhance communication, coordination, collaboration, and resource sharing among teams and workgroups, see Figure 11-9. We revisit the technologies used to enable information sharing and communication in Chapters 13 and 14.

Groupware software to support and enhance the communication, coordination, and collaboration among networked teams and workgroups, including software tools for electronic communications, electronic conferencing, and cooperative work management

```
                    ┌──────────────┐
                    │  Groupware   │
                    │     for      │
                    │  Enterprise  │
                    │Collaboration │
                    └──────┬───────┘
         ┌─────────────────┼─────────────────┐
         ▼                 ▼                 ▼
┌─────────────────┐ ┌─────────────────┐ ┌──────────────────────┐
│   Electronic    │ │   Electronic    │ │ Collaborative Work   │
│ Communications  │ │  Conferencing   │ │     Management        │
│(E-Mail, Voice   │ │(Data, Voice &   │ │(Calendaring, Task    │
│Mail, Text and   │ │Video Conferencing│ │and Project Mgt       │
│MM Messaging     │ │Discussion Forums &│ │Workflow Systems,     │
│Web Publishing)  │ │Electronic Meetings)│ │Knowledge Mgt        │
│                 │ │                 │ │Document Sharing)     │
└─────────────────┘ └─────────────────┘ └──────────────────────┘
```

Figure 11-9
Collaboration tools

©iStockphoto.com/Georg Winkens

Video conferencing equipment, an example of groupware

Technology (telecommunications and software applications) can overcome geographic barriers enabling the capture of information about business transactions from remote locations; time barriers – providing information to remote locations immediately after it is requested; overcome cost barriers, reducing the cost of more traditional means of communication and can support linkages for competitive advantage (overcome structural barriers).

Knowledge

Knowledge and information are closely related and, as was the case with data and information concepts, on occasions the two terms are used interchangeably, see Figure 11-10. The definition of knowledge is still a live debate for philosophers. However, for our purposes we only require a simple working definition. Many see knowledge as the understanding, awareness, or familiarity acquired through education or experience. Others see knowledge as applying experience to problem solving. The source of knowledge as education or experience has led many to divide the concept in two classes: it may be about 'knowing-that' (explicit) or 'know-how' (tacit). Explicit knowledge is 'knowledge and understanding which is codified, expressed and available to anyone'; the knowledge that deals with objective, rational, and technical knowledge (data, policies, procedures, software, documents, etc.). Tacit knowledge (also termed 'sticky' knowledge), on the other hand, is mainly intangible knowledge that is typically intuitive and not recorded since it is part of the human mind; the knowledge that is usually in the domain of subjective, cognitive, and experiential learning. It is highly personal and hard to formalize. Thus, explicit knowledge is more easily confused with information; tacit knowledge with skills, abilities and competencies.

Knowledge what people understand as a result of what they have been taught or have experienced; knowledge may then be applied to solve problems

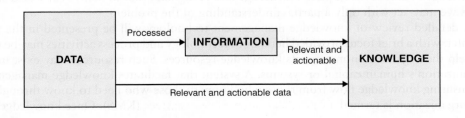

Figure 11-10
Data, information and knowledge relationships

The new, global economy is driven by what people and organizations 'know' and not only by capital and labour, see Figure 11-11. The knowledge-creating company is a firm that consistently creates new business knowledge, disseminates it widely throughout the company, and quickly builds this new knowledge into their products and services (O'Brien 2002).

Figure 11-11

Key organizational resources

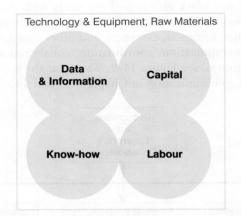

Knowledge comes from learning. The way we learn from our experiences and develop our knowledge is conceptualized in the famous learning cycle model presented by Kolb (see Figure 11-12). We may start with a concrete experience which is then reviewed (reflection). At this stage we may ponder and analyze the experience. We may think things through and assimilate disparate facts into coherent theories. We may use explicit knowledge sources to make sense of our experiences or to identify alternative theories to be tested in new situations.

Figure 11-12

Kolb's learning cycle (Kolb 1976)

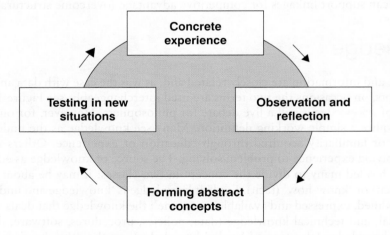

Aside from tacit or explicit, knowledge may also be described as situated or partial. Situated knowledge, often generated by trial and error or through experience, is knowledge specific to a particular situation. Situational knowledge is often embedded in language, culture, or traditions. Explicit knowledge, on the other hand, is often generated by scientific method which typically seeks to create general theories for wider application. Partial knowledge concerns incomplete knowledge and recognizes that in many real world situations we may act with only a partial understanding of the problem.

A detailed review of knowledge management technology will be presented in the next chapter, with a brief focus provided here. Both technology and process activities may be used to help the organization manage its knowledge resources. Such resources may exist in the organization's human capital or systems. A system that facilitates knowledge management by ensuring knowledge flow from those who know to those who need to know throughout the organization is termed a Knowledge management system (KMS). Once knowledge can

Knowledge management systems a system that facilitates knowledge management by ensuring knowledge flow from those who know to those who need to know throughout the organization

be captured, the issue of where and how to store it arises. There are two knowledge management models (one for tacit and one for explicit knowledge) – the knowledge network and knowledge repository model (hybrid models also exist). In some cases databases may be used to simplify the task of identifying where knowledge exists (more likely when the knowledge is tacit), and in other cases the databases may be used to actually store knowledge (more likely when the knowledge is explicit). Technology is crucial to the success of the knowledge management system. Knowledge management systems are developed using three sets of technologies:

- communication;
- collaboration; and
- storage.

Communication technologies allow users to access the knowledge they need and to communicate with each other – especially with experts (e-mail, the Internet, corporate intranets and other web-based tools provide communication capabilities). Collaboration technologies provide the means to perform group work. Groups can work together on common documents at the same time (synchronous) or at different times (asynchronous); in the same place, or in differing locations. Technologies allow us to create a virtual space, so that individuals can work online anywhere and at any time. The knowledge management system challenge is to identify and integrate these three technologies to meet the knowledge management needs of an organization. There are many challenges associated with knowledge and its use within the international organization. Many organizations assign responsibility to manage knowledge to a person, *see* the chief knowledge officer (CKO). Knowledge, when locked into systems or processes, has higher inherent value than when it can 'walk out of the door' in people's heads. Consequently organizations embark on knowledge management programmes in an attempt to ensure knowledge can be accessed, shared and retained. Knowledge management seeks to understand the way in which knowledge is used and traded within organizations.

A global company's skill at transferring knowledge across subsidiaries gives these subsidiaries the added benefit of innovations created by their peers (Gupta and Govindarajan 2001). By minimizing, if not altogether eliminating, counterproductive reinvention of the wheel, product and process innovations are accelerated across the entire global network. Since significant geographic, linguistic, and cultural distances often separate subsidiaries, the potential for knowledge transfer can easily remain buried under a sea of ignorance. Companies face the management challenge of creating mechanisms to uncover both systematically and routinely the opportunities for knowledge transfer. Gupta and Govindarajan (2001) suggest that organizations can evaluate their performance in knowledge transfer across locations by answering the following questions:

- How good are we at routinely and systematically uncovering the opportunities for knowledge transfer?
- How enthusiastic are our subsidiaries to share knowledge with other units?
- How eager are our subsidiaries to learn from any and all sources including peer subsidiaries?
- How good are we at codifying the product and process innovations generated by our subsidiaries? Have we built efficient communication mechanisms for the sharing of codified know-how across locations?
- How good are we at keeping codified knowledge proprietary to our company?
- Have we built effective mechanisms (e.g. people transfer, face-to-face interchange) for the transfer of tacit knowledge across locations?

Look forward
See chapter 12

Think back to the opening case study. Evaluate Duckworth's knowledge transfer needs and initiatives.

STOP & THINK

We devote the next chapter of this book to knowledge management and will explore the business need to manage intellectual resources in more detail. For now, we turn our attention to the construct at the top of the DIKW hierarchy: wisdom.

Wisdom

While data and information may exist outside of the person and certain knowledge types exist both externally and internally, wisdom can only be found in people – not technology. Managers frequently find themselves in situations where the capacity to assess shrewdly those situations or circumstances and to draw sound conclusions is an important skill. **Judgement** is a cognitive process of reaching a decision or drawing conclusions.

Sound judgement may be based on specialized knowledge or common sense. Small (2004) discusses high-profile mistakes made at top management level, all of which point to an absence of what common sense would probably call 'wise' behaviour; good judgement. Meacham, cited in Sternberg (1990, p. 187), argued that the essence of wisdom was not in what was known, but rather in the manner in which knowledge was held and how that knowledge was put to use. Birren and Fisher cited in Sternberg (1990, p. 324) described wisdom as 'an integrative aspect of human life'. Wisdom brought together experience, cognitive abilities, and affect, and allowed good decisions to be made at an individual and societal level. Wisdom is often considered to be a trait that can be developed by experience, but not taught. Many regard wisdom to be an ability to use one's experience and knowledge to make sensible decisions and judgements. Later in this chapter we explore decision-making and judgement in detail, identifying it to be one of the most important of managerial activities.

Throughout this section we have explored the differences between data, information, knowledge and wisdom. We have also identified the role of technology in managing such resources within the international organization. In the next section we focus on the use of information in the vertical and then in the horizontal organization before considering decision-making.

Judgement a balanced weighing up of evidence (data, and information) from multiple sources, preparatory to making a decision

Look back
See chapter 9

Supporting international business

Information flow is the major differentiator for every business – the lifeblood of your company.
(GATES 1999)

Figure 11-13
Information flows

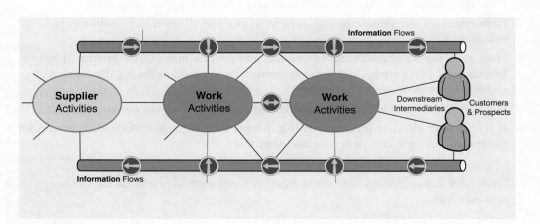

Earlier we recognized that structure and culture can impact upon information flow within the organization and in the previous chapter we distinguished between traditional (bureaucratic and hierarchical) and process (horizontal) organizations that reflect a particular approach to organization and work design. In this section we consider the use of information resources by such organizations. Traditional organizational designs are based on the creation of functional groupings within the organization (refer back to Chapter 9). Typical (functional) groups include finance, accounting, HR, sales and marketing, manufacturing, etc. Each group is both a consumer and creator of organizational information.

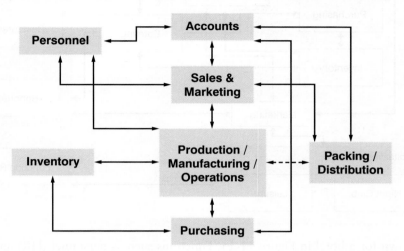

Figure 11-14

Information flows between the typical business functions

Like the blood circulatory or nervous system in the body, an organization needs information flows (see Figure 11-13 and Figure 11-14) to link up its parts and create the whole (see the concept of holism – the idea that the whole is greater than the sum of the parts). As an example, consider how information may flow in a hotel business.

Holism the idea that the whole is greater than the sum of the parts

STOP & THINK

The Plaza is a medium sized hotel. House Services are the busiest team. The House Services are responsible for the main reception area, the housemaids, and porters. The catering team is responsible for servicing the restaurants, room service and the needs of the banqueting and function rooms. Hospitalities, the smallest team, support the booking and servicing of the banqueting and function rooms and the running of the hotel's nightclub and the leisure suite.

Create a diagram to show the information flows within the organization.

There are many examples of information flow within and between functions and other organizational groups. Employees throughout the organization typically complete time sheets and expense claims to be processed by finance and HR. Departments report expenditures to finance for cost accounting and sales report orders for receivables and cash flow management. Within business processes such as order management, one department may take the order; another may prepare it while others are responsible for shipment and distribution. Each activity uses data and information provided by the other. In the order management activities, information typically flows upstream. This information is used to manufacture and source products or adapt services; during fulfilment, information typically flows downstream towards the customer.

The information flow diagram (IFD) is a simple diagram showing how information is routed between different parts of an organization. It has an information focus rather than a process focus (Kelly 2005). Such diagrams enable the identification of entities which send and receive data and information within a business information system. An example

Look back
See p. 318

Figure 11-15

Hotel information flows

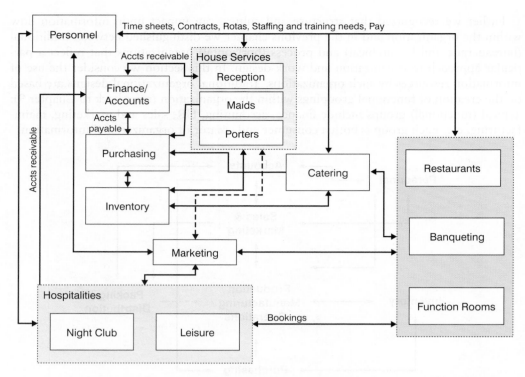

IFD is shown for a hotel in Figure 11-15. Functions such as personnel (HR) and finance are shown as rectangles and the flow of information with connecting lines and directional indicators (arrow heads). In some cases the connecting line may be annotated with detail of the data/information and media type that flows between the business functions. The IFD reveals stakeholders and the inputs/outputs they rely upon or provide for operations and function. Using this model we can investigate how functions receive or share information within the business information system (BIS) and the purpose to which that information is put.

Typically (historically), functions develop their own (functional) information systems in support of their parochial goals. We will revisit the associated problems with such systems toward the end of the chapter. A functional MIS is an information system developed for a functional area, such as a marketing information system. Business applications have traditionally served the functional areas of an organization, such as:

- human resources;
- accounting;
- production;
- inbound and outbound logistics;
- marketing and sales.

As was highlighted in the previous two chapters, there are many problems associated with organizations that structure according to function and consequently may have functional information systems. It has been argued (see Sandoe, Corbitt and Boykin 2001) that such organizations focus on discrete tasks and individuals, not processes and teams. The functional structure and associated systems can act as a barrier to information flow. Consequently, functions tend to be parochial with little sense of the bigger picture.

Throughout this chapter we have discussed the application of information by managers and workers. Managerial work was described by Henri Fayol who identified six key activities:

- forecasting (predicting the future);
- planning (devising a course of action);
- organizing;

■ commanding;

■ coordinating; and

■ controlling.

Interestingly, information resources are required for each of them. The activities also require decision-making, a concept we address in the next section.

Decision-making flows

Mintzberg felt that decision-making was possibly the most important of all of the managerial activities.

Consider Mintzberg's comment. Do you feel he is right?

STOP & THINK

Decision-making is the process of making choices from among several options. Decisions are made at all organizational levels – from strategic to operational. Some of the strategic decisions whose successful outcomes depend on the availability of good information include:

■ market selection and targeting;

■ new investments;

■ location of factories and offices;

■ new product development and launch;

■ pricing and promotion.

Decisions can lead a company to success or failure. Decision-making has been studied in order both to understand how decisions are actually made in practice and to advise managers how to make better decisions. Classical decision theory assumes that decision-makers are objective, have complete information and consider all possible alternatives and other consequences before selecting the optimal solution. The traditional approach to understanding individual decision-making is based upon classical decision theory and the rational economic model. The rational economic model (see Figure 11-16) assumes that decision-making is and should be a rational process consisting of a sequence of steps that enhance the probability of attaining a desired outcome.

Decisions may be classified or categorized in many ways such as by the organizational level and the degree of structure to the decision, i.e. repetitive, routine, and require judgements. Some decisions are semi-structured – in such cases, only part of the problem has a clear-cut answer provided by an accepted procedure. Decisions (selecting the right action from a series of choices) can be structured (decision rules are known) or unstructured (not known – highly uncertain/ambiguous situations) and may be made/taken at a variety of levels (operational/tactical/strategic) within the organization. In the case of structured decision-making the organization may formulate decision/business rules specifying what action is required in a given situation. Decision trees may be used to show the sequence of events, decisions and consequent actions that occur in a decision-making process. Decision tables are another tool to show the alternative outcomes of different decisions.

■ *Operational decisions* tend to be structured, frequently with more certainty, often relying on data/information from within the organization.

■ Strategic decisions on the other hand are unstructured, made less frequently and may use more information sourced form outside the organization.

Decision-making the process of making choices from among several options

Semi-structured decisions decisions where only part of the problem has a clear-cut answer provided by an accepted procedure

Structured decisions decisions that are repetitive, routine, and have a definite procedure for handling them

Unstructured decisions unstructured decisions tend to involve complex situations, where the rules governing the decision are complicated or unknown. Such decisions tend to be made infrequently and rely heavily on the experience, judgement and knowledge of the decision-maker

Business rule a rule defines the actions that need to occur in a business when a particular situation arises. For example a business rule may state that if a customer requests credit and they have a history of defaulting on payments, then credit will not be issued

Decision tree a diagram showing the sequence of events, decisions and consequent actions that occur in a decision-making process

Strategic decision-making determining the long-term objectives, resources, and policies of an organization

Figure 11.16
Rational economic decision-making model

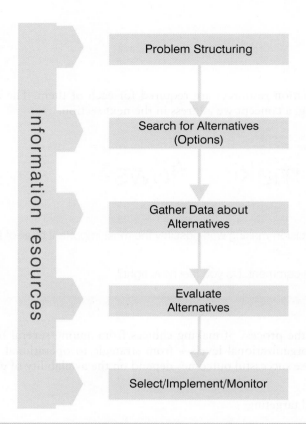

STOP & THINK

Consider the problem at PTC. How could you improve credit decision making so that you only accepted customers likely to pay their bills without losing them.

Example: Structured/operational decision

Credit decisions are made by employees in banking and finance organizations when considering a loan or mortgage application or in telecommunications when a customer seeks a subscription-based mobile phone. In each case the prospective customer could turn out to be a good paying customer or may default on payments. In the case of the former the company will accrue revenues and profits whereas costs and losses will result from bad customers. It is therefore in the interests of the company to assess customer risk when making credit decisions. Decision rules, external, internal and customer data can all be used in a model to support this structured decision. Data from the customer is collected on an application form. External credit databases are used to assess the customer's credit history and verify contact and personal data. Analysis of bad customer data is used to identify characteristics of non-payers. This is then combined in a model that weights data according to rules.

Table 11-1.

Factor	Weighting	Score
Home owner	10	
Salary	10	
Negative information (previous bad debts)	−20	
Age	10	
Total		Σ (above)

Consider James, an unemployed home owner aged 30 with a good credit history. He would score 20 points. Helen, aged 35 years, a well paid professional, home owner with no credit history would score 30 points. Whereas Tom (20 years), an unemployed student in temporary accommodation and with a history of bad debt would have no points. Companies analyze their customers to determine the optimum score at which to filter out bad prospects and improve the quality of their decision-making.

Consider the MNC, can the credit checking activity and decision be a centralized role or do culture, local knowledge and other factors present the argument to decentralize it?

STOP & THINK

A variety of models and processes have been offered to suggest ideally how people should or describe how they actually do make decisions. Some writers discuss rational models where decision-makers adopt value maximizing calculations and pursue alternatives that best meet the organizational goals while other writers recognize real-world situation and cognitive decision-maker constraints where rationality may be bounded. The rational model, depicted in Figure 11-16, has a number of inherent weaknesses. For example, it is rarely possible to consider all alternatives since there are too many and some alternatives will not have occurred to the decision-maker. It may be impractical to consider all consequences and accurate information may not be available; furthermore generated or purchased information has a cost. Consequently decisions are often made on incomplete, insufficient and only partially accurate information. Finally decision-makers as individuals may lack the mental capacity to store and process all the information relevant to a decision and frequently lack the mental ability to perform the mental calculations required.

Descriptive models of decision-making investigate how individuals actually make decisions. Each decision made by an individual or group is affected by a number of factors. These include: individual personality, group relationships, organizational power relationships and political behaviour, external environmental pressures, organization strategic considerations and information availability (or lack of). Bounded rationality refers to individuals making decisions by constructing simplified models that extract the essential features from problems without capturing all their complexity. Research suggests that decisions may be subject to bias (prejudiced predisposition or a systematic distortion caused by the application of heuristics – simple rules used to solve problems). With turbulent environments there is greater uncertainty and a lack of information available for decision-making. Consequently rational decision-making may be seen as more appropriate in a stable environment whereas intuitive and subjective decision-making may dominate in turbulent environments. A similar issue concerns the programmability of decisions. Routine decisions

Look back
See chapter 10

are made according to established procedures and rules whereas adaptive decisions require human judgement.

Three sets of decision rules (heuristics) may be adopted in the *simple* strategy:

■ *Satisficing* is simply about choosing the first alternative that meets the minimal problem requirements.

■ *Analogizing* (metaphorical thinking) is about seeing a current event as analogous to a similar historical event (which gives a single and very limited perspective of the situation and also raises issues about what it is in memory and how easily it is recalled (see availability heuristics).

■ *Nutshell briefings*, ask someone else, who has looked into the problem, to give you a briefing, and then decide.

All of the above decision rules (heuristics) may allow for speedy decisions with little effort but can lead to ill-conceived and poor quality decisions.

Janis (1989) discusses the quality of the decision-making process and presents two decision-making strategies:

1 'simple' based on cognitive (heuristic), decision-rules; and

2 vigilant.

Decision-making starts with a challenge (trigger) that may be framed as an opportunity or a threat. The first activity for the decision-maker becomes an assessment as to whether the matter is important or not; a number of factors may influence the importance-judgement: constraints and attributes of both the problem and the solution. There are two main constraints that may prevent a new problem from being classified as important

1 time; and

2 resources.

In the time constraint, there are two-dimensions, first does the problem require a speedy resolution and second does the decision-maker have the necessary time to allocate to the problem. In determining the answer to the latter issue, the decision-maker is likely to compare this new problem with those that presently occupy his or her agenda; it must compete for priority and attention. In considering the attributes of the problem, judgements about importance will be influenced by whether or not the decision-maker believes that the problem will occur when it may happen and how harmful or beneficial the event may be. In considering these latter attributes of the presented problem, the decision-maker may compare predictions with desired and tolerable outcomes, calculating the size of discrepancy. Finally, the way in which the decision-maker treats this new problem may be influenced by beliefs on whether or not the problem can be managed. Should the problem not be classified as important, the simple strategy adopting decision-rules or delegation will be chosen. Despite the problem being considered important, if there are any affiliative (needed for acceptability or consensus) or egocentric constraints (self-serving criteria), the decision-maker may relegate the problem for treatment by a simple strategy. If there are no anticipated issues and the problem is considered important, the issue is managed using a vigilant decision-making strategy (process).

So far we have recognized that decision-makers may make decisions in different ways and may be more or less reliant on information resources to improve decision quality. Technology has also been applied to support the decision-making process, providing information to assist with problem structuring and the evaluation of alternative choices/ solutions. Whereas the management information system may 'provide information about the performance of the organization' decision support systems are used to provide analysis for specific problems or opportunities. With the management information system, information is produced by extraction/manipulation, whilst in the decision support system, information is produced by analytical modelling of business data.

The MIS is backward looking while the DSS has its orientation in the future. Decisions concern the future – where to allocate resources, what the organization should and should

Decision support system (DSS) a computer-based information system that combines models and data in an attempt to solve semi-structured problems with extensive user involvement

not do. Consequently, strategic decisions are surrounded in uncertainty and ambiguity. Dickson (1995: 49) informs us that 'it is our lack of knowledge which is really at the root of the uncertainty and no matter what we do we will never have perfect knowledge. The best we can do is to increase our knowledge by reducing the imperfections'. Information can improve the quality of decision-making and other managerial activities. One of the challenges for the international organization is to make information available to decision-makers that may be located in the corporate or subsidiary headquarters or in a local operation. In some cases this will manifest as a competitive advantage. In the next section we specifically consider how information resources (data and information in particular) might provide a competitive advantage; knowledge resources will be considered in the next chapter.

Competing with information resources

Competing and sources of competitive advantage was discussed in Chapter 3. Thus far we have described information resources (DIKW) and their application to business activities and decision-making within organizations. We now turn to the application of such resource (building on Chapter 3) in generating competitive advantage. Porter and Millar (1985) in their landmark article – how information gives you competitive advantage, discuss the impact of information and technology on the business we do and the way in which we do it. Defining information technology as 'more than just computers [it] encompasses the information that businesses create and use as well as a wide spectrum of increasingly convergent and linked technologies that process the information'. They review impact on internal operations (processes to create products – see the value chain) and relationships with other organizations (suppliers, customers, rivals, etc.).

Porter and Millar also examine how such resources alter industry structures, support cost or differentiation strategies and spawn entirely new businesses (competition). Internal operations are conceptualized as the value chain (linked business activities), which exists in a wider system – the value system (to include supplier and channel value chains). Value is measured by the 'amount that buyers are willing to pay for a product or service' and 'a business is profitable if the value it creates exceeds the cost of performing the value activities'. According to Porter and Millar (1985: 151), 'to gain competitive advantage over its rivals, a company must either perform these activities at a lower cost or perform them in a way that leads to differentiation and a premium price (more value)'. A company's cost position is 'the collective cost of performing all [the companies] value activities, relative to rivals' and differentiation is concerned with the fulfilment of buyer needs. Information resources and technology may therefore enable the organization strategy by reducing cost or enabling it to add value and do things differently. However, while in the 1980s, companies tended to develop their own (differentiated) systems, they are now more likely to acquire systems off-the-shelf. Such systems are therefore available to competitors and may, therefore, be less likely to provide a competitive advantage. The challenge to companies is to source cost-effective solutions.

Organizations pursuing a differentiation strategy must also find systems that are difficult to imitate if a sustainable advantage is to be created. The value chain is a set of linked, interdependent activities (one impacts upon the other), which may be primary, concerned with the physical creation of products (inbound logistics, operations, outbound logistics, marketing and sales, services) or secondary 'support' activities (firm infrastructure, human resources management, technology and procurement). Porter and Millar believe the careful management of linkages (coordination/trade-off management/control) in both the value chain and system is an important source of competitive advantage. The authors examine the role of information in the way work is done (activities/operations), the product and

Look back
See p. 13

competition. Information has always been the glue holding value chains together argue BCG (1999). Porter and Millar (1985: 152) believed that, 'every value activity creates and uses information of some kind'. Dividing value activities into two components (physical and information) they note the industrial revolution focused on physical components (substituting people with machines), whereas the information revolution focused on the information component (the move from paper ledgers and dependence on people for decisions to computers). Information technology affects how activities are performed and exploits linkages to give better coordination.

To compete effectively in global markets, exporters need to develop the capabilities to produce high value-added products and to target their marketing efforts more closely. This requires closer linkages with suppliers and with customers (Campbell 1998). Although researchers have employed different definitions of cooperation, a common consensus is that cooperation is a process by which individuals, groups and organizations come together, interact and form psychological relationships for mutual gain or benefit (Smith *et al.* 1995 cited in Campbell (1998)). Since cooperation rests on norms of behaviour which may differ in differing countries, there are significant challenges in achieving cooperation when dealing with foreign cultures. Exploring cooperation in the context of an international value chain can reveal issues faced by exporters which may not be faced by firms in a strictly domestic context (Campbell 1998). Partnerships in a value chain encourage a joint approach to problems and lead to cost reductions and quality improvements. The assumption underlying buyer–seller partnerships is that value chains can be optimized so that at each stage value is added at minimum cost. This is achieved through vertical collaboration in which each firm recognizes that their performance depends upon a series of upstream and downstream relationships which they are dependent upon for resources.

Optimizing a value chain through balancing, resource auditing and relationship management has been given various names such as supply chain management or pipeline management. While the cooperation necessary to achieve the full optimization of a value chain is difficult to establish in a domestic context, Campbell (1998) argues it is even more problematic in international settings. According to Rainbird (2004), an important element of the new economy is the focus becoming less on organizations as standalone entities and more on the business networks within which they operate. More recently the emphasis is on changes in inter-organizational relationship management giving rise to the concept of the 'virtual organization' and with it 'virtual integration'. Drucker notes that the traditional response to market pressures was vertical integration – in contrast the new successful corporations are adopting models based on virtual integration. Arguably if the new structures are to be made effective then an additional factor is also necessary – coordination. Managers need to be good at mobilizing, managing, and using resources rather than at formally acquiring and owning resources. The ability to reconfigure, i.e. to use more effectively resources inside and particularly outside the boundaries of the traditional corporation becomes a mandatory skill for management (Normann 2001 cited in Rainbird 2004). In the preceding text we have focused on the value system, next we turn our attention from external matters to the value chain and internal operations.

The international organization has to develop and maintain smooth, seamless coordination across locations (Gupta and Govindarajan 2001); the worldwide business team needs to foster operational coordination between units performing similar activities (e.g. two R&D labs or two production centres), as well as those performing complementary activities (e.g. manufacturing and procurement and manufacturing and marketing), and the transfer of knowledge and skills across locations. The pursuit of seamless coordination along these dimensions requires creating eagerness among those managers whose cooperation is essential, and setting up mechanisms that will put the desired cooperation into practice. Gupta and Govindarajan (2001) offer several mechanisms to make cooperation feasible:

- Formal rules and procedures that enhance communication.
- Global or regional business teams, functional councils, and similar standing committees bringing key managers from various subsidiaries into routine face-to-face communication with each other.

Supply chain all of the activities related to the acceptance of an order from a customer and its fulfilment. In its extended format, it also includes connections with suppliers, customers, and other business partners

■ Corporate investment in cultivating interpersonal familiarity and trust among the key managers of various subsidiaries. Managers from different subsidiaries can be brought together in executive development programmes, managers can be rotated across locations, and language skills can be developed among these managers so that these 'get-acquainted' encounters have high leverage.

Thus far we have focused on the use of information resources in value adding activities (that may be globally dispersed). The outputs of the value chain (the primary activities of the organization) are products and services. There is an unmistakable trend towards expanding the information content in products suggested Porter and Millar (1985: 154). The *product information component* may include product characteristics, or information about how to obtain and use the product. It may also be reflected in the diagnostic/control systems of products (see for example, the new Internet fridge).

The Internet fridge …

'Watch TV, listen to music or surf the Internet using this titanium finish, state-of-the-art fridge freezer. It's the ultimate in kitchen technology with a built-in MP3 player for downloading and playing music from the Internet, e-mail and video mail using a built-in camera and microphone. It even has full Internet access so you can re-stock the refrigerator on-line or check on the latest news and weather – all without leaving the kitchen. And it's great for storing food too.'

http://www.lginternetfamily.co.uk/fridge.asp

Industry structures

In Chapter 3 we highlighted two fundamental approaches to strategy: RBV and positioning. In the previous paragraphs we have discussed the role of information resources in creating value (RBV) and in the following paragraphs consider how information supports positioning strategies. Information resources and technology may determine industry structure (see five forces), competitive advantage (lower costs/enhanced differentiation) and new business. IT can increase buyer-power (making product information more readily available, enabling comparisons to be made between suppliers); raise or lower barriers-to-entry (dependent on the needs and cost technology investments); make it easier to create substitute products and increase rivalry. Throughout the 1980s and 1990s we have witnessed many examples of technology driven product substitutions. The video gave way to the DVD and the record to the CD and then the MP3. Aside from the threat of losing market share to a new product, organizations face the threat of new organizations entering their market. Technology may lower the cost of entry to a given industry.

> Estimate the cost of setting up and running a physical book store in a city centre. Now estimate the costs of setting up and running an online book store. Compare and contrast the cost and benefits of each business model.

STOP & THINK

While it might cost around £50 000 to set up a physical book store the online shop could be established for around 10 per cent of the costs. Why then is it so much cheaper to set up the online store? First, the lease (rent) on a building is expensive when looking for a city high street property. The physical shop requires space to store books (stock) and allow customers to browse. The e-shop requires only cyberspace and no stock. Books can be ordered from the supplier the second a customer order is received electronically. The physical shop requires furnishing and staff during opening hours.

© Ambrits | Dreamstime.com

Table 11-2

Example cost of physical store vs. online store

Costs (month)	Physical store	Online store
Lease (building/web space)	2000	10
Payroll	3000	1000
Utilities	500	100
Furnishings	500	0
Advertising	500	500
Total	6500	1610
One-off set-up costs		
Stock	50000	0
Computing	3000	3000
Furnishings	5000	500
Total	58000	3500
Grand Total	64,500.00	5,110.00

Aside from being lower on cost, making entry by new companies easier, there are other benefits for the online shop or e-tailer. First, there is *reach*. The online shop can reach every person with Internet access around the globe, while the physical shop relies on the people walking past the building each day. Second, there is the issue of *opening hours* to manage. Typically 9–5, six days per week for the physical store but 24 × 7 for the online trader. Aside from the advantages mentioned so far, perhaps the biggest benefit to the online trader concerns product searching. The online trader can make use of database technologies and Internet search engines to direct its prospective customers immediately to the product they want immediately and from the comfort of their homes. Furthermore, the online trader can give more information about the product at very little cost. Finally, the successful online trader may spawn new business by selling marketing space on their websites.

In our previous example we examined how information technologies may make market entry more or less costly. Next we consider the factors affecting bargaining power. When purchasers buy goods they evaluate the product or service attributes and price. In the physical world this can be a time-consuming exercise and may be limited to the geographical area of the purchaser. The Internet, however, allows purchasers to search further afield and compare, with relative ease, prices and product characteristics (see for example price comparison websites such as: www.pricerunner.co.uk; www.kelkoo.co.uk). Consequently, purchasers can seek out the best value and price deals or use the information obtained to negotiate the sale in their favour.

STOP & THINK

How do you think this technology affects business?

According to Porter (2001), the Internet tends to weaken industry profitability. If average profitability is under pressure in many industries influenced by the Internet, it becomes all the more important for individual companies to set themselves apart from the pack–to be more profitable than the average performer (Porter 2001). The only way to do so is by achieving a sustainable competitive advantage – by operating at a lower cost, by commanding a premium price, or by doing both.

In the opening paragraphs of this section we once again made use of the value chain as a means to analyze organizations and where information resources may be created and used. The value chain represents the key processes (Chapter 10) within the firm – describing what the organization actually does (Rainbird 2004). The view of the chain may, however, be misleading to the extent it gives the impression such links are, as a matter of course, neatly sequential – that inputs are turned into outputs and value created in a neat and ordered series of links or events. The value chain should be seen as dynamic. Conceptually, Michael Porter's classic model addresses the physical supply chain and the value-building process from the context of a logistical materials flow. His value system traces products from the original producer to the ultimate consumer, argues Eustace (2003). For a long time, we thought the only possible value configuration for organizations was the value chain developed by Porter (1985). Insights emerged, however, that many organizations have no inbound or outbound logistics of importance, they do not produce goods in a sequential way, and money-making does not only occur at the end of their value creation (Gottschalk 2006). Therefore, alternative value configurations have been identified such as the 'value shop' and 'value network'.

One approach to understanding the organization is to define the value configuration. To comprehend the value that information resources provide to organizations, we must first understand the way a particular organization conducts business and how information systems affect the performance of various component activities within the organization. A value configuration describes how value is created in a company for its customers. A value configuration shows how the most important business processes function to create value for customers. The best-known value configuration is the value chain, typical examples are found within manufacturing industries (see the Duckworth case study). Attention is on performing chain activities in the most efficient and effective ways.

> **Value configurations** describes how value is created in a company for its customers

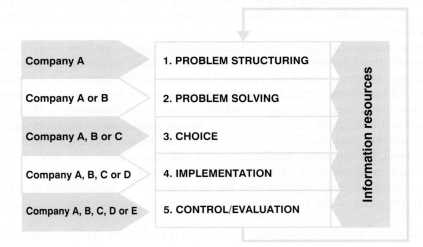

Figure 11-17
Value shop configuration

Imagine yourself working for an international consultancy firm. What are the information and knowledge flows used to create value and enable competition?

STOP & THINK

A value network is a company (e.g. telecoms, mediating firms, marketplace providers) that creates value by connecting clients and customers that are, or want to be, dependent upon each other – they act as the conduit between people. Depending upon the *value configuration*, information systems might create competitive advantage in different ways (with the traditional approach you may focus on making production more efficient whereas information systems in the value shop will create competitive advantage by implementing improved solutions to client problems. Information systems in the value network will create competitive advantage by enabling more users to share more services at a lower price on the common infrastructure) Gottschalk (2006).

Enterprise and global information needs

Responsive strategies and time-based competitive advantage, structural changes, empowerment strategies, coordination and control needs, all place new requirements on and arguments for the way information resources are managed. The information needs of large organizations differ greatly from those of small organizations; similarly, the needs of process oriented organizations differ from traditional organizations. In the case of the horizontal (process oriented) organization there is a greater dependency on integrated systems and wider access to information resources. In the case of the international organization there are also likely to be differences in local and corporate needs. And as was discussed in Chapter 3, it is important that corporate headquarter resources (such as a centralized information systems group) add value and not simply costs to do business globally. One way of adding value is through central management of certain information resources.

Aside from processing larger amounts of transaction data in support of primary activities, large organizations also tend to be more formal organizations. The MNC must not only deal with the problem of how to make information available to a larger set of people but must face additional challenges such as language barriers, incompatible systems, time zone differences, different legal systems and privacy or tax laws, currency, etc. There is a greater need for coordination and control in the large and the dispersed organization (refer back to Chapter 9).

Typically, organizations have multiple information systems that have evolved over time. Unfortunately, there are often problems encountered when trying to link them (integration) together. However, there are potential benefits, for the international organization, to be derived from some central control over information resources. The international organization may benefit from the re-usability of information resources, thus obtaining scale benefits. Information resources created in one subsidiary or business unit may be re-used in another without that other unit incurring the costs to create such resources. At a basic level, the corporate headquarters can help the organization meet its needs for group finance and accounting data and information (see Chapter 17). However, in more developed (transnational) organizations the key role for the information systems group is to unify the parts of the organization and enable information resources to be widely shared.

The traditional information systems approach was to develop separate systems for each functional area – this resulted in information islands – silos within the organization and therefore fragmented information and a lack of information flow. Sandoe *et al.* (2001) discusses the motivation for integration, arguing that enterprise systems seem to offer a vehicle for enhancing competitive performance, increasing responsiveness to customers, and supporting strategic initiatives. As business becomes increasingly global, integrated systems show promise for tying together the geographically dispersed organization. By far the largest intangible benefit to enterprise integration is the improved availability of information about the organization that is widely available throughout the company. This increased information visibility that results from integrated information systems enables managers and senior executives to make informed decisions in a timely manner. Integrated information systems are often achieved using enterprise resource planning (ERP) software (such as SAP).

Integration information systems integration involves bringing together previously isolated information systems with the goal of providing a more whole or complete information resource for the organization

Enterprise system an information system that integrates information from all functional areas of an organization with the goal of providing a more whole or complete information resource for the organization

Enterprise resource planning (ERP) complex software package commonly used to implement an enterprise information system. Major ERP vendors include SAP, PeopleSoft, Oracle, etc.

Since the 1970s, organizations have pursued integrated systems – unified systems to support transaction processing in all parts of the organization. Most enterprise systems use commonly available relational database management systems (e.g. Oracle, DB2, and SQL Server) and are based on standard network protocols (e.g. TCP/IP). This unbundling allows enterprise systems to run in heterogeneous computing environments and coexist with the widest possible range of hardware and operating system platforms.

Example: SAP

Worldwide the Core Enterprise Applications market accounts for approximately $16.4 billion in software revenues (2006) – SAP receives approximately 25 per cent of the market's business.

Founded in 1972 as **S**ystems **A**pplications and **P**roducts in Data Processing, SAP is the recognized leader in providing collaborative business solutions for all types of industries and for every major market. Serving more than 36 200 customers worldwide, SAP is the world's largest business software company and the world's third-largest independent software provider overall. Headquartered in Walldorf, Germany, SAP employs approximately 40 000 people in more than 50 countries. SAP is the world's leading provider of business software (enterprise resource planning and related applications such as supply chain management, customer relationship management, product life-cycle management and supplier relationship management). Customers in more than 120 countries run SAP® applications – from distinct solutions addressing the needs of small and midsize enterprises to suite offerings for global organizations.

Source: http://www.sap.com (October 2006)

STOP & THINK

Compare and contrast the enterprise information needs and strategies of Bosch (see learning case on below) and the Duckworth Group.

Active learning case

The Bosch Group

The global orientation of the Bosch Group is almost as old as the Bosch company itself. The first international Bosch branches were set up at the end of the 19th century, and work on the construction of a Bosch factory in the United States began in 1909. Today, Bosch is active on every continent and has subsidiaries and associated companies in more than 50 countries (the Bosch Group employs approx. 271 000 people). Bosch operates roughly 270 production sites worldwide, of which nearly 210 are located outside Germany – in Europe, North and South America, Africa, Asia and Australia. The name Bosch is closely associated with the automotive industry. But Bosch is not just famous for automotive technology products like gasoline, diesel and chassis systems and car electronics. Bosch also supplies other products and services, including industrial technology, power tools, security solutions and household appliances[1].

Photo: Bosch

Bosch diesel works in Hallein, Austria

This is a factual, problem-oriented case that will allow you to explore complex multi-disciplinary problems in a real world setting. The target organization is a large international company. Issues of managing information resources are presented and the opportunity for students to engage with a variety of problems presented. The case is centred on a large scale information systems project undertaken around 2003/4.

The Bosch Group has grown strongly in recent years, has succeeded with pioneering innovations and has a global network of customers and suppliers.

Like any contemporary large MNC operating in the manufacturing (power tools, household appliances and automotive equipment) industry, Bosch need to be flexible and responsive, efficient and effective. Their large size, international presence and diverse product portfolio have created a complex organization with inherent coordination and control problems. They face several related and significant problems due to their structure, processes and systems. Such problems make them less effective and efficient and inhibit their ability to meet challenges posed by their global business environment. To the outside world they must appear as one, commonly branded, organization if fruitful supplier and customer relationships are to be maintained and grown. Aside from considering weaknesses born out of legacy systems, structures and processes, the Bosch Group is also presented with opportunity. In particular there are significant opportunities to share resources across its subsidiaries and production plants resulting in synergistic benefits[2].

	2003[1]	2004[2]	2005[2]	2006	2007
Sales revenue	36 357	38 954	41 461	43 684	46 320
Percentage share of sales revenue generated outside Germany	71	72	73	74	75
Annual average number of associates (thousands)	229	234	249	261	271
located in Germany	105	107	110	110	112
located outside Germany	124	127	139	151	159
Capital expenditure	2 028	2 435	2 923	2 670	2 634
Research and development cost[3]	2 650	2 898	3 073	3 348	3 583
Profit after tax	1 100	1 675	2 450	2 170	2 850

Currency figures in millions of euros
[1] Before 2004, figures pursusant to the provisions of the German commercial code
[2] With the exception of profit after tax, figures apply to continuing operations only
[3] Including development work charged directly to customers

Historically, their numerous subsidiaries and production plants developed information systems individually and were suitable for their specific needs. This led to a decentralized heterogeneous IS architecture comprising legacy systems, varied business processes and ways of doing business. Unfortunately, this became a weakness in the context of a global organization. Recognizing the need for change, their aim is to become more flexible, to improve coordination, control and decision-making, to exploit synergy through resource sharing, reduce IS costs and develop their corporate identity through a group portal. Goals were to be achieved through a large scale change programme involving the streamlining, updating and integration of systems, processes and structures. Central to its integration programme was the development of a homogeneous IS architecture (a standardized integration architecture named the 'business bus'). Certain legacy systems were migrated over to SAP which was to be used to harmonize its internal IS architecture. Intra (between business units) and then inter (suppliers and customers) organizational processes as well as integrating the companies' EC (SCM and CRM) systems. Furthermore, the standardized integration architecture was to be controlled centrally. At the time of the project, anticipated benefits included cost savings, improved coordination and control. Specifically, the company will be able to develop its corporate identity through a group portal strategy. At the time of the project, present customers placed orders across differing business units. The project team identified potential improvements in the areas of procurement, inventory management, production, warehousing and a variety of stakeholder relationships.

Sources:
1 http://www.bosch.com/
2 Puschmann, T. and Alt, R. (2004) Enterprise application integration systems and architecture – the case of the Robert Bosch Group, The Journal of Enterprise Information Management, 17 (2):105–116.

Information resource strategy

As the previous case revealed, the global management of information resources is a significant challenge. Previous sections have highlighted the importance of *information resources* to the international organization. At the beginning of this chapter we noted that a goal of today's organization is having the right information, in the right place, in the right format, at the right time and at the right cost. We also suggested that a significant contemporary challenge concerns exploiting an organization's proprietary information resources as strategic assets (refer back to the RBV). In this final section we outline key aspects of the strategic management of information resources. It is widely agreed that the information and knowledge strategy should support ('fit') the organizational strategy. The information strategy concerns approaches to the organization, control and application of organizational information resources through coordination of people and technology resources in order to support the organizational strategy and processes (Chaffey and Wood 2005: 180). The authors argue the need to manage information, people and technological resources together in support of the organizational strategy; the relationship between such organizational elements was discussed in Chapter 5. Many organizations, however, fail to manage information as an important resource.

Look back
See chapters 3 and 5

Without a strategy, organizations can run into problems with data confidentiality, availability and quality, leading to legal and regulatory problems and an inability to compete. Aside from a focus on problems we should also consider the benefits. Integrating information activities improves information and knowledge flow and therefore timely decision-making, enabling agile and responsive organizations. Attention from the top of the organization will also impact upon culture development, fostering an open communications climate and knowledge-sharing thus facilitating innovation and creativity. There will also be benefits associated with visibility and employees appreciating the 'bigger picture' focus i.e. not a parochial focus. Furthermore, empowerment strategies, certain organizational and work designs and quality decision-making are critically dependent upon the availability of information resources.

Look back
See chapter 5, p. 148

We have noted that the organizational design may facilitate or impair information flow. Structurally, there is often a need for a champion, someone with responsibility for corporate information and technology. There will normally be an organizational unit responsible for information and knowledge that is distinct from the IT function. In larger international organizations this unit may exist in both corporate and regional headquarters while in the SME there is more likely to be a single information systems group addressing company-wide needs.

The structuring of information management and IT specialists is likely to be dependent upon whether the organization is global or multi-domestic. Ultimately, information management is everyone's responsibility. However, certain tasks require specialist knowledge and a specialist group is needed in order to focus on information quality and availability and the need to safeguard information (security) and assure information resources are used in a legally and ethically compliant manner.

The information strategy may be more or less formal and may emerge or be created (as a result of a planned activity). The *process* for developing an information resource management strategy has much in common with the approach for developing a corporate strategy i.e. establish where you are now, where you want to be and a means to get there. Typically, organizations assess information relevancy, value and quality, security and the information management skills of employees in the first stage of strategy formulation (an information resource audit). Consideration will be given to where information resources are located, how they flow, are handled and used. They also determine legal constraints and the organizational significance of information resources – how they support the creation of value and the achievement of the organization's objectives. Having assessed organizational information management strengths, weaknesses and needs, requirements will be generated and alternative solutions evaluated. Among such solutions are knowledge management systems (Chapter 12), enterprise systems (Chapter 13), Internet and other communications and collaboration software and systems (Chapter 14).

Throughout this chapter we have identified and demonstrated the strategic importance of information resources to the international organization. Such resources must therefore be protected if organizations are to benefit from them, retain a sustainable competitive advantage and function as planned. In protecting their information resources, organizations typically pursue three security goals: confidentiality, integrity and availability (CIA). Confidentiality (also known as secrecy and concerned with privacy) measures seek to ensure that the computing or information system's assets or data can be read only by authorized parties. Integrity controls seek to ensure that data is truthful while the availability goal ensures that information resources are accessible to authorized parties in a timely manner (Kelly 2005: 107).

Summary of key learning points

Information resources include data, information, knowledge, and wisdom (DIKW). Data refers to raw facts and information is the summarization of data. Technology and information/knowledge represent 'hard' and 'soft' resources available to the organization. Unlike most resources which deplete when used, information and knowledge can be shared, and actually grow through application. It is now widely accepted that winning strategies are more often grounded in the accumulation and creative exploitation of intangibles that are more difficult to replicate.

Key factors of production include – knowledge, collaboration and engagement assets, and time (how quickly value is created). These are the four key resources from which economic activity and competitive advantage are primarily derived and delivered. Improved information flows can improve the quality of decision-making, collaboration, planning, coordination and control and internal operations. A firm's resources will be a source of competitive advantage if the resources are valuable, rare, inimitable and not substitutable.

Structure and culture may impact upon the free flow of information within the organization. There are also geographical and time barriers, language and technology barriers and legal constraints. All may impair communications and the sharing of information resources.

There are many challenges associated with knowledge and its use within the international organization. Knowledge, when locked into systems or processes, has higher inherent value than when it can 'walk out of the door' in people's heads. Consequently organizations embark on knowledge management programmes in an attempt to ensure knowledge can be accessed, shared and retained. A global company's skill at transferring knowledge across subsidiaries gives these subsidiaries the added benefit of innovations created by their peers.

To compete effectively in global markets, exporters need to develop the capabilities to produce high value-added products and to target more closely their marketing efforts. This requires closer linkages with suppliers and with customers. Partnerships in a value chain encourage a joint approach to problem-solving and lead to cost reductions and quality improvements. The international organization has to develop and maintain smooth, seamless coordination across locations. The worldwide business team needs to foster operational coordination between units performing similar activities as well as those performing complementary activities and the transfer of knowledge and skills across locations.

As business becomes increasingly global, integrated systems show promise for tying together the geographically dispersed organization. By far the largest intangible benefit to enterprise integration is the improved availability of information about the organization that is widely available throughout the company. This increased information visibility enables organizations to make informed decisions in a timely manner.

Given the importance of information resources they should be strategically managed. It is widely agreed that the information and knowledge strategy should support ('fit') the organizational strategy.

Review questions

Consider the opening chapter case study:

1 Using the stakeholder analysis approach list the senior internal roles at the headquarters and within the subsidiaries. Identify the important decisions they must make. Finally, consider, with particular reference to data, information and knowledge resources, how the quality of decision-making may be improved.

2 Look back at Chapter 8 (organizational design) and draft a probable organizational chart for the the Duckworth Group. How might the structure impact upon the flow of information resources throughout the organization?

3 How important is knowledge management to this company? Explain your answer.

4 What challenges and issues may be posed by the geographical, cultural, language, technological and time difference barriers within the group? In particular, consider the impact on planning, decision-making, coordination and control and business activities.

When considering cultural differences and similarities it may help to consider the data presented by Hofstede (1984) in his landmark work on international differences. Scores for the Power Distance Index (PDI),Uncertainty Avoidance Index (UAI), Individualism (IDV) and Masculinity (MAS) follow: PDI – India (77), South Africa (49) and Great Britain (35); UAI – India (40), South Africa (49) and Great Britain (35); IDV – India (48), South Africa (65) and Great Britain (89) and MAS – India (56), South Africa (63) and Great Britain (66).

5 Finally, assess how technology may be deployed to enable information resource sharing and allow Duckworth a competitive advantage over its rivals.

The takeover

In 2004, Cargill (the largest private company in the US) acquired the Duckworth Group:

The Manchester-based food flavourings company was acquired by Cargill of the US for about £40m. In an article, Duckworth Flavours stated that following its acquisition by Cargill at the start of the year it would now be focusing on supplying ingredients to the eastern European markets in a bid to increase its position in the European ingredients market. 'Although we are keeping the Duckworth name, we have now made the jump from a family business to become part of a huge multinational operation', said Jack Proctor, key accounts manager at UK-based Duckworth Flavours. 'What this means is that our pockets are now a lot deeper and that there is more potential for us to invest in new and expanding markets.'

Consider the integration issues faced by the two companies following the acquisition. How could each company benefit from the resources held by the other? Focus, in particular, on information and knowledge resources and identify the possible technological, cultural and other challenges they would face.

Sources of competitive advantage

Read and précis the article by Porter, M. E. and Millar, V. E. (1985), 'How information gives you a competitive advantage' – next, consider the Duckworth case study or an organization with which you are familiar:

1 Assess information intensity

- How is information being used by the organization and its customers?
- Where are the priority areas for its investment?

2 Examine how information resources and IT provides competitive advantages.

3 What are the possibilities for information resources and IT providing competitive advantage?

■ Where are the opportunities to reduce cost and differentiate services?

4 Can IT enable relationships with other industries?

5 Can IT spawn new business?

References

Bierly, P., Kessler, E. and Christensen, E. (2000) 'Organizational learning, knowledge and wisdom', *Journal of Organizational Change Management* 13(6):595–618.

Blumberg, R. and Atre, S. (2003) 'The Problem with Unstructured Data', *DM Review Magazine*, February 2003 Issue.

BCG (1999) 'How value chains are starting to dissolve', *The Antidote from C|S|B|S* 1999 23:23–25.

Campbell, A. (1998) 'Cooperation in international value chains: comparing an exporter's supplier versus customer relationships', *Journal of Business & Industrial Marketing* 13(1):22–39.

Chaffey, D. (2007) *E-Business and E-Commerce Management* (3 ed), Harlow: Prentice Hall.

Chaffey, D., Bocij, P., Greasley, A. and Hickie, S. (2003) *Business Information Systems – Technology, Development and Management for the e-business* (2 ed), Harlow: FT Prentice Hall.

Chaffey, D. and Wood, S. (2005) *Business Information Management*, Harlow: FT Prentice Hall.

Dickson, G. C. (1995) *Corporate Risk Management*, London: Witherby & Co.

Drucker, P. (1955) '"Management Science" and the Manager', *Management Science* (January 1955) 1(2):115–126.

Drucker, P. (1994) 'The Theory of the Business', *Harvard Business Review* (September/October 1994) 72(5):95–104.

Duncan, R. (1972) 'Characteristics of Organizational Environments and Perceived Environmental Uncertainty', *Administrative Science Quarterly* 17(3):313–327.

Eustace, C. (2003) 'A new perspective on the knowledge value chain', *Journal of Intellectual Capital* 4(4):588–596.

Gates, B. (1999) *Business © the Speed of Thought: Using a Digital Nervous System* (1 ed), New York: Warner Business Books.

Gottschalk, P. (2006) 'Information systems in value configurations', *Industrial Management & Data Systems* 106(7):1060–1070.

Gupta, A. K. and Govindarajan, V. (2001) 'Converting global presence into global competitive advantage', *Academy of Management Executive* (May 2001) 15(2).

Handy, C. B. (1995) *Beyond Certainty*, London: Hutchinson.

Hofstede, G. (1985) *Culture's Consequences: International differences in work-related values* (abridged), Newbury Park, CA: Sage.

Hofstede, G. (1997) *Cultures and Organizations*, New York: McGraw-Hill.

Huczynski, A. and Buchanan, D. (2007) *Organizational Behaviour* (6 ed), Harlow: Financial Times, Prentice Hall.

International Trade Centre (ITC) http://www.intracen.org/tis/ accessed 17 October 2006.

Janis, I. L. (1989) *Crucial Decisions*, New York: Free Press.

Jones, C. (1994) 'Improving Your Key Business Processes', *The TQM Magazine* 6(2):25–29.

Kelly, P. (2005) *Information Systems Risk*, London: Witherbys.

Kolb, D. A. (1976) *The Learning Style Inventory: Technical Manual*, Boston, Ma: McBer.

Laudon K. C. and Laudon, J. P. (2007) *Management Information Systems: Managing the Digital Firm* (10 ed), Upper Saddle River, NJ: Prentice Hall.

O'Brien, J. A. (2002) *Management Information Systems – Managing Information Technology in the E-Business Enterprise* (5 ed), New York: McGraw-Hill Higher Education.

Pantzar, E. (2000) 'Knowledge and wisdom in the information society', *Foresight* (April 2000) 2(2):230–236.

Porter, M. E and Millar, V. E. (1985) 'How information gives you a competitive advantage', *Harvard Business Review* (July–August 1963):149–174.

Porter, M. E. (2001) 'Strategy and the Internet', *Harvard Business Review* (March 2001):62–78.

Pugh, D. S. (1997) *Organization Theory* (4 ed), Harmondsworth: Penguin.

Puschmann, T. and Alt, R. (2004) 'Enterprise application integration systems and architecture – the case of the Robert Bosch Group', *The Journal of Enterprise Information Management* 17(2):105–116.

Rainbird, M. (2004) 'A framework for operations management: the value chain', *International Journal of Physical Distribution & Logistics Management* 34(3/4):337–345.

Robson, W. (1997) *Strategic Management of Information Systems* (2 ed), Harlow: FT Prentice Hall.

Sandoe, K., Corbitt, G. and Boykin, R. (2001) *Enterprise Integration*, New York: Wiley.

Simon, H. A. (1960) *The new science of management decision*. New York: Harper and Row.

Simons, R. (1995) *Levers of Control*, Boston, Mass: Harvard Business School Press.

Skyrme, D. (1994) 'Ten Ways to Add Value to Your Business', *Managing Information* (March 1994) 1(3):20–25.

Small, M. W. (2004) 'Wisdom and now managerial wisdom: do they have a place in management development programs?', *Journal of Management Development* 23(8):761–774.

Sternberg, R. J. (1990) 'Wisdom: Its Nature, Origins, and Development', Cambridge: Cambridge University Press.

Syed, H. and Akhter, F. R. (2006) 'Leveraging internal competency and managing environmental uncertainty – Propensity to collaborate in international markets', *International Marketing Review* 23(1):98–115.

Turban, E., McLean, E. and Wetherbe, J. (2002) *Information Technology for Management – Transforming Business in the Digital Economy* (3 ed), Hoboken, NJ: Wiley International.

World Bank (2006) www.worldbank.org/data.

Suggestions for further reading

Journals

Management Information Systems Quarterly (MISQ) – The editorial objective of the *MIS Quarterly* is the enhancement and communication of knowledge concerning the development of IT-based services, the management of IT resources, and the use, impact, and economics of IT with managerial, organizational, and societal implications. http://www.misq.org/.

The *International Journal of Information Management* (IJIM) is an international, peer-reviewed journal which aims to bring its readers the very best analysis and discussion in the developing field of information management. http://www.sciencedirect.com/science/journal/02684012

Key articles

Scholars of this subject area have often read the following:

1 Porter, M. E. and Millar, V. E. (1985) 'How information gives you a competitive advantage', *Harvard Business Review* (July–August 1963):149–174.

2 Evans, P. and Wurster, T. (1997) 'Strategy and the New Economics of Information', *Harvard Business Review* (September/October 1997) 75(5):70–82.

3 Benjamin, B. and Wigand, R. (1995) 'Electronic Markets and Virtual Value Chains on the Information Superhighway', *Sloan Management Review* (Winter 1995) 36(2):62–72.

4 Rayport, J. F. and Sviokla, J. J. (1996) 'Exploiting the virtual value chain', *McKinsey Quarterly* 1:20–36.

5 Stabell, C. B. and Fjeldstad, O. D. (1998) 'Configuring Value for Competitive Advantage: On Chains, Shops, and Networks', *Strategic Management Journal* (May 1998) 19(5):413–437.

6 Sambamurthy, V., Bharadwaj, A. and Grover, V. (2003) 'Shaping Agility Through Digital Options: Reconceptualizing The Role Of Information Technology In Contemporary Firms', *MIS Quarterly* (June 2003) 27(2):237–263.

Chapter 12

Managing knowledge resources

Introduction

Learning, knowledge and intellectual capital

Organizational learning and learning organization

KM infrastructure

Cross-border learning and KM

··

Key concepts

- ■ Knowledge ■ Human (tacit) knowledge ■ Structured (explicit) knowledge
- ■ Knowledge integration ■ Codification ■ Learning ■ Learning organization
- ■ Knowledge acquisition ■ Knowledge transfer ■ Communities of practice
- ■ Personalization strategy

By the end of this chapter you will be able to:

- ■ Discuss KM processes

- ■ Explain the roles of technology, people, structure, culture and processes in knowledge management

- ■ Explain how the KM infrastructure contributes to organizational effectiveness

- ■ Explain how knowledge is managed within the MNC and between alliances, partnerships and joint ventures

- ■ Explain what is meant by the knowledge-based view (KBV) and evaluate the role of knowledge resources in developing sustainable competitive advantage

Active learning case

Unilever

Teleos, an independent knowledge management and intellectual capital research firm, administer the *Most Admired Knowledge Enterprises* (MAKE) programme. The European MAKE study was established in 1999 to recognize organizations for their ability to create shareholder wealth by transforming new as well as existing enterprise knowledge into superior products, services or solutions. European MAKE finalists are ranked against each of the eight knowledge performance dimensions which form the MAKE framework and are the visible drivers of wealth creation[1]: creating an enterprise knowledge-driven culture; developing knowledge workers through senior management leadership; delivering knowledge-based products/services/solutions; maximizing enterprise intellectual capital; creating an environment for collaborative knowledge sharing; creating a learning organization; delivering value based on customer knowledge, and transforming enterprise knowledge into shareholder value. The 2006 winners included Unilever (Netherlands/UK) one of the world's leading suppliers of fast-moving consumer goods. The company has two global divisions: foods, and home and personal care, generating annual sales of approximately €40 billion, employing around 180 000 people worldwide and operating in 100 countries. Unilever believes that its long-term success requires a total commitment to exceptional standards of performance and productivity, working together effectively, and a willingness to embrace new ideas and learn continuously. The 2006 European MAKE panel recognized Unilever for its enterprise-wide collaborative knowledge sharing (1st place). Unilever is a six-time European MAKE Finalist and four-time European MAKE Winner (see also Gorelick and Tantawy-Monsou 2005).[2]

KM is also about combining existing knowledge to make new products and services. 'For instance,' he says, 'Unilever was the first company to make a moisturising lipstick, because a cosmetics manager was inspired by an internal presentation on margarine showing how it structures fats to contain water. KM brings clarity on how such combinations might be encouraged,' said Sam Marshall, a KM specialist at Unilever R&D.[3]

Unilever has developed knowledge strategies for creating and transferring knowledge, Nonaka, Von Krogh and Aben (2001). Knowledge relies not on technology but on people, who have knowledge, develop it and act on the basis of it. David Smith, head of knowledge management at Unilever, stated that 'Knowledge management is the only long-term, sustainable source of competitive advantage.'[4] At the heart of Unilever's corporate purpose is the ambition to be a truly 'multi-local', multinational company – understanding and anticipating the everyday needs of people everywhere and meeting these needs with branded products and services.[5] Having recognized the importance of knowledge as a key differentiator and the source for sustainable competitive advantage, Unilever has made significant investments in IT over the past decades. However, the company recognize most knowledge in the organization is not explicit, but tacit, residing in the heads of its employees. In light of continuous restructuring, it is this tacit knowledge that is most under threat. Trying to capture or transfer this tacit knowledge is not easy, as it stems from personal experience and individuals are not always aware of the value of the knowledge they hold. Moreover, knowledge is not static. In fact, it is the continuous creation of new knowledge and learning, rather than static knowledge assets that will produce a sustainable advantage.

Cathy Bautista, head of knowledge management at Unilever, speaking on the BBC's 'Nice Work' programme (2005) described how Unilever practised knowledge management (KM). Bautista suggested that KM is accomplished in a combination of ways. At Unilever, KM is about bringing

In a history spanning three centuries, Unilever, a multi-local multinational, has created products to help people get more out of life – cutting time spent on household chores, improving nutrition, enabling people to enjoy food and take care of their homes, their clothes and themselves. Around 150 million times a day, someone somewhere chooses a Unilever product. With 400 brands spanning 14 categories of home, personal care and food products, no other company touches so many people's lives in so many different ways.

Formed in 1930 from two companies, Margarine Unie (Netherlands) and Lever Brothers (UK), Unilever produced goods made of oils and fats, principally soap and margarine. By the 1980s Unilever was one of the world's biggest companies, its success based upon understanding consumer requirements and valuing the role of science, technology and knowledge in delivering solutions. Fostering an 'open approach to innovation' allowed Unilever to 'unlock creativity from many sources'. Working with partners all over the world, Unilever has developed new opportunities and translated them into better ways of meeting people's needs. The company is constantly enhancing its brands, investing €1 billion every year in cutting edge research and development. Its five laboratories around the world explore new thinking and techniques to help develop their products.

Dammtorwall 15

Unilever

people together to share and apply what they know; it's also about communication and making information and knowledge available to the wider organization in the form of reports and IT tools. KM is about sharing best practice through formal and informal networks. However, Unilever formalize the network, bringing people together through workshops, etc. They facilitate groups coming together and recommend people at least meet face-to-face once. By bringing people together, elements of trust are developed and then participants can choose whether they're going to continue with their relationship through virtual ways such as collaborative work space on the Internet or how they manage their e-mail, etc.[6]

Over the past few years, Unilever has established numerous knowledge-management initiatives across the company. At the outset, in order to capture what was known and identify what was not (knowledge gaps), knowledge workshops were organized and continue to be used. At such workshops, key experts and practitioners from around the world discuss a specific, strategically relevant knowledge domain. The workshops aim to develop a common understanding about the knowledge strengths and weaknesses of the company as a whole. Existing good practices are captured and rolled out to the wider community. At the same time, innovation and R&D programmes are initiated to address the knowledge gaps identified.[5] From these workshops, communities of practice (CoP) emerge – groups of experts acting as the custodians of a specific knowledge domain; CoPs bring together and network the most highly talented people in their area. Networks have been interwoven with Unilever's organization for many decades, both on a personal, informal level and on a more structured, organizational level. However, as the organization becomes leaner it is apparent that communities of practice depend on careful management and the appropriate allocation of resources if they are to survive. For this reason, the Knowledge Management Group (KMG) has devised a more formal framework to help ensure the effective and efficient operation of the firm's communities of practice. The roles and responsibilities of CoP members are identified and ground rules laid as the basis for creating an open and trusting culture in which members feel safe to share and create knowledge. As part of its launch, each community defines these ground rules itself, including the ICT support needed to ensure effective ongoing communication and knowledge sharing. Initiatives also ensure knowledge flows not just within but also in and out of the CoP. The KMG works closely with activists and champions who are in the process of setting up a community of practice. Typically, a champion identifies the need for networking and knowledge development in their part of the business. The next step is then to clarify objectives, and determine whether setting up a CoP is the most effective way of realizing these objectives.

Iske (2002) discusses the 'learning organization' as a key concept in the integration of business units and in Unilever's ongoing strategy to continue as a focused, efficient and entrepreneurial 'multi-local, multinational'. To help Unilever to become a learning organization, the company has developed a number of initiatives. Unilever does not restrict the scope of knowledge sharing to that of an intracompany only initiative. Iske (2002) argues the core benefit of a CoP is the exchange of ideas and experiences; 'organizations do learn from each other'. Recognizing KM to be a new discipline he suggests we are all struggling with questions like: How do we start our KM efforts? How can senior management be convinced that an investment in KM is worthwhile? What technology should we use? How do we measure the benefits of KM? and what are the best practices? Iske (2002) identifies several topics that have been discussed within the community, which include: people finders/Yellow-Pages systems for the identification of experts within the organization; the use of customer-relationship-management tools to capture and leverage knowledge from and about customers; new technology, such as portals, search engines and e-learning; the development and facilitation of knowledge communities; issues around sharing of knowledge and information (such as privacy); the organization of KM (do you need a separate department or a CKO?); the relationship between KM, HR and training and development and the relationship between KM and e-business. He argues that, in practice, organizations learn from each other indirectly, via case studies, conferences, books and, most of all, through the use of consultants.

Sources:

1 Teleos (2006) European most Admired Knowledge Enterprises – Executive Summary www.knowledgebusiness.com.
2 Gorelick, C. and Tantawy-Monsou, B. (2005) 'For performance through learning, knowledge management is critical practice', The Learning Organization, 12(2):125–139.
3 Lelic, S. (2003) 'Your Say: KM in research and development', Inside Knowledge, Ark Group Ltd, posted 23 Jan 2003, 6(5).
4 first.emeraldinsight.com/knowledge_management/management_briefings.htm.
5 Pos, A., Linse, K. and Aben, M. (2005) 'Unilever: Leveraging community value', Inside Knowledge, Ark Group Ltd, 14 Jan 2005 in 8(4).
6 www.bbc.co.uk/radio4/news/nicework/transcripts/20050329_nice_work.pdf Iske, P. (2002) 'Building a corporate KM community', Inside Knowledge, Ark Group Ltd, posted 9 Dec 2002 in 6(4).

Introduction

In the previous chapter we differentiated between the various information and knowledge resources and explained aspects of information processing, collecting data inputs, data transformation and processing and the dissemination of information outputs. We then linked Chapter 11 with Chapters 9 and 10, explaining the role of data and information in support of business functions, processes and decision-making. Throughout the chapter we considered how information can deliver a competitive advantage. However, it is questionable whether a sustainable advantage is obtained. As information technology becomes more 'open' and 'standard' it becomes readily available in a similar guise for competitors to implement (imitate). We noted that we now live in a 'knowledge society' and must therefore ask how organizations process knowledge and, more importantly, how they create new knowledge (Nonaka 1994).

One of the challenges we address in this chapter concerns how an organization can develop in such a way that it uses its knowledge to the strategic advantage of the international business. This challenge is made greater, given the nature of the organization's external environment (Chapter 2). The turbulent nature of the environment forces organizations to constantly adapt to change. Consequently, the search for new knowledge is ever present and the need to constantly integrate and utilize it to add value. Davenport and Völpel (2001) identify knowledge management as the key success factor of today's business leaders; it has become a mainstream business function.

Knowledge management (KM) is a complex and multidisciplinary concept bringing together people, processes, technology, strategy, structure and culture; much of what has been covered in previous chapters. Nonaka (1994) argues that at a fundamental level, knowledge is created by individuals. An organization cannot create knowledge without individuals. The organization supports creative individuals or provides a context for such individuals to create knowledge. Bartlett and Ghoshal (2002) argue there is value in attracting and developing individuals who hold specialized knowledge and there is value in the social networks enabling sharing of such knowledge. Indeed, unless a company actively links, leverages and embeds the pockets of individual-based knowledge and expertise, it risks underutilizing or losing its knowledge. As companies seek the best ways to convert individual expertise into embedded intellectual capital, they frequently allocate the task to the chief information officer or chief knowledge officer. However, people with a background in information-systems focus immediately on the task of mapping, modelling and codifying knowledge.

Under their leadership, companies have developed databases and intranets to help capture and make accessible the company's most valuable information and explicit knowledge. Yet in many companies, managers do not take full advantage of the 'softer' knowledge-management systems. At the heart of the problem is a widespread failure to recognize that although knowledge management can be supported by an efficient technical infrastructure, it is operated through a social network. Information technologists may help in organizing data and making it accessible, but they must be teamed up with – and operate in support of – those who understand human motivation and social interaction. Only then can individual roles and organizational processes be designed to ensure the delicate conversion from available information to embedded knowledge. Thus, a core strategic role of the HR executive is to take the lead in developing the social networks that are vital to the capture and transfer of knowledge. Because that requires an understanding of organizational design, process management, interpersonal relationships and trust-based culture, it calls for leadership from sophisticated human-resources professionals who also have a strong understanding of the business, see Figure 12-1.

Increasingly, managers are becoming aware of the importance of knowledge resources in pursuing international business strategy (Massingham 2004). Knowledge provides the capability to identify, examine and capture market opportunities. It develops competence in important activities and helps resolve problems. Knowledge is also changing the way

Knowledge management (KM) The strategic use of information and knowledge resources to an organization's best advantage and includes a system or framework for managing the organizational infrastructure that obtains, creates, stores, distributes and promotes the use of knowledge within and between organizations

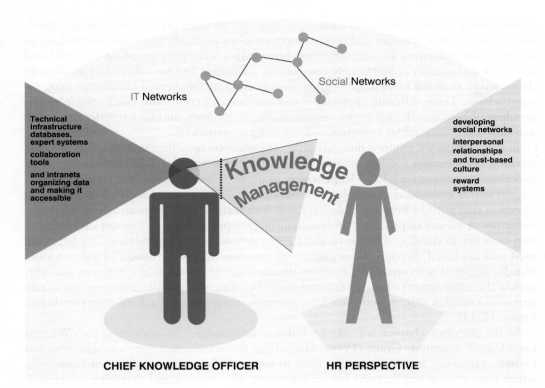

Figure 12-1

Perceptions of KM

organizations compete, particularly in the international business arena where opportunities for creating value are shifting from managing tangible assets to managing knowledge-based strategies. Indeed, Ghoshal, Bartlett, and Moran (2000) argue that managing knowledge is a key to international business success. Massingham (2004) suggests that knowledge resources can create a sustainable competitive advantage in dynamic, changing international markets through the creation of knowledge barriers to imitation in key knowledge components. Organizations can use these knowledge resources to establish competitive advantage by developing competence in key value creating activities. In fact, a growing number of executives, consultants, and management theorists have declared in recent years that knowledge now represents the major source of competitive advantage for organizations.

This knowledge-based view of the firm (KBV) argues that creating, organizing, and using knowledge resources is at the core of organizational value-adding activities and competition. Effectiveness in these activities determines performance, relative to the competition. As a consequence, many companies have launched major programmes to manage knowledge and become learning organizations. In this chapter we provide an overview of the literature on knowledge management and organizational learning. We highlight the significance of networks, alliances and inter-organizational relationships for organizations; and consider the importance of learning in and through such relationships. We also examine aspects of the KM infrastructure and determine how it can lead to enhanced organizational performance. We close the chapter with a focus on the KM strategy and processes to develop such a strategy.

Knowledge-based view of the firm a view that knowledge should be the resource on which to base strategy

Learning knowledge and intellectual capital

There are many concepts associated with knowledge. Indeed, knowledge has been studied by scholars from many disciplines: finance and accounting have developed theories to value knowledge as an asset; HR seek to acquire, attract, motivate and facilitate the utilization of knowledge to improve organizational performance through the transformational activities of people; ICT scholars and practitioners seek out methods to employ technology to facilitate the utilization of organizational knowledge; strategists adopting the RBV and KBV seek out sources of sustainable competitive advantage and yet others may be directly dedicated to studying knowledge through membership of a dedicated knowledge management school. These differing approaches and perspectives contribute much to our understanding of how people, networks, organizations, economies, and societies depend upon, and deal with, 'intangibles resources' – knowledge in particular.

In this section we explore this vast array of concepts: organizational learning and the learning organization focuses on knowledge acquisition and development and diffusion processes on making such knowledge widely available. There are different types of knowledge resource embedded in people, systems, culture, routines and formal procedures and direction that must be bundled and integrated with further knowledge and other company resources. A variety of processes and mechanisms are put in place to support such integration in order to develop difficult to imitate competencies and capabilities. The latter are used and deployed through the organization structure and work design in value adding transformational activities. This leads to the creation of products and services and ultimately the achievement of organizational goals. For now we consider each concept as one part of a complex system and then later integrate them through a KBV framework (see Figure 12-14).

In the previous chapter we asked, 'What is knowledge?' In answering the 'What is knowledge?' question, Grant (1996: 110) offers the simple tautology of 'that which is known'. However, he recognizes the need to establish those characteristics of knowledge which have critical implications for management. The concept and definition of 'knowledge' itself is complex and disputed (Beeby and Booth 2000). A number of authors have commented that what we call knowledge embodies a wide range of different meanings and attributes. The Greeks distinguished valid information (eidos) from opinions or beliefs (doxa), truth (noesis) from perception (pistis), abstractions (episteme) from practical skills (techne), political and social sense (phronesis) from cunning (metis). It is common to make distinctions between knowing what and knowing how, and between knowledge in our heads and knowledge in a book.

Senge (1998a) considers the difference between 'knowing about things,' which is really information, versus 'knowing how'. De Long and Fahey (2000) discuss types of knowledge such as human knowledge, what individuals know or know how to do and structured knowledge – knowledge embedded in an organization's systems, processes, tools, and routines. Kogut and Zander (1992) distinguish between two categories of knowledge – information and know-how. By information, they mean knowledge which can be transmitted - knowledge as information implies knowing what something means. Know-how is, as the compound words state, a description of knowing how to do something. Know-how, like procedural knowledge, is a description of what defines current practice inside the international organization.

Most scholars identify two types of knowledge: tacit, which is embedded in the human brain and cannot be expressed easily, and explicit knowledge, which can be easily codified (Nonaka 1991); Polanyi (1966), however, argues all knowledge is either tacit or rooted in tacit knowledge. According to Davenport and Völpel (2001) both types of knowledge are important, but Western firms have focused largely on managing explicit knowledge. Thomas and Allen (2006) recognize problems with the definition of explicit knowledge and the confusion with information. Knowledge is mainly embedded in people; it can be written down and made 'explicit', but rarely without losing a good deal of its richness and applicability. Consequently, explicit knowledge is often also relegated to the lowly title of information. Machlup (1980) identifies 13 different 'elements of knowing', including: being acquainted with, being familiar with, being aware of, remembering, recollecting, recognizing, distinguishing, understanding, interpreting, being able to explain, being able to demonstrate, being able to talk about, and being able to perform.

From our discussions so far we note that knowledge may be *located* in many places: in people (human capital) and in organizational systems. Diefenbach (2006) treats human

© Monkeybusinessimages | Dreamstime.com

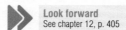

Look forward
See chapter 12, p. 405

Human knowledge what individuals know or know how to do. Human or individual knowledge is manifested in skill or expertise and usually combines both explicit and tacit knowledge (may be sentient or cognitive)

Structured knowledge knowledge embedded in an organization's systems, processes, tools, and routines. Knowledge in this form is explicit and rule-based (exists independently of human knowers it is an organizational resource)

capital as tacit knowledge and individual competence. Individuals often interact with others, i.e. act within social relationships. Hence, intangible resources can and do reside in more than one person, for example: social norms and traditions. The common characteristic of these intangible resources is that they are 'between' or shared by people; this category is called social capital. As Gant *et al.* (2002: 296) explains, the term social capital refers 'both to the network of relationships that exist among individuals in some group and to the assets that are mobilized through the network of social relationships'. Furthermore, intangible resources can exist that are shared by two or more people but are not linked to particular individuals, for example: language, cultural traditions and heritage, corporate culture, working climate, informal rules, social norms, values, rules; and law. Even if certain people leave the system, or individuals change, the intangible resources remain – because they are deeply embedded in all kinds of institutions and routines of this social group or culture. Such intangible resources are transferred to new members via different means such as teaching and learning.

This category of intangible resources can be called cultural capital. There are other intangible resources that are transferable: information, explicit knowledge, intellectual property (company's name and logo, trademarks, drawings, formulas, software programs, copyrights, patents, licences, quota, internet domains, portals) and contractually regulated aspects of formal relations between parties (rights and duties). Finally, there is embedded capital; infrastructure (hierarchies, controlling structures and processes), organizational knowledge embedded in technologies, models and routines; and knowledge embodied in goods are examples. Categorical systems, like the one developed above, make it possible to identify and locate both precisely and efficiently different types of intangible resources. Furthermore, it helps clarify how we can manage different types of intangible resources, i.e. how to gather, create, use, share, and develop them more appropriately.

Knowledge and competitive advantage

Having identified what knowledge is we now turn briefly to its role in strategy and the organization. The 'knowledge-based view' focuses upon knowledge as the most strategically important of resources; it is an outgrowth of the RBV. Beeby and Booth (2000) discuss the 'knowledge-based-view of the firm', where knowledge is seen as the resource upon which organizations base their competitive strategies. Many scholars investigate the utilization of knowledge within the organization to create value. The international organization can create value in two ways. By *production* inputs which are physically transformed into outputs where the outputs have greater value than the inputs. And by arbitrage, either across place (trade) or time (speculation), firms create value by moving a product from one market to another, but without physically transforming it. The focus of this chapter is upon the role of knowledge among international organizations which engage in production – the most important and complex means of value creation (Grant 1996). Grant considers the knowledge requirements of production, arguing that all human productivity is knowledge dependent, and machines are simply embodiments of knowledge (1996: 112).

There are two fundamental processes associated with the utilization of knowledge in production (knowledge integration and transfer). In many cases goods or services are produced by many individuals working collectively. Such individuals are often differentiated by role, skill, ability, etc., i.e. they are specialized and work on their respective activity, with their task often being knowledge dependent. In such cases, the organization must integrate their knowledge in order to create the desired output. Knowledge integration is one of the fundamental processes associated with knowledge utilization. In many organizations, more than one person will be required to know how to do some particular task or activity. In some cases people may work together and in other cases they may work on different shift patterns

Look back
See chapter 3

Arbitrage the purchase and sale of an asset in order to profit from a difference in the price

Knowledge integration is the process of incorporating know-how from a variety of sources in order to achieve a common goal

Knowledge transfer includes the movement of knowledge from its point of generation or codified form to the point of use

Figure 12-2

Fundamental organizational knowledge processes

(separated by time) or in different locations (separated by space). In such cases there is an organizational need to facilitate the transfer and diffusion of knowledge within the organization. Knowledge transfer is the second fundamental process. Both processes become more complex in the international organization, see Figure 12-2, and are discussed later.

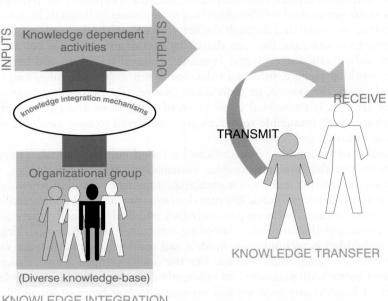

Durso (2007: 92) asks whether knowledge is generally integrated or fragmented. Historically, scholars have discussed 'individual parcels of knowledge' – what have been referred to as 'ideas' and the pathways connecting them. Within organizations, such 'parcels' of know-how may exist in several individuals (a team) connected through the task, routines, rules and procedures. Grant (1996) discusses the mechanisms through which knowledge is integrated within organizations in order to create capability.

Explicit knowledge involves few problems of integration because of its inherent communicability. Advances in information technology have greatly facilitated the integration of explicit knowledge through increasing the ease with which explicit knowledge can be codified, communicated, assimilated, stored, and retrieved. However, the most interesting and complex issues concern the integration of tacit knowledge. The literature points to two primary integration mechanisms: direction and organizational routines. Direction seeks to embody knowledge in standard operating rules. With complex activities occurring in a number of locations, in which that activity must be replicated under more stringent performance specifications the greater is the reliance on knowledge integration through direction (a formal mechanism). Direction involves codifying tacit knowledge into explicit rules and instructions. But since a characteristic of tacit knowledge is that 'we can know more than we can tell' (Polanyi 1966), converting tacit knowledge into explicit knowledge in the form of rules, directives, formulae, expert systems, and the like inevitably involves substantial knowledge loss.

Codifiability the ability of the firm to structure knowledge into a set of identifiable rules and relationships that can be easily communicated

Direction knowledge codified in explicit (standard operating) rules

Organizational routine knowledge and experience embodied within an informal procedure

An organizational routine provides a mechanism for coordination which is not dependent upon the need for communication of knowledge in explicit form. Within our knowledge-based view, the essence of an organizational routine is that individuals develop sequential patterns of interaction which permit the integration of their specialized knowledge without the need for communicating that knowledge. The observation of any work-team reveals closely coordinated working arrangements, where each team member applies his or her specialist knowledge, but where the patterns of interaction appear automatic (consider the medical team in theatre or the racing car team in a pit-stop). This coordination relies heavily upon informal procedures in the form of commonly understood roles and interactions established through training and constant repetition, supported by a series of explicit and implicit signals. The advantage of routine over direction is in economizing on communication and providing greater flexibility.

Teece (1998) discusses knowledge and competitive advantage. It has long been recognized that economic prosperity rests upon knowledge and it useful application. According to Teece (1998: 76), knowledge, competence and related intangibles have emerged as the key drivers of competitive advantage in developed nations. The key sources of wealth creation lie with the exploitation of technological know-how, intellectual property, and brands. He also argues the emphasis on the development and exploitation of knowledge assets shifts the focus of attention from cost minimization to value maximization. An organization may focus on the creation of knowledge assets or on their deployment and use. Knowledge assets are often inherently difficult to copy and may therefore act as a source of sustainable competitive advantage, particularly when they have been integrated with other resources. While knowledge assets are grounded in the experience and expertise of individuals, international organizations provide the physical, social, and resource allocation structure so that knowledge can be shaped into competences. How these competences and knowledge assets are configured and deployed will shape competitive outcomes dramatically and the commercial success of the enterprise (Teece 1998: 62).

Once created or acquired, the international organization will want to share its knowledge resources company wide. In doing so, economies of use benefits are conferred. The copying and re-use of knowledge assets is both an internal and external issue. On the one hand the organization may generate value through the use of such assets in other parts of the organization yet on the other hand there remains the threat of imitation by competitors. Others have described this as the *'knowledge conversion dilemma'* i.e. the trade-off between the need to share and transfer knowledge internally and the risk of exposing the knowledge to imitation. Teece (1998: 65) discusses replicability and imitability as related issues. To the extent that the capabilities in question are relevant to customer needs elsewhere, replication can confer value. *Replication* involves transferring or redeploying competences from one concrete economic setting to another. At least two types of strategic value flow from replication. One is simply the ability to support geographic and product line expansion (refer back to the Duckworth case study – starting from a strong UK R&D capability they set out to export their core competence, expanding abroad to allow knowledge re-use). Another is that the ability to replicate indicates the firm has the foundations in place for learning and improvement.

As was stated earlier, knowledge may also be copied (imitation) by competitors. Imitation is simply replication performed by a competitor. If self-replication is difficult, imitation is likely to be even harder. In competitive markets, it is the ease of imitation that determines the sustainability of competitive advantage. The resource-based view of the firm recognizes the transferability of a firm's resources and capabilities as a critical determinant of their capacity to confer sustainable competitive advantage (Barney 1986). With regard to knowledge, the issue of transferability is important, not only between firms, but even more critically, within the firm, see Figure 12-3. Distinguishing between the two different types of knowledge (explicit and tacit) enables a focus upon the mechanisms for transfer across individuals, across space, and across time. Grant recognizes the relative immobility of tacit knowledge but notes explicit knowledge is revealed by its communication. This ease of communication is its fundamental property. Tacit knowledge is revealed through its application. If tacit knowledge cannot be codified and can only be observed through its application and acquired through practice, its transfer between people is slow, costly, and uncertain.

Know-how the accumulated practical skill or expertise that allows one to do something smoothly and efficiently ('accumulated', implies that know-how must be learned and acquired)

Competencies clusters of skills, abilities and knowledge needed to perform work tasks

Imitation replication performed by a competitor

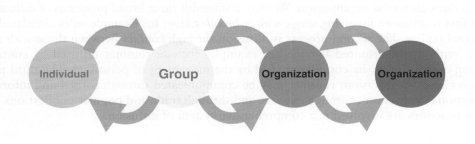

Figure 12-3
Knowledge transfer levels

In today's global market, competitive advantage also requires dynamic capabilities. This is the ability to sense and then to seize new opportunities, and to reconfigure and protect knowledge assets, competencies, and complementary assets and technologies to achieve sustainable competitive advantage (Teece 1998: 72). Knowledge assets underpin competencies, and competencies in turn underpin the organizations product and service offerings to the market. The international organization's capacity to sense and seize opportunities, to reconfigure its knowledge assets, competencies, and complementary assets, to select appropriate organization forms, and to allocate resources astutely and price strategically all constitute its dynamic capabilities. Competitive advantage can be attributed not only to the ownership of knowledge assets and other assets complementary to them, but also to the ability to combine knowledge assets with other assets needed to create value.

Dynamic capabilities dynamic capabilities are an organization's abilities to develop and change competencies to meet the needs of rapidly changing environments

Organizational learning and learning organization

As was highlighted in the previous section, in a changing environment the organization must constantly seek out new knowledge if it is to stay ahead of competition and perform value adding activities in an efficient and effective manner. In this section we consider how the organization meets this challenge – how it learns by trial and error (experience) – internal learning – and by imitation – external learning. We also consider how the organization ensures knowledge diffuses throughout the company – worldwide. We start by considering how we learn from our own and the experiences of others. We then consider mechanisms for the diffusion of knowledge. Having considered learning processes we consider the attributes of the learning organization as an entity.

Learning the development of knowledge

Organizations may learn through two major mechanisms: the first is trial-and-error experimentation (learning by doing/experiential learning); the second mechanism is organizational search. An organization draws from a pool of alternative routines, adopting better ones when they are discovered. Inferences drawn from experience are recorded in documents, accounts, files, standard operating procedures, and rule books; in organizational structures and relationships; in standards of good professional practice; in the culture of organizational stories; and in shared perceptions of 'the way things are done around here'. Not everything, however, is recorded. The transformation of experience into routines and the recording of those routines involve costs. Unless the implications of experience can be transferred from those who experienced it to those who did not, the lessons of history are likely to be lost through turnover of personnel.

Learning from the experience of others has been a persistent theme in the organizational learning literature; 'others' include competitors and suppliers; training and development; external benchmarking; consultants, customers and suppliers; factory visits, trade shows, online databases, magazines and journals; mergers, acquisitions, strategic alliances, licensing and franchises. Organizations capture the experience of other organizations (see imitation) through the transfer of encoded experience in the form of technologies, codes, procedures, or similar routines.

As was the case with information in the previous chapter, knowledge must be disseminated throughout the organization. We may distinguish three broad processes of diffusion. The first is diffusion involving single source *broadcasting*; for example rules circulated by external bodies. The second process is diffusion through *contact* between those with and those without the required knowledge; examples include routines diffused by contacts among organizations, by consultants, and by the movement of personnel. The third process is two-stage diffusion; routines may be communicated through formal and informal educational institutions, through experts, and through trade and popular publications. All three processes are involved in a comprehensive system of diffusion.

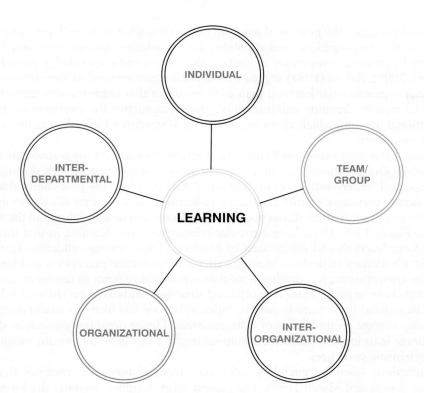

Figure 12-4
Levels of learning

Learning is typically associated with individuals but may also be associated with groups of individuals, see Figure 12-4. The organization represents a large group of individuals and is comprised of various sub-groups such as teams and departments. Peter Senge, who popularized learning organizations in his book *The Fifth Discipline*, described them as places where people continually expand their capacity to create the results they truly desire, where new and expansive patterns of thinking are nurtured, where collective aspiration is set free, and where people are continually learning how to learn together. The concept of the learning organization is that the successful organization must continually adapt and learn in order to respond to changes in environment.

But what is a learning organization? Surprisingly, a clear definition of learning has proved to be elusive over the years. According to Garvin (1993: 80), a learning organization is an organization skilled at creating, acquiring, and transferring knowledge, and at modifying its behaviour to reflect new knowledge and insights. He suggests learning organizations are skilled at five main activities: systematic problem solving, experimentation with new approaches, learning from their own experience and past history, learning from the experiences and best practices of others, and transferring knowledge quickly and efficiently throughout the organization. Systematic problem solving, the first activity, rests heavily on the philosophy and methods of the quality movement, an area discussed in Chapter 10. We will review the other activities throughout the remainder of this chapter. We focus on learning from others later in the chapter when we discuss learning within the MNC and from IJVs.

Change, learning, and adaptation have all been used to refer to the process by which organizations adjust to their environment (refer back to Chapter 5). The problem is that these terms have not been used consistently with the same meanings. Fiol and Lyles (1985: 803) attempted to define, develop, and differentiate organizational learning and its components. Learning is the development of insights, knowledge, and associations between past actions, the effectiveness of those actions, and future actions. Learning concerns the ability to acquire and integrate knowledge (Beeby and Booth 2000). Learning, most fundamentally, is the process of acquiring knowledge or skill (Locke and Jain 1995). Learning may be confused with adaptation but the concepts are different.

Adaptation is the ability to make incremental adjustments as a result of environmental changes, goal structure changes, or other changes. A distinction is often made between

Learning organization an organization skilled at creating, acquiring, and transferring knowledge, and at modifying its behaviour to reflect new knowledge and insights

Organizational learning the process of improving actions through better knowledge and understanding

Adaptation the ability to make incremental adjustments as a result of environmental changes, goal structure changes, or other changes

content and process – the process of learning rather than what is learned, meaning that the capacity to develop organizational capability (in knowledge management) may be more important in creating competitive advantage than the specific knowledge gained (Beeby and Booth 2000). Rahim (1995) argued that 'there is a greater need to improve our knowledge about organizational learning than ever before so that organizations can effectively respond to rapidly changing environments'; this encapsulates the contingency theory of organizational learning which views organizations as systems which adapt continuously to their environments.

Fiol and Lyles also make distinctions between *individual* and *organizational* learning (1985: 804). Organizational learning is the process of improving actions through better knowledge and understanding. Four contextual factors affect the probability that learning will occur: corporate culture conducive to learning, strategy that allows flexibility, an organizational structure that allows both innovativeness and new insights, and the environment, see Figure 12-5. These have a circular relationship with learning in that they create and reinforce learning and are created by learning. Thus strategy influences learning by providing a boundary to decision making and a context for the perception and interpretation of the environment. A centralized, mechanistic structure tends to reinforce past behaviours, whereas an organic, more decentralized structure tends to allow shifts of beliefs and actions. Functional organizations may be efficient but are less likely to adapt; questions of adaptability emerge around issues of differentiation. Hence organizations can be designed to encourage learning and reflective action-taking, but this generally means moving away from mechanistic structures.

Organizations learn by encoding inferences from history into routines that guide behaviour (Levitt and March 1988). The generic term 'routines' includes the forms, rules, procedures, conventions, strategies, and technologies around which organizations are constructed and through which they operate. It also includes the structure of beliefs, frameworks, paradigms, codes, cultures, and knowledge that buttress, elaborate, and contradict the formal routines. Routines are transmitted through socialization, education, imitation, professionalization, personnel movement, mergers, and acquisitions.

Look back
See chapter 9

Figure 12-5
Contextual factors affecting learning

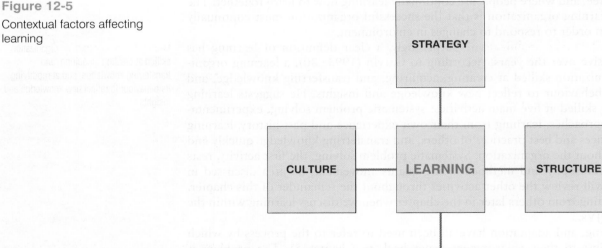

With regard to learning, Fiol and Lyles (1985: 807) differentiate between lower and higher levels of learning. Lower-level learning is focused learning that may be mere repetition of past behaviours – usually short term, surface, temporary, but with associations being formed; such learning captures only a certain element – adjustments in part of what the organization does. Argyris and Schön (1978) refer to this as 'single-loop learning'. Single-loop learning is concerned with the detection and correction of errors in pursuit of existing goals within existing structures in a manner akin to the routine operation of a thermostat (Beeby and Booth 2000). In contrast to these repetitions double-loop learning is non-routine in character and based in cognitive processes. Double-loop learning results in changes to underlying mental frameworks such as: theories in use; assumptions; organizational strategies and norms; and the ways in which competencies and environments are construed. By surfacing and changing theories in use double-loop learning can lead to transformational shifts towards the openness, flexibility and autonomy of the learning organization. Higher-level learning aims at adjusting overall rules and norms rather than specific activities or behaviours. Considerable evidence suggests that some type of crisis is necessary for changes in higher-level learning – for example, a new strategy, a new leader, or a dramatically altered market. Argyris and Schön (1978) refer to this higher level as 'double-loop learning': resolving incompatible organizational norms by setting new priorities and weighing of norms or by restricting norms altogether.

Learning organizations are not built overnight (Garvin 1993: 91). The first step is to foster an environment that is conducive to learning. In addition Garvin recommends opening up boundaries which inhibit knowledge flows and the use of programmes or events designed with explicit learning goals in mind (refer back to the initiatives conducted by Duckworth when exporting their core competencies); see also the opening case study and the use of communities of practice by Unilever. Davenport and Völpel (2001) also discuss communities of practice, an idea, which developed in the 'organizational learning' movement and posits that knowledge flows best through networks of people who may not be in the same part of the organization, but have the same work interests (Brown and Duguid, 1991).

Some firms (like Unilever) have attempted to formalize these communities. Central to the concept of a learning organization is both organizational learning (the intentional use of learning processes to continuously transform the organization) and the related concept of knowledge (Thomas and Allen 2006). Learning organizations have the capability to create, integrate and apply knowledge. Such capability is critical to firms developing sustainable competitive advantage. However, a criticism of the knowledge-based approach is the lack of evidence suggesting that learning does in fact lead to improved organizational performance. Despite a need for more empirical evidence, there is a general consensus in literature that organizational learning can help achieve sustained competitive advantage.

In summary, the terms organizational learning and learning organization, while used interchangeably are not the same. Organizational learning refers to learning processes which occur within organizations whereas the learning organization refers to an entity with particular characteristics and capabilities (Beeby and Booth 2000). The learning organization's main characteristics are:

■ the presence of environmental monitoring mechanisms;

■ their tendency towards organic, decentralized structures; and

■ their permeation by cultures that value learning.

The learning organization concept is about building learning and knowledge creating capacity in individuals and enabling the effective dissemination of this knowledge through the organization. In essence then, the learning organization is the product or result of a critical combination of internal change mechanisms concerned with structure, process and human capability allied to continuous environmental reviews intended to maintain or improve performance. Conversely, organizational learning might be described simply as the capacity or processes to get to that product or result.

A functional view of organizational learning considers the three stages of knowledge acquisition, knowledge sharing or dissemination, and knowledge utilization. The purpose of knowledge management is to enhance organizational performance by explicitly designing

Communities of practice an idea that knowledge flows best through networks of people who may not be in the same part of the organization, but have the same work interests

and implementing tools, processes, systems, structures, and cultures to improve the creation, sharing, and use of knowledge, critical for decision-making. In the next section we turn our attention to the tools, processes, systems, structures, and cultures that comprise the KM infrastructure and management initiatives aimed at making KM work.

KM infrastructure

Infrastructure people, systems, and procedures

Organizations may need to develop their infrastructure before seeking to implement specific knowledge management initiatives and becoming a learning organization. Three key infrastructures, technical, structural, and cultural, enable the creation, sharing, and use of knowledge. In order to leverage infrastructure, KM processes must also be present in order to store, transform, and transport knowledge throughout the organization. These processes enable the organization to capture, bring together, and transfer knowledge in an efficient manner (Gold, Malhotra and Segars 2001). Within this section we consider KM processes, technology, structure and culture. Knowledge infrastructure and knowledge process architecture are essential organizational 'preconditions' for effective knowledge management.

KM processes

Knowledge generation includes all processes involved in the acquisition and development of knowledge

Knowledge codification involves the conversion of knowledge into accessible and applicable formats

Many scholars have identified processes and sub-processes (activities) associated with knowledge management. Grover and Davenport (2001) identify three knowledge processes: knowledge generation, knowledge codification, and knowledge transfer/realization. Knowledge generation includes all processes involved in the acquisition and development of knowledge. Knowledge codification involves the conversion of knowledge into accessible and applicable formats. Knowledge transfer includes the movement of knowledge from its point of generation or codified form to the point of use. The process of knowledge management (knowledge management cycle) begins with knowledge creation (Davenport and Völpel (2001) and progresses to knowledge capture and storage, knowledge refinement, knowledge distribution, knowledge use, and monitoring of the entire process, which should then impact upon the beginning of the process, see Figure 12-6.

Figure 12-6

The knowledge management cycle

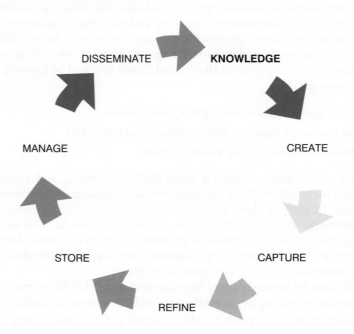

Acquisition-oriented knowledge management processes are directed at obtaining knowledge. Innovation, an aspect of acquisition, is the creation of new knowledge. Two examples of acquisition-oriented knowledge management processes are *benchmarking* and *collaboration*. Through benchmarking, an organization identifies outstanding practices from organizations, and then assesses the current state of a particular process to identify gaps and problems. Once these practices and variances have been identified, the organization can then capture the knowledge for use internally. The creation of organizational knowledge requires the sharing and dissemination (i.e. collaboration) of personal experiences.

Collaboration takes place within and between organizations. Collaboration between individuals brings together individual differences and can be used to create knowledge; this assumes that interaction between the individuals will promote learning. Collaboration between individuals is also the basis for the socialization of knowledge. Collaboration between organizations is also a potential source of knowledge and will be discussed later. Conversion-oriented knowledge management processes are those oriented towards making existing knowledge useful. Sub-processes that enable knowledge conversion are an organization's ability to organize, integrate, combine, structure, coordinate or distribute knowledge.

Nonaka (1994) argues knowledge is created through conversion between tacit and explicit knowledge; he postulates four different 'modes' of knowledge conversion, see Figure 12-7:

1 From tacit knowledge to tacit knowledge, 'socialization' i.e. interaction between individuals; the key to acquiring tacit knowledge is experience. Without some form of shared experience, it is extremely difficult for people to share each other's thought processes. Apprentices work with their mentors and learn craftsmanship by observation, imitation, and practice – see also on-the-job training (OJT) – socialization is connected with theories of organizational culture.

2 From explicit knowledge to explicit knowledge, 'combination'. The reconfiguring of existing information through the sorting, adding, re-categorizing, and re-contextualizing of explicit knowledge can lead to new knowledge – combination is rooted in information processing.

3 From tacit knowledge to explicit knowledge, 'externalization'.

4 From explicit knowledge to tacit knowledge, 'internalization', i.e. learning – internalization has associations with organizational learning.

Innovation implementation of a new idea

©iStockphoto.com/Chris Schmidt

Dissemination of knowledge is a key part of knowledge management

Look back
See chapter 8

Figure 12-7

Four modes of knowledge conversion (adapted from Nonaka)

	TO	
	Tacit	Explicit
FROM Tacit	SOCIALIZATION	EXTERNALIZATION
Explicit	INTERNALIZATION	COMBINATION

Socialization may start with the building of a 'team' or 'field' of interaction where members' experiences and perspectives can be shared; *externalization* is triggered by successive rounds of meaningful 'dialogue' used to enable team members to articulate their own perspectives, and thereby reveal hidden tacit knowledge that is otherwise hard to communicate; *combination* is facilitated by such triggers as 'coordination' between team members and other sections of the organization and the 'documentation' of existing knowledge. Through an iterative process of trial and error, concepts are expressed and developed until they surface in a concrete form. This 'experimentation' can trigger *internalization* through a process of 'learning by doing'. Co-workers share explicit knowledge that is gradually translated, through interaction and a process of trial-and-error, in to different aspects of tacit knowledge (Nonaka 1994).

Knowledge infrastructure: KM technologies

Knowledge management technology is not a single technology, but rather a broad collection of technologies that need to be adopted and integrated.

DAVENPORT AND VÖLPEL (2001)

In this section we continue to focus on KM infrastructure, building on KM process aspects of infrastructure, turning attention to the technology dimension. We outline technology used to support the aforementioned KM activities and processes. The technical systems within an organization determine how knowledge is obtained, stored and disseminated (flows) – see Figure 12-8. Through the linkage of information and communication systems in an organization, previously fragmented flows of information and knowledge can be integrated. These linkages can also eliminate barriers to communication that naturally occur between different parts of the organization.

The technological dimensions that are part of effective knowledge management include business intelligence, CRM, collaboration, distributed learning, knowledge discovery, knowledge mapping, opportunity generation, as well as security: Business intelligence technologies (see Chapter 13) enable a firm to create knowledge regarding its competition and broader economic environment; collaboration and distributed learning technologies allow individuals within the organization to collaborate, thereby eliminating the structural and geographical barriers that may have previously prevented such interaction; knowledge discovery technologies allow the firm to find new knowledge that is either internal or external to the firm; knowledge mapping technologies allow the firm to track sources of knowledge effectively, creating a catalogue of internal organizational knowledge; knowledge application technologies enable a firm to use its existing knowledge and opportunity generation technologies allow the firm to track knowledge about its customers, partners, employees, or suppliers. In addition to these aspects of creating, transferring, and storing knowledge through technological infrastructure, the organization must take steps to ensure that knowledge is not stolen or used inappropriately (Gold, Malhotra and Segars 2001).

Figure 12-8 highlights three key elements in the organization's KM system. Enterprise systems not only contain explicit company knowledge about customers, products and services but also have policies, rules, routines and procedures encoded within their technology. In the previous chapter we discussed the relationship between data, information and knowledge; see Figure 11-10. Organizations increasingly view attempts to transform raw data into usable knowledge as part of their knowledge management initiatives. Approaches typically involve separating data in a 'warehouse' for access and the use of statistical analysis or data mining and visualization tools. Their goal is to create data – derived knowledge, (Grover and Davenport 2001).

Database technologies are used to create repositories for knowledge and may store structured or unstructured knowledge or may identify the people (tacit-knowledge-holders) recognized as knowledge-holders within the organization. In addition there are supporting technologies. Portals and search engines help practitioners find the knowledge they wish to use and the collaboration technologies support knowledge creation and integration.

In Chapter 13 we discuss enterprise systems in detail and then in Chapter 14 focus on communication and collaboration technologies. A knowledge repository is a database storing knowledge; the objective of the knowledge repository is to capture knowledge for later use and for broader access by others (Grover and Davenport 2001). Familiar repository technologies include Lotus Notes, web-based intranets and Microsoft's Exchange, supplemented by search engines, document management tools, and other tools that allow editing

Look back
See chapter 11, p. 355

Knowledge repository a database storing knowledge

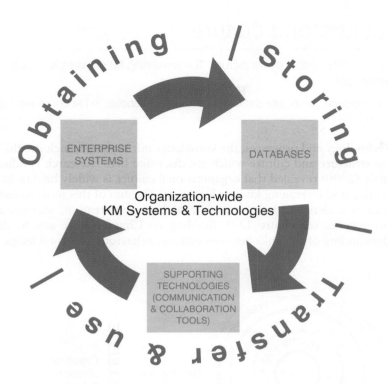

Figure 12-8

Organizational KM systems and technologies

and access. The repositories typically contain a specific type of knowledge for a particular business function or process. Although most knowledge repositories serve a single function, it is increasingly common for companies to construct an internal 'portal' so that employees can access multiple different repositories and sources from one screen. It is also possible and increasingly popular for repositories to contain not only knowledge, but also pointers to experts within the organization on key knowledge topics. Called 'knowledge Yellow Pages' these systems facilitate contact (expertise location system) and knowledge transfer between knowledgeable people and those who seek their knowledge (see Davenport and Völpel 2001 or more recently, Criscuolo, Salter and Sheehan 2007). For a selection of case studies describing the use of Yellow Pages systems, see Iske (2002).

Example

Knowledge management creating a sustainable Yellow Pages system

Chris Collison (2005) asks, How can I 'know who knows'? None of us can personally know more than around 250 people, yet we want our companies to be smart, learning organizations where it's easy to find the right person to talk to. This is why many organizations create 'Yellow Pages' applications, which enable employees to find and contact other staff with particular expertise and skills. Collison identifies ten key steps involved in creating and sustaining a successful, employee-owned Yellow Pages system.

Printed with the permission of Chris Collison, www.chriscollison.com

De Long and Fahey (2000) believe that to enhance effectively an organization's capacity to create, share, and use knowledge, managers ultimately must take into account all knowledge types. Consequently we will discuss KM structure and culture before turning our attention to the specific challenges of KM in an international organization context.

KM structure and culture

'Technology is only 20 per cent of the picture. The remaining 80 per cent is people. You have to get the culture right.'

Roger Chaddock, associate director, Computer Sciences, in De Long and Fahey (2000)

Look back
See chapter 8

Aside from technology and processes, the knowledge infrastructure includes the additional dimensions of structure and culture which are discussed here. Research conducted by De Long and Fahey (2000) revealed that organizational culture is widely held to be the major barrier to creating and leveraging knowledge assets. The aim of this section, consequently, is to help readers understand how cultures can shape the creation, sharing, and use of knowledge in general, see Figure 12-9. Building on Chapter 8 we aim to develop the reader's understanding of the links between culture, behaviour and knowledge.

Figure 12-9

Culture and knowledge management

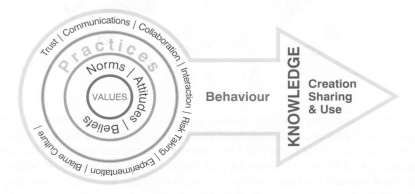

Managers need frameworks to categorize the links between culture and knowledge so they can design the interventions needed to create behaviours that will support their knowledge management objectives. De Long and Fahey (2000) identify how organizational culture influences behaviours central to knowledge creation, sharing, and use; culture creates the context for social interaction that ultimately determines how effective an organization can be at creating, sharing, and applying knowledge. Culture shapes assumptions about which knowledge is important, thus influencing what is perceived as useful, important, or valid knowledge in an organization. Culture shapes what a group defines as relevant knowledge, and this will have a direct affect upon the knowledge a unit will focus upon. Furthermore, culture dictates what knowledge belongs to the organization and what knowledge remains in control of individuals or subunits.

This is most evident when management tries to convince individuals to share the human knowledge they possess so that it can be converted into more structured knowledge, which the organization will control. A common instance of this occurs when management tries to convince sales people to contribute their knowledge about individual customers to a common customer database. De Long and Fahey (2000) argue human knowledge transferred into databases is really information until interpreted by others with the experience and skills to apply it in a different context. In essence, cultural norms and practices determine who is expected to control what knowledge, as well as who must share it, and who can hoard it.

Interaction between individuals is essential in the innovation process; dialogue between individuals or groups is often the basis for the creation of new ideas and can therefore be viewed as having the potential for creating knowledge. Employee interaction should be encouraged, both formally and informally, so that relationships, contacts, and perspectives are shared by those not working side by side. This type of interaction and collaboration is important when attempting to transmit tacit knowledge between individuals or convert tacit knowledge into explicit knowledge, thereby transforming it from individual to organizational level. The corporate vision and values have a bearing upon KM. when properly articulated explicitly stated visions, including value statements, can encourage the growth of knowledge within the organization. Trust and openness are commonly cited as two of these explicitly stated values that promote knowledge management behaviours (Gold, Malhotra and Segars 2001).

Example IWMI

Headquartered in Sri Lanka, IWMI is a non-profit research organization that works with national and international partners in Africa and Asia to improve water and land management in developing countries. Their vision is to be, 'a world-class knowledge center on water, food and environment. [they will] generate knowledge on better water and land management in developing countries, through strategic research alliances with a set of core partners throughout Asia and Africa, and with advanced research institutes in developed countries. This knowledge is held and maintained as global public goods for the benefit of all mankind.' Their core values include excellence, impact-orientation, partnerships, teamwork, knowledge sharing and respect for diversity.

Source: www.iwmi.cgiar.org/pubs/AReps/2005_2006/index.html

Low-trust cultures constrict knowledge flow and status differences may impede cross-functional knowledge sharing. A culture that clearly values some units over others is more likely to undermine the cross-functional sharing of any type of knowledge, in part by supporting subcultures that seek to defend their own knowledge assets (De Long and Fahey 2000). A silo mentality where employees spend unproductive time defending their unit's perspective may be observed when some parts of the organization are more valued than others. In some organizations, middle and senior managers are more approachable than others; this enables vertical interactions helping create a context for effective knowledge sharing. Cultures with norms and practices that discourage open and frank exchanges between levels in the hierarchy create a context for communication that undermines effective knowledge sharing. Aside from vertical interaction, there is a clear need to consider horizontal interactions and interactivity. Culture determines the patterns of interaction used to accomplish work.

An organization may rely on formal communication processes and meetings designed to bring individuals together periodically, while a more informal culture may observe frequent, unplanned and unstructured interactions among employees. Formal and informal interactions are valued differently in organizations resulting in different patterns of knowledge creation and sharing (De Long and Fahey 2000). Even though the Internet and other new technologies are greatly reducing communication barriers, unless cultural norms and practices support higher levels of interactivity between the right individuals or groups, these new channels will have relatively little impact upon knowledge use. Another way that culture shapes the context for horizontal interactions is through norms and practices which promote collaboration (analyze the Duckworth and Unilever case studies to identify what they do).

Knowledge management is about managing and creating a corporate culture that facilitates and encourages the sharing, appropriate utilization, and creation of knowledge resulting in a corporate strategic competitive advantage (Walczak 2005). Structure and culture are linked in that a knowledge-based management structure may facilitate the development and maintenance of an organizational knowledge culture; similarly, organizational structure is an important factor in leveraging technology. Organizational structures must be flexible to encourage sharing of knowledge and collaboration across traditional organizational boundaries, thus promoting knowledge creation. Organizational culture is formed and reinforced through the interrelated elements of strategy, structure, people and process.

People work within the organizational structure that supports organizational processes to accomplish the overall business strategy. While organizational structure and corporate culture are interrelated, both have been identified as necessary elements for knowledge management initiative success. Traditional hierarchical management structures allow vertical knowledge transfer through typical chain-of-command, but inhibit horizontal knowledge transfer that must cross the organization's functional boundaries. Increasing competition and ever shortening rates of technological change necessitate better transfer of knowledge across organizational boundaries, with organizational structure identified as one of five factors contributing to knowledge transfer performance (Walczak 2005).

The KM structural dimensions include an organization's formal organizational structure and incentive systems. An inappropriate structure may inhibit collaboration and sharing of knowledge across internal organizational boundaries. For example, structures that promote individualistic behaviour where people or groups are effectively rewarded for 'hoarding' information can inhibit effective knowledge management across the organization. In essence, it is important that organizational structures be designed for flexibility so they encourage sharing and collaboration across boundaries within the organization and across the supply chain. Along with policy and process, an organization's system of rewards and incentives can determine the channels from which knowledge is accessed and how it flows. Incentive systems should be structured so that workers are motivated and rewarded for taking the time to generate new knowledge (i.e. learn), share their knowledge and help others outside their own group (Gold, Malhotra and Segars 2001).

A key aspect KM in organizations is the development of an organizational structure to perform knowledge-oriented tasks (Davenport and Völpel 2001). While many existing functions are already concerned with aspects of knowledge – including R&D and market research – in most companies there has been no group with broad responsibility for knowledge management. However organizations are beginning to create such groups. They involve the establishment of new roles and responsibilities, new skills, new relationships. At the most senior, and visible, level is the chief knowledge officer (CKO) or equivalent role. The CKO's primary role is to convert knowledge into profit by leveraging the corporation's intellectual asset (Guns 1997). This is achieved by creating the corporation as a learning organization and developing a knowledge infrastructure. The first of these dimensions deals more directly with the human dynamics of the organization; the second is more concerned with technology. A balance is needed between these two dimensions. The specific responsibilities of the CKO include:

- ensuring the right kind of technology is in place;
- maintaining a knowledge inventory;
- uniting people through information systems, telecommunications and knowledge management;
- identifying valued skills, knowledge, and expertise in the corporation;
- collecting best practices; and
- providing the necessary human support to back up the knowledge management system.

The CKO should set knowledge management strategic priorities; ensure a knowledge (best practices) database is up and running; gain commitment of business leaders to better support a learning environment; establish a process for managing intellectual assets and globalize knowledge management. As much as the CEO, the CKO needs to command a broad perspective of the business, and integrate all the relevant sectors within that perspective in order to leverage intellectual capital (Guns 1997). Managers also need to understand knowledge and its use in various aspects of the business, the motivational and attitudinal factors necessary to get people to create, share, and use knowledge effectively, and the ways technology can be used to enhance knowledge activities. Knowledge managers perform a broad collection of tasks, including:

- facilitation of knowledge-sharing networks and communities of practice;
- creation, editing, and pruning of 'knowledge objects' in a repository;
- building and maintaining technology-based knowledge applications;
- incorporating knowledge-oriented job descriptions, motivational approaches, and evaluation and reward systems into the human resource management processes of the organization; and
- redesigning knowledge work processes and incorporating knowledge tasks and activities into them.

We have summarized the structure, culture and technological factors impacting upon knowledge sharing and use within organizations in Figure 12-10. Whereas the KM processes and infrastructure may make the organization able to create, transfer and utilize knowledge there is a reliance on the behaviour of individuals and their propensity to engage in KM activities. This sharing propensity is influenced by structure, culture, reward mechanisms and motivation. Organizational culture may be regarded as a form of common knowledge, one of the functions of which is to facilitate knowledge integration within the company. Efficiency of knowledge integration requires economizing upon the amount of communication needed to effect integration. Organization structures need to be designed with a view to organizing activities such as to reduce the extent and intensity of communication needed to achieve knowledge integration. Bureaucracy is a structure which (under certain circumstances) maximizes the efficiency of knowledge integration in an organization where direction is the predominant integrating mechanism, Grant (1996).

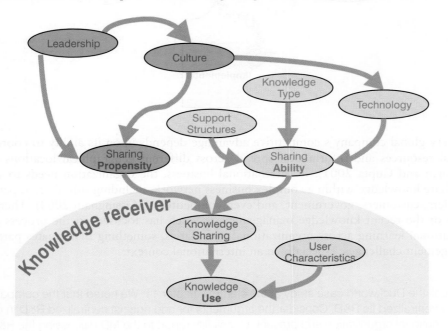

Figure 12-10

Factors impacting upon knowledge sharing and use within organizations

Cross-border learning and KM

Thus far we have identified and defined foundation constructs and discussed the KM infrastructure, linking it with organizational performance. We now build on this work by turning to the international context. Indeed we first considered knowledge back in Chapter 7 when we discussed international assignments. Knowledge acquired by individuals in international assignments can be diffused across the organization; the international assignment is both an opportunity to teach and learn (Kamoche 1997). The MNC can be thought of as a network of capital, product and knowledge transactions among the subsidiary units located in different countries argue Gupta and Govindarajan (1991). Each transaction may vary in magnitude and direction. In this section we focus on the knowledge flows. Intracorporate knowledge flows involve the transfer of expertise (e.g. skills or capabilities) or explicit information or knowledge resources. Gupta and Govindarajan (1991) identify four types of subsidiary according to the nature of the knowledge flows within the MNC see Figure 12-11:

1 global innovator – the knowledge provider;
2 integrated player – the knowledge provider and user;
3 implementer – knowledge user; and
4 local innovator – the contained, self-creator and user (see the multidomestic MNC).

Figure 12-11

Knowledge flow variations within the MNC (Adapted from Gupta and Govindarajan 1991)

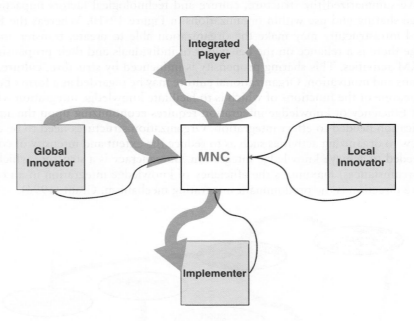

Every global company's competitive advantage depends upon its ability to coordinate critical resources and information spread across different geographical locations (Govindarajan and Gupta 2001). In international business, the organization needs to source and share knowledge within a complex business network, including subsidiaries, partners, suppliers, customers, government, and even competitors (Massingham 2004). Therefore, much of the recent knowledge management research has focused on the process of organizational learning across organizational boundaries, something that creates particular management challenges, especially in an international context.

STOP & THINK

Recall the Duckworth case study at the start of Chapter 11. We noted that the company had centralized its R&D. Consider the arguments for and against centralized R&D in the international organization and present a feasibility report to the MD discussing the R&D decentralization decision at Duckworth. Finally, critically review the mechanisms used for knowledge transfer at Duckworth.

Sanna-Randaccio and Veugelers (2007) ask whether subsidiaries should have a role in R&D – the R&D decentralization decision (R&D internationalization). Evidence suggests that while most research is carried out at headquarters, there is a trend to carry out R&D abroad; there are trade-offs to be made when deciding however. Decentralization avoids having to adapt centrally developed innovations to local markets (being able to use the specific know-how of the subsidiary); centralized R&D, on the other hand, may benefit from synergistic and economies-of-scale gains. Decentralized R&D may be motivated from the demand side – more responsive/close to customers, or the supply side – access to a wide range of scientific and technological skills (human capital). Furthermore, there may be opportunity for reverse intra-company knowledge transfer. However, amongst the disadvantages associated with decentralized R&D is the potential for know-how to spill over to local competitors and added costs associated with duplicated effort.

Earlier we discussed internal people and ICT networks to enable knowledge creation, storage and utilization. Such networks may also be used between companies. Beeby and Booth (2000) explore the significance of networks, alliances and inter-organizational relationships for companies and consider the nature and importance of learning in and through such relationships. Networks and other partnership arrangements are a means of transferring and exchanging knowledge between organizations – see strategic networks; strategic alliances; cooperative strategies; joint ventures; collective strategies and value-adding partnerships in the literature. Firms enter into different forms of strategic alliances for a wide range of reasons, most of which are driven primarily by economic and technological change.

The perceived benefits of alliances may be divided into two main categories – those concerned with building new businesses or with introducing new products, and those concerned with improvement of the current business. Primary reasons for entering into strategic alliances include: to achieve economies of scale and of learning, to gain access to the benefits of other firms' assets (such as production capacity, technology, market access, capital, products, or workforce), to reduce risk by sharing the capital requirements of new product development, to reach new markets, to enjoy first mover advantage by exploiting speed to market, and to achieve transformative synergies via process rationalization, systems improvement and other benefits of learning. However, one of the widely cited 'pitfalls' of alliances and networks is that alliances may lead to the diffusion of a firm's strategic assets and to the appropriation of competences and capabilities by their partners. Similarly, it is argued that alliances create dependency relationships which lead to a narrowing of expertise and to limitations on creativity and competitiveness. These issues have particular resonance in considering learning and knowledge management within strategic alliances and networks.

In their 'decade award winning article' Lyles and Salk report on a study of IJV (foreign) parental involvement and support and the consequences for knowledge acquisition. They start by reiterating a key message from Nonaka, namely that individuals create knowledge but organizations create a context for that creation and then augmentation or amplification to take place. They found IJV knowledge acquisition, building local competence, impacted upon performance (1996: 899) and therefore investigated the factors that might have a, positive or negative, affect upon knowledge acquisition. Factors that may help the acquisition process include:

1 the IJV's capacity to learn – some organizations are better than others at absorbing, circulating and utilizing knowledge. In particular, organizations with flexible structures (non-bureaucratic) and flexible management approaches seem to be better learners;

2 similarly, organizations with well articulated visions, missions, goals and milestones make good learners; and

3 parental support and involvement can help in several ways, foreign parents can provide technology and share administrative management know-how.

Through active involvement they point to sources of knowledge and may help to train local employees in the IJV. Training programmes not only transmit explicit knowledge but build networks, the 'conduit', enabling knowledge dissemination. However, conflict and misunderstandings may inhibit knowledge flows. Cultural differences (see Hofstede 1980), disagreement over goals, ownership type and structure all have the potential to impact negatively upon knowledge acquisition in the IJV. Continuing with the problem of how organizations access and transfer knowledge across organizational boundaries, Inkpen and Dinur (1998) examine knowledge management in an alliance context. In particular they explore how organizations access and exploit alliance-based knowledge, i.e. how the parent can learn and gain knowledge from the new joint venture (JV) and the other parents; the direction of knowledge flow is from child (JV) to parent and between parents (partners) see Figure 12-12. They identified four key processes to transfer knowledge: technology sharing, alliance – parent interaction, personnel transfers and strategic integration. Each of the processes is shown to provide an avenue for managers to gain exposure to knowledge and ideas outside the traditional organizational boundaries and create connections with people to communicate the alliance experience with others.

Figure 12-12

Knowledge transfers within an alliance context

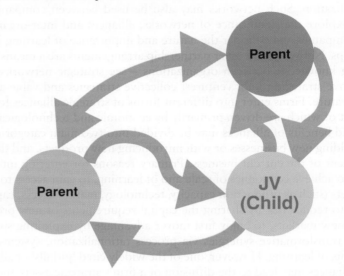

It is widely accepted that alliances provide a platform for organizational learning. An alliance may generate idiosyncratic knowledge but may also generate knowledge that can be used by parent companies to enhance their own strategy and operations. Knowledge useful to a parent may be knowledge transferred by an alliance partner to the alliance. Alternatively the knowledge may be created independently by the alliance through its interactions with customers, competitors and other organizations. Inkpen and Dinur (1998: 460) found that knowledge was shared through structured meetings between joint venture and parent managers; direct links – such as a visit to parent facilities and work secondment. Employees from the parent or child organization may work temporarily in one of the other organizations (personnel transfers).

This was seen as a means of mobilizing personal (tacit) knowledge. Transfers and rotation of personnel help members of an organization to understand the business from a multiplicity of perspectives, which in turn make knowledge more fluid and easier to translate into practice. Clearly the risk with personnel transfers is that if the knowledge remains individual the learning opportunity may be lost. Once back at the organization, mechanisms are used to facilitate internal knowledge transfer and diffusion. In some cases JV managers were promoted to positions within the parent organization.

STOP & THINK

Consider an organization with which you are familiar:

How good is this organization at routinely and systematically uncovering the opportunities for knowledge transfer? How enthusiastic are their subsidiaries to share knowledge with other units? How eager are their subsidiaries to learn from any and all sources including peer subsidiaries? How good are they at codifying the product and process innovations generated by their subsidiaries? Have they built efficient communication mechanisms for the sharing of codified know-how across locations? How good are they at keeping codified knowledge proprietary to their company? Have they built effective mechanisms (e.g. people transfer, face-to-face interchange) for the transfer of tacit knowledge across locations?

Questions sourced from Gupta and Govindarajan (2001).

Having considered knowledge management and explored knowledge sharing options we now consider strategic issues more closely. Throughout this chapter we have focused on two types of knowledge: tacit (or human knowledge) and explicit (or structured knowledge) and argued the need for a supporting infrastructure of people, processes and technology. We have also identified several alternative approaches organizations may wish to consider. Hansen, Nohria and Tierney (1999), ask, what is your organizational strategy for managing knowledge? Some companies automate while others rely on their people to share knowledge through more traditional means. The authors refer to two knowledge management strategies: codification (a technology enabled strategy focusing on explicit knowledge) and personalization (based on face-to-face contact). In the case of the former, knowledge is codified (the person-to-document approach) and then stored in a database before reuse. Such an approach enables recipients to access knowledge without having to contact the person who originally developed it; such an approach achieves scale benefits. The personalization strategy may also be reliant on databases but for different reasons. In this strategy, knowledge is transferred through one-to-one conversations and databases are used to help people find each other and then a technology is used to support the communication process thereafter. The emphasis is on building and supporting people networks and sharing knowledge face-to-face. Companies should focus on a single strategy but consider using the alternative in support (more an 80:20 split) advise Hansen, Nohria and Tierney (1999).

The knowledge management strategy should fit the competitive strategy. Choice is dependent upon whether the primary business is based on novel (inventors) or similar/repeat (implementers) problems. Codified knowledge enables companies to deal with similar problems over and over again – in this scenario, knowledge objects are like Lego bricks to be reused when building solutions. Such strategy provides economies of reuse. This saves work and reduces communication costs, allowing companies to take on more work. By contrast, the personalization strategy (1999: 110) relies on the logic of expert economics; the knowledge is shared in an often time-consuming and costly process. The approach is more associated with tacit knowledge transfer. Hansen, Nohria and Tierney (1999: 115) offer further questions to help companies choose the primary knowledge management strategy:

1 Do you offer standardized or customized products? The authors argue that standardized products benefit from the reuse model, i.e. codification.

2 Do you have a mature or innovative product? Since the mature products are based on well-established approaches they benefit from a reuse model.

3 Do your people rely on explicit or tacit knowledge to solve problems? The knowledge management strategy requires HR and IT support and mechanisms to encourage the sharing of knowledge within the company.

We need to incentivize the approach pursued argue Hansen, Nohria and Tierney (1999). The codification model relies on a system that encourages people to write down what they know. Similarly, with the personalization strategy, there is a need to reward sharing knowledge directly with each other. The two strategies vary in the level of IT use with the codification model relying more heavily on technology. Strategies rely on communication and database technologies but in different ways. While the codification model is much like the online library, the personalization strategy makes use of the database to find people within the organization; communication technology is then used to share the relevant knowledge. Whichever strategy is chosen, companies should ensure appropriate leadership and coordination to minimize 'silo' type problems.

The KM goals and infrastructure do not happen by chance but through planned activity or a pattern of decisions resulting in an emergent strategy. A framework for KM strategy development is shown in Figure 12-13. This process is based on the generic strategy formulation process which starts with analysis of where you are now, where you want to be and what is presently missing. Organizations must determine where their current knowledge is inadequate or underutilized. After justifying the need to improve KM the organization essentially determines whether to focus on its explicit or tacit knowledge; the former driving

Codification approach a knowledge management strategy with primary reliance on repositories of explicit knowledge

Personalization approach a knowledge management strategy where the primary mode of knowledge transfer is direct interaction among people

a codification and the latter a personalization strategy. A series of KM projects, comprising the KM programme, are then implemented and resources allocated to deliver the strategy. Managers attempting to develop an international knowledge strategy must:

1 clarify the firm's strategy;
2 identify the unique, value creating activities necessary to achieve this strategy;
3 identify knowledge resources necessary to perform these activities well;
4 prioritize the knowledge components underlying each knowledge resource; and
5 decide upon how to access these knowledge resources (Massingham 2004).

> **Knowledge strategy** the employment of knowledge processes to an existing or new knowledge domain in order to achieve strategic goals

Figure 12-13

KM strategy process

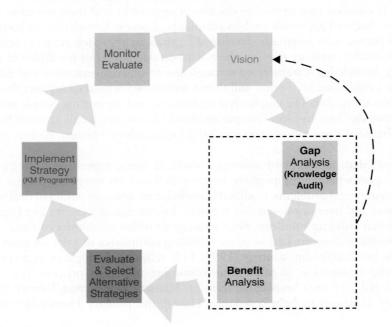

In concluding this chapter we note that, on their own, resources do not create any value for the organization. For example, human resources may sit idle at their desks unless given something to do and armed with tools and processes to work with. Resources need to be combined with other resources to create capabilities (Grant 1996). These capabilities are employed to enable the organization to perform activities. Knowledge and its management involve effort on many fronts to be successful, conclude Grover and Davenport (2001). Within this chapter we have reviewed the contribution of knowledge resources, through competitive and sustainable competitive advantage, to corporate success.

Summary of key learning points

The theories and concepts presented throughout this chapter are identified in the framework shown in Figure 12-14. In turbulent environments and in the face of competition, (learning) organizations must develop and access knowledge resources continuously and then diffuse throughout the organization.

Organizations may learn from others by imitation or may learn from their own history, experimentation, trial and error. They may also recruit talented individuals into their pool of knowledge capital. Quality management processes (TQM and BPM) enable learning through a continuous improvement culture, tools and techniques. Organizations learn so that they can adapt to new environmental challenges. We distinguished between learning

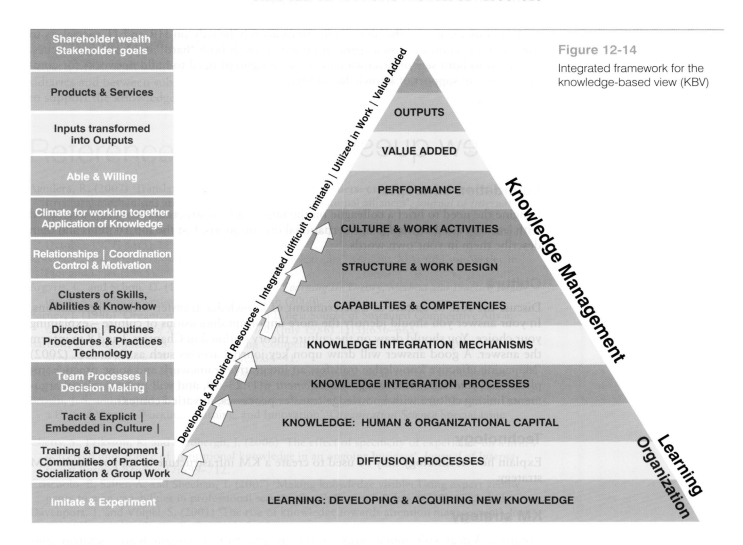

Figure 12-14

Integrated framework for the knowledge-based view (KBV)

processes, the learning climate and culture and the content of learning. It is the latter which exists as a resource to be used by the organization. This resource may exist in the heads of individuals, culture, procedures, and routines and may be tacit or explicit.

Given that no one person holds all of the organizational knowledge required for transformational processes, integration processes and mechanisms are required in order to bring a range of knowledge resources together and integrate them as difficult to imitate capabilities and competencies. Integration is supported by structure, culture, processes and technology – the organization's knowledge management infrastructure. Knowledge is also transferred and integrated through group work and decision-making and may be transferred between individuals, groups and organizations.

Capabilities and competencies represent the clusters of knowledge and other resources used in work, in the transformation process. However, not only must capabilities exist, human resources must be motivated to develop, share, integrate and use knowledge resources in value adding activities. In some cases the organizational and national culture may support or inhibit the use of such resources.

Resources are used in work activities, the output of which may be products or services. Ultimately, knowledge resources ensure organizational goals are attained in an effective and efficient manner. They may also be rare and difficult to imitate; in which case they may confer a sustainable competitive advantage to the organization. However, when knowledge only exists in employees it may leak out of the company to competitors.

Ghoshal, S., Bartlett, C. A. and Moran, P. (2000) 'Value creation: the new millennium management manifesto', *Management 21C*, Edinburgh: Prentice Hall, in Massingham, P. (2004).

Gibbert, M., Leibold, M. and Voelpel, S. (2001) 'Rejuvenating corporate intellectual capital by co-opting customer competence', *Journal of Intellectual Capital* 2(2):109–126.

Goh, S. C. (2002) 'Managing effective knowledge transfer: an integrative framework and some practice implications', *Journal of Knowledge Management* 6(1):23–30.

Gold, A., Malhotra, A. and Segars, A. (2001) 'Knowledge Management: An Organizational Capabilities Perspective', *Journal of Management Information Systems* 18(I):183–214.

Govindarajan, V. and Gupta, A. (2001) 'Building an Effective Global Business Team', *MIT Sloan Management Review* 42(4):63–71.

Grant, R. (1996a) 'Toward a Knowledge-Based Theory of the Firm', *Strategic Management Journal* (Special Issue) 17:109–122.

Grant, R. (1996) 'Prospering in Dynamically-Competitive Environments: Organizational Capability as Knowledge Integration', *Organization Science* (July–August 1996) 7(4):375–387.

Grover, V. and Davenport, T. (2001) 'General Perspectives on Knowledge Management: Fostering a Research Agenda', *Journal of Management Information Systems* (Summer 2001) 18(1):5–21.

Guns, R. (1997) 'The Chief Knowledge Officer's Role: Challenges and Competencies', *Journal of Knowledge Management* 1(4):315–319.

Gupta, A. and Govindarajan, V. (1991) 'Knowledge Flows and the Structure of Control within Multinational Corporations', *The Academy of Management Review* (October 1991) 16(4):768–792.

Haesli, A. and Boxall, P. (2005) 'When knowledge management meets HR strategy: an exploration of personalization-retention and codification-recruitment configurations', *International Journal of Human Resource Management* (November 2005) 16(11):1955–1975.

Hansen, M., Nohria, N. and Tierney, T. (1999) 'What's your strategy for managing knowledge?', *Harvard Business Review* (March/April 1999) 77(2):106–116.

Hofstede, G. (1980) 'Motivation, leadership and organization: do American theories apply abroad?', *Organizational Dynamics* (Summer 1980):42–63.

Inkpen, A. C. and Dinur, A. (1998) 'Knowledge Management Processes and International Joint Ventures', *Organization Science* (July/August 1998) 9(4):454–468.

Inkpen, A. C. (1998) 'Learning and knowledge acquisition through international strategic alliances', *Academy of Management Executive* (November 1998) 12(4):69–80.

Inkpen, A. C. (1998) 'Learning, knowledge acquisition, and strategic alliances', *European Management Journal* (April 1998) 16(2):223–230.

Iske, P. (2002) 'Building a corporate KM community', Inside Knowledge, Ark Group Ltd, posted 9 Dec 2002 in 6(4).

Kamoche, K. (1997) 'Knowledge creation and learning in international HRM', *International Journal of Human Resource Management* (April 1997) 8(2):213–226.

Kaplan, R. S. and Norton, D. P. (1996) *The Balanced Scorecard,* Boston, Mass: HBS Press.

Kelly, P. (2005) *Information Systems Risk*, London: Witherbys.

Kogut, B. and Zander, U. (1992) 'Knowledge of the Firm, Combinative Capabilities, and the Replication of Technology', *Organization Science* (Focused Issue) 3(3):383–397.

Kotabe, M., Dunlap-Hinkler, D., Parente, R. and Mishra, H. (2007) 'Determinants of cross-national knowledge transfer and its effect on firm innovation', *Journal of International Business Studies* 38:259–282.

Levitt, B. and March, J. G. (1988) 'Organizational Learning', *Annual Review of Sociology* 14:319–340.

Locke, E. and Jain, V. (1995) 'Organizational Learning And Continuous Improvement', *International Journal of Organizational Analysis (1993–2002)* (January 1995) 3(1):45–68.

Lyles, M. and Salk, J. (1996) 'Knowledge Acquisition from Foreign Parents in International Joint Ventures: An Empirical Examination in the Hungarian Context', *Journal of International Business Studies* 27:877–903.

Lyles, M. and Salk, J. (2007) 'Knowledge Acquisition from Foreign Parents in International Joint Ventures: An Empirical Examination in the Hungarian Context', *Journal of International Business Studies* 38:3–18.

Machlup, F. (1980) *Knowledge: Its Creation, Distribution, and Economic Significance, Volume* 1. Princeton, NJ. Princeton University Press. In Grant (1996a).

Markus, M. (2001) 'Toward a Theory of Knowledge Reuse: Types of Knowledge Reuse Situations and Factors in Reuse Success', *Journal of Management Information Systems* 18(1):57–93.

Massingham, P. (2004) 'Linking business level strategy with activities and knowledge resources', *Journal of Knowledge Management* 8(6):50–62.

Meyer, K. (2007) 'Contextualising organizational learning: Lyles and Salk in the context of their research', *Journal of International Business Studies* 38:27–37.

Nonaka, I. (1991) 'The knowledge-creating company', *Harvard Business Review* (November/December):96–104.

Nonaka, I. (1994) 'A Dynamic Theory of Organizational Knowledge Creation', *Organization Science: A Journal of the Institute of Management Sciences* 5(1):14–35.

Nonaka, I., Von Krogh, G. and Aben, M. (2001) 'Making the Most of Your Company's Knowledge: A Strategic Framework', *Long Range Planning* 34(4):421–439.

Polanyi, M. (1966) 'The Logic of Tacit Inference', *Philosophy* (January 1996) 41(155):1–18.

Rahim, M. A. (1995) 'Issues in organizational learning', *International Journal of Organizational Analysis* 3:5–9.

Sanna-Randaccio, F. and Veugelers, R. (2007) 'Multinational knowledge spillovers with decentralised R&D: a game-theoretic approach', *Journal of International Business Studies* 38:47–63.

Schulz, M. (2001) 'The Uncertain Relevance of Newness: Organizational Learning and Knowledge Flows', *The Academy of Management Journal* 44(4):661–681.

Senge, P. M. (1997) 'Creating learning communities', *Executive Excellence Provo* 14 (3):17–18.

Senge, P. M. (1998a) 'Sharing knowledge', *Executive Excellence* 15(6):11–12.

Senge, P. M. (1998b) 'The knowledge era', *Executive Excellence* 15(1):15–16.

Spender, J. C., Grant, R. (1996) 'Knowledge and the Firm: Overview', *Strategic Management Journal* (Special Issue) 17:5–9.

Sveiby, K. (1997) *The New Organizational Wealth, Managing and Measuring Knowledge-Based Assets,* San Francisco, CA: Berrett-Koehler.

Teece, D. J. (1998) 'Capturing Value from Knowledge Assets: The New Economy, Markets for Know-how, and Intangible Assets', *California Management Review* (Spring 1998) 40(3):55–79.

Thomas, K. and Allen, S. (2006) 'The learning organization: a meta-analysis of themes in literature', *The Learning Organization* 3(2):123–139.

Walczak, S. (2005) 'Organizational knowledge management structure', *The Learning Organization* 12(4):330–339.

Vignali, C. (2001) 'McDonald's: "think global, act local" – the marketing mix', *British Food Journal* 103(2):97–111.

Yahya, S. and Goh, S. C. (2002) 'Managing human resources toward achieving knowledge management', *Journal of Knowledge Management* 6(5):457–468.

Suggestions for further reading

Journals

While many journals publish articles on this subject area, we have identified specific titles below:

Journal of Intellectual Capital

The *Journal of Intellectual Capital* brings together current thinking, research case studies and experience to help you create and manage a coherent and effective policy on intellectual capital in your business – www.emeraldinsight.com/info/journals/jic/jic.jsp.

Journal of Knowledge Management

The Journal of Knowledge Management is dedicated to the exchange of the latest academic research and practical information on all aspects of managing knowledge in organizations – www.emeraldinsight.com/info/journals/jkm/jourinfo.jsp.

The Learning Organization: *The International Journal of Knowledge and Organizational Learning Management*

This journal explains the conceptual underpinnings and practices; most beneficial to companies pursuing learning strategies – www.emeraldinsight.com/info/journals/tlo/tlo.jsp.

Key articles

Scholars of this subject area have often read the following:

1 Fiol, C. M. and Lyles, M. (1985) 'Organizational Learning', *The Academy of Management Review* (October 1985) 10(4):803–813.

2 Grant, R. (1996) 'Toward a Knowledge-Based Theory of the Firm', *Strategic Management Journal* (Special Issue) 17:109–122.

3 Grant, R. (1996) 'Prospering in Dynamically-Competitive Environments: Organizational Capability as Knowledge Integration', *Organization Science* (July/August 1996) 7(4):375–387.

4 Nonaka, I. (1994) 'A Dynamic Theory of Organizational Knowledge Creation', *Organization Science: A Journal of the Institute of Management Sciences* 5(1):14–35.

5 Hansen, M., Nohria, N. and Tierney, T. (1999) 'What's your strategy for managing knowledge?', *Harvard Business Review* (March/April 1999) 77(2):106–116.

6 Levitt, B. and March, J G. (1988) 'Organizational Learning', *Annual Review of Sociology* 14:319–340.

7 Teece, D. J. (1998) 'Capturing Value from Knowledge Assets: The New Economy, Markets for Know-how, and Intangible Assets', *California Management Review* (Spring 1998) 40(3):55–79.

8 Spender, J. C. and Grant, R. (1996) 'Knowledge and the Firm: Overview', *Strategic Management Journal* Special Issue 17:5–9.

9 Davenport, T., Jarvenpaa, S. and Beers, M. (1996) 'Improving Knowledge Work Processes', *Sloan Management Review* (Summer 1996) 37(4):53–65.

10 Argyris, C. (1977) 'Double loop learning in organizations', *Harvard Business Review* (September/October 1977) 55(5):115–125.

Chapter 13

Global business and enterprise systems

Introduction
Computerized business information systems
Classifying CBIS
Acquiring CBIS
Enterprise systems
Global ES strategies

Key concepts

- Business information system (BIS) ■ Functional BIS ■ Systems acquisition
- Systems development ■ Feasibility study ■ Enterprise system ■ ERP software
- Systems architecture ■ Systems integration ■ Implementation ■ ES strategy

By the end of this chapter you will be able to:

- Identify the various types of computer-based information systems

- Evaluate alternative approaches for acquiring and developing business information systems for the international organization

- Identify what an enterprise systems is and the arguments for and against adoption

- Explain why it is important for the international organization to make information resources widely available

- Critically evaluate approaches used to enable the international organization to achieve its goal of integrated information

- Evaluate the role of IT as a strategic resource for the international organization

Active learning case

Omega

ERP Project

Omega (the fictionalized name for a Danish multinational production company) with more than 1000 employees, began its ERP journey in 1995. The company was over 40 years old and a significant player in both the Danish and world markets. In 1995, the parent company was divided into four functional departments, each with its own management structure and each more or less autonomous. The company had no tradition for outsourcing activities and was horizontally integrated (i.e. differing activities producing different goods or services for sale on the market, carried out in parallel with each other). IT systems were commissioned individually by the different departments and subsidiaries, which all had their own software solutions. The IT department supported the different systems and departments with development, maintenance and updates. The IT function's skill base was technical and viewed as the prime owner of IT issues, but it had never developed solutions from scratch and normally responded to requirements set by the different departments.

With growth came the problem of intra unit coordination and process management at the Danish MNC – Omega. In pursuit of integration, better control and coordination, the company sought a new IT system. The desired system would address existing problems, reduce business costs and improve customer service. In a traditionally IT-lead project the company identified a need for an ERP system and conducted a cost-benefit analysis and feasibility study. This proved difficult as many of the associated benefits and costs are intangible and difficult to measure. Any investment decision would therefore be difficult to justify on a quantitative bases. During their investigations they observed additional benefits such as reduced inventory costs due to improved planning, enhanced coordination with suppliers and customers, better integration between purchasing, production and sales

© Rusm/Dreamstime.com

and shorter order cycle times. Costs, however, were high and included not only the cost of the software but also hardware, consultancy, business process re-engineering activities and the use of employees (an opportunity cost). Omega decided to purchase an off-the-shelf solution – an ERP with modules for sales and distribution, material and production planning and finance. A project team, led by the IT manager, and the steering committee was established. A big bang (direct-cut-over) strategy was chosen to implement the system in all departments.

Many problems arose during the early stages of the project and the project manager was replaced with an external SAP consultant. Initially the project was seen primarily as technical with no consideration given to organizational and process change. At the outset the company assumed the ERP system had been chosen to meet its needs, not that the company might need to change in order to fit with the system. The ERP system was viewed as an administrative tool which should support existing processes and procedures. Their assumptions turned out to be the source of many problems such as widespread process confusion and user dissatisfaction. Business capabilities were hindered and financial performance significantly impacted. The three months following the go-live date were chaotic with many unable to use the system resulting in a large backlog of production orders and late deliveries. The financial result was a deficit for the first year in the history of the company.

Omega concluded that ERP implementation cannot be managed as a traditional IT project – that the ERP system was a strategy enabler and resource that must be congruent with business processes, culture and structure. Given a limited ability to change the off-the-shelf ERP software, they had to consider changes to other organizational elements so that Omega could fit the system and not the other way round (ERP systems are pre-programmed). Omega learned that such projects should be business led as an organizational change initiative – changes to business processes, human resources,

© Enjoylife25/Dreamstime.com

culture, structure, software and hardware are likely in such cases. Furthermore, they learned that ERP implementation should be seen as an evolutionary not traditional planned change process. System implementation requires a focus on organizational and business issues and less on technical aspects.

Sources:

(A) Jeremy Rosea and Pernille Kræmmergaardb (2006) 'ERP systems and technological discourse shift: managing the implementation journey', *International Journal of Accounting Information Systems* (September 2006) 7(3):217–237. Sixth International Research Symposium on Accounting Information Systems (IRSAIS) and (B) Pall Rikhardsson, and Pernille Kræmmergaard (2006) 'Identifying the impacts of enterprise system implementation and use: Examples from Denmark', *International Journal of Accounting Information Systems* (March 2006) 7(1):36–49.

Introduction

Recognizing the strategic role of enterprise systems resources and the need for the business (not a parochial IT manager) to lead such projects, we believe enterprise and system resource management knowledge is essential for each and every international manager. As was seen in the opening case study, enterprise systems are strategic resources which may be used as part of the competitive strategy of the international organization. As company-wide systems, they are tightly linked with strategy, structure, culture and the transformational work activities of the organization. They can have significant impact upon company performance and as a consequence are reviewed in this chapter. In Chapters 11 and 12 we identified how organizations compete through their information resources, a matter we expand upon, within this chapter, through a focus on *technology* and business information systems. Whereas Chapter 11 presented foundation concepts, focusing on information resources, this chapter considers specific systems (supported by technology) in detail, enterprise systems in particular.

An organization must establish which business information systems (BIS) and technology resources are essential for competing in its given market; it must also identify the complementary resources needed to create capabilities in a given area. In some cases investment in such technologies and systems is essential to keep up with competitors (to avoid being disadvantaged by competitor actions). In other cases investment may lead to sources of competitive and sustainable competitive advantage. The information system(s), associated technology, acquisition, development and implementation methods and overall IS strategy must be aligned with corporate strategy. The way in which information systems are used in organizations and indeed the organizations themselves have changed considerably over the past three decades.

In the 1980s, Porter discussed the role of information in providing competitive advantage (*see* section: Competing with information resources). Throughout the 1980s the use of IT spread throughout the value chain. IT not only affects how individual activities are performed but, through new information-flows, it also greatly enhances a company's ability to exploit linkages between activities, both within and outside the company. Technology helps manage linkages between activities, allowing companies to coordinate their actions more closely with those of their buyers and suppliers. Information systems allow companies to coordinate value activities in far-flung geographic locations and create many new interrelationships among businesses. While Porter and Millar (1985) noted the role of IT/IS in support of activities and linkages between such activities, the 1980s was characterized by a greater focus on the activities (a functional orientation), identifying the ways systems could either replace or complement employee activity. Furthermore, the focus was much more intra-organizational rather than interorganizational.

The way IS/IT systems supported the functions of the traditional organization led to the creation of information islands or 'silos' within the organization. This in turn created co-ordination and control problems and contributed to problems associated with responsiveness and adaptation to the environment. Not only was the organization fragmented but, through outsourcing and global competition, so too was the supply chain. In the 1990s the BPR movement focused on the linking of activities and company-wide processes through horizontal flows (process integration). Organizations became flatter, more global in scope and employees more autonomous. Such changes drove a need for systems to better support the linkages of activities undertaken by various functions. There was a need for systems to support cross-functional processes and inter-organizational collaboration and deliver information widely throughout the organization. Consequently, *enterprise systems* evolved throughout the 1990s to replace the functional systems emanating in the 1980s.

In the new millennium we have witnessed the growing scope of such systems as back-office systems take on more front-end roles and vice versa. We have also witnessed such systems operating in support of more senior managers with business intelligence systems complementing decision-making. Advances in database and communication and collaboration (Internet) technologies and the evolution of open standards have all facilitated the evolution of information systems in the global organization. The popularity of ERP/ES

Information system a system designed to produce information that can be used to support the activities of managers and other workers

Look back
See chapter 11, p. 365

is attributed to its potential to improve the profitability potential of an organization by reducing the time and costs of completing business activities. Such systems are particularly useful in providing management with the type of information necessary for making critical decisions. ES acquisition and implementation represents a strategic capital investment decision, with company-wide implications.

The ERP/ES system is a business solution and not another IT project. Acquisition decisions are difficult since there is a degree of uncertainty associated with estimating savings, and it is difficult to anticipate developments because of constant changes. Furthermore, intangible benefits of an ERP system are difficult to portray in monetary terms. The ERP/ES has a greater impact on the organization than traditional system changes. ERP systems are used by small, medium and large corporations as well as government agencies and non-profit organizations. In order to take advantage of the competitive capabilities of ERP systems, managers and employees must understand the basic principles of ERP/ES so that such systems can be used to their full potential.

Significant time and investment is needed to implement enterprise systems and associated project failure rates are relatively high and which can lead to bankruptcy of the organization. Commitment by management is therefore essential. This commitment needs to be incorporated into the business culture and is likely to result in changes to organizational designs, process and technical infrastructure (see Chapters 9 and 10). Managers must understand global business information system challenges from a multi-stakeholder perspective if they are to work with others in delivering such solutions (see Chapter 5); they will need to know how to communicate with IT specialists within and external to the company. This requires a high-level understanding of the systems, how they are acquired, developed and implemented.

This chapter builds on Chapter 11, considering the holistic BIS in the context of the international organization. We start by considering BIS classification approaches and then describe a range of functional business systems. We demonstrate how the traditional approach led to a lack of integration – silos or islands of information and knowledge throughout the organization. After identifying a range of functional systems we confront the problem of how to acquire such systems. We consider alternative approaches such as off-the-shelf acquisition and software development and the methods used to manage systems projects. We then turn our attention to problems associated with functional systems and the needs of the global organization – the need for integration and seamless information and knowledge flows throughout the organization. Enterprise systems are discussed as a solution to corporate needs. We consider enterprise resource planning, business intelligence, e-business and customer relationship management systems. Finally, we link with Chapter 3 – Strategy, discussing the relationship between technology, business information systems, IT and the corporate strategy.

Throughout the chapter we focus on the links between people (structure and culture), processes and technology as interrelated aspects of the organizational (enterprise) infrastructure. Implicit is a continued reference to contingency theory – the corporate strategy fits the environment, functional strategies fit with the corporate strategy and the structure and culture fit with processes and technology. This was partly reflected in models presented in Chapters 5 and 11; see for example Figure 11-2 Business information resource perspectives. This chapter has three parts:

Look back
See chapter 11, p. 368

1 considers the traditional (functional) approach to information systems;

2 considers the contemporary enterprise (integrated) systems approach; and

3 considers the application of enterprise systems in the context of the international company and its environment.

Computerized BIS

The aim of this section is to outline traditional approaches to the use of computer-based information systems (CBIS) within international organizations; to explore what they are, how organizations acquire, develop and implement such systems to meet organizational functional needs and the resultant shortcomings of functional (silo) approaches. This section not only lays down key foundation concepts and systems development frameworks but also provides the rationale for the enterprise system discussed later. Information system foundation concepts are derived from general systems theory. A system is a set of interrelated or interacting elements; typically the elements or components work together towards a collective goal (see the concept of holism).

The system functions by virtue of the interdependence of its component parts. Business professionals rely upon many types of information system, and they are explored later. Managers should be able to recognize the fundamental components of information systems and be able to identify the resources they use, types of information they produce, and the way they operate. There are many ways of categorizing information systems, yet the primary roles concern support for business processes and operations, decision-making and strategies for competitive advantage. At this point we might ask, 'What is a *business information system*?' An information system is a system designed to produce information that can be used to support the activities of managers and other workers; or 'Interrelated components working together to collect, process, store, and disseminate information to support decision-making, coordination and control in an organization. Similarly it is:

1 a set of people, procedures, and resources that collects, transforms, and disseminates information in an organization; and

2 a system that accepts data resources as input and processes them into information products as output (O'Brien 2002).

Sandoe, Corbitt and Boykin (2001) consider the information system to be a unique configuration of IT resources with organizational processes whereby the IT resources (and the information they provide) are applied to support specific organizational processes. Indeed, Porter and Millar (1985) commented on information technology in a similar vein – declaring it to be more than just computers, it includes the information that businesses create and use as well as a wide spectrum of increasingly convergent and linked technologies that process the information. In addition to computers, communications technologies, factory automation, and other hardware and services are involved. While many scholars may use the terms IT and IS interchangeably, most consider IT to be a subset of IS. We have represented system resources in Figure 13-1. In summary, a business information system is an IS that supports business, making use of a variety of resources such as people, hardware, software, data and communications.

Holism the total of a system is greater than the sum of its parts.

Information technology the hardware and software that are used to store, retrieve, and manipulate information

Figure 13-1
Business information system resources

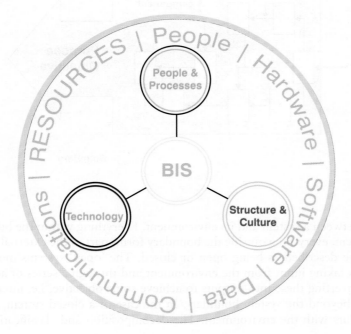

At the highest level we might distinguish two types of information system: formal and informal. Formal systems rest on accepted and fixed definitions of data and procedures, operating with predefined rules while *informal systems* are unstructured, i.e. 'office gossip networks' that use unstated rules of behaviour. With informal systems there is no agreement on what constitutes information or on how it will be stored and processed. In many ways, the use of the terms 'formal' and 'informal' is consistent with the way such terms have been used previously within this book. It is common to subdivide the *formal system* into:

1 manual (i.e. paper and pencil); and

2 computer-based systems.

We focus on the latter in this chapter. CBISs rely on computer hardware and software technology (the technical foundation) to process and disseminate information. In subsequent sections we further categorize computer-based information systems. We have described the CBIS as a set of interrelated parts bound together through common goals. We may describe system parts in terms of a particular resource type (hardware, software, data) or as a collection of resources bound through some sub-goal; for example we might discuss the part of a system responsible for interfacing with other systems or the part responsible for processing bookings rather than payments. Parts are related in as much as they may share data inputs or the outputs of one part become the inputs of another. Parts may also come together in order to fulfil some higher order goal (see holism).

In the opening case study we discussed 'modules' of the ERP system – these represent system 'parts'. The relationship between components is shown in Figure 13-2. As an example, consider a hotel management system. One part of the system will manage the reservation process and allocate rooms; another may take and process payments and yet another may allocate goods and services to guests enabling them to charge a restaurant meal to their room. However, the charging of services to a room is dependent upon the guest being registered in the system and a room having been allocated. Similarly, invoice generation is dependent upon customer details having been entered.

While we have described systems according to the resources they use we must also consider their *boundaries* and their relationship with the environment. Figure 13-2 describes

Figure 13-2

Characteristics of a system

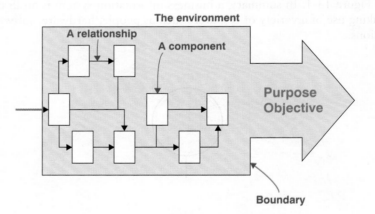

the interface between a system and its environment. Everything within the boundary forms part of the system, everything outside the boundary forms part of the external environment. Systems may be described as being open or closed. The 'open' systems model views the organization as taking input from the environment and through a series of activities transforming or converting these into outputs to achieve some objective, i.e. interaction occurs with elements beyond the system boundary. In the case of a closed system, no or limited interaction occurs with the environment. The decomposition and classification of systems and their parts enables us to focus specifically on how systems are used within the organization and identify areas where improvements may be made. Having established what we mean by a CBIS we are now in a position to identify the several ways used to classify them.

Classifying CBIS

Classification schemes are not definitive and represent merely one way of grouping and dividing a complex field.

BODDY *ET AL.* (2002: 13).

Classifying computer-based information systems is not unlike classifying cars. Cars have a series of common components no matter what the make or model: wheels, engine, fuel, steering and seats. In some cases a car may be placed in more than one category and in some cases it is difficult to categorize. Information systems also have common components: inputs, processes and outputs and sometimes storage. They tend to be categorized according to their use, the user and purpose. When distinguishing systems it is useful to consider the following attributes and properties:

- *Components* – may be concrete (physical, such as stock held in a warehouse) or abstract (such as a telephoned purchase order). Information and data are abstract and their display properties may be *hard* (properties which can be defined or measured) *or soft* (properties that depend upon personal values, opinions, tastes or ethics).

- *Connection* – the components of a system are connected in some way. The connection may be either physical (as in the cabling between components of a computer system), or abstract (as in interactions between team members).

- *Structure and hierarchy* – the components are organized and relate to each other in particular ways.

- *Process and interaction* – system components interact to achieve something.

Earlier we discussed formal and informal, paper and computer-based systems. When classifying CBIS we may also consider: function (goal or purpose) i.e. decision support; expert system; communications; operational and monitoring or reach – individuals, departmental, intra or inter-company.

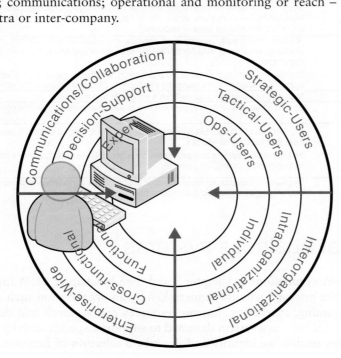

Figure 13-3

Classifying business information systems

Methods for classifying BIS are summarized in Figure 13-3. A system may serve strategic, tactical or operational users who may be individuals or groups. In some cases users may span more than one organization. Users may reside in a functional group or be spread throughout the company and finally, the system may assist with a particular activity such as decision-making, or collaboration. A selection of common CBIS types can be seen in Figure 13-4. In the next section we focus on functional systems before considering how organizations may acquire and develop them.

Figure 13-4

Types of information system

Accounting Information Systems	Information systems that record and report business transactions, the flow of funds through an organization, and produce financial statements. This provides information for the planning and control of business operations, as well as for legal and historical record-keeping
Business Intelligence (BI) Software	BI software is a general term used to describe analysis software which makes use of functions available in data warehouses, data marts and data mining
Customer Relationship Management (CRM)	Technology that includes collecting the required customer data, maintaining this data, and providing tools to analyze and report the data, CRM systems involve the collection and recall of large amounts of customer information and the integration of all this customer information throughout the entire supply chain. CRM attempts to address all of the customer touch points, such as face-to-face, Internet, or phone. CRM allows an organization's employees and its customers to collaborate on a variety of levels, such as product inquiry, contract information, past order history, product repair and service, and account details
Decision Support System (DSS)	A computer-based information system that combines models and data in an attempt to solve semi-structured problems with extensive user involvement
Enterprise Collaboration Systems	The use of groupware tools and the Internet, intranets, extranets, and other computer networks to support and enhance communication, coordination, collaboration, and resource sharing among teams and workgroups
Enterprise Resource Planning (ERP)	Complex software package commonly used to implement an enterprise information systen; typically integrates all functions of the enterprise, such as manufacturing, sales, finance, marketing, inventory, accounting, and human resources
Enterprise Systems	Organization-wide information systems that integrate key business processes so that information can flow freely between different parts of the company
Executive Information Systems (EIS)	Systems used by senior management to select, retrieve and manage information that can be used to support the achievement of an organisation's business objectives. They need not be directly concerned with decision-making activities, but can help senior managers to become more efficient and productive in a number of other ways, for example by helping them to manage their time more efficiently
Expert Systems	(also Knowledge-based systems) Intelligent computer programs that use knowledge and inference procedures to solve problems that are difficult enough to require significant human expertise for their solution
IHRM System	A set of distinct activities, functions and processes that are directed at attracting, developing and maintaining human resources
Just-In-Time Systems	Methods of managing inventory (stock) in which items are delivered when they are needed in the production process instead of being stored by the manufacturer
Knowledge Management Systems (KMS)	Systems that facilitate knowledge management throughout the organization by ensuring knowledge flow from those who know to those who need to know. KMSs are centred on a corporate knowledge base or depository
Management Information Systems (MIS)	Systems designed to provide past, present, and future routine information appropriate for planning, organizing, and controlling the operations and functional areas in an organization
Office Systems	Computer systems such as word processing, electronic mail systems, and scheduling systems, designed to increase the productivity of data workers in the office
Payment Systems	Methods of transferring funds from a customer to a merchant
Process Control Systems	Systems that deal with the large volume of data generated by production processes
Telecommunications System	A collection of compatible hardware and software arranged to communicate information from one location to another
Transaction Processing System (TPS)	An information system that processes an organization's basic business transactions such as purchasing, billing, and payroll
Work Management Systems (WMS)	Systems that distribute, route, monitor, and evaluate various types of work by controlling and managing all related information flow

Functional business systems

Look back
See chapter 9, p. 277

Functional business system a system designed to support a specific primary activity of the organization

We discussed business functions in Chapter 9 and then in Chapter 11. A functional structure is based on the primary activities undertaken by an organization such as production, finance and accounting, marketing, human resources and research and development. A functional business system is a system designed to support a specific activity of the organization. Within this section we identify and describe a selection of functional systems, see

Figure 13-5, and then consider functional system issues, particularly in the context of the international organization and with reference to Porter and Millar's (1985) requirement for systems to link up primary activities.

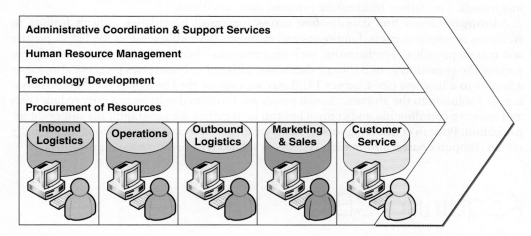

Administrative Coordination & Support Services

Human Resource Management

Technology Development

Procurement of Resources

| Inbound Logistics | Operations | Outbound Logistics | Marketing & Sales | Customer Service |

Figure 13-5

Functional business information systems (silos)

Business applications have traditionally served the functional areas of an organization, such as: production; inventory; purchasing; accounting; human resources; inbound and outbound logistics and marketing and sales; a selection of functional systems are described below:

- *Accounting information systems* – are used to record and report business transactions, the flow of funds through an organization, and produce financial statements. This provides information for the planning and control of business operations, as well as for legal and historical record-keeping.

- *Sales and marketing systems* – are used to record customer information; process sales orders; manage product pricing information; provide sales forecast information and manage market research and analysis information; track competitor data; support telemarketing and may include a geographical information system.

- *Inventory systems* – are used for stock control and may link with the sales order processing (SOP) or supplier information systems.

- *Production and manufacturing systems* – include production control, computer aided manufacturing and workflow management systems.

- *Packaging and distribution systems* – include logistical planning and customer database – labelling systems.

- *HR systems* – include payroll database, skills, training and development, employee record and payroll systems.

- *Purchasing systems* – include product pricing information, market research and analysis information and supplier information systems.

Functional systems serve the specific and local needs of parts of the organization and are developed using specific programming languages. Typically they have their own database(s), data structures, operating systems and other idiosyncrasies.

Silo problems

In Chapter 11 we discussed information and its flow between the value chain activities and within the value system. Organizations that grouped activities by function tended to develop separate information systems to support the specific goals of that function. Functional parts often operate in relative isolation – as if there were some brick wall between them. In many cases, functional departments would acquire or develop their information systems with little collaboration. Consequently, functional systems within the same organization

Functional parts often operate in relative isolation, this poses problems for connection and communication

may utilize differing technologies, data structures and standards. This poses problems for connection and communication and as a consequence, information is said to exist on islands within the organization – systems are fragmented along functional lines (they are not integrated). This failure to integrate presents many problems.

Silo organizations find coordination across functional boundaries difficult leading to weakness in responsiveness. Employees and managers have little sense of the bigger picture and remain parochial. Furthermore, such organizations often duplicate systems in different parts of the organization or duplicate data entry. This not only increases costs but also acts as a barrier to e-business (see Chapter 14). Later we explore the concept of the enterprise system as a solution to the aforementioned problems. Integrated systems not only reduce costs and improve coordination and control but can tie together the geographically dispersed organization. Prior to considering such systems we first review how organizations traditionally obtain computer-based information systems as solutions to organizational problems.

Acquiring CBIS

UK wasting billions on IT projects (22 April 2004)

Billions of pounds are wasted every year on new IT systems, according to a report published by the Royal Academy of Engineering and BCS.

'Even conservative estimates put the cost of such failures into tens of billions of pounds across the EU.'

Source: www.bcs.org. Printed with permission

Many IT or CBIS implementation projects fail by either taking too long to deliver, overspending or failing to deliver a solution that actually meets users' needs. It is therefore in the organization's interest to approach such projects using frameworks and methods that incorporate the lessons (knowledge) of the past. Pitfalls in systems development projects, mistakes commonly encountered, stem from users having unrealistic expectations or having little involvement; low cross-functional involvement; requirements with a lack of 'fit' with the organization; poor cost-benefit analysis (CBA) and poor resourcing of projects.

Figure 13-6

Acquisition process

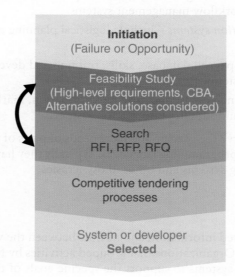

Thus far we have identified business information system types but have not yet explained how they find their way into the organization. We address this challenge in this section.

First we ask, Why do organizations initiate IS projects? In some cases projects are 'failure driven', i.e. faults in existing system(s) and in other cases may be 'aspiration driven', i.e. new opportunities are presented. The CBIS may be obtained from within or outside the organization and may exist already or be specially developed for the organizational problem at hand. Acquiring a CBIS is not unlike purchasing a new suit of clothes. In some cases the suit fits perfectly but costs more, takes time to create and may have particular flaws. Acquisition refers to the approach for sourcing the CBIS. Alternative acquisition methods include:

- procurement off-the-shelf – purchased from a software vendor;
- bespoke development – built from scratch; and
- end-user-developed – either built by the IT department (internal developers) or by the end-user themselves.

The acquisition methods cited may be compared using criteria such as delivery time, cost, quality (bugs) and how closely they meet needs, i.e. are fit for purpose. Bespoke solutions score better with this latter criterion but are poor when judged against the others. The standard off-the-shelf solution tends to be the opposite, i.e. good on all criteria except the fit with business needs. Acquisition method is therefore linked with generic strategy – a tailor-made system supporting a differentiation and an off-the-shelf supporting a cost advantage.

Consider two organizations: (A) is an international hotel chain seeking a hotel management system – an all-in-one seamlessly integrated property management software solution – online reservations, front desk, sales, restaurant and retail POS, back office accounting; and (2) is a specialized consultancy delivering innovative solutions to clients. They require a fully integrated system to support consultants in all aspects of their work, worldwide.

Critically discuss the likely preferred acquisition methods for the two organizations.

STOP & THINK

In cases other than end-user development or development by the IT department, the organization will either search for and select an off-the-shelf solution or find a developer to build one for them. In such cases, the organization will typically conduct a feasibility study (to include a cost-benefit analysis) in order to justify and secure funding for the project. Interactions with external suppliers often take the form of the request for information (RFI); request for proposals (RFP) or request for quote (RFQ), see Figure 13-6. The purpose of the RFI and RFP is to identify possible solutions to the IS problem; they typically constitute a detailed list of questions submitted to vendors of packaged software or other computer services to determine if the vendor's product can meet the organization's specific requirements.

The RFQ is a request for pricing quote(s) specifications related to a required product, by a prospective purchaser. Such requests mark the beginning of the selection process. From here, as with the generic problem solving process, companies will select their preferred solution through a competitive tendering process and mechanisms to identify the solution that most meets their requirements. A variety of stakeholders may become involved in the acquisition process, depending upon the culture of the organization. In some cases this

Consider the centralized (IT led) versus the decentralized (sponsoring unit) approach to systems acquisition.

What are the relative advantages and disadvantages of the two approaches?

STOP & THINK

may be a centralized and in other cases a decentralized activity. External consultants and consultants from the solution provider may also support the process.

While the centralized approach may be informed by the IT and corporate strategy and will consider integration issues, support and maintenance, the decentralized approach ensures requirements are best understood and met and that change has a greater chance of success through problem ownership, involvement and commitment.

Development

Systems development the activities that go into producing an information systems solution to an organizational problem or opportunity

Systems development life cycle the traditional methodology used to develop, maintain, and replace information systems; it is the sequence in which a system is created from initiation, analysis, design, implementation, build and maintenance

When a system does not already exist it must be developed. Systems development concerns the activities that go into producing an information system solution to an organizational problem or opportunity. While there are many development *models*, mostly based on generic problem-solving approaches (refer back to decision-making, Chapter 11), we focus on the best known here, the systems development life cycle (SDLC), also known as the waterfall or stepwise model. Developed in the 1950s and 1960s, this is the traditional methodology used to develop, maintain, and replace information systems; it is the sequence in which a system is created from initiation, analysis, design, implementation, build and maintenance. The model may be applied in different ways. For example, more detail and rigour may be evident for the development of a more expensive system or one that is to be built from scratch as opposed to one that may have already been developed. End-user development tends to neglect the feasibility, analysis, design and testing phases and the design and build phases are relatively insignificant for off-the-shelf acquisition. The traditional information systems development cycle (see Figure 13-7) is based upon the following stages:

Figure 13-7

Systems development life cycle (SDLC)

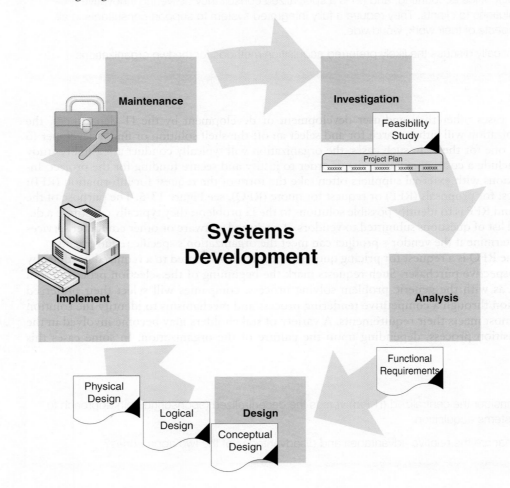

- *Systems investigation*. This stage seeks to answer the question, What system do we need and why? Typically, this stage includes a cost-benefit analysis as part of a feasibility study.

- *Systems analysis*. This stage seeks to answer the question, What exactly should the system do? This stage includes a detailed analysis of the information needs of end users, the organizational environment, and any system currently used to develop the functional requirements of a new system.

- *Systems design*. This stage develops specifications for the hardware, software, people, network, and data resources of the system. The information products the system is expected to produce are also designated.

- *Systems implementation*. Here the organization develops or acquires the hardware and software needed to implement the system design. Testing of the system and training of people to operate and use the system are also part of this stage. Finally, the organization converts to the new system. Four options are generally considered when changing over from the old system (paper or computer-based) to the new system:

  1 parallel conversion – the old and new systems are used concurrently until the new system is demonstrably stable and reliable;

  2 pilot conversion – the system is trialled in a limited area before it is deployed more extensively across the business;

  3 phased conversion – this changeover method involves introducing different modules of the new system sequentially; and

  4 direct cut-over strategy – where the new system completely replaces the old one on an appointed day.

  Conversion methods vary in the amount of associated risk, cost and complexity.

- *Systems maintenance*. In this stage, management uses a post implementation review process to monitor, evaluate, and modify the system as needed.

It is important to note the different roles and responsibilities throughout the project. The first two stages may be undertaken by non-technical people: the investigation stage typically makes use of employees from the target department, i.e. where the users are located and the analysis stage by systems analysts. The design stage is typically undertaken by IT specialists while implementation tasks may be shared between the users and the IT function.

Consider the changeover (conversion) methods/strategies discussed above. Identify the advantages and disadvantages of each.

Which approach might you consider for the two organizations (a hotel and a consultancy) discussed earlier?

STOP & THINK

The SDLC and variants allows a structured and disciplined approach to be taken in the design, development and implementation of information systems. While it seeks to ensure a close fit with business needs (through thorough requirement capture and modelling) it has been criticized for being implementation as a linear sequence of steps, such that requirements may have changed before the system is built and will therefore no longer be fit for purpose by the time the system is built. Many other systems development methods have been considered, see structured systems analysis and design method (SSADM), rapid application development (RAD), agile software development, etc.

Consider Chapter 5 *Change management* covered earlier in this book. What are the challenges and initiatives typically associated with a large scale systems implementation project?

STOP & THINK

Feasibility study the activity that occurs at the start of the project to ensure that the project is a viable business proposition. The feasibility report analyzes the need for and impact of the system and considers different alternatives for acquiring software. The study outputs include the feasibility report and recommendation to proceed

Functional requirements describes the functionality desired of a problem solution; fully describes what the software will do

Systems analysts specialists who translate business problems and requirements into information requirements and systems, acting as liaison between the developer and the rest of the organization

Organizations typically consider the need for a new organizational design and changes to other dimensions of structure (see Chapter 9); processes may need re-engineering (see Chapter 10); they consider the existing culture (see Chapter 8) when assessing the feasibility of the proposed system and may make use of measurement and reward mechanisms, training and education to motivate adoption. Furthermore, user involvement is encouraged to obtain buy-in and motivate acceptance of the new system. Recognizing employee fear of the unknown and new initiatives, aside from training and involvement, there may be frequent communication with stakeholders and support must be made available. The design and development of a business information system should include the provision of user support both during the implementation stage and on an ongoing basis.

We started the section by introducing systems theory and methods to classify systems and then described a range of functional systems, noting the problem of information silos and resultant coordination problems. We then introduced a method to manage IS/IT projects and considered acquisition, conversion methods and change management issues. In many cases such projects may be managed by the area of the company most affected with help from the IT department. However, such approaches may not be appropriate for cross-functional systems that have a major impact upon the organization. We therefore consider *enterprise systems* in the next section.

Enterprise systems

If a company's systems are fragmented, its business is fragmented.

DAVENPORT 1998

The concept of enterprise systems (ES) can be traced backed to the mid-1970s when database technology allowed, at least in principle, all applications to be supported by a common, centrally controlled database (Sandoe, Corbitt, and Boykin 2001). An ES is an organization-wide information system that integrates key business processes so information can flow freely between different parts of the organization. Enterprise systems, considered by many to be the most important development in the corporate use of IT in the 1990s, presented a new model of corporate computing. In the form of ERP systems they allowed companies to replace their existing information systems, which are often incompatible with one another, with a single, integrated system. An ES streamlines a company's data flow and provides management with direct access to a wealth of real-time operating information. Unlike business information systems of the past, which were typically developed in-house and with a company's specific requirements in mind, enterprise systems (in the form of ERP systems) tend to be off-the-shelf solutions. They impose their own logic on a company's strategy, culture, and organization, often forcing companies to change the way they do business. Enterprise systems are designed to solve the problem of fragmented information in large business organizations.

> **Enterprise system (ES)** an organization-wide information system that integrates key business processes so information can flow freely between different parts of the organization

Every large company collects, generates, and stores vast quantities of data. In most companies, though, the data is not kept in a single repository. Rather, the information is spread across dozens or even hundreds of separate computer systems. Each of these so-called legacy systems may provide invaluable support for a particular business activity; considered collectively, however, they are inefficient. Maintaining many different computer systems leads to enormous costs – for storing and rationalizing redundant data, for re-keying and reformatting data from one system for use in another, for updating and debugging obsolete software code and for programming interfaces between systems to automate the transfer of data.

> **Legacy systems** older systems that have become central to business operations and may still be capable of meeting these business needs

There are also indirect costs to consider. If a company's sales and ordering systems cannot communicate with its production-scheduling systems, then its manufacturing productivity and customer responsiveness suffer. If its sales and marketing systems are incompatible with its financial-reporting systems, then management is left to make important decisions by instinct rather than according to a detailed understanding of product and customer profitability; if a company's systems are fragmented, its business is fragmented (Davenport 1998).

Møller (2005) presents a succinct overview of enterprise systems and how they have evolved. The concept of enterprise systems (ES) is often explained through the evolution of ERP and has evolved over the past 50 years. The fundamental structure of ERP has its origin in the 1950s and 1960s with the introduction of computers into business. The first applications automated manual tasks such as bookkeeping, invoicing and ordering. The early inventory control systems (ICS) and similar systems progressively became material requirements planning (MRP) systems. The development continued in the 1970s and 1980s with the evolution of MRP II. This development peaked in the early 1990s with the advent of the ERP systems often embodied in SAP R/3 along with the other major vendors.

Although the ERP systems were influenced by the needs of accounting, planning and control, their philosophy is entrenched in manufacturing. ERP is standardized software designed to integrate the internal value chain of an enterprise; based on an integrated database, the ERP consists of several modules each designed for specific business functions. ERP is a method for the effective planning and controlling of all the resources needed to take, make, ship and account for customer orders in a manufacturing, distribution or service company. ERP systems represent a significant investment (typically costing 3–5 per cent of revenue) necessitating a thorough consideration of the benefits that such systems provide. Companies adopt ERP systems for many reasons such as legacy system problems; globalization; an enabler of business process reengineering (BPR), process integration and optimization (see Chapter 10); the pursuit of saleable and flexible infrastructures; and to enable collaboration with others in the supply chain.

Earlier in the book we noted global competition and outsourcing have caused the fragmentation of the supply chain. Managing information in an inter-organizational context has become critical and the emergence of the Internet and the range of related e-business technologies created new opportunities and threats to supply chain managers. The concept of the extended enterprise (EE) has been used to characterize the global supply chain of a single product in an environment of dynamic networks of agile companies engaged in various complex relationships. The inter-organizational network may be defined as a virtual enterprise of all the relevant functions of a company, its suppliers and its customers, who together are termed the EE. The EE introduces the idea of the loosely coupled supply chain.

ERP applications

ERP systems are information systems that integrate all manufacturing and related applications for an entire enterprise; they are applications used by large organizations (though getting smaller) to manage inventory, resources, and business processes across departments in the enterprise. More recently, ERP is considered as business software for running every aspect of a company including managing orders, inventory, accounting, and logistics. ERP systems may be referred to as fully integrated software (FIS) – a software package with a number of integrated modules to cover a range of functions and requirements, see Figure 13-8. Well-known ERP software providers include BAAN, Oracle, PeopleSoft and SAP. The advantages of an ERP system include: the creation of a more uniform organization (does business the same worldwide); efficiency and customer driven; improved decision-making and the creation of a process understanding and consequently better control throughout the organization. The system may also drive inventory and staff reduction or productivity improvements. Disadvantages and problems may also be encountered. Implementation is costly and takes considerable time; there is often a need for BPR (see Chapter 10) and in the cases of the wall-to-wall option, users are limited to the proprietary system where not all parts are best of breed.

CRM applications

Whereas the ERP (traditionally) is oriented towards back-office activities (systems not dealing directly with the customer such as inventory management and accounts payable) of the organization, the CRM supports the work of the front-office (systems that deal directly

Back-office the internal operations of an organization that are not accessible or visible to the general public

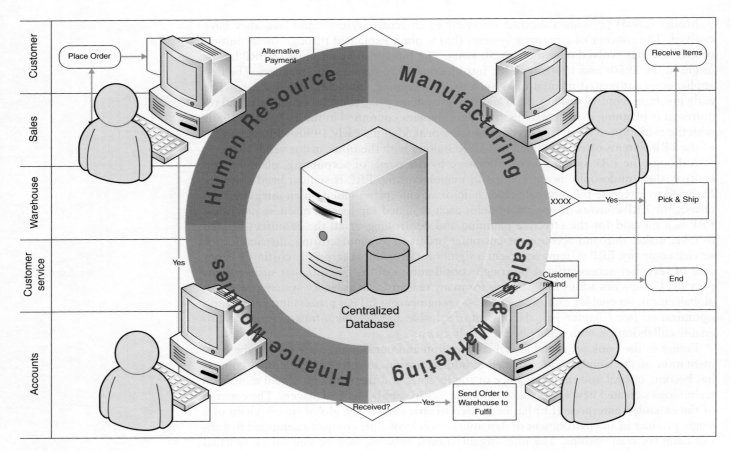

Figure 13-8
ERP system model

with the customer such as order processing). CRM can be used to build a sustainable long-term business with customers. The aim of CRM technology is to provide an interface between the customer and the employee – to replace or facilitate direct interaction. Ideal CRM systems support multichannel communications, needs of customers (product information, order placement, post sales support) and the core needs of employees (placing orders received by phone, fax or face-to-face and to answer a customer's questions). Databases lie at the heart of such systems, which may also make use of expert knowledge technologies. Combined, the ERP and CRM systems contribute to the backbone of the overall enterprise system, see Figures 13-9 and 13-10. We will discuss middleware, the software necessary to build distributed applications, in more detail later.

Look back
See chapter 11, p. 370

ERP systems themselves have evolved over the last decade. Functionality has been added and the overall scope of the systems enlarged. Over time, businesses extended their enterprise systems into the supply chain with 'bolt on' SCM systems. This led to substantial benefits and the next generation of ERP (ERP II) systems. Gartner Group defines ERP II as a business strategy and a set of industry-domain-specific applications building customer and shareholder value by enabling and optimizing enterprise and inter-enterprise, collaborative-operational and financial processes. Thus far we have identified what constitutes an ES and how they have evolved. Initially, the fully integrated ERP was implemented as a wall-to-wall ES but this business solution was not without problems.

Aside from not providing a complete solution (i.e. lacking in certain up and downstream functionality and inter-organizational collaboration) it forced organizations to re-engineer processes and lose competitive advantage through differentiation, mainly providing cost

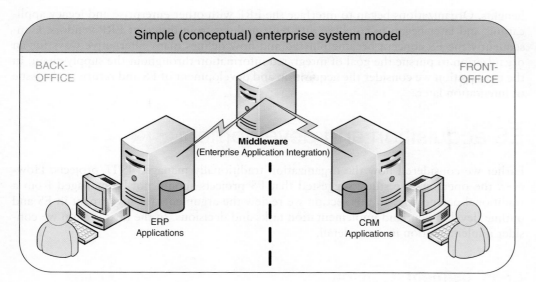

Figure 13-9

Simple model of an enterprise system

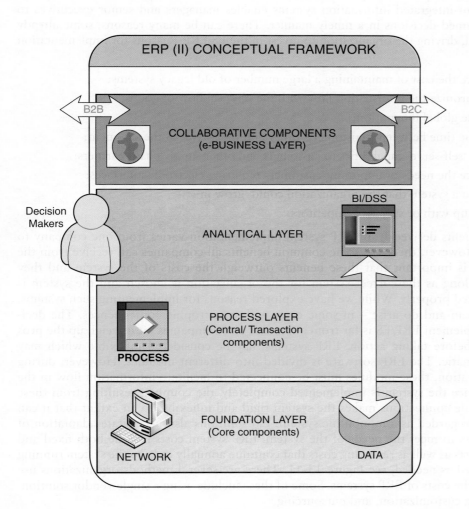

Figure 13-10

ERP (2) Conceptual framework

benefits. Organizations began to interface the ERP with other enterprise and legacy applications and later began to combine different modules from different ERP vendors. Consequently the ES concept became blurred and now defines many alternative ways for an organization to pursue the goal of integrated information throughout the supply chain. In the next section we consider the acquisition and development of ES and return to the issue of integration later.

ES acquisition and development

Earlier we considered how the organization traditionally managed IS/IT projects. However, the opening case study suggested that ES projects should not be managed from a traditional perspective. In this section we review the arguments for investment in ES and outline development and implementation tasks and decisions. In the next section we consider implementation in more detail.

ES investment decision

As business becomes increasingly global, integrated systems show promise for tying together the geographically dispersed organization. The increased information visibility that results from integrated information systems enables managers and senior executives to make informed decisions in a timely manner. There can be many reasons, some already highlighted, driving the organization to invest in the ES/ERP. Reasons for implementation include:

- to reduce the cost of maintaining a large number of old legacy systems;
- to synchronize the information flow with the physical flow of goods;
- to enable global integration;
- to cut the time between a customer's order and the arrival of the shipment;
- to offer 'self-serve' capabilities to customers and other supply chain partners;
- to service the needs of important customers requiring electronic interfaces;
- to obtain a system that the organization could 'grow in';
- to keep up with or surpass competitors.

The benefits derived from ERP system implementation varies from one company to another. However, there are some common benefits all companies can receive from the system. It is important that these benefits outweigh the costs of the system and they should as long as the correct system for the organization is chosen and the system is implemented properly. While we have explored reasons for implementing such systems, problems can and do arise – in some cases with catastrophic consequences. The decision to implement ERP/ES is far from automatic and companies must weigh up the pros and cons before taking action. ERP systems may be considered inflexible which may be problematic. The ERP software is divided into different modules. However, during implementation, these modules must be connected to facilitate information flow in the system. Once the system is implemented completely, the coupling resulting from these inter-module connections makes the system rigid and inflexible to an extent that it can almost be regarded as a monolithic system. FIS solutions also necessitate adaptation of the business to meet the needs of the system. ERP system costs include both fixed and upfront costs as well as recurring costs that continue annually to keep the system running and updated as needed, see Figure 13-11. There are several methods organizations use to reduce the costs of ERP systems. Some of these include using a single vendor solution, eliminating customization, and outsourcing.

Enterprise system implementation costs

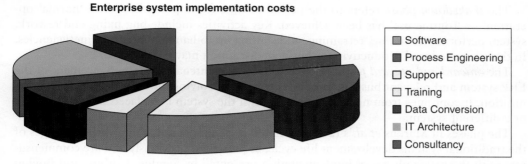

Figure 13-11

ES implementation costs

Having decided to invest in an ES, the organization must then decide whether to invest in a FIS (wall-to-wall) or develop their own solution by interfacing components that may be sourced from ERP vendors as components, other software providers or in-house legacy systems. This latter approach is termed the best-of-breed approach and we will revisit this decision later. For now we consider ES development and implementation. Throughout the next section we make comparisons with the traditional approaches to systems development and implementation discussed earlier in this chapter.

Developing ES

When developing information systems in the past, companies would first decide how they wanted to do business and then choose a software package that would support their proprietary processes, see previous. They often rewrote large portions of the software code to ensure a tight fit. With enterprise systems (FIS: ERP), however, the sequence is often reversed. The business must be modified often to fit the system. An off-the-shelf enterprise system is a generic solution. Its design reflects a series of assumptions about the way companies operate in general. Vendors try to structure the systems to reflect best practices, but it is the vendor, not the customer, who defines what 'best' means.

Some degree of ES customization is possible. Since the systems are modular, for instance, companies can install only those modules most appropriate to their business. However, the system's complexity makes major modifications impracticable. As a result, most companies installing enterprise systems will need to adapt or even completely rework their processes to fit the requirements of the system. Previously we introduced the SDLC but noted its role as a framework for managing systems development. In the case of the off-the-shelf ERP, little development is required and a variation on the SDLC may be used to manage the project.

Markus *et al*. Tanis (2000) identified four phases in an ERP life cycle:

1 chartering;
2 project;
3 shakedown; and
4 onward and upward.

The *chartering phase* comprises decisions leading to funding of the ERP system project. A variety of stakeholders (internal and external) engage in activities that include initiation of the idea to adopt an ERP/ES system, developing the business case, the decision on whether to proceed or not, searching for the project leader/champion, selecting the software and implementation partner, and project planning and scheduling.

The *project phase* activities include software configuration, system integration, testing, data conversion, training, and rollout. In this phase, the implementation partners must not only be knowledgeable in their area of focus, but also work closely and well together to achieve the organizational goal of ERP implementation.

The *shakedown phase* refers to the period of time from 'going live' until 'normal operation' or 'routine use' has been achieved. Key activities include bug fixing and rework, system performance tuning, retraining, and staffing up to handle temporary inefficiencies. In this phase reduced productivity or business disruption may be observed.

The *onward and upward phase* refers to ongoing maintenance and enhancement of the ERP system and relevant business processes to fit the evolving business needs of the organization. It continues from normal operation until the system is replaced with an upgrade or a different system.

The phases in Markus *et al.*'s (2000) ERP life cycle model are in line with the stages of the traditional systems development life cycle, as presented previously and are commensurate with the major phases of implementation presented by Sandoe, Corbitt, and Boykin (2001). Their model comprises six stages – the first three of which (initiation, planning, analysis and design) are similar to the chartering phase described above. See also Sumner (2005: 42) for a similar approach. The key differences with the SDLC is that the organization must adapt to the system rather than vice versa. Consequently there is a need for business process re-engineering, system configuration and customization. In the next section we consider key choices and alternative strategies for implementing ES in the context of the international organization.

Enterprise system implementation

Thus far we have considered what enterprise systems are and in this section will consider implementation issues. ES implementation is the one task likely to impact upon all managers of the organization. It includes hardware and software installation, system configuration, customization, integration, user-training, data migration, testing and more. Processes, structure and culture are likely to be changed through a wide range of activities, see Figure 13-12. Implementation continues until the new system is embedded into the organization. The implementation literature shows that many organizations have

Figure 13-12

ES implementation

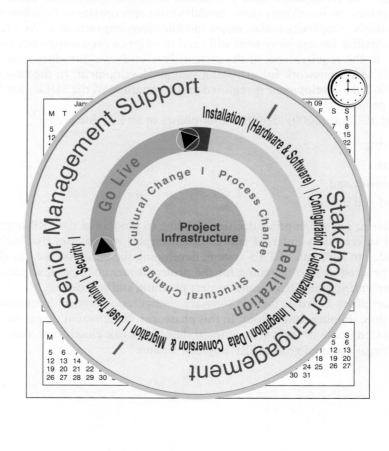

been able to install ES, in the sense that the system is available for use, but failed in their efforts to diffuse and incorporate it throughout the organization's daily practices. This difficulty with embedding technology into organizational processes and culture is not new. It is, of course, widely documented in the implementation of many other kinds of information systems. When can implementation be said to have occurred? Many believe the process finishes when the use of the technology is encouraged as a normal activity – i.e. routinized.

As was discussed earlier, the organization has options with regard to how the system is rolled out. Recent research suggests that system features such as the number of sites and users, the level of complexity of the business processes, the level of customization, the mix of ERP modules chosen, and the existence of legacy systems can be critical in determining the success of a firm's roll-out strategy. These factors can lead to varied approaches to ERP system roll-out. However, there is good support for two general approaches to ERP roll-outs:

1 the 'big bang' approach; and

2 the phased implementation approach.

Firms have used the 'big bang' approach for a variety of reasons such as where a business strategy required worldwide capability to promise product availability to customers. On the other hand, firms have used a phased approach for their international ERP roll-outs.

The high failure rate of ERP implementation calls for a better understanding of the pitfalls and success factors. What are the best strategies for setting up an ERP system? What are its special risks? And how can problems be avoided? First we focus on enterprise change generally before turning to the specifics of ERP implementation. A key issue at the outset concerns the amount of knowledge of enterprise systems managers and the project team should have when seeking to manage change. A *functional (black box) perspective* focuses on what the system is required to do; knowledge about the system's design and internal operation is not required. The *constructional (white box) perspective* is concerned with how the system is to be designed and built.

Here, knowledge about the system's internal operation is essential; concepts such as operating channels, resource deployment, process orientation, culture or management practices play a role. The distinction between both perspectives, see Figure 13-13, becomes clear when observing the difference between managing a system and changing a system. Change without knowledge about the system's operation and design seems not to be a sensible approach and is often disastrous. Business and organizational change thus necessitates a constructional perspective. The *enterprise architecture* is a concept that bridges the two perspectives. In its customary meaning, the term 'enterprise' refers to a (commercial) business organization. Enterprise integration has more facets than just technology. Making technology *work* thus requires a wider perspective than technology only, whereby contextual aspects are included in the design perspective such that the context and technology are optimally matched and integrated.

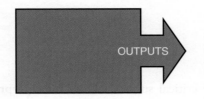 

Figure 13-13

Functional (black box) and constructional (white box) perspective

Dimensions of the enterprise include: business, organization, information, and technology. The concept of architecture can be used to describe the design of each dimension. The *business architecture* – concerns the strategic intentions and mission, the set of principles and standards that guide how a particular field of (commercial) endeavour will be exploited and explored; the business model. The *organizational architecture* describes the means to produce the desired outcome of purposeful activities; it is about the processes, events, people and culture, learning and competencies. Finally, the *information architecture* refers to a set of principles and standards that guide how information is to be managed (Hoogervorst 2004). An understanding of the enterprise architecture is essential throughout the change process as changes in one area are likely to affect other areas. This presents one argument against making ES implementation a traditional IT project; refer back to the Omega case study.

Look back
See chapter 13, p. 412

In addition to being expensive, ERP systems are complex, difficult to implement, and often very time consuming. A typical ERP system is likely take over one year to implement and benefits may not accrue until a number of years thereafter. ERP projects, encompassing people, business, technology, and process issues, are complex since there are a large number and variety of stakeholders; implementation is expensive; they integrate business functions and necessitate subsequent configuration of software. It has been argued that people, structure, realignment and change management will prove important to attain an effective ES. Earlier in this chapter we discussed the SDLC and other system development methods. However, implementing enterprise systems such as ERP, etc. necessitates non-traditional systems development and implementation frameworks. This point is demonstrated well in the Omega case study.

To implement an ES system successfully and thus avoid failure, the firm must conduct a careful preliminary analysis and develop a plan for system acquisition and implementation (Beheshti 2006). The most important success factors for implementation include senior management support, effective project management, extensive user training, and viewing ERP or ES as a business solution. Prior to system implementation, a company may need to make changes to organizational structure, corporate culture (Chapter 8), and business processes (Chapter 10) because of an ES's profound business implications Davenport (1998) cautions against shifting responsibility for its adoption to technologists. Only a general manager will be able to mediate between the imperatives of the system and the imperatives of the business.

The technical challenges are not the main reason enterprise systems fail. The biggest problems are business problems. Companies fail to reconcile the technological imperatives of the enterprise system with the business needs of the enterprise itself. An enterprise system, by its very nature, imposes its own logic on a company's strategy, organization, and culture; it pushes a company toward generic processes even when customized processes may be a source of competitive advantage.

One method of managing change effectively is the establishment of an ES planning and implementation team. This team is comprised of representatives from all major functional areas and senior management. Formation of a team provides a structure for determining the impact of ES on the organization. Choosing, implementing, maintaining, and updating an ERP/ES system takes an extraordinary amount of time. Company time is a huge opportunity cost of ERP and related systems. Along with the time that it takes to train employees and keep them up-to-date with the newest innovations within their present system, much time is invested in determining which system to choose, implementing and maintaining the system.

Success factors

Fui-Hoon Nah *et al.* (2001) summarized the critical success factors for enterprise integration. They included senior-level support, adequate business plan, business process re-engineering, collaborative teamwork, effective communication, appointment of a project champion, and capable project management. Shore (2006) adds to this work by considering the additional challenge imposed by global integration. While creating an integrated enterprise environment is certainly challenging for the organization whose business units are geographically concentrated and centrally controlled, it becomes even more challenging when these units are geographically dispersed (multi-site implementations) and individuals from around the globe must work together.

The international organization must consider the social structure of business units and the challenges these structures impose upon the implementation process. Many ERP implementation studies have concluded that organizational culture is the differentiator between successful and failed ERP implementations. They suggest that implementation success increases when the culture supports open communication and when the company recognizes employees as the primary source of ideas. However, a wider variation in organizational culture is expected when implementation spans the globe. This can be attributed to differences in national culture. Cultural factors may add another layer of complexity to the role of organizational/management issues in the integration process. International companies faced with global integration challenges have found face-to-face collaboration within a structured framework that combined a top-down centralized focus with a bottom-up collaborative environment to be very effective.

Look back
See chapter 9

When an integration project must span geographic and cultural boundaries, consideration should be given to the creation of a working team of international managers. Given the complexities of global integration there is a distinct need to choose the right champion. This person must have the skills necessary to balance technological business process and managerial/organizational issues including the complexities brought on by a diverse cultural group. Further, this individual must open the process to international collaboration, while maintaining tight project control. Less social control but more project control is the real paradox in managing the global integration, argues Shore (2006). Recognizing that employees are often reluctant to share information, companies embarking on ERP projects should be aware of the dimension of cultural change and prepare managers and other employees to deal with it.

Some organizations need to make long-term plans to begin to change the culture long before ERP is implemented. Re-engineering (BPR) may form the preliminary part of the implementation of the project. However, the combined effects of cultural and process changes in ERP projects can produce serious detrimental effects on employee attitudes. BPR and ERP projects inspire a transition from a function oriented to a process-oriented view. Employees may be uncomfortable with the process perspective, as it does not provide the familiarity and togetherness of working in a traditional functional departmental environment. Additional factors include overcoming user resistance through user involvement; gaining user acceptance and having, on the project team, a good balance of hybrid skills available.

User resistance an unwillingness to accept changes that are perceived to be damaging or threatening to the individual

Integrating

If you're not careful, the dream of information integration can turn into a nightmare.

DAVENPORT (1998)

All large organizations have complex heterogeneous IT systems and a need to integrate them. Integration converts many smaller applications into a larger application. A key goal of the organization is to get incongruent organizational parts to act as a harmonious whole. Many argue that integration across the enterprise is one of the most significant issues facing today's organizations. Functional differentiation must be countered with appropriate integration to bring the differentiated parts together for effective operation of the business processes. Aside from the problem of ensuring groups of people work together (refer back to Chapters 9 and 10), there is the difficulty of dealing with heterogeneous applications (systems) that use different formats (syntax) and apply different meanings (semantics) to data (Giachetti 2004). The problem of how to integrate these heterogeneous systems will be considered here. Integration is a common term in the enterprise systems literature. Loosely speaking, there is a general consensus that integration refers to the process of making applications work together that were never intended to work together, by passing information through some form of interface.

Integration bringing applications together to create a 'whole'

Large scale integration implies that all relevant data for a particular bounded and closed set of business processes is processed in the same software application. Updates in one application module or component are reflected throughout the business process logic, with no complex external interfacing. Data is stored once, and it is shared instantaneously by all business processes enabled by the software application. This implies 'one source of truth' for those business processes that are enabled by core ERP solutions; if all data is stored once and shared, then integrity issues are less likely to occur (Gulledge 2006). The total cost of ownership (TCO) is significantly less, since interfaces across application components are not required. Furthermore, complexity is significantly reduced. However, for reasons stated, organizations typically have other enterprise applications to be interfaced with each other. The fundamental goal of the ES is information integration. Whereas a fully integrated ERP automatically meets this goal, fragmentation remains when legacy and additional enterprise applications exist in the IS infrastructure. Earlier we listed several components of the ES: ERP (and modules); CRM, SCM, BI, legacy system, etc. Organizations must determine how to integrate such components.

In some cases systems (applications) may simply share a common data set over a network, see Figure 13-14. There are many types of integration such as database-to-database integration; data warehouse integration; enterprise application integration (EAI); and business-to-business (B2B) integration. Database-to-database integration requires the sharing of information at the database level; there are companies that provide middleware to accelerate this process but data integrity problems are likely.

Total cost of ownership (TCO) the total cost of owning technology resources, including initial purchase costs, the cost of hardware and software upgrades, maintenance, technical support, and training

Figure 13-14

Shared data approach (Adapted from Giachetti (2004))

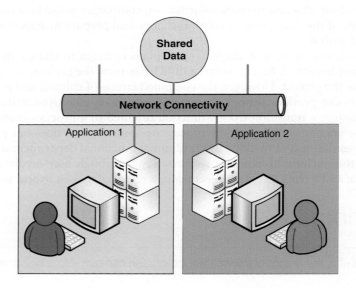

Enterprise application integration (EAI) is about loosely *coupling* applications and data stores together to solve intra-enterprise business problems. Application integration is a strategic activity and technology; it is a common approach to bind systems together. Its strength is facilitating the free flow of information from any system to any other system. EAI typically integrates ERP packages in addition to customer relationship management (CRM) packages, databases, legacy systems and older mainframe systems. EAI also allows organizations to externalize existing enterprise application information to interested parties, including real-time B2B information exchanges and web-enabled applications (we first introduced EAI in the Bosch case study).

The software used to facilitate communication between business applications including data transfer control, is known as *middleware*. A contemporary goal of the large and international organization is to integrate a range of *enterprise applications* as shown in Figure 13-15. This goal is related to the need to make information available throughout the organization and shared with other entities in the value system in near real time.

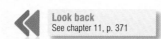

Look back
See chapter 11, p. 371

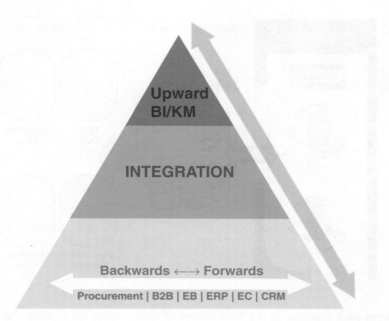

Figure 13-15
Enterprise systems: integration

Many organizations integrate backwards in order to extend the supply chain. The supply chain is more than just flows of materials, supplies and services; it also involves the flow of information, both logistical and financial. It is the efficient coordination of these two flows (physical and informational) that gives the enterprise a competitive advantage (Sandoe, Corbitt, and Boykin 2001). Information systems need to deliver supply chain visibility to different parties who need to access the supply chain information of an organization, whether it is employees, suppliers, logistics service providers or customers. Typically, ERP systems (e.g. SAP), through Internet technologies provide personalized views of information for different parties. Similarly, many organizations integrate forward to better meet demand and manage customers. The relationship between the organization and its customers is discussed in Chapter 15 with a focus on the creation of customer value.

The process of getting the product or service to the customer has changed from a basic order fulfilment/delivery process to one involving management of the entire customer experience. This customer experience is an integral part of the information flow in the extended supply chain – the forward integration of the supply chain has created a need to have accurate and real-time information on customers (see CRM) (Sandoe, Corbitt and Boykin, 2001).

Organizations also aim to integrate upwards. By integrating its information systems, an organization gains enhanced visibility into its internal processes. This visibility allows managers and executives to make more informed and often better decisions. When considering upward integration we should consider the information needs of senior managers. Executives need to review organizational performance from a firm-wide perspective, to detect problems with an ability to get to detail (drill down); they need simplified representations of the data, timely and accurate information. ERP and related systems generate much data, but the data is often not in the form managers can use to make decisions. Business intelligence (BI) tools and systems play a key role in the strategic planning process of the corporation; they allow a company to gather, store, access and analyze corporate data to aid in decision-making, see Figure 13-16. BI tools are used in areas such as customer profiling/support, market research/segmentation, product profitability, statistical analysis, and inventory/distribution analysis. BI applications include decision support systems, query and reporting; online analytical processing (OLAP), statistical analysis, forecasting, and data mining (refer back to Chapter 11). Many writers make the link between the use of BI tools and the creation of knowledge (refer back to Chapter 12).

Throughout this chapter we have presented numerous alternatives associated with the way the international organization may use systems. There are design alternatives (FIS or BoB); integration alternatives, information architecture alternatives and choices about how

Online analytical processing capability for manipulating and analyzing large volumes of data from multiple perspectives (see slice and dice)

Figure 13-16

Data warehouse and analysis

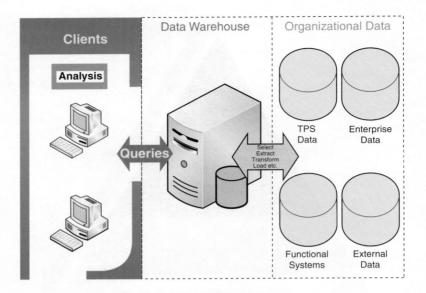

to implement such systems. In the final section of this chapter we explore the fundamental decisions associated with ES acquisition and implementation in the global enterprise.

Global ES strategies

In this final section we review key strategic decisions associated with ES and the international organization. A number of questions should be answered before any decisions are made. How might an ES strengthen or erode competitive advantage? What will be the system's effect on organization and culture? Does the system need to extend across all functions, or should only certain modules be implemented? Would it be better to roll the system out globally or to restrict it to certain regional units? Are there alternatives to the ES for information management? (Davenport 1998). For a multinational corporation, enterprise systems raise another important organizational question: How much uniformity should exist in the way business is done in different regions or countries? Some large companies have used their enterprise systems to introduce more consistent operating practices across their geographically dispersed units. For most companies, however, differences in regional markets remain so profound that strict process uniformity would be counterproductive.

If companies in such circumstances do not allow their regional units to tailor their operations to local customer requirements and regulatory structures, they risk sacrificing key markets to more flexible competitors. To preserve local autonomy while maintaining a degree of corporate control a very different approach to enterprise systems needs to be taken. Rather than implement a single, global ES, these companies need to roll out different versions of the same system in each regional unit, tailored to support local operating practices. Because of the increasingly complex nature of global operations, success of the multinational enterprises' strategy depends on its ability to capture, manipulate, distribute, and use real-time information. MNEs have increasingly invested in enterprise resource planning (ERP) systems to meet these needs. In an international context, ERP systems also facilitate the integration of information flows across national boundaries. Research has highlighted the importance of aligning information technology (IT) with the international strategy of the organization – refer back to the McKinsey 7S model and Figure 5-2, the organizational system model.

Misalignment of a organization's global ERP system with its international strategy is one of the primary reasons for delayed or failed ERP implementations. Evidence suggests these misalignments can hinder an organization's efforts to effectively control and coordinate its business activities, and in so doing, can negatively affect its bottom line. Several factors contribute to such misalignments. For example, ERP vendors would like

Look back
See chapter 5, p. 148

organizations to adopt a 'one-size-fits-all' solution that is built on industry best practices. However, this requires organizations to conform, at least partially, to industry best practices; such transitions can adversely influence their performance. Alignment becomes even more challenging when one factors in the diverse national environments that confront the international organization. In a dynamically changing external environment, achieving and sustaining ERP configuration-international strategy alignment is an extremely challenging task (Madapusi and D'Souza 2005). In this section we will consider two fundamental and strategic problems faced by the international organization. First we consider the arguments surrounding the choice between FIS or BoB and then consider how to align the IS or enterprise IS infrastructure and system with the corporate strategy.

Strategic alternatives: re-engineer or customize

There are two fundamental approaches to ES implementation:

1 acquire an off-the-shelf solution and re-engineer the organization around it; or
2 engineer (customize) the software to meet the needs of the organization.

This is referred to as the re-engineering versus customization approach (fully integrated or BoB). In the re-engineering approach the team selects a commercial fully integrated off-the-shelf package and then adapts business processes. In the customization approach the team selects and then customizes solutions to meet business needs, i.e. adapts the software. Not all international companies implement enterprise systems in the same way.

One factor that impacts upon such decisions is the company size and scope. Madapusi and D'Souza (2005) suggest there is a need to view the ERP systems employed by small multinational enterprises (SMNEs) as different from those of larger multinational enterprises (LMNEs). For SMNEs, ERP implementation costs have always been a major barrier. SMNEs prefer ERP systems that are simple, easy to use, and upgradeable. To cater to this SMNE demand, ERP vendors offer slimmed-down versions of ERP systems (refer to the Duckworth case study). The offerings are web enabled, user friendly, provide functionalities and options required by SMNEs, and are upgradeable to the fully fledged ERP systems traditionally implemented by LMNEs. ERP vendors also increasingly prefer to address the SMNE market through the application service provider (ASP) model by web-enabling their software. The Internet, through the use of XML and web services, has also brought the ability to create standardized data that can be used across supply-chain partners. SMNEs have been quick to adopt XML-based ERP systems because these systems are cheaper and faster to build.

Enterprise resource planning (ERP) software is the dominant strategic platform for supporting enterprise-wide business processes. However, while, as standard packages, they have the advantage of easy maintenance, they have been criticized as inflexible and not meeting specific organization and industry requirements. The implementation of single vendor systems results in broadly similar business process and IT infrastructures; this has considerable implications for competitive advantage. Consequently, some organizations have developed their own customized suite of enterprise applications known as a *best of breed (BoB)* IT strategy; see Light, Holland and Wills (2001). The objective is to develop enterprise systems that are more closely aligned with the business processes of an organization. BoB aims to provide greater flexibility and closer alignment of software with the business processes of the organization. BoB, an alternative approach to enterprise IT infrastructure development, recognizes context as key to successful BPR. This is because organizational members can select IT components on the basis of how well they think they will support business processes; the aim is for enterprise integration and a process orientation. BoB is based on the integration of standard software from a variety of vendors. For example, General Motors has linked the SAP financial and Peoplesoft human resource applications (Zygmont 1999).

Some companies have also developed custom components due to the absence of best in class standard software. The strengths of BoB centre on the ability of organizations to benefit from the most appropriate software functionality. The approach also provides an infrastructure that accommodates the implementation of new or improved applications and business processes, thereby providing companies with a constant state-of-the-art capability. A further benefit of BoB is the extent to which it can facilitate BPR. In pursuit of competitive advantage through differentiation, some organizations are implementing strategies such as customer relationship management systems and web enabled developments.

Organizations at this stage need to decide whether to stay with the single vendor approach. If the vendor offers a product, organizations need to assess its strength. If a product does not exist, organizations must either wait for it or implement a component from another source. BoB deals with this problem by componentizing single vendor ERP systems to allow for integration within their enterprise infrastructure. BoB offers other advantages over single vendor systems. Each BoB component can be implemented as a stand-alone application. The rapid delivery of functionality can mean a payback from the project throughout implementation rather than at the end. The incremental approach also subjects the organization to smaller amounts of change, thereby reducing organizational trauma. Additionally, BoB increase flexibility in business process (re)design.

The main difficulties of BoB relate to the complexity of implementation and the costs associated with maintenance generally and specifically related to the links between the software (which are costly to build – see the Bosch case study). ERP requires a clean slate approach, whereas BoB offers the chance for organizations to recognize existing ways of work and make trade-offs with stakeholders. This is an important distinction as the BPR associated with BoB can facilitate implementation and the management of complexity. Another important difference is that ERP systems do not offer the same levels of flexibility, and potentially, the responsiveness associated with BoB. BoB approaches have the potential to require higher degrees of maintenance due to the complex connections made between different components, whereas maintenance of components and connections between components, of single vendor ERP systems is largely outsourced to the vendor. Companies typically compare ERP (fully integrated software) with best of breed solutions on four aspects:

- *The time, cost and resources for implementation*
  The overall cost and time required will generally be less for a fully integrated ERP than implementing the equivalent best of breed packages. Best of breed packages give the option to spread the implementation over a longer time scale but will take more time overall and may actually cost more in the end. Implementing best of breed packages can be spread over a longer time period. Each package may only affect one department so can be implemented at a time when that department is available.

- *Degree of fit*
  Because a best of breed package can be selected to fit a particular need, they tend to better fit organizational requirements. Every ERP package has its strengths and weaknesses; an ERP package that has good financials may be poor on process manufacture and so on.

- *Simplicity of use*
  Task by task, best of breed is generally simpler to use but from an overall company perspective ERP is simplest.

- *Implementation management*
  With only one supplier to deal with, management of the fully integrated software is easier. There is one company providing the training and support and only one system for the technical professionals to understand.

The ERP II conceptual framework encapsulates the BoB and EAI strategy by componentizing the concept. Therefore ERP II is able to capture the application architecture independently of vendors or systems. The BoB strategy is competing head to head with a single ERP vendor strategy. Dell uses the Internet in combination with their ES to create a rapid-responding supply chain consisting of customers, Dell and Dell's suppliers. Thus Dell is able to purpose-build computers by synchronizing supply and demand. Dell abandoned a SAP project and implemented their 'G2 strategy' based on an open flexible architecture and EAI middleware.

Strategic alignment

Look back
See chapter 3

Businesses typically adopt one of three types of international strategies: multinational, global, or transnational. MNEs that achieve an appropriate fit between their ES systems and international strategies have been found to achieve better business performance. Therefore, managers must align ES systems with their organization's international strategy, see Figure 13-17. The multinational strategy gives priority to local responsiveness (differentiation) in each international location. National units have considerable autonomy (decentralized) and typically have local, independently run IT operations and ERP systems. However, installations are linked to HQ for financial and production reporting purposes. At the enterprise level, organizations implementing a multinational strategy tend to select a 'multi-financials/multi-operations' logical structure for their ERP systems. Such a structure is appropriate for the loose-knit inter-relationships between the national units.

Typically, each national unit manages it own ERP operations. These organizations prefer a high degree of customization of ERP functionality to meet local market needs; they opt for distributed information architectures with stand-alone local databases. Each local unit is autonomous. HQ linkage occurs primarily through financial reporting structures. The preferred roll-out option would be a phased implementation of application modules at the national level, with integration primarily through financial reporting modules. Although phased implementation is time consuming, it involves less risk compared with the 'big bang' approach.

Organizations that adopt a multinational strategy face unique challenges. The near absence of centralized control and standardization often results in multiple and varied ERP/ES configurations across national units. Application functionality can also vary across multiple platforms, making it difficult to obtain an integrated/holistic view of crucial business data.

Organizations that use a global strategy place high priority on operational efficiency and standardization. They typically require high levels of control and low levels of coordination.

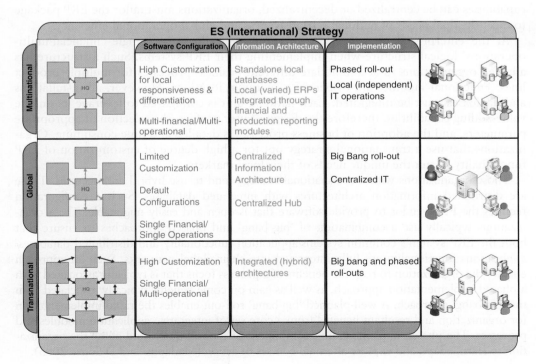

	ES (International) Strategy			
	Software Configuration	**Information Architecture**	**Implementation**	
Multinational	High Customization for local responsiveness & differentiation Multi-financial/Multi-operational	Standalone local databases Local (varied) ERPs integrated through financial and production reporting modules	Phased roll-out Local (independent) IT operations	
Global	Limited Customization Default Configurations Single Financial/Single Operations	Centralized Information Architecture Centralized Hub	Big Bang roll-out Centralized IT	
Transnational	High Customization Single Financial/Multi-operational	Integrated (hybrid) architectures	Big bang and phased roll-outs	

Figure 13.17

Enterprise system and international strategy alignment

These organizations are structured around centralized 'hubs', with strategic decision-making concentrated at HQ. HQ drives IT activities with an eye towards maximizing operational efficiency. The national units have limited freedom to adopt the strategies, products, and services passed down (integrated) to them by HQ. At the enterprise level, organizations that implement a global strategy tend to use a 'single-financial/single-operation' logical structure. HQ manages and distributes ERP operations to national units through interfaces. Cost savings are achieved using vendor-recommended default configurations for user profiles, parameters, and business processes.

Global standardization affords further savings by requiring only limited customization of ERP functionality. Organizations that use a global strategy typically follow centralized information architectures with HQ appropriately linked to national units. The installation of a centralized database also affords stronger HQ control. The downside is that local (national) data storage may not entirely reflect local practices. The adoption of 'best practices' embedded in ERP packages serves to enhance organizational integration and control. These organizations prefer a 'big bang' approach to ERP implementation. Such an approach allows the organization to roll out a set of ERP application modules across its worldwide operations simultaneously.

The 'big bang' strategy is much riskier than the phased implementation strategy and may lead to short-term disruptions in operations and drops in productivity. However, a well-executed 'big bang' approach would enable a organization to efficiently transition from a set of disparate legacy systems to an enterprise-wide integrative and standardized system (Madapusi and D'Souza 2005).

Organizations that adopt a transnational strategy are structured as integrated networks with specialized but interdependent strategic and operational decision-making functions; they embrace the dual need for efficiency (integration) and being local (differentiation). These organizations create competitive advantages that are location specific and efficiency driven. They gain location advantages by dispersing their value-creating activities wherever this can be best done and at the cheapest cost. They gain economic efficiencies by leveraging their worldwide knowledge base and by acquiring economies of scale. These organizations tend to adopt an integrated global IT approach that emphasizes common systems and core applications for shared worldwide functionality. They also encourage adaptation to meet local requirements. Organizations that adopt a transnational strategy have found it difficult to meet effectively worldwide needs for coordination and integration. Since resources and capabilities can be centralized or decentralized, organizations must tailor the ERP package to meet the dual needs of national responsiveness and global operational efficiency.

At the enterprise level, these organizations typically use a 'single- financial/multi-operations' logical structure when implementing their ERP systems. Such a structure has allowed organizations to accommodate different business processes for multiple product lines. Functional modules are dispersed to national locations. However, all installations and databases must be integrated. Each national unit is configured to leverage its unique value-adding capabilities, therefore the design of user profiles, the selection of appropriate parameters, and the adoption of business processes is detailed and time consuming. Organizations that use a transnational strategy opt for a high degree of customization of ERP functionality to suit the unique needs of their local markets.

Those organizations with a transnational strategy tend to use hybrid architectures. These are distributed information architectures with integrated databases. Such a configuration requires the ERP vendor to provide software that is open and easily migratable. These organizations typically use a combination of 'big bang' and phased approaches to ensure that both the ERP system's common systems/application functionality and distributed databases/ applications functionality are fully integrated into their global networks. Such an approach enables the organization to reap the benefits of a process focus that is typically associated with a phased implementation approach, as well as gain outcome benefits typically associated with the 'big bang' approach. A well-planned 'big bang' roll-out enables the rapid implementation for organization and resultant benefits from a core set of integrative application modules and processes. The phased implementation component of the roll-out would allow the organization to learn, adapt, and explore alternate courses of action (Madapusi and D'Souza 2005).

Not only must managers consider alignment of the ES with the international strategy, the ES must also fit with other dimensions of the enterprise. Managers must understand that implementing an ERP system is not merely a technological challenge; it involves significant and radical changes to other components of the business. Neither the 'one-size fits-all' configuration nor the configuration that emphasizes heavy customization of the ERP package is likely to be successful unless it is aligned with the international strategy of the organization. Therefore, careful planning of an organization's ERP-strategy alignment should always precede the ERP investment. Once managers have decided on the broad parameters of their organization's ERP/ES strategy alignment, they should draft a configuration for the ERP system. Here, managers should plan their ERP configuration so it addresses all the three major configuration issues – software configuration, information architecture, and system rollout – all the while ensuring that they are compatible and aligned with the international strategy of the organization.

The remaining chapters of the book build upon the work presented here. In the next chapter we provide more detail on collaborative technologies, e-business and commerce then return to the supply chain in Chapter 15 (upstream activities) and CRM activities in Chapter 16 (downstream). Finally, in Chapter 17 we consider international finance.

Summary of key learning points

Computer-based information systems are used to support all roles at all levels of the organization. They improve information access but not necessarily the flow of information within the whole organization. Traditionally, the business functions acquired and developed computer-based information systems to help them meet their localized goals. A functional business information system is used to support a specific organizational activity. The value chain can be used to match such systems against the primary and secondary activities of the company. Historically, computer-based information systems were used within the organization. Traditional approaches created silos (information islands) and a fragmented organization. This resulted in coordination, communication and control problems leading to increased cost and poor responsiveness.

Systems may be acquired, developed and implemented in many ways. Each has relative strengths and weaknesses in terms of strategic fit, timeliness, cost and quality. Historically, systems were developed to meet the unique needs of the organization. Development projects were typically led by the IT manager who would follow a linear, command and control approach to implementation (such as the systems development life cycle). Such approaches are less appropriate for the implementation of an enterprise system.

Developments in database, Internet and middleware technologies paved the way for integrated systems and resultant information flows. As a result, software developers and vendors created enterprise resource planning software as single software solutions, available off the shelf for purchase by large multinational corporations. This fully integrated software (FIS) utilized a single monolithic database which enabled the organization to integrate its primary activities. With time, vendors have added (integrated) additional components and functionality to such systems, upstream and downstream within the organization.

Fully integrated ERP software and associated hardware is typically available off-the-shelf and therefore easily imitated. An alternative, best of breed approach presents an opportunity to develop a unique enterprise system for the organization. Furthermore, whether a fully integrated or best of breed approach, the enterprise system is seen as a bundle of resources which include people, technology, processes and culture which may be configured in a manner to enable organizational strategy and provide a sustainable, hard to imitate, competitive advantage (see the RBV). This is particularly true, when the parts are congruent and the whole system aligned with strategy. For the international organization among the many advantages to an enterprise system is the ability to 'tie' together organizational parts, regardless of geographical location, thus providing benefits associated with an integrated organization. Among such benefits is the ability to support time-based competitive advantage and integrate the supply chain through interorganizational linkages. The implementation of such a system is costly and necessitates a business not IT-led approach.

Small, global organizations or those in pursuit of a cost advantage are more likely to adopt a fully integrated system. The transnational, larger organization or organization, pursuing a differentiation strategy, is more likely to adopt a best of breed approach. This latter approach will enable the company to make the system fit the existing organization. The fully integrated system approach requires the organization to embark on a business process re-engineering programme and make both structural and cultural changes so that the organization fits the system. In many cases, the smaller multinational corporation is likely to adopt an enterprise system to avoid competitive disadvantage. Whereas the fully integrated system may be simpler to use, the best of breed will be better aligned with the organization and its strategy.

Review questions

Enterprise information systems

Read the Duckworth case study – For the purpose of this task you should imagine that Duckworth has not yet implemented SAP.

1 In search of sustainable competitive advantage Duckworth are now considering the procurement of an enterprise system. In recent years their business has become increasingly global and they believe integrated systems show promise for tying together the geographically dispersed subsidiaries forming the present organization. The board would now like you to help them plan and prepare for the implementation of an enterprise system.

   You should create a briefing report sensitizing the board to key issues, helping them consider options for a way forward. Specifically, you should: analyze the current (as is) data, information and knowledge management situation at Duckworth, discuss core processes and determine the high level information needs for the future and discuss the feasibility of implementing an ERP system at Duckworth – focusing in particular on the business case issues (drivers).

2 You should critically evaluate and recommend approaches aimed at enabling broad team participation, information and knowledge sharing within Duckworth and with partners. The MD believes in the need to focus not just on the value chain and system but also on value networks (the human and technical resources in a business that work together to form relationships and add value to a product or service – the context within which a firm identifies and responds to customers' needs, solves problems, procures input, reacts to competitors and strives for profit).

   You must research and analyze the business problem posed and then consider and evaluate possible solutions and initiatives that support their goal to share skills and knowledge throughout the group of companies worldwide.

   Your problem analysis and possible solutions/initiatives should be presented to the senior management at Duckworth.

Enterprise systems – case comparison

Create a feasibility study for ERP implementation at Duckworths, focusing on the cost-benefit analysis in particular.

Enterprise systems – Omega

Consider the Omega case study at the start of this chapter.

1 Justification for implementation – identify the reasons for implementing the ES in Omega.

2 Determination of appropriate functionality – how would you go about identifying the appropriate functionality?

3 What problems are inherent with nice-to-have functionality?

4 Compare and contrast several leading ERP vendor products, discussing their relative advantages and disadvantages.

5 Development of a business case – what should be included in the business case?

6 What organizational changes resulting from the implementation of such a system would you expect? (You should draw on Chapter 4 to help inform your answer.)

7 Many consider the ES a combination of software, hardware, persons, and work processes where the sum is greater than the individual parts. Discuss this statement with reference to the concept of holism and the article by Porter (1985).

In order to give depth to your answer it is encouraged that the source references for the case study are read. You should also cite other work to present a critical aspect to your answer.

References

Aladwani, A. (2001) 'Change management strategies for successful ERP implementation', *Business Process Management Journal* 7(3):266–275.

Boddy, D., Boonstra, A. and Kennedy, G. (2002) *Managing Information Systems: An Organizational Perspective*, Harlow: Pearson Education.

Beheshti, H. (2006) 'What managers should know about ERP/ERP II', *Management Research News* 29(4):184–193.

Davenport, T. (1998) 'Putting the Enterprise into the Enterprise System', *Harvard Business Review* (July/August 1998) 76(4):121–131.

Davenport (2000) cited in Skok, W. and Legge, M. (2002) 'Evaluating enterprise resource planning (ERP) systems using an interpretive approach', *Knowledge and Process Management* 9(2):72–82.

Davenport, T. and Brooks, J. (2004) 'Enterprise systems and the supply chain', *The Journal of Enterprise Information Management* 17(1):8–19.

Giachetti, R. (2004) 'A framework to review the information integration of the enterprise', *International Journal of Production Research* 42(6):1147–1166.

Gulledge, T. (2006) 'What is integration?', *Industrial Management & Data Systems* 106(1):5–20.

Holland, C., Shaw, D. and Kawalek, P. (2005) 'BP's multi-enterprise asset management system', *Information and Software Technology* 47:999–1007.

Hoogervorst, J. (2004) 'Enterprise Architecture: Enabling Integration, Agility And Change', *International Journal of Cooperative Information Systems* (September 2004) 13(3):213–233.

Laudon, K. C. and Laudon, J. P. (2007) *Management Information Systems: Managing The Digital Firm* (10 ed), Upper Saddle River, NJ: Pearson.

Lee, S. M. and Kim, B. (1996) 'Developing the information systems architecture for world-class organizations' *Management Decision* 34(2):46–52.

Light, B., Holland, C. and Wills, K. (2001) 'ERP and best of breed: a comparative analysis', *Business Process Management Journal* 7(3):216–224.

Madapusi, A. and D'Souza, D. (2005) 'Aligning ERP systems with international strategies', *Information Systems Management* (Winter 2005) 22(1):7–17.

Markus, M., Tanis, C. and van Fenema, P. (2000) 'Multisite ERP Implementations', *Communications of the ACM* (April 2000) 43(4):42–46.

Møller, C. (2005) 'ERP II: a conceptual framework for next-generation enterprise systems?', *Journal of Enterprise Information Management* 18(4):483–497.

Nah, F., Lau, J. and Kuang, J. (2001) 'Critical factors for successful implementation of enterprise systems', *Business Process Management Journal* 7(3):285–296.

O'Brien, J. A. (2002) *Management Information Systems – Managing Information Technology in the E-Business Enterprise* (5 ed), New York: McGraw-Hill Higher Education.

Porter, M. E. and Millar, V. E. (1985) 'How information gives you a competitive advantage', *Harvard Business Review* (July–7August 1963):149–174.

Sandoe, K., Corbitt, G. and Boykin, R. (2001) *Enterprise Integration*, New York: Wiley.

Scheer, A. and Habermann, F. (2000) 'Making ERP a success', *Communications of the ACM* (April 2000) 43(4):57–61.

Scott, J. and Vessey, I. (2002) 'Managing risks in enterprise systems implementations', *Communications of the ACM* (April 2002) 45(4):74–81.

Sheth, J. (1981) 'Psychology of innovation resistance', *Research in Marketing* 4:273–282.

Shore, B. (2006) 'Enterprise integration: Across the Globally Disbursed Service Organization', *Communications of the ACM* (June 2006) 49(6):102–106.

Sikora, R. and Shaw, M. J. (1998) 'A Multi-Agent Framework for the Coordination and Integration of Information Systems', *Management Science* (November 1998) 44(11), (Part 2 of 2):65–78.

Skok, W. and Legge, M. (2002) 'Evaluating enterprise resource planning (ERP) systems using an interpretive approach', *Knowledge and Process Management* 9(2):72–82.

Sumner, M. (2005) *Enterprise Resource Planning*, Upper Saddle River, NJ: Pearson Prentice Hall.

Zygmont J. (1999) 'Mixmasters find an alternative to all-in-one ERP software', 'Datamation', cited in Light, Holland and Wills (2001).

Suggestions for further reading

Journals

The evolution of enterprise systems, enterprise resource planning (ERP) and next-generation enterprise systems (ES) along with models to analyze and design complex enterprise systems architecture is presented in Møller, C. (2005) ERP II: a conceptual framework for next-generation enterprise systems?, *Journal of Enterprise Information Management*, 18(4):483–497.

Journal of Enterprise Information Management

The *Journal of Enterprise Information Management* (previously published as *Logistics Information Management*) strives to publish articles of key interest and practical relevance to anyone operating in the field of logistics. Specific matters were presented in Issue 4, 2005, Special issue: ERP and enterprise application and Issue 1 2004, Special issue: Enterprise systems integration and management.
www.emeraldinsight.com/info/journals/jeim/jeim.jsp

Communications of the ACM

Communications of the ACM is the flagship publication of the ACM – it is frequently cited in the computing field. The October issue focuses on ICT-led globalization.
www.acm.org/pubs/cacm/homepage.html

Key articles

Scholars of this subject area have often read the following:

1 Davenport, T. (1998) 'Putting the Enterprise into the Enterprise System', *Harvard Business Review* (July/August 1998) 76(4):121–131.
2 Nah, F., Lau, J. and Kuang, J. (2001) 'Critical factors for successful implementation of enterprise systems', *Business Process Management Journal* 7(3):285–296.
3 Skok, W. and Legge, M. (2002) 'Evaluating enterprise resource planning (ERP) systems using an interpretive approach', *Knowledge and Process Management* 9(2):72–82.
4 Møller, C. (2005) 'ERP II: a conceptual framework for next-generation enterprise systems?', *Journal of Enterprise Information Management* 18(4):483–497.
5 For a comprehensive overview of integration readers should review Giachetti, R. (2004) 'A framework to review the information integration of the enterprise', *International Journal of Production Research* 42(6):1147–1166.

Chapter 14

Global digital business

Introduction
Net technologies and opportunity
E-commerce and e-business
Virtual markets and organizations
Strategic and net-technologies
Global challenges

Key concepts

- Digital organization ■ E-commerce ■ E-business ■ Reach ■ Disintermediation
- Reintermediation ■ Intranet ■ Extranet ■ Internet ■ E-procurement
- E-marketing ■ Virtual organization ■ EB strategy ■ Virtual organizing
- Business model

By the end of this chapter you will be able to:

■ Explain what is meant by e-commerce and e-business

■ Identify ways the use of the Internet and how Internet (net) technologies can help the international organization compete, create wealth and add value

■ Discuss common electronic business models and their components

■ Understand how e-commerce and the associated technologies affect strategy and strategies applicable to e-commerce

■ Evaluate the challenges associated with global EC

Figure 14-1

Internet activities (Adapted from Zwass (2003))

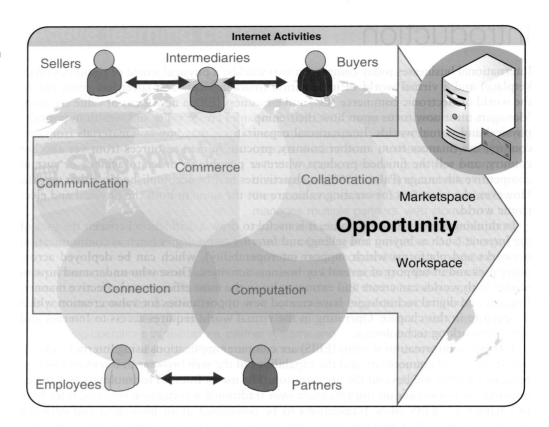

connectivity of the Internet enables m-commerce. The innovation potential of m-commerce stems from its ability to offer location-sensitive services. Important access devices employed by individuals include: PCs and mobile telephones; access is also made with personal digital assistants, and laptops, and with the emerging wearable devices. Beyond this, a number of more recent products, from cars to refrigerators, have the capability to communicate over the Internet as part of a development known as ubiquitous computing, which aims ultimately to equip a great variety of devices with URLs. EC as we know it today is based not only on developments pertaining to the Internet, but on prior technological and organizational developments arising from the combination of telecommunications and computing.

The effectiveness and efficiency of organizational information systems (*see* Chapters 11–13) can be enhanced significantly by a move to Internet technologies. The spread of Internet-centric applications has created a universal development platform for organizational systems. Enterprise-level systems like ERP or CRM can be introduced into a firm with the expectation that they will be able to interact with the systems of the firm's business partners. Interoperability of web services permits the creation of enterprise-wide information-system architectures (*see* Chapter 13) that link all the corporate core business systems to the firm's website.

Business software, including web services, can be reused and amortized across multiple user organizations and locations. Development environments and methodologies can be applied across the business units of an enterprise and across enterprises. The Internet makes vast numbers of computers accessible along with the associated resources of software and data. These resources can be harnessed for distributed computing and problem-solving on a very large scale, with the Internet becoming a virtual computing platform; see for example grid computing. Through coordinated sharing of available computing capacity, grid computing has enabled such computationally demanding tasks as simulation, visualization, and data analysis. In the EC domain, grid computing will enable data mining and also access to federated databases for CRM and supply-chain management as well.

This chapter builds upon previous chapters, focusing on the business utilization of the Internet and Internet technologies which offer a wide range of opportunities to rethink strategic business models, processes and relationships in international companies. Their impact on the business organization is discussed and several domains of e-opportunity are explored. The scale and pervasiveness of today's technological change require a fundamental review of business strategy.

We have divided the chapter into four parts to provide a structure for understanding. First, we consider the Internet as a technology and discuss its enabling role in more detail before general sources of opportunity are identified. We consider what is meant by e-commerce and e-business and how an organization transforms itself through the use of the technologies described. We then focus on the strategic use of such technologies and investigate their role in value creation and competing through a range of business models. Finally, we complete the chapter with a discussion on the global challenges associated with implementing such technologies. An overall model for the knowledge presented within this chapter is shown in Figure 14-2.

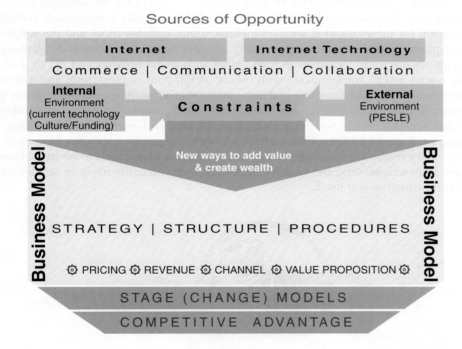

Figure 14-2
Global digital business model

Net technologies and opportunities

In this section we explore the opportunities presented by the Internet and web technologies before discussing what is meant by e-commerce and by e-business. In previous chapters, we introduced information systems, defining what was meant by an information system and describing various types of system found in organizations. Laudon and Laudon (2007) discuss 'the widening scope of information systems' observing that, over time, information systems have come to play a larger role in the life of organizations. They note that 'information systems extend far beyond the boundaries of the firm to encompass vendors, customers and even competitors'. They introduce the concept of the digital organization, an 'organization where nearly all significant business processes and relationships with customers, suppliers, and employees are digitally enabled, and key corporate assets are managed through digital means'. Included in information systems technology is *communications*, which link hardware and software and transfer data between locations. The linking of two or more computers to share data or resources creates a *network*. The world's largest and most widely used network is the Internet, which is reshaping the way information systems are used in business life.

Digital organization an organization where nearly all significant business processes and relationships with customers, suppliers, and employees are digitally enabled and key corporate assets are managed through digital means

The Internet, the primary technology for the digital firm, offers many new possibilities for doing business. Organizations that use the Internet for communication, coordination and the management of the organization are considered to be conducting business electronically and the term e-business is used to describe such technology use. The Internet and other networks have made it possible for businesses to replace manual and paper-based processes with the electronic flow of information. Net technologies manifest in the form of the Inter, intra and extra-nets.

The key to understanding the Internet is the concept of connectivity. The Internet is simply a global network of interlinked computers, operating on a standard protocol which allows data to be transferred between otherwise incompatible machines. The word itself simply means a 'network of networks'. The Internet can be a powerful source of competitive advantage in global markets and companies develop Internet-based strategies to support overall business development.

Protocol a set of rules and procedures for the control of communications in a communications network

An *intranet* is a network inside an organization that uses Internet technologies (such as web browsers and servers, TCP/IP network protocols, HTML hypermedia document publishing and databases, and so on) to provide an Internet-like environment within the organization for information sharing, communications, collaboration, and the support of business processes. Intranets can significantly improve communications and collaboration within an organization. Examples include: using an Intranet browser and PC to send and receive e-mail and to communicate with others within your organization, and externally through the Internet and extranets and using intranet groupware features to improve team and project collaboration with services such as discussion groups, chat rooms, and audio and videoconferencing. The comparative ease, attractiveness, and lower cost of publishing and accessing multimedia business information internally via intranet websites have been one of the primary reasons for the explosive growth in the use of intranets in business. Intranet software browsers, servers, and search engines can help you easily navigate and locate the business information you need.

Figure 14-3

The role of internet technologies

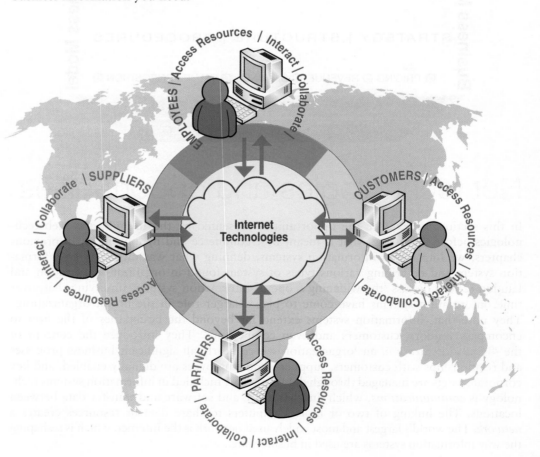

Enterprise information portals are a growing trend in the design and deployment of intranets in business. An enterprise information portal (EIP) is a web-based interface and integration of intranet and other technologies that gives all intranet users and selected extranet users access to a variety of internal and external business applications and services. Business benefits of enterprise information portals include providing easy access to key corporate intranet website resources. A company's intranet can also be accessed through the intranets of customers, suppliers, and other business partners via extranet links.

Extranets are network links that use internet technologies to interconnect the intranet of a business with the Intranets of its customers, suppliers, or other business partners. Extranets enable a company to offer new kinds of interactive web-enabled services to their business partners. Thus, extranets are another way that a business can build and strengthen strategic relationships with customers and suppliers; they enable and improve business collaboration with its customers and other business partners and facilitate an online, interactive product development, marketing, and customer-focused process that may bring better designed products to market more rapidly.

In summary we have outlined the 'net technologies': the Internet, which connects everyone; extranets, which connect companies to one another; and intranets, which connect individuals within companies. The Internet and Internet-like networks inside the enterprise (intranets), between an enterprise and its trading partners (extranets), and other types of networks are now the primary information technology infrastructure of many organizations. The internet-worked e-business enterprise enables managers, business professionals, teams, and workgroups to electronically exchange data and information with other end users, customers, suppliers, and business partners anywhere in the world. E-business *applications* rely on telecommunications networks that include the Internet, intranets, extranets, and other types of networks. Electronic business applications of an internet-worked enterprise can conceptually be grouped into three major categories. These categories include:

- Electronic commerce (applications supporting the buying and selling of products, services, and information over the Internet and extranets, e.g. web retailing).
- Internal business systems (applications of an Internet-worked e-business enterprise support a company's internal business processes and operations, e.g. CRM, ERP etc.).
- Enterprise communications and collaboration (applications support communication, coordination, and collaboration among the members of business teams and workgroups. Examples include e-mail).

We discuss e-commerce, business and collaborative technologies in the next section but first outline the business opportunities presented by the Internet and net technologies. The main business uses of the Internet include: communications; globalization; to achieve competitive advantage; inter-firm collaboration; as an information search and retrieval tool; for marketing and sales promotion; and the transmission of any type of data. Broadly speaking, the Internet presents three distinct types of opportunity. First, it links companies directly to customers, suppliers, and other interested parties. Second, it lets companies bypass other players in an industry's value chain. Third, it is a tool for developing and delivering new products and services to new customers.

Downstream advantages from effective Internet marketing include: improved corporate image; improved customer and investor relations; finding new prospects (customers); increased visibility; cost reduction; market expansion; and improved internal communications (Hamill and Gregory 1997). Sources of competitive advantage include: cost/efficiency savings achieved through substituting the Internet for other communications channels; performance improvements from the widespread internal use of the Internet to integrate information resources; market penetration which can be achieved from high external connectivity with customers; and product transformation, including the development of Internet-based products and services that redefine the company's strategic position.

The World Wide Web (WWW) makes it easier for small companies to compete on a worldwide basis. Global advertising costs, a traditional barrier to entry, are significantly reduced as the web provides relatively cheap access to a global audience. Small companies

Portal a website that acts as a gateway to information and services available on the Internet by providing search engines, directories and other services such as personalized news or free e-mail

Telecommunications the exchange of information in any form (e.g. voice, data, text and images) over networks

offering specialized niche products can find the customers necessary to succeed through the worldwide reach of the Internet. Overall, the Internet's low cost communications permits organizations with limited capital to become global marketers at an early stage in their development. Further international marketing implications of the Internet include: the increasing standardization of prices across borders, or at least, the narrowing of price differentials as consumers become more aware of prices in different countries; connecting end-users and producers directly will reduce the importance of traditional intermediaries in international marketing (i.e. agents and distributors); the Internet is a powerful tool for supporting networks, both internal and external to the organization; the 'Net' is an efficient medium for conducting worldwide market research, e.g. gaining feedback from customers; establishing online consumer panels; tracking individual customer behaviour, etc.

E-marketing strategy leverages new technology to get more effective ways of selling a business's product to existing or new customers. Opportunities presented for marketing include: enhancing the selling process (making the sales effort more effective through better product and market targeting or by more successfully expressing the characteristics and benefits of the product); enhancing the customer's buying experience (providing support services that make the product easier to buy or better matched to the customer's needs); and enhancing the customer's usage experience (providing support services that increase customer satisfaction over the life cycle of product use).

Opportunities presented for *operations* include: automating administrative processes; re-engineering of the primary infrastructure – leading to faster turnaround of customers' orders, enhanced customer support and shorter time to market for new products; shared learning; competitive procurement through electronic buying and supply-chain reconfiguration and integration and the virtualization of enterprise components. Feeny (2001) suggests companies examine the role of information on three different dimensions: the information content of the product, information intensity along the supply chain, and information dispersion across the value chain. The opportunity for increased parenting value is greatest when there is a high level of information dispersion across the value chain – for example, when one or more of the company's activities are performed at multiple geographical locations. High levels of information dispersion are becoming more common as more businesses become global. A parent-company initiative to coordinate information across replicated activities can lead to shared learning, scale economies and company-wide consistency in the way an activity is performed.

Despite the benefits, there are several limitations associated with the application of Internet technology in business:

■ customers cannot physically examine products;

■ learning about suppliers and customers is limited by the lack of face-to-face contact which also makes 'selling' more difficult and limits the ability to take advantage of the low-cost, non-transactional functions performed by sales forces (such as performing limited service and maintenance functions at a customer site);

■ there may be delays, due to shipment, in providing the goods or services to the end customer who cannot always simply walk out of the e-shop with them;

■ extra logistical costs are required to assemble, pack, and move small shipments;

■ the absence of physical facilities reduces a means to reinforce image and attracting new customers is difficult given the enormity of the available information and buying options.

E-commerce and e-business

Commerce arrangements through which goods and services are offered in the marketplace

In the introduction to this chapter, see Figure 14-1 Internet activities, we identified commerce as a key activity supported by the web. Managers cannot avoid the impact of electronic commerce on their businesses. They need to understand the opportunities available to them and recognize how their companies may be vulnerable if rivals seize those opportunities first (Ghosh 1998). Many see e-commerce as simply buying and selling using the Internet; for some, e-commerce is more than electronic financial transactions, extending it to all electronically mediated transactions between organizations, and any third party with which it deals. Others have defined E-commerce with a broad scope, as the exchange of information across electronic networks, at any stage in the supply chain, whether within an organization, between businesses, between businesses and consumers, or between the public and private sector, whether paid or unpaid.

E-commerce all electronically mediated information exchanges between an organization and its external stakeholders (see sell-side and buy-side e-commerce)

We must understand traditional approaches to supply chain management in order to understand how e-commerce can be used to make enhancements. Supply chain management (to be discussed further in the next chapter) incorporates both e-procurement, upstream activities and sell-side e-commerce, downstream activities; it involves the coordination of or supply activities of an organization from its suppliers and delivery of its products to its customers. The 1960s and 1970s were typified by a focus on the management of finished goods (stock management, warehousing, order processing and delivery) using manual (paper-based) information systems.

The just-in-time philosophy (JIT) was the philosophy of the 1970s and 1980s. Efficiency was seen to derive from flexibility; holding limited stock while ensuring customer orders were met in a timely manner. Undersupply and oversupply can impact significantly upon an organization's profitability. In the 1980s and 1990s we witnessed much closer integration between the supplier, customer and intermediaries. During this period, the Internet became an enabling technology especially for smaller players who could now globally source raw materials and therefore improve competitiveness. During this period, new integrated information systems such as the SAP enterprise resource planning system helped manage the entire supply chain. Technology enabled the introduction of faster, more responsive and flexible ordering, manufacturing and distribution systems. Early supply chain thinking was *manufacturing-led* whereby the first consideration was product development, followed by market identification (push supply chain).

Just-in-time (JIT) methods of managing inventory (stock) whereby items are delivered when needed in the production process instead of being stored by the manufacturer

An alternative approach focuses on customer needs and starts with analysis of their requirements. This latter approach relies on greater communication within the supply chain (pull supply chain). The objectives of supply chain management (SCM) include:

1 maximize efficiency and effectiveness of the total supply chain for all players; and

2 maximize the opportunity for customer purchase by ensuring adequate stock levels at all stages of the process.

Internet and associated technologies are vital to SCM since managing relationships with customers, suppliers and intermediaries is based on the flow of information and the transactions between these parties. Organizations seek to enhance the supply chain in order to provide a superior value proposition (quality, service, price and fulfilment times), which they do by emphasizing cost reduction, increased efficiency and consequently increased profitability. Not only can we conceive of the supply chain as an opportunity to increase profits, it may also be viewed as a sequence of events intended to satisfy customers. Typically, it will involve procurement, manufacture, and distribution together with associated transport, storage and information technology. In order to improve understanding we unpack EC and first discuss *upstream* and then *downstream* activities before considering the unifying concept of e-business.

E-procurement (upstream B2B activities)

In this section, we take a more detailed look at one aspect of the supply chain, buying/procurement; we review the procurement process and examine how technology (Internet technologies and information systems) can reduce costs and improve responsiveness. E-procurement is not a neat concept and there are many ways in which it may be implemented. Some organizations adapt existing systems and take a piecemeal approach while others have implemented total e-procurement systems.

Procurement the act of getting possession of something from a supplier

E-procurement the use of Internet technologies and information systems to manage all procurement activities including purchase request, authorization, ordering, delivery and payment between a purchaser and a supplier

and satisfaction comes the threat of defection; worse still, dissatisfied customers may actually deter other prospects and customers from doing business with the organization. Consequently it is important for companies to identify, measure and track loyalty drivers and implement plans for improvements.

How can organizations encourage repeat visits? One method is to regularly update content. Personalization and mass customization can be used to tailor information. While the two concepts are similar, personalization aims to tailor content to an individual's needs while mass customization tailors content to a group with similar interests (see also collaborative filtering). Such techniques take advantage of the dynamic possibilities of web content. Users' preferences are stored in and content is taken from a database.

Other techniques to retain customers and increase the site visits include the creation and management of online communities. Such communities help users with shared or similar purposes, positions, interests or professions. Customers generate revenue for companies from one-off or continued purchases. Continued purchases (referred to as extension selling) may be of the same or different (cross-sales) products and services. The combined revenue attributable to a customer during their relationship with a company is termed the lifetime value (LCV). Customer extension is about activities to deepen the relationship with customers through increased interaction and product transactions. Some organizations find and then focus upon their most profitable customers. Together, e-procurement, e-marketing and selling defines e-commerce.

Earlier in this chapter we defined e-business, considering it to be more than simply 'business conducted over the Internet' (Amit and Zott (2001). E-business is the transformation of key business processes (see Chapter 9) through the use of Internet technologies; the buy-side, e-commerce transactions with suppliers and the sell-side e-commerce transactions with customers can also be considered key business processes, see Figure 14-4.

Dynamic webpage a page that is created in real time, often with reference to a database query, in response to a user request

E-business using Internet technologies as the platform for internal business operations, electronic commerce and enterprise collaboration

Figure 14-4
E-business

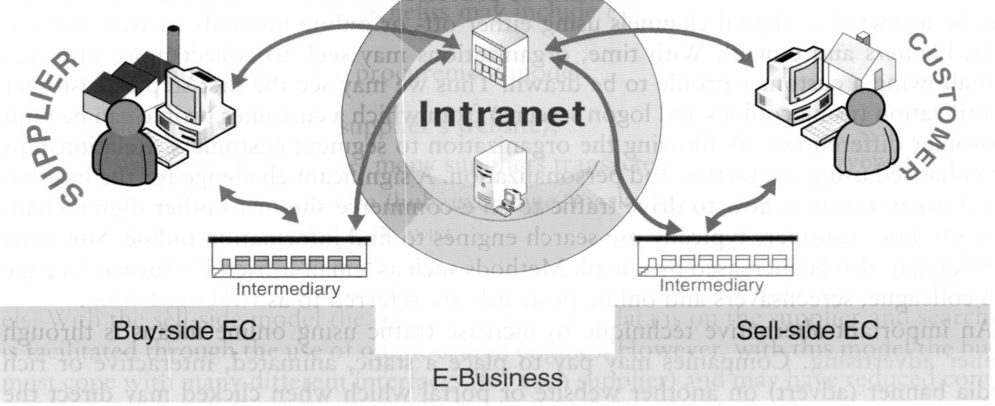

Virtual markets and organizations

Virtual market settings in which business transactions are conducted via open networks based on the fixed and wireless Internet infrastructure

Not only do net technologies impact upon commerce and the way business is carried out but they also affect market and organizational structure. In this section we introduce two concepts – the virtual market and the virtual organization. The word virtual tends to be used with reference to things that imitate their 'real' counterpart. A market is a mechanism which allows people to trade; historically a public place where goods and services are traded, purchased and sold. The characteristics of virtual markets combined with the vastly reduced costs of information processing allow for profound changes in the way companies operate and in how economic exchanges are structured. Virtual markets refer to settings in which business transactions are conducted via open networks based on the fixed and wireless Internet infrastructure. These markets are characterized by a focus on transactions, the importance of information goods and networks and high reach – reach is increased through the Internet not just because of the electronic channels that may connect entities, but because the information-based, navigation function (catalogue) is separated from the physical function (inventory) – and richness of information. Richness is defined by three aspects of the information itself:

Richness the depth and detail of information that can be accumulated, offered, and exchanged between market participants

- the amount of information that can be moved from sender to receiver in a given time;
- the degree to which the information can be customized; and
- interactivity.

The richness of information benefits the retailer and customer. Retailers have always been well-positioned to collect and use information about their customers, but the Internet greatly enhances their ability to do so; retailers can better target customers, personalize and customize their services when operating through the Internet. Customers, on the other hand, benefit from more information about more products from a greater number of suppliers to inform their purchase decisions and help them get the most out of their products and services. Virtual markets have unprecedented *reach* because they are characterized by a near lack of geographical boundaries. There still exist certain barriers to business, due, for example, to local languages and tastes, or to cross-border logistics. However, the importance of geographical boundaries is vastly reduced relative to the traditional 'bricks-and-mortar' world.

As an electronic network with open standards, the Internet supports the emergence of virtual communities and commercial arrangements that disregard traditional boundaries between firms along the value chain. Business processes can be shared among firms from different industries, even without any awareness of the end customers. As more information about products and services becomes instantly available to customers, and as information-goods are transmitted over the Internet, traditional intermediary businesses and information brokers are circumvented (disintermediated) and the guiding logic behind some traditional industries begins to disintegrate. At the same time, new ways of creating value are opened up by the new forms of connecting buyers and sellers in existing markets (reintermediation) and by innovative market mechanisms (e.g., reverse market auctions) and economic exchanges.

Disintermediation the process of doing away with 'middlemen' from business transactions

Reintermediation the reintroduction of an intermediary between end users (consumers) and a producer/manufacturer

There are several other characteristics of virtual markets that, when considered together, have a profound effect on how value-creating economic transactions are structured and conducted. These include the ease of extending one's product range to include complementary products, improved access to complementary assets (resources, capabilities, and technologies), new forms of collaboration among firms (e.g. affiliate programmes), the potential reduction of asymmetric information among economic agents through the Internet medium, and real-time customizability of products and services. Industry boundaries are thus easily crossed as value chains are redefined. This in turn may affect the scope of the firm as opportunities for outsourcing arise in the presence of reduced transaction costs and increased returns to scale; for example, many companies now find it economically viable to outsource their IT services.

A virtual organization is one which uses information and communications technology to allow it to operate without clearly defined physical boundaries between different functions. It provides customized services by outsourcing production and other functions to third parties. Features of the virtual organization include: processes transcend the boundaries of a single organization and are not controlled by a single organizational hierarchy; production processes are flexible with different parties involved at different times; parties involved in the production of a single product are often geographically dispersed; and given this dispersion, coordination is heavily dependent on telecommunications and data networks. The process of a company developing more of the characteristics of the virtual organization is termed virtualization. Electronic communications have enabled a shift to outsourcing, enabling the transfer of information necessary to create, manage and monitor partnerships. Partners may exist on the supply (wholesalers, distributors) and sell side. In some companies, primary or core VC activities may be outsourced to partners.

Virtual organization uses information and communications technology to operate without clearly defined physical boundaries between different functions

Communication and collaboration

Virtual markets and organizations, the dispersed organization, groups or teams separated in time and space depend upon tools to bring them together when working towards common goals. In the introduction we identified communication and collaboration as key activities supported by the Internet and its associated technologies (refer back to Figure 14-1). Communication and collaboration technologies were first introduced in Chapter 11 and we expand upon earlier work here. Enterprise collaboration systems provide tools to help us collaborate – to communicate ideas, share resources, and coordinate our cooperative work efforts as members of the many formal and informal processes, project teams and workgroups that make up many of today's organizations. Such tools enable the KM processes discussed in the previous chapter.

Figure 14-5

Groupware for enterprise collaboration

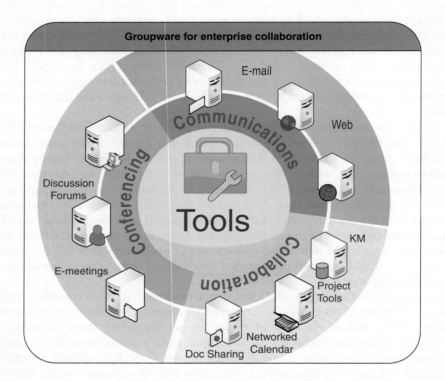

Enterprise collaboration systems (see Figure 14-5), enable us to work together more easily and effectively by helping us to: communicate (share information with each other), coordinate (coordinate our individual work efforts and use of resources with each other) and collaborate (work together cooperatively on joint projects and assignments). The enterprise collaboration system is an information system. Therefore, it uses hardware, software, data, and network resources to support communication, coordination, and collaboration among the members of business teams and workgroups.

Groupware can be defined as collaboration software which helps workgroups and teams work together in a variety of ways to accomplish joint projects and group assignments. Groupware is designed to make much easier the communication and coordination of workgroup activities and cooperation amongst end users, no matter where the members of a team are located. It helps the members of a team collaborate on group projects, at the same or different times, and at the same place, or at different locations. Many industry analysts believe the capabilities and potential of the Internet, as well as intranets and extranets, are driving the demand for enterprise collaboration tools in business. On the other hand, it is Internet technologies like web browsers and servers, hypermedia documents and databases, and intranets and extranets that are providing the hardware, software, data, and network platform for many of the groupware tools for enterprise collaboration wanted by business users. Groupware provides software tools for: electronic communication, electronic conferencing and collaborative work management.

Electronic communication tools include electronic mail, voice mail, bulletin board systems, and faxing. They enable documents and files in data, text, voice, or multimedia form to be sent electronically over computer networks. This helps the sharing of everything from voice and text messages to copies of project documents and data files with team members. Collaborative work management tools help people accomplish or manage group work activities (e.g. calendaring and scheduling tools, task and project management, workflow systems and knowledge repositories). As a result of such tools, members of different organizations and people at different locations are able to work together on business projects as members of *virtual teams* to develop, produce, market, and maintain products and services.

Strategy and net technology

Thus far we have introduced net technologies, identified the business opportunities they present and described the concepts of EC and EB. In this section we focus upon:

Look back
See chapter 3

- the way net technologies and EC impact upon the strategic planning process;
- how net technologies help organizations to compete;
- the organizational design and structural issues associated with implementing digital technologies;
- new business models; and
- value propositions and stage models for net technology adoption prior to consideration of the global challenges associated with EC in the final section of this chapter.

Strategy was discussed in Chapter 3 and so we focus on specific e-business issues here. Throughout this book we have made reference to contingency theory – a concept of importance when planning and aligning strategic e-business initiatives. EC/EB strategies should 'fit' with the corporate strategy and the IS strategy in particular but will also need to fit with other functional strategies, see Figure 14-6, i.e. there is a need to align strategies within the international organization. Additionally, the EB strategy should fit and enable the KM strategy discussed in the previous chapter.

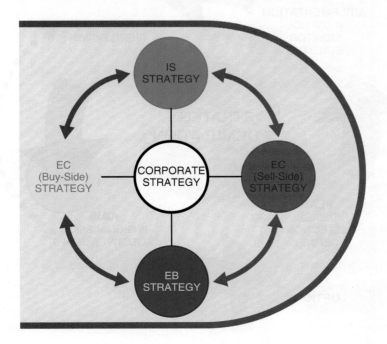

Figure 14-6

Aligning strategies

EB strategy is formulated in a similar manner as any strategy, see Figure 14-7. Many argue that identifying opportunity is the first task for the strategist and we opened this chapter with a discussion of the opportunities presented through both the Internet and Internet technologies. In this section we build on previous chapters and consider the strategic role of IT and IS in the contemporary international organization. The Internet and digital technologies have created new opportunities for firms to create value. However, international organizations operate in rapidly changing business environments and competitive advantage is short-lived because organizations launch competitive actions continually to disrupt their rivals' positions.

Organizations must undertake a series of actions to recreate competitive advantage continuously. The fundamental question in the field of strategic management is how firms achieve and sustain competitive advantage. We confront this question here, focusing in particular on how and why certain firms build competitive advantage in regimes of rapid change. Traditional models of strategy and structure are considered by many as inadequate to meet the challenges of the information and knowledge age, i.e. the appropriateness of traditional business models, rooted in the industrial economy are questionable. International organizations face new strategic questions such as:

■ How do we market products and services in the information/knowledge age?

■ How can we interact with customers, suppliers and partners, i.e. how can we best use the web's power to create superior linkages with all stakeholders?

■ Should we make-to-sell or adopt a make-to-order philosophy?

The challenge for companies in information-intensive markets is to manage the rate of shift from physical to electronic infrastructures and compete effectively against those entrants who do not have the constraints of a physical infrastructure.

Organizations considering an e-business strategy may pose questions in order to determine the size of opportunity (present and future demand), and its impact on their organization and industry. Organizations need to determine their response, levels of investment and

E-business strategy the use of Internet technologies in support and influence of corporate strategy

Figure 14-7
E-strategy formulation process

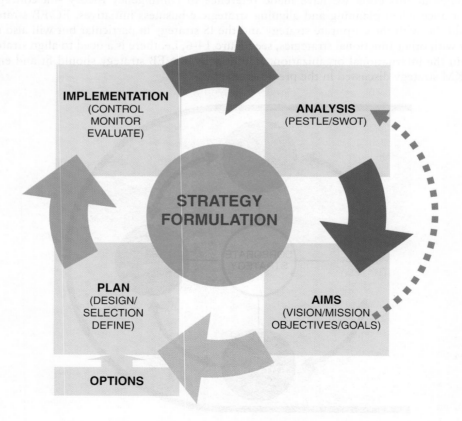

action and will need to prioritize decisions. They will therefore attempt to forecast and predict associated market variables. E-business strategies may be conceived (intended) or may emerge through everyday routines, activities and processes in organizations. E-strategies are influenced by information technology strategies, which determine the most appropriate technological infrastructure (hardware, networks and software applications) for the organization. There are two broad *drivers* influencing organizations to adopt e-business: opportunity for increased revenue and competitive advantage and opportunity to reduce costs and be more efficient.

Internet technologies may enhance customer loyalty, bringing repeat business and opportunity for cross-selling; increase reach, opening up new markets and support efforts to offer a full product range. On the other hand, sales, purchasing and operating costs may be reduced, while the organization becomes more efficient, able to obtain supplier and dispatch goods in a more timely manner. Among the *barriers* to e-business are cost, access to resources, channel cannibalization costs and a lack of customer demand.

One of the main aims of this section is to inform strategists about the options and choices they face when creating their e-strategy or supporting the corporate strategy. The changing economics of information have required virtually every company to rethink its strategy – not incrementally, but fundamentally (Evans and Wurster 1997). Net technologies both serve and inform organizational strategy – they serve by enabling the organizational strategy, by providing the means to carry it out (delivering low cost information in the form and place required) but also shape organizational strategy through new business models and ways of doing business. International organizations may approach strategic problems from a variety of contextual standpoints. Some will be mature and established traditional organizations, some may only be online; they will vary on their dependence upon the physical world – some migrating between worlds and others seeking to join the two. For the international organization, becoming a digital organization is an enormous challenge, necessitating from the outset the need to make many strategic decisions:

- Should they move first or follow and learn from others (technology adoption)?
- In which industries and areas shall it compete and what should it do for itself rather than leave to suppliers and partners (corporate scope)?
- Is there a need to restructure the marketplace (disintermediation)?
- Should the organization integrate or separate the online business (structural alternatives)?
- What traditional strengths may be used to compete online – is there a need for a separate brand?
- What will be the pricing strategy?
- Which opportunities will be exploited and how will they be seized?
- What will be the online value proposition and which business model will drive profit?

Following primary strategic choices, important consequential challenges arise such as channel or offline/online conflict. The organization will also need to build a network of alliances and redesign business processes. We will answer such questions throughout the remainder of this chapter, turning first to the challenge of competing with net technologies.

Competing with technology

While the Internet presents new opportunities it also intensifies competition and shifts power to buyers. In this section we recap theories of *competitive advantage* and apply them to EC and EB.

The general discussion on approaches to strategy outlined thus far, act as a backdrop for the specific focus on e-strategies to be considered next. We discussed the competitive use of information in Chapter 10 where we drew, in particular, on theories presented by Porter

Channel cannibalization the decrease in sales through an existing channel due to the introduction of a new channel

throughout the 1980s. Porter (2001) considers the consequences of the Internet, presenting arguments for the changing nature of competition and the resultant challenges for strategy formulation. The Internet has created new industries; however, its greatest impact has been to enable the reconfiguration of existing industries previously constrained by high costs for communicating, gathering information, or accomplishing transactions.

Internet technology provides buyers with easier access to information about products and suppliers, thus strengthening buyer bargaining power. The Internet mitigates the need for such things as an established sales force or access to existing channels, reducing barriers to entry. Marketplaces automate corporate procurement by linking many buyers and suppliers electronically. The benefits to buyers include low transaction costs, easier access to price and product information, convenient purchase of associated services and sometimes, the ability to pool volume. The benefits to suppliers include lower selling costs, lower transaction costs, access to wider markets, and the avoidance of powerful channels. By enabling new approaches to meeting needs and performing functions, it creates new substitutes. As an open system, companies have more difficulty maintaining proprietary offerings, thus the rivalry among competitors is intensified. On the Internet, buyers can often switch suppliers with just a few mouse clicks, and new web technologies are systematically reducing switching costs even further.

The use of the Internet also expands the geographic market, bringing many more companies into competition with one another. A number of businesses are able to increase revenue through network effects which can create demand-side economies of scale and raise barriers to entry. However, the openness of the Internet makes it difficult for a single company to capture the benefits of a network effect. Online companies have found it more difficult to build Internet brands, perhaps because of the lack of physical presence and direct human contact. Despite advertising, product discounts, and purchasing incentives, most dot-com brands have not approached the power of established brands, achieving only a modest impact on loyalty and barriers to entry.

While partnering is a well-established strategy, the use of Internet technology has made it much more widespread. In EC, *complements* (products that are used in tandem with another industry's product) have proliferated as companies seek to offer broader arrays of products, services, and information. As partnerships proliferate, companies tend to become more alike, which increases rivalry. Instead of focusing on their own strategic goals, moreover, companies are forced to balance the many potentially conflicting objectives of their partners. Another common form of partnering is outsourcing. Internet technologies have made it easier for companies to coordinate with their suppliers, giving widespread currency to the notion of the 'virtual organization' – a business created largely out of purchased products, components, and services. While extensive outsourcing can reduce near-term costs and improve flexibility, it can erode company distinctiveness.

Outsourcing often lowers barriers to entry because new entrants need only assemble purchased inputs rather than build their own capabilities. In addition, companies lose control over important elements of their business, and crucial experience in components, assembly, or services shifts to suppliers, enhancing their power in the long run. Internet technologies tend to reduce variable costs and tilt cost structures toward fixed cost, creating much greater pressure for companies to engage in destructive price competition. In general, new Internet technologies erode profitability by shifting power to customers. The great paradox of the Internet is that its very benefits – making information widely available; reducing the difficulty of purchasing, marketing, and distribution; allowing buyers and sellers to find and transact business with one another more easily – also make it more difficult for companies to capture those benefits as profits. Much of the value, however, is absorbed by customers and may not result in expected wealth creation for the business.

The Internet is an enabling technology – a powerful set of tools which rarely offers a direct competitive advantage. Internet technology, itself is not as a source of advantage because it is readily available to all. Competitive advantages arise from traditional strengths fortified through Internet technology, by tying a company's activities together in a more distinctive system (Porter 2001). It becomes all the more important for individual companies to operate at a lower cost, command a premium price, or do both. Cost and price advantages can be achieved in two ways.

The first is *operational effectiveness* – doing the same things your competitors do but doing them better. Operational effectiveness advantages can take myriad forms, including better technologies, superior inputs, better-trained people, or a more effective management structure. By easing and speeding the exchange of real-time information, it enables improvements throughout the entire value chain, across almost every company and industry. As an open platform with common standards, companies can often tap into its benefits with much less investment than was required to capitalize on past generations of information technology. The nature of Internet applications (openness) makes it difficult to sustain operational advantages. When companies develop similar types of Internet applications, through generic packages offered by third-party developers, the resulting improvements in operational effectiveness will be broadly shared. Very rarely will individual companies gain durable advantages from the deployment of 'best-of-breed' applications. Whereas out of the box applications will not, in themselves, provide a sustainable competitive advantage, the Internet architecture and standards make it possible to build truly integrated and customized systems that reinforce the fit among activities. To gain these advantages companies need to tailor their deployment of Internet technology to their particular strategies.

The second way to achieve advantage is *strategic positioning* – doing things differently from competitors, in a way that delivers unique value to customers. This can mean offering a different set of features, a different array of services, or different logistical arrangements.

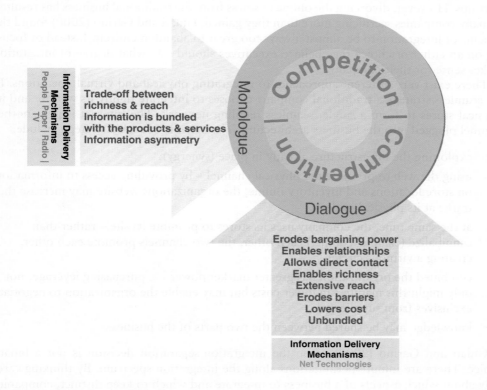

Figure 14-8

The importance of ICT in competition

Structural alternatives

Should the organization integrate or separate the online business?

International organizations which operate in both the physical and electronic world face difficult decisions about structuring. Evans and Wurster (1999) argue a need to separate the new venture as much as possible from the established organization, perhaps even to spin it out, because of the consequences of deconstructed value chains. Gulati and Garino (2000) investigate how incumbent companies move onto the web. Alternatives include:

1 clicks-and-mortar strategies with a separate Internet businesses;
2 clicks-and-mortar strategies, tightly integrating website and physical stores – the *seamless strategy*;
3 partnering with another company; or
4 simply remaining as a bricks-and-mortar, traditional (physical) organization.

The clicks-and-mortar strategies bridge the physical and the virtual worlds. The web presents an additional channel to market which may complement or compete with existing channels. If customers desire flexibility, creating a new channel may provide added value to them. If their primary concern is buying at lowest price, a new channel merely creates additional competition for existing outlets. Organizations considering such strategic alternatives may decide whether to integrate the Internet business with their traditional business, or keep the two separate. Despite the obvious benefits that integration offers – cross-promotion, shared information, purchasing leverage, distribution economies, etc. – some executives believe that to thrive Internet businesses need to be separate. They believe the traditional business will smother any Internet initiative.

Separate Internet businesses may find it easier to create an entrepreneurial culture, to attract quality management, and to tap into the vast pool of capital available to Internet start-ups. However, divorcing the online business from the traditional business has resulted in many companies sacrificing more than they gained. Gulati and Garino (2000) found the benefits of integration to be almost always too great to abandon entirely. Instead of focusing on an either/or choice they believe executives should ask, what degree of integration makes sense for their company.

There exist very different approaches to integrating physical and virtual operations. In the seamless strategy a traditional company chooses to integrate tightly its website and its physical stores to form a single, seamless retailing network. The Internet is just another channel plugged into the business architecture. The benefits of such a strategy include:

1 exploiting the infrastructure already in place (synergy);
2 using the web to promote the physical channel – by providing access to information on store locations and inventory online, the organizations website may increase the traffic at its physical outlets;
3 at the same time, the company uses its stores to promote its site – rather than cannibalize (channel conflict) each other, the two channels promote each other, creating a virtuous circle;
4 combined the organization has greater market power i.e. purchasing leverage; not only might this manifest in lower costs but may enable the organization to negotiate exclusives from suppliers;
5 knowledge may be shared between the two parts of the business.

Gulati and Garino (2000) argue the integration-separation decision is not a binary choice. There are infinite permutations along the integration spectrum. By thinking carefully about which aspects of a business to integrate and which to keep distinct, companies can tailor their clicks-and-mortar strategy to their own particular market and competitive situation, dramatically increasing the odds of e-business success. They recommend examining four business dimensions – brand, management, operations, and equity – and determining the degree of integration that makes sense along each. The organization must decide whether or not to integrate brands or keep them separate.

Extending a company's current brand to the Internet may give instant credibility to a site leading to immediate traffic and revenue and new consumers will know that the site is legitimate. Furthermore, brand integration can result in a virtuous circle, sending online customers to the stores and bricks-and-mortar customers online, all the while continuing to build the brand. However, in integrating a brand, a company often loses flexibility. An online store may be forced to offer the same products and prices as its physical counterparts – or risk leaving customers confused. With a shared brand, it also becomes more difficult to use the Internet to target different customer segments. An integrated management team can better align its strategic objectives, find and exploit areas of synergy, and share knowledge. Separate teams can focus more sharply, innovate more freely, and avoid contaminating one business model with another. However, as has been stated, companies need not make an all-or-nothing decision – they can integrate particular functions and leave others separate.

Decisions about integrating operations should be based on the strength of a company's existing distribution and information systems and their transferability to the Internet. Integration can provide significant cost savings, a more compelling and informative site, and a competitive advantage. Separation allows a company to build state-of-the art, customized systems without the flaws of legacy systems and develop sophisticated Internet-specific distribution capabilities that could provide a superior customer experience. Finally, managers must decide whether to own or to 'spin off'? Integration allows the parent to capture the entire value of its Internet business; on the other hand separation can help attract and retain talented managers and provide access to outside capital. On all counts there is a need to manage the trade-offs between separation and integration. By avoiding an either/or choice and considering each aspect of its business on its own, a company can strike the right balance between the freedom, flexibility, and creativity that come with separation and the operating, marketing, and information economies that come with integration (Gulati and Garino 2000).

Organizational separation has often undermined company ability to gain competitive advantages, argues Porter (2001). By creating separate Internet strategies instead of integrating the Internet into an overall strategy, companies failed to capitalize on their traditional assets. Online and traditional methods can benefit each other. For example, many companies have found websites that supply product information and support direct ordering make traditional sales forces more, not less, productive and valuable. The sales force can compensate for the limits of the site by providing personalized advice and after-sales service, for instance. The site can make the sales force more productive by automating the exchange of routine information and serving as an efficient new conduit for leads.

Ultimately, strategies that integrate the Internet and traditional competitive advantages and ways of competing should win in many industries. On the demand side, most buyers will value a combination of online services, personal services, and physical locations over standalone web distribution. They will want a choice of channels, delivery options, and ways of dealing with companies. On the supply side, production and procurement will be more effective if they involve a combination of Internet and traditional methods, tailored to strategy. The value of integrating traditional and Internet methods creates potential advantages for established companies. It is not enough, however, just to graft the Internet onto historical ways of competing in simplistic 'clicks-and-mortar' configurations. Established companies will be most successful when they deploy Internet technology to reconfigure traditional activities or when they find new combinations of Internet and traditional approaches. While a new means of conducting business has become available, the fundamentals of competition remain unchanged. Only by integrating the Internet into overall strategy will this powerful new technology become an equally powerful force for competitive advantage.

In many cases, the Internet complements, rather than cannibalizes, companies' traditional activities and ways of competing. Virtual activities do not eliminate the need for physical activities, but often amplify their importance argues Porter (2001). The complementarity between Internet activities and traditional activities arises for a number of reasons. First, introducing Internet applications in one activity often places greater demands on physical activities elsewhere in the value chain. Direct ordering, for example, makes warehousing and shipping more important. Second, using the Internet in one activity can have systemic consequences, requiring new or enhanced physical activities that are often unanticipated. Suppliers are able to reduce the transactional cost of taking orders when they move online, but they must often respond to many additional requests for information and quotes, which, again, places new strains on traditional activities. Such systemic effects emphasize the fact that Internet applications are not standalone technologies; they must be integrated into the overall value chain.

STOP & THINK

Identify a selection of companies that seem to be exploiting a clicks-and-mortar configuration as a complementary approach (consider TV advertisements for companies suggesting you order online but collect from the store). How does this provide the company with an advantage over a clicks only business?

Business models

Understanding how e-business firms create wealth

The ideas to exploit net technology opportunities are encapsulated within business models. In this section we outline what is meant by a business model and the components and related concepts associated with an understanding of EC and EB. The business model concept is unclear and open to a number of interpretations. Most show how the organization will meet customer needs (value proposition); how the organization will earn money (revenue model); how the organization will compete and be structured. There are many ways for the international organization to earn revenue through EC such as from sales, subscriptions, transaction fees and advertising.

We explore alternatives in this section. Much of the value created by e-business is due to the more effective use of information. Value creation is often explored within the theoretical views of the value chain framework (Porter 1985) – also see value configuration models, Stabell and Fjeldstad (1998) discussed in Chapter 11; Schumpeter's theory of creative destruction (Schumpeter 1942), the resource-based view of the firm (Barney 1991), strategic network theory (e.g., Dyer and Singh 1998), and transaction costs economics (Williamson 1975) – discussed earlier in this chapter. In Schumpeter's theory, innovation is the source of value creation. The RBV states that marshalling and uniquely combining a set of complementary and specialized resources and capabilities, which are difficult to imitate, may lead to value creation. A firm's resources and capabilities 'are valuable if, and only if, they reduce a firm's costs or increase its revenues compared to what would have been the case if the firm did not possess those resources' (Barney 1997: 147).

One of the main effects of transacting over the Internet is the reduction in transaction costs. The emphasis of transaction cost economics is on efficiency, i.e. cost minimization. Transaction costs (the cost associated with buying or selling) include the time spent by managers and employees searching for customers and suppliers, communicating with counterparts in other companies regarding transaction details, the cost of travel, physical space for meetings, and processing paper documents. Each theoretical framework discussed makes valuable suggestions about possible sources of value creation.

More recently, in the context of virtual markets, Amit and Zott (2001) identify four primary and interrelated value drivers of e-businesses: novelty (new methods), lock-in (prevents the migration of customers and strategic partners to competitors – switching costs), complementarity (offering bundles of complementary products), and efficiency (increases when the costs per transaction decrease) that provide further insight into aspects of value creation in e-business. They go on to propose the business model construct as a unifying unit of analysis that captures the value creation arising from multiple sources. The business model depicts the design of transaction content, structure, and governance so as to create value through the exploitation of business opportunities.

Each of the primary drivers are discussed next. Amit and Zott (2001) suggest that no single theoretical framework (i.e., value chain analysis, Schumpeterian innovation, RBV, strategic network theory, transaction cost economics) should be given priority over others when examining the value creation potential of e-businesses. Their analysis calls for an integration of the various frameworks, in particular for the linking of strategic management and entrepreneurship theories of value creation. They propose the business model as a unit of analysis. A business model refers primarily to value creation whereas a revenue model is primarily concerned with value appropriation.

The business model of a profit-oriented organization explains how it consistently generates revenue and profit. For some there are two basic business models: companies either compete on price, or they compete on quality. The business model may be described more precisely with attention to specific model components. The components of a business model may include:

1 *pricing model* (e.g. no-frills service);

2 *revenue model*;

3 *channel model* (the traditional bricks and mortar as a single channel, clicks and mortar combining the web with traditional channels, clicks only as a .com and other variants based on the use or absence of intermediaries, i.e. direct-to-customer);

4 *commerce process* model (e.g. auction);

5 *organizational form* (standalone business unit, integrated internet capability); and

6 *value proposition* (less value and very low cost, more value at the same cost, much more value at greater cost).

Many e-business models are improvements, not radical departures from traditional business models. Among other benefits, the Internet does give new reach and radically improved cost structures compared with old models. Furthermore, the ecommerce model may offer a more convenient option for the consumer. For most organizations, business models are under constant change. Innovations in technology, changes in the law or competition, or change in consumer preferences can erode an operating model's profitability. In response, organizations revamp their business models in a wide variety of ways.

We explore key model components in the following sections. We have already discussed channel models and structural alternatives; in the next section we consider Internet business models. There are several strategies that Internet-based businesses can use to improve their value propositions (Lumpkin and Dess 2004). These include Internet-specific activities that are providing organizations with new capabilities – *search* (gathering information and identifying purchase options), *problem-solving* (identifying problems or needs), *evaluation* (considering alternatives and comparing the costs and benefits of various options) and *transaction* (completing the sale, including negotiating and agreeing contractually, making payments and taking delivery). These value-adding activities are enhanced further by managing three different types of Internet content – customer feedback, expertise, and entertainment programming. Second, these value-adding strategies are best understood in the context of business models specific to the Internet environment.

We consider a variety of popular Internet business models that have emerged and proven successful, and outline how value-adding activities and content are best used in the context of each. At this point we ask, how are firms using the Internet to add value and therefore gain competitive advantage? Portals, online retail stores (e-tailer), content providers, transaction brokers, market creators, service providers and community providers are examples of Internet models. In this section, drawing on the work of Lumpkin and Dess (2004), we discuss Internet business models that account for the vast majority of business conducted online.

■ In the direct-to-customer model, buyer and seller communicate directly creating the potential for the provider to develop a primary relationship with customers.

■ *Commission-based models* are used by businesses that provide services for a fee. The business is usually a third-party intermediary and the commission charged is often based on the size of the transaction.

Revenue model the specific modes in which a business model enables revenue generation (subscription fees, advertising fees, and transactional income)

Business model the organization's essential logic for consistently achieving its principal objectives – explains how it consistently makes money, highlights the distinctive activities and approaches that enable the firm to succeed – to attract customers and deliver products and services profitably

Reach the number of people and products that are reachable quickly and cheaply in virtual markets

Direct to customer provides goods or services directly to the customer

■ *Advertising-based models* are used by companies that provide content and/or services to visitors and sell advertising to businesses that want to reach those visitors.

■ *Markup-based models* are used by businesses that add value in marketing and sales (rather than production) by acquiring products, marking up the price, and reselling them at a profit – resellers.

■ *Production-based models* are used by companies that add value in the production process – the Internet adds value by lowering marketing costs and facilitating customization and problem-solving.

■ *Referral-based models* are used by firms steering customers to another company for a fee.

■ *Subscription-based models* are used by businesses charging a flat fee for providing either a service or proprietary content. Internet service providers are one example of this model.

■ *Fee-for-service-based models* are used by companies providing ongoing services; the fee-for-service model involves a pay-as-you-go (metered) system.

■ The full-service provider adds value by providing a full range of products, sourced both internally and externally, and consolidated into the channel(s) chosen by the customer.

■ A content provider is an organization that creates and provides information or digital products to customers via a third party. These third parties generally pay the content provider for its product or information, and pass product or information along to their own customers.

■ The *virtual-community model* brings together a group of members around a common interest.

Full service provider provides a full range of services in one domain (e.g. financial, health) from own products and best of breed, attempting to own the primary customer relationship

Content provider provides content (information, digital products and services) via intermediaries

Stage models

Aside from alternative business models, organizations may be categorized according to the extent of technology adoption. Stage models can describe the logical evolution of e-commerce involving different stages of development, each stage being better in some sense than the previous stage; such models can be useful in providing to companies a roadmap for improvement. A stage is a set of descriptors that characterize the evolutionary nature of e-commerce. Rao, Metts and Monge (2003) (see Figure 14-9) propose e-commerce development takes place in four stages:

1 presence;
2 portals;
3 transactions integration (TI); and
4 enterprises integration (EI).

It is important to note that in later stages of the model, cost, technological demands, and complexity increase. In the following paragraphs we describe each stage.

■ The *presence stage* the company has a website that provides information about products and services, contact information, and other relevant information in a static manner.

■ The *portals stage* is viewed as the introduction of two-way communication, customer or supplier order placing, the use of profiles and cookies. The information provided in the presence stage can be coupled with facilities for ordering, product feedback, and product and/or quality surveys.

■ The *transactions integration stage* (TI) is differentiated from the portals stage mainly by the presence of financial transactions between partners – ordering and payment facilities in a secure environment to purchasers. This in turn will require higher technical capabilities and IT infrastructure. Interactions can be for selling as well as buying.

■ *Enterprises integration (EI)* refers to complete integration of business processes; this involves high levels of collaboration between customers and suppliers. Enterprise integration includes full integration of B2B and B2C business including value chain integration and utilizes the e-commerce systems to manage customer relationships (CRM) and the supply chain (SCM).

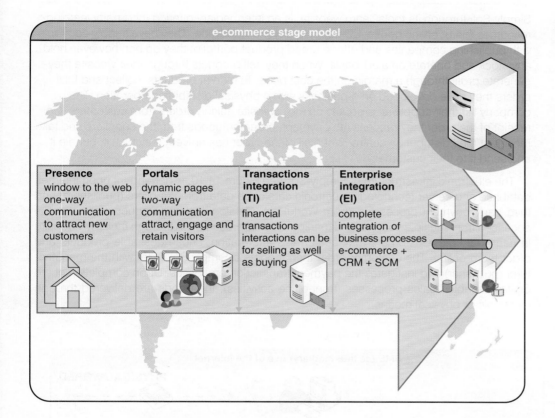

Figure 14-9
E-commerce stage model

Larger MNCs tend to progress at least to the TI stage and will be located, to varying degrees in the EI stage. Smaller MNCs and SMEs are likely to be located in an earlier stage. The stage model approach can be used to assess the extent of technology utilization and to establish the goals and vision for future initiatives.

Small medium enterprise (SME) and the small MNE

The power of the Internet in enabling SMEs to globalize has attracted a great deal of scholarly attention. For small medium enterprise (SMEs), effective use of the Internet can provide a low cost 'gateway' to international markets and help overcome many of the barriers or obstacles to internationalization commonly experienced by such firms. An Internet connection can substantially improve communications with actual and potential customers, suppliers and partners abroad; generate a wealth of information on market trends and developments worldwide; provide an 'ear to the ground' on the latest technology and R&D; and be a very powerful international promotion and sales tool. Earlier, we introduced the concept of disintermediation but noted that, given the large volumes of information about products and services on the Internet, reintermediation may take place in virtual markets. The following case study examines a SME intermediary utilising internet technologies to compete worldwide.

Small medium enterprise (SMEs) generally a business with a headcount of fewer than 250 is classified as medium-sized; a business with a headcount of fewer than 50 is classified as small, and a business with a headcount of fewer than 10 is considered a microbusiness

Active learning case

Simply-Sol

Simply-Sol.com Ltd was conceived from a partnership formed in 2002 that draws upon some 30 years' collective experience in the IT and computer aided learning sector. The company is an SME, which offers, among other things, learning products online. Through Tools2Learn.co.uk, a source for distance learning content, books, DVDs and online courses are sold. Learning materials are sold to home users, businesses, schools and colleges.

Simply-Sol.com Ltd was nominated for best use of technology, category, at the business 'Start-ups Awards 2004' – UK. They have kindly allowed us to use their company as a case study.

Simply-Sol, through its tools2learn website, is an intermediary offering third-party learning-resources (on or offline books, CDs etc.) to anyone worldwide. They have supply contracts with publishing companies and offer a broad product portfolio; they do not, however, hold any stock and operate on a JIT basis. When they sell products through their website they generate profit through a margin on the cost price. To market products, collect and fulfil orders they have developed an e-business with a physical distribution operation. The company list their suppliers' products on their website, taking orders from customers. On receipt of the order they process the payment, order the goods from the suppliers and take receipt at their distribution centre. When all of the order has arrived, they pick it, bundle it and send it to their customer.

The electronic infrastructure of Simply-Sol, see Figure 14.10, is dependent upon Internet, database and server technology, electronic catalogue data from suppliers (publishers) and third party payment processing (from WorldPay). Catalogue data (product information) is accessed from multiple sources and manipulated for presentation through their own website in near real time. Customers may search this information, chose desirable products and order them online. The customer order then triggers a Simply-Sol order with the manufacturer (publisher) and instigates the payment transaction processes. Upon completion of the digitally enabled sales processes (front-office activities), the goods are delivered through electronic or physical means.

Figure 14-10

SME (as intermediary) use of the internet

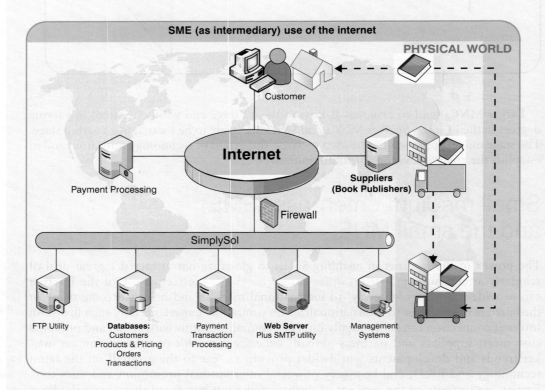

Sources: (1) http://www.simply-sol.com (2) http://www.tools2learn.co.uk/

As is typical of many hi-tech SMEs the number of employees is small – often below 20. This keeps costs down, as does having no inventory and limited costs associated with physical space.

Describe the Simply-Sol value proposition and their sources of competitive advantage

STOP & THINK

Global challenges

In previous sections we introduced the EC concept and corporate scope. The major advantage of EC is the ability to undertake business at any time, from anywhere and at low cost. Corporate scope describes the range of business activities measured along vertical, horizontal and geographic dimensions. Corporate level scope choices overlay strategy and contribute to success and failure. Scope not only refers to how many parts there are in the business but also where those parts and customers may be located. Parts must be connected and customer needs serviced, presenting challenges to the organization.

Within this section we focus mainly on *geographic scope* and implications for EC. There will of course, be additional challenges for EB, drawing dispersed parts of the business together; such challenges are more complex when the parts transcend country boundaries. Net technologies facilitate global trade and create a global marketplace. However, organizations must make decisions about the scope of globalization and meet associated challenges. This section briefly examines the problems for the international company when using EC for global expansion.

Ghemawat (2001) considers the barriers created by *distance*. Distance is not restricted to geographic separation, but also has cultural, administrative or political, and economic dimensions. The CAGE framework of distance presented by Ghemawat (2001) considers four attributes:

- cultural **distance** (religious beliefs, race, social norms, and language that are different for the target country and the country of the company considering expansion);
- administrative (or political) **distance** (colony-colonizer links, common currency, and trade arrangements);
- geographic **distance** (the physical distance between the two countries, the size of the target country, access to waterways and the ocean, internal topography, and transportation and communications infrastructures); and
- economic **distance** (disparities in the two countries' wealth or consumer income and variations in the cost and quality of financial and other resources).

Distance types influence business in varying ways. Geographic distance, for instance, affects the costs of transportation and communications, so it is of particular importance to companies that deal with heavy or bulky products. Cultural distance, by contrast, affects consumers' product preferences. While the Internet arguably brings people and business closer, connecting them, a country's cultural attributes also determine how people interact with one another and with companies and institutions. Differences in culture are capable of creating distance between two countries. In general, the farther you are from a country, the harder it will be to conduct business in that country. Geographic distance is not simply a matter of how far away the country is in miles or kilometres. Other attributes that must be considered include the physical size of the country, average within-country distances to borders, access to waterways and the ocean, and topography. Man-made geographic attributes must also be taken into account – most notably, a country's transportation and communications infrastructures. Geographic attributes influence transportation costs. Technology may indeed be making the world a smaller place, but it is not eliminating the very real-and often very high-costs of distance (Ghemawat 2001).

Corporate scope the range of business activity measured along vertical, horizontal and geographic dimensions

The challenges and problems associated with global EC manifest with a need to authenticate buyers and sellers, build trust and fulfil orders among other things. Large-scale global e-commerce initiatives may require country-specific websites and large expenditure for customization and ongoing management. Organizations that wish to compete in the global marketplace must understand 24-hour order taking and customer service response capability; possess regulatory and customs-handling experience to ship internationally and an in-depth understanding of foreign marketing environments to assess the advantages of its own products and services. Before conducting EB globally, web-enabled enterprises must consider an array of international economic, technological, social, and legal issues.

There are intra-firm considerations such as access to technology, availability of appropriate skills, core competencies of the organization, and senior-management commitment. At the inter-firm level, there is competition and the nature of the supply chains to consider. Economic considerations regarding EC include the cost justification of projects, the number of sellers and buyers and their access to the Internet, the issues connected with infrastructure upgrade, and the question of skill shortage. One major area of concern in global EC is the construction of a telecommunications infrastructure to support its explosive growth. The current infrastructure is inadequate to support the full potential of EC. Many countries need to revamp their telecommunication networks and equipment completely in order to take advantage of this new medium. The technical considerations concerning EC are security, reliability, communication protocols, bandwidth availability, and integration with existing applications, see Figure 14-11.

As the internet evolves into a global information infrastructure, the issue of security becomes a major concern. Consumers are distrustful about the safety of the information they give out on the web. Threats come from hackers, viruses, saboteurs, extortionists and the environment to name but a few. Unfortunately, in their haste to implement EC solutions, corporations do not pay enough attention to security. Reliability is another significant concern in electronic commerce. Network infrastructure and application systems must be continuously upgraded, fine-tuned, and maintained to keep the systems running. There

Figure 14-11

Challenges facing global e-commerce (Adapted from Bingi, Mir and Khamalah (2000))

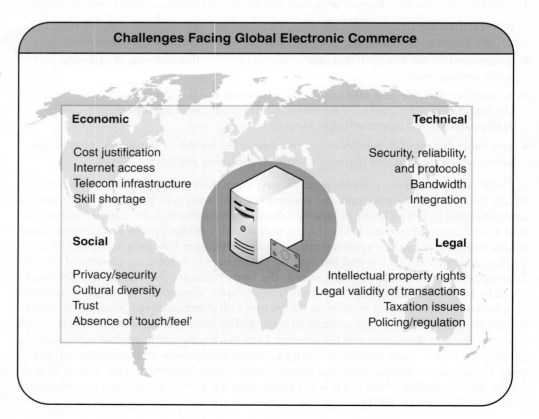

Challenges Facing Global Electronic Commerce

Economic

Cost justification
Internet access
Telecom infrastructure
Skill shortage

Technical

Security, reliability, and protocols
Bandwidth
Integration

Social

Privacy/security
Cultural diversity
Trust
Absence of 'touch/feel'

Legal

Intellectual property rights
Legal validity of transactions
Taxation issues
Policing/regulation

are difficulties in integrating Internet and EC software with some existing applications and databases. Many of the integration solutions are provided by middleware designed to work with popular software systems, but many organizations have home-grown applications or other commercial software for which they develop their own interfaces. Integration software is also difficult to maintain, and organizations often expend an inordinate amount of ongoing resources to maintain them.

Many legal issues have yet to be resolved. Digital media is vastly different from traditional media such as books. It is far more amenable to replication, transmission, and alteration. They are compact and easy to store. It is, however, difficult to classify, categorize and catalogue. These characteristics significantly alter the terrain concerning intellectual property rights. The issue becomes even more complicated in the international arena. Typically, different countries have different attitudes toward intellectual property rights, and, despite attempts by global bodies such as the World Trade Organization, the debate around these rights is far from resolved.

Furthermore, the manner in which information is obtained and presented on the web challenges intellectual property protections. A web page can be constructed in such a way that each one of its components can come from different sources, making the issue of ownership complicated. A further issue concerns the legal validity of electronic transactions. Traditional means of conducting commerce was in person and was based on paper documentation and 'wet' signatures. Existing laws in many countries require that contracts be evidenced by written documents (in physical media). For EC to flourish, this recognition must be extended so that electronic documents and signatures evidencing contracts can have the same legal validity as written signatures and documents. It is widely believed in the EC community that digital signatures and other forms of electronic authentication can provide greater security and certainty regarding the identity of individuals and the content of important documents than traditional written and printed documents.

Appropriate legislation is also required to address other aspects of electronic transactions. Currently, it may be difficult to say with certainty where a commercial EC transaction actually takes place and which jurisdiction may have regulatory authority over the transaction. Taxation in the EC environment is another important issue. A related issue of concern for many corporations is the sale of commodities that are restricted or illegal by the laws of the country in which the product or service is being sold.

The ability to fulfil orders from wherever they are placed was a key challenge identified in this section and we consider this problem in more detail in the next chapter, international operations management.

Summary of key learning points

International businesses compete in two worlds: a physical and a virtual world. The latter has given rise to the world of electronic commerce (EC) and e-business (EB), a new locus of value creation. Much of the value created by e-business is due to the more effective use of information. Managers must now focus upon how their companies create value in both worlds alike.

The effectiveness and efficiency of organizational information systems can be enhanced significantly by a move to Internet technologies. Internet technologies enable EC and EB. The opportunities presented by EC fall into five broad domains: commerce, collaboration, communication, connection, and computation. The web provides the connective tissue for information flow within and between organizations anytime – anyplace. Interoperability of web services permits the creation of enterprise-wide information-system architectures linking all the corporate core business systems to the firm's website. Information systems extend far beyond the boundaries of the organization to encompass vendors, customers and even competitors.

The Internet links companies directly to customers, suppliers, and other interested parties; it lets companies bypass other players in an industry's value chain and is a tool for developing and delivering new products and services to new customers. Furthermore, it enables low-cost communication and broad reach both up and downstream. Opportunities presented for operations include automating administrative processes, leading to faster turnaround of customer orders, enhanced customer support and shorter time to market for new products; shared learning; competitive procurement through electronic buying and supply-chain reconfiguration and integration and the virtualization of enterprise components. Not only do net technologies impact upon commerce and the way business is carried out but they also affect market and organizational structure.

There are limitations associated with the application of Internet technology in business. Customers cannot physically examine products; learning about suppliers and customers is limited by the lack of face-to-face contact which also makes 'selling' more difficult and limits the ability to take advantage of the low-cost, non-transactional functions performed by sales forces. There may be delays, due to shipment, in providing the goods or services to the end customer who cannot always simply walk out of the e-shop with them; extra logistical costs are required to assemble, pack, and move small shipments; the absence of physical facilities reduces a means to reinforce image and attracting new customers is difficult given the enormity of the available information and buying options.

The internet has both created new industries and enabled the reconfiguration of existing industries. While the Internet presents new opportunities it also intensifies competition. Internet technology provides buyers with easier access to information about products and suppliers, thus strengthening buyer bargaining power. The Internet mitigates the need for such things as an established sales force or access to existing channels, reducing barriers to entry. Marketplaces automate corporate procurement by linking many buyers and suppliers electronically. The benefits to buyers include low transaction costs, easier access to price and product information, convenient purchase of associated services, and, sometimes, the ability to pool volume. The Internet is an enabling technology – a powerful set of tools which rarely offers a direct competitive advantage. Internet technology, itself is not as a source of advantage because it is readily available to all. Competitive advantages arise from traditional strengths fortified through Internet technology – by tying a company's activities together in a more distinctive system.

Review questions

Opening case study

1 Individually or in groups, brainstorm and discuss why you think GSI commerce has been so successful?

2 Compare and contrast buying and selling on and offline from a customer and retailer's perspective – what are the similarities and differences and how does the buyer's experience differ?

3 With reference to Chapter 13, discuss how technology enables the GSI business model. Consider integration of the GSI and partners' systems, processes and infrastructure.

4 Select several large, predominantly traditional, retailers and discuss the arguments their boards might voice when considering outsourcing their e-commerce channel (to a company like GSI) as a strategic alternative.

5 Should traditional companies separate out or integrate their e-commerce business? What are the arguments for and against such decisions?

6 Do you believe a well established offline brand will help or hinder the respective companies' online commercial goals?

Using Internet technologies to gain a competitive advantage

Select companies from three different industries. With reference to traditional business, the digital organization, e-business, e-commerce and competitive strategies, discuss how Internet technologies may support the organizations in achievement of their strategic goals. You should discuss:

1 how the Internet can be used to create value;

2 the impact on operational effectiveness;

3 the extent to which the Internet will replace or complement conventional ways of undertaking business;

4 whether the Internet and IT can provide a sustainable competitive advantage; and

5 the limitations of the Internet for business.

Global e-commerce

Identify three organizations with large scale global e-commerce operations and several country specific websites.

■ **Discuss** the challenges in relation to each organization.

■ **Compare** and contrast their different country web pages.

Business models

Consider the business models listed in this chapter. Individually or in groups, identify at least one real world example of each model (a variety of recent examples are listed in Lumpkin and Dess (2004)); be prepared to discuss or present your findings to the rest of the class or business colleagues. You should identify how the organization adds value through the use of the Internet or digital technologies. You may also assess sources of competitive advantage.

Look back
See p. 468

Competitive advantage

Critically evaluate the Internet and net technologies as potential sources of competitive advantage. You should ascertain whether each is a source of competitive advantage, presenting arguments and examples to justify your stance.

References

Amit, R. and Zott, C. (2001) 'Value Creation in E-Business', *Strategic Management Journal* (Special Issue) 22(6/7):493–520.

Barney, J. (1991) 'Firm Resources and Sustained Competitive Advantage', *Journal of Management* (March 1991) 17(1):99–120.

Barney, J. (1996) 'The Resource-based Theory of the Firm', *Organization Science* (September/October 1996) 7(5):469.

Barney, J. (1997) *Gaining and Sustaining Competitive Advantage*, Reading, MA: Addison-Wesley.

Benjamin, B. and Wigand, R. (1995) 'Electronic Markets and Virtual Value Chains on the Information Superhighway', *Sloan Management Review* (Winter 1995) 36(2):62–72.

Bingi, P., Mir, A. and Khamalah, J. (2000) 'The Challenges Facing Global E-Commerce', *Information Systems Management* (Fall 2000) 17(4):26–34.

Chaffey, D. (2007) *E-Business and E-Commerce Management* (3 ed), Harlow: FT Prentice Hall.

Chang, K., Jackson, J. and Grover, V. (2003) 'E-commerce and corporate strategy: an executive perspective', *Information & Management* 40(7):663–675.

Dyer, J. H. and Singh, H. (1998) 'The Relational View: Cooperative Strategy and Sources of Interorganizational Competitive Advantage', *The Academy of Management Review* 23(4):660–679.

Evans, P. and Wurster, T. (1997) 'Strategy and the New Economics of Information', *Harvard Business Review* (September/October 1997) 75(5):70–82.

Evans, P. and Wurster, T. (1999) 'Getting Real About Virtual Commerce', *Harvard Business Review* (November/December 1999) 77(6):84–94.

Feeny, D. (2001) 'Making Business Sense of the E-Opportunity', *MIT Sloan Management Review* (Winter 2001) 42(2):41–51.

Ghemawat, P. (2001) 'Distance Still Matters. The Hard Reality of Global Expansion', *Harvard Business Review* (September 2001) 79(8):137–147.

Ghosh, S. (1998) 'Making Business Sense Of The Internet', *Harvard Business Review* (March/April 1998) 76(2):126–135.

Gulati, R. and Garino, J. (2000) 'Get the Right Mix of Bricks and Clicks for your company', *Harvard Business Review* (May–June, 2000):107–114.

Hamill, J. and Gregory, K. (1997) 'Internet Marketing in the Internationalisation of UK SMEs', *Journal of Marketing Management* (January–April 1997) 13(1–3):9–28.

Kobrin, S. (2001) 'Symposium: Electronic Commerce and Global Business Territoriality and the Governance of Cyberspace', *Journal of International Business Studies* (4th Quarter 2001) 32(4):687–704.

Laudon, K. C. and Laudon, J. P. (2007) *Management Information Systems: Managing the Digital Firm* (10 ed) Upper Saddle River, NJ: Prentice Hall.

Linder, J. and Cantrell, S. (2000) 'So What Is a Business Model Anyway?' *Accenture – Institute for Strategic Change* (March 2 2000).

Lord, C. (2000) 'The practicalities of developing a successful e-business strategy', *Journal of Business Strategy* (March/April 2000) 21(2):40–44.

Lumpkin, G. and Dess, G. (2004) 'E-Business Strategies and Internet Business Models: How the Internet Adds Value', *Organizational Dynamics* (May 2004) 33(2):161–173.

Palvia, P. (1998) 'Developing a model of the global and strategic impact of information technology', *Information & Management* 32(5):229–244.

Porter, M. E. and Millar, V. E. (1985) 'How information gives you a competitive advantage', *Harvard Business Review* (July–August 1963):149–174.

Porter, M. E. (2001) 'Strategy and the Internet', *Harvard Business Review* (March 2001):62–78.

Rao, S., Metts, G. and Monge, C. (2003) 'Electronic commerce development in small and medium sized enterprises: A stage model and its implications', *Business Process Management Journal* 9(1):11–32.

Rayport, J. F. and Sviokla, J. (1995) 'Exploiting the Virtual Value Chain', *Harvard Business Review* (November/December 1995) 73(6):75–85.

Rayport, J. F. and Sviokla, J. (1996) 'Exploiting the virtual value chain', *McKinsey Quarterly* 1:20–36.

Sambamurthy, V., Bharadwaj, A. and Grover, V. (2003) 'Shaping Agility Through Digital Options: Reconceptualising The Role Of Information Technology In Contemporary Firms', *MIS Quarterly* (June 2003) 27(2):237–263.

Schumpeter (1934) cited in Amit, R. and Zott, C. (2001) 'Value Creation in E-Business', *Strategic Management Journal* (Special Issue) 22(6/7):493–520.

Schumpeter, J. (1942) *Capitalism, Socialism and Democracy*, New York: Harper.

Stabell, C. B. and Fjeldstad, O. D. (1998) 'Configuring Value for Competitive Advantage: On Chains, Shops, and Networks', *Strategic Management Journal* (May 1998) 19(5):413–437.

Suarez, F. and Lanzolla, G. (2005) 'The Half-Truth of First-Mover Advantage', *Harvard Business Review* (April 2005) 83(4):121–127.

Teece, D. J., Pisano, G. and Shuen, A. (1997) 'Dynamic Capabilities and Strategic Management', *Strategic Management Journal* (August 1997) 18(7):509–533.

Venkatraman, N. and Henderson, J. C. (1998) 'Real Strategies for Virtual Organizing', *MIT Sloan Management Review* (Fall 1998) 40(1):33–48.

Weill, P. and Vitale, M. (2002) 'What IT Infrastructure Capabilities are Needed to Implement E-Business Models?', *MIS Quarterly Executive* (March 2002) 1(1):17–34.

Werbach, K. (2000) 'Syndication: The Emerging Model for Business in the Internet Era', *Harvard Business Review* (May/June 2000) 78(3):84–93.

Williamson, 1975 cited in Amit, R. and Zott, C. (2001) 'Value Creation in E-Business', *Strategic Management Journal* (Special Issue) 22(6/7):493–520.

Zwass, V. (2003) 'Electronic Commerce and Organizational Innovation: Aspects and Opportunities', *International Journal of Electronic Commerce* (Spring 2003) 7(3):7–37.

Suggestions for further reading

Journals

Articles feature in a range of journals from the *Strategic Management Journal* or *Sloan Management Review* through the more general, HBR to more specialist IT or process management journals such as the *International Journal of Electronic Commerce*.

International Journal of Electronic Commerce

The Journal is devoted to advancing the understanding and practice of electronic commerce. http://www.gvsu.edu/business/ijec/

Key articles

Scholars of this subject area have often read the following:

1 Amit, R. and Zott, C. (2001) 'Value Creation in E-Business', *Strategic Management Journal* (Special Issue) 22(6/7):493–520.
2 Benjamin, B. and Wigand, R. (1995) 'Electronic Markets and Virtual Value Chains on the Information Superhighway', *Sloan Management Review* (Winter 1995) 36(2):62–72.
3 Rayport, J. F. and Sviokla, J. (1996) 'Exploiting the virtual value chain', *McKinsey Quarterly* 1:20–36.
4 Evans, P. and Wurster, T. (1997) 'Strategy and the New Economics of Information', *Harvard Business Review* (September/October 1997) 75(5):70–82.
5 Evans, P. and Wurster, T. (1999) 'Getting Real About Virtual Commerce', *Harvard Business Review* (November/December 1999) 77(6):84–94.
6 Gulati, R. and Garino, J. (2000) 'Get the Right Mix of Bricks and Clicks for your company', *Harvard Business Review* (May–June, 2000):107–114.
7 Ghosh, S. (1998) 'Making Business Sense of the Internet', *Harvard Business Review* (March/April 1998) 76(2):126–135.
8 Stabell, C. B. and Fjeldstad, O. D. (1998) 'Configuring Value for Competitive Advantage: On Chains, Shops, and Networks', *Strategic Management Journal* (May 1998) 19(5):413–437.
9 Venkatraman, N. and Henderson, J. C. (1998) 'Real Strategies for Virtual Organizing', *MIT Sloan Management Review* (Fall 1998) 40(1):33–48.
10 Porter, M. E. (2001) 'Strategy and the Internet', *Harvard Business Review* (March 2001): 62–78.

Part IV Summary

This part of the book has focused on the role of information resources in enabling strategy and operational effectiveness and ensuring the organization is able to meet its goals. We also considered how such resources are used to create value by enabling the organization to do things differently or at lower cost. Information resources rarely exist or are used in isolation. Knowledge may be embedded in culture or human capital or in organizational systems; data may be stored in databases (software) located on the hardware and accessible through networks. Information is generated by processing data and knowledge through data mining and other sophisticated forms of analysis. Systems theory and holism can be used to explain the relationship between information resources: people, hardware, software, data and communication technologies.

We recognized knowledge as an important intangible resource, difficult to imitate in many cases, and therefore a potential source of sustainable competitive advantage. Consequently, organizations, in dynamic environments, constantly seek out new knowledge (learning and adapting) and look to create, store, transfer, access and use knowledge throughout the company. Knowledge management processes may operate over borders and are enabled by technology—particularly in the form of databases and communication networks. The re-use of knowledge throughout the international organization provides economies of use benefits. More importantly we recognized the role of HR specialists in knowledge management. Two types of knowledge (tacit and explicit) were distinguished and we argued the need to bring people together, to enable transfer. We linked this to two specific strategic approaches to knowledge management, codification and personalization. The latter relies more on person-to-person transfer but can still be enabled with collaborative technologies.

Information, when accessible, supports the international organization at the corporate headquarter level, subsidiaries and specific business units. Traditionally, organizations have been less responsive because information systems were fragmented (silos). Advances in database technology, business process knowledge and web technologies have manifested in enterprise systems; some of which are developed logically as single monolithic systems and therefore fully integrated. Others are integrated through middleware and the web, enabling the creation of digital organizations where information flows freely. This is essential to support time-based competitive advantage, e-commerce and empowerment strategies. Consequently a key role for information systems technology is to unify the dispersed parts of the global organization. Information resources facilitate commerce, unify organizational parts and partners, reduce uncertainty, and improve the quality of decision-making, planning, coordination and control. Such resources also enable more effective and efficient management of the supply chain both upstream (e-procurement) and downstream (e-marketing). While such technologies, in isolation, are unlikely to deliver a sustainable advantage, opportunities are possible when information resources are bundled with other resources to create capabilities and competencies. Altogether they can impact significantly on the way work is undertaken in the international organization; sometimes enabling tasks to be completed more efficiently, sometimes enabling new business models and different ways of working.

In the final part we considered how the capabilities and competencies derived from human and information resources (coupled with financial capital, building facilities and other assets) can help the organization to add value through primary activities of production, marketing and sales – international business and trade.

Part V

International business

This book has five parts, this is the final one. At the outset of the book we described the context for international business and management and used this, in Part II, to focus on the scope of the organization (strategy) – the purpose, goals and mission; the business the company is in and the development of a plan of action. Through this, and leadership, managers come to understand how they ought to develop, allocate and utilize resources to business advantage. Parts III and IV focused on resource management. Resourcing encompasses the acquisition, development and deployment of human, technological and other resources to create capabilities; an ability to achieve the mission. In this final part we focus on the actual work that is done; bringing together the resources and capabilities to provide the goods and services for consumers and thus generate a financial return. In this part we seek to make optimum use (productivity) of the resources discussed in Parts III and IV and to administer the whole business effectively and efficiently and in accordance with the strategy. Our focus is on the primary tasks and processes that cut across management, to add value and realize goals. As a consequence, financial resources are also acquired, utilized and generated; they too must be managed.

As can be seen from the figure, the contents of this book part include:

- international operations management
- international marketing
- international finance.

In this part we explore the primary activities of operations (using capabilities to add value and create offerings) and marketing (exchanging offerings for revenue) and finish with the supporting financial processes and associated challenges for the international organization.

Chapter 15

International operations management

Introduction

International operations management

IOM strategy

Establishing the infrastructure

Production-related processes

Forecasting demand

Sourcing strategies

Managing production

Logistics

Key concepts

- Manufacturing ■ Operations ■ International operations management ■ Economies of scale
- Inventory management ■ Focused factory ■ Time to market ■ Product development process
- Production process ■ Sales and operations planning ■ Batch manufacturing ■ Job shop
- Capacity ■ Logistics ■ Just-in-time production ■ Lean production

By the end of this chapter you will be able to:

- Discuss what is meant by international operations management and supply chain management

- Explain the importance of international operations management to international business competitiveness

- Describe key decisions associated with international operations management

- Identify major operations management and supply chain management activities

- Evaluate how international operations management contributes to international business success

Active learning case

Dyson

Starting in 1978, James Dyson set to work on the world's first bagless vacuum cleaner[1] which was launched in 1993 and stormed British homes in the 1990s, despite retailing at almost double the price of more established brands[2]. Throughout the 1990s, the company enjoyed significant growth in turnover, Dyson invested £44m of his own money in a new UK factory (1995); but the economics of running it did not add up[3]. Until 2002, the Dyson vacuum cleaner company was widely regarded as a rather unusual British business. Its owner had resisted moving operations abroad, despite the fact that labour and land costs would certainly be cheaper elsewhere. Choosing instead to keep his manufacturing plant in the UK, a sub-optimum location; Dyson was often portrayed by the media as a patriotic figure, given that his reluctance to relocate was increasing the firm's operating costs and reducing potential profits. His location decision was more behaviouralist than rational economical. 'In 2002 we were presented with a difficult decision. We were unable to get permission to extend our Malmesbury factory, and increasingly our suppliers were based in the Far East. And so we were forced to move production elsewhere. It was a hard choice[4].'

In 2002, Dyson made the decision to switch production from the UK factory; 'Increasingly in the past two to three years our suppliers are Far East-based and not over here', he said[6], 'and our markets are there too. We're the best selling vacuum cleaner in Australia and New Zealand, we're doing well in Japan and we're about to enter the US. And we see other Far Eastern countries as big markets as well.' Although Dyson already has a plant in Malaysia, other countries – including China – are viewed as possible sites. Whatever decision is made, research and development will remain at the firm's base in Malmesbury, Wiltshire, which has received £32m of investment in the past two years. That makes Dyson products still 'British-engineered', Mr Dyson said.

New Dyson factory is built in Malaysia – why did Dyson change his mind? There were several arguments supporting the relocation of production facilities. Arguments for the move included rising employment costs, the strong pound, high research and development costs and the decline in British component makers[6]. Labour content was quite high and the company's suppliers (such as aluminium tubing and switches) were not located in the UK[6].

Furthermore, the company was not allowed to expand the existing UK manufacturing site at a critical time in the company's growth. They were producing 900 000 machines a year back then, but it's now more than four million, further supporting the need to move. Their switches and flex were coming from Taiwan; tubing was coming from Germany, motors from Japan, polymers from Korea and so on. In Malaysia, almost all suppliers were within a 10-mile radius of the factory. The costs of a UK worker amounted to £9 per hour compared with the Malaysian worker who earned £3 per hour; similarly UK office rent amounted to £114 sq m a year, while Malaysian office rent was £38 sq m a year[7].

Dyson also commented on logistical costs, 'we import a lot of components from the Far East, and it makes sense to manufacture out there so we do not have the added expense of flying them around'. In a different interview Dyson[8] stated, 'Europe is almost the most expensive place in the world to manufacture anything.

www.press.dyson.com

Dyson Limited is a large company, headquartered in the UK, and founded in 1993 by Sir James Dyson. The company manufactures electric domestic appliances. Products include vacuum cleaners, washing machines and hand driers. In 2005, revenue was approximately GB£0.5 billion – and the total number of employees was less than 2000. Dyson developed and built his first prototype vacuum cleaner, the G-Force in 1983 and in 1986, a production version of the G-Force was first sold in Japan. Using the income from the Japanese licence, James Dyson set up the Dyson Company, opening a research centre in England, in June 1993. His first production version of a dual cyclone vacuum cleaner, featuring constant suction, was the DC01, sold for £200. Initially, all Dyson vacuum cleaners and washing machines were made in England. In 2002, the company transferred vacuum cleaner production to Malaysia.

▶ ▶ ▶

The lower labour cost in Malaysia is important but, having moved our manufacturing there, quality has gone up enormously. Also, whereas we used to have sub-contractors scattered around the world, now they are all within 10 miles of the factory. This has helped to improve scheduling – and product development has been easier too.' – If you have a problem within manufacturing you can nip down the road to see the supplier to sort out that problem.

Global growth: *It appears the new locational strategy is working …*

The company now makes three times as many cleaners at a lower cost[9] and profits rose 137 per cent on revenues up 54 per cent to £426m. Traditionally manufacturers have taken the view that research and development should take place close to production so that the communications channels are as short as possible. So has moving the manufacturing to Malaysia while retaining research and development in the UK had any affect? 'None at all, really', according to Dyson. 'People circulate between the UK and Malaysia, where we have 80 to 90 people, so we retain good feedback and communications[10].' Relocating allowed Dyson to stay competitive while doing what they do best – designing and engineering new technology; highly skilled work continued to be performed at the UK Research, Design and Development centre.

Before 2002, less than a third of sales were made overseas, now 75 per cent come from outside the UK. Reflecting on the decision they believed Malaysia was perfect; English was widespread and it had an established and reliable manufacturing base upon which to build. One of the biggest global challenges was and is communication. When Dyson started in 1993 they only sold machines in the UK. Now they operate in approximately 50 countries, from Canada to New Zealand. Although they make use of various information and communication technologies none are a replacement for face-to-face discussion. Many of their Malmesbury-based engineers now spend a few months of the year in Malaysia or China to oversee the last steps of the manufacturing process. It is important that decisions are not made in a distant ivory tower. 'Manufacturing goes beyond making things in a factory. For us, assembly comes at the very end of a long period of research, design and development.'

Dyson plan is to come out with products that use better technology, better design and better engineering for which they can charge a premium price to fund research and development to help bring out more products[11].

Sources:

Website www.dyson.co.uk

1. www.international.dyson.com 7 October 2007;
2. BBC News (2003) 'Dyson's domestic dilemma', Thursday, 2 October 2003, //news.bbc.co.uk/1/hi/business/3113002.stm 06/10/2007;
3. Shelley, T. (2005) 'Combining product design with engineering is key', *eurekamagazine* 14/11/2005, www.eurekamagazine. co.uk/article/3324/Combining-product-design-with-engineering-is-key.aspx 06/10/2007;
4. Geographyinthenews (2005) 'Gold dust', 8 March 2005, www.geographyinthenews.rgs.org/news/article/?id=331 06/10/2007;
5. *Engineer Live*, 'James Dyson: Invention and frustration', www.engineerlive.com/european-design-engineer/opinion/12240/ james-dyson-invention-and-frustration.thtml 06/10/2007;
6. BBC News (2002) 'Dyson to move to Far East', Tuesday, 5 February 2002, //news.bbc.co.uk/1/hi/business/1801909.stm 06/10/2007;
7. Tran, M. (2002) 'Dyson to shift manufacturing operations to Asia', *Guardian Unlimited*, Tuesday, 5 February 2002, www. guardian.co.uk/recession/story/0,,645405,00.html 06/10/2007;
8. From the *Swindon Advertiser*, first published Friday, 14 June 2002. //archive.thisiswiltshire.co.uk/2002/6/14/185729.html 06/10/2007;
9. telegraph.co.uk (2005) 'Far Eastern promise has paid off, says Dyson', 23/02/2005, www.telegraph.co.uk/money/main. jhtml?xml=/money/2005/02/23/cndys23.xml 06/10/2007;
10. telegraph.co.uk (2005) 'Dyson's chip with everything', 27/02/2005, www.telegraph.co.uk/money/main.jhtml?xml=/ money/2005/02/27/ccdys27.xml 06/10/2007;
11. *The Engineer*, 11 April 2007, www.latest-science-news.com/news/a-move-in-the-right-direction-5777.htm 06/10/2007.

Introduction

Creating value through operations

Primary activities and core organizational processes aim to produce the goods and services customers desire. Collectively, such activities add value, transforming materials into finished goods, see Figure 15-1. In order to create products and services, the international organization must overcome many challenges – greater and more complex than their domestic counterparts. International supply chains must operate over greater geographic distances and time differences, multiple national markets, multiple operational locations, making use of a wider set of transportation strategies and more complex sourcing and logistical decisions, as was highlighted in the opening case study.

Costs associated with manufacture and the movement of goods must be considered along with costs associated with product adaptation and customization (see differentiation strategies), taxes and subsidies, exchange rates and other overheads. In the case of the international organization, the distance increases between customers and production or distribution facilities. Organizations respond by expanding their global logistics and distribution networks. They must position inventories strategically so that products are available when customers want them, in the right quantity and for the right price. Decisions about sourcing, stock, production process, facility location, distribution and transportation become strategically important because of their role in determining cost, quality, dependability and responsiveness.

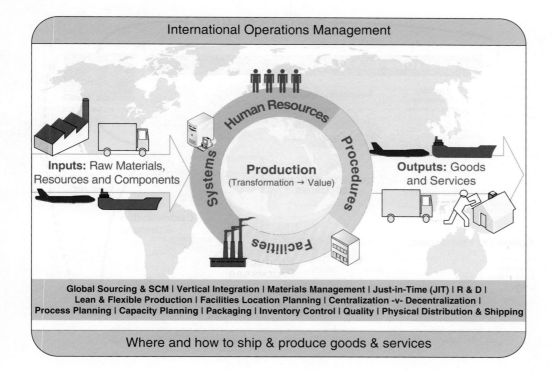

Figure 15-1

The international operations management (IOM) process

This chapter builds upon previous chapters, focusing on the role of people and information and technology resources as transformational resources. We also build upon earlier work concerning business processes and business process improvement and total quality management. The chapter examines how the international organization may undertake interrelated activities and processes associated with making and supplying goods and services – from research and development to procurement, manufacture and shipment. We

Look back
See p. 322

consider resource acquisition, logistics, production, inventory control, capacity planning, packaging, distribution and shipment; considering associated problems such as determining where and how to obtain raw materials and inputs and associated make or buy (vertical integration and outsourcing) decisions; where to make or create goods and services and through what process; whether to centralize or decentralize operations and how to ensure worldwide distribution of goods and services to customers. Like all organizations, multinational corporations and international organizations are concerned with the efficient use of labour and capital; they need to organize their production to minimize cost. A key challenge faced by all organizations is the speed with which they develop and move new products and services to market (speed to market).

This chapter has been structured in line with the IOM models shown in Figure 15-2. There is a need for the international organization to:

- create an IOM strategy that 'fits' with the corporate strategy;
- establish an operational infrastructure (acquire and maintain operational assets such as production facilities, buildings and machinery);
- design the products and services and offerings generally sought after by customers;
- forecast the demand for such offerings;
- develop sourcing strategies for inputs (raw materials and components) – deciding what should be made in-house and what should be procured from other businesses;
- manage production by matching capacity with demand, identifying what to produce and when and the materials and transformational resources required;
- manage logistics and the supply chain.

Figure 15-2

Model for IOM

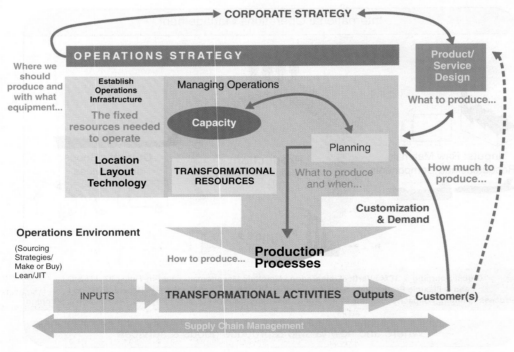

Such activities are conceived and executed with competitive strategies in mind, i.e. to deliver what the customer requires – quality, dependability, responsiveness and at low cost. We therefore structure this chapter in the following sections:

- IOM strategy;
- establishing the operational infrastructure;
- production processes;

- forecasting demand;
- sourcing strategies;
- managing production;
- logistics and the supply chain.

International operations management

We open this chapter by asking what international operations management (IOM) is and why study it? Once an organization has designed a product that satisfies market need, it must decide how best to produce it. Companies need to develop an operational infrastructure to meet demand, consider what production method is best for the organization and the product; whether to produce it by themselves or contract with someone else to produce it; the volumes that should be produced and the quality level desired.

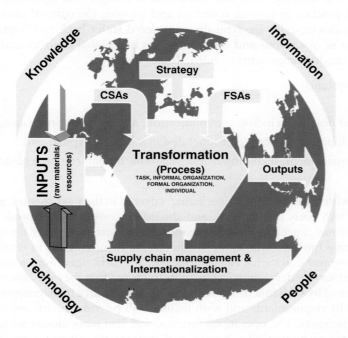

Figure 15-3
International operations management

The collection of people, knowledge, technology, and systems within an organization that has primary responsibility for producing and providing the organization's products or services is referred to as operations; the traditional way to think about operations is as a *transformation process* which takes a set of inputs and transforms them in some way to create outputs (goods or services – offerings) that a customer values, see Figure 15-3.

Operations the core activities of a business

The mechanisms transforming inputs into outputs are called processes, discussed in Chapter 10. Operations management (OM) is the planning, scheduling, control and coordination of the activities that transform inputs into finished goods and services. Operations management is important because it can reduce costs, differentiate the organization's products and services and impact upon quality and therefore may increase revenue through increased customer satisfaction. The traditional view of OM takes an internal perspective, focusing on the organization's own value-adding activities (see for example, Porter's primary activities). However, many now believe in the need to consider the operations of suppliers, intermediaries and customers also – the supply chain.

Operations management the planning, scheduling, and control of the activities that transform inputs into finished goods and services

Operations management is associated with supply chain management, quality, productivity, information technology, materials management and logistics, transportation options, location options, make or buy decisions, inventory, packaging and facilities design. Such activities may take place in the home or another country. *International operations management* (IOM) is essentially concerned with the transformation of inputs into goods or services by the international firm-creating value. Lawrence and Rosenblatt (1992) say that topics relevant to the study of international operations can be classified into six broad categories:

1 international operations strategy;

2 national comparisons of operations;

3 issues critical to global operations;

4 operational issues affected by globalization;

5 risk management; and

6 international cross-functional coordination.

The international operational strategy category is comprised of topics that broadly define and characterize the scope of global operations. We consider IOM strategies in the next section. When studying IOM it is also useful to compare the operating environment and operational practice in various countries and regions; the cultural context of operations and management styles are typically considered (refer back to Chapter 8). Finally, the coordination of operations and other functions in a global environment is frequently included in the taught components of IOM. Topics include:

■ information systems;

■ marketing;

■ organizational design, including communication, and coordination issues;

■ product development, including product design and prototyping; and

■ workforce management, including labour relations, human resource management, and incentives.

Such topics, with the exception of marketing, covered in the next chapter, were explored in the previous two parts of this book and should be considered alongside this chapter. Operations constitute a primary function within the organization. They must work closely with the marketing function who can provide market requirements; in return, the operations function communicates what can be achieved. Similarly, operations must work closely with product and service development functions to ensure that they are able to produce the new ideas generated by such functions. With the human resource management function they can determine HR requirements and with finance will provide the information necessary for investment decisions. The operations function will also work closely with the technical function to source technological solutions and appropriate computer-based information systems. International operations networks are comprised of supplier, manufacturing, warehouse and transportation facilities and the connections between these facilities. Managers of these organizations are grappling to find efficient and effective techniques for coordinating the resulting collection of geographically dispersed facilities (Boone *et al.* 1996).

Operations are typically conceived as the primary internal activities of the value chain. However, such activities rely upon raw materials, which may be sourced from upstream suppliers, and relationships downstream. The supply chain is a network of manufacturers and service providers that work together to convert and move goods from the raw materials stage through to the end user. These manufacturers and service providers are linked together through physical, information and monetary flows, see Figure 15-4. Supply chain management (SCM) involves the active management of supply chain activities and relationships in order to maximize customer value and achieve a sustainable competitive advantage. It represents a mindful effort by an organization or group of organizations to develop and run supply chains in the most effective and efficient way possible.

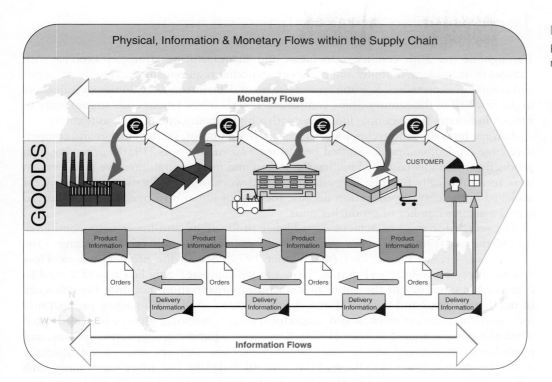

Figure 15-4

Physical, information and monetary flows

Internationalization, globalization, increasing competition, EC and relationship management has increased the importance of OM and SCM to managers working within international organizations. Major IOM and SCM activities include: running overseas plants or coordinating international activities, selection of transformation processes; forecasting; capacity planning; inventory management; planning and control, purchasing and logistics. From a practical standpoint, one of the attractions to developing international operations is the low labour cost available in many of the less developed nations. However, the low labour cost is not enough to offset the low labour productivity in some of these nations. In an article based on labour productivity data and public labour rate data, Xiao, Vargas, and Whybark (1996) show that extremely low wages do not offset the differences in labour productivity in some of the reforming economies. This would indicate a fairly sophisticated understanding of international differences is necessary to be an effective international operations manager. Thus far we have identified what is generally meant by IOM and discussed the need to consider the supply chain in its entirety when managing operations. Next we turn to IOM strategy.

IOM strategy

The fundamental role of operations is to implement corporate strategy. In some cases the operations function may hold the organization back while in other organizations operations may support or even drive strategy. It is important for the organization to align the corporate, operations, marketing and information systems strategies. Management must decide what it is going to make and what it will buy; how many plants to have, how big they should be, and where to place them; what processes and equipment to buy; what the key elements are which need to be controlled and how they can be controlled; and what kind of management organization would be most appropriate. Finally, implementation programmes are determined as are controls, performance measures, and review procedures. This section starts with a historic review of strategy and then describes contemporary approaches to IOM.

The evolution of operations strategy

Throughout the 20th century, operations and manufacturing strategies evolved with changes in technology, mobility and transport, customer requirements, corporate strategies and competitive pressures. Scientific management and Taylorism were dominant influences in the first half of the century. Some companies used their low labour costs to gain entry to various industries (for example industries with a high labour content such as textiles).

As wage rates rose and technology became more significant, i.e. advantages and competitive edge eroded, companies shifted first to *scale-based strategies* (1950s) achieving high productivity and low costs by building the largest and most capital-intensive facilities that were technologically feasible; investment boosted workforce productivity – savings were achieved in the cost of production because the cost of initial investment could be spread across a greater number of producing units.

The search for ways to achieve even higher productivity and lower costs continued. And in the mid-1960s, it led companies to a new source of competitive advantage – the focused factory, see Figure 15-5 (see Skinner 1974). Seeing the problem not as 'How can we increase productivity?' but as 'How can we compete?' Scholars argued a need to consider the efficiency of the entire manufacturing organization, not only the efficiency of the direct labour and the workforce. A factory that focused on a narrow product mix for a particular market niche would outperform the conventional plant, which attempted a broader mission argued Skinner (1974). Because its equipment, supporting systems, and procedures concentrated on a limited task for one set of customers, its costs and especially its overheads were lower than those of the conventional plant. But, more importantly, such a plant became a competitive weapon because its entire apparatus was focused to accomplish the particular manufacturing task demanded by the company's overall strategy and marketing objective. The focused factory did a better job because repetition and concentration in one area allowed its workforce and managers to become effective and experienced in the task required for success (Skinner 1974).

Factory costs were very sensitive to the variety of goods a plant produced. Reduction of the product-line variety by half, for example, raised productivity by 30 per cent and cuts costs by 17 per cent. In manufacturing, costs fall into two categories: those that respond to volume or *scale* and those driven by *variety*. Scale-related costs decline as volume increases, usually falling 15 per cent to 25 per cent per unit each time volume doubles. Variety-related costs, on the other hand, reflect the costs of complexity in manufacturing: set-up, materials handling, inventory and many of the overhead costs of a factory. In most cases, as variety increases, costs increase, usually at a rate of 20 per cent to 35 per cent per unit each time variety doubles. The sum of the scale – and variety-related costs represents the *total cost of manufacturing*. With effort, managers can determine the optimum cost point for their factories – the point where the combination of volume and variety yields the lowest total manufacturing cost for a particular plant. When markets are good, companies tend to edge towards increased variety in search of higher volumes, even though this will mean increased costs. When times are tough, companies cut variety to reduce costs.

Traditional batch manufacturing has always had inherent limitations. Work in process levels are high and machine utilization is low. Jobs spend a high proportion of time waiting for something to happen to them, waiting for a machine to be set up, waiting to be moved or waiting for other jobs on the machine to be completed. Batch production often requires a mass of expediters or progress chasers in order to keep jobs flowing through the manufacturing facilities. It was recognized that some means of automatically routing jobs through the manufacturing system from one machine to the next was required and some way of greatly reducing the set-up time of jobs on a machine. These requirements were met with the aid of computer and numerical control techniques and this led to the development of the basic concept of a flexible manufacturing system (FMS) (Buzacott and Yao 1986).

Among the options for competition are price (cost), quality, delivery, service, and flexibility. In the late 1970s variety became a competitive weapon. Japanese companies exploited *flexible manufacturing* to the point that a new competitive thrust emerged – the *variety*

Focused factory a factory that focuses on a narrow product mix for a particular market niche

Batch manufacturing a type of manufacturing process where items are moved through the different manufacturing steps in groups, or batches

war. The advantage of flexible manufacturing – a flexible factory enjoys more variety with lower total costs than traditional factories, which are still forced to make the trade-off between scale and variety. In a flexible factory system, variety-driven costs start lower and increase more slowly as variety grows. Scale costs remain unchanged. Thus the optimum cost point for a flexible factory occurs at a higher volume and with greater variety than for a traditional factory. The advent of just-in-time production brought with it a move to flexible factories (1970/80s), as leading Japanese companies sought both low cost and great variety in the market.

Thus far we have discussed competing through price (cost), quality, service, flexibility and variability. Since the 1980s, companies have capitalized on 'time' as a critical source of competitive advantage. They managed structural changes to speed up operational processes. Such companies competed with flexible manufacturing and rapid-response systems, expanding variety and increasing innovation. A company that builds its strategy on this cycle is a more powerful competitor than one with a *traditional strategy* based on low wages, scale, or focus (Stalk 1988). Older, cost-based strategies require managers to do whatever is necessary to drive down costs: move production to or source from a low-wage country; build new facilities or consolidate old plants to gain economies of scale; or focus operations down to the most economic subset of activities. These tactics reduce costs but at the expense of *responsiveness*. Generally, the organization's major strength was flexibility of product (able to make changes in the product easily) or flexibility of volume (able to absorb large shifts in demand easily). Organizations that are able to do this are said to have flexible capacity, the ability to operate manufacturing equipment at different production rates by varying staffing levels and operating hours, or starting and stopping at will. Companies are systems; time connects all the parts.

Traditional manufacturing requires long lead times to resolve conflicts between various jobs or activities that require the same resources. The long lead times, in turn, require sales forecasts to guide planning. But sales forecasts are inevitably wrong; by definition they are guesses, however informed. Naturally, as lead times lengthen the accuracy of sales forecasts declines. With more forecasting errors, inventories bulge and the need for safety stocks at all levels increases. Time delays may be reduced in many ways, for example, in the flow of information and products through the system. When it comes to lot size, for instance, traditional factories attempt to maximize production runs whilst time-based manufacturers try to shorten their production runs as much as possible.

Factory layout also contributes to time-based competitive advantage. Traditional factories are usually organized by process. Time-based factories, however, are organized by product. In traditional factories, scheduling is also a source of delay and waste. Most traditional factories use central scheduling, however, in time-based factories, local scheduling enables employees to make more production control decisions on the factory floor. The combination of the product-oriented layout of the factory and local scheduling makes the total production process run more smoothly. These differences between traditional and time-based factories add up argues (Stalk 1988).

Flexible factories enjoy big advantages in both productivity and time: labour productivity in time-based factories can be as much as 200 per cent higher than in conventional plants; time-based factories can respond eight to ten times faster than traditional factories. Flexible production means significant improvements in labour and net-asset productivity; these, in turn, yield reductions of up to 20 per cent in overall costs and increases in growth for much less investment. Time-based competition is not restricted to production processes and time compression may be applied to sales and distribution activities also. Companies aim to cut delays in sales and distribution, reduce costs, and improve customer service. The evolution of production strategies is summarized in Figure 15-5.

Economies of scale a decrease in the per unit cost of production as a result of producing large numbers of the good

Lot size the number of units of product or item to be manufactured at each set-up

Production run completion of all tasks is associated with a production order

Time compression reducing the time required to produce and deliver a product or service

Contemporary operation strategies

In the relatively stable environment of the 1960s and early 1970s, the prime strategic focus was to find an attractive industry position (offer the lowest cost or the highest quality)

Figure 15-5

Evolution of international operations management strategies

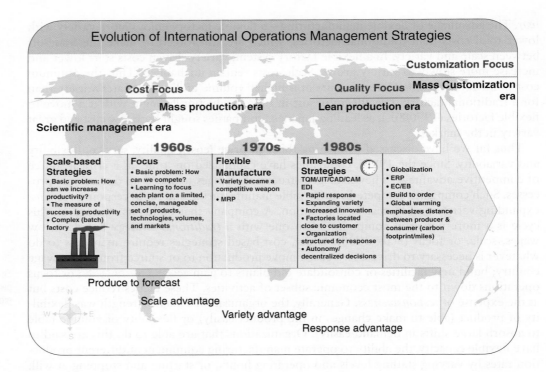

and build a competitive fortress around it. A good manufacturing strategy was one that defended a company's position through a narrowly focused set of capabilities. Hayes and Pisano (1994) discussed the 'new manufacturing strategy' arguing companies need strategies for building critical capabilities to achieve competitive advantage – the key to long-term success is being able to do certain things better than your competitors can. The problem is that simply improving manufacturing – by, for example, adopting JIT, TQM, or some other three-letter acronym – is not a strategy for using manufacturing to achieve competitive advantage. Neither is aspiring to lean manufacturing, continuous improvement, or world-class status.

In today's turbulent competitive environment, a company more than ever needs a strategy that specifies the kind of competitive advantage that it is seeking in its marketplace and articulates how that advantage is to be achieved. If managers pin their competitive hopes on the implementation of a few best-practice approaches, they implicitly abandon the central concept of a strategy in favour of a generic approach to competitive success. How can a company expect to achieve any sort of competitive advantage if its only goal is to be 'as good as' its toughest competitors? In turbulent environments, however, the goal of strategy becomes strategic flexibility. Being world-class is not enough; a company also has to have the capability to switch gears – from, for example, rapid product development to low cost – relatively quickly and with minimal resources. The job of manufacturing is to provide that capability.

From discussions presented thus far we note that the international organization typically develops an OM and SCM strategy that supports its business strategy. The operations and supply chain strategy is a functional strategy indicating how structural (tangible resources, such as buildings, equipment, and information systems) and infrastructural elements (includes the policies, people, decision rules, and organizational design) within the operations and supply chain areas will be acquired and developed to support the overall business strategy. Organizations must determine the amount and type of capacity, facilities and technology required. Similarly they must make sourcing decisions, organize human resources, and manage inventory and production. Both OM and SCM impact significantly upon business performance – quality, delivery speed and reliability, flexibility and cost may all be affected. For many organizations it is important to be able to deliver quality products and services when promised; similarly, they need to be capable of responding quickly to the needs of customers. Cost is always a concern. In particular, labour, materials, engineering and quality related costs are managed through OM and SCM processes and decisions.

The contemporary operations strategy is both planned and emergent. Influenced by the corporate and other functional strategies such as marketing and by a desire to maintain desirable competencies such as responsiveness and dependability; strategy emerges from decisions such as where to locate and which technology to use (establishing the infrastructure); important decisions concerning processes for producing goods and services and other related decisions. Similarly, organizations must decide where they will source raw materials from or whether to create their own inputs. Such decisions are considered in the following sections.

Establishing the infrastructure

Operational managers are responsible for providing sufficient capacity to meet the organization's needs. Facilities decisions are of significant strategic importance to the international organization and the operations function in particular. Such decisions place physical constraints on the amount that can be produced and may require large amounts of capital investment (refer to Chapter 17). Such decisions often affect many parts of the organization and may be made at the highest levels of management. Such decisions have a long lead time due to construction. Decisions are influenced by many factors such as the total capacity required, when and where capacity is required, cost, quality, flexibility, dependability and responsiveness. In many cases, the organization's operations strategy will contain a facilities strategy. In this section we consider three key aspects of infrastructure development: the location and layout of production facilities and the selection and application of technology.

Location and layout decisions

The strategic importance of location

One of the most important strategic decisions made by some companies is where to locate their operations. Such decisions are encompassed in the development of operations strategy. Location has a major impact upon the overall risk and profit of the company. In particular it may impact on transportation costs, taxes, wages, raw material costs and rents – refer back to the opening 'Dyson' or the previous Burberry case study in Chapter 7.

Look back
See chapter 15, p. 485
chapter 7, p. 204

Location decisions are not made frequently and may concern the location of a new facility or the relocation of an existing facility. In the case of an existing operation, capacity issues, shifts in customer demographics, exchange rates, cost reduction and other factors may incentivize relocation. Location options include:

1 expanding an existing facility instead of moving;
2 continuing with the current and adding a further facility elsewhere; or
3 closing the existing facility and moving to another location.

In some cases different aspects of the value chain are either outsourced or respective activities moved to a lower cost location. The move to provide or produce different parts of goods and services in different countries, see Figure 15-6, before they are combined into final goods is termed the fragmentation process. Decisions will be influenced according to the nature of the facility to be located. For example, a warehouse location strategy will differ from a factory location strategy. In each case, however, the corporate strategy will drive the location strategy. For example, a strategy emphasizing cost reduction will influence location choice in a different way than a strategy emphasizing the need for creativity and innovation. In the case of the latter, the presence of specialized talent in the workforce, a

Fragmentation process different parts of goods and services are provided in different countries before they are combined in final goods

sophisticated local market and the presence of related and supporting industries will influence the location decision.

Figure 15-6

Fragmented production process

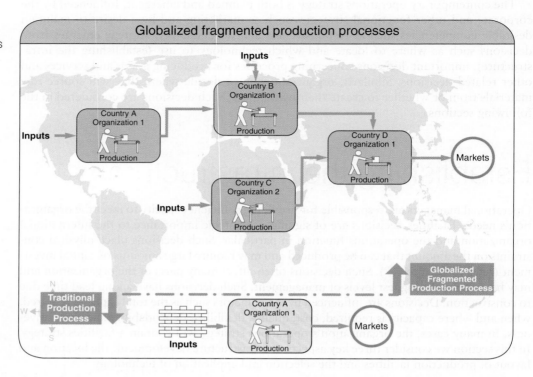

One of the first tasks for the international organization is to determine which countries in which to operate. Frequently, the organization will identify the critical success factors needed to achieve competitive advantage. Factors such as political risk, cultural and economic issues, availability of talented human resources, the availability of supplies and energy, communication and transportation network and financial risks such as exchange rate in currency may all be considered when evaluating possible countries within which to locate (refer back to Chapter 2). After selecting the country (or countries), the next step will be to narrow down options by selecting particular regions and will then focus on a specific site. Proximity to market, suppliers and competitors and transportation systems will influence such decisions.

When deciding upon a location, local (low) wage rates are often a powerful driver but should not be considered in isolation. In some cases, a low wage rate may be accompanied by low labour productivity. Dividing the labour cost per day by productivity (units produced that day) indicates the cost per unit. A country with high labour costs and a high productivity rate may well be a better option than one with a low labour costs.

Furthermore, location decisions may create ethical situations (refer back to Chapter 4). Is it ethical for developed countries to exploit undeveloped countries where sweatshops and child labour are commonly used? Work attitudes need to be considered as they may impact upon flexibility and dependability goals particularly with regard to employee loyalty, absenteeism and unions. For many organizations it is extremely important to locate near customers. Manufacturing firms find it useful to be close to customers when transporting finished goods is expensive or difficult. Similarly, firms locate near their raw materials and suppliers because of transportation costs and also perishability. Some companies also like to locate near competitors (clustering).

Look back
See chapter 4

STOP & THINK

Discuss the factors you believe influenced the location decision for Burberry or Dyson. In each case, sort them in order of importance.

Layout

Once a location has been selected, decisions about layout must be made. The layout of an operation is concerned with the physical location of the *transforming resources*. The organization must make decisions such as where to put facilities, machines, equipment and people. While many factors will impact upon such decisions, decision-makers will frequently consider safety issues, the flow of resources and materials, noise, accessibility, the use of space and flexibility. The layout will typically depend upon the type of process employed. Layout decisions determine operational efficiency and can help an organization achieve a strategy that supports differentiation, low-cost or response. The layout design should ensure efficient space utilization, the flow of information, materials or people, desired customer interaction and should be flexible and motivating (see Figure 15-7). Layout *types* include the office, retail and warehouse and may be driven by the production process selected. Office layouts require the grouping of workers and their equipment, focusing mainly on the flow of information; retail layouts try to expose customers to as many products as possible whereas the objective of warehouse layout is to find the optimum trade-off between handling cost and costs associated with warehouse space.

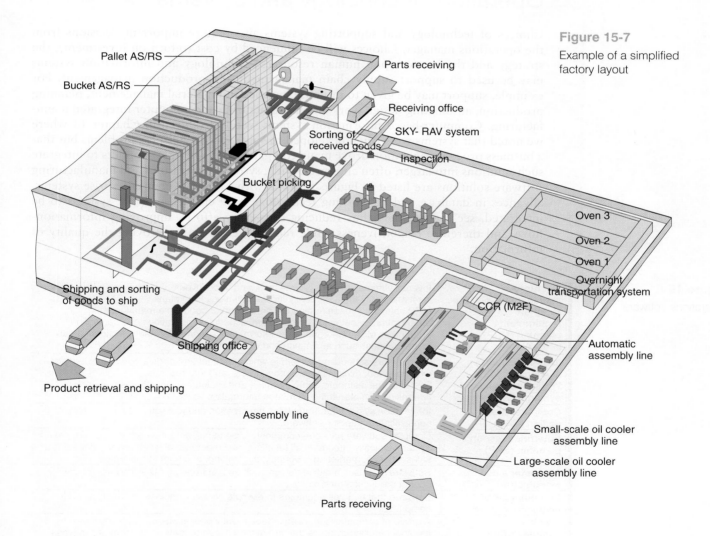

Figure 15-7

Example of a simplified factory layout

Frequently occurring layout types include:

1 the fixed-position layout – where the position of the product is fixed; materials, equipment, and workers are transported to and from the product;

2 process layout – locating similar transforming resources together so that different products or services with different processing needs will take different routes through the operation;

3 cellular layout – locating transforming resources with a common purpose such as processing the same types of product, serving similar types of customer, etc.; and

4 functional layout – a type of layout where resources are physically grouped by function.

Other layout types described include the product-based layout – a type of layout where resources are arranged sequentially according to the steps required to make a product. As was mentioned earlier, technology assets are among the resources that must be considered in the layout of the facility. In the next section we consider alternative technologies and systems used in operations.

Operations technology and systems

Choices of technology and supporting systems also require important decisions from the operations manager. Choices will be influenced by cost (return on investment), the strategy and the impact upon human resources. Technology and information systems may be used to support supply chain management and production management. For example, support may be given to in-house logistics and material management, planning production, automating design work and manufacturing and computer integrated manufacturing. Computer-based information systems were introduced in Chapter 13 where we noted that systems were often developed to solve specific business problems but that a business process orientation drove many companies and software suppliers to integrate such solutions into larger, often enterprise-wide, systems. Operations and manufacturing software solutions are listed in Figure 15-8. As with ERP and other enterprise systems, advances in database and networking technology have enabled separate systems to be integrated, see Figure 15-9, thus reducing data-entry efforts, improving information-flows and therefore responsiveness while reducing costs and improving the quality of information.

Figure 15-8
Operations software

Inventory management systems	Inventory management systems track and trace inventory globally on a line-item level and notify the user of significant deviations from plans.
Materials requirements planning (MRP) software	MRP software is used to plan the production of goods in a manufacturing organization by obtaining components, scheduling operations and controlling production. MRP II integrates the information system with other functional areas in the business such as finance and marketing.
Just-in-time (JIT) systems	An inventory scheduling system in which material and parts arrive at a workplace when needed, minimizing inventory, waste, and interruptions.
Work management systems (WMSs)	Systems that distribute, route, monitor, and evaluate various types of work by controlling and managing all related information flows.
Computer-aided design (CAD)	Information system that automates the creation and revision of designs using sophisticated graphics software.
Enterprise resource planning (ERP)	Complex software package commonly used to implement an enterprise information system; typically integrates all functions of the enterprise, such as manufacturing, sales, finance, marketing, inventory, accounting, and human resources.
Computer aided manufacture (CAM)	Software that uses a digital design such as that from a CAD system to directly control production machinery.
Computer aided engineering (CAE)	Software that enables engineers to execute complex engineering analysis on a computer.
Flexible manufacturing systems (FMS)	A group of computer-controlled independent workstations or machines linked by material handling systems that are able to accommodate wide variations in types and quantities of products.
Computer integrated manufacturing (CIM)	A term used to describe the integration of computer-based monitoring and control of all aspects of a manufacturing process, often using a common database and communicating via some form of computer network; integrates several computerized systems, such as CAD, CAM, MRP, and JIT into a whole, in a factory.

Figure 15-9

Integrated manufacturing systems

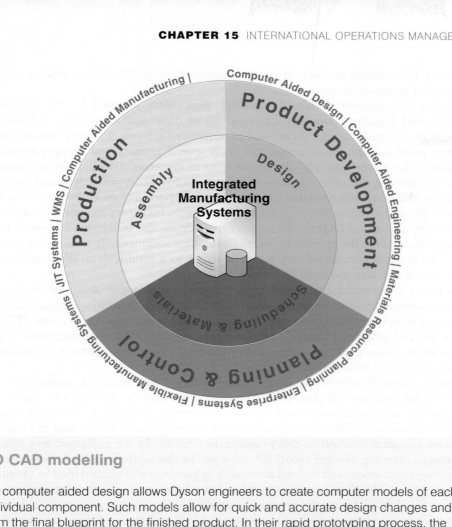

3D CAD modelling

3D computer aided design allows Dyson engineers to create computer models of each individual component. Such models allow for quick and accurate design changes and form the final blueprint for the finished product. In their rapid prototyping process, the CAD model is computer sliced into horizontal layers which are then built in a fusion deposition modelling (FDM) machine; the machine builds the layers in ABS thermoplastic to create a prototype. Parts can then be assembled by model makers to create fully working prototype products. These can then be tested.

SOURCE: (1) HTTP://WWW.INTERNATIONAL.DYSON.COM/TESTHOUSE/TESTHOUSE2.ASP

An important activity in the value chain is the design of products, services and processes. Computer aided design is a system that provides the computer with an ability to create and modify product, service or process drawings; engineers can develop, modify, share, and test designs in a virtual world.

CAD systems help organizations avoid the time and expense of paper-based drawings and physical prototypes. Their ability to rotate or create movement in the design allows testing and subsequently reduces the cost of prototyping. Subsequent modifications are quick and easy for the designer. This capability enhances designer productivity and speeds up the design process while reducing design errors. Once CAD work has been completed a designer can use computer aided engineering software to analyze the design and determine whether it will work as the designer predicted. Data generated through computer aided design or engineering may then be used in computer aided manufacturing (CAM).

CAM involves the direct use of computers to control production equipment and indirectly to support manufacturing operations. CAM software may be used to facilitate planning, operation and control on a production facility. Workflow management is the automation of a business process, in whole or part during which documents, information or tasks are passed from one participant to another for action, according to the set of procedural rules. Workflow systems are used to automate business processes, enabling tasks to be assigned to people. Different types of workflow system exist according to the work supported. Examples of production systems include those used in call centres, for example, for assessing insurance claims.

Logistics management deals with ordering, purchasing, inbound logistics (receiving), and outbound logistics (shipping) activities. All of these activities can be supported by information systems – see for example e-procurement systems. In-house logistics activities are a good example of processes that cross several primary and support activities in the value chain. Three costs play important roles in inventory management decisions: the cost of maintaining inventory, the cost of ordering (a fixed cost per order), and the cost of not having inventory when needed (the shortage or opportunity cost). Two basic decisions are made by operations: when to order and how much. Inventory models such as the economic order quantity (EOQ) model support these decisions. Where the inventory falls to a certain level, called the reorder point, the computer automatically generates a purchase order. The order is transferred electronically either to a vendor or to the manufacturing department if restocking is done in-house.

Computer integrated manufacturing is a concept or philosophy about the implementation of various integrated computer systems in factory automation, see Figure 15-9. For example, it may integrate technologies such as flexible manufacturing systems, JIT, MRP, CAD, CAE, and group technology. The computer integrated manufacturing model support families of processes used in product and process definition, manufacturing planning and control and factory automation.

Large amounts of information are generated and used during the management of operations. This information will also be used in many if not all other parts of the organization. Consequently, a technical solution is required to integrate disparate systems and make the information widely available. Enterprise resource planning software discussed in Chapter 13 represents the main solution to this problem. In Chapter 13 we explained how materials requirement planning evolved into ERP software. In this section we have focused on the acquisition of and investment in fixed assets such as buildings and systems used by operations. In Chapter 12 we identified people, systems and procedures as elements of infrastructure and in the next section we discuss the processes associated with the operations environment. First we consider processes associated with product and service design and then consider production (transformational) processes.

Production-related processes

Look back
See chapter 10

New-product or service development is an essential part of business. A process represents a way of doing something such as designing or producing products and services; in this section we consider such processes. We discussed business processes in Chapter 10 and consider operations and related processes in more detail here. It is important to note that process design and product/service design are interrelated. People often treat the design of products and services and the design of the processes which make them as separate activities. Once a product has been designed, operational managers must make important decisions concerning processes for producing those goods or services. The choice of production process is discussed following the section on product and service design. Finally in this section we review another process choice – whether the product is made-to-order or to stock, i.e. customer or supply led and the processes associated with the customization of the designed products and services.

Designing and developing offerings

Operations managers may not have direct responsibility for product and service design but will provide information and advice upon which product or service development will depend. It is important to note that the design activity is itself a process, arguably the most important, see Figure 15-10. End products are the final goods and services produced by the organization based on utilizing the competences that it possesses. Product design can be thought of as the characteristics or features of a product or service that determine its ability to meet the needs of the user. In contrast the product development process is the overall process of strategy, organization, concept generation, product and marketing plan creation and evaluation, and commercialization of a new product, see Figure 15-10. In order to reach a final design of a product or service, the design activity must pass through several stages. Stages are not, however, necessarily followed in a linear fashion.

Designers frequently return to previous activities. While there are many ways to describe the product development process, the first phase of a product development effort is typically termed the *concept development phase*. Here a company identifies ideas for new or revised products and services. Ideas for new products or services can come from many different sources inside and outside the organization. New ideas may come from customers,

Product development process the overall process of strategy, organization, concept generation, product and marketing plan creation and evaluation, and commercialization of a new product

Figure 15-10

Development and production processes

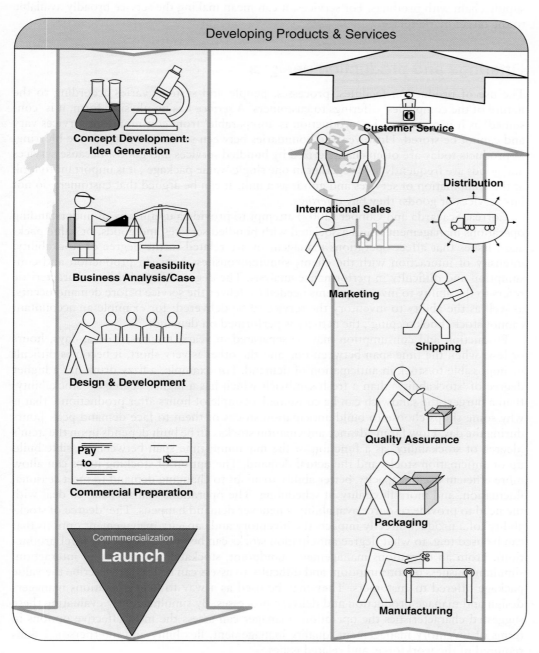

competitors, front office staff or the research and development department. Not all concerns will be developed into products and services.

The second (*screening and planning*) phase of a product development effort begins to address the feasibility of a product or service. Organizations will assess the ability of an operation to produce a product or service (feasibility), the acceptability of the product or service (will customers want it?) and the associated risks.

Having created a feasible, acceptable and viable product or service concept, the next stage is to create a *preliminary design*. The company invests heavily in the development effort and builds and evaluates prototypes (*design and development phase*). Preliminary designs are evaluated and improved upon.

In the fourth phase of a product development effort (*commercial preparation phase*) the organization invests heavily in the operations and supply chain resources (infrastructure) needed to support the new product or service. The final phase of a product development effort is termed the *launch phase*. For physical products, this usually means 'filling up' the supply chain with products. For services, it can mean making the service broadly available to the target marketplace.

Offerings and production designs

The use of production facilities, processes, people and systems varies according to the nature of the companies' offerings to customers. A *service* has no physical form, it is 'consumed' as it is produced, i.e. production is 'inseparable' from consumption; services vary and cannot be stored. However, the boundaries between services and goods are blurring, as products today are often characterized by bundled services and goods. Because services and goods are frequently sold together in one single 'value package', it is important to look at the combination of services and goods as a unit. It can be argued that customers do not buy services or goods: they buy *offerings*.

Corrêa, Scavarda and Cooper (2007) attempt to provide a useful way of understanding operations management issues associated with bundled services and goods, or value packages. Issues that affect operations management are related to the degree of stockability; intensity of interaction with the client; simultaneousness between production and consumption and difficulty in performance analysis. The degree of *stockability* characteristic refers to the ability to inventory items needed to deliver the service before demand occurs, as well as the ability to inventory the service to be delivered; for example an accountant cannot stock 'bookkeeping', the activity is performed on demand.

Production and consumption may be separated in years, months, weeks, days, hours or less; when the time span between one and the other is very short, it becomes difficult or impossible to stock in anticipation of demand. For example, a fizzy drink has a higher degree of 'stockability' than a fresh sandwich which has a higher degree of 'stockability' than a burger; the sandwich can be consumed a couple of hours after production – that is why some shops choose to build anticipation stocks of them to face demand peak hours during the day. How far in advance anticipation stocks can be built depends upon the item's 'degree of stockability' as a function of the maximum time span between possible build up of anticipation stocks and the actual demand. The option of stocking items can allow more efficient use of capacity, better ability to adapt to changing demand to meet seasonal fluctuation, and more flexibility in scheduling. The operations manager has to deal with the need to provide resource availability whenever demand happens. The 'degree of stockability' of a product directly impacts the inventory and capacity management options that can be used (e.g. to what degree anticipation stocks can be built up to better level production). From an operations management standpoint, stockability, intensity of interaction, simultaneousness of consumption, and difficulty to assess can be used to describe the value package offered to customers. They may be used as a way to help operations managers design and manage production and delivery processes. By simultaneously evaluating these suggested characteristics the operations manager can assess the most effective options in terms of inventory management, quality management, flexibility and interpersonal skills required of the workforce, and related issues.

This can help with planning of operations to better understand requirements before a change is implemented, allowing for anticipation of changes in the cost and process structure of the operations. It can help with the execution of change by identifying the options and limitations associated with each value package characteristic. This proposed approach can also help to identify and provide insights into day-to-day management issues, such as the skill sets required of employees (Corrêa, Scavarda and Cooper 2007). In the next section we consider production process decisions.

Process choice

Operations managers must make important decisions concerning processes for *producing* goods and services (the right-hand side of Figure 15-10) selected for launch. They must select and improve processes and related technologies. Process selection decisions tend to be strategic in nature, requiring a long-term perspective and cross-functional coordination. Various process selection decisions are encountered. In this section we focus on two types of process – product flow and by type of customer order (e.g. make-to-order or make-to-stock). Organizations may have to do produce very high volumes of products or services or very low volumes; consequently there are different processes to support different requirements. Different operations, even those in the same organization, may adopt different types of processes. A manufacturing plant may be designed with a large area for mass production to make their high-volume best selling products but in another part of the plant may have an area set to one side for the production of wider variety products in smaller volumes. Several types of production process exist, see Figure 15-11.

The way international businesses create products and services is known as the production process. Ultimately, the objective of the production process is to create goods and services that meet customer requirements. The needs of customers will be met if a business can produce the correct number of products, in the shortest possible time, to the best quality and at low cost. The process architecture may be an important component in the organization's strategy for building competitive advantage.

Production process the way that businesses create products and services

Figure 15-11
Production processes evaluated

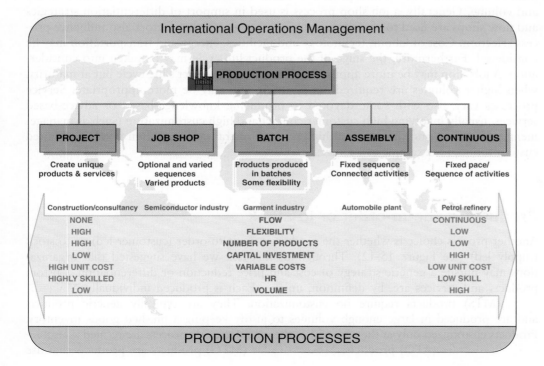

		International Operations Management		
		PRODUCTION PROCESS		
PROJECT	**JOB SHOP**	**BATCH**	**ASSEMBLY**	**CONTINUOUS**
Create unique products & services	Optional and varied sequences Varied products	Products produced in batches Some flexibility	Fixed sequence Connected activities	Fixed pace/ Sequence of activities
Construction/consultancy	Semiconductor industry	Garment industry	Automobile plant	Petrol refinery

NONE	FLOW		CONTINUOUS
HIGH	FLEXIBILITY		LOW
HIGH	NUMBER OF PRODUCTS		LOW
LOW	CAPITAL INVESTMENT		HIGH
HIGH UNIT COST	VARIABLE COSTS		LOW UNIT COST
HIGHLY SKILLED	HR		LOW SKILL
LOW	VOLUME		HIGH

PRODUCTION PROCESSES

The production process is concerned with transforming a range of inputs into those outputs that are required by the market. Two sets of resources are needed – the transforming resources (the facilities, machinery, technology, and people to carry out the transforming processes – see Parts III and IV of this book), and the raw material inputs (transformed resources). At each stage value is added in the course of production. Adding value involves making a product more attractive to a consumer so they will pay more for it. Adding value is not restricted to operations, but may relate to all supply chain processes such as marketing, etc. that make the final product more desirable. There are several key types of production process – project, job shop, batch, assembly line and continuous flow, see Figure 15-11.

- Project processes deal with discrete, usually highly customized, products.

Job shop a type of (flexible) manufacturing process used to make a wide variety of highly customized products in quantities as small as one

- Jobbing processes deal with high variety and low volumes, although there may be some repetition of flow and activities. The 'job shop' is a type of (flexible) manufacturing process used to make a wide variety of highly customized products in quantities as small as one. Job shops are characterized by general-purpose equipment and workers who are broadly skilled.

Production line a set of sequential operations established in a factory whereby materials are transformed to produce an end-product or components are assembled to make a finished article

- A production line is a set of sequential operations established in a factory whereby materials are transformed to produce an end-product or components are assembled to make a finished article. The production line is a type of manufacturing process used to produce a narrow range of standard items with identical or highly similar designs.

Continuous flow process a type of manufacturing process that closely resembles a production line process

- Closely resembling the production line process is the continuous flow process – a type of manufacturing process that closely resembles a production line process. The main difference is the form of the product, which usually cannot be broken into discrete units. Examples include yarns and fabric, food products, and chemical products such as oil or gas.

- Mass processes produce goods in high volume and relatively low variety.

- Batch manufacturing is a type of manufacturing process where items are moved through the different manufacturing steps in groups or batches.

Process flow structures impact upon facility layout, technology decisions and work methods. We have identified types of production process and now consider how the organization determines the optimal process. Process selection is influenced by product variety and volume. Generally, a job shop process is used in support of differentiation strategies and flow shops are used to support cost-based strategies. Other factors also influence process selection. Cost of labour, technology and facilities, energy and transportation may be considered. Furthermore, the stage of the product life cycle may be taken into consideration. A job shop may be more appropriate early in the product's life cycle but at maturity, when higher volumes are required, an assembly line may be more appropriate. Service processes vary also with some devoted to producing knowledge-based or advice-based services, usually involving high customer contact and high customization (such as management consultants) and those with a high number of transactions, often involving limited customization, for example call centres.

Make-to-stock a supply chain model that focuses on producing goods and restocking the finished goods inventory based upon estimates of customer demand

Products made-to-order or to-stock

Assemble-to-order a production environment where a product or service can be made after receipt of a customer's order

Another process choice is whether the product is made-to-order (customer led) or to stock (supply led) (see Figure 15-12). Throughout this text we have suggested that organizations may pursue a generic strategy of cost and price reduction or differentiation. Custom products and services are, by definition, unique. Each is produced individually. Make-to-stock (MTS) products require no customization. They are typically generic products and are produced in large enough volumes to justify keeping a finished goods inventory. Products customized only at the very end of the manufacturing process are termed assemble-or finish-to-order (ATO) products. Make-to-order (MTO) products are products that use

Make-to-order the production of goods or components to meet an existing order – make-to-order products are made to the customer's specification, and are often processed in small batches

standard components, but the final configuration of those components is customer-specific. Finally, products that are designed and produced from the start to meet unusual customer needs or requirements are called engineer-to-order (ETO) products. They represent the highest level of customization. When customization occurs early in the supply chain, organizations have more flexibility to respond to customer needs but costs increase and lead times lengthen. When customization occurs late in the supply chain, flexibility is limited but lead times and cost may be less.

Engineer-to-order products that are designed and produced from the outset to meet unusual customer needs or requirements – they represent the highest level of customization

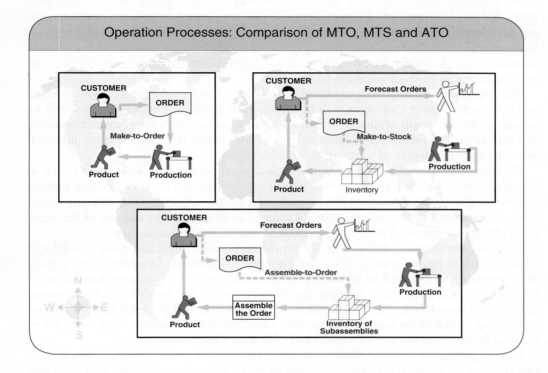

Figure 15-12

Make-to-order and make-to-stock processes

> What production and customization models might you expect at Burberry, Dell or Dyson?

STOP & THINK

Forecasting demand

Thus far we have focused on the operations strategy and infrastructure – creating production capacity and (supply) capabilities. *Planning and control* is concerned with operating resources on a day-to-day basis, ensuring availability of materials and other resources in order to supply the goods and services to fulfil customers' demands. The purpose of planning and control is to match supply with demand through the effective and efficient management of the operations processes. Planning is about preparing for the future and makes use of demand forecasts for the near, medium and possibly long term. Control is an ongoing process which either seeks to correct actions and assure the plan is achieved or involves activities of re-planning to cope with unforeseen events and change.

We have noted that planning relies upon forecasts of demand yet throughout this text-book we have commented on the turbulent nature of the business environment. With constant change comes uncertainty, making planning and control more difficult. Some operations can predict demand with more certainty than others. Consequently, within business we may observe a variety of responses to demand. Certain organizations will only buy in resources and produce their goods and services following the receipt and order from a customer. This approach has been labelled resource-to-order. In such cases, the organization is unlikely to maintain an inventory of raw materials. Other organizations, facing less uncertainty in demand, may maintain stocks of raw materials but will only produce products upon receipt of a customer order, i.e. they create or make-to-order. Finally, organizations that face least uncertainty may produce products before orders are received. Some operations (called make-to-stock operations) produced their product and services in advance of any demand – see previous section. Organizations with operations of this type will require make-to-stock planning and control.

The organizational approach to planning and control will impact upon responsiveness and the length of time customers wait to receive their product. The waiting time will be influenced by the length of time it takes the organization to obtain the resources, produce and deliver the product or service (throughput time). Clearly, the make-to-stock approach indicates a greater degree of speculation, i.e. risk-taking.

Planning and control requires the reconciliation of supply and demand in terms of volumes, timing and quality. One of the planning problems and areas of decision-making is concerned with the amount of work a particular centre will undertake. The amount of work allocated to a work centre is termed *loading*. Loading must take account of the maximum capacity of the work centre and periods of unavailability (holidays, etc.).

A second key decision and activity within planning and control addresses the order in which work is to be performed. This activity is termed *sequencing*. Sequencing may depend on a variety of factors such as physical constraints; sometimes a customer priority factor may influence the sequencing as might the date the item is due for delivery. Some operations serve customers in exactly the sequence they arrive; this is called first-in first-out sequencing or first-come first-served. In other cases operations schedule the longest job to be done first so as to occupy its work centres for longer periods.

If an organization has cash flow problems they may well tackle the short jobs first so that they can be invoiced and payment received faster. Job sequencing rules may therefore impact upon dependability (meeting the due date), speed and cost. Some organizations require a detailed timetable showing at what time or date jobs should start and when they should end. This is termed *scheduling* (as an example, imagine a bus schedule or time-table). Scheduling is a complex task. There are different approaches governing when work may start. Work may start as soon as it arrives (forward scheduling) or at the last possible moment to prevent it being late (backward scheduling). Forward scheduling provides for more flexibility and higher labour utilization while backward scheduling results in lower material costs and can more easily accommodate changing customer requirements.

Employee work times are also scheduled (staff rosters) to ensure that sufficient numbers of people are working at any point in time to provide appropriate capacity for the level of demand at that point in time. Having created a plan for the operation through *loading*, *sequencing* and *scheduling,* each part of the operation is monitored to ensure that planned activities take place. Information is an essential part of managing operations and supply chains. Information is used to support the development of long-range plans, coordinate activities in the supply chain, support routine decision-making, and record transaction data.

Forecasting and managing capacity

How much product is needed, where and when?

The availability of transformational resources and raw materials will impact upon the level of value added activity of which an operation is capable in any given period (capacity).

Organizations typically operate below capacity because of a lack of demand or intentionally so that the operation can respond quickly to new orders. In some cases, one part of an organization may be operating at their capacity ceiling but this may constrain other parts of the organization that may be reliant upon their outputs. Capacity planning and control is the task of setting the effective capacity of the operation so it can respond to the demands placed upon it.

Long-term capacity strategies will consider transforming assets such as buildings, large machinery and staffing levels whereas other capacity strategies may be determined within the constraints of the physical capacity limits set by the operation's long-term capacity strategy. Operations managers may also make decisions to adjust capacity in the medium and short term. Capacity strategies have an impact on cost. Capacity levels in excess of demand could mean underutilization of capacity and therefore high unit cost. If demand is higher than capacity then revenue may be lost. Building up inventories may diminish working capital, hiring temporary staff may impact upon the quality of goods produced and as we have mentioned previously, speed, dependability and flexibility may be affected.

Capacity planning and control activities are typically decomposed to three steps:

1 forecast demand;

2 identify alternative capacity strategies; and

3 select the most appropriate strategy.

A forecast is an estimate of the future level of some variable. Common variables forecasted include demand levels, supply levels, and prices. Forecasting is a critical business process for nearly every organization; it is often the first step in planning future business activities. Forecasting is often the responsibility of the sales and marketing function that is a key input to capacity planning and control.

Demand forecasts should be as accurate as possible and expressed in terms which are useful for capacity planning and control. Many organizations experience seasonal demand fluctuations which may be forecast to some extent. However, unexpected variations in the weather and economic conditions make forecasting problematic. Whereas some fluctuations occur on a longer (annual) cycle, others may occur in a shorter cycle, i.e. daily or weekly patterns. For some organizations these patterns may be predictable, i.e. the organization may be busier in the afternoon rather than the morning, etc. In any event, capacity adjustments may need to be made.

Not only should demand be measured as effectively as possible so too should capacity – both can be difficult to measure. Capacity is the capability of a worker, machine, work centre, plant, or organization to produce output per time period. Some of the most important strategic decisions revolve around capacity – how much is needed and when? Capacity planning is concerned with satisfying demand and identifies how many customers can be served at any given time. Capacity decisions are made to accommodate expected growth in demand or product lines.

There are three common capacity strategies: the lead capacity strategy is a capacity strategy in which capacity is added in anticipation of demand; in contrast the lag capacity strategy is a capacity strategy in which capacity is added only after demand has materialized. A capacity strategy that strikes a balance between the lead and lag capacity strategies by avoiding periods of high under- or overutilization is named a match capacity strategy. Such capacity alternatives vary in their cost (fixed and variable) benefits. The percentage of a resource's capacity that is used in production is termed utilization. For example, an organization's production may be reduced because of time lost waiting for materials. This might result in a labour utilization of below 100 per cent.

The organization may respond to demand fluctuations by either doing nothing (level capacity planning), adjusting capacity to reflect demand or may attempt to manage demand itself. The methods used to adjust capacity include: varying the size of the workforce, using part-time staff, paying existing staff overtime and subcontracting. Similarly there are different approaches to managing demand. An organization may lower its prices in order to stimulate demand. Discounts may be used during quieter periods in order to attract custom. Organizations can also attempt to increase demand in low periods by appropriate

Capacity the maximum production possible – the amount of work a production unit, whether individual or group, can accomplish in a given amount of time

Lead capacity strategy a capacity strategy in which capacity is added in anticipation of demand

Lag capacity strategy a capacity strategy in which capacity is added only after demand has materialized

Match capacity strategy a capacity strategy that strikes a balance between the lead and lag capacity strategies by avoiding periods of high under- or overutilization

Utilization the percentage of a resource's capacity that is used in production

advertising. Alternatively, the organization could develop alternative products that may be produced using existing processes but have different demand patterns throughout the year.

Sales and operations planning a business process that helps organizations plan and coordinate operations and supply chain decisions over a tactical time horizon

Sales and operations planning (S&OP) is a business process to help organizations plan and coordinate operations and supply chain decisions over a tactical time horizon (usually 4 to 12 months). S&OP indicates how the organization will use its capacity to meet demand and serves as a coordinating mechanism for the various supply chain partners. There are two major approaches to S&OP: top-down planning and bottom-up planning. Top-down planning is an approach to S&OP where a single, aggregated sales forecast drives the planning process. For top-down planning to work, the mix of products or services must be essentially be the same from one time period to the next, or the products or services to be provided must have very similar resource requirements. The process of generating a top-down plan consists of three steps:

- develop the aggregate sales forecast;
- translate it into resource requirements; and then
- generate alternative production plans.

Bottom-up planning is an approach to S&OP used when the product/service mix is unstable and resource requirements vary greatly across the offerings. Under such conditions, managers will need to estimate the requirements for each set of products or services separately and then add them up to get an overall picture of the resource requirements. Whichever approach is taken, the support of suppliers is often critical.

Sourcing strategies

Should we make or buy the raw materials and inputs?

High-level, often strategic decisions regarding which products or services will be provided internally and which will be provided by external supply chain partners are referred to as sourcing (make-or-buy) decisions. Insourcing concerns the use of resources within the organization to provide products or services as opposed to outsourcing where supply chain partners provide products or services. Such decisions are not without consequences. Insourcing provides for greater control and opportunity for scale advantages but may require high levels of investment and a loss of access to superior products. Outsourcing may enhance flexibility, improve cash flow and allow access to state-of-the-art products and services but creates communication and coordination challenges, reduces control and introduces the possibility of selecting an ineffective bad supplier.

Sourcing method used to obtain raw materials or component parts

Insourcing a service performed in-house

Outsourcing the practice of having goods or services provided by an outside organization

Several sourcing strategies are recognized. In single sourcing, a single supplier is relied upon as opposed to a sourcing strategy in which the buying organization shares its business across multiple suppliers. A sourcing strategy in which the company uses a single supplier for a certain part or service in one part of the business and another supplier with the same capabilities for a similar part in another area of the business is known as cross-sourcing. Each supplier is then awarded new business based on its performance, creating an incentive for both to improve. Finally, a sourcing strategy in which two suppliers are used for the same purchased product or service is termed dual sourcing. Purchasing concerns the activities associated with identifying needs, locating and selecting suppliers, negotiating terms, and following up to ensure supplier performance. The purchasing process and procurement was discussed in Chapter 14 (refer to e-procurement).

Sourcing may take place within or outside the home country. Global sourcing is the process of identifying, evaluating negotiating and configuring supply across multiple geographies. When evaluating global sourcing opportunities, the organization should consider the purchase price, transportation costs, inventory carrying costs, cross-border taxes, tariffs and duty costs, supply performance and risks. Operations may also seek to ensure they only deal with ethical suppliers (refer back to Chapter 4).

Managing production

Operations managers make decisions that are frequently oriented toward efficiency goals. Efficiency is concerned with the relationship between the result achieved and the resources used. Productivity is an economic measure of efficiency that summarizes the value of outputs relative to the value of inputs used to create them. The three factors critical to productivity improvements are labour, capital and management. Management are responsible for ensuring labour and capital are used effectively to increase productivity. Organizations often find it helpful to compare their business processes with those of competitors or even other organizations with similar processes. This activity is known as benchmarking (*see* Figure 10-14 Tools and techniques for improvement) – the process of identifying, understanding, and adapting outstanding practices from within the same organization or from other businesses to help improve performance. In Chapter 10 we discussed strategies for business process improvement; *see* continuous improvement – a principle of TQM that assumes there will always be room for improvement, no matter how well an organization is doing and business process re-engineering (BPR) – a procedure that involves the fundamental rethinking and radical redesign of business processes to achieve dramatic organizational improvements in such critical measures of performance as cost, quality, service, and speed. Production management decisions are also made with the company's competitive strategy in mind.

Earlier we discussed time-based competition and the need to compress activities in order to improve responsiveness. The total elapsed time needed to complete a business process is called cycle time also throughput time; for a line process, it is the actual time between completion of successive units on a production line. Contemporary international organizations seek out methods constantly to reduce cycle times. While there are many ways to reduce cycle times, the reduction of the time required to execute a task or produce a product is often achieved through the use of information technologies (see Chapter 13 – the functional business systems section). Companies also compete on quality and the operations manager must be mindful of the impact of transformational activities on quality.

Quality, also discussed in Chapter 10, refers to the characteristics of a product or service that bear on its ability to satisfy stated or implied needs (fitness for use). Acceptable quality level (AQL) represents the maximum defect level a consumer would accept. Internal failure costs are costs caused by defects that occur prior to delivery to the customer, including money spent on repairing or reworking defective products, as well as time wasted on these activities. In order to reduce costs and better satisfy customers, the international organization attempts to manage quality within and across the supply chain. Total quality management (TQM) is a managerial approach in which the entire organization is managed so that it excels in all quality dimensions important to customers. Core ideas associated

Productivity an economic measure of efficiency that summarizes the value of outputs relative to the value of inputs used to create them

Look back
See chapter 10, p. 331

Cycle time the time it takes a product to go from beginning to end of a production process; i.e. the time it is work-in-process

Throughput (the rate of production) the output rate of a production process

Look back
See chapter 10, p. 323

with the TQM business philosophy include: customer focus, leadership involvement, continuous improvement, employee empowerment, quality assurance, supplier partnerships and a strategic quality plan. Continuous improvement tools and techniques were discussed earlier. Managing quality throughout the supply chain may be facilitated through the use and adoption of quality standards. For example, ISO 9000 is a family of standards, supported by the International Organization for Standardization, representing an international consensus on good quality management practices. ISO 9000 addresses business processes rather than specific outcomes.

Managing production across the supply chain

Scheduling decisions (see previous section) allocate, over time, available capacity or resources to jobs, activities or customers and their orders. Scheduling is an *allocation decision* which follows many of the key decisions discussed thus far. Planning and control concerns a set of tactical and execution-level business activities that include master scheduling, material requirements planning, and some form of production activity control and vendor order management. Planning and control begins where S&OP ends. The first step in planning and control is *master scheduling* in which the overall resource levels established by S&OP are developed further. Master scheduling is a detailed planning process that tracks production output and matches this output to actual customer orders.

The master schedule states exactly when and in what quantities specific products will be made. It also links production with specific customer orders, allowing the organization to tell the customer exactly when an order will be filled. The master schedule is used to track demand, orders, inventory levels and units available to meet customer needs (*available to promise*, ATP). ATP is shown on the master schedule and is used to make delivery promises to customers. It is calculated by subtracting from each point of supply (master schedule receipt) actual customer's orders up to the next point of supply. Together with capacity planning and S&OP, master scheduling provides a set of planning tools for the operations manager.

Material requirements planning (MRP) takes the process one step further; it is a planning process that translates the master production schedule into planned orders for the actual parts and components needed to produce the master schedule items. The complexity of MRP demands that such systems be computerized. Furthermore, for an MRP system to work properly, it must have accurate information.

At the lowest level are two further systems: production activity control (PAC) and vendor order management. The former assures that in-house manufacturing takes place according to plan and the latter assures that materials ordered from supply chain partners are received when needed. PAC may make use of job sequencing rules – rules used to determine the order in which jobs should be processed when resources are limited and multiple jobs are waiting to be done. Other useful technologies for monitoring and tracking include radio frequency identification (RFID), bar coding, and online order tracking systems developed to trace the movement and location of materials in the supply chain. Throughout the processes discussed thus far is a need to manage raw materials, work-in-process and finished goods. We finish this chapter with discussion about logistics.

Logistics

Logistics the management of both inbound and outbound materials, parts, supplies and finished goods

The management of the physical flow of products from the point of origin as raw materials to end-users as finished products is termed logistics. Logistics is that part of the supply chain process that plans, implements, and controls the efficient, effective flow and storage of goods, services, and related information from the point of origin to the point of consumption in order to meet customer requirements. Logistics covers a wide range of business activities such as: transportation, warehousing, material handling, packaging, inventory management and logistics information systems. Logistical operations impact upon costs, flexibility and delivery performance and are critical to many international organizations. Transportation *modes* include the roads, water, air, rail and pipeline. Each has its own advantages and disadvantages. Road transport is flexible but costly, water transport is typically slow but cheap and air transport is both the quickest and most expensive. Many organizations adopt a multimodal system i.e. they seek to exploit the strengths of multiple transportation modes through physical, information, and monetary flows that are as seamless as possible. The logistics strategy is a functional strategy ensuring an organization's logistics choices – transportation, warehousing, information systems, and even form of ownership are consistent with its overall business strategy and support the performance dimensions most valued by targeted customers. As logistics becomes more globalized and information-intensive, more organizations are outsourcing the logistics function to specialists, most notably third-party logistics providers (3PLs).

Transportation systems represent just one part of the physical flow of goods and materials – the other is *warehousing*; any operation that stores, repackages, stages, sorts, or centralizes goods or materials. Organizations use warehousing to reduce transportation costs, improve operational flexibility, shorten customer lead times, and lower inventory costs. A form of warehousing that pulls together shipments from a number of sources (often plants) in the same geographical area and combines them into larger – and hence more economical – shipping loads is known as *consolidation warehousing*. There are several other types of warehousing. A form of warehousing in which large incoming shipments are received and then broken down into smaller outgoing shipments to demand points in a geographic area is termed *cross-docking*. This combines the economies of large incoming shipments with the flexibility of smaller local shipments. Those stocks or items used to support production (raw materials and work-in-process items), supporting activities (maintenance, repair, and operating supplies) and customer service (finished goods and spare parts) are known as inventory. In general, using slower and cheaper transportation modes will cause inventory levels within the supply chain to rise, while using faster and more expensive modes enables organizations to lower inventory levels.

The international organization must identify where its customers are located and in what quantity; they need to consider export volumes, the value density of their products and whether or not customers require rapid delivery. Such factors will influence distribution channel, transportation and storage decisions. Several alternative distribution channel strategies or models exist such as:

1 *direct* – on receiving an order a manufacturer, without the aid of intermediaries, may seek to transport goods directly to the customer. This may result in higher transportation costs and longer lead times;

2 *transit* – using this model, the international organization will have exports sent to a warehouse in another country;

3 *classical* – in such cases each country will have its own separate warehouse; and

4 *multi-country* – a depot may serve several particular countries.

Material handling and packaging are important because of the impact they can have on transportation, warehousing, logistics and information systems. Material handling systems include the equipment and procedures needed to move goods within a facility, between a facility and a transportation mode, and between different transportation modes (e.g., ship-to-truck transfers). From a logistics perspective, packaging refers to the way goods and materials are packed in order to facilitate physical, informational, and monetary flows through the supply chain.

Managing inventory

Inventory management remains an important function with some organizations arguing for less and others more inventory. Dell prefers less inventory, Li & Fung see it as the

Inventory stock on hand; often divided between raw materials inventory, work-in-process and finished goods inventory

Inventory management controlling stock levels within the physical distribution function to balance the need for product availability against the need for minimizing stock holding and handling costs

Cycle stock the stock that is ordered from a supplier to meet the demand for a certain time period. It is based on a forecast for an item and is reordered at a point where the next delivery will occur just in time to meet demand for the next cycle

Safety stock safety stock or buffer stock exists to counter uncertainties in supply or demand

Just-in-time production a method of operating production facilities in such a way that production only takes place when customers place an order

root of all evil. Too much may result in waste while too little and the organization may be caught out by a surprise. Inventory may be classified in a number of ways. Components or products that are received in bulk by a downstream partner, gradually used up, and then replenished again in bulk by the upstream partner are referred to as cycle stock.

Extra inventory held by companies to protect themselves against uncertainties in either demand or replenishment time is called safety stock – it is there just in case. Safety stock or buffer stock exists to counter uncertainties in supply or demand. For example, a supplier may deliver their product late, the warehouse may be on strike or a number of items may be of poor quality. In addition, a competitor may be sold out on a product, increasing demand. Safety stocks enable organizations to satisfy customer demand in the event of these possibilities.

Anticipation inventory is held in anticipation of customer demand. It allows instant availability of items when customers want them. Inventory that is moving from one link in the supply chain to another is termed transportation inventory. Inventory, while useful in meeting demand, ties up space and capital and may become obsolete. Organizations may be exposed to both upstream and downstream risks. There is a risk that component flows may be interrupted thus delaying operations. On the downstream side, organizations face demand uncertainty.

Just-in-time (JIT) popularized in the late 1980s and closely aligned with TQM, is a philosophy of manufacturing based on planned elimination of all waste and on continuous improvement of productivity. JIT is an inventory strategy companies employ to increase efficiency and decrease waste by receiving goods only as they are needed in the production process, thereby reducing inventory costs. The central concept of JIT is about reducing inventories by working closely with suppliers to coordinate delivery of materials just before their use in the manufacturing or supply process. Goods arrive when needed (just in time) for production or use rather than becoming expensive inventory that occupies costly warehouse space. In the broad sense, it applies to all forms of manufacturing and to many service industries as well. Lean production (to do more with less) is a term commonly used to refer to just-in-time production.

Waste according to the JIT perspective is any activity that does not add value to the good or service in the eyes of the consumer. There are many sources of waste such as: overproduction, unnecessary transportation or inventory, underutilization of employees, defects or inappropriate ways of working. The JIT perspective on inventory places strong emphasis on reducing raw materials, work-in-process, and finished goods inventories throughout the system.

In summary, JIT is both a business philosophy and a specific approach to production control. A good example would be a car manufacturer that operates with very low inventory levels, relying on their supply chain to deliver the parts they need to build cars. The parts needed to manufacture the cars arrive just as they are needed. This inventory supply system represents a shift away from the older 'just in case' strategy where producers carried large inventories in case higher demand had to be met. The main downside to JIT is capacity utilization. With the JIT approach there is lower capacity utilization but no surplus product goes into inventory and this in turn exposes problems for early consideration leading to less production stoppages; the overall focus is on producing only when needed as opposed to the traditional approach which focuses on high capacity utilization. Key aspects of the lean philosophy include the elimination of waste, the involvement of everyone and continuous improvement.

Summary of key learning points

The collection of people, knowledge, technology, and systems within an organization that has primary responsibility for producing and providing the organization's products or services is referred to as operations; the traditional way to think about operations is as a transformation process which takes a set of inputs and transforms them in some way to create outputs (goods or services – offerings) that a customer values. The mechanisms transforming inputs into outputs are called processes.

Operations management (OM) is the planning, scheduling, control and coordination of the activities that transform inputs into finished goods and services. Operations management is important because it can reduce costs, differentiate the organization's products and services and impact upon quality and therefore may increase revenue through increased customer satisfaction. The fundamental role of operations is to implement corporate strategy.

Operational managers are responsible for providing sufficient capacity to meet the organizations' needs. Facilities decisions are of significant strategic importance to the international organization and the operations function in particular. Such decisions place physical constraints on the amount that can be produced and may require large amounts of capital investment.

One of the most important strategic decisions made by some companies is where to locate their operations. One of the first tasks for the international organization is to determine which countries in which to operate. Frequently, the organization will identify the critical success factors needed to achieve competitive advantage. Factors such as political risk, cultural and economic issues, availability of talented human resources, the availability of supplies and energy, communication and transportation network and financial risks such as exchange rate in currency may all be considered when evaluating possible countries within which to locate.

After selecting the country(ies), the next step will be to narrow down options by selecting particular regions and will then focus on a specific site. Once a location has been selected, decisions about layout must be made. Choices of technology, production process and supporting systems also require important decisions from the operations manager.

The product development process is the overall process of strategy, organization, concept generation, product and marketing plan creation and evaluation, and commercialization of a new product. Operations managers must then decide upon which process to adopt when producing such goods and services. Process selection decisions tend to be strategic in nature, requiring a long-term perspective and cross-functional coordination. The way international businesses create products and services is known as the production process. Ultimately, the objective of the production process is to create goods and services that meet customer requirements. A related process choice is whether the product is made-to-order (customer led) or to stock (supply led).

Planning and control is concerned with operating resources on a day-to-day basis, ensuring availability of materials and other resources in order to supply the goods and services to fulfil customers' demands. The purpose of planning and control is to match supply with demand through the effective and efficient management of the operations processes. The availability of transformational resources and raw materials will impact upon the level of value added activity of which an operation is capable in any given period (capacity). Operations managers make decisions that are frequently oriented toward efficiency goals.

Productivity is an economic measure of efficiency that summarizes the value of outputs relative to the value of inputs used to create them. The three factors critical to productivity improvements are labour, capital and management. The management of the physical flow of products from the point of origin as raw materials to end users as finished products is termed logistics. Logistics covers a wide range of business activities such as: transportation, warehousing, material handling, packaging and inventory management.

Review questions

Opening case study

1 Compare and contrast this location decision with that at Burberry.
2 How important is it to locate R&D near to production? How important is it to locate production near to suppliers or customers?

3 With reference to the technologies and systems introduced in Part IV of this book, what resources may help the organization manage the differences between locations (e.g. R&D and production) in time and space?

4 Discuss arguments for a spatial division of labour in the context of globalization; identify advantages that Malaysia has as a manufacturing location. What advantages are there in having the UK as an R&D location?

5 What is the relationship between R&D, product development and production?

Production process

Evaluate and recommend production processes for (1) the Dyson vacuum cleaner and (2) the wing of a now obsolete aeroplane – only five are required.

You should explain the factors considered, i.e. what influenced your choice of process.

Discuss how an organization could best manage production when initially they expect low demand for standard products but that success will follow and high demand will be observed?

Critical decisions in international operations management

Identify and describe the most important decisions made in international operations management.

Product development

Describe how products are typically developed in the international organization. Identify who is typically involved with each stage and explain why. Explain why a cross-functional approach is critical for success.

What are the advantages of computer aided design?

Location strategies

Describe the factors that affect location decisions at the country, regional and site level. Why shouldn't low wage rates alone act as the sole decision criterion for relocation to a different country?

Capacity planning

Discuss the circumstances or conditions that might determine whether or not an organization pursues a lag or a lead capacity strategy.

Inventory management

Describe the different types of inventory.

Critically discuss cost implications associated with the inventory system.

References

Ansari, A., Lockwood, D. and Modarress, B. (1992) 'Characteristics of periodicals for potential authors and readers in production and operations management', *International Journal of Operations & Production Management* 12(6):56–62.

Barman, S., Tersine, R. J. and Buckley, M. R. (1991) 'An empirical assessment of the perceived relevance and quality of POM related journals by academicians', *J. Oper. Mgmt.* 10(2):194–212.

Boone, T., Johnson, S. P., Sisk, M. and Whybark, D. C. (1996) 'An analysis of research on international operations networks', *International Journal of Production Economics* (December 1996) 46–47:477–488.

Boudreau, J., Hopp, W., McClain, J. O. and Thomas, L. J. (2003) 'On the interface between operations and human resources management', *Manufacturing & Service Operations Management* 5(3):179–202.

Buzacott, J. A. and Yao, D. D. (1986) 'Flexible Manufacturing Systems: A Review of Analytical Models', *Management Science* (July 1986) 32(7):890–905.

Collier, D. A. and Meyer, S. M. (1998) 'A service positioning matrix', *International Journal of Operations & Production Management* 18(11/12):1223–1244.

Cook, D. P., Goh, C. H. and Chung, C. H. (1999) 'Service typologies: a state of the art survey', *Production and Operations Management* 8(3):318–338.

Corrêa, H. L., Scavarda, A. J. and Cooper, M. C. (2007) 'An operations management view of the services and goods offering mix', *International Journal of Operations & Production Management* 27(5):444–463.

Dunning, J. H. (1980) 'Toward an Eclectic Theory of International Production: Some Empirical Tests', *Journal of International Business Studies* (Spring–Summer 1980) 11(1):9–31.

Dunning, J. H. (1998) 'Location and the Multinational Enterprise: A Neglected Factor?', *Journal of International Business Studies* (1st Qtr. 1998) 29(1):45–66.

Fisher, M. L., Hammond, J. H., Obermeyer, W. R. and Raman, A. (1994) 'Making supply meet demand in an uncertain world', *Harvard Business Review* (May/June 1994) 72(3):83–93.

Fisher, M. L. (1997) 'What is the right supply chain for your product?', *Harvard Business Review* 75:105–116.

Hayes, R. H. and Wheelwright, S. G. (1979) 'Link manufacturing process and product life cycles', *Harvard Business Review* 57(1):133–140.

Hayes, R. H. and Pisano, G. (1994) 'Beyond World-Class: The New Manufacturing Strategy', *Harvard Business Review* (January/February 1994) 72(1):77–87.

Hayes, R. H. (2002) 'Challenges posed to operations management by the new economy', *Production and Operations Management* 11(1):21–32.

Johnston, R., Silvestro, R., Fitzgerald, L., Brignall, T. J. and Voss, C. A. (1992) 'Towards a classification of service processes', *International Journal of Service Industry Management* 3(3):62–75.

Lawrence, S. R. and Rosenblatt, H. (1992) 'Introducing International Issues Into Operations Management Curricula', *Production and Operations Management* 1(1):103–117.

Lee, H. L., Padmanabhan, V. and Whang, S. (1997) 'Information Distortion in a Supply Chain: The Bullwhip Effect', *Management Science* (April 1997) 43(4):546–558.

Skinner, W. (1969) 'Manufacturing – missing link in corporate strategy', *Harvard Business Review* (May/June 1969) 47(3):136–145.

Skinner, W. (1974) 'The focused factory', *Harvard Business Review* (May/June 1974) 52(3):113–121.

Stalk, G. (1988) 'Time – The Next Source of Competitive Advantage', *Harvard Business Review* (July/August 1988) 66(4):41–51.

Vargas, V. A., Whybark, D. C. and Xiao, C. Z. (1996) 'Comparing manufacturing output and practices in China, Hungary, the USSR and USA', *International Journal of Production Research* (May 1996) 34(5):1429–1445.

Vargo, S. L. and Lusch, R. F. (2004) 'Evolving to a new dominant logic for marketing', *Journal of Marketing* 68(1):1–17.

Vesey, J. T. (1991) 'The New Competitors Think in Terms of 'Speed-to-Market', *SAM Advanced Management Journal* (Fall 1991) 56(4):26–34.

Whybark, D. C. (1997) 'GMRG survey research in operations management', *International Journal of Operations & Production Management* 17(7):686–696.

Whybark, D. C. (1994) 'Marketing's Influence on Manufacturing Practices', *International Journal of Production Economics* 37(1):41–50.

Wise, R. and Baumgartner, P. (1999) 'Go downstream: the new profit imperative in manufacturing', *Harvard Business Review* 77(5):133–141.

Xiao, C. Z., Vargas, V. A. and Whybark D. C. (1996) 'Comparing Manufacturing Output and Practices in China, Hungary, the USSR and USA', *International Journal of Production Research* 45(1–3):271–278.

Suggestions for further reading

Journals

Ansari *et al.* identified the characteristics of 100 journals publishing articles of interest to operations management researchers or practitioners. Barman *et al.* undertook an empirical evaluation of the perceived relevance and quality of a variety of operations management journals. They ranked 20 journals according to the journals' academic relevance as outlets for research and the perceived academic quality of the articles published. Top ranked journals identified as relevant to POM researchers worldwide were:

Academy of Management Journal, Academy of Management Review, Decision Sciences, European Journal of Operations Research, Harvard Business Review, TIE Transactions Interfaces, International Journal of Operations and Production, Management, International Journal of Production Economics, International Journal of Production Research, International Journal of Technology Management, Journal of International Business Studies, Journal of Management, Journal of Operations Management, Management Science, Omega, Operations Research, SAM Advanced Management Journal, Sloan Management Review and Strategic Management Journal.

Journal of Operations Management

The mission of the *Journal of Operations Management* is to publish original, high-quality research papers in the field of operations management. http://www.elsevier.com/wps/find/journaldescription.cws_home/523929/description?navopenmenu=1.

International Journal of Operations and Production Management

IJOPM looks at the managerial problems of developing and implementing operation systems.
http://www.emeraldinsight.com/info/journals/ijopm/ijopm.jsp

Production & Operations Management (POM Journal)

Research journal in operations management in manufacturing and services – see also Production and Operations Management Society (POMS), an international professional organization representing the interests of POM professionals from around the world. http://www.poms.org/journal/

Key articles

Scholars of this subject area have often read the following:

1 Lee, H. L., Padmanabhan, V. and Whang, S. (1997) 'Information Distortion in a Supply Chain: The Bullwhip Effect', *Management Science* (April 1997) 43(4):546–558.
2 Stalk, G. (1988) 'Time – The Next Source of Competitive Advantage', *Harvard Business Review* (July/August 1988) 66(4):41–51.
3 Fisher, M. L., Hammond, J. H., Obermeyer, W. R. and Raman, A. (1994) 'Making supply meet demand in an uncertain world', *Harvard Business Review* (May/June 1994) 72(3):83–93.
4 Hayes, R. H. and Wheelwright, S. C. (1979) 'Link manufacturing process and product life cycles', *Harvard Business Review* (January/February 1979) 57(1):133–140.
5 Skinner, W. (1969) 'Manufacturing – missing link in corporate strategy', *Harvard Business Review* (May/June 1969) 47(3):136–145.
6 Hayes, R. H. and Pisano, G. (1994) 'Beyond World-Class: The New Manufacturing Strategy', *Harvard Business Review* (January/February 1994) 72(1):77–87.
7 Skinner, W. (1974) 'The focused factory', *Harvard Business Review* (May/June 1974) 52(3):113–121.

8 Wise, R. and Baumgartner, P. (1999) 'Go Downstream: The New Profit Imperative in Manufacturing', *Harvard Business Review* (September/October 1999) 77(5):133–141.

9 Buzacott, J. A. and Yao, D. D. (1986) 'Flexible Manufacturing Systems: A Review of Analytical Models', *Management Science* (July 1986) 32(7):890–905.

10 Welch, J. A. and Nayak, N. P. (1992) 'Strategic sourcing: a progressive approach to the make-or-buy decision', *Academy of Management Executive* (February 1992) 6(1):23–31.

Chapter 16

International marketing

Introduction

What is international marketing

International marketing strategy

Marketing mix

Enabling technologies

Customer acquisition management

Customer retention

Key concepts

- ■ International marketing ■ Segmentation ■ Marketing research ■ Marketing mix
- ■ Marketing intelligence ■ Market share ■ Brand ■ Product portfolio analysis
- ■ Market penetration ■ Marketing plan ■ Product life cycle ■ Marketing communication
- ■ Customer satisfaction ■ Direct marketing

By the end of this chapter you will be able to:

- ■ Outline the principal activities and processes associated with international marketing

- ■ Identify and describe the main strategic marketing decisions

- ■ Critically evaluate alternatives for the international organization's strategic marketing approach

- ■ Specify the key elements of the international marketing mix and discuss how to balance these elements

- ■ Critically discuss the appropriateness of standardization through the marketing strategy and mix

Active learning case

VIRGIN

At the launch of his cola drink the Chair of the Virgin Group, Richard Branson, burst into New York's Times Square astride a Second World War tank. For the Virgin Brides' wedding service launch he donned a $10 000 white silk bridal gown. When introducing his mobile phone company in Australia he flew into the press conference, hanging from a helicopter promising to save Australians from their money-grabbing mobile contractors. For this wily UK entrepreneur, publicity stunts and, for that matter, brand extensions have become a way of life[6]. In 2006, NTL agreed to pay Branson £255m for permission to use the Virgin brand on media offerings over the next 30 years[5]. Virgin Media was the rebranded name for NTL after it bought the mobile phone group Virgin Mobile and rival Telewest in 2006, creating the first British company to offer a 'quadruple-play' package of television, broadband, fixed-line and mobile telecom services. Branson holds a 10.5 per cent stake in NTL, making him the largest single shareholder.

As part of the Virgin Mobile takeover, NTL entered into a 30-year exclusive brand licence for the use of the Virgin brand[2]. NTL's reputation for customer service 'has taken a beating in recent years'[3] whereas the Virgin brand is perceived more favourably and has widespread presence in the UK, including an airline and train service. However, buying Virgin Mobile – in conjunction with a side deal to license the Virgin brand in other areas – is seen as significant because it will enable NTL to sell broadband access, cable television, fixed-line telecommunications and wireless calling to UK customers in a single bundle and under a single brand[4].

The Virgin brand is essentially a projection of a personality; a sympathetic one suggests Sanghera (2006). Sometimes without consciously realizing it brands have emotional effects on us and we pre-dispose ourselves to purchase certain brands over others. Virgin has discovered to its advantage that those consumers with a positive perception of a brand are far more likely to sample a brand extension than choose a completely unfamiliar brand in that product category[6]. Virgin is one of the best-known brands of the last two decades, the signature of restless entrepreneur Sir Richard Branson. Yet defining the brand is virtually impossible; and it is equally hard to determine exactly what it is worth. Almost all of Virgin's businesses are joint ventures, and it would appear that as many lose money as make it. So what exactly does the Virgin brand stand for?

A recent independent research study (conducted by HPI Research April 2007) has shown that the UK public vote Virgin as their most admired brand. Conceived in 1970, the Virgin Group has gone on to grow very successful businesses in sectors ranging from mobile telephony, to transportation, travel, financial services, leisure, music, holidays, publishing and retailing[1]. Virgin has created more than 200 branded companies worldwide, employing approximately 50 000 people, in 29 countries. Revenues around the world in 2006 exceeded £10 billion. Virgin stands for value for money, quality, innovation, fun and a sense of competitive challenge.

When Virgin start a new venture, it is based on hard research and analysis. Typically, they review the industry and put themselves in the customer's shoes to see what improvement can be made. They ask fundamental questions: is this an opportunity for restructuring a market and creating competitive advantage? What are the competitors doing? Is the customer confused or badly served? Is this an opportunity for building the Virgin brand? Can Virgin add value? Will it interact with other Virgin businesses? Is there an appropriate trade-off between risk and reward?

New ventures are often steered by people seconded from other parts of Virgin, who bring with them the trademark management style, skills and experience. Virgin frequently creates partnerships

© jim forrest / Alamy

Led by adventurous founder, chairman, and owner Sir Richard Branson, Virgin Group Ltd is a conglomeration of separately run companies, each making use of the Virgin brand. The core business areas are travel, entertainment and lifestyle, among others.

Founded in the UK (1989) the group has revenues of US$20 billion (2006), generated through a workforce of approximately 50 000 employees. Branson retains complete ownership and control of the Virgin brand, however, the commercial set-up of companies using the brand is varied and complex. The group is sometimes perceived as a conglomerate, but this is not in fact the case. Each of the companies operating under the Virgin brand is a separate entity, with some wholly owned by Branson, while in others he holds minority or majority stakes. Occasionally, he simply licenses the brand. Many of the companies began as wholly owned Virgin subsidiaries.

▶ ▶ ▶

with others to combine skills, knowledge, and market presence. Virgin is one of the most diverse brands in the world. 'All the markets in which Virgin operate tend to have features in common: they are typically markets where the customer has been "ripped off" or under-served, where there is confusion and/or where the competition is complacent.' The Virgin brand values define what Virgin is all about, they are:

- value for money;
- good quality;
- brilliant customer service;
- innovation;
- competitive challenge; and
- fun.

The inconsistency of Sir Richard's offering is part of the appeal[5]. It shows that Virgin's brand values are not enforced in a corporate way, and not-being-corporate is a quality that the people's capitalist, who has managed to succeed in business without resorting to RAC membership and golf, has always projected. For Virgin, brand extensions form a key part of overall strategy and so treading carefully is vital[6]. One mistake and there is a tangible danger of brand damage and dilution. According to *Forbes Magazine*[7], 'a customer enjoying a massage on a Virgin Atlantic flight may be pre-disposed into drinking Virgin Cola or staying in a Virgin hotel, but a customer who has a bad enough experience with any one of the product lines may shun all the others'. As well as this risk, over-extending into a variety of unrelated areas can in some instances dilute a brand. There is a danger that people fail to understand what the brand actually stands for. Virgin is not alone in its brand extension success – other examples include Caterpillar, Stelios Haji-Ioannou's Easy Group (the name behind leading European low-cost airline easyJet) or Yahoo!

Sources:
Website www.virgin.com Sources:
(1) www.virgin.com
(2) rawstory.com/news/afp/Virgin_Media_says_bid_for_company_r_07022007.html
(3) www.abcmoney.co.uk/news/1720061741.htm
(4) http://www.ecommercetimes.com/story/49750.html accessed 16 November 2007
(5) Sanghera, A. (2006) 'Testing the Virgin brand', FT.Com, Published: May 4 2006 www.ft.com
(6) Anon. (2002) 'Virgin flies high with brand extensions', *Strategic Direction* 18(10):21–24.
(7) Wells, M. (2000) 'Red Baron', *Forbes Magazine* 166(1):150.

Introduction

Several key marketing issues and challenges are evident in the Virgin case study presented above. The case raises questions such as: how to communicate with customers; the role and value of the brand; how to identify markets and then enter them; what products to offer and the content of the business and product portfolio; and, how to price offerings. We address such issues in this chapter. The previous chapter examined the primary value adding activities of production and identified a number of links with marketing. The marketing function must identify how best to meet customer needs, sources of advantage and must estimate demand for products and services – all of which impact upon the operations function and processes. Few could doubt the importance of international marketing in contemporary business but there are differences in beliefs concerning the knowledge and skills required by international marketing managers and international business students.

Many scholars and practitioners have asked what should be taught in an international marketing curriculum (see Philip 1995). Lundstrom and White (1997) found the following to be highly rated: knowledge of culture and language, overall management and marketing competence, regional cultural differences, and general business knowledge of specific world regions. Practitioners consider knowledge of assessing country and market potential and the development of international marketing skills to be significantly more important than academicians; academics tend to focus on general issues of globalization and the environment. Additional topics include environmental issues, market entry strategies, channel strategies, pricing strategies, product development, market segmentation, promotion and advertising and branding strategies.

In this chapter the reader will be introduced to the concepts of international marketing, enabling an appreciation of the complexities of marketing on an international basis and how this differs from operating solely in domestic markets. In the following sections we will define international marketing, examine the important trends in the global marketing environment and introduce the reader to the international marketing management process. Knowledge and an understanding of the markets in which companies operate are important for all business activities. In international markets, because of geographical distances and the complexities of operating in a number of dissimilar markets where risk and uncertainty are high, the need for knowledge and understanding becomes of vital importance. This chapter builds upon previous work and has strong links with other parts of the book, especially Chapters 2 and 3.

Figure 16-1 identifies the major decisions in the international marketing process and is used, to some extent, to organize the content of the chapter. The first problems concern the identification of target markets and whether or not to internationalize. Having assessed global market opportunities they must then decide which markets to enter, how to enter and compete. The ability of the product to meet customer needs, the price, promotional communications and distribution network (the marketing mix) will all impact upon sales. The international organization must make decisions about what to standardize and what to adapt to the local market – should they change the product, the price, the message or the distribution network in each of the countries within which they operate? All of the decisions require information derived from analysis and analytical tools. Such information may drive strategic, tactical and operational decisions. To help explain key concepts we have organized the chapter in three sections: international marketing strategy, the (tactical) marketing mix and technology-enabled international marketing.

What is international marketing?

Later in this chapter we consider how organizations market their products and services worldwide but first identify what is meant by international marketing. Marketing is the management process responsible for identifying, anticipating and satisfying customer

Marketing the processes associated with the transfer of goods from and the relationships between producer and consumer. It is also concerned with anticipating the customers' future needs and wants. Marketing involves researching, promoting, selling, and distributing products or services

Figure 16-1

Major decisions in the
international marketing
process

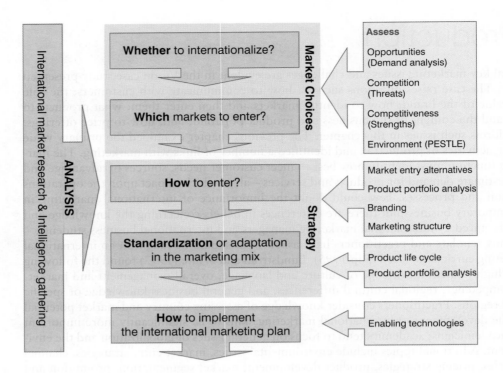

requirements profitably. International marketing may be approached in different levels (such as corporate or business) and there are more uncontrollable elements in the marketing environment. International marketing involves the organization making one or more marketing mix decisions across national boundaries. The international marketing scope may be extended to include the establishment of operational facilities overseas (see Chapter 15) and the coordination of marketing strategies across the globe. Whereas domestic marketing involves the company manipulating a series of controllable variables such as price, promotion, distribution and products, international marketing involves operating across a number of foreign country markets in which not only do the controllable variables differ from country to country, but the uncontrollable factors are also likely to differ significantly. This makes international marketing more complex than domestic marketing. The key difference between domestic marketing and marketing on an international scale is the multidimensionality and complexity of the many foreign country markets within which a company may operate in and the number of companies that may comprise the MNC.

An international manager needs a knowledge and awareness of these complexities and the implications they have for international marketing management. Key factors include diverse, multicultural, widespread and sometimes fragmented markets with different governments, politics, economics and financial systems; there are also different stakeholders and business rules to contend with and a need for control and coordination across markets. International marketing makes use of domestic marketing processes but the marketing decisions require consideration to be given to a greater number of factors. Key decisions concern the extent of standardization and adaptation of practices, products, prices and promotional messages. The development of successful international marketing strategies is based upon a sound understanding of the similarities and differences that exist in countries around the world.

Culture may influence the consumer's perception, attitudes and understanding of products and marketing communications which determine aspects of consumer behaviour. The culture that we live in establishes norms of behaviour that may impact upon eating and shopping habits, the way we use products and the benefits we derive from them. The buying process may differ from country to country. National culture and values (see uncertainty avoidance) may impact upon the willingness of customers to try out new products and services for example. When analyzing cultures and the implications for consumer behaviour we must consider the needs that are fulfilled by products in the minds of members of the particular culture and attributes of that culture's purchasing behaviour. We must also consider the broader cultural values relevant to the product and evaluate promotion methods appropriate for the culture in question.

International marketing strategy

There are many ways in which to study international marketing. One useful approach is to consider the field in terms of the major decisions and activities involved. First, the international Organization must determine which markets to enter and how to enter the selected markets (refer back to market entry strategies). Such decisions are typically made at the corporate level and are directly influenced by the corporate strategy (the marketing strategy must be aligned with other strategies) which might dictate growth requirements. These decisions are supported by country level analysis which seeks to identify where opportunities exist worldwide, i.e. favourable places for the organization to sell its goods and services.

Opportunity may be assessed using the tools and techniques described in Chapters 2 and 3, such as through SWOT and PESTLE analysis; competitor and internal resource and capability analysis. In Chapter 3, we also discussed market entry strategies, direct or indirect and the geographical scope – choice of countries in which to do business. Having identified the selected the opportunity space (market) the company will simultaneously consider its offerings to that market, determining what to sell and how to sell it; such decisions will also be based on analysis. The latter decision will require the organization to identify appropriate structure, processes, policies and systems (drawing on the knowledge presented in Parts III and IV). Decisions will also be made about pricing, channel strategy, branding and marketing communications. Marketing specialists in the corporate headquarters of the global or transnational organization will then need to consider the extent to which marketing is standardized throughout the whole organization.

In Chapter 1 we commented on the issue of convergence noting that global organizations (convergent) favour centralization, consolidating power under central control. Such companies, are therefore more likely, to centralize the strategic marketing decisions discussed so far.

Global companies emphasize the advantages of integration and standardization particularly in terms of coordination, control and cost benefits. In the global company, standard products are sold under a global brand through standard practices, leaving less to be decided by local operations. The multidomestic (divergent), on the other hand, prioritizes differentiation advantage and argues the need to be local, i.e. decentralized. Consequently, more of the marketing decision-making will be left to subsidiaries and local business units. Rather than managing the local product portfolio, the multidomestic focuses more on managing the company portfolio. As was noted, in Chapter 1, companies tend to lie somewhere between these two extreme stances.

The transnational will standardize some of its marketing plan and activities, making certain decisions from the corporate centre, but allowing for degrees of adaptation where locally demanded – the 'glocal' approach. Consequently certain marketing decisions are made at the corporate (centre) and others at the business unit (local) level. The marketing mix describes a set of variables (product, place/distribution, promotion/marketing communication and price) that an organization can control in order to appeal to the target market. In some cases the decisions about certain of these variables may be viewed as strategic and in other cases tactical. Therefore, in some cases the decision may be made by corporate marketing specialists in the global organization and in other cases (the transnational and multidomestic) such decisions may be made by the marketing specialists in the local subsidiary or business unit. A variety of arguments

Look back
See chapter 3, p. 91

Market an aggregate of people with a need for certain products and the means to purchase such products

Marketing plan the written document specifying an organization's marketing activities and marketing mixes

Figure 16-2

Developing market strategy

Look back
See chapter 3

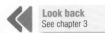

Marketing strategy a plan indicating the opportunities to pursue, specific target markets to address, the types of competitive advantages that are to be developed and exploited and maintenance of an appropriate marketing mix that will satisfy those people in the target market(s)

International marketing process the interlinked activities of analysis, planning and marketing programme formulation which identifies the best way of using company resources to satisfy the needs of foreign and domestic customers to the greatest benefit of such customers and the international organization

Marketing programme process of determining tactics to be carried out to achieve the objectives and goals established in the marketing strategy

Figure 16-3

International marketing

(standardization versus adaptation, political or legal, economic or cultural, the need for congruence and decision-maker attitudes) govern such decisions.

So far we have outlined the major strategic marketing decisions but are yet to define what we mean by the marketing strategy. The marketing strategy is a plan indicating the opportunities to pursue, specific target markets to address, the types of competitive advantages that are to be developed and exploited and maintenance of an appropriate marketing mix that will satisfy those people in the target market(s). In some cases, the marketing strategy is intentionally formulated (a planning approach) while in other cases it may emerge from a set of choices and actions. Strategy is concerned with the optimal application of the resources and organization possesses relative to competitors. The international marketing strategy then, is developed from an analysis of the internal and external environment, see Figure 16-2; the classic approach to strategy formulation begins with an appraisal (analysis) of organizational competencies and resources (Andrews 1971 cited in Peteraf 1993), see Figure 16-3, and considers the organization's capabilities and offerings relative to those of competitors (competitive position).

The international marketing process is concerned with how work is done to create marketing strategies and plans. There are three essential stages in the process: analysis, planning and the development of the marketing programme, see Figure 16-3. *Analysis* focuses on the four Cs – customers, competitors, the causal-environment (environmental forces) and internal capabilities. The organization requires intelligence about the four Cs to analyze and then

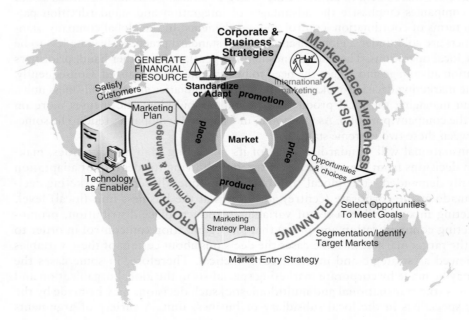

develop strategies. The international organization must select opportunities to be followed (marketing opportunity analysis) and devise associated target marketing strategies. Analysis is used to support *planning*. The marketing strategy, guided by the corporate mission and goals, identifies opportunities, target markets to address, methods to enter target markets and the competitive advantages to be developed. This plan communicates how best to use the organization's resources in order to achieve marketing and corporate goals. The plan is also used to coordinate the activities of other parts of the organization and their associated resources such as production – to include human and technical resources (see Chapter 15) and finance (see Chapter 17). The development of competitive advantage is necessary if the organization is to persuade customers to purchase its products and services.

Opportunity analysis

In Chapter 3 we discussed external, industry analysis, understanding of the competitive environment, and internal analysis – the analysis of resources and capabilities – and in this section we consider how to assess opportunity and target markets from a marketing perspective. Decisions about whether to internationalize and which *markets* to enter are not taken in isolation. When evaluating potential markets to enter, organizations typically make use of environmental analysis (refer back to Chapter 2), market research and intelligence alongside information gleaned from internal resource and capability analysis. In any marketing situation, there will normally be a need to segment any identified market as it is unlikely the organization's products will appeal to the entire market in the same way.

Segmentation refers to a process of identifying different groups within a target market in order to develop different offerings for the groups. Market segmentation is a process of dividing a heterogeneous market into segments which are relatively homogeneous and identifiable for the purpose of designing a marketing mix to meet the needs of consumers in segments which are attractive to the organization. Segmentation results in a number of customer groups, some of which will be served, others may be unattractive. Segments may be evaluated in terms of their volume, accessibility, urgency of need and profitability. If a company is to survive in the international marketplace, it is important that it searches for methods to reduce, as far as possible, the risk of making a wrong decision. Segmentation may improve the relevance of analysis and the information used in decision-making. At the end of the chapter we discuss how database technologies support segmentation and how e-commerce technologies enable one-to-one marketing.

Markets may be segmented on the basis of demographic, psychographic or behavioural variables. With the increasing globalization of the business world, *international segmentation* becomes an ever more important concept in marketing. Marketing mix (product, price, etc.) offerings have typically been made at a country level, thereby assuming that customers in a particular country are all alike and ignore similarities between segments across countries. In fact, nothing could be farther from the truth argues Kale (1987). This approach ignores the differences between customers within a country and ignores the similarities across boundaries. Heterogeneity among consumers within a country is more a rule than an exception and it is the responsibility of the international marketer to take this heterogeneity into account. Further, significant advantages accrue to the geocentric firm by recognizing similarities across national boundaries in the markets it services. Consequently, arguments have been put forward for segmentation on the basis of consumers, not countries.

Earlier we recognized the role of marketing in determining what to make and sell. This requires an understanding of the needs of international customers. Customer requirements may be assessed through market research – the systematic gathering, recording, analysis and interpretation of data on problems relating to the marketing of goods and services. The research process is typically described in six stages, see Figure 16-4. The marketing intelligence system is used to gather, process, assess, and make available marketing data

Segmentation the process of grouping customers in heterogeneous markets into smaller, more similar or homogeneous segments – customers are aggregated into groups with similar needs and buying characteristics

Segment a collection of entities sharing one or more similar characteristics that cause them to have relatively similar product needs and buying characteristics

Marketing research the process of gathering, interpreting and disseminating information to help solve specific marketing problems or take advantage of marketing opportunities

Marketing intelligence information about buyer needs and competitor activities compiled, analyzed, and/or disseminated in an effort to provide insight and assistance in decision-making

Figure 16-4
The research process

Step 1	Step 2	Step 3	Step 4	Step 5	Step 6
problem definition	approach	research design	implementation/ data gathering	data analysis	report

and information in a format that allows marketing managers to function more effectively. International environments and different products may be monitored with the resultant marketing intelligence used for planning, policy making, and decision purposes.

Data may be routinely collected from within and outside of the organization or may be collected as a one-off research activity. Sales statistics may provide a useful internal information source for the international marketing manager. The international marketing research process may be in or outsourced but starts with a problem definition phase. Information needs are assessed and a research project designed and implemented. Data is then analyzed and presented to the target audience. This may then help the organization with decisions such as where to invest or divest and how to position the company and its offerings. From an international perspective, projects may seek to compare countries while in other cases the unit of analysis may be a factor within a given country such as market share or brand preference.

It is important to recognize that information may come from within or outside the organization and may involve primary (new and specific) or secondary data (already available). Secondary data is normally cheaper to collect and available sooner. Primary data is typically collected through surveys (mail, online telephone or through personal interviews). The collected and analyzed data must then be carefully interpreted. Frequently, the interpretation of data gathered on an international level demands a high level of cultural understanding. There is a tendency to believe that other people perceive things in the same way as us, see Figure 8-3 The process of perception. Consequently, those interpreting data and intelligence from a particular region should be well acquainted with the culture of the region (refer back to Chapter 8).

The organization uses research to determine if there is *demand* (information required by the producers of the organization – see Chapter 15) for its products elsewhere and if there is, seeks to estimate potential market share so that the opportunity can be quantified. Determining opportunity is a complex challenge and requires analysis of end customers' needs and buying behaviour, intermediaries, competitors and the industry as well as the wider environment. Given the large number of countries worldwide there is a need to focus attention. Researchers typically scan markets to identify which countries have the potential for growth. Identified countries are then qualified through assessment of accessibility, profitability and market size (country attractiveness). The scanning stage identifies countries where marketing opportunities exist.

Opportunities may exist in countries already serviced by existing suppliers (existing markets); in countries where no company has yet offered a product of potential (latent market) and where a future opportunity may exist in the future (incipient markets). At the scanning stage, the manager researching international markets is identifying and then analyzing opportunities in order to evaluate which markets to prioritize for further research and development. When country attractiveness is high and the company's products, services and capabilities are highly compatible, a significant opportunity exists, see Figure 16-5.

Opportunity is also hunted by competitors. Competitor analysis starts with an assessment of the competitive environment. Relevant competitors are identified and primary competitors determined. A common measure of their relative competitive strength is their respective market share, i.e. the proportion of total sales volume they have captured. Next, information is gathered about the strengths and weaknesses and capabilities of the most

Look back
See chapter 8

Look back
See chapter 8, p. 248

Market share the company's sales of a product stated as a percentage of industry sales of that product

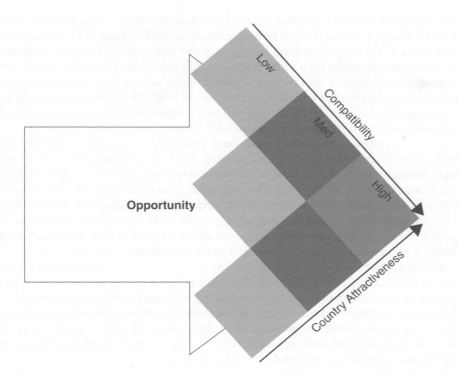

Figure 16-5

Country-based classification system

important competitors in relation to the identified success factors. For each competitor, the marketer may compare:

a strategy (see Chapter 3) and operations (see Chapter 15);

b leadership (see Chapter 6);

c elements of structure and business processes (see Chapters 9 and 10); and

d the organization's information systems and technology (see Chapter 13).

It is also useful to consider access to financial resources (Chapter 17) and the availability of talented HR (Chapters 7 and 8).

Served markets

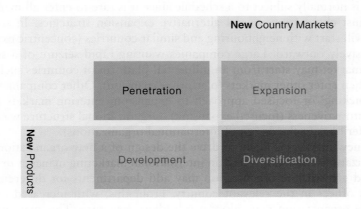

Figure 16-6

Portfolio options (Ansoff matrix)

Having assessed the attractiveness of potential product and country markets and the organization's competitive position in the markets under consideration, the organization decides which markets should be served. The Ansoff growth matrix is a tool to help organizations determine their product and market growth strategy; **product portfolio analysis**

Product portfolio analysis a strategic planning tool that takes a product's market growth rate and its relative market share into consideration in determining a marketing strategy

enables organizations to analyze market attractiveness and competitive position simultaneously and includes consideration of both opportunities and threats. International portfolio analysis starts at the corporate level, where country and product markets, must be compared. Such analysis can be used to determine market priorities. A company can be involved in a current country market with current or new products or may be considering new country markets. The product/market grid has two dimensions: products and markets, see Figure 16-6. Four options may be considered such as product market penetration, geographic expansion, product market development and diversification.

Market penetration (sell more of the same products or services in current markets) involves increasing market share of an existing product, or promoting a new product, through strategies such as bundling, extensive advertising, lower prices, or volume discounts. It is a marketing strategy used by an organization to increase the sales of a product within an existing market through the employment of more aggressive marketing tactics. Geographic expansion is a marketing strategy that seeks to expand operations to new geographic areas – sell more of the same products or services in new markets. Selling new products or services in current markets is a marketing strategy termed product development and finally, the most risky type of strategy is diversification – selling new products or services in new markets. Ansoff's product/market grid is a model proven to be very useful in business unit strategy processes for determining business growth opportunities.

This section highlighted how the attractiveness of international markets can be assessed and how comparisons with competitors can help identify where a company may do well by virtue of its capabilities and success factors. Such assessment supports decision-making and the formulation of international marketing strategy.

Alternative strategic responses

Four high level strategic responses were considered in the previous paragraph. Once a marketplace has been identified, the organization must plan to operate within it, to satisfy customers and win business. The marketing mix variables are used to achieve this and the variables themselves are dependent upon internal strengths, i.e. organizational resource utilization, competencies and capabilities (see the RBV). The marketing mix variables are discussed after this section. International market expansion impacts upon the organization and the way its resources are distributed and used. Following entrance into new markets or the development of new products, resource allocation decisions must be made. Organizational processes and structures may need to be reshaped and new facilities, technology and systems acquired and developed.

Expansion is normally subject to a schedule since it is rare to enter all markets at once. Companies must chose from several alternative expansion strategies. In some cases an organization will start with neighbouring and similar countries (concentric expansion) and move progressively outward. Large companies wanting rapid seizure of a sizeable share of the global market may start from an influential platform of countries such as the triad markets and then enter other markets (platform expansion). Other companies adopt more of a 'cherry-picking' or focused approach to expansion, entering markets according to their level of attractiveness (focused expansion). Organizational structure was discussed in Chapter 9 (refer back to the design of international organizations).

Look back
See chapter 8

Entry into new markets is likely to drive the design of a new organizational structure. Smaller organizations may simply add an international marketing manager or department. With increased growth, the organization may add departments for different markets or resource sales offices in the relevant country. From this, with increased foreign direct investment the organization may adopt a subsidiary structure. This may evolve into an international divisional structure. In such cases the company may be divided into two divisions – the national and the international. Finally, with decreased dependence upon home country sales, the organization may adopt a global structure. At this point, the organization is fragmented and decisions on standardization come to the forefront of the senior marketing manager's mind.

Market penetration a strategy of increasing sales of current products in current markets

Geographic expansion a marketing strategy that seeks to expand operations to new geographic areas

Product development a strategy of increasing sales by improving present products or developing new products for current markets

Diversification a strategy that takes the organization into both new markets and products or services

Buzzell (1968) recognized 40 years ago that the international company may view its strategy in each country strictly as a local or global problem; there are real potential gains to consider in standardizing various elements of the marketing programmes used in different areas (see also Elinder 1961). These gains range from substantial cost savings and more consistent dealings with customers to better planning, control, and exploitation of ideas with universal appeal. An international marketing strategy identifies the served product markets, general marketing objectives and policies, such as branding, product line management, or distribution channel decisions. The problem organizations face is determining which aspects of international activity to standardize and which to adapt. This leads to organizations adopting a variety of global strategies, from those that are very similar from country to country to those that are substantially different in each country in which the organization operates.

Through globalization, it has been argued the worldwide marketplace has become so homogenized that multinational corporations can market standardized products and services all over the world, by identical strategies, with resultant lower costs and higher margins. Standardization of international marketing strategy refers to using a common product, price, distribution, and promotion programme on a worldwide basis. The decision on standardization is not a dichotomous one between complete standardization and customization. Rather, there can be degrees of standardization. Most of the literature on standardization, especially the earlier studies, addresses the standardization of the marketing programme – various parts of the marketing mix. The standardization decision is situation-specific, requiring reference to a particular target market for a particular product. Differences in environment (see Chapter 2) are an important concern affecting the feasibility of standardization – for example culture influences every aspect of marketing.

Cultural differences influence consumer acculturation which, in turn, affects acceptance of standardized products. If customer behaviour and lifestyle are similar then we should expect a high degree of standardization; similarly the higher the cultural compatibility of the product across the host countries, the greater the degree of standardization. As the difference in physical, political, and legal environments between home and host countries grows, we should expect to see the degree of standardization to reduce. Standardization is more feasible for industrial goods than for consumer goods. Studies have shown that industrial and high technology products (e.g. computer hardware, airliners, photographic equipment, heavy equipment, and machine tools) are considered most appropriate for global brand strategies. Confections, clothing, food, toiletries, and household cleaners are considered much less appropriate.

Regardless of the drivers for standardization, such decisions are made by people who are predisposed to think in certain ways. Perlmutter (1969) identified among international executives three primary orientations toward building multinational enterprises: ethnocentric (home-country oriented), polycentric (host-country oriented), or geocentric (world-oriented). An organization having either an ethnocentric or a geocentric orientation is likely to standardize its marketing programme. Ultimately, the decision on standardization should be based on economic payoff, which includes financial performance and competitive advantage; scale effects that transcend national boundaries can provide cost advantages to companies selling to the world market. The decision on standardization also should be examined for its impact on competition, measured in terms of the competitive advantage it may provide.

In addition to financial performance and competitive advantage, standardization should be considered for coherent international image, rapid diffusion of products and ideas internationally, and greater central coordination and control. A standardization strategy is more effective if worldwide customers, not countries, are the basis of identifying the segment(s) to serve (Jain 1989).

While there are many forces driving organizations towards achieving a global strategy through standardizing as many marketing activities as possible, there are also very important arguments persuading companies that they can also achieve an effective worldwide strategy through a multidomestic approach. Such an approach recognizes the high costs to harmonize standards; customer demand for locally differentiated products; perceived country of origin issues and the difficulties in managing global organizations). In practice, organizations adopt a combination of standardization and adaptation of the various elements of the marketing programme and processes by standardizing some elements and globalizing others. Different elements of marketing management may be at different points of the standardization continuum, whereby pricing and distribution are more difficult to standardize and therefore more likely to be adapted to the local environment.

Thus far we have considered the strategic process stages of market analysis through to the choice of alternatives with regard to products offered, countries in which to operate in and extent of internationalization and the consequences for resource allocation. Such strategic decisions develop a framework for managers to act within. Managers need to ensure that trade can occur and that customer orders can be taken in the right place and time; they must chose distribution channels; arrange for the local provision of services; integrate communication activities and set prices.

We turn our attention to such matters in the remainder of this chapter. Next we consider, in detail, the marketing mix. We discuss product management, pricing decisions, promotions and distribution (place). Some marketing mix decisions may be described as strategic, others tactical. For example, product standardization and branding may be considered as strategic decisions while others discuss product life cycle decisions as more tactical. It is important to recognize that international organizations vary in what is typically treated as a strategic or tactical, a group or central versus a local marketing issue. We will discuss each component of the marketing mix and the issue of standardization in the next section.

Marketing mix

The organization determines how it will satisfy customers in the target markets through the marketing mix variables (such as product, price, place, promotion and people). The international marketing manager must consider how such variables are to be managed internationally and locally; in each case arguments are considered for standardization or adaptation. When marketing their products, firms need to create a successful mix of: the right product, sold at the right price, in the right place and using the most suitable promotion. The marketing mix is the tactical 'toolkit' of the marketing programme; variables that an organization can control in order to appeal to the target market and facilitate satisfying exchange.

Optimizing the marketing mix is the primary responsibility of marketing. By offering the product with the right combination of the four Ps, marketers can improve their results and marketing effectiveness. Making small changes in the marketing mix is typically considered to be a tactical change. Making large changes in any of the four Ps can be considered strategic. The *marketing mix* is probably the most famous marketing term and its elements are the basic components of a marketing plan. The offer made to the customer can be altered by varying the mix elements. Each aspect of the marketing mix is described in the following sections. First we consider products, then promotion, place and price.

International product management

How are products managed internationally?

Product a good, service or idea

We discussed product development in the previous chapter. The international organization must make many decisions about its products and services. It must first make sure it has identified exactly who the target customers or purchase decision-makers are; knowledge of customers will help with designing customer value-creation. The marketer must assess what constitutes its product from the customer's perspective. Product decisions include determining the brand name, functionality, level of quality, warranty, accessories and ancillary services. It is important to recognize that customers may purchase products for their own use or for the use of others, such as family members, friends and relatives and the employees within their work organization (organizational buyers).

Different customers may engage in different buying processes and their emotional involvement may also vary. Business customers differ from the residential customer. For example, a business customer may require exact specifications to be met as input materials may be critical to the quality design of their offering. Potential customers may not only have varying expectations but may also derive different benefits. Customer's expectations may be similar across countries allowing a product to be standardized. In some cases an organization will simply offer an already developed product or service into new markets with no adaptation while in other cases a product may be developed to a standard that will meet the needs of the most demanding customers and will then be offered in other countries.

International marketers have, for decades, debated the issue of product adaptation versus standardization as a mechanism for serving global markets. Levitt (1983) asserts that well-managed companies have moved from emphasis on customizing items to offering globally standardized products that are advanced, functional, reliable – and low priced – 'Companies must learn to operate as if the world were one large market – ignoring superficial regional and national differences'. However, it is important to recognize that product standardization does not work everywhere and that a need for product adaptation (customization) may be apparent. This is necessary to meet with local customer needs. Different approaches to customization were identified in the previous chapter. In some cases it may be necessary to treat every single customer as a market segment with specific requirements that must be fulfilled. The arguments for and against standardization are summarized in Figure 16-7.

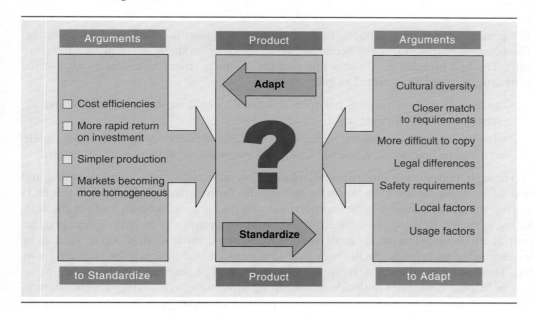

Figure 16-7

Product standardization arguments

International organizations need to develop and maintain a competitive combination of products and/or services – a **product portfolio**. Portfolios will vary in terms of the number of product lines, the age structure of products, and the number of variations of the total products. The marketer must ensure a sufficiently large number of products exist in order to generate sufficient cash flow to finance new product development or penetration and expansion strategies. Portfolios may be analyzed, with the company's product evaluated according to the attractiveness of served product markets and the relative competitive position. In order to maintain a balanced portfolio, new products are developed continually and introduced into markets (see Figure 16-9). Groups of people from within and outside the organization, influenced by market requirements, will generate ideas for new products

Product portfolio the variety of products manufactured or supplied by an organization

Look forward
See chapter 16, p. 534

Look back
See chapter 8

and services. Any teams involved in this process should be aware of cultural diversity and the team itself may be heterogeneous with regard to employee nationality (refer back to multicultural teams discussed in Chapter 8).

International product management is a complex task, drawing upon resources from many functions within and outside the organization. In some cases, such resources may be centralized and in other cases the organization may encourage locally operating business units to drive their own innovation. International marketing success is dependent upon satisfying the demands of customers through the product or services offered. Included within the product definition are the additional elements of packaging, warranties, after sales service and branding (see later) that make up the total product offer.

The satisfying of customer needs, whatever and wherever they are, necessitates an identification and understanding of the customer or prospect. In meeting the needs, the marketer will consider the benefits of the products offered; product attributes (features and specifications) and support services such as delivery, after sales and guarantees. A variety of product standardization strategies exist from which the international marketing manager may choose:

1 product *extension*, promotion *adaptation* – this strategy offers the standard product to customers in other countries but adapts the promotional effort (see later section) for individual countries;

2 product *adaptation*, promotion *extension* – makes use of a standard promotional campaign but adapts the product to local needs; and

3 dual adaptation is a strategy where both the marketing communication and the product are adapted for each market.

Product portfolio analysis

The process of managing groups of brands and product lines is called portfolio planning. The business portfolio is the collection of businesses and products that make up the company. The best business portfolio is one that fits company strengths and helps exploit the most attractive opportunities. The company must:

1 analyze its current business portfolio and decide which businesses should receive more or less investment; and

2 develop growth strategies for adding new products and businesses to the portfolio, while at the same time deciding when products and businesses should no longer be retained.

Through analysis, the international organization must clarify its strategic position and that of its competitors. Like Ansoff's matrix, the Boston matrix (also called the BCG matrix, the growth-share matrix and portfolio analysis) is a well known tool for the marketing manager. Developed by the large US consulting group, it is an approach to product portfolio planning. The matrix analyzes the success of a company's products or services by looking at the percentage of sales they have in the market and how fast the sales are growing. The Boston matrix was developed in the 1970s by The Boston Consulting Group as a way of helping companies to decide on an appropriate investment strategy for their future. Figure 16-8 shows how different products or parts of a company can be compared in terms of market growth and market share. It has two controlling aspects, namely relative market share (meaning relative to your competition) and market growth.

Understanding the Boston matrix requires an understanding of how market share and market growth interrelate. Market share is the percentage of the total market serviced by the company, measured either in revenue terms or unit volume terms. A high market share allows high market control. Market growth is used as a measure of a market's attractiveness. Markets experiencing high growth reflect expansion of the total market share available with plenty of opportunity for all to make money. By contrast, competition in low growth markets is often bitter and while a company may enjoy high market share in the short term, given a few months or years the situation might be very different; this makes low growth markets less attractive.

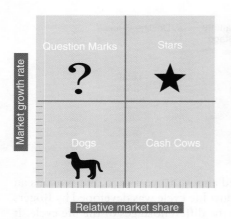 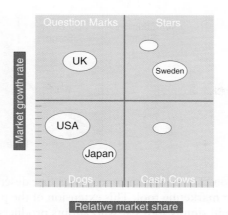

Figure 16-8
Boston matrix

Having considered relative share and growth rates, the organization may consider one of four possible strategies:

1 build share: the company can invest to increase market share (for example turning a 'question mark' into a star);

2 *hold*: the company invests just enough to remain in its present position;

3 *harvest*: the company reduces the amount of investment in order to maximize the short-term cash flows and profits. This may have the effect of turning stars into cash cows; and

4 *divest:* the company can divest – in order to use the resources elsewhere (e.g. investing in the more promising 'question marks').

The application of the portfolio approach to international business, i.e. comparing the strength of a portfolio across a variety of markets, becomes difficult. One away to use the matrix in international marketing is to focus on a single product range and make the circles in the matrices represent country sales instead of product sales, see Figure 16-8. Thus, product management includes the introduction of new products, marketing of existing products and the elimination of others. Resources and the marketing system may not cope with the introduction of too many products over a short space of time. Analysis on a global basis may reveal a product to be a cash cow in one country and a question mark in another. Consequently, decision-making is more complex in international product management.

The product life cycle (PLC), see Figure 16-9, is a theory based upon the biological life cycle (we first considered it in Chapter 3 when discussing industries); it is a marketing tool for evaluating products – a model that provides a framework for thinking in detail about product policy, product introduction and product elimination. After a period of development a product is introduced or launched into the market; it gains more and more customers as it grows; eventually the market stabilizes and the product becomes mature; then after a period of time when the product is overtaken by development and the introduction of better competitors, it goes into decline and is eventually withdrawn.

A variety of strategies for the differing stages of the PLC may be considered. During growth, advertising spend is high and there is a focus upon building brand. In mature markets, producers attempt to differentiate products (brands are key to this). Price wars and intense competition occur. At this point the market reaches saturation. Producers begin to leave the market due to poor margins. Promotion becomes more widespread and uses a greater variety of media.

Marketing managers of organizations have long been concerned with how to launch new products more efficiently. One reason for this interest is the high failure rate of new consumer products. Products are adopted by different consumer groups at different times. Diffusion is the process by which a new idea or new product is accepted by the market; the extent and pace at which a market is likely to adopt new products. The rate of diffusion refers to the speed the new idea spreads from one consumer to the next. Adoption is similar

Stars products with a dominant share of the market and good prospects for growth

Cash cow products with a dominant share of the market but low prospects for growth

Question mark(s) (or problem child) is a business unit or product in a growing market, but without a high market share

Product life cycle the four major stages through which products move: introduction, growth, maturity and decline

Figure 16-9

Product life cycle (PLC)

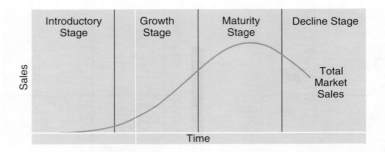

to diffusion. The adoption process was first described almost 50 years ago, but remains an important marketing tool. This extension of the product life cycle was developed by Rogers in 1962 and simply looks at who adopts products at the different stages of the life cycle. It describes the behaviour of consumers as they purchase new products and services. The diffusion model aided understanding of the consumption of new products (Rogers 1976). The individual categories of innovator, early adopter, early majority, late majority and laggards are described below:

- *Innovators* – the first people to adopt a new product; they want to be ahead, and be the first to own.
- *Early adopters* – among the first to get hold of items or services, are key opinion leaders.
- *Early majority* – people who adopt products just prior to the average person.
- *Late majority* – tend to purchase the product later than the average person, sceptical but eventually adopt because of economic necessity or social pressure.
- *Laggards* – the last people to adopt, suspicious of new products and oriented towards the past.

Various scholars and practitioners argue the marketer should focus on one group of customers at a time, using each group as a base for marketing to the next group. The most difficult step is making the transition between early adopters and early majority. This is the *chasm* shown in Figure 16-10. If a successful organization can create a 'bandwagon' effect then momentum builds and the product becomes a de facto standard.

Figure 16-10

The adoption process

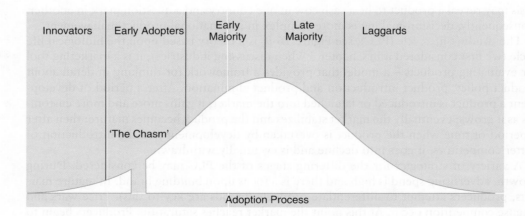

Despite the benefits as an organizing framework, there are problems with using the PLC. In reality very few products follow such a prescriptive cycle. Where they do, the length of each stage varies enormously and not all products go through each stage; some go from introduction to decline. At this stage we might also ask how the PLC is affected by international business. The introduction stage can be shortened due to other competitors from around the globe copying the product; the decline stage can be extended, by exporting beyond your existing markets. The international product life cycle can be a valuable tool for multinational companies to market new products abroad; products in international markets can have consecutive lives in different countries.

In this section we have discussed product management, first discussing arguments for standardizing products worldwide, and then discussing the Boston matrix and product life cycle, product diffusion and portfolios. Product decisions represent one aspect of the traditional marketing mix but product issues impact upon the other components – price, place and promotion. Product management will often determine pricing, the choice of distribution channels and market communication strategies. We will discuss such matters in the remainder of this section but first explain what is meant by branding.

International branding

A strong brand provides competitive advantage

Closely linked with the image of the product is the issue of branding. In the opening case study we recognized the importance of branding. Buyers use information from a variety of sources in order to evaluate the product they may wish to purchase. The design performance and quality of the product itself provide intrinsic cues (signals) whereas brand names and the country of origin, among other factors, present extrinsic cues. Different factors will play a greater or lesser role, i.e. influence in the buyer decision-making process in different situations and context. In some cases, customer perceptions of the company will be influenced by national stereotypes. Customers make generalizations about products and services based on their generalizations about the country of origin. For example, Japanese products tend to be 'X', American products tend to be 'Y' and Chinese products are 'Z'. Such generalizations tend to be based on quality and reliability, cost, use of technology, originality and so on; as a consequence, when making judgements, decision-makers may perceive one product to be inferior to another.

Furthermore, people tend to associate certain products with certain countries, for example Germany may be associated with motorcars and machinery. Overcoming such stereotypes is a key challenge for the international marketer. Increasingly, however, a product may be designed in one country and produced in another for sale in yet another country (see, for example, the Burberry or Dyson case studies described previously). Brands allow customers to identify products or services and their promised benefits allowing the organization to differentiate itself from competition.

A brand can be many things; it may be a legal instrument, an identity system, differentiator, relationship or image in the mind of a customer. They evoke feelings and convey both tangible and intangible benefits. Companies may choose from several branding strategies – different types of branding exist:

1 All branding may occur at the organizational level – corporate brand (see for example Disney or Virgin). A corporate brand increases the attractiveness of the entire company, building trust, loyalty and even commitment among stakeholders. Through a corporate brand, a consistent appearance is maintained. This approach is common among related product lines but may be problematic as product variety and market diversity increase.

2 When products or customer expectations vary, an alternative branding approach, house branding, may be adopted. In such cases, the company name may be used in conjunction with the product name.

3 Finally in some cases it may be beneficial to engage in separate branding.

Many international organizations target various customer segments through different brand names. Furthermore, brands may be global, regional or local. Global brands have worldwide recognition and as such can increase cross and extension sales while providing economies of scale and a concentration on communication budgets, see Figure 16-11. However, there can be adverse consequences also with the possibility of negative spillover

Branding the process of creating and developing successful brands

Brand a name, term, design, symbol or any other feature that identifies one seller's good or service as distinct from those of other sellers

Look back
See chapter 7, p. 204 and chapter 15, p. 485

Corporate brand the application of product branding at the corporate level, reflected visibly through the company name, logo and visual presentation, and in the underlying values of the business

effects leading to a global reduction in sales. Creating a global brand necessitates consistent positioning across the world, resulting in a universally shared meaning of the brand's core concept. Global brands are more effective in homogeneous markets. However, when differences exist between country markets it may be more appropriate to consider local branding. Local brands exist in one country or in a limited geographical area. They represent a custom approach which may result in higher trust levels with customers. This may develop customer loyalty. Periodically or upon start-up, a marketer must assess the brand identifying what the meaning and purpose should be (the intention) and what it is actually (the reality).

Figure 16-11

Top brands (Source: Interbrand 2007)

Interbrand

2007 Rank	2006 Rank	Brand		Country of origin	Sector	2007 Brand Value ($m)	Change in brand value
1	1	Coca-Cola		US	Beverages	65,324	-3%
2	2	Microsoft		US	Computer Software	58,709	3%
3	3	IBM		US	Computer Services	57,091	2%
4	4	GE		US	Diversified	51,569	5%
5	6	Nokia		Finland	Consumer Electronics	33,969	12%
6	6	Toyota		Japan	Automotive	32,070	15%
7	5	Intel		US	Computer Hardware	30,954	-4%
8	9	McDonald's		US	Restaurants	29,398	7%
9	8	Disney		US	Media	29,210	5%
10	10	Mercedes		Germany	Automotive	23,568	8%

International marketing communication

Marketing communication the diffusion of persuasive information about a product aimed at key stakeholders and consumers within the target market segment

The brand is one way of communicating with prospects and customers. Marketing communication is the transmission of persuasive information about goods, services or an idea, aimed at key stakeholders and consumers within the target market segment. Marketing communication aims to raise product visibility and awareness and, at the same time to differentiate the company's products and services from its competitors. While a variety of communication tools exist, such as advertising, sponsoring, sales promotion and direct communication, their use by the international marketer may be influenced by a range of factors – local culture in particular. We discussed perception, culture, communication and negotiation in Chapter 8.

Communication is concerned with a sharing of meaning through the transmission of information. Many organizations will typically develop a central message to be communicated to all stakeholders; for example 'I'm lovin' it' is a trademark of McDonald's Corporation and its affiliates. To ensure consistency of communications, guidelines of corporate design are often developed (see Figure 16-12). Such guidelines may determine the logo, use of colour, and writing styles. If an internationally standardized identity is important to the organization then there will be a greater need to coordinate market communication activities.

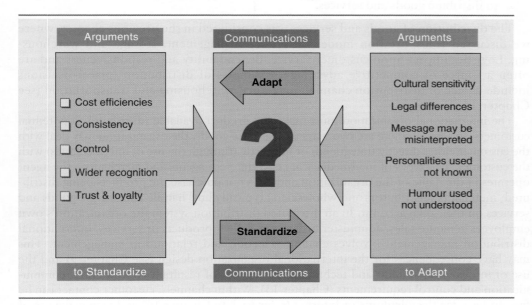

Figure 16-12

International marketing communications – standardization

McDonald's advertising on a streetcar in Shanghai

One of the communication tools which maybe standardized or adapted for local markets is advertising. Advertising is a paid-for form of non-personal communication transmitted through mass media (television, radio, newspapers, magazines, direct mail, outdoor displays and the Internet). It is used to stimulate interest in products and services and promote their benefits. The availability of media, legal restrictions on advertising and cultural differences will be considered by the international marketer when deciding which parts of any campaign to standardize or adapt locally. Standardization presents cost advantages that may result in the message failing to be conveyed. Readers should refer to Chapter 8 and consider the determinants of effective communication across cultures.

Advertising may take place using broadcast media, cinemas, billboards, on taxicabs, etc. One of the problems with advertising is information overload. This has led some marketers to use sponsorships as a means to promote the company and its products. Sponsorship describes the provision of resources by an organization to a person, company, event, cause or activity in exchange for association with the sponsored entity. One of the main objectives of sponsoring is to raise customer awareness. An alternative to sponsorship may be direct marketing communications such as direct mailings which can, like sales calls, be made more effective and efficient through the use of database technologies. The interest and attention of prospects and customers may also be gained through use of *sales promotion*. Sales promotion activities aim to stimulate sales and typically have a short-term focus. Promotion activities may be directed at customers, employees or intermediaries. The sales promotion tools (coupons, discounts, samples, displays, competitions, events and product demonstrations) most often applied in international marketing have differing communication target groups and different objectives.

Advertising a paid-for form of non-personal communication that is transmitted through mass media (television, radio, newspapers, magazines, direct mail, outdoor displays and the Internet)

Sponsorship the financial or material support of an event, activity, person, organization or product by an unrelated organization or donor

Direct marketing the use of non-personal media, the Internet or telesales to introduce products to customers, who then purchase the products by mail, telephone or the Internet

International distribution management

What channels will be used to distribute goods and services?

Another element of the marketing mix is *place*. Place is also known as channel, distribution, or intermediary. It is the mechanism through which goods and/or services are moved from the manufacturer/ service provider to the user or consumer. The distribution system exists for two prime reasons:

1 to establish and maintain customer relationships; and

2 to distribute goods and services.

The distribution of goods and services was considered in the previous chapter, where we discussed transportation modes, inventory management, storage and warehousing. Logistics impact upon customer service, dependability and responsiveness and are often a source of competitive advantage. Examples of distribution (place) decisions include choice of distribution channel, inventory, warehousing and transportation (see Chapter 15).

The international organization must make the product available (distribute) to potential customers. In general, there are two ways to distribute goods; the organization may deal with the customer either directly (integrated) or indirectly (through the use of intermediaries) with the customer. Two types of intermediary are encountered: agents and merchants – the agent operates in the name of the organization and does not purchase the products being distributed; merchants (distributors and wholesalers) typically buy, handle and sell the goods and services on their own account. In an integrated distribution system the organization's own employees generate sales, administer orders and deliver products or services. International distribution management involves channel selection and relationship management. This may have consequences for the international organization design (see Chapter 9) and the use of information systems and technology in support of resultant coordination, communication and control requirements (Chapter 13). Within channels, customer contact can be face-to-face, via the telephone or Internet (refer back to Chapter 14) and may make use of mail order selling.

The integrated distribution alternative may be preferred in the following situations; when a marketing success depends upon specialized product or application knowledge; a high level of service is necessary; product know-how is needed to advise customers adequately; or where there is a need to control local marketing practice or it has not been possible to find appropriate distribution partners. Integrated distribution demands access to human and facility resources in the target country. Thus far we have recognized different channels, however, organizations generally rely on a mix of channels.

Different channels may vary in location and access to customers. Intermediaries (middlemen) may perform a variety of functions such as: the physical handling of products (from import through assembly and inventory to delivery); product promotion, sales and customer acquisition; the development and management of business relationships and may also assume certain business risks. The distribution of power between the organization and its intermediaries varies from one country to another and from one product market to another. Power relationships impact upon the organization's ability to control the implementation of marketing mix decisions in the channel. International distribution decisions influence product management but can also impact upon pricing (intermediaries require a margin).

International sales management

Every commercial organization must acquire customers. The customers of an international marketer may be final customers or intermediaries – both require relationships to be built and maintained. Such relationships are managed by customer contact resources. Such resources must be knowledgeable about product features and benefits, how the product is used by different customer segments and how to communicate with potential buyers (see Figure 16-13). In the case of the international organization, knowledge of culture and its relationship with communications and negotiations will also be required. Customers in other countries often need more information for their buying decision and may experience communication problems due to language barriers and differences in meanings. Activities associated with managing the sales function will include resource allocation, target setting and the development of policies, processes and procedures which specify how work should be carried out.

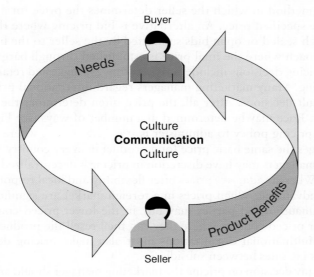

Figure 16-13
Buyer-seller 'fit'

A variety of sales techniques may be employed. Techniques can be individualized and personal or not. Many believe that personal selling is the most effective way to sell in any market due to the nature of communication. A salesperson has the flexibility to modify the message and the offer there and then and can match the product with buyer needs. However, individualized communication and sales costs money, consequently organizations may also rely on less-expensive sales techniques such as the Internet, catalogue sales or self service. Other ways to reduce sales costs include the use of processes to target and qualify prospects.

Potential customers (prospects) can be found using both internal and external sources. The sales force will have developed market knowledge and collected market information about customers and prospects. In some cases, the customer takes the initiative in searching for a product or service and may make inquiries of suppliers through letters, telephone calls, e-mail, faxes, the Internet, request for proposals (RFP), request for information (RFI), request for quotation (RFQ) or invitation to tender. In such cases, the supplying organization must decide whether it is able and willing to quote or make an offer. In some cases they may need to simply dispatch sales literature while in other cases they need to tailor responses to specific requirements. In many cases, initial contact will be through a sales call. A customer database and contact management system enables such activities. Product information is communicated and attempts are made to deliver benefits to the prospect. This usually starts the negotiation process. More complex sales may need several interactions and follow up sessions. Again, there are a number of software solutions that will support this process; they will be discussed in the final section of the chapter. There are also after sale activities, such as providing service, handling claims and disputes. The manager of the international sales force will have to recruit and select human resources, train and develop them. Such resources, on an ongoing basis, require motivation and compensation.

Personal selling the task of informing and convincing customers to purchase through personal communication

Request for proposal Publication of a request for information related to any required product, by a prospective purchaser. The RFP goal is to attract offers by companies to supply the intended purchase. A request for proposal is the beginning of the selection process

Request for quotation a formal request for suppliers to prepare bids based on the terms and conditions set by the buyer

International pricing

Should products be priced the same in each country?

Price the value placed on what is exchanged

Pricing strategy an approach to influencing and determining pricing decisions

Standard pricing (uniform geographic pricing) – pricing in which the same price is charged to all customers regardless of geographic location

Adaptive pricing pricing in which a different price is charged to customers dependent upon geographic location

In this section we explain the importance of international pricing decisions and the factors which influence the final price. Product pricing is important because it may be used by the buyer to judge quality, attractiveness and general value (cues). Pricing may be used as a competitive strategy and will interact with distribution. In short, proper pricing of goods and services can be a key to success for the international organization. The marketing manager may select from several alternative pricing methods and strategies. Administered pricing is a method in which the seller determines the price for a product and the customer pays the specified price. An alternative is bid pricing where the determination of prices is through sealed or open bids submitted by the seller to the buyer. Negotiated pricing is an approach where the final price is established through bargaining.

Examples of pricing decisions include: pricing strategy, suggested retail price, discounts and seasonal pricing. Many marketing managers regard international pricing decisions to be the most difficult decisions. After all, the price often determines the attractiveness of a company's offer. Price may be determined in a number of ways (see Figure 16-14). Perhaps the simplest pricing policy to administer is standard pricing where the international organization charges the same basic price for a product in every country market served. In other cases, local managers may have discretion in pricing – decentralized pricing decisions enable flexibility. Whereas adaptive prices offer flexibility and local responsiveness they are not without a disadvantage. When prices in a foreign market are significantly lower than another market, unauthorized parties may buy in the lower-priced country and import them to the higher-priced country where they can then resell the product at higher prices (grey markets). Multinational organizations must also make pricing decisions for intra company transfers i.e. sales between subsidiaries.

Before making any decision on pricing the marketing manager should analyze competitor pricing, cost and market structure alongside the corporate strategy. The marketing manager will evaluate different strategic pricing options and select the most appropriate approach which is then implemented throughout the organization. A critical factor to be considered when developing a pricing strategy in international markets is the response of customers and competitors. The organization may consider a range of objectives for pricing such as:

1 rate of return or cost plus pricing or mark-up pricing;

2 competition-led pricing;

3 market or price-skimming is a pricing strategy whereby a company charges the highest possible price that buyers will pay;

4 market penetration – a pricing strategy of setting a price below the prices of competing brands in order to penetrate a market and produce a larger unit sales volume;

5 demand led – the level of demand for a product, resulting in a high price when demand is strong and a low price when demand is weak;

6 premium pricing;

7 pricing an item in the product line low, with the intention of selling a higher-priced item in the line (bait pricing);

8 pricing together two or more complementary products and selling them for a single price (bundle pricing); and

9 early cash recovery.

The marketing manager may have less influence over pricing of some products compared with others. Commodities and commoditized products have an established market price – the mechanisms of supply and demand dictates that price when products are undifferentiated. A variety of factors influence price setting. Costs determine a product's

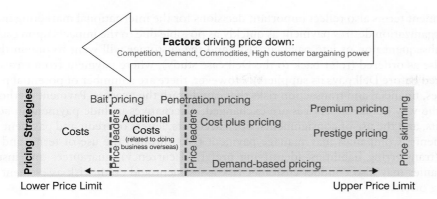

Figure 16-14

Basis for pricing

lower-price limit. The attractiveness of a product to the target customers determines the theoretical price ceiling in a given market. However, the purchasing power of customers, itself influenced by income distribution, exchange rates and inflation will drive price down. Furthermore, additional costs must be accounted for when selling in another country, Figure 16-15. There are additional costs of doing business (travel expenses), longer distribution channels, additional packaging and labelling, taxes, tariffs and administration fees.

The bargaining power of customers and intermediaries must also be considered. The prices of competitor products and customer satisfaction with the products will strongly influence what the customer is willing to pay. In some countries, particular retail organizations may be very powerful and can therefore dictate the price they are prepared to pay for products and services from suppliers.

Finally there are cultural considerations and factors that impact upon pricing decisions. It may be desirable to end the price with a digit '9' since Western societies typically round down such figures and believe the goods are cheaper than they really are. Numbers have different meanings in other cultures and these meanings should be considered. The international organization, when forced to lower price, may resort to strategies such as modifying the product, replacing costly materials with less expensive ones to reduce cost; shifting production or component assembly to the served country or shifting production to lower wage countries. In other cases, the international organization may attempt to increase unit sales and attain cost reduction through economies of scale benefit.

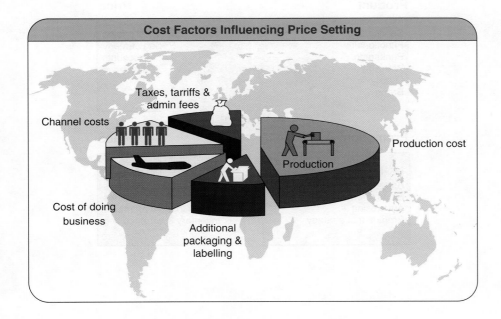

Figure 16-15

Pricing products to be sold in another country – cost factors

Look back
See chapter 10, p. 306

Payment terms also reflect important decisions for the international marketing manager. The organization desires payment as quickly as possible due to the impacts upon cash flows and subsequent non or late payment risks and the customer will want to obtain the merchandise as ordered (refer back to the Dell case study), where payment from customers is collected before Dell pays its suppliers). However, there are a number of potential payment disputes, financial and transaction risks that can disturb the process. Payment methods regulate the way goods or services are exchanged. Alternatives include payment in advance, deposits, and the use of consignments, open accounts, letters of credit and payment against documents. Companies may manage payment risks through the use of terms and conditions (transferring liabilities, identifying preferred currency), guarantees and insurance. Companies may also conduct customer risk assessment and credit risk assessment before making offers.

The marketing plan

A key output of the marketing process is the marketing plan. The specific content of any marketing plan varies from organization to organization. A common structure for the marketing plan is as follows:

Marketing plan the written arrangements for specifying, implementing and controlling an organization's marketing activities and marketing mixes

1 introduction – this section will include the reasons for the plan, target audience and key assumptions;

2 executive summary – in this section the main results of analysis and conclusions drawn are presented;

3 actual situation – in this section the internal and external situations are analyzed, strengths and weaknesses, opportunities and threats presented;

4 objectives – target customer segments and the means to differentiate the company's offerings from competitors are identified along with market share and financial objectives. An activity plan based on the marketing mix and the proposed organizations are also included; and

5 budgets – the costs of planned activities are presented.

A summary of the marketing mix decisions is shown in Figure 16-16. In the next and final section we consider how technology may enable marketing and related decision-making.

Figure 16-16

Summary of marketing mix decisions

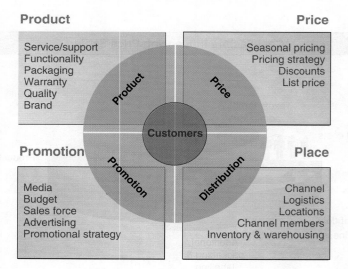

Enabling technologies

MNCs and SMEs alike are now critically dependent upon marketing technologies to enable their marketing processes and activities. International marketing is evolving as the marketplace becomes increasingly global. It can be argued that many of the changes taking place, such as the greater homogenisation of consumer demand (refer back to Chapter 2) and the increasing speed and intensity of competition have accelerated due to of advances in technology. Technology facilitates the collection, analysis and dissemination of information for marketing purposes worldwide. Not only does technology make such processes faster but it also allows achievement at lower cost. Integrated technologies enable the organization to be both adaptive and responsive.

In previous chapters we have considered integrated technologies such as enterprise systems (Chapter 13) and communication (Chapter 14) based on Internet technologies. In this section we revisit the role of technology in providing solutions to international marketing problems. Technologies of particular interest include those associated with e-business and e-commerce, technologies used in operations (in Chapter 15) database technologies and electronic communication tools. We briefly introduced CRM in Chapter 13.

Look back
See chapter 13, p. 436

In this section we focus on the concept in more detail, considering technologies, processes and philosophies associated with winning and retaining customers; such approaches seek to build a sustainable long-term business with customers. Three phases of CRM are typically described: acquisition (magnetism/attraction), retention (stickiness) and extension (elastic); in essence we may consider CRM to really be about M-CARE – managing customer acquisition retention and extension. Traditional marketing places emphasis on the marketing mix and individual transactions whereas relationship marketing focuses on winning and retaining customers.

Relationship marketing requires a different philosophy in the organization and is reliant upon database technologies to support customer acquisition, retention and continued selling activities, see Figure 16-17. The aim of CRM technology is to provide an interface between the customer and the employee to replace or facilitate direct interaction. Ideal CRM systems support multichannel communications, needs of customers (product information, order placement, post sales support) and the core needs of employees (placing orders received by phone, fax or face-to-face and answer a customer's questions). Databases lie at the heart of such systems, which may also make use of expert knowledge technologies.

The Internet, discussed in Chapter 14, is both a communication and a transaction vehicle which presents opportunity for domestic and cross-border activity in both areas (Prahalad and Hamel 1990). Consequently it impacts upon international marketing and may be used to build a brand image, provide product support, win business and interact with prospects and customers. Transaction capabilities can have both revenue generation and cost reduction potential. The dissemination of information via the Internet can also reduce costs, replacing expensive alternative and less efficient communication channels.

Some organizations use the web primarily as a communication tool while others use it to reach and sell to (transact) consumers who may be inaccessible. In some cases, the organization will use the Internet to communicate with domestic audiences only while in other cases the international audience will be targeted. The Internet impacts upon the marketing mix in a variety of ways. It enables the adaptation of *price* to the level of the individual user but transparency makes comparative pricing possible at low cost for the consumer. Consequently, the buyer power is increased and there is a tendency for the standardization of prices online. Web-based technologies lower barriers to entry and increase rivalry through the transparency of product pricing. *Distribution channels* are affected through the process of disintermediation as the Internet makes direct contact between end-users and producers more feasible. However, problems of information overload drive reintermediation.

The Internet will also impact upon *product management*. Announcements on the Internet will spawn immediate demand and companies may find it easier to test multiple new product variations simultaneously. Small companies offering specialized niche products should be able to find customers more easily. The Internet also enables the customization of marketing *communications* to the level of the individual. It offers an efficient medium for conducting worldwide market research (see online surveys, web visitor tracking, advertising measurement, customer identification systems and e-mail) and the understanding of global consumers.

The Internet can also be used to make markets through vehicles such as auctions and exchanges. Furthermore, Internet technologies may be applied within the organization (intranet) to facilitate communications and transactions. With database technologies it can be used to facilitate knowledge management while also linking front-office and back-office systems, processes and activities. Cost savings can be made in many areas of the supply chain and organizations may use such technologies to mass customize their offerings, treating customers as individuals. It is evident that information technology and management systems are now critical to the success of many international organizations. As was mentioned in Chapter 13, the key challenge is to integrate customer facing (front-office) systems with operational (back office) and management systems throughout the organization. Technology can be used to support a custom-led approach and improve coordination and communications.

Figure 16-17

Technology-enabled customer relationship management

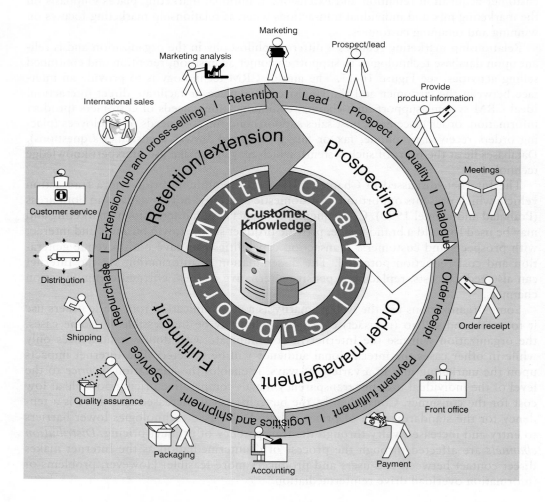

Customer acquisition management

Both databases and the Internet enable companies to acquire customers. The aim of customer acquisition management (CAM) is to gain *leads* which generate new sales (see the prospecting phase in Figure 16-17). With e-commerce such leads are normally processed via digital channels. Customers may be attracted to digital channels using either off or online methods (search engines, links, banners and e-mail). While simply having an e-mail address may be sufficient to engage a prospect in an online relationship, ideally what we need is a qualified lead (additional contact information and information indicating they are likely to make a purchase). Better still, and with time, organizations may seek to collect more information allowing creation of a customer profile. Thus we may see the first step as *customer identification* (using cookies and logon screens) and will then build a profile (customer differentiation) allowing the organization to segment customers. Relationships are enhanced using interaction and personalization.

A concern, for the international organization is how to drive traffic to an e-commerce site. Web-users use search engines to find information online. It is therefore important for an organization to be registered with a search engine. Not only should a company be registered, it will want to optimize its position in the listings (ranking). Site visits (traffic) may also be increased by e-mail. Methods such as 'email-a-friend' – forward a page to a colleague, screensavers and online postcards are referred to as viral marketing. Finally, the last major technique of increasing traffic using online means is through banner advertising. Companies may pay to place a static, animated, interactive or rich media banner (advert) on another website or portal which when clicked, may direct the visitor to their site or collect their e-mail address. Banners can be used to generate revenue, deliver content, shape attitudes and build brand awareness, solicit response and encourage retention. They are used much more with business-to-consumer than the business-to-business e-commerce.

Mixed mode buying behaviour

Understanding why customers shop online can help organizations devise means to encourage prospects to engage in buying. Customers may buy offline, online or may engage in

Lead a potential sales contact (prospect): an individual or organization that expresses an interest in your goods or services. Leads are typically obtained through the referral of an existing customer, or through a direct response to advertising

Customer profile information that can be used to segment a customer

Viral marketing E-mail is used to transmit a promotional message to another potential customer

Banner advertising a rectangular graphic displayed on a webpage for the purposes of advertising. It is normally possible to perform a click-through to access further information

Figure 16-18
Buying behaviour

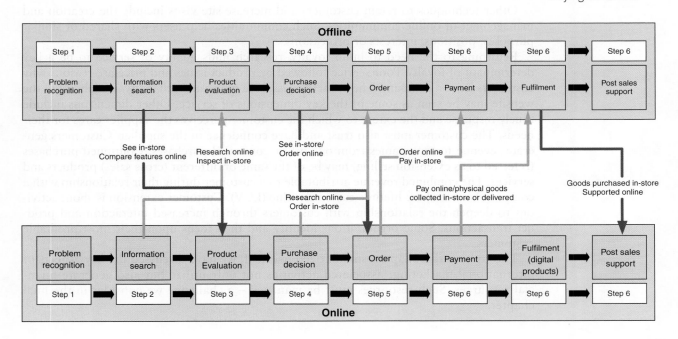

multimode buying, i.e. will use different channels for different stages of the buying process. Companies who understand how customers use new media in their purchase decision-making can develop integrated communications strategies which support their customers at each stage of the buying process, see Figure 16-18.

The simple buying process may be broken down into stages of problem recognition, information search, evaluation, decision, purchase and post sales support. Companies must consider how they can use technology to support each stage. Aside from differences in buying behaviour in target markets, we might consider the differences between B2C and B2B buying behaviour. There tend to be far fewer but larger buyers in business-to-business which means that efforts to promote the website using banner advertising or listing in search engines is less important. Business purchases typically involve a more complex decision-making process since more people are involved (users, influences, and buyers, deciders and the gatekeepers).

Customer retention

Companies typically want to keep customers so that they continue buying from them. This is a challenge for organizations as today's customers are more empowered, impatient with short attention spans, facing lots of choice and able to switch easily from one supplier to another. In many industries, profitability is seen to be dependent on loyalty and loyalty on satisfaction. With reduced loyalty and satisfaction comes the threat of defection; worse still, dissatisfied customers may actually deter other prospects and customers from doing business with the organization. Consequently it is important for companies to identify, measure and track loyalty drivers and implement plans to make improvements. In e-commerce, a range of tools to generate repeat visits are used. One method is to regularly update content. Personalization and mass customization can be used to tailor information. While the two concepts are similar, personalization aims to tailor content to an individual's needs while mass customization tailors content to a group with similar interests (see also collaborative filtering). Such techniques take advantage of the dynamic possibilities of web content. User's preferences are stored in and content is taken from a database.

Other techniques to retain customers and increase site visits include the creation and management of online communities. Such communities help users with shared or similar purposes, positions, interests or professions.

Returning to the need to build loyalty, research finds quality of service to be a key determinant of loyalty. Poor service followed by product issues and price are reasons why customers leave a company. The attractiveness, ease of use and reliability/availability of the website may be seen as some of the key dimensions of service. Other dimensions include timely response and the extent to which the customer perceives the supplier cares for their needs. The customer must also trust and have confidence in the supplier. Customers generate revenue for companies from one-off or continued purchases. Continued purchases (referred to as extension selling) may be of the same or different (cross-sales) products and services. The combined revenue attributable to a customer during their relationship with a company is termed the lifetime customer value (LCV). Customer extension is about activities to deepen the relationship with customers through increased interaction and product transactions. Some organizations identify and then focus upon their most profitable customers.

Throughout this chapter, summarized overleaf, we have discussed the key aspects of international marketing; associated activities not only utilize but also generate financial resources. Such resources must be managed – a challenge we consider in the final chapter.

Customer satisfaction when an exchange meets the needs and expectations of the buyer

Personalization structuring marketing communications in response to a user's particular interests or usage pattern

Summary of key learning points

Marketing is the management process responsible for identifying, anticipating and satisfying customer requirements profitably. The key difference between domestic marketing and marketing on an international scale is the multidimensionality and complexity of the many foreign country markets within which a company may operate. An international manager needs a knowledge and awareness of these complexities and the implications they have for international marketing management. Key factors include: diverse, multicultural, widespread and sometimes fragmented markets with different governments, politics, economics and financial systems; there are also different stakeholders and business rules to contend with and a need for control and coordination across markets.

The international marketing process is concerned with how work is done to create marketing strategies and plans. There are three essential stages in the process: analysis, planning and the development of the marketing programme. Analysis is used to support planning. The organization may analyze its environment to identify opportunities and specific markets to enter and will identify customers and buyer behaviour. One of the first tasks for the international marketing manager is to assess potential for success. The organization uses research to determine if there is demand for its products elsewhere and if there is, seeks to estimate potential market share so that the opportunity can be quantified. Determining opportunity is a complex challenge and requires analysis of end customers' needs and buying behaviour, intermediaries, competitors and the industry as well as the wider environment. Given the large number of countries worldwide there is a need to focus attention. The marketing intelligence system is used to gather, process, assess, and make available marketing data and information in a format that allows marketing managers to function more effectively. External and internal analyses are the basis of good strategy formulation.

Marketing strategy indicates the opportunities to pursue, specific target markets to address, and the types of competitive advantages that are to be developed and exploited when meeting marketing goals. Strategy is concerned with the optimal application of the resources a firm possesses relative to competitors. When marketing their products, firms need to create a successful mix of: the right product, sold at the right price, in the right place and using the most suitable promotion. Marketing mix variables (such as product, price, place, promotion and people) are specified. The international marketing manager must consider how products, price, promotion and place (channels) are to be managed internationally; in each case arguments are considered for standardization or adaptation in the marketing mix. The marketing mix is the tactical 'toolkit' of the marketing programme; the 4Ps are variables that an organization can control in order to appeal to the target market and facilitate satisfying exchange.

International marketing is evolving as the marketplace becomes increasingly global. It can be argued that many of the changes taking place, such as the greater homogenization of consumer demand and the increasing speed and intensity of competition have accelerated due to of advances in technology. Technology facilitates the collection, analysis and dissemination of information for marketing purposes worldwide. Not only does technology make such processes faster but it also allows achievement at lower cost. Integrated technologies enable the organization to be both adaptive and responsive.

Review questions

Virgin case study:

1 What does the cable company (NTL) get for money spent on a licence to use the Virgin brand?

2 How does Virgin's product diversification strategy impact upon the brand? Will numerous brand extensions threaten the inherent value of the Virgin brand?

3 What other risks may be associated with the brand? What would happen if Branson left the Virgin Group – retiring or making a sudden departure?

4 The basic idea behind 'extending' a brand is to develop a new product or service which can piggyback on the perceptions and feelings associated with a parent brand. Identify examples of companies who have had success with brand extension.

Burberry case study

Refer back to the Burberry case study, at the start of Chapter 7.

Internationalization and market entry strategies

1 How important is it for Burberry to have control over:
   a. Product development?
   b. Sourcing?
   c. Manufacturing?
   d. Distribution (place)?

Explain your answers for each section.

2 Identify alternative means for Burberry to control distribution, commenting on preferred approaches.

Marketing strategy

In their IPO Prospectus (2002), Burberry clearly identify the importance of active marketing communications in the development of an image and lifestyle that is capable of 'generating interest among retail customers, wholesale buyers and the media' (p. 34).

3 Would you advise Burberry to centralize or decentralize management of marketing? Explain your answer.

Burberry communications

4 Discuss the marketing communications options open to Burberry – which approaches do you favour and why?

Branding

Earlier in the chapter we suggested that a brand can be many things but that branding concerns activities directed at influencing customers and stakeholders through communication and brand objects.

5 How might you go about rebranding the company?

Pricing

6 Should Burberry adopt an ethnocentric (standard) or adaptive approach to pricing – explain your answer.

References

Andersen, O. (1993) 'On the Internationalization Process of Firms: A Critical Analysis', *Journal of International Business Studies* 24(2):209–231.

Barney, J. (1986) 'Organizational Culture: Can it be a Source of Sustained Competitive Advantage?', *The Academy of Management Review* (July 1986) 11(3):656–665.

Bartlett, C. and Ghoshal, S. (1987) 'Managing Across Borders: New Organizational Responses', *International Executive* (Fall 1987) 29(3):10–13.

Buzzell, R. D. (1968) 'Can You Standardize Multinational Marketing?', *Harvard Business Review* (November/December 1968) 46(6):102–113.

Collis, D. (1991) 'The Resource-Based Analysis of Global Competition: The Case of the Bearings Industry', *Strategic Management Journal* (Special Issue: Global Strategy) 12:49.

Day, G. S. and Wensley, R. (1988) 'Assessing Advantage: a Framework for Diagnosing Competitive Superiority', *Journal of Marketing* (April 1988) 52(2):1–20.

Elinder, E. (1961) 'How International Can Advertising Be?', *International Advertiser* (December): 12–16.

Hofstede, G. (1994) 'The Business Of International Business Is Culture', *International Business Review* 3(1):1–14.

Hunt, S. D. and Morgan, R. M. (1995) 'The Comparative Advantage Theory of Competition', *Journal of Marketing* (April 1995) 59(2):1–15.

Interbrand (2007) www.ourfishbowl.com/images/surveys/Interbrand_BGB_2007.pdf.

Jain, S. C. (1989) 'Standardization of International Marketing Strategy: Some Research Hypotheses', *Journal of Marketing* (January 1989) 53(1):70–79.

Johanson, J. and Wiedersheim-Paul, F. (1975) 'The Internationalization Of The Firm – Four Swedish Cases', *Journal of Management Studies* (October 1975) 12(3):305–322.

Kale, S. (1987) 'A Strategic Approach to International Segmentation', *International Marketing Review* (Summer 1987) 4(2):60–71.

Kahan, R. (1998) 'Using database marketing techniques to enhance your one-to-one marketing initiatives', *The Journal of Consumer Marketing Santa Barbara* 15(5):491–493.

Levitt, T. (1983) 'The Globalization Of Markets', *Harvard Business Review* (May/June 1983) 61(3)92–102.

Lundstrom, W. J. and White, D. S. (1997) 'A Gap Analysis of Professional and Academic Perceptions of the Importance of International Marketing Curriculum Content and Research Areas', *Journal of Marketing Education* 19(2):16–25.

Mcgahan, A. and Porter, M. E. (1997) 'How Much Does Industry Matter, Really?', *Strategic Management Journal* (Summer Special Issue) 18:15–30.

Moore, C. M. (2004) 'The Burberry business model: creating an international luxury fashion brand', *International Journal of Retail & Distribution Management* 32(8):412–422.

Perlmutter, H. (1969) 'The Tortuous Evolution of the Multinational Corporation', *Columbia Journal of World Business* (January/February 1969) 4(1):9–19.

Peteraf, M. A. (1993) 'The Cornerstones of Competitive Advantage: A Resource-Based View', *Strategic Management Journal* (March 1993) 14(3):179–191.

Philip, N. E. (1995). 'Which International Business (IB) Courses Do IB Faculty Consider the Most Important?', *Journal of Teaching in International Business* 6(3):87–100.

Porter, M. E. (2001) 'Strategy and the Internet', *Harvard Business Review* (March 2001): 62–78.

Prahalad, C. and Hamel, G. (1990) 'The Core Competence Of The Corporation', *Harvard Business Review* (May/June 1990) 68(3):79–91.

Quelch, J. A., and Harding, D. (1996) 'Brands Versus Private Labels: Fighting To Win', *Harvard Business Review* (January/February 1996) 74(1):99–109.

Rogers, E. M. (1976) 'New Product Adoption and Diffusion', *The Journal of Consumer Research* (March 1976) 2(4):290–301.

Stalk, G., Evans, P. and Shulman, L. E. (1992) 'Competing On Capabilities: The New Rules Of Corporate Strategy', *Harvard Business Review* (March/April 1992) 70(2):54–66.

Suggestions for further reading

Journals

Marketing literature is vast. Readers are advised to consider the journals, textbooks and well-known articles shown below.

Journal of Marketing

Journal of Marketing's primary objectives are (1) to lead in the development, dissemination, and implementation of marketing concepts, practice, and information and (2) to probe and promote the use of marketing concepts by businesses, not-for-profits, and other institutions for the betterment of society.

http://www.marketingpower.com/content1053.php

International Marketing Review

The International Marketing Review provides a platform for contemporary ideas in international marketing, the thinking, theory and practice. It is not a home for general marketing papers, but delivers research based on empirical studies of marketing strategy issues as well as comparative studies of markets and marketing practice with a purely 'international' flavour.

http://www.emeraldinsight.com/info/journals/imr/imr.jsp

International Journal of Research in Marketing

The International Journal of Research in Marketing is an international journal for marketing academics and practitioners. Building on a great tradition of global marketing scholarship, IJRM aims to contribute substantially to the field of marketing research by providing a high-quality medium for the dissemination of new marketing knowledge and methods.

http://www.elsevier.com/wps/find/journaldescription.cws_home/505550/description# description

Key articles

Scholars of this subject area have often read the following:

1 Andersen, O. (1993) 'On the internationalization process of firms: a critical analysis', *Journal of International Business Studies* 24(2):209–231.
2 Barney, J. (1986) 'Organizational culture: can it be a source of sustained competitive advantage?', *The Academy of Management Review* (July 1986) 11(3):656–665.
3 Collis, D. (1991) 'The resource-based analysis of global competition: the case of the bearings industry', *Strategic Management Journal* (Special Issue: Global Strategy) 12:49.
4 Day, G. S. and Wensley, R. (1988) 'Assessing advantage: a framework for diagnosing competitive superiority', *Journal of Marketing* (April 1988) 52(2):1–20.
5 Hunt, S. D. and Morgan, R. M. (1995) 'The comparative advantage theory of competition', *Journal of Marketing* (April 1995) 59(2):1–15.

6 Levitt, T. (1983) 'The globalization of markets', *Harvard Business Review* (May/June 1983) 61(3):92–102.

7 Mcgahan, A. and Porter, M. E. (1997) 'How much does industry matter, really?', *Strategic Management Journal* (Summer Special Issue) 18(15–30).

8 Peteraf, M. A. (1993) 'The cornerstones of competitive advantage: a resource-based view', *Strategic Management Journal* (March 1993) 14(3):179–191.

9 Prahalad, C. and Hamel, G. (1990) 'The core competence of the corporation', *Harvard Business Review* (May/June 1990) 68(3):79–91.

10 Stalk, G., Evans, P. and Shulman, L. E. (1992) 'Competing on capabilities: the new rules of corporate strategy', *Harvard Business Review* (March/April 1992) 70(2):54–66.

Chapter 17

Managing global financial resources

Key concepts

- Finance ■ Economics ■ Accounting ■ Capital budgeting ■ Cost of capital ■ Foreign exchange risk
- Transfer pricing tariff ■ Multilateral netting ■ Fronting loan ■ NPV ■ IRR ■ ROI
- Investment appraisal ■ Centralized depository ■ Financial statements ■ Consolidated accounts
- Agency ■ Corporate governance ■ Auditing ■ Internal control

---

By the end of this chapter you will be able to:

- Identify factors in the global economic environment likely to impact upon international financial management goals and accountancy practice

- Describe the techniques used by international organizations to manage working capital

- Evaluate capital budgeting techniques used by international organizations

- Discuss sources of investment capital available to international businesses

- Evaluate the need for international harmonization of accounting practice

- Explain what is meant by corporate governance and why the international organization strives to achieve it

Active learning case

First Pacific

Founded in 1981, First Pacific began as a small Hong Kong-based financial services company. The First Pacific group began building a portfolio of acquisitions. By the mid-1980s, the company had acquired 23 companies, with activities spread across industries from dry goods (Hong Kong's Dragonseed), to computer products in Australia, soap and shoe polish distributorships in Thailand, to coffee in Saudi Arabia and office properties in Hong Kong. First Pacific also amassed extensive holdings in the Philippines. The company adopted a policy of identifying undervalued companies in the Pacific Rim and hiring new management to build them. Managers for the individual companies were given near-complete autonomy to run the companies.

The company changed direction in 1991. First Pacific was refocused on its four core areas of marketing and distribution, telecommunications, real estate, and banking. In just a decade and a half, First Pacific had grown from a tiny company to one of Asia's largest **conglomerates**, which posted a profit of HK\$1.57 billion (US\$202 million) on turnover of HK\$54.8 billion (US\$7.03 billion) in 1996. First Pacific continued to seek out investment opportunities throughout the 1990s taking a controlling stake in the Philippines' leading telecomms company, PLDT, towards the end of the decade. They also invested in Fort Bonifacio, an urban development in Taguig City, Metro Manila, Philippines – also known as the Bonifacio Global City.

The company recorded revenues of \$2054.6 million during the fiscal year ended December 2004, a decrease of 5 per cent from 2003. The decrease was primarily attributable to the depreciation of rupiah (Indonesian currency). The operating profit of the company during fiscal year 2004 was \$229.6 million, an increase of 3.9 per cent over fiscal year 2003. The net profit was \$179.0 million during fiscal year 2004, an increase of 32.6 per cent over 2003. By 2006, the company, once a sprawling conglomerate, had shed holdings and sharpened its focus, maintaining interests primarily in consumer food products and telecommunications. The company claims to be among Asia's first professionally managed investment companies with governance benchmarked to world class standards. Headquartered and listed in Hong Kong, investment strategy focuses on emerging markets in Asia and opportunities for long-term value creation. Investing in telecomms, consumer foods and infrastructure (property); these are seen as the three core businesses with strong cash flows. Investments are primarily in the Philippines and Indonesia. Goals for First Pacific in 2007 included: 'Evaluate new investment opportunities in telecoms, consumer food products and infrastructure in the emerging markets in Asia; continue to enhance value in our current operating businesses and to strengthen the balance sheet in support of new investment opportunities'.

©iStockphoto.com/Oktay Ortakcioglu

Principal investments

■ The Philippine Long Distance Telephone Company (PLDT) is the leading telecommunications service provider in the Philippines. It has one of the largest **market capitalizations** among Philippine **listed companies**. Through its three principal business groups, PLDT offers a wide range of telecommunications services: wireless (principally through wholly owned

First Pacific (HKEx: 00142) is a Hong Kong-based investment and management company with operations located in Asia. Its principal business interests relate to telecommunications, consumer food products and infrastructure.

Listed in Hong Kong, First Pacific's shares are also available in the United States through American Depositary Receipts. The company has its head office in Hong Kong and Registered Office in Bermuda. Ernst & Young act as auditors for the group.

Description: communications investment and management company involved in consumer food products, telecommunications and property operations in South-East Asia.

Key numbers for fiscal year ending December 2006:
Sales: \$2474.8m
One-year growth: 24.6%
Net income: \$221.7m
Income growth: 59.7%

Conglomerate a firm operating in several industries

Market capitalization the aggregate value of a company or stock (obtained by multiplying the number of shares outstanding by their current price per share)

Listed company firm whose shares are listed (quoted) on a stock exchange for public trading

▶ ▶ ▶

First Pacific principal investments

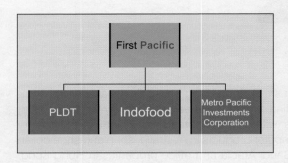

subsidiary company Smart Communications, Inc.); fixed line (principally through PLDT); and information and communications technology (principally through wholly owned subsidiary company ePLDT). PLDT has developed the Philippines' most extensive fibre optic backbone, cellular, fixed line and satellite networks.

- PT Indofood is the premier processed-foods company in Indonesia. It is based in Jakarta, and is listed on the Jakarta and Surabaya Stock Exchanges. Through its four strategic business groups, Indofood offers a wide range of food products: consumer branded products (noodles, nutrition and special foods, snack foods and food seasonings), bogasari (flour and pasta), edible oils and fats (plantations, cooking oils, margarine and shortening) and distribution. Indofood is one of the world's largest instant noodle manufacturers by volume, and the largest flour miller in Indonesia. Indofood's flourmill in Jakarta is one of the largest in the world in terms of production capacity in a single location. It also has an extensive distribution network in the country.

- Metro Pacific Investments Corporation is a Philippine-based, publicly listed, investment and management company with holdings in water utility, real estate development and healthcare enterprises.

Introduction

The opening case study will be used throughout this chapter to explore the challenges of managing financial resources across country and company borders. Trade, discussed in the introductory chapter, allows consumers to buy from foreign sources. Organizations involved with international trade are exposed to more competitors but are also able to export goods themselves, tap into foreign investors, and relocate to foreign markets, increasing their competitive position by avoiding trade barriers and transportation cost, or by benefiting from local resources. International trade creates both opportunities and threats. Trade in different countries creates issues associated with currency and exposes organizations to new challenges associated with where production or trade takes place.

In the previous two chapters we have considered the primary activities of the value chain, production and marketing, associated with trade. In previous chapters we also considered the use of human (labour) and technical resources in such activities. As yet, we have not discussed the management of financial resources in the international organization, a matter we address in this chapter. Economic and international economic theory provides insights and explanations for matters discussed in previous chapters such as operations and marketing and for the chapters which considered human and technological resources. The global economy refers to the expansion of economies beyond national borders, in particular, the expansion of production by transnational organizations to many countries around the world. The global economy includes the globalization of production, markets, finance, communications, and the labour force.

Finance is the branch of economics which studies *the management of money* and other assets; the commercial activity of providing funds and capital. Finance studies the ways in which organizations raise, allocate, and use monetary resources over time, taking into account the risks entailed. Financial management is the term used to describe the raising of capital to finance an organization's operations and the decisions of source and use of the financial resources. Finally, the system for recording and summarizing business transactions and activities designed to accumulate, measure, and communicate financial information about economic entities for decision-making purposes is termed accounting.

Accounting refers to the overall process of identifying, measuring, recording, interpreting, and communicating the results of economic activity; tracking business income and expenses and using these measurements to answer specific questions about the financial and tax status of the business, i.e. it is a system that provides quantitative information about finances. Where as financial accounting is the use of accounting information for reporting to parties outside the organization, management accounting is concerned with the provisions and use of accounting information to managers within organizations, to provide them with the basis for making informed business decisions to allow them to be better equipped in their management and control functions. In previous chapters we have considered human, knowledge and technical resources and in this chapter we discuss the use and management of monetary (financial) resources.

Much of what is taught in international financial management constitutes applications of the principles of domestic financial management. The common thread linking all the topics of an international course considers those matters that are peculiarly international, and the opportunities open to a firm has by virtue of its international status. Giddy (1977) considers the distinguishing features of international financial management to be:

1 doing business across national boundaries means dealing with more than one currency and therefore involves exchange risk; and

2 international business is subject to capital and credit controls.

More recently, Brakeman *et al.* (2006) argue that central topics in international finance and business cannot be understood without knowledge of international economics. They analyze how international businesses are affected by the global economic environment. Consequently, our first section considers such matters.

Economics a social science concerned chiefly with description and analysis of the production, distribution, and consumption of goods and services

Finance a branch of economics concerned with resource allocation as well as resource management, acquisition and investment; deals with matters related to money and markets.

Accounting the overall process of identifying, measuring, recording, interpreting, and communicating the results of economic activity

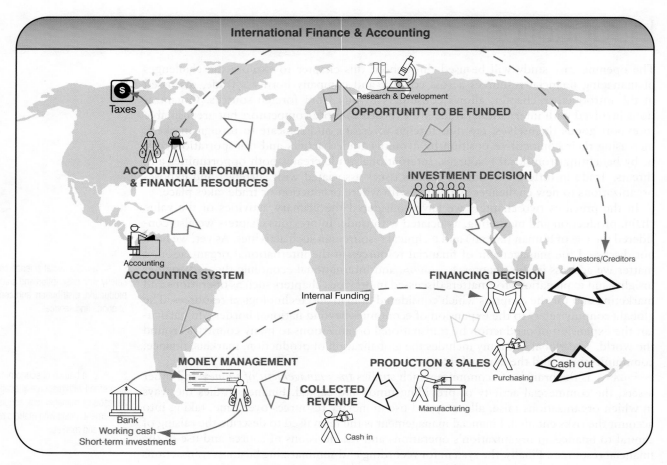

Figure 17-1

International finance and accounting

Figure 17-1 summarizes and highlights the key areas where knowledge of finance and accounting is required in the international organization. Organizations constantly face alternative investment opportunities for which funding needs to be provided and may indeed compete with each other for financial resources. The organization may be funding R&D, new operations, improvements, staff development or maintaining existing assets. Decision-makers identify priorities and appropriate investment opportunities and determine how they will be funded: either from internal or external capital. Cash then flows out of the company as investments are made in the hope of future cash in-flows. This will often be associated with sales and receivables but other benefits such as cost savings may also be considered. Collected revenue must be managed and accounted for. Collectively, transactions are recorded and aggregated into financial reports forming accounting information used by a variety of stakeholders. Once taxes and liabilities are settled and working capital assigned the organization may repeat the cycle, and may invest some of the profit back into new investment opportunities.

In this chapter we discuss the international economic environment, financial decisions, investment appraisal, international accounting, corporate governance and internal control systems. The chapter has strong links with all of the chapters presented thus far. Many of the earlier chapters consider initiatives such as HRM, BPR, systems implementation and marketing promotion; all require capital. This chapter considers investment appraisal techniques which can be used to evaluate such initiatives and related projects.

Throughout this chapter we draw up on the opening case study to provide examples of real world finance and accounting challenges. We consider both local and global issues: how to raise capital and fund investment, how to report financial performance both locally and as a larger group of companies through consolidated accounts and how to assure investor confidence through good corporate governance and the provision of accounting information. First we provide the context for such challenges by exploring the financial environment – a source of capital, opportunity and threat. International organizations may have increased opportunity to raise money at low cost but in doing so, may expose themselves to a variety of political and economic risks such as currency value and exchange rate fluctuations. We also use the case study to demonstrate challenges associated with international trade. To provide structure and aid learning we have organized this chapter into four sections:

■ the international finance environment;

■ finance management in the international organization;

■ accounting in the international organization;

■ financial controls and corporate governance.

The financial environment

In Chapter 2 we explored the economic and political environment in which the international organization may operate and in the introduction to this chapter we outlined the scope of international economics. Any organization operating in at least two countries must appreciate and manage differences in the financial and political environments of those countries. As has already been noted, differences exist in tax systems, currency, accounting standards, the availability of capital, and investor expectations. However, there is also a need to move beyond specific issues and consider the global economic environment. Organizations must raise capital (money) to fund investment opportunities and are therefore concerned with investment availability in both the domestic environment and overseas (for a discussion on international capital mobility see Feldstein and Horioka 1980). The lowering of transportation and communication costs has provided a strong stimulus for cross-border financial transactions and the development of new financial products has stimulated international capital mobility. The global and local political and economic environment presents several key challenges for the international finance and accounting department(s):

■ Currency issues: when trading internationally, the organization must determine which currency to accept in the exchange process. Consequential issues then emerge and a necessity to manage exchange rate risk may become necessary.

■ Financial flows: fragmenting the value chain and the creation or acquisition of subsidiaries creates challenges associated with the movement of funds. Should working capital be centrally managed and should funds be moved to locations which are more tax efficient? In considering such problems, the organization must be aware of the political environment and associated rules.

■ Capital markets: the international organization must consider how to raise funds for investment and from where such funds may originate.

■ Financial accounting: variations in accounting standards impact upon how accounting information is created and presented.

In Chapter 2 we introduced financial challenges but explore them in more detail in the remainder of this chapter. The issues identified above exist as challenges to all international organizations including First Pacific, the organization featured in the opening case study. As was noted in the opening case study, First Pacific is a Hong Kong-based investment and management company with operations located in Asia. Its principal business interests relate to telecommunications, consumer food products and infrastructure. The company invested heavily in the Philippines (telecomms and property) towards the end of the 1990s and was reliant on revenues generated from its Indonesian investments.

The First Pacific Annual Report (2000) stated that:

'During a period in which entrenched political issues adversely affected the rupiah … [and] Similarly, PLDT [Philippines] contended with a volatile peso and an unstable political climate …

Darya-Varia absorbed escalating costs for imported raw materials as the rupiah weakened ... However, economic uncertainty, prompted by political instability, had the inevitable effect of eroding currency exchange rates and, reported results as a consequence. We recorded some US$143 million in largely unrealized exchange losses.'

Tariff a tariff is a tax imposed on goods and services imported into a country.

Aside from currency issues, the international organization may also face trade and capital restrictions. Despite the obvious advantages of free trade flows and a gradual reduction of trade barriers since the 1980s, there are still many policy-induced barriers to trade, such as tariffs, quotas and minimum standards. A tariff is a tax imposed on goods and services imported into a country (the words tariff, duty, and customs are generally used interchangeably). The tax is most often calculated as a percentage of the price charged for the good by the foreign supplier. A tariff may be assessed directly, at the border, or indirectly, by requiring the prior purchase of a licence or permit to import specified quantities of the goods.

Imposing trade restrictions in this way will benefit specific interest groups such as domestic producers or the government. A tariff may be imposed as a source of revenue for the government; however, a more common purpose of tariffs is protection against foreign competition. By raising prices of imported goods relative to the prices of domestic goods, tariffs encourage consumers to buy domestic rather than foreign products. This practice allows domestic producers either to charge higher prices for their goods or to capitalize on their own lighter taxes by charging lower prices and attracting more customers.

Tariffs are often used to protect 'infant industries' or to safeguard older industries in decline. They are sometimes criticized for imposing hidden costs on domestic consumers and encouraging inefficiency in domestic industries. Tariffs are subject to negotiation and treaties among nations (see GATT General Agreement on Tariffs and Trade an international agreement to encourage trade by the reduction of tariffs and quotas on foreign goods and services).

Throughout this chapter we will make reference to the challenges posed by the economic and political environment. In the next section we consider financial management and key decisions such as how to manage the global cash resources of the international organization and in the following section we turn to accounting challenges.

Finance management in the MNC

In the preceding discussion and in Chapter 2 we explored the environment as a source of opportunity and threat – a source of capital, investors and buyers but also a place where rules are made that can impact upon what the organization does and how it does it. This may reduce revenues or increase costs. We also discussed operations and the fragmentation of the value chain and resultant need to invest in different countries that may offer a comparative advantage. The overall focus of this chapter is to manage financial resources. Financial management involves making decisions about investment, sources of finance and how to manage the financial resources of organizations most efficiently. Such decisions are complicated by different currencies, tax regimes, regulations concerning the flow of capital across borders, norms regarding the financing of business activities and levels of economic and political risk. It is important to note that good financial management can be an important source of *competitive advantage*.

Creating a competitive advantage may be achieved essentially through cost reduction. The international finance manager may be able to reduce the cost of capital for the organization, eliminate foreign exchange losses, minimize tax burdens, reduce exposure to risk and manage the cash flows and reserves in a more efficient manner. Consequently, the finance function can reduce the cost of creating value. The international organization typically exists to maximize shareholder wealth and this normally means generating revenues and profit. To do this the organization must create outputs that have added value.

Output (production), discussed in Chapter 15, is a function of inputs such as capital and labour and the production process and technology; to some extent, employee(s) can produce more if they have more tools and equipment available with which to work. Consequently, there can be many different types of investment in many different types of physical, human and knowledge capital. In most cases the organization must make an initial investment in productive assets, however purchased capital regularly depreciates and so to maintain a given capital/labour ratio the organization must replace depreciated capital. Furthermore, if the labour force increases then the capital/labour ratio declines, necessitating further investment.

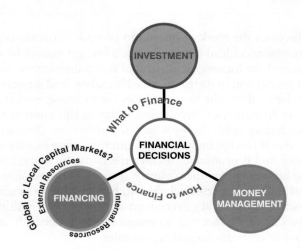

Figure 17-2

Financial decisions

Recognizing the important role of finance, international organizations vary in the degree of central control they exert over such operations and decisions (see Figure 17-2). Throughout this book we have made use of the ethno-, poly- and geocentric categories to describe models of control and influence in international organizations. For example, we discussed staffing policies when managing human resources. Here, we consider different approaches to managing financial resources. International organizations must determine who makes what decisions concerning the management of finances. Where there is a need to coordinate operations carefully the organization may opt for a more centralized approach. In such an approach, the ethnocentric approach, financial decisions and control are generally performed by the parent company.

Centralized approaches enable the formation of specialized groups and therefore improved decision-making. Such approaches provide economies of scale advantages and should better align financial decisions with corporate goals. Should there be a need for speedy responsive decision-making and a good understanding of the local financial environment and accounting rules then a more decentralized polycentric approach may be adopted. In some cases, however, there may be benefit in coordinating financial planning and decisions on a global basis (the geocentric approach).

Several factors will influence the overall parent–subsidiary relationship when managing finance. In some locations there may be an expectancy of decentralization; reward mechanisms and staffing policies may follow a similar approach. However, in some cases there may be a need for tight control over spending. However, as will be seen later, there have been significant attempts to harmonize finance and accounting standards, systems and markets in recent years. This should reduce but has not yet eliminated the need for and importance of local knowledge.

Financial decisions may therefore be made at the centre or locally in the subsidiary. We have structured the remainder of this section around three important financial decisions:

1 what to invest in;

2 how to fund investments; and

3 how to manage the international organizations global cash resources.

We consider the issues associated with such decisions next before turning attention to international accounting – how business financial transactions are recorded and reported.

Investment decisions

The organization must establish mechanisms for developing, screening and selecting projects in which to invest

Markusen (1995) discusses the work of international trade economists and two key questions: first, what circumstances lead a firm to serve a foreign market by exports versus foreign production? Second, he focuses on horizontal direct investment, meaning the foreign production (not just investment in distribution, wholesaling, and servicing) of products and services roughly similar to those the firm produces for its home market. Horizontal direct investment is different from vertical investment which in this context means fragmenting the production process geographically, by stages of production. Discussing Dunning's OLI framework he notes that if foreign multinational enterprises are exactly identical to domestic firms, they will not find it profitable to enter the domestic market. After all, there are added costs of doing business in another country, including communications and transport costs, higher costs of stationing personnel abroad, barriers due to language, customs, and being outside the local business and government networks. The multinational enterprise must, therefore, arise due to the fact that it possesses some special advantage such as superior technology or lower costs due to scale economies.

Investment decisions generally concern outlays of cash, the acquisition and development or use of assets and speculation, i.e. risk and reward. A decision to invest in activities in a given country must consider the risks; threats and opportunities in that country's macro environment (see previous section – see also Vernon (1966) for a discussion of economic advantages associated with production location). One role of the international financial manager is to quantify the various benefits, costs and risks that are likely to flow from an investment in a given location. This is done by using capital budgeting techniques which enable managers to compare different investment alternatives within and across countries so that they can make informed choices about where the organization should invest its scarce resources.

Projects should be appraised from both the subsidiary and parent company perspective since cash flows to the parent company may differ from those to the subsidiary. When evaluating foreign investment opportunity, the parent should be interested in the cash flows it will receive as opposed to those the project generates. Furthermore, the parent company, when analyzing a foreign investment opportunity, must consider the political and economic risks stemming from the foreign location. Changes in a country's business environment may impact upon the profits derived from subsidiaries operating in that country.

When political risk is high, there is a high probability that change will occur in the country's political environment which will endanger foreign organizations there. Negative consequences include the possibility of assets being expropriated or devalued and taxes increased. Political and social unrest may also lead to economic risk which manifests as higher inflation and possible currency devaluation. This will impact upon the value of cash flows from the country concerned thus decreasing the attractiveness of that country. The multinational organization can manage location risk in a number of ways. For example it might apply a higher discount rate to potential investments to reflect greater perceived political and economic risks in that country. The higher the discount rate, the higher the projected net cash flows must be for the foreign investment to have a positive net present value. An alternative approach might be to revise future cash flows downwards to reflect potential risk.

Capital budgeting the process of analyzing and selecting various proposals for capital expenditures

STOP & THINK

List examples of the investment decisions you might expect to have been considered at PLDT over the past decade.

While there are many possible answers, you may have considered decisions such as company acquisitions; the establishment of greenfield operations; headquarter or other building relocations; whether to invest in specific information systems or technology; maintenance of existing plant and networks; training and development of people; quality improvement initiatives; new product development, etc. However, the organization does not have limitless funds to invest and opportunities must be carefully considered if resources are not to be wasted and goals achieved. Consequently we discuss investment appraisal techniques next.

Investment appraisal techniques

The essence of good investment is to buy assets for less than they are worth

Investment decisions are important for all organizations. International organizations must raise finance (money) from various sources (see next section) which is then invested in assets such as plant, machinery and systems. Cash flows out of the organization when investments are made; however, the purpose of investment is to increase value and ultimately cause cash to flow into the organization. There is normally a time lag between flows and the organization must choose the most appropriate opportunities in which to invest, i.e. those that will increase shareholder wealth. In this section we consider how investment decisions are made by both parent and subsidiary companies alike. The overall process of investment appraisal is based upon the rational economic decision-making process and is summarized in Figure 17-3.

Asset anything that has value to the organization

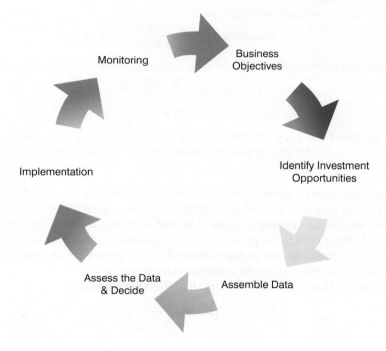

Figure 17-3
Investment appraisal decision-making process

Investments are made to help the organization achieve its goals. Since there may be many ways to achieve goals there are often many initiatives and assets in which to invest to attain such goals. Investment opportunities arise in many ways either intentionally or by chance. Once an idea emerges it must be evaluated. To do this, the organization must describe the problem to be overcome by the investment, quantify the benefits of the investment and explain why investment is necessary to attain goals. Numerous quantitative approaches for evaluating investments ('assess the data and decide' in Figure 17-3) are available, such as net present value, internal rate of return, payback period and pay-off tables which are discussed below. The main goal of such techniques and investment appraisal is to assess the profit (increase in wealth) for a given period. In the next section we consider the main investment appraisal techniques before considering options for funding such investments.

Net present value

Net present value (NPV) an investment appraisal technique that determines the amount of money an investment is worth, taking into account its cost, earnings and the time value of money

The net present value (also called discounted cash flow) measures the worth of a stream of cash flows, taking into account the time value of money. The concept is based on the idea that money today is worth more than money in the future. The net present value (NPV) is a logical, quantitative, practical evaluation procedure that evaluates opportunities which seek to maximize shareholder wealth.

Time value of money explained ...

One thousand of any currency is worth more now than it is one or more years into the future, i.e. we would not lend some person or entity that amount now and expect the same amount back one year later because of risk, inflation and interest foregone. The fact that money has a 'time value' makes investment appraisal more complicated. We need to be able to make comparisons between money now and money that may be paid out or flow into the company at some point in the future. In order to work out the value of a future cash sum we need to discount the sum by the amount of interest we could have earned over the period concerned and calculate the present value of the sum. Example: A consultancy company will be paid €1 000 000 after one year – what is the present value of the receivable?

The present value of a future amount of income is:

$$\text{Present value} = \frac{\text{Future value}}{(1 + \text{Discount rate})}$$

If we assume the interest (discount) rate to be 10 per cent then the present value of

$$€ 1\,000\,000 = \frac{€\,1\,000\,000}{1.1}$$
$$= €\,909\,091$$

That is to say that if we had €909 091 today and invested it with a bank offering 10 per cent interest we would turn our €909 091 investment into €1 000 000 over one year.

The net present value of an investment is calculated by using a discount rate and a series of future payments (negative values) and income (positive values). The calculation of NPV involves three simple yet non-trivial steps. The first step is to identify the size and timing of the expected future cash flows generated by the project or investment. The second step is to determine the discount rate or the estimated rate of return for the project. The third step is to calculate the NPV using the equations shown below:

The net present value is calculated using the following formula:

$$NPV = \sum_{i=1}^{n} \frac{values_i}{(1 + rate)^i}$$

The process of converting future cash flows to their present value is known as discounting. The NPV is typically calculated using a spreadsheet.

Example Consider PLDT, discussed at the beginning of the chapter. Telecomms companies are vulnerable to fraud such as customers dishonestly using their networks without intention to pay for calls made etc. A PLDT department submits an expenditure proposal to procure, from an external vendor, a fraud detection system that will enable PLDT to reduce its fraud losses by detecting patterns indicative of fraudulent use. Imagine that the system and related costs amounted to €100 000 and that the system returned benefits of € 30 000 at the end of year 1; € 50 000 at the end of year 2 and so on. Should PLDT invest in the system?

The head of department consults with the finance director who informs her that the cost of capital is 10 per cent. Benefits were computed using data from the system vendor and internal data.

	Rate 10.00%	Initial cost – € 100 000	Year 1 € 30 000	2 € 50 000	3 € 40 000	4 € 40 000
Total expenditure	– €100 000					
Total income/benefit	€160 000					
Net difference	€60 000					
NPV	€23 607					

Note: the initial cost is payable at the end of the first year.
For simplicity we have shown cash flows in the euro currency.

The above fictitious example of a financing decision shows both costs and benefits over time. The discount rate is the rate used to discount future cash flows to their present values and is a key input of this process. Choosing an appropriate discount rate is crucial to the NPV calculation. Simply subtracting costs from benefits, as we can see form the example, does not indicate the true value of the decision. We must first discount future benefits. If NPV > 0, the investment would add value to the firm and the project should be accepted, depending upon whether or not the project is competing with other investment alternatives for the organization's limited financial resources. The NPV is a logical way of assessing or evaluating investment opportunities, with the objective of maximizing shareholder wealth and taking into account the timing of cash flows. While it is probably the most common investment appraisal technique, there exist other techniques which are discussed next. Such techniques have differing strengths and may complement the NPV approach.

Decisions involving a single alternative

Many decisions involve a choice of whether to accept or reject a single alternative. The internal rate of return may be used to help with such decisions. IRR is sometimes referred to as 'economic rate of return (ERR)'. The internal rate of return for an investment is the discount rate which makes the present value of the income stream total zero; the interest rate *received* for an investment, consisting of payments (negative values) and income (positive values) that occur at regular periods. In general, if the IRR is greater than the project's cost of capital, or hurdle rate, the project will add value for the company. To find the internal rate of return:

Internal rate of return (IRR) the internal rate of return (IRR) is the discount rate which delivers a net present value of zero for a series of future cash flows. It is a discounted cash flow (DCF) approach to valuation and investing

IRR is defined by the equation: NPV(C, t, IRR) = 0.
In other words, the IRR is the discount rate which sets the NPV of the given cash flows made at the given times to zero.

Example
$$\text{Year/Cash Flow: 0 } (-100); 1 (+30); 2 (+35); 3 (+40); 4 (+45)$$

Internal rate of return (IRR)
$$IRR = -100 + 30/[(1+i)^1] + 35/[(1+i)^2] + 40/[(1+i)^3] + 45/[(1+i)^4]$$
$$IRR = 17\%$$

The IRR can be calculated using Microsoft Excel.

As a decision tool, the calculated IRR should not be used to rate mutually exclusive projects, but only to decide whether a single project is worthy of investment. IRR is closely related to NPV, the net present value function. The major difference is that whilst net present value is expressed in monetary units, the IRR is the true interest yield expected from an investment expressed as a percentage.

Decisions involving non-mutually exclusive alternatives

In many cases, an organization will consider numerous investment options. In some cases the options may seek to solve the same problem and compete with each other to the extent that only one of the options should be selected (mutually exclusive). In other cases, options may compete with each other for internal capital, i.e. the company may have only so much money (the budget) to spend. When there are a number of non-mutually exclusive alternatives considered, various ranking criteria, such as return on investment (ROI) or a more general cost-benefit ratio provide a basis for evaluation. The rate of return (ROR) or return on investment (ROI), or sometimes just return, is the ratio of money gained or lost on an investment relative to the amount of money invested. ROI is usually expressed as a percent rather than a decimal value. To calculate ROI, the benefit (return) of an investment is divided by the cost of the investment:

$$\text{ROI} = (\text{Gain from investment}) - (\text{Cost of investment}) / \text{Cost of investment}$$

Or

$$\text{ROI} = (\text{Annual revenue}) - (\text{Annual costs}) / \text{Initial investment}$$

Or

$$\% \text{ROI} = (\text{Benefits} / \text{Costs}) \times 100$$

Another way of looking at ROI is to calculate how many months it will take before benefits match costs and the investment pays for itself. This is called the payback period:

$$\text{Payback period} = \text{Costs} / \text{Monthly benefits}$$

The payback technique simply asks how long will it take for the investment to pay for itself out of the expected cash inflows. Proposals are typically ranked in order of highest ROI first and are selected until total initial investment exceeds a budget. Benefits can be quantified as revenues or cost savings. In either case, they should be converted to present values in order to take account of the time value of money. Ratios greater than one generally indicate that a proposal should be adopted if sufficient resources exist to support it.

Decisions involving mutually exclusive alternatives

Many decisions involve a choice amongst several mutually exclusive alternatives. When only one alternative can be selected from many, the best choice can usually be identified by evaluating each alternative according to some criteria. The NPV or IRR may be used to choose between competing projects/choices. For decisions involving multiple criteria, simple scoring models are often used. The scoring model is a qualitative assessment of a decision alternatives value, based on a set of attributes. For each decision alternative, a score is assigned to each attribute (which might be weighted), and the overall score as a basis for selection.

Decisions involving uncertainty and risk

Many decisions involve a selection from a small set of mutually exclusive alternatives with uncertain consequences. In this scenario we must also define the outcomes, or events, that may occur once a decision is made and over which the decision-maker does not have control. These outcomes provide a basis for evaluating risk associated with decisions. A useful tool for making decisions under uncertain conditions is the pay-off table, discussed below.

Mutually exclusive options may be seeking to solve the same problem and competing with each other

Return on investment (ROI) the percentage return on an investment in a project, computed as Net return ± Required investment

Payback period an investment appraisal technique that assesses how long it takes for initial cash investment to be repaid from cash receipts generated by the investment

Pay-off tables

Financial decision-making is easy when only a single choice can be made (take it or leave it) if there is only one alternative (Hobson's choice). However, rather than only one alternative, most of the time a set of choices exist. It is also relatively easy to make decisions when the precise outcome of the decision is known. However this is rarely the case with contemporary management business decisions. Such decisions normally involve highly uncertain outcomes. In such cases a pay-off table can help to decide which alternative is best; a pay-off table is a tool for organizing what is known about each alternative.

Hobson's choice no choice at all – the only option being the one that is offered to you

Hobson's choice

Thomas Hobson ran a carrier and horse rental business in England, around the turn of the 17th century. Hobson rented horses but refused to let customers choose their own (as the stable contained slow and fast horses); instead they were offered one. The choice his customers were given was 'this or none'.

A memorable example of the application of Hobson's choice in the 20th century was Henry Ford's offer of the Model-T Ford in 'any colour so long as it's black'.

Consider an artificial example where the organization is thinking of investing in a particular product initiative. Suppose the organization is considering four alternatives, these are the four choices that are within the control of the organization; choices require different levels of investment. The consequences of each investment alternative, in terms of profit or loses, are dependent on the market and beyond the control of the organization. Once the question posed is known, the next step is to organize data. Possible choices are listed down the left-hand side of a table (one per row), and possible futures then detailed across the top (one per column). Where a row and column intersect, we can insert the outcome of that choice for that future. We might draw up a pay-off table as follows:

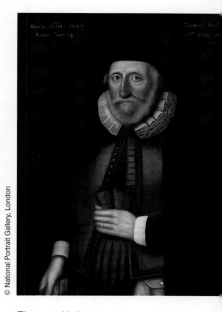

© National Portrait Gallery, London

Thomas Hobson

		Possible futures	
	Product does well	Product does OK	Product is a failure
D₁ (Alternative/Choice 1)	€100 000	€6 000 000	– €200 000
D₁ (Alternative/Choice 2)	€800 000	€7 000 000	€0
D₃ (Alternative/Choice 3)	€900 000	€500 000	– €100 000
D₄ (Alternative/Choice 4)	€400 000	€350 000	– €50 000

Although the possible returns of the investment are beyond the control of the decision-maker, the decision-maker may or may not be able to assign probabilities to them. If no probabilities are assigned to the possible consequences, then the decision situation is called 'decision under uncertainty'. If probabilities are assigned then the situation is called 'decision under risk'. This is a basic distinction in decision theory. Decision theory treats decisions against nature. This refers to a situation where the result (return) from a decision depends on the action of other entities (nature). A *state of nature* is a term used to refer to a possible future situation for which the decision-maker has little or no control. In business it might concern the uptake of a particular product or may concern impacts of the external political environment, etc. In one state the product might be well received while in another case it may be purchased by only a few people; alternatively we might be concerned with one future where the economic environment is stable whilst in another the currency may be devalued. An *alternative* is a course of action or strategy available to the decision-maker. For each combination of a state of nature and a course of action a pay-off or outcome exists. The fundamental piece of data for decision theory problems is a pay-off table, see Figure 17-4.

Figure 17-4

Pay-off table

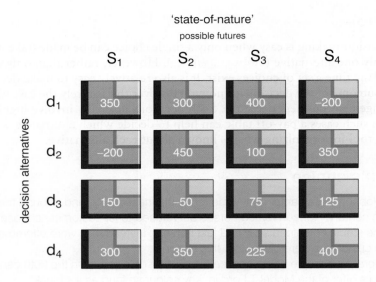

There are different ways of looking at the data in the pay-off table, and reaching decisions (decision strategies/rules):

- If we are *optimistic*, we look at only the best outcome for each alternative (without worrying about which futures we are talking about). This rule is also called maximax or best-of-the-best – upper pay-off (optimistic). In the example shown in Figure 17-4 where there are four alternatives (d_1 to d_4) we can see that (if the outcomes were profit) d_1 could deliver 400 (this could be thousands, millions or other), d_2 could deliver 450; d_3 could deliver 150 and d_4 could deliver 400. The best-of-the-best is therefore d_2.

- A *conservative* person may consider the worst that could happen. This rule is called maximin, i.e. the best-of-the-worst (pessimist). This time the lowest number is selected from each row – lower pay-off (conservative).

  In the example shown in Figure 17-4 we can see that d_1 could deliver -200, d_2 could deliver -200; d_3 could deliver -50 and d_4 could deliver 225. The best-of-the-worst is therefore d_4. It is useful to compare the B of B and the B of W for each alternative (the range) and calculate the mid point between the two.

- An alternative decision rule/strategy might be to take the *average* of the outcomes for each alternative. This is determined by summing the values in a given row, for an alternative, and then dividing by the number of values/states of nature (four in this case). In the example we can see that d_1 could deliver 212.5, d_2 could deliver 175; d_3 could deliver 75 and d_4 could deliver 318.75. The best average is therefore d_4.

  Thus far we have treated each state of nature (possible future) as equally likely. They may not be and we may be able to assign probabilities to each of the states S_1 to S_4. For example, we might believe that S_3 is the most likely outcome. If there were a 50 per cent chance that this state became reality then we would say it had a probability of 0.5. Assume for this example probabilities of: S_1 (0.25); S_2 (0.2); S_3 (0.5) and S_4 (0.05). Note that probabilities add up to 1.

- The *expected (monetary) value* (EMV) is calculated by multiplying the weights for each state-of-nature by the respective pay-offs for that alternative and then summing them. For d_1, that would be $(0.25 \times 350) + (0.2 \times 300) + (0.5 \times 400) + (0.05 \times -200) = 337.5$

  The EV or EMV for each alternative is d_1 (337.5); d_2 (72.5); d_3 (71.25) and d_4 (277.5). Using this rule alone might direct us to choose D_1. As with all the other rules, whilst the ranking offers us a little assistance, we learn more by comparing the rules.

- **A** final rule to consider here is the 'regret' rule, also known as the minimax (opportunity loss) or *minimize maximum regret*. Calculating regret is always a measure of distance, so it is always reported as a positive number. A separate regret table is built. For minimax regret (MMR), we commence by looking at the columns, the states-of-nature – refer to the S_1 column. Identify the best pay-off for this state-of-nature (350) i.e. d_1. If alternative d_1 is chosen and state of nature (future) S_1 becomes reality then there is gratification with the decision. However, if d_2 is selected and S_1 occurs the result is disappointing. Since d_2 has a pay-off (under S_1) of -200, 200 is lost rather than 350 gained. There would therefore be regret with this decision. The amount of regret is the distance between the pay-off gained (-200) and the best pay-off that could have been gained (350), a distance of $350 - (-200)$ or 550. Repeat the calculation for each alternative for S_1, finding the distance of each pay-off from the best pay-off in the first state-of-nature. Repeat the procedure for S_2, S_3 and S_4. Figure 17-5 shows the results. The next step is to consider the rows of the table and select the maximum regret for each alternative. We use the maximum regret because we are setting up a conservative rule, so we look at the worst case, the most we would ever regret each alternative. These maximum regrets are then placed in a column attached to the pay-off table. Under the minimax regret rule, the *lowest* number in the column is the best choice (d_4) and the highest number is the worst (d_1).

Figure 17-5

Pay-off table

	Pay-off table				**Decision strategies/rules**					
	S1	S2	S3	S4	BoB	BoW	mid point	Av	EMV	MMR
	0.25	0.2	0.5	0.05						
d1	350	300	400	-200	**400**	-200	**100**	**212.5**	**337.5**	600
d2	-200	450	100	350	**450**	-200	**125**	175	**107.5**	550
d3	150	-50	75	125	150	**-50**	50	75	71.25	500
d4	300	350	225	400	**400**	225	312.5	318.75	277.5	175
	350	450	400	400						

	Regret table							Key		
d1	0	150	0	600					Preferred choice	
d2	550	0	300	50					Worst Choice	
d3	200	500	325	275						
d4	50	100	175	0						

Build the table shown in Figure 17.5 in MS Excel.

To determine the BoB values use the 'MAX' function, e.g. =MAX(C6:F6)
To determine the BoW values use the 'MIN' function, e.g. =MIN(C6:F6)
To determine the mid point values add BoB to BoW and divide by 2, e.g. =(G6+H6)/2
To determine the Av values use the 'AVERAGE' function, e.g. =AVERAGE(C6:F6)
To determine the EMV values multiply each decision outcome by the probability of it occurring and then sum the weighted values, e.g. =(C6×C5)+(D6×D5)+(E6×E5)+(F6×F5)

To determine the MMR values:

1 use the 'MAX' function, e.g. =MAX(C6:C9) to determine the best alternative in a given state of nature, e.g. S1. Enter this value in cell C10 (it is the score in bold above the regret table in Figure 17.5).

2 Create the regret table from the instructions given in the text above.

3 Create an MMR column. Use the 'MAX' function, e.g. =MAX(C14:F14) to identify the MMR from the regret table assuming the D1_S1 cell is C6 in the spreadsheet.

STOP & THINK

The different ways of looking at the data: optimistic (BoB), conservative (BoW), simple average (Av), weighted average (EMV), and avoiding regret (MMR) can be seen in Figure 17-5. The additional information (rules) is present to aid understanding of the data in the pay-off table. In some cases the analysis of alternatives will be undertaken by the person making the decision; however in many business cases involving large expenditure a group of decision-makers may be involved. Decisions may be based on information prepared by others. Decision makers need to be wary of when information is furnished by individuals or departments in their attempt to sell something, i.e. where they may attempt to convince others their point of view is the correct one. In doing so, they often gloss over the bad points and emphasize the good points. Reporting means presenting information in a non-prejudicial fashion, suppressing personal opinions and giving the reader all the information s/he needs to make his/her own decision. Refer back to Figure 17-3. In terms of the investment appraisal decision-making process we have assembled the data and now need to assess it in order to make or recommend a decision. At this point, we might ask how we can analyze the alternatives presented in Figure 17-5. One of the first steps, having computed values for decision rules, is to summarize the data for each alternative in text format. Thus for d_1 we might say:

Best-of-the-Best (BoB) gives us the second highest score on the table at 400, while

Best-of-the-Worst (BoW) gives us the worst score on the table at −200.

There is a wide possible data range, which may be a cause for concern. The midpoint of the data range is 100 and the average outcome (Av) score of 212.5 is above that, indicating that pay-offs are grouped to the higher end of the range. The expected value (EV) score of 337.5 is the highest on the table and is significantly higher than the Av score of 212.5. The 600 regret score was the worst on the table, which coincides with the ranking of the other conservative rule, BoW, where the score of −200 was also the worst on the table. Thus, from a conservative point of view, we have reservations about this alternative.

The best pay-off for d_1 is 400, and the worst payoff is −200, as shown in the BoB and BoW rules. The remaining two payoffs are 350 and 300, rather at the high end in the middle range of scores, which explains why the Av of 212.5 was above the midpoint of the data range. The probability of getting the highest score of 400 is 50 per cent, the most likely future on the table, while the probability of losing the −200 is only 5 per cent, the least likely future on the table. This match up of weights and pay-offs accounts for the EMV score of 337.5 being so much higher than the Av of 212.5. The remaining two pay-offs, 350 and 300, have probabilities of 25 per cent and 20 per cent respectively. The regret score of 600 was caused by the −200 loss, which is why the two conservative scores being so closely aligned.

This alternative has a high pay-off of 400, clearly a reward; yet two other alternatives have pay-offs as high or higher. Conversely, a risk for this alternative is the loss of −200. The chance of earning the 400 pay-off is 50 per cent, a further reward, while the chance of losing the −200 is only 5 per cent, which offsets the risk to some degree. There is a 95 per cent chance of a positive pay-off, the lowest of which would be 300 – itself a relatively high return, which is a reward. Overall, this alternative represents a low risk, despite the high regret score.

STOP & THINK

Summarize the data for each of the remaining alternatives in text format (as above). Which alternative would you choose?

There are a variety of ways to choose the 'best' alternative but the choice will ultimately be influenced by decision-maker preferences, values, personality and attitudes to risk, among other things.

Attitudes to risk:

- *Risk averse* – a person who prefers the certain prospect to any risky prospect.
- Risk aversion principle – principle that one should take the action that produces the least harm or incurs the least cost.

- *Risk neutral* – the risk neutral person exhibits a reaction to risk in line with its statistical probability.
- *Risk seeker* – risk seekers choose among the risks that have negative consequences.

We can compare two alternatives by looking at similar risks or rewards, however the decision-makers' level of risk tolerance will impact upon which data to compare or emphasize. A pessimist or conservatist (risk averse) may prefer d_4 with its lower MMR and higher BoW. An optimist or risk seeker might prefer d_2 with the highest BoB and a risk neutral person may favour d_1 which has the highest utility value. Typically, decision-makers will recognize that the data is reliant and based upon many assumptions about chance and consequences and will factor in other concerns of a political and personal nature. Such important decisions, made under uncertainty, are rarely based purely on rational and economic processes and calculations (as outlined in this section).

Recognizing that ultimately, risk decisions are made by people, it becomes important to explore decision-maker characteristics and their possible implications for risk decisions. A range of decision-maker characteristics such as age, gender, experience, attitudes, beliefs and personality have been studied. Such factors are mediated through judgement and perception (refer to Chapter 8) which may then manifest in risk and decision-making behaviour. Decision-makers must make judgements; judgement is the cognitive process (the capacity to assess situations or circumstances) of reaching a decision or drawing conclusions. Bazerman (2002) argues that organizational decisions are often flawed through cognitive error, how we process information, or motivational biases such as doing what we want rather than should do.

Rational decision-making or problem solving is a process typically involving stages where the situation is defined, criteria are identified and weighted, alternatives are generated and rated and then the optimal solution is computed and selected (as was shown in Figure 17-3). The ability to make considered decisions or reach sensible conclusions is judgement which may be tarnished through a variety of irrationalities. 'Cognitive' or 'judgmental' or 'general' heuristics, 'rules-of-thumb', are used by managers to simplify and speed up decisions. Bazerman discusses three types of heuristic – availability, representativeness and anchoring – that may be used to estimate likelihood (a key component of our pay-off tables). The availability heuristic is about memory and the ease of recall. Vivid or recent events will be recalled more easily and people are more likely to overestimate unlikely events. The representative heuristic is concerned with stereotypes and generalizations: do people draw conclusions from small sample sizes or have misconceptions of connectedness, leading to false conclusions. Finally, the anchoring heuristic recognizes problems with 'starting points' which influence the estimation process.

Throughout this section we have considered investment (risk: reward) decision-making. We have noted the existence of a variety of rational analytical approaches to aid such decision-making, but recognized that in many cases it is people who are at the centre of such decision-making. Any investment appraisal technique is reliant upon forecasts of costs and sales or benefits and some techniques are dependent on the assignment of probabilities to outcomes. It is important to note that organizations vary in the emphasis they place upon different approaches, some favouring rational or objective over subjective and intuitive approaches. Such preferences are rooted in culture at organizational and country levels. In all organizations, decisions are made about in what to invest, by whatever approach and this necessitates the related decision of how to fund, i.e. finance the investment. Once again there are choices and alternatives to be considered and we explore these in the next section.

Financing decisions

Expansion, maintenance, creativity and innovation require funds. In the previous section we discussed investment decisions – what activities to finance, i.e. invest in. A project that requires financial resources, i.e. funding, necessitates decisions about financing options.

The organization may make use of internal or external financial resources; external finances may come from within the host country or from global capital markets. The latter represents a larger pool of investors and is therefore typically associated with a lower cost of capital (the rate of return).

Organizations obtain money from external sources in a number of ways such as by issuing bonds or equity offerings (such as shares); they may also make use of commercial credit, short or long-term bank loans. A bond is a debt instrument issued for a period of more than one year with the purpose of raising capital by borrowing. Generally, a bond is a promise to repay the principal (the original investment) along with interest (coupons) on a specified date (maturity). When an investor buys a bond, he/she becomes a creditor of the issuer. However, the buyer does not gain any kind of ownership rights to the issuer, unlike in the case of equities.

Bonds may be classified in a number of ways. Eurobonds are bonds placed in countries other than the one in whose currency the bond is denominated; fixed-rate bonds offer a fixed set of cash pay-offs each year until maturity, when the investor also receives the face value of the bond in cash. Foreign bonds are bonds sold outside the borrower's country and denominated in the currency of the country in which they are issued.

Equity is ownership interest in a corporation in the form of common stock or preferred stock. An *equity loan* occurs when a corporation sells stock (shares) to an investor. Equity also refers to the value of assets remaining once debt has been accounted for. A company's debt, divided by its equity is described as the debt-to-equity ratio. This ratio is used as a relative measure of debt. It is a measure of the extent to which an organization's capital is provided by owners or lenders and is also, a measure of a company's ability to repay its obligations. If ratios are increasing – more debt in relation to equity – the company is being financed by creditors rather than by internal positive cash flow. When an organization borrows money it is termed in *debt*, i.e. it has an obligation to pay something. A debtor is a person who owes a creditor: someone who has the obligation of paying a debt.

Financing decisions are therefore influenced by many factors such as the availability of the different sources of finance, the availability of internal funds, rates of return and the cost of capital, repayment terms and risk.

Money management decisions

Investments should generate revenue (money). The multinational organization must attempt to manage the organization's global cash resources – its working capital – most efficiently. This involves minimizing cash balances and reducing transaction costs. Rather than simply sitting on its cash reserves, the organization will invest money in return for interest payments. However, the rate of interest is typically associated with liquidity – the higher the rate of interest the lower the liquidity, i.e. cash resources must be placed in longer-term financial instruments where the organization cannot withdraw its money before such instruments mature otherwise financial penalties are incurred.

One technique to manage global money is through centralized depositories. The international organization can pool cash reserves centrally thus reducing day-to-day cash needs. The international organization will also make attempts to reduce transaction costs (such as commissions paid to foreign exchange dealers) and transfer fees for moving cash from one location to another. Multilateral netting can reduce the number of transactions between the organization's subsidiaries, thereby reducing the total transaction costs arising from foreign exchange dealings and transfer fees. A further source of efficiency may stem from tax reduction.

Different countries have different tax regimes. For the international business with activities in many countries, the various tax regimes and tax treaties have important implications for how the organization should structure its internal payment systems amongst the foreign subsidiaries and the parent company. The multinational organization can use transfer pricing and fronting loans to minimize its global tax liability. In addition, the form in which income is remitted from a foreign subsidiary to the parent company (royalty payments and fees and dividends) can be structured to minimize the organization's global tax liability.

Bond long-term debt instrument issued by companies to raise funds

Working capital short-term assets, net of short-term liabilities

Centralized depositories the practice of centralizing corporate cash balances in a single depository

Multilateral netting a technique used to reduce the number of transactions between subsidiaries of the organization, thereby reducing the total transaction costs arising from foreign exchange dealings and transfer fees

Transfer pricing the type of pricing used when one unit in a company sells a product to another unit within the same company

Fronting loan a loan between a parent company and a foreign subsidiary that is channelled through a financial intermediary (e.g. bank)

Dividend payments are probably the most common method by which organizations transfer funds from foreign subsidiaries to the parent company. However, this approach will be influenced by the rate of tax levied on dividends by the host country.

Royalties and fees have certain tax advantages over dividends and are additional mechanisms used to move money efficiently across borders. It is common for a parent company to charge its foreign subsidiaries royalties for the technology, patents or trademarks it has transferred to them. Royalties may be levied as a fixed or variable amount.

Transfer prices can also be used to position funds within an international business. For example, funds can be moved out of a particular country by setting high transfer prices for goods and services supplied to the subsidiary in that country and by setting low transfer prices for the goods and services sourced from that subsidiary, see Figure 17-6. While this has benefits in terms of tax reduction and financial risk management significant problems may be associated with transfer pricing policies as these are not favoured by governments. Many governments now limit international business's ability to manipulate transfer prices in the manner described. Some consider the correct transfer price to be the arm's-length price. Furthermore transfer pricing is inconsistent with a policy of treating each subsidiary in the organization as a profit centre. A final method used to move money across borders is the fronting loan: this is a loan between a parent company and a foreign subsidiary that is channelled through a financial intermediary (e.g. bank).

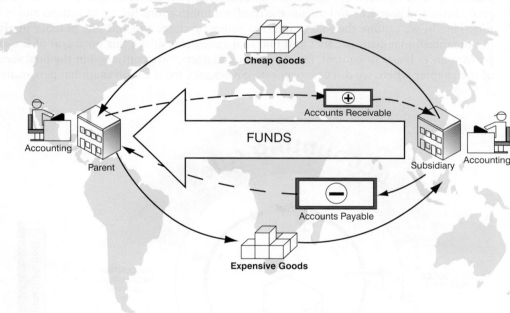

Figure 17-6

Transfer pricing and funds positioning

Managing money in the international organization also necessitates a consideration of risk. Such organizations not only face traditional investment and credit risks but must also consider political, economic and exchange rate risks. Political risk refers to the likelihood of political forces causing dire changes in a country's business environment that will adversely affect the profit and other goals of a particular organization. Economic risk concerns the probability that events, including economic mismanagement, will cause drastic changes in a country's business environment which again adversely affect the profit and other goals of a particular organization.

Foreign exchange risk is the risk that changes in exchange rates will harm the profitability of a commercial transaction. Risks are normally assessed in terms of their probability (chance) and the consequences of any event (typically adverse, i.e. harmful). The expected monetary value (EMV) of a risk is thus computed as the potential loss or gain multiplied by the probability of that loss or gain. A significant risk is any risk that may threaten the survival of the group, or could seriously weaken it. While there are a variety of techniques employed to manage financial risks they fall out of the scope of this text.

Political risk the likelihood that political forces will cause dire changes in a country's business environment that will adversely affect the profit and other goals of a particular organization

Economic risk the probability that events, including economic mismanagement, will cause drastic changes in a country's business environment which adversely affect the profit and other goals of a particular organization

In this section we considered three important financial decisions: what to invest in, how to fund investments and how to manage money. The transactions associated with financing and the costs and receivables they generate must be recorded and reported by the international organization and we therefore turn our attention to international accounting in the next section.

Accounting for internationals

In this section we consider the accounting system, see Figure 17-7, and how financial transactions are recorded and information generated for a range of stakeholders (see Figure 17-8). We start by exploring the differences between management (internal) and financial (external) accounting and then consider financial statements as the information outputs of the accounting process. The three main financial statements (income, balance sheet and cash flow) are described as typical components of the company annual report. Next we evaluate how parent companies aggregate and bring together the accounts of its subsidiaries and introduce the concepts of the consolidated account. Having focused, primarily, on local issues we next turn our attention to international accounting practices and the similarities and differences between countries. We consider evolving global standards for accounting procedures and practices and discuss the resultant implications for organizations and investors. Finally, we outline the role of internal control systems and auditing practice in assuring organizational goals are met and financial statements give a fair portrayal of financial performance. Issues of control, fair reporting and agency are continued in the final section of the chapter where we discuss corporate governance from an international perspective.

Figure 17-7

Accounting system

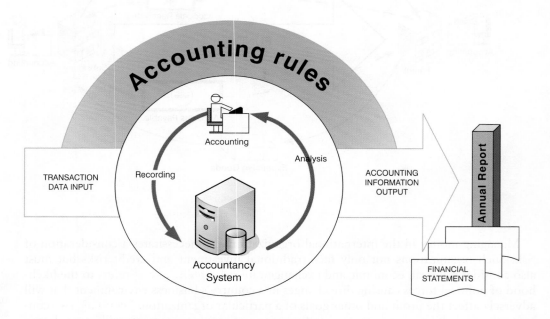

Accounting is the recording of financial or money transactions. Accounting is the systematic recording, reporting and analysis of financial transactions of a business

We start by asking: what is accounting? It is not easy to provide a concise definition of accounting since the word has a broad application within businesses. A simple definition is the recording of financial or money transactions. Accounting is the systematic recording, reporting, and analysis of the monetary financial transactions of a business; it is a system that provides quantitative information about finances. Accounting and accountancy also refers to the occupation of maintaining and auditing records and preparing financial reports for a business. Accounting refers to processes involved in providing information about a company's financial situation. This includes recording financial information and compiling it into financial statements for public use in assessing the financial soundness of a company. With the various influences on accounting, many *accounting systems* have been developed over the years. However, the differences between countries typically lie in a few key areas.

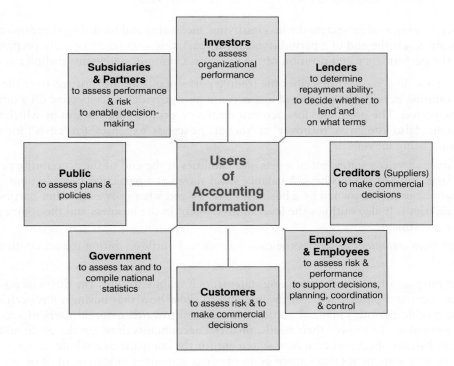

Figure 17-8

Users of accounting information

Accounting is typically split into two key branches: financial accounting and management accounting. Put simply, management accounting can be defined as the provision of information required by management for planning, organizing and control. According to the Chartered Institute of Management Accountants (CIMA), management accounting is 'the process of identification, measurement, accumulation, analysis, preparation, interpretation and communication of information used by management to plan, evaluate and control within an entity and to assure appropriate use of and accountability for its resources'. Management accounting is concerned with information for management purposes: it is internal information for the organization itself and is very rarely made public, unlike financial accounting information. Techniques such as costing, budgetary control, marginal costing, and the preparation of management and financial ratios may be used in the practice of management accounting. It is the design, implementation, and management of the internal systems which allow effective decision support, planning, and control over the organization's value-creating operations.

Management accounting is focused on operations and the value chain, the indicators of financial results, as opposed to the historical activities of external financial reporting. It is forward-looking and focused on seeking opportunities for growth and improvement. Management accounting focuses on the internal running of the organization. Management accountants therefore help with strategy formulation, planning and decision-making and the safeguarding of assets.

The key difference between managerial and *financial accounting* is that managerial accounting information is aimed at helping managers within the organization make decisions. In contrast, financial accounting is aimed at providing information to parties outside the organization. Financial accountancy (or financial accounting) is concerned with the preparation of financial statements for decision-makers, such as stockholders, suppliers, banks, government agencies, owners, and other stakeholders. The fundamental need for

Financial accounting reporting of the financial position and performance of a firm through financial statements issued to external users on a periodic basis

Management accounting the process of identifying, measuring, analyzing, interpreting, and communicating information for the pursuit of an organization's goals

financial accounting is to reduce the principal–agent problem (see next section) by measuring and monitoring agents' performance and reporting the results to interested users.

Financial accounting statements

Financial accounts are concerned with classifying, measuring and recording the transactions of a business. At the end of a period (typically a year), financial statements are prepared to show the performance and position of the business. Common statements include:

Financial statements presentation of financial data including balance sheets, income statements and statements of cash flow, or any supporting statement intended to communicate an entity's financial position at a point in time and its results of operations for a period then ended

Profit and loss account a statement that sets the total revenues (sales) for a period against the expenses matched with those revenues to derive a profit or loss for the period

- Profit and loss account describes the trading performance of the business over the accounting period; the profit and loss account also provides a perspective on a longer time period. The profit and loss account measures 'profit' – the amount by which sales revenue (also known as 'turnover' or 'income') exceeds 'expenses' (or 'costs') for the period being measured.

- *Balance sheet* is a statement of assets and liabilities at the end of the accounting period (a 'snapshot') of the business. A balance sheet shows at a particular point in time what resources are owned by a business ('assets') and what it owes to other parties ('liabilities'). It also outlines the level of investment in the business and the sources of that investment.

- *Cash flow statement* describes the cash inflows and outflows during the accounting period.

The purpose of financial accounting statements is mainly to show the financial position of a business at a particular point in time and to show how that business has performed over a specific period. Financial accounts are geared towards external users of accounting information. To answer their needs, financial accountants draw up the profit and loss account, balance sheet and cash flow statement for the company as a whole.

An income statement (also known as an earnings statement or statement of operations) is a standard financial document that summarizes a company's revenue and expenses for a specific period of time such as the entire fiscal year; it itemizes the past revenue and expenditure which led to current profit or loss.

The income statement is a simple and straightforward report on a business's cash-generating ability. The income statement illustrates just how much a company makes or loses during the year by subtracting cost of goods and expenses from revenue to arrive at a net result, which is either a profit or a loss. It is based on a fundamental accounting equation (Income = Revenue − Expenses) and shows the rate at which the owners equity is changing for the better or worse. Along with the balance sheet and cash flow statement (discussed in the next section) it forms the core financial information required to manage the organization.

The balance sheet summarises the assets, liabilities and shareholders' equity of the organization. *Assets* describe the property owned by the business. Tangible assets include money, land, buildings, investments, inventory, vehicles, or other valuables. Intangibles such as goodwill are also considered to be assets. It is normal practice to categorize assets as current or fixed (non-current).

A *fixed asset* (capital asset) is a long-term, tangible asset, held for business use and not expected to be converted to cash in the current or upcoming fiscal year, such as manufacturing equipment, buildings, and furniture. Fixed assets are sometimes collectively referred to as 'plant'. Assets expected to be converted into cash within one year are termed *current assets*. These include assets a company has at its disposal which can be easily converted into cash such as accounts receivable, work in process and inventory.

Liabilities are obligations that legally bind an organization to settle a debt; a liability is a financial obligation, debt, claim, or potential loss. Liabilities are reported on a balance sheet and are usually divided into two categories: '*current liabilities*' the term given to a balance sheet item which equals the sum of all money owed by a company and due within one year (also called payables or current debt) and *long-term liabilities* – (non-current

Contribution Summary

Figure 17-9

First Pacific Company Limited – Extract from financial reports 2000

	Turnover		Contribution to Group profit	
	2000 US$m	1999 US$m	2000 US$m	1999 US$m
CONSUMER				
Indofood*	1,490.3	440.4	55.7	16.4
Berli Jucker	281.3	294.2	9.9	15.6
Darya-Varia	50.5	45.7	5.0	5.6
	1,822.1	780.3	70.6	37.6
TELECOMMUNICATIONS				
PLDT*	1,334.5	1,184.7	25.6	18.5
Smart [1]	80.5	307.2	(9.0)	13.9
Escotel*	35.7	21.6	(11.8)	(12.6)
China Telecom ventures [2]	–	–	–	7.6
	1,450.7	1,513.5	4.8	27.4
PROPERTY				
Metro Pacific	240.0	317.5	(6.4)	(4.4)
FPDSavills/Savills [3]	37.2	167.4	6.0	7.7
SPORTathlon [4]	5.1	10.3	(0.4)	(0.2)
	282.3	495.2	(0.8)	3.1
BANKING				
First Pacific Bank	114.3	89.2	13.9	3.5
Subtotal	3,669.4	2,878.2	–	–
Non-consolidated operations*	(2,860.5)	(1,646.7)	–	–
CONTRIBUTION FROM OPERATIONS BEFORE EXCHANGE DIFFERENCES [5]	808.9	1,231.5	88.5	71.6
Corporate overhead			(11.8)	(16.0)
Finance (charges)/income: net bank interest			(1.4)	10.5
convertible bonds			(24.3)	(24.7)
Recurring profit before exchange differences			51.0	41.4
Gain on disposal/dilution less provision for investments [6]			143.7	92.6
Exchange (losses)/gains [7]			(143.5)	4.2
PROFIT ATTRIBUTABLE TO ORDINARY SHAREHOLDERS			51.2	138.2

liabilities) these liabilities are reasonably expected not to be liquidated within a year. They usually include issued long-term bonds, notes payables, long-term leases, pension obligations, and long-term product warranties.

The accounting equation relates assets, liabilities, and owner's equity:

$$\text{Assets} = \text{Liabilities} + \text{Owner's equity}$$

The accounting equation is the mathematical structure of the balance sheet.

The income statement, discussed previously, differs from a *cash flow statement* because the income statement does not show when revenue is collected or when expenses are paid. In financial accounting, a cash flow statement is a financial statement that shows a company's incoming and outgoing money (sources and uses of cash) during a specified time period (often monthly or quarterly). The statement shows how changes in balance sheet and income accounts affected cash and cash equivalents, and breaks the analysis down according to operating, investing, and financing activities. As an analytical tool the statement of cash flows is useful in determining the short-term viability of a company, particularly its ability to pay bills.

The balance sheet is a snapshot of a firm's financial resources and obligations at a single point in time, and the income statement summarizes a firm's financial transactions over an interval of time. These two financial statements reflect the accrual basis accounting used by firms to match revenues with the expenses associated with generating those revenues.

The cash flow statement includes only inflows and outflows of cash and cash equivalents; it excludes transactions that do not directly affect cash receipts and payments. The cash flow statement is intended to provide information on a firm's liquidity and solvency.

If the company is a 'parent company' (in other words, the company also owns other companies – subsidiaries) then 'consolidated accounts' (a consolidated financial statement) must also be prepared. Consolidated accounts are financial statements which factor the holding company's subsidiaries into its aggregated accounting figure. It is a representation of how the holding company is doing as a group. Such statements bring together all assets, liabilities, and operating accounts of a parent company and its subsidiaries. Consolidated accounts present the financial position and results of operations of the parent company and its subsidiaries as if the group were a single company with one or more branches. The technique for preparing consolidated financial statements is to take the individual statements to be consolidated and combine them on a worksheet after eliminating all intercompany transactions and intercompany relationships. Most firms prepare consolidated statements when more than 50 per cent of the subsidiary's stock is held.

In the opening case study we considered the First Pacific group as the 'parent' or major investors in PLDT and other telecomms companies such as SMART, Metro Pacific, Indofoods and others. Part of the group's consolidated accounts can be seen in Figure 17-9. Large corporations publish financial information, typically in an annual report. For most companies this will be an audited document required by law or some other rule. The annual report typically contains the financial results for the year (including the balance sheet, income statement, cash flow statement and description of company operations) and comments on the outlook for the future. The term sometimes refers to the glossy, colourful brochure and sometimes to specific forms submitted to relevant authorities.

Consolidated account financial statement combining the accounts of two or more companies in a group

Annual report document detailing the business activity of a company over the previous year, and containing the three main financial statements: income statement, cash flow statement, and balance sheet

STOP & THINK

Visit the websites identified in the opening case study and download a selection of annual reports. Compare and contrast the selected reports.

International accounting practices

We need accounting and its products such as an organization's annual report as a platform upon which to build many other decisions and activities. Organizations must follow specific rules and formats of presentation for their annual reports and financial statements. However, countries may adopt differing accounting procedures. For some time there has been worldwide support for a single set of accounting standards and practice; see for example the study by Tarca (2004) which demonstrated considerable support for 'international' standards. Organizations such as the International Accounting Standards Board (IASB) have taken a lead role in developing global standards for accounting procedures and practices (Stanko (2000) examined the need for greater comparability and uniformity in international financing reporting).

The key accounting event for any organization is the publication of the annual report which records the organization's (financial) performance over a book year. The construction of the annual report is subject to country-specific regulations. Organizations operating internationally must decide how to account for foreign currency transactions and must take care of cross-country financial management, involving such issues as exchange-rate risk management and fiscal optimization. National differences exist in accounting procedures though attempts have been made to harmonize approaches through accounting standards.

Accounting data is collected, stored and then analyzed and manipulated (processed) according to accounting standards – rules for preparing financial statements. Differences in national accounting standards make it difficult to compare the financial reports from one country to another. Differing accounting practices make it very difficult for investors to compare the

Accounting standards rules for preparing financial statements

financial statements of organizations based in different countries. Accounting systems around the world vary in a number of ways such as their treatment of goodwill, etc.

The variance in accounting systems worldwide may be attributable to culture (see for example uncertainty avoidance), the level of economic development, political and economic ties with other countries and relationships with other stakeholders – Salter and Niswander (1995) explain cross-national differences in accounting structure and practice. From an international business theory perspective, building on the work of Gray (1988) they provide additional credence to the view that culture is the building block of cross-national differences in business practice and performance across nations.

In recent years there have been attempts to harmonize accounting standards in order to develop an internationally acceptable accounting convention. For example, companies whose stock is publicly traded on European stock exchanges are required to issue financial accounts in a format agreed upon by the International Accounting Standards Board (IASB). The IASB and the financial accounting standards board, in the United States, are two influential bodies promoting international standards.

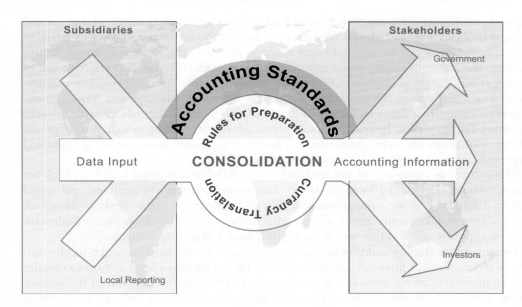

Figure 17-10

Multinational accounting system

Subsidiary organizations produce accounting information for local consumption and for the parent company. A consolidated financial statement combines the separate financial statements of two or more companies to yield a single set of financial statements as if the individual company were really one. Although subsidiaries may be separate legal entities they are not separate economic entities. Economically, all the companies in a corporate group are interdependent. The purpose of consolidated financial statements is to provide accounting information about a group of companies while recognizing their economic interdependence. Preparing consolidated financial statements is becoming the norm of multinational organizations. Investors realize that without consolidated financial statements, a multinational organization might hide losses in an unconsolidated subsidiary, thereby concealing the economic status of the entire group.

Foreign subsidiaries of multinational organizations normally keep their accounting records and prepare their financial statements in the currency of the country in which they are located. When a multinational prepares consolidated accounts, it must convert all these financial statements into the currency of its home country. There are two main methods to determine what exchange rate should be used when translating financial statements: the current method (adopts the exchange rate applicable on the date the balance sheet is created) and the temporal method which adopts the exchange rate applicable at the time assets were purchased.

In recent years the International Accounting Standards Board (IASB) and US Financial Accounting Standards Board (FASB) have been coordinating their work programmes. Their aim is to eliminate differences between International Financial Reporting Standards (IFRS) and US GAAP Generally Accepted Accounting Principles to such an extent that the SEC would no longer require foreign registrants to prepare a reconciliation from IFRS to US GAAP (ICAEW 2007a).

Listed companies are obliged to publish their accounts in order to show their owners (shareholders) and potential investors how they are performing. Furthermore, because companies are often managed on behalf of shareholders, the organization must make efforts to both safeguard and accurately report on the organization's assets. The remainder of the chapter considers such obligations in more detail. In particular we consider the role of control systems, auditing and other financial controls in the fulfilment of such goals.

Control systems and auditing practice

Control theory was discussed earlier (refer back to Chapter 9) when we noted that control systems (policies and procedures) implemented to help the organization meet its goals. In some cases control has an internal focus whereas in others the focus is external. In this context, the control system should not only encourage the efficient and effective use of resources but should also ensure compliance with applicable laws and regulations, safeguard assets and ensure the reliability of financial reporting. Management has a responsibility to ensure that financial information is fairly prepared in accordance with relevant reporting requirements. Internal controls – procedures or systems designed to promote efficiency or assure the implementation of a policy or safeguard assets, avoiding fraud and error, etc. are implemented to achieve such goals.

Many controls make use of the feedback loop as the fundamental building block for action (Wiener 1948 cited in Klein 1989). Inputs and outputs are analyzed and tested against a standard; if the comparison reveals a discrepancy, an error signal is generated, and the system takes some action via the effector to reduce the discrepancy. Budgetary controls typically work in this way as do performance and quality controls.

Organizations employ auditors to assure control systems are working and typically outsource the auditing of financial statements to third-party (independent) auditors to ensure that financial statements are a fair representation of the financial position of the organization. However, the responsibility for adopting sound accounting policies, maintaining adequate internal control and making fair representations within financial statements rests with management. The auditor(s) must obtain, through audits, reasonable assurance that the financial statements are free of error. When company account, financial statements are prepared, management make assertions about them. For example, they assert whether assets included in the balance sheet actually exist and whether all transactions and accounts that should be represented in the financial statements are included (completeness). Similar assertions are made about the value of assets and other issues concerning how the statements were prepared. Auditors make use of the financial statements and management assertions when conducting audits.

The auditors of the First Pac accounts were named in the opening case study. You can see the independent auditors report in the First Pac (see for example 2006: 57) annual report. In their report they state, 'In our opinion, the Financial Statements give a true and fair view of the state of affairs of the Company and of the Group as at 31 December 2006 and of the Group's profit and cash flows for the year then ended in accordance with Hong Kong Financial Reporting Standards and have been properly prepared in accordance with the disclosure requirements of the Hong Kong Companies Ordinance'. They address their report to the shareholders of First Pacific Company Limited and note that their responsibility is to express an opinion on the financial statements based on their audit; their report is made solely to the shareholders. The First Pac annual report (2006: 41) also contains a corporate governance report. Like many international companies, First Pacific is committed to building and maintaining high standards of

Generally Accepted Accounting Principles (GAAP) a widely accepted set of rules, conventions, standards, and procedures for reporting financial information, as established by the Financial Accounting Standards Board

corporate governance practices and we explore what this means in the final section of this chapter.

Corporate governance

'The governance of companies is more important for world economic growth than the government of countries'

James Wolfensohn, President of the World Bank

Corporate governance is an area that has developed very rapidly in the last decade; much of the recent emphasis has arisen from high-profile corporate scandals, globalization and increased investor activism. Put simply, corporate governance deals with the ways in which suppliers of finance, to commercial organizations, assure themselves of getting a return on their investment. Previously we discussed the importance of assuring financial statements are reported fairly. Corporate governance consists of the set of processes, customs, policies, laws and institutions affecting the way people direct, administer or control an organization.

According to the Institute of Chartered Accountants in England & Wales (2007) corporate governance is commonly referred to as a *system* by which organizations are *directed and controlled*. It is the process by which company objectives are established, achieved and monitored. Corporate governance is concerned with the relationships and responsibilities between the board, management, shareholders and other relevant stakeholders within a legal and regulatory framework. One of the key goals of corporate governance is to reduce the principal agency problem. Corporate governance aims to:

- protect shareholder rights;
- enhance disclosure and transparency;
- facilitate effective functioning of the board; and
- provide an efficient legal and regulatory enforcement framework.

Corporate governance is a key element in enhancing investor confidence, promoting competitiveness, and ultimately improving economic growth. There is no 'one size fits all' approach to corporate governance and a number of countries have developed approaches that seek to address agency problems. However, while approaches may differ, there is global appreciation of the OECD's generic corporate governance principles of responsibility, accountability, transparency and fairness. Good corporate governance plays a vital role in underpinning the integrity and efficiency of financial markets. In 1999, the OECD published its Principles of Corporate Governance, the first international code approved by governments.

These Principles focus on publicly traded companies and are intended to assist governments in improving the legal, institutional and regulatory framework that underpins corporate governance; principles are not prescriptive or binding, but rather take the form of recommendations that each country can respond to as best befits its own traditions and market conditions. The principles, for example, suggest that company boards should be truly accountable to shareholders and to take ultimate responsibility for their organizations' adherence to a high standard of corporate behaviour and ethics (refer back to Chapter 4). For board members, this means fostering the best interests of both the company and the shareholders who have invested their money in the company which they oversee. The revised OECD Principles address a range of aspects from the internal preparation of financial reports and internal controls through to the role of the board in approving the disclosure, the accounting standards being used and the integrity of the external audit process.

The OECD (2007) argues that markets work best when information is available to all. They believe that companies have a responsibility in this area. The degree to which corporations observe basic principles of good corporate governance is an increasingly important factor for investment decisions. Of particular relevance is the relation between corporate governance practices and the increasingly international character of investment. International flows of capital enable companies to access finance from a much larger pool of investors. If countries are to reap the full benefits of the global capital market, and if they are to attract long-term capital, corporate governance arrangements must be credible, well understood across borders and adhere to internationally accepted principles. Even if corporations do not have a primary reliance on foreign sources of capital, adherence to good corporate governance practices will help improve the confidence of domestic investors, reduce the cost of capital, underpin the good functioning of financial markets, and ultimately induce more stable sources of financing.

The OECD (2004) suggests that a strong disclosure regime can help to attract capital and maintain confidence in the capital markets. By contrast, weak disclosure and non-transparent practices can contribute to unethical behaviour and to a loss of market integrity at great cost, not just to the company and its shareholders but also to the economy as a whole. Shareholders and potential investors require access to regular, reliable and comparable information in sufficient detail for them to assess the stewardship of management, and make informed decisions about the valuation, ownership and voting of shares. Insufficient or unclear information may hamper the ability of the markets to function, increase the cost of capital and result in poor allocation of resources. In summary, good corporate governance promotes economic activity and prosperity by inspiring trust in companies so that people have confidence to do business and invest.

Summary of key learning points

The key issues and concepts discussed in this chapter are shown in Figure 17-11. Finance studies the ways in which organizations raise, allocate, and use monetary resources over time, taking into account the risks entailed. The raising of capital to finance an organization's operations and the decisions of source and use of the financial resources is termed financial management.

The system for recording and summarizing business transactions and activities designed to accumulate, measure, and communicate financial information about economic entities for decision-making purposes is termed accounting. Accounting refers to the overall process of identifying, measuring, recording, interpreting, and communicating the results of economic activity; tracking business income and expenses and using these measurements to answer specific questions about the financial and tax status of the business, i.e. it is a system that provides quantitative information about finances. Whereas financial accounting is the use of accounting information for reporting to parties outside the organization, management accounting is concerned with the provisions and use of accounting information to managers within organizations, to provide them with the basis for making informed business decisions that will allow them to be better equipped in their management and control functions.

Corporate governance consists of the set of processes, customs, policies, laws and institutions affecting the way people direct, administer or control an organization. It is the process by which company objectives are established, achieved and monitored. Corporate governance is concerned with the relationships and responsibilities between the board, management, shareholders and other relevant stakeholders within a legal and regulatory framework. One of the key goals of corporate governance is to reduce the principal–agency problem.

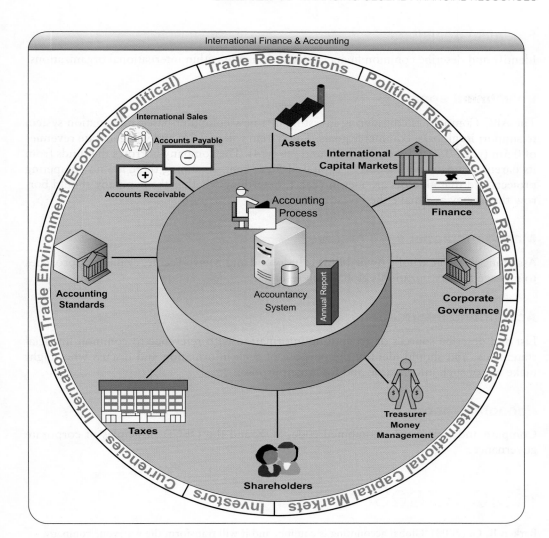

Figure 17-11

Summary – international finance and accounting

Review questions

Economic theory 1

Explain why organizations fragment their value chains, establishing operations in different countries. Your answer should draw on a range of economic theories.

International transactions – exposure to risk

Describe the four main exposures associated with international transactions and list mechanisms to reduce risk.

International trade restriction

Explain why countries attempt to restrict trade and identify the typical mechanisms used. Evaluate the benefits and problems associated with international trade restriction from a multi-stakeholder perspective.

Competitive advantage

Evaluate how financial management can be an important source of competitive advantage.

Financial decisions

Identify and describe common financial decisions made within international organizations.

Investment appraisal

The ABC Company is considering investing in a new computer-based information system to support its global e-commerce goals. The system will cost 2m and will generate revenues of 0.5m (yr1); 0.75m (yr2); 2m (yr3) and 2m (yr4). The company borrows the funds from its parent company with a cost of capital of 5 per cent. Assuming there are no competing projects and that all costs are met in year 1, determine whether the company should borrow the money and make the investment.

Managing global cash reserves

Assuming First Pac wholly owned PLDT, Indofood and Metro Pacific, evaluate approaches to manage the organization's global cash reserves.

Accounting information

List and describe sources of accounting information with reference to common financial statements. You should identify the purpose of such information and discuss who might make use of such information and for what purpose.

Economic theory 2

Compare and contrast the combined code, SOX and the OECD principles of corporate governance.

References

Barker, R. G. (2003) 'Global accounting is coming: and it will transform the way your company reports profits', *Harvard Business Review* 81(4):24–25.

Bazerman, M. H. (2002) *Judgment in Managerial Decision Making,* New York: John Wiley & Sons.

Block, S. (2000) 'Integrating Traditional Capital Budgeting Concepts Into An International Decision-Making Environment', *Engineering Economist* 45(4):309–326.

Brakeman, L., Garretsen, H., Marrewijk, C. and Witteloostuijn, A. (2006) *Nations and Firms in the Global Economy,* Cambridge: Cambridge University Press.

CIMA, The Chartered Institute of Management Accountants www.cimaglobal.com accessed 27 December 2007.

Eisenhardt, K. M. (1989) 'Agency Theory: An Assessment and Review', *Academy of Management Review* 14(1):57–74.

Feldstein, M. and Horioka, C. (1980) 'Domestic Saving and International Capital Flows', *The Economic Journal* (June 1980) 90(358):314–329.

Ghosh, A. R. (1995) 'International Capital Mobility Amongst the Major Industrialised Countries: Too Little or Too Much?', *The Economic Journal* (January 1995) 105(428):107–128.

Giddy, I. H. (1977) 'A Note on the Macroeconomic Assumptions of International Financial Management', *The Journal of Financial and Quantitative Analysis* (November 1977) 12(4):601–605.

Gray, S. J. (1988) 'Towards a Theory of Cultural Influence on the Development of Accounting Systems Internationally', *Abacus* 24(1):1–15.

Hagelin, N. and Pramborg, B. (2004) 'Hedging Foreign Exchange Exposure: Risk Reduction from Transaction and Translation Hedging', *Journal of International Financial Management & Accounting* 15(1):1–20.

Hague, I. P., Jones, K., Milburn, A. and Walsh, M. (2006) 'New Developments in the Framework for Financial Reporting: The Role of National Standard Setters and the Canadian Contribution to Research on Measurement on Initial Recognition and a Framework for Disclosure of Financial Information', *Journal of International Financial Management & Accounting* 17(3):256–270.

Hope, O. (2003) 'Firm-level Disclosures and the Relative Roles of Culture and Legal Origin', *Journal of International Financial Management & Accounting* 14(3):218–248.

Institute of Chartered Accountants in England & Wales (2007) www.icaew.com/ accessed 28 December 2007

Institute of Chartered Accountants in England & Wales (2007a) 'Emerging Issues paper', ICAEW available as a pdf file from www.icaew.com/

Kahneman, D. and Tversky, A. (1979) 'Prospect theory: An analysis of decisions under risk', *Econometrica* 47:262–291.

Klein, H. J. (1989) 'An Integrated Control Theory of Work Motivation', *Academy of Management Review* 14(2):150–172.

Markusen, J. R. (1995) 'The Boundaries of Multinational Enterprises and the Theory of International Trade', *The Journal of Economic Perspectives* (Spring, 1995) 9(2):169–189.

Markusen, J. R. (1998) 'Multinational firms and the new trade theory', *Journal of International Economics* (1 December 1998) 46(2):183–203.

McGregor, W. and Street, D. L. (2007) 'IASB and FASB Face Challenges in Pursuit of Joint Conceptual Framework', *Journal of International Financial Management & Accounting* 18(1):39–51.

OECD (2004) 'OECD Principles of Corporate Governance', OECD accessible from the OECD website.

OECD (2007) 'Improving Business Behaviour: Why we need Corporate Governance', www.oecd.org/document/37/0,3343,en_2649_34813_31838821_1_1_1_1,00.html accessed 20 December 2007.

PriceWaterhouseCoopers (2007) 'Sarbanes-Oxley and strategies for compliance', www.pwc.com/ accessed 28 December 2007.

Salter, S. B. and Niswander, F. (1995) 'Cultural Influence on the Development of Accounting Systems Internationally: A Test Of Gray's [1988] Theory', *Journal of International Business Studies* 26(2):379–397.

Smith, A. (1776) *An Inquiry into the Nature and Causes of the Wealth of Nations*, Book IV, Chapter II, London: Methuen and Co., Ltd., ed. Edwin Cannan, 1904. [Online] available from www.econlib.org/LIBRARY/Smith/smWN13.html; accessed 17 December 2007; Internet.

Stanko, B. (2000) 'The Case for International Accounting Rules', *Business & Economic Review* (July–September 2000) 46(4):21–26.

Tarca, A. (2004) 'International Convergence of Accounting Practices: Choosing between IAS and US GAAP', *Journal of International Financial Management & Accounting* 15(1):60–91.

Vernon, R. (1966) 'International Investment and International Trade in the Product Cycle', *The Quarterly Journal of Economics* (May 1966) 80(2):190–207.

Suggestions for further reading

Journals

Journal of International Financial Management & Accounting

The Journal of International Financial Management & Accounting publishes original research dealing with international aspects of financial management and reporting, banking and financial services, auditing and taxation. Providing a forum for the interaction of ideas from both academics and practitioners, the JIFMA keeps up-to-date with new developments and emerging trends.

http://www.blackwell-synergy.com/loi/JIFM

Readers may also wish to consider work published in the following journals: *The Economic Journal; The Quarterly Journal of Economics; Journal of International Economics; The Journal of Economic Perspectives; Business & Economic Review and The Journal of Financial and Quantitative Analysis.*

Key articles

Scholars of this subject area have often read the following:

1 Feldstein, M. and Horioka, C. (1980) 'Domestic Saving and International Capital Flows', *The Economic Journal* (June 1980) 90(358):314–329.

2 Vernon, R. (1966) 'International Investment and International Trade in the Product Cycle', *The Quarterly Journal of Economics* (May 1966) 80(2):190–207.

3 Eisenhardt, K. M. (1989) 'Agency Theory: An Assessment and Review', *Academy of Management Review* 14(1):57–74.

4 Markusen, J. R. (1995) 'The Boundaries of Multinational Enterprises and the Theory of International Trade', *The Journal of Economic Perspectives* (Spring, 1995) 9(2):169–189.

5 Markusen, J. R. (1998) 'Multinational firms and the New Trade Theory', *Journal of International Economics* (1 December 1998) 46(2):183–203.

6 Ghosh, A. R. (1995) 'International Capital Mobility Amongst the Major Industrialised Countries: Too Little or Too Much?', *The Economic Journal* (January 1995) 105(428):107–128.

7 Salter, S. B. and Niswander, F. (1995) 'Cultural Influence on the Development of Accounting Systems Internationally: A Test of Gray's [1988] Theory', *Journal of International Business Studies* 26(2):379–397.

8 Hope, O. (2003) 'Firm-level Disclosures and the Relative Roles of Culture and Legal Origin', *Journal of International Financial Management & Accounting* 14(3):218–248.

9 McGregor, W. and Street, D. L. (2007) 'IASB and FASB Face Challenges in Pursuit of Joint Conceptual Framework', *Journal of International Financial Management & Accounting* 18(1):39–51.

10 Tarca, A. (2004) 'International Convergence of Accounting Practices: Choosing between IAS and US GAAP', *Journal of International Financial Management & Accounting* 15(1):60–91.

Part V Summary

Within Part V we focused on the primary activities of the organization and the management of financial resources. We concluded that operations management (OM) refers to the planning, scheduling, control and coordination of the activities transforming inputs into finished goods and services. In order to do this they must utilize the organization's resources and capabilities.

Operations management is important because it can reduce costs, differentiate the organization's products and services and impact upon quality and therefore may increase revenue through increased customer satisfaction. The fundamental role of operations is to implement corporate strategy. Working closely with operations, marketing is the management process responsible for identifying, anticipating and satisfying customer requirements profitably. The organization may analyze its environment identifying opportunities and specific markets to enter and categorizing customers and buyer behaviour.

One of the first tasks for the international marketing manager is to assess potential for success. Marketing strategy indicates the opportunities to pursue, specific target markets to address, and the types of competitive advantages to be developed and exploited when meeting marketing goals. Strategy is concerned with the optimal application of the resources a firm possesses relative to its competitors. When marketing their products, firms need to create a successful mix of the right product, sold at the right price, in the right place and using the most suitable promotion. As a result of sales, the organization generates financial resources. Prior to this, the organization must acquire and utilize such resources in order to develop capabilities, source raw materials and transform them into finished goods and services.

Finance studies the ways in which organizations raise, allocate, and use monetary resources over time, taking into account the risks entailed. There are many challenges associated with managing worldwide the international organization's financial resources and activities in this area can also be a source of advantage.

International business and management is about managing HRM, operations, strategy, marketing, finance, information systems and technology, in an international context. For some, such management will emanate from the corporate centre, while for others, decisions will be made in the subsidiaries or more local business units. This text has identified the theories, concepts and challenges which provide the understanding needed by the manager working in the international organization. This understanding must be complemented by personal skills, abilities, competencies and sound judgement if such managers are to contribute towards a high performing and responsible organization.

Index